THE REAL GUIDE

IRELAND

John M. Gaffney

REAL GUIDE CREDITS

Series Editor: Mark Ellingham
U.S. Text Editors: Marc Dubin, Greg Ward, and Jamie Jensen
Editorial: Martin Dunford, John Fisher, Jack Holland, Jonathan Buckley
Production: Susanne Hillen, Kate Berens, Andy Hilliard, Gail Jammy
Typesetting: Greg Ward
Design: Andrew Oliver

Many thanks to all the regional and local offices of the **Irish Tourist Board** and the **Northern Irish Tourist Board** who helped with the research of this book: in particular Mark Rowlette (London), Ellen Redmond (Dublin) and Anne Moore (Belfast), and to Naudi O'Sullivan of Shannon Development.

Thanks also to **Aer Lingus**, the **Youth Hostel Association of Northern Ireland**, **An Óige**, **Budget Hostels**, and to Vary Knovett of the **Independent Hostel Owners** co-op.

For their invaluable help, encouragement and advice: Luke Dodd, Frank and Rosemarie Kennan, Tom Joyce, Charles and Geraldine O'Kane, Clare Coyle, Marleen, Jenny and Brian Nuttall, German Pump, Eamonn and Pauline Keenan, Padraig Sugrue, Mary Hughes, Sara Hillen, Catherine Mulvenna, Michael O'Sullivan, Veronica O'Driscoll, Anne and Frank Greenwood, Maire Molloy, Charles Hueston, Juliana MacGregor, Mick and Nuala O'Driscoll, Ian McNicholl, Jack and Fidelis, Alice and John and Ben, Mary Hillen, George Gavan Duffy, Sean of Derrylahan, Elke and Karsten, Jean and Michael, Cillian Rodgers and family, Mike Gerrard, Jessica, and to Mark Ellingham.

Thanks also to the *Real Guides* crew: Wendy Ferguson, Mick Sinclair, Jack Holland, Kate Berens, Dan Richardson, Jules Brown, and John Gawthrop—and especially to the indefatigable trio of Jonathan Buckley, Greg Ward, and Susanne Hillen.

And, of course, to the unflappable John Fisher.

Published in the United States and Canada by Prentice Hall Trade Division
A division of Simon & Schuster, Inc., 15 Columbus Circle, New York, NY 10023.

Typeset in Linotron Univers and Century Old Style.
Printed in the United States by R.R. Donnelley & Sons.

Illustrations in Part One and Part Three by Ed Briant; Basics illustration by Gila
Contexts illustration by Andrea McMordie

© Seán Doran, Margaret Greenwood, and Hildi Hawkins 1990

576pp
includes index

Library of Congress Cataloging-in-Publication Data

Ireland : the real guide
(The Real Guides)

1. Ireland—Description and Travel—1981—Guide-books
   I. Doran, Seán II. Greenwood, Margaret III. Hawkins, Hildi IV. Title V. Series
   DA980.D67 1990   914.15'04824   89-26585
   ISBN 0–13–783614–7 : $12.95

THE REAL·GUIDE

IRELAND

written and researched by

SEÁN DORAN, MARGARET GREENWOOD,
and **HILDI HAWKINS**

With additional contributions by
Joe O'Connor, Brian Trench, Luke Dodd, Jo O'Donoghue,
Lin Coghlan, Tom Joyce, and Richard Nairn

Contributing Editors
Susanne Hillen, Greg Ward, Jules Brown,
Wendy Ferguson, and John Gawthrop

Edited by
JOHN FISHER and JONATHAN BUCKLEY

■ PRENTICE HALL ■
NEW YORK LONDON TORONTO SYDNEY TOKYO SINGAPORE

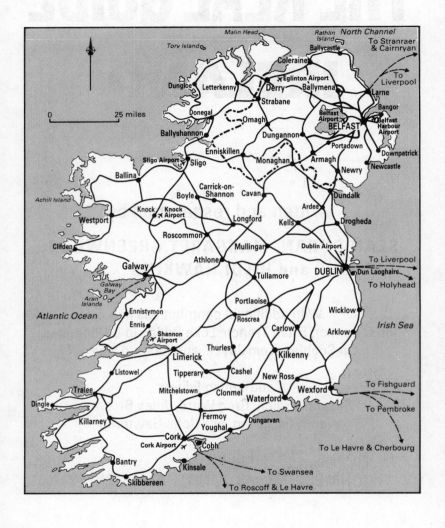

CONTENTS

INTRODUCTION

L andscape and people are what bring most visitors to Ireland – South and North. And once there, few are disappointed by the reality of the stock Irish images: the green, rain-hazed loughs and wild, bluff-staggered coastlines, the inspired talent for talk and conversation, the easy pace and rhythms of life. What is perhaps more of a surprise is how much variety this very small land packs into its countryside. The limestone terraces of the stark, eerie Burren seem separated from the fertile flatlands of Tipperary by hundreds rather than tens of miles, and the primitive beauty of the west coast, with its cliffs, cove,s and strands, seem almost a country apart from the rolling plains of the central cattle-rearing counties.

The greatest attractions of the place are, with a few fine exceptions, rural. Ireland is becoming increasingly integrated with the industrial economies of western Europe, yet the modernization of the country has to date made little impact: the countryside appears startlingly unspoiled and unpopulated if you have come over from England. It's a place to explore slowly, roaming through agricultural landscapes scattered with farmhouses, or along the endlessly indented coastline, where the crash of the sea against the cliffs and myriad islands is often the only sound. It is perfect if you want spaces to walk, bike, or (with a bit of bravado) swim; likewise, if you want to fish, sail, or spend a week on inland waterways. In town, too, the pleasures are unhurried: evenings over a Guinness or two in a pub, listening to the conversation around a blood-orange turf fire.

This said, there are sights enough. In every corner of the island are traces of a culture established long before the coming of Christianity; sites such as **Newgrange** in County Meath or the cliff-top fortress of **Dun Aengus** are among the most stupendous Neolithic remains in Europe, while in some areas of Sligo almost every hill is capped by an ancient cairn. In the depths of the so-called Dark Ages the Christian communities of Ireland were great centers of learning, and the ruins of **Clonmacnoise**, the **Rock of Cashel**, and a score of other **monasteries** are evocative of a time when Ireland won its reputation as a land of saints and scholars. Fortifications raised by the chieftains of the Celtic clans and the Anglo-Norman barons bear witness to an early period of turbulence, while the ascendancy of the Protestant settlers has left its mark in the form of vast mansions and estates.

But the richness of Irish **culture** is not a matter of monuments. Especially in the Irish-speaking *Gaeltacht* areas, you'll be aware of the strength and continuity of the island's oral and musical traditions. **Myth-making** is for the Irish people their most enduring and fascinating entertainment. The ancient classics are full of extraordinary stories—Cúchulainn the unbeatable hero in war, Medb the insatiable heroine in bed, or Finn Mac Cumaill chasing Diarmuid and Gráinne up and down the country—and tall tales, superstition-mongering and "mouthing off" (boasting) play as large a part in day-to-day life as they did in the era of the *Táin Bó Cuailnge*, Europe's oldest vernacular epic. As a gullible foreigner inquiring about anything from a beautiful lake to a pound of butter, you're ideally placed to trigger the most colorful responses. And the speech of the country—molded by the rhythms of the ancient tongue—have fired such twentieth-century greats as Yeats, Joyce, and Beckett.

Music has always been at the heart of Irish community life. Virtually every village has a pub that hosts **traditional** music sessions—some of it might be of dubious pedigree, but the *Gaeltacht* areas, and others too, can be counted on to provide authentic renditions. Side by side with the traditional circuit is a romping **rock** scene, largely Dublin-based, that has spawned the Undertones, "Saint" Bob's Boomtown Rats, U2, and more recently the Hothouse Flowers. And ever-present are the country-and-western performers, fathoming and feeding the old Irish dreams of courting, emigrating and striking it lucky; there's hardly a dry eye in the house when the guitars are packed away.

The lakes and rivers of Ireland make it an angler's dream, but the **sports** that raise the greatest enthusiasm amongst the Irish themselves are speedier and more dangerous. Horse-racing in Ireland has none of the socially divisive connotations present on the other side of the Irish Sea, and the country has bred some of the finest thoroughbreds—the most recent hero being the lamented Shergar. Hurling, the oldest team game played in Ireland, requires the most delicate of ball-skills and the sturdiest of bones. Gaelic football, which commands a larger following, bears a superficial resemblance to soccer, but allows a wider range of violent contact. And, in Sean Kelly and Stephen Roche, Ireland has produced two of the supermen of professional bicycling, the cruellest of endurance tests.

No introduction can cope with the complexities of Ireland's **politics**, which permeate every aspect of daily life, most conspicuously in the North. However, throughout the guide we have addressed the issues wherever they arise, and at the end of the book, in the *Contexts* section, we have included pieces that give a general overview of the current situation. Suffice it to say that, regardless of partisan politics, Irish hospitality is as warm as the brochures say, on both sides of the border.

Where to Go

The area that draws most visitors is the **west coast**, where the demonically daunting peninsulas of its northern reaches are immediately contrasted a little inland by the mystical lakes of the **Donegal highlands**. The **midwest coastline** is even more strangely attractive, combining vertiginous cliffs, boulder-strewn wastes, and violent mountains of granite and quartz. In the **south**, the melodramatic peaks of the **Ring of Kerry** fall to tarns and seductive seascapes. Less talked about, but no less rewarding in their way, are the gentle sandy coves that **Cork** and **Kerry** share.

In the **north** of the island, the principal attraction is the weird basalt geometry of the **Giant's Causeway**, not far from the lush **Glens of Antrim**. To the south of Belfast lies the beautiful walking territory of the softly contoured **Mountains of Mourne**, divided by **Carlingford Lough** from the myth-drenched **Cooley Mountains**.

The **interior** is nowhere as spectacular as the fringes of the island, but the southern heartland of pastures and low wooded hills, and the wide peat bogs of the very middle are the classic landscapes of Ireland. Of the **inland water-ways**, the most alluring are the island-studded **Lough Erne** complex of Fermanagh, and the **Shannon River**, with its string of huge lakes.

Offshore Ireland has some of the country's wildest scenery: west-coast **Aran** is the best known of the islands, but equally compelling are storm-battered **Tory Island**, to the far northwest; the savage **Skelligs**, off the south-west coast; and the sequestered **Scattery**, in the mouth of the Shannon.

For anyone with strictly limited time, one of best options must be to combine a visit to **Dublin** with the mountains and monastic ruins of **County Wicklow**. Dublin is an extraordinary combination of youthfulness and tradi-tion, a human-scale capital of decaying Georgian squares and vibrant pubs. **Belfast**, victim of a perennially bad press, vies with Dublin in the vitality of its nightlife, while the cities of **Cork**, **Waterford**, and **Galway**, too, have a new-found energy about them.

When to Go

Determined by the pressure systems of the Atlantic, Ireland's **climate** is notoriously variable, and cannot be relied upon at any time of the year. Each year produces weeks of beautiful weather—the problem lies in predicting when they are likely to arrive. In recent years **late spring** and **early autumn** have proved the sunniest, with May and September as the pleasantest months.

Geographically, the **southeast** is the driest and sunniest part of the coun-try, and the **northwest** is the wettest. But regional variations are not partic-ularly pronounced, the overall climate being characterized by its mildness in comparison with that of Britain, which doesn't benefit so much from the Gulf Stream. Even in the wetter zones, mornings of rain are frequently followed by afternoons of blue sky and sun—and besides, a downpour on a windswept headland can be exhilarating, and provides as good a pretext as any for a warming shot of whiskey.

HELP US UPDATE

We've gone to considerable effort to ensure that this edition of the **Real Guide: Ireland** is up-to-date and accurate. However, things do change, and any suggestions, comments, or corrections you can offer for the next edition would be much appreciated. We'll credit all contributions, and send a copy of the new book (or any other Real Guide, if you prefer) for the best letters. Send them along to:

John Fisher, The Real Guides, Prentice Hall Trade Division, A Division of Simon and Schuster Inc., 15 Columbus Circle, New York, NY 10023.

THE

BASICS

GETTING THERE

Ireland is easily accessible from the USA by a number of airlines that offer direct flights to either Dublin or Shannon, the country's two major gateways. Since the deregulation of Ireland's air transport and the opening of a number of additional regional airports, there's been a proliferation of cheap flights available from other parts of the British Isles. Together with the number of rail/ferry and bus/ferry options, this makes Ireland easily accessible as part of a wider European travel itinerary.

DIRECT FROM THE USA

Aer Lingus (☎800/223-6537), the national airline of Ireland, flies out of **Boston**, **New York**, and **Chicago** (Sunday only) to **Dublin** and **Shannon**. The fares from New York and Boston to Dublin are the same: the APEX ticket, requiring a fourteen-day advance purchase and permitting a maximum stay of six months, is $459 in the low season and $663 in the high, with fares to Shannon approximately $30 less. **From Chicago** the fares are $697 in the low season and $797 in the high. A cheaper option are the promotional fares *Aer Lingus* offers throughout the year, including such offers as a Tuesday-to-Tuesday round-trip fare from New York for $359. These are liable to change, so it's well worth inquiring about the latest promotion when calling.

Of the US airlines that fly direct to Ireland, *Pan Am* (☎800/221-1111) flies only from New York to Shannon, offering a low-season APEX ticket for $429, high-season $633. *Delta* (☎800/221-1212) flies from Atlanta to both Shannon and Dublin. Their APEX fares range from $642 low season to $846 in the high, with a mid-season return costing $742. If you are connecting from another US city however, fares can be a good deal more reasonable. **From Los Angeles** for example, the APEX fare is $698 low season, $856 in the high season.

DISCOUNT FLIGHTS

There is a good variety of **discount flights** available to Ireland. *STA* for example (☎800/777-0112) has a high-season fare of $530 from New York, with cheap connections from other US cities, or more economically, *Council Travel* offers low-season round trips starting at $403. Among the range of other discount companies worth checking out are *Nouvelles Frontières* (☎212/779-0600), *Access International* (☎800/333-7280), *McTravel* (☎800/333-3335), *International Travel Specialists* (☎800/444-6064), *Voyages Cuts* in Canada (☎416/979-2406), or any similar companies advertising in the travel sections of the Sunday papers.

Airhitch (☎212/864-2000) sells last minute standbys to Europe from several US cities for one low price ($160 from New York, $229 from Los Angeles). However, precise dates and destinations cannot be guaranteed. Instead you tell them what range of days you want to fly on, and where you want to fly to, and a few days prior to the time you want to leave you will be offered a choice of flights. Naturally this form of travel is very unpredictable, and while you are almost sure to leave at the time you specified, it is not certain you will fly to the exact place you wanted to.

GROUP/STUDENT TRAVEL

A variety of short excursions and specialized tours to Ireland are available from a variety of organizations, including *Aerlingus*, which offer a range of **fly-drive packages**. Other special interest operators in this field include *Forum Travel International* and *Backroads*, who both offer a range of bicycling tours, and *Equitours*, who lead horseback-riding trips.

For students, programs combining work and study with travel to many destinations including

CIEE IN THE U.S.

Head Office: 205 E. 42nd St., New York, NY 10017; ☎800/223-7401

CALIFORNIA
2511 Channing Way, Berkeley, CA 94704; ☎415/848-8604
UCSD Student Center, B-023, La Jolla, CA 92093; ☎619/452-0630
5500 Atherton St., Suite 212, Long Beach, CA 90815; ☎213/598-3338
1093 Broxton Ave., Los Angeles, CA 90024; ☎213/208-3551
4429 Cass St., San Diego, CA 92109; ☎619/270-6401
312 Sutter St., San Francisco, CA 94108; ☎415/421-3473
919 Irving St., San Francisco, CA 94122; ☎415/566-6222
14515 Ventura Blvd., Suite 250, Sherman Oaks, CA 91403; ☎818/905-5777

GEORGIA
12 Park Place South, Atlanta, GA 30303; ☎404/577-1678

ILLINOIS
29 E. Delaware Place, Chicago, IL 60611; ☎312/951-0585

MASSACHUSETTS
79 South Pleasant St., 2nd Floor, Amherst, MA 01002; ☎413/256-1261

729 Boylston St., Suite 201, Boston, MA 02116; ☎617/266-1926
1384 Massachusetts Ave., Suite 206, Cambridge, MA 02138; ☎617/497-1497

MINNESOTA
1501 University Ave. SE, Room 300, Minneapolis, MN 55414; ☎612/379-2323

NEW YORK
35 W. 8th St., New York, NY 10011; ☎212/254-2525
Student Center, 356 West 34th St., New York, NY 10001; ☎212/661-1450

OREGON
715SW Morrison, Suite 1020, Portland, OR 97205; ☎503/228-1900

RHODE ISLAND
171 Angell St., Suite 212, Providence, RI 02906; ☎401/331-5810

TEXAS
1904 Guadalupe St., Suite 6, Austin, TX 78705; ☎512/472-4931
The Executive Tower, 3300 W. Mockingbird, Suite 101, Dallas,TX 75235; ☎214/350-6166

WASHINGTON
1314 Northeast 43rd St., Suite 210, Seattle, WA 98105; ☎206/632-2448

STA IN THE U.S.

BOSTON
273 Newbury St., Boston, MA 02116; ☎617/266-6014

HONOLULU
1831 S. King St., Suite 202, Honolulu, HI 96826; ☎808/942-7755

LOS ANGELES
920 Westwood Blvd., Los Angeles, CA 90024; ☎213/824-1574
7204 Melrose Ave., Los Angeles, CA 90046; ☎213/934-8722

2500 Wilshire Blvd., Los Angeles, CA 90057; ☎213/380-2184

NEW YORK
17 E. 45th St., Suite 805, New York, NY 10017; ☎212/986-9470;☎ 800/777-0112

SAN DIEGO
6447 El Cajon Blvd., San Diego, CA 92115; ☎619/286-1322

SAN FRANCISCO
166 Geary St., Suite 702, San Francisco, CA 94108; ☎415/391-8407

NOUVELLES FRONTIÈRES

In the United States
NEW YORK 19 W. 44th St., Suite 1702, New York, NY 10036; ☎212/764-6494
LOS ANGELES 6363 Wilshire Blvd., Suite 200, Los Angeles, CA 90048; ☎213/658-8955
SAN FRANCISCO 209 Post St., Suite 1121, San Francisco, CA 94108; ☎415/781-4480

In Canada
MONTREAL 1130 ouest, bd de Maisonneuve, Montréal, P.Q. H3A 1M8; ☎514/842-1450
QUEBEC 176 Grande Allée Ouest, Québec, P.Q. G1R 2G9; ☎418/525-5255

Ireland are available from: *The Council on International Education Exchange*, 205 East 42nd Street, New York, NY 10017 (☎212/661-1414); *The Humanities Institute*, PO Box 18B, Belmont, MS 02178 (☎800/327-1657), and *The American Institute of Foreign Study*, College Summer Division, 102 Greenwich Avenue, Greenwich, CT 06830. For general information and publications about studying abroad, try contacting the *Institute of International Education*, 809 U.N. Plaza, New York, NY 10017 (☎212/883-8200).

VIA BRITAIN

As an alternative to a direct flight, a combined trip taking in Ireland via England is a viable option. While flying to Ireland from England is easy (though relatively expensive), there are also regular ferry crossings from Liverpool, Holyhead, and Fishguard to Dublin, Belfast, and Cork.

FLIGHTS

With a flight time from England to the Republic of only an hour to an hour and a half, flying is again the fastest option, and the most convenient: *Aer Lingus* flies from eleven British airports, and *Ryanair*, its main competitor, from six. While seasonal price variations are minimal, a complex fare structure is in operation, and its advisable to

check with the airlines or travel agents for the latest offers. Most price differences arise from how much you're prepared to commit yourself in advance to travel dates.

The cheapest fares from **London to Dublin** start at around £32 one-way, offered by all the major carriers—*Aer Lingus, British Airways*, and *British Midland*—with varying restrictions. *Capital* divides their planes into three fare sections of £32, £42 and £52 and sell on a first-come, first-served basis. *Ryanair* operate a similar scheme but with fewer available seats and slightly higher fares. Both companies however, only allow seats to be booked the day before flying. While an *Aer Lingus* one-way fare is slightly more expensive (£43), they have the advantage of flying to several regional airports, including Cork, Kerry, Shannon, Waterford, Knock, Galway, Sligo, and Derry. All the airlines also offer a range of APEX and budget round-trip fares, with a typical SuperAPEX flight, reservable fourteen days in advance and including at least one Saturday night in Ireland, costing around £74 round-trip. If you're not visiting Dublin, it's worth considering *Aer Lingus* SuperAPEX flights to the regional airports (although you will have to change planes in Dublin), which are around £85 to Kerry, Cork, Shannon, Waterford, Knock, Galway, and Sligo.

If you're **flying from outside London** you can expect to pay a bit more: a *Ryanair* round-trip flight from Leeds, Bradford, or Coventry to Knock, for example, costs £90.

The easiest way of flying from **London to the North** is by the hourly *British Airways* or *British Midland Shuttle* and *Diamond* services to Belfast. These are currently priced at £46 one-way, £84 APEX round-trip (which you must book fourteen days in advance). Flying from other parts of Britain, however, these two airlines are generally the most expensive (£90 round-trip from Manchester, £105 from Birmingham), and other carriers such as *Air UK* or *Dan-Air* will offer better deals.

FERRIES

The traditional way of getting to Ireland from Britain, ferries are now being outclassed by cheap air travel. With some crossings stretching to three to four times the average flight duration, the only real advantage is that you can take a car over with you (car rental in Ireland is among the most expensive in Europe). In summer reservations should be made in advance as all sailings are "controlled" and may not allow passengers on without reservations. Prices again vary all the time, though as an indication a round-trip ticket from **Pembroke** to **Rosslare** with *B&I* or *Sealink* for a car and four people will cost around £119, with similar fares on the **Holyhead–Dublin**

TRAVEL OPERATORS TO IRELAND

AIRLINES

Aer Lingus, 223 Regent Street, London W1 (☎01-569 5555).

Air UK, Stansted House, Stansted Airport, Essex (☎0345-666777).

Britannia Airways, Luton Airport, Luton, Beds LU2 9ND (☎0582-405737).

British Airways, PO Box 10, Heathrow Airport, Hounslow, Middlesex TW6 2JA (☎01-897 4000).

British Midland, Donington Hall, Castle Donington, Derby DE7 2SB (☎01-589 5599).

Capital Airlines, Northair House, Leeds/Bradford Airport, Leeds LS19 7YG (☎0345-800777).

Dan-Air, Newman House, Victoria Street, Horley, West Sussex (☎0345-100200).

Ryanair, 150 New Bond Street, London W1 (☎01-435 7101).

FERRY COMPANIES

B & I Line, Reliance House, Water Street, Liverpool L2 8TP (☎051-227 3131).
Holyhead ☎0407-50222 or 50223.
Fishguard ☎0348-872881.
Dublin ☎01-724711.
Rosslare ☎053-33311.
Cork ☎021-273024.
After-hours information lines
England ☎061-236 3936.
Ireland ☎01-606666.

P & O European Ferries, Cairnryan, Stranraer, Wigtownsrent DG9 8RF (☎05812-276).
Central reservations ☎0304-203388
Larne ☎0574-74321

Sealink British Ferries, Charter House, Park Street, Ashford, Kent TN24 8EX (☎0233-4707).
Dublin ☎01-808844.
Dun Laoghaire ☎01-774206.
Rosslare ☎053-33115.

Belfast Car Ferries, North Brocklebank Dock, Bootle, Merseyside L20 1DB (☎051-922 6234).

Swansea–Cork Ferries, 55 Grand Parade, Cork (☎021-271166).

Irish Ferries, 2/4 Merrion Row, Dublin 2 (☎01-610511).

Brittany Ferries, 42 Grand Parade, Cork (☎021-277801).

STUDENT/YOUTH OPERATORS, TRAINS AND BUS COMPANIES

Campus Travel/USIT, 52 Grosvenor Gardens, London SW1W 0AG (☎01-730 3402).
Other offices throughout Britain and Ireland
STA Travel, 86 Old Brompton Road, London SW7 (☎01-937 9921).
Other offices throughout Britain

Eurotrain, 52 Grosvenor Gardens, London SW1W 0AG (☎01-730 3402).

Wasteels, 121 Wilton Road, London SW1V 1JZ (☎01-834 7066).

Slattery's Bus Service, 162 Kentish Town Road, London NW5 (☎01-485 2778).

route. The round-trip fare for individual foot passengers is £29.

As for other routes, *Belfast Ferries* operates an eight-hour **Liverpool–Belfast** crossing, with round-trip fares for foot passengers starting at £45, and *Swansea–Cork Ferries* runs a ten-hour Swansea–Cork trip. The shortest crossing is from **Stranraer** or **Cairnryan** to **Larne** (2hr 20min), operated by *Sealink* and *P&O*, with foot passenger round-trip fares at £26. Alternatively, *Irish Ferries* and *Brittany Ferries* between them connect **Rosslare** to **Le Havre** and **Cherbourg**, and **Cork** to **Le Havre** and **Roscoff**.

Students, IYHF members and Eurail and InterRail travelers are entitled to discounts of up to fifty percent with some carriers.

TRAINS
Combined rail and sea tickets can be booked at British Rail stations and travel agents. The round-trip fare from **London** to **Dublin** is £52, or £41 from Manchester; London to Belfast (via Liverpool) is £66; Birmingham to Belfast (via

Stranraer) is £59. Eurail and InterRail travelers get fifty percent off these fares, while anyone under 26 can get discount tickets from *Eurotrain* or *Wasteels*, a round-trip ticket to Dublin costing £36, or £52 to the west coast (with stopovers on the way).

BUSES
Getting to Ireland by bus is a slog, but has the advantage of being cheap. *Slattery's* offers an off-peak **London–Dublin** round-trip for £29, with a "family" ticket (two adults and two children) for £58. At peak times however, special offers may not apply, in which case the adult round-trip fare goes up to £45–50. Journey time is around twelve hours, leaving London's Victoria bus station at 8:30am. *National Express's Supabus* fares also start at £29 from London, with additional departures from all over Britain, reservable through most travel agents. Buses to the North are more expensive, a London–Belfast round-trip ticket from *Scottish Citylink* costing £50, Birmingham–Belfast £47.

RED TAPE AND VISAS

American and Canadian nationals don't need a visa to travel to Ireland, and can stay in the country for up to three months on production of a passport.

Anyone intending to stay longer than this period must apply to the Department of Justice in Dublin (39 Anne's Lane, Dublin 2; ☎01-714811). In the North British regulations apply; thus, again, a passport is sufficient to secure a stay of up to three months.

IRISH CONSULATES ABROAD

Australia, 20 Arkana Street, Yarrulumla, Canberra 2600 A.C.T. (☎62/733-022).

Canada, 170 Metcalfe Street, Ottawa K2P 1P3, Ontario (☎613/233-6281)

Germany, Godesberger Allee 119, 5300 Bonn 2 (☎228/37-69-37).

Great Britain, 17 Grosvenor Place, London SW1X 7HR (☎01-235 2171).

Netherlands, 9 Dr Kuperstraat, 2514 BA The Hague (☎70/63-09-93).

United States, Embassy, 2234 Massachusetts Avenue N.W., Washington DC 20008 (☎202/462-39-39).

COSTS, MONEY, AND BANKS

One thing Ireland is not is a cheap place to travel. The least expensive bed, in a hostel, will rarely be less than $6.50 per night, while Bed and Breakfast generally amounts to $13–16. Reckon on about $5 for a decent meal, and on spending more than you expect on drink, partly because it's expensive (around IR£1.40 a pint), and partly because so much social life and entertainment revolves around the pubs.

In short you're likely to spend a minimum of $25 a day if you're watching the pennies, and it's easy to find yourself getting through more like $40. As always, if you're traveling in a group you may be able to save some money by sharing rooms and food.

The **currency** in the **Republic** is the Irish pound, also known as the *punt*, which is divided into 100 pence. If coming via Britain and you have a supply of pounds sterling, don't fall for the myth that there is no need to exchange them; the Irish may well accept English pounds but this is due to the favorable exchange rate (£1=IR£1.15). For the best rates (IR£1 is currently worth $1.39) change your money either in banks or in exchange bureaux, located in major cities and the larger tourist offices.

The best way of carrying the bulk of your money is in **travelers' checks**, available from almost any bank (whether or not you have an account) for a usual fee of one percent of the amount ordered.

Banks in the Republic are open Mon–Fri 10am–12:30pm and 1.30pm–3pm; most are also open until 5pm on Thursday. It makes sense to change your money while in the cities since many small country towns are served by sub-offices open only certain days of the week.

Foreign exchange counters are open at all main **airports**: Dublin (daily summer 7am–9:30pm, winter 7:30am–8:30pm); Shannon (summer daily 6am–5:30pm, winter Mon–Fri 7am–5:30pm, Sat & Sun 7am–4:30pm); Cork (Mon–Fri summer 10am–12:30pm & 1:30–5pm, winter 10am–1pm); Connaught (Horan International, located in the tourist office, 9am–12:30pm & 1:30–5pm).

Credit cards are accepted in large department stores, gas stations, hotels and upscale restaurants. *Visa* cards can be used to withdraw cash from branches of the *Allied Irish Bank*.

THE NORTH

In the North the currency is pounds sterling (£1=$1.60). Main banks in large towns are open Monday to Friday 10am–3:30pm; elsewhere they close from 12:30–1:30pm. In very small villages the bank may open on only two or three days a week—so, as in the Republic, aim to get your cash in the bigger centers.

There are a couple of places in Belfast where you can change money outside banking hours: *Thomas Cook*, 11 Donegall Place (Mon–Fri 9am–5:30pm, Sat 9am–noon); and 7 Shaftesbury Square (Mon–Fri 9am–5:30pm, Sat 9am–12:30pm). Large hotels may also change money, although the exchange rate is generally poor.

Access/Mastercard and *Visa/Barclaycard* are the most commonly accepted credit cards, and can be used, as in the Republic, in upscale restaurants and hotels, gas stations, and department stores. *Diners' Club* and *American Express* are not widely accepted.

HEALTH AND INSURANCE

There are no inoculations required for travelers to Ireland, nor any particular health hazards to beware of beyond the usual ones when traveling in an unknown place.

However, there's no free medical treatment for North Americans in Ireland, so some form of **travel insurance** is essential. Before you purchase any insurance, however, check what you have already, whether as part of a family or student policy. You may find yourself covered for medical expenses and loss, and possibly loss of or damage to valuables, while abroad.

For example, **Canadians** are usually covered for medical expenses by their provincial health plans (but may only be reimbursed after the fact). Holders of **ISIC** cards are entitled to $2000 worth of accident coverage and 60 days ($100 per diem) of hospital in-patient benefits for the period during which the card is valid. University **students** will often find that their student health coverage extends for one term beyond the date of last enrollment.

Bank and charge **accounts** (particularly *American Express*) often have certain levels of medical or other insurance included. **Homeowners' or renters'** insurance may cover theft or loss of documents, money, and valuables while overseas, though exact conditions and maximum amounts vary from company to company.

SPECIALIST INSURANCE

Only after exhausting the possibilities above might you want to contact a **specialist travel insurance** company; your travel agent can

usually recommend one—*Travelguard* and *The Travelers* are good policies.

Travel insurance offerings are quite comprehensive, anticipating everything from charter companies going bankrupt to delayed (as well as lost) baggage, by way of sundry illnesses and accidents. **Premiums** vary widely—from the very reasonable ones offered primarily through student/youth agencies (though available to anyone), to those so expensive that the cost for two or three months of coverage will probably equal the cost of the worst possible combination of disasters.

A most important thing to keep in mind—and a source of major disappointment to would-be claimants—is that *none* of the currently available policies insure against **theft** of anything while overseas. North American travel policies apply only to items lost from, or damaged in, the custody of an identifiable, responsible third party, i.e. hotel porter, airline, luggage consignment, etc. Even in these cases you will still have to contact the local police to have a complete report made out so that your insurer can process the claim.

BRITISH POLICIES

If you are **transiting through Britain**, policies there cost considerably less (under £20/$32 for a month) and include routine cover for theft. You can take out a British policy at almost any travel agency or major bank. ISIS, a "student" policy but open to everyone, is reliable and fairly good value; it is operated by a company called *Endsleigh*, and is available through any student/youth travel agency.

REIMBURSEMENT

All insurance policies—American or British—work by **reimbursing you** once you return home, so be sure to keep all your receipts from doctors and pharmacists. Any thefts should immediately be reported to the nearest police station and a police report obtained; no report, no refund.

If you have had to undergo serious medical treatment, with major hospital bills, contact your consulate. They can normally arrange for an insurance company, or possibly relatives, to cover the fees, pending a claim.

MAPS AND INFORMATION

There's plenty of information published on Ireland, much of it free; before you leave it's worth contacting the nearest office of the Irish Tourist Board (*Bord Fáilte*), and/or the Northern Ireland Tourist Board.

The *Bord Fáilte* office in New York is located at 757 Third Avenue (☎212/418-0800), while the NITB can be found at 40 West 57th Street, Third Floor, New York, NY 10019 (☎212/765-5144), as well as 230 North Michigan Avenue, Chicago, Illinois 60061 (☎312/726-9356), and 625 Market

Street, San Francisco, California 94105 (☎415/957-0985). In Britain, the main *Bord Fáilte* office is at Ireland House, 150 New Bond Street, London W1Y 0AQ (☎01/439-3201), and the NITB is at 11 Berkeley Street, London W1 (☎01/493-0601).

Once in Ireland, you'll find some kind of tourist office anywhere that gets a reasonable number of tourists. Most of these are listed in the relevant sections of the guide, and again most are extremely helpful—with local maps and leaflets, as well as advice on where to stay.

MAPS

There is a great variety of road maps of Ireland, none of them adequate for much more than driving. The *Michelin* 10km=1cm map is clear, and detailed enough for cycling, but doesn't give much idea of hills. For serious hiking, tourist boards or bookshops in Ireland may have excellent maps unavailable elsewhere; in Connemara for instance, the best maps are the locally-produced *Folding Landscapes* series, available at the Galway tourist office. For the Ulster Way the route guides published by the *Sports Council for Northern Ireland* (House of Sport, Upper Malone Road, Belfast BT9 5LA; ☎0232/381-222; four sections), are invaluable.

GETTING AROUND

Travel between major centers in the Republic is generally straightforward, with reliable—albeit infrequent and slow—public transit operated by the state-supported *CIE* train and bus company (*Irish Rail* and *Bus Éireann*). There are, however, glaring anomalies, and you should never assume that two major, local towns are going to be connected. It pays to think and

plan ahead. Once off the main routes this becomes particularly important since it's quite usual for small towns and villages to be served by a couple of buses a week and no more. It can be a time-consuming and frustrating business; here, it seems, there's no such thing as a hurry, and the only way to handle it is to slow down to the local pace.

Transport in the **North** is slightly more efficient, though again infrequent in rural areas. *Ulsterbus* is generally regular and dependable, as is the (limited) train network.

TRAINS

In the **Republic** *Irish Rail* (*Iarnrod Éireann*) operates **trains** to many major cities, and towns en route; on direct lines it's by far the fastest way of covering long distances, but the network is by no means comprehensive—Donegal, for instance

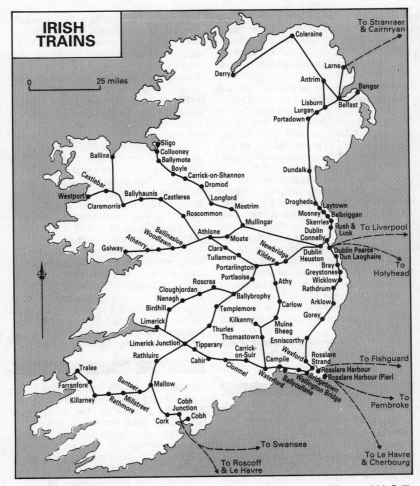

IRISH TRAINS

0   25 miles

To Stranraer & Cairnryan

Coleraine

Derry

Larne

Antrim

Bangor

Lisburn
Lurgan
Portadown

Belfast

Sligo
Collooney
Ballymote
Boyle

Ballina

Carrick-on-Shannon
Dromod

Dundalk

Castlebar

Westport
Claremorris

Ballyhaunis
Castlerea

Longford

Roscommon

Mostrim

Drogheda
Mosney
Skerries

Laytown
Balbriggan

Rush &
Lusk

To Liverpool

Ballinasloe
Woodlawn

Athlone

Mullingar

Dublin
Connelly

Athenry

Clara
Tullamore

Moate

Newbridge
Kildare

Dublin
Heuston

Dublin Pearse
Dun Laoghaire

Galway

Portarlington

Portlaoise

Athy

Bray
Greystones
Wicklow

To
Holyhead

Roscrea

Cloughjordan
Nenagh

Birdhill

Ballybrophy

Templemore

Kilkenny

Carlow

Rathdrum

Arklow
Gorey

Limerick

Thurles
Thomastown

Muine
Bheag

Enniscorthy

Limerick Junction

Rathluirc

Tipperary

Carrick-
on-Suir

Wexford

Rosslare
Strand

Cahir

Clonmel

Campile

Waterford

Bridgetown
Wellington Bridge
Ballycullane

Rosslare Harbour
Rosslare Harbour (Pier)

To Fishguard

Tralee

Farranfore

Killarney

Banteer

Millstreet
Rathmore

Mallow

Cobh
Junction

Cork

Cobh

To
Pembroke

To Swansea

To Roscoff
& Le Havre

To Le Havre
& Cherbourg

---

has no service at all. In general, rail lines fan out from Dublin, with few routes running north–south across the country. So although you can get to the west easily by train, you can't rely on the railroads if you hope to explore the west coast.

Train travel is by no means cheap either. For example, a Dublin–Galway return ticket will cost around £21 (singles from £16 on certain trains). As always, there's a complex system of peak and off-peak fares, and the time and day on which you travel can significantly affect the cost of the ticket. It's always worth asking about any special fares that may be on offer.

If you're looking for a **rail pass**, *Irish Rail's Rambler Ticket* buys unlimited rail travel on any eight days out of fifteen for £52; a fifteen-day ticket valid over thirty days costs £77. A ticket buying unlimited rail *and* bus travel in the Republic costs £66 (8 days out of 15) or £95 (15 days out of 30). For unlimited rail and bus travel throughout Ireland (North and South) an *Overlander* ticket (valid 15 days in 30) costs around £109. Unfortunately, the nature of travel in Ireland is such that you very rarely stick to your carefully drawn itinerary—thus the constraints of the rail pass may outweigh its advantages.

If you are a **student** with an *International Student Identity Card* (*ISIC*) you can buy a *Travelsave Stamp* (£7 from any *USIT* office—Dublin, Cork, Galway, Limerick, Maynooth, Waterford, Belfast, Coleraine, Jordanstown, and Derry) which entitles you to discounts of 50 percent off one-way *CIE* rail and bus tickets and 33 percent off round-trip bus and rail tickets in the Republic. These savings also apply to Dublin–Belfast rail tickets. An **under-26** *Farecard* (£8 plus passport from any *USIT* office or train station) gets you a 33 percent reduction on train fares. The cost of taking **bikes** on trains varies, but it's never more than £6 each way.

The **North** has only three short rail routes, but these are efficient and surprisingly cheap: a Belfast–Derry ticket will cost you £6.10 one-way, £8.85 round-trip; a Belfast–Dublin ticket costs £10.80 one-way, £13.80 round-trip. The *Rail Runabout Ticket* is a **rail pass** (seven days unlimited travel; summer only) costing around £27, and *Irish Overlander* tickets (as above) are available from main Northern Ireland railroad stations.

Taking a **bike** on a train is pretty cheap—a quarter of the one-way fare. If you are a student with an *ISIC* card and have bought a *Travelsave Stamp*, you'll get savings of up to 50 percent on the standard fares.

The only service **between the Republic and the North** is the non-stop Belfast–Dublin express (six each way daily, 2hr).

BUSES

CIE buses (*Dublin Buses* in the capital, *Bus Éireann* elsewhere) operate throughout the **Republic**, and are reliable, if infrequent. It's possible to travel by bus between all major towns, but the routings can be complex, involving several connections, and hence very slow. Fares are generally far lower than the train, especially during midweek—a one-way ticket bought on Tuesday, Wednesday, or Thursday gives you the return journey free (if you travel again Tues–Thurs). This system operates on short local journeys too, so it's always worth hanging on to your midweek bus tickets, even if you don't think you'll use them—they remain valid for a month. Also look out for occasional special fare offers.

A *Rambler* ticket (£49 for any 8 days out of 15; £73 for 15 days out of 30) gives unlimited bus travel throughout the Republic; **students** can also buy a *Travelsave Stamp* for large reductions (see under "Trains"). If you are going to be using

buses a lot, it makes sense to buy a **timetable** from any major bus station (around 50p), or at least to pick up the relevant information for the area you intend to explore before you leave; remote villages may only have a couple of buses a week, so knowing when they are is essential. Carrying a **bike** on a bus will cost you £4.

Private buses, which operate on many major routes, are often cheaper than *Bus Éireann*, and almost always faster. Companies, timetables, and pick-up points are listed in "Travel Details" at the end of chapters. They're very busy on weekends, so reserve ahead if you can; during the week you can usually pay on the bus. Prices for parts of their journeys are often negotiable, and bikes can be carried if booked with your seat. Some of these companies are unlicensed and have no insurance so that in the event of an accident you would not be covered: if this bothers you, ask when you book your ticket.

In the **North** *Ulsterbus* runs regular and reliable services throughout the six counties, particularly to those towns not served by the rail network. A *Freedom of Northern Ireland Ticket*, for daily (£6) or weekly (£17) unlimited travel on all scheduled *Ulsterbus* services, is available at the main bus station in Belfast, as is the 15-day *Overlander* ticket (see above), valid on all Irish bus and rail services except Belfast *Citybus* services.

DRIVING

Uncongested roads in the **Republic** make driving a very relaxing option—if you can afford the IR£2.80 per gallon for gas. The national speed limit is 55mph/88kph, except where posted otherwise. Front-seat occupants must wear seat belts, and motor cyclists and their passengers must wear helmets. In remote areas wandering cattle, unmarked junctions, and appallingly potholed minor roads are all potential dangers, particularly for motorbikes. Other hazards to watch out for include drunk drivers late at night; despite high accident rates, the police have a lax attitude, and little seems to be done about the problem.

Ireland is very slowly converting to metric measures, and on the main roads the new (green) signs are in **kilometers**. In rural areas, however, you'll find mostly the old black-and-white fingerpost signs in miles. Most people continue to think and talk in miles too. There is also such a thing as an "Irish mile"—shorter than the standard imperial one—though this is rare and found only on very old signposts. You drive on the left.

Only occasional filling stations stock **unleaded gasoline**, so if you're going to need it, pick up a list of where they are from a major tourist office. In all large towns a **disc parking** system is in operation: discs can be bought at newsstands and have to be displayed on the vehicle when parked in a designated area. The *Automobile Association* has offices in Dublin (☎01-779481), and in Cork (☎021-505155), and they're the people to call for any driving queries.

Large international **car rental** companies such as *Hertz* have outlets in all the major cities, airports and ferry terminals: they're expensive at around IR£340 a week, although if you book in advance all sorts of special offers apply which can come close to halving this price. If you haven't booked, then the smaller local firms can almost always offer better deals. Some companies insist you have held a full, valid, endorsement-free driving licence for two years, some for one year. Generally only drivers over the age of 23 are eligible to rent a car, though for some of the larger companies, this age limit is lowered to 21 years. If you intend to drive **across the border**, you should inform your rental company beforehand to check that you are fully insured.

If you do cross the border, note that there are twenty **approved border crossing points**, marked on all recent road maps. Although it is possible to drive across in other places, you are strongly advised to use these.

Roads in the **North** are in general notably superior to those in the Republic. Driving is on the left and rules of the road are as in mainland Britain. Cars bearing large red 'R' (Restricted) plates identify drivers who have passed their driving test within the past 12 months and are meant to keep to low speeds. Most towns have "**control zones**" in the center, indicated by prominent yellow signs: "Control zone—no unattended parking." These are to prevent car-bombs being left in busy commercial and populated areas. A parked car in a control zone is considered a security risk (and likely to be blown up by police) unless someone is sitting in it. **Gasoline prices** in the North are much the same as in Britain—far cheaper than in the Republic at around £1.80 a gallon.

Renting a car in the North involves much the same cost and age restrictions as in the Republic. There are far fewer outlets, but rental is available in all the major cities, Belfast airport, and Larne ferry terminal. Again, the cheapest deals are reserved ahead, and here too you must inform the rental company if you plan to cross the border.

HITCHING

The **Republic** has to be one of the easiest countries in Europe to hitch in; for locals it's almost as normal as using the buses and trains, and for the visitor the human contact makes it one of the best ways to get to know the country. Knowing the shortcomings of public transportation, many drivers readily give lifts, and it's not unusual to see single women with babies and shopping, or whole families waiting for a ride. The chief problem is a lack of traffic, especially off the main roads, and in the tourist-swamped areas of the west, you may find a reluctance to pick up foreigners. That said, without transportation of your own you may well *have* to hitch if you want to see the best of Ireland's wild, remote places.

Women shouldn't be lulled into naive notions of security. The Irish women who hitch alone know what cars they should and should not get into. Chances are you'll get lifts easily and be subjected to no more than a reactionary discussion about marriage and divorce; but no hitching is risk-free, and you can be unlucky anywhere. If you're hitching alone (though it's best not to), simply remember that you don't have to get in a car just because it stops for you.

The best way to hitch in the **North** is to look like a tourist. Even then, it's never easy. Men traveling alone or in pairs are viewed with suspicion, and may find it impossible to get a lift. Once in the car, you can expect conversation at some time to come around to the Troubles; most people want to know how their situation is viewed from outside the country. Be cautious in your response; even if you think you have managed to ascertain where the owner of the car stands on the subject, as with all social encounters in the North, you can never be sure who you are talking to. Someone else's car is the last place you want to get into a political argument. Getting a lift **across the border** can be very difficult since it's risky for both hitcher and driver. There is the possibility of getting a ride from someone who is under military observation—which could bring you under surveillance throughout your stay.

BICYCLING

If you are lucky enough to get decent weather, bicycling is one of the most enjoyable ways to see Ireland, ensuring you're continually in touch with the landscape. Roads are generally empty, though very poor surfaces may slow you down.

If you don't want to cycle long distances, it's easy and relatively cheap to **rent a bike** in most towns in the **Republic**, and at a limited number of places in the **North** (many outlets are listed in the text); you can't take a rented bike across the border. *Raleigh*, which operates a national rental scheme, are the biggest distributors (£6 per day, £25 per week plus around £30 deposit; collection and delivery service £6–10; in the North £5 a day, £22 a week); but local dealers (including some hostels) are often less expensive. Wherever you rent your bike, it makes sense quickly to check the tires and brakes, and request a pump and repair kit before you set off. You should also consider the terrain: if you plan on mountain riding, make sure your machine has enough gears to cope.

At high season it's best to collect a bike early in the day (or reserve it the day before) as supplies frequently run out. If you arrive with your own bike, it's easy to carry it long distances by train or bus. Finally, a problem you may encounter— particularly in the west—is that of farmers' dogs chasing and snarling at your wheels. Should you be fortunate enough to be heading downhill at the time, freewheeling silently past cottages and farm entrances is perhaps the only humane way of minimizing the risk of savaged wheels.

SLEEPING

The cheapest way to sleep in Ireland, as anywhere, is to camp, though here the distinct possibility of continual rain somewhat detracts from its appeal. You'll also find that some of the terrain is very tricky— especially the areas of bog and rock in Clare, Galway, Mayo, and Donegal. Next on the list, in terms of price, come hostels. These vary a lot, but all offer the essential basics of a bed and somewhere to wash and to cook, and some are very good indeed. Above these, in more or less the following order, come bed and breakfasts, guesthouses, town houses, country houses, and hotels, all officially graded by the tourist boards on a set formula which, most of the time, gives a fair idea of what to expect.

CAMPING

The cost of staying on **organized campgrounds** varies—from about £1–6 a night depending on the facilities, the number of people sharing etc.— but unless you want washing facilities, shops and the like, there is rarely any need to use them. There's usually no problem if you ask to camp in a field, and in out-of-the-way places nobody minds where you pitch a tent (the only place you definitely can't camp is in a state forest—but these are usually dark pine woods anyhow). The farmer may ask you for a pound or two if his field happens to be in a heavily touristed region such as Kerry, and if there's an organized site nearby you'll probably be directed to it, but other than this, expect to camp for free. Should you want a site, they're included in the Guide, and it's worth knowing that most hostels will let you camp on their land, and the overnight price may well include the use of kitchen facilities and showers.

Whatever your budget, remember that in **July and August** the big tourist centers get booked up well in advance, and during **festivals** things get even more hectic. For the really big festivals—like the *Fleadh de Cheoil* and the Cork Jazz Festival—there's often an extra accommodation office to cope with the overload, but you may still end up sleeping in a different town, or perhaps just reveling your way through to morning. The less famous festivals can be equally difficult for the spontaneous traveler. Since festivals take place all over Ireland throughout the summer, it's worth checking out where and when they are before you head off—see box on p.21.

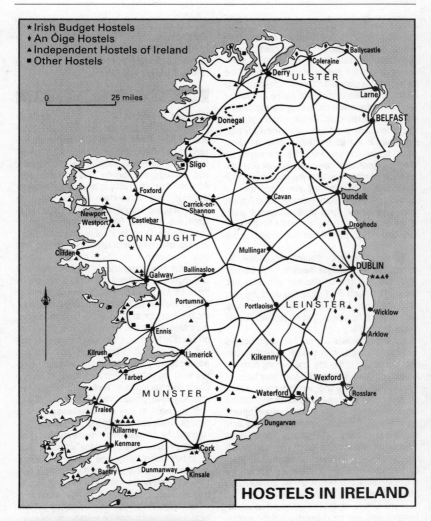

★Irish Budget Hostels
♦An Óige Hostels
▲Independent Hostels of Ireland
■Other Hostels

0 ——— 25 miles

HOSTELS IN IRELAND

HOSTELS

Until recently staying in hostels in Ireland meant—as it does almost anywhere else—subjecting yourself to the strictly disciplined regime of **An Óige** (the official Irish Youth Hostel Association) or the **Youth Hostel Association of Northern Ireland**. In recent years, however, the growth in the Republic of the **Independent Hostel Owners** group and **Budget Hostels**, both run along far more relaxed lines, has opened up cheap and attractive alternatives. As well as having traditional dormitory accommodation, an increasing number of the independent hostels have private double and family rooms. You can rent a sheet sleeping bag at most hostels, but if you are going to be using them extensively, it makes sense to take your own.

In the **Republic**, Independent and Budget hostels have the best of the cheap accommodation. **Independent hostels** are all privately owned, and they're all different, each reflecting the character and interests of the owner. Some are on organic farms, some are tucked away in such beautiful countryside that they're worth staying in for the setting alone. Very often the atmosphere is cosy and informal: you can stay in all day if you want and there are no curfews or chores. On the downside, such is their popularity that some hostels cram people in to the point of discomfort. July and August are particularly bad, especially in the major cities and on the west coast, as are festival times. If you're relying on them it's worth phoning ahead to check what the situation is; most won't let you reserve over the phone, but some may hold you a bed up to a certain time in the early evening. Some hostels offer **bike rental**, some **food**: details are given in the text. Expect to pay around £4 for a dormitory bed; £5–6 per person for private rooms where available.

Similarly informal, though not always as homey, are the **budget hostels**. The best of these are very comfortable and efficiently run, the worst, though *Bord Fáilte* approved, are cold and impersonal. Again, there are no membership requirements, no chores, and no curfews. Expect to pay around £4.

An Óige hostels are run like youth hostels throughout Europe, with shared "duties", premises closed during the day, and evening curfews. At least officially. In fact you'll find many far more flexible than the rule book would suggest, particularly in out-of-the-way places. Once again, some are worth visiting simply for the location; others, especially in the mountains, may be the only places you *can* stay. International Youth Hostel Association Membership (also valid for YHANI membership in the North) is required at most hostels, costing £7.50. If transiting via Britain, you can contact the *YHA* at 14 Southampton Street, London WC2; ☎01/836-1036.

If you turn up at an *An Óige* hostel as a non-member, you will be charged a nightly supplement of £1.25, which accumulates so that after paying six such supplements you become a full member. On top of this the Dublin hostels charge £6.50 October to May (non-members £7), £7 June and September (£7.50), £7.50 July to August (£8). Hostels outside the capital are graded A, B, and C, and charge accordingly: October to May £4.30, £3.80, and £3 respectively; June to September £4.90, £4.30, and £3.50. *An Óige* also offer special accommodation and travel deals, which

you should ask for details of on arrival: a "one night stopover," for instance, buys you one night's accommodation and a single rail journey to any destination in the Republic for £14.50 (£16.50 if you are in Dublin).

B&B, GUESTHOUSES, AND HOTELS

Bed and breakfast accommodation, available throughout Ireland, is the next most affordable option. B&Bs vary enormously, but most are welcoming, warm, and clean, with huge breakfasts including cereal, massive fry-ups of bacon, egg, sausage, and tomato, plus tea and toast. Afternoon tea can usually be arranged, and can be delicious, with home-made scones and soda bread—costing around £3–4. *Bord Fáilte* registered and approved B&Bs are generally pretty good, though it's not an absolute guarantee. Don't assume that non-registered places will be less good—inclusion in the official guide is voluntary, and a fair few simply choose not to bother. You can expect to pay from around £10 per person (from £8 for non-registered houses) and out of season you may be able to negotiate bed without the breakfast for as little as £6. Reservations for registered B&Bs can be made through tourist offices (50p for local, £1.50 long distance), or you can do it yourself. Many phone numbers and addresses are given in the text of this guide, but if you want the complete list then buy *Bord Fáilte's Guest Accommodation* book (£2), which has comprehensive, graded lists of B&Bs and hotels.

If you want to stay in a **farmhouse**, or in a cottage, these can be arranged through the tourist board; for all their simple rooms and turf fires, almost all "Rent-an-Irish-Cottage" cottages cluster in tiny tourist villages, so it's worth checking out exactly what the set-up is if you're after real solitude. **Hotels** are generally more expensive but not always. Certainly if you get stuck in a small village it's always worth checking out any local hotels, which may be surprisingly inexpensive. Virtually all hotels have bars and provide meals to residents and non-residents alike.

Bed and breakfast accommodation is far less prominent in the **North**, and you will need to phone ahead if you want to guarantee somewhere to stay during the summer months. Addresses and phone numbers for B&Bs in all of the main centers are given in the Guide, while the Northern Ireland Tourist Board's *All the Places to Stay* gives extensive, highly detailed lists.

EATING AND DRINKING

One thing you won't be going to Ireland for is a wonderful gastronomic experience. The country has no real tradition of eating out, and the food you'll find as a traveler will tend to be (at best) simple and hearty. Often the best bet is to fill up with a good pub lunch in the middle of the day, and concentrate on drinking in the evening—few pubs serve food at night.

MEAT AND POTATOES

Irish food is generally highly meat-orientated, and you don't have to be a vegetarian to find this becomes wearing after a while. For carnivores, there's nothing wrong with Irish meat—steaks, in particular, are excellent—but after a while you do begin to long for some variety in your diet, and for something which hasn't been fried.

If you're staying in B&Bs, it's almost impossible to avoid the "traditional" Irish **breakfast** of sausages, bacon, and eggs, although this usually comes accompanied by generous quantities of delicious soda bread. Pub **lunch** staples are usually meat and two vegetables, with plenty of gravy, although you can almost always get freshly made sandwiches (sometimes excellent, but often sliced white and processed cheese) and a sustaining soup as well. Most larger towns have good, simple **cafés** (open daytimes only) where you can get soup, sandwiches, cakes, and the ubiquitous apple pie as well as slightly more ambitious and filling dishes. In the North in particular, they all seem to serve enormous portions of meat and thoroughly overcooked

vegetables that will ground you for the rest of the afternoon. It's worth remembering that **hotels** are obliged to offer food to all comers—so you can always find a sandwich and a cup of coffee, at any reasonable hour; you can generally order a plate of sandwiches and a pot of tea in pubs, too.

Many traditional Irish dishes are based on the **potato** and, all jokes aside (like the one that describes an Irish five-course meal: four pints of Guinness and a potato), you do get an awful lot of them—often served up in several different forms in the same meal. Potato cakes can be magnificent—a flour and potato dough fried in butter—as can potato soup. **Irish stew** of varying quality will be available almost everywhere; and **colcannon**, cooked potatoes fried in butter with onions and cabbage, or leeks, can also be very good. Colcannon is a traditional dish for Hallowe'en, as is **barm brack**, a sweet yeast-bread with spices and dried fruits in which a gold ring is traditionally concealed; the person who finds the ring in their slice of barm brack will be the next to marry.

Much is made of Ireland's recent **gastronomic revolution**, but in practice you're likely to find that its effects are restricted to the more expensive restaurants. Far more noticeable is the **fast-food** revolution, which has brought kebabs and burgers everywhere—old-fashioned fish and chips are always a safer bet. For the occasional binge, however, there are some very good **seafood restaurants**, particularly along the west coast, serving freshly caught seafood and, often, home-grown vegetables. Irish **oysters** are famous; the season opens with a grand oyster festival at Clarinridge on Galway Bay. **Salmon** and trout can also be fabulous, but be warned that they may not be all they seem, especially away from the coast: fish-farming is becoming big business in Ireland, and your fish may have spent all its life in cages and be pumped full of hormones.

Some **guesthouses**, particularly if they're historic buildings, serve very good food, in what can be very grand surroundings. **Health-food** restaurants or cafés are very thin on the ground outside Dublin, Belfast, and the more tourist-influenced areas in the west; some of the hostels here have very good, locally-grown food. We've included them in the Guide, where they exist; but if you really want to avoid traditional food, you're better off staying in hostels where you can cook for yourself.

Cooking for yourself, at least some of the time, may in fact be the best option. Produce available in Ireland is limited in range—you won't find any exotic fruit or vegetables—but generally excellent. Irish potatoes, cabbages, and carrots are delicious (though surprisingly hard to buy in rural areas, where people grow their own); meat is very good; bread and scones are wonderful; and if you're traveling around the coast, you can often buy seafood very cheaply direct from the fishermen. Sometimes you'll be able to find more unusual things in this way—spider crabs and monkfish, for example—that you would never find in local fish shops; it's generally all exported. In many places you can gather your own mussels from the rocks too—but be sure to check locally in case there's a sewage outlet nearby.

Dairy products, especially cheese, can also be excellent. The past decade has seen a revolution in the Irish cheese business, which now produces delicious, often unpasteurized cheeses such as Cashel Blue. There's no need to go to a smart restaurant for these—you can often find them in grocery stores, alongside freshly baked soda bread. Fill up with this, and you're unlikely to need to eat again for at least half a day. **Cream** is also served everywhere, with everything.

PUBS

To travel through Ireland without visiting a **pub** would be to miss out on a huge chunk of Irish life. Especially in rural areas, the pub is far more than just a place to drink. It's the social and conversational heart of any Irish village, and often the political and cultural center too. If you're after food, advice, or company, the pub is almost always the place to head for; and very often they'll be the venues for local entertainment too, especially traditional and not-so-traditional music (see "Festivals and Entertainment," following).

Along with Mass and market day, the pub is the center of Irish social activity: a cliché, perhaps, but one that wears very well. Talking is an important business here, and drink is the great lubricant of social discourse. Even so, it doesn't pay to arrive with too romantic a notion of what this actually means. Away from the cities and the touristed west coast, there are plenty of miserable, dingy bars where the only spark of conviviality is the dull glow of the TV. But in major cities you'll find bars heaving with life (they're actually very similar to English pubs), and out in remote country villages it can be great fun drinking among the fig

rolls and trifle sponges of the ancient grocery shops-cum-bars you'll find dotted around.

While women will always be treated with genuine (unreconstructed) civility, it's true to say that most bars are a predominantly male preserve. In the evening, especially, women travelers can expect occasional unwanted attention, though this rarely amounts to anything too unpleasant. Should your first encounters be bad ones, persist—the good nights will come, and will probably rank amongst the most memorable experiences of your trip.

In the Republic, **opening hours** are 10am–11:30pm from Monday to Saturday (12:30–2pm and 4–10pm on Sun); some pubs, especially in the cities, may close for a couple of hours in the afternoon ("holy hour"), while illegal lock-ins remain something of an after-hours institution in rural parts. In the North pubs are open Monday to Saturday 11:30am–11pm, but are closed altogether on Sunday (though you may be able to find a drink in a hotel bar).

DRINKS

The classic Irish drink is of course **Guinness** ("a Guinness" is a pint; if you want a half of any beer, ask for "a glass") which, as anybody will tell you, is simply not the same as the drink marketed as Guinness outside Ireland. For one thing, good Guinness has to be kept properly, something non-Irish pubs abroad tend not to do; it has to be poured gradually (you don't pour a pint, you build one—the ultimate gaffe in a pub is to ask them to hurry this process); and even across Ireland you'll taste differences—it's best in Dublin where it's brewed. A proper pint of Irish Guinness is a dream, far less heavy than you may be used to, though still a considerable, filling drink. Other local stouts, like *Beamish* and *Murphy's* (a Cork stout, far sweeter and creamier), make for interesting comparison; they all have their faithful adherents.

If you want a pint of English-style **bitter**, then try *Smithwicks*; and, of course, **lager** is also increasingly popular—mostly *Harp* (made by Guinness) or *Heineken*. Whatever your tipple, you're likely to find drinking in Ireland an expensive business at around IR£1.40 a pint.

Irish **whiskeys**—try *Paddy's, Powers* or, from the North, *Bushmills*—also seem expensive, but at least the measures are large. If you've come in from the cold you can have your whiskey served warm with cloves and lemon. Asking for Scotch in an Irish pub is asking for trouble, and in any case anyone here will tell you that the Irish version is infinitely superior.

Non-alcoholic drinks are limited to the usual soft drinks and bottled fruit juices, but,

unless the bar is extremely busy, you can always get **coffee** (served with a dollop of full cream) or **tea**. You can usually get **Irish coffee** too (with whiskey and cream), which is delicious if not very traditional—it was invented at Shannon airport.

COMMUNICATIONS: POST, PHONES, AND MEDIA

Ireland can often seem isolated when you're trying to get in touch with home. Mail from the Republic, especially, is notoriously unreliable; if you have anything important or urgent to say, best do it by phone.

PHONES

In towns throughout Ireland you'll find fully automatic **payphones** in booths; instructions for use are on display, and internal and international calls can easily be made. A local call costs 10p minimum but, as you might imagine, long-distance daytime calls are expensive. International calls are cheapest if dialled direct, or after 8pm. In rural areas in the Republic you

may well come across the old-style 'button A' telephones. To operate these insert a minimum of 10p and dial the number. When you get a reply, press button A—this will cause the machine to swallow the coin; if you can't get through, press button B and the coin will be returned. These phones only accept 5p and 10p pieces, and are fairly useless for international calls. If you make calls from a hotel or the like, expect a hefty premium charged on top of the normal price.

Dialing the Republic from the North is, peculiarly, not the same as dialling the Republic from mainland Britain (except in the case of Dublin, for which the code from both is 0001), and you'll have to check in the local phonebook or call Directory Enquiries.

MAIL

Mail to or from the Republic is slow and unreliable, and parcels sent to the country seem to have little better than a 50 percent chance of reaching their destination. If it's something important, it's worth spending the extra for recorded or registered mail. To send a letter within Ireland (and to all other EC countries) costs 28p, postcards 24p; to anywhere else in the world, the surface mail letters charge is 30p, postcards 28p; airmail postage costs 39p. Main post offices are open Monday to Saturday 9am–5:30pm. Mail from the North is more efficient. Letters and postcards travel for 20p first class anywhere in the EC, between 32p and 37p for the rest of the world.

OPERATOR SERVICES

In the Republic:	In the North:
Operator ☎10	Operator ☎100
Directory Enquiries ☎190	Directory Enquires ☎192
Long Distance Calls ☎10	Long Distance Calls ☎100
International Calls ☎114	International Calls ☎155
Telegrams ☎115	Telegrams ☎190/193

MEDIA

The most widely read **papers** in the Republic are the *Irish Times*, the *Irish Press*, and the *Irish Independent*—good, but remarkably slim, they really bring home just how small (and conservative) the population is. There are also lots of local and regional papers which can be useful for checking on what's happening in your area. British newspapers are generally available the same day in Dublin and other cities.

In the North, all the British papers are sold: based in Belfast is also the *Belfast Telegraph*, the biggest-selling evening paper in the North, which attempts to steer a middle course in terms of Northern Irish politics. The morning papers are the *Irish News*, read by the Nationalist community, and the loyalist *News Letter*, which is a tabloid.

In the Republic, *RTE* (*Radio Telefís Éireann*) runs two state-sponsored **television** channels and two radio stations; both services are imaginatively known as RTE1 and RTE2. Programming on all of them is, for the most part, fairly dull. In the north and east you can also pick up programs from Britain (or the North). You'll find more interesting fare on local radio stations around the country (including all Gaelic stations in Connemara and tiny Ring, County Waterford)—worth tuning in to for the traditional music and for insights into local issues. In the North you get the BBC and *Ulster Television*, and you can also pick up plenty of broadcasts from the South.

FESTIVALS AND ENTERTAINMENT

A festival in Ireland is never a half-hearted affair. Whatever the pretext for the celebration, it's always also an excuse for serious partying. Well established ones like the Cork Jazz Festival and the Wexford Opera Festival are big international events, and getting tickets for top performances can be well nigh impossible without advance planning—but if you fail to get into the concert you came for, chances are you'll stumble across wild merriment in some poky bar nearby.

The very word 'festival' seems to act as a magnet for all sorts of musicians, and many events are wonderfully overwhelming—no matter what the size of the town, there's rarely enough room for all that's going on, with music and dancing bursting out of the official forums into surrounding streets and bars. The biggest of the annual events are listed here, but pick up a calendar of events at any major tourist office and you'll soon get a picture of the huge range of celebrations.

MUSIC

The most enjoyable aspect of Irish festivals—sheer exuberance apart—is probably the **traditional music**. Many festivals (known as *Fleadh*) are devoted almost exclusively to this: the biggest of them is the *Fleadh Cheoil Nah Éireann* (see box), which includes the finals of the All Ireland music and dance contests.

However, you don't have to go to a festival to experience this; music in Irish **pubs** is similarly legendary, and again there's a huge range to experience, only a relatively small proportion of it "traditional." **Country and western**, for example, is extremely popular, and there are a frightening number of middle-of-the-road pop bands lurking in country areas, with regular country-and-western nights at pubs across Ireland. **Ballads** are another well-developed Irish music form. The term "ballad" is a bit of a catch-all, and open to countless interpretations—it's generally some form of dull crooning, and essentially middle-aged in spirit. Brace yourself for the worst, and from time to time you'll be very pleasantly surprised.

The best of pub music, however, has to be the **traditional folk sessions** of fiddles, accordions, *bodhran* (a drum), and singing. Interest from abroad and tourism have a lot to do with the resurgence of this musical culture—but this hardly matters, since the music can be phenomenal. The west coast (especially around Clare and Galway) has the best of the traditional scene. Pointers as to where to find sessions are given in the text, but really the locations of the best sessions are hard to pin down. The thing to do is to ask around and keep your ears open for local tips.

Traditionally Sunday evening was the night for sessions—a throwback to restrictions on holy days that meant partying on Saturday had to stop at midnight—but Friday and Saturday are becoming equally important, and you may find something happening any night of the week. Things generally don't get going till late, and a bar that's still empty at 10pm may be a riot of music by half-past. While it's all extremely convivial and relaxed, if you're a musician yourself and want to join in, then do so tactfully. The first thing to do is sit and listen for a while—to make sure you can play to a high enough standard—and then work out who the leader is and ask. If you're not playing, don't crowd the musicians; the empty seats around them are for others who may join in.

Comhaltas Ceoltoiri Éireann is an organization that exists purely to promote traditional music and culture, and evenings organized by them (not always in bars), though by their nature not spontaneous, are well worth looking out for. Run by real enthusiasts, the standard of playing is usually pretty high.

SPORT

Fishing attracts many people to Ireland, and there really are superb opportunities for virtually every form, from seasonal salmon- and trout-angling on the rivers, to coarse fishing in the Loughs and deep-sea-fishing all year round. Both *Bord Fáilte* and the NITB publish detailed leaflets on fishing, including the best times and places and how and where to apply for permits.

Other big participatory sports are also mostly water-based (unless you count **pony-trekking**, easily arranged in most of the bigger tourist centers). Sailing, and especially **windsurfing**, are both increasingly popular. Small dinghies can often be rented in seaside resorts and—as long as you have a wetsuit—there is magnificent windsurfing all around the coast, and several new windsurfing centers. For details of these write to the *Irish Board Sailing Association*, 5 East Beach, Cobh, County Cork (☎021-811237).

As for watching, **horseracing** is a national obsession, constantly on the TV and enormously popular live too. The biggest races are mostly at

---

MAJOR ANNUAL FESTIVALS AND EVENTS

Saint Patrick's Day (March 17): celebrations in all the big cities for several days roundabout.

Irish Grand National (April): horseracing at Fairyhouse (Meath).

Cork International Choral and Folk Dance Festival (April/May): one of the big ones.

Killarney Pan Celtic Week (May): traditional music and traditional sports.

Irish FA Cup Final (May): climax of the soccer year, in Dublin.

An Fleadh Nua (May): traditional music, song and dance in Ennis (Clare).

Festival of Music in Great Irish Houses (June): just what it says, at mansions around the country.

Listowel Writers' Week (June): literary festival at Listowel (Cork).

Irish Derby (July): and other important race meets at the Curragh (Kildare).

Rose of Tralee International Festival (August): another big one, with a beauty contest as its (rotten) heart.

Fleadh Cheoil na Éireann (August): the most important of all the traditional music festivals; currently held in Sligo, the venue changes regularly.

Kilkenny International Arts Week (August): includes recitals, poetry readings, art exhibitions.

Lisdoonvarna Matchmaking Festival (September): plenty of traditional entertainment accompanies the lonelyhearts side.

All Ireland Hurling Final (September): the biggest event of the hurling year, in Dublin.

Cork Jazz and Film Festival (September/October): actually two separate events, but they often run into one another. Enormously popular.

Wexford Opera Festival (October): another really big one, of international renown.

courses around Dublin—in counties Kildare and Meath—during the summer; it's worth going for the atmosphere alone. Even more fun, perhaps, are local events at festivals—races along the beach, for example—where both horses and riders may be amateurs.

Other traditional sports—**hurling** and **Gaelic football**—also remain tremendously well-supported. Even if you don't understand a thing to begin with, the atmosphere of the big games is again at least as much an attraction as the sports themselves. Irish **rugby** is in something of a decline at the moment, though still wholeheartedly physical, while **soccer** is on the ascendant, inspired by qualification for the finals of the 1990 World Cup.

OPENING HOURS AND HOLIDAYS

Business and shop opening hours, North and South, are approximately 9am–5:30pm, Monday to Saturday, with a smattering of late openings (usually Thurs or Fri) and half days.

In the South, however, particularly once you get away from the bigger towns, hours tend to be more varied, with later opening and closing times. In rural areas, though, you can generally find someone to sell you groceries at any reasonable hour, even if they have to open their shop to do it—and very often the village shop doubles as the local pub. For banking hours see "Costs, Money, and Banks."

There's no pattern to the opening hours of **museums, archaeological sites,** and the like, though most are closed for at least one day a week. Wherever possible, hours are listed in the guide. The bigger attractions are normally open all day, while smaller places may open only in the afternoon. Many sites off the main tourist trails—especially houses which are also private homes—are open only during the summer. **Churches**, at least if they're still in use, are almost always open, and if they're locked there's usually someone living nearby (often the priest himself) who has a key; otherwise, opening times follow religious activity fairly closely.

PUBLIC HOLIDAYS

In the Republic:	In the North:
New Year's Day	**New Year's Day**
St Patrick's Day, March 17	**St Patrick's Day**, March 17
Good Friday	**Good Friday**
Easter Monday	**Easter Monday**
First Monday in June	May 1
First Monday in August	Last Monday in May
Last Monday in October	**Orange Day**, July 12
Christmas Day	Last Monday in August
December 26 (**Boxing Day** to Protestants,	**Christmas Day**
St Stephen's Day to Catholics)	December 26

SECURITY AND THE POLICE

The Republic has to be one of the safest countries in Europe to travel in. You might be robbed on the street in Dublin—the city has a big heroin problem and a lot of poverty—but beyond this nothing much is likely to happen to you. In the North, of

course, the problems are very different, and security will never be far from your awareness. You need to be careful where you go, and when. Nonetheless personal security, and crimes against the individual, are less of a problem.

POLICE

In the Republic, people generally have a healthy indifference to law and red tape, perhaps in part a vestige of pre-Independence days, when any dealings with the police smacked of collusion with the British. The **police**—known as **Garda** or **Gardai** (pronounced "gar-dee")—accordingly have a low profile. In rural areas the low level of crime is such that policing is minimal and, should you need them, you might spend an entire afternoon waiting for the Garda to arrive. If you have any dealings with the Garda at all, the chances are you'll find them affable enough.

In the **North** the **Royal Ulster Constabulary** (RUC) deal with all general civic policing, and are the people you should go to if in difficulties. Security at police stations is tight and they're generally covered in barbed wire. The North is subject to British law and heavily policed, with several "emergency measures" permanently in effect that seriously restrict personal freedom. You may well find yourself being quizzed about where you are going, what you are doing, and so forth, especially in border areas. Be cooperative and polite and you should have no difficulties. Again, whatever their reputation, you'll find that the RUC are helpful enough in matters of everyday police activity. The emergency number in both North and South is ☎**999**.

SECURITY IN THE NORTH

If you are British or Irish it's likely you'll have a strong response to the sight of **British troops**, tanks, and weaponry on the streets in the North. Like the police, armed soldiers may stop and question you. Whatever your thoughts on the presence of the army, it really isn't a good idea to share them with the soldier on the street. Travelers from the Republic may experience more troublesome dealings with both the RUC and the army, as anyone with an Irish accent will tell you. All you are obliged to tell the army is your name, address, date of birth, and where you're going. The more open you are with them, of course, the less likely you are to have trouble; but in certain areas you may want to weigh against this the fact that appearing to be on good terms with the army will not endear you to the local population.

Road checks are common—tedious, but nothing to worry about. **Crossing the border** into the Republic, you *must* use official border crossing points, marked on all up-to-date maps, and clearly signposted. Security is such that there are no public places to leave luggage anywhere in the North, and you should never leave baggage unattended. All towns and cities, and even some small villages, have **security zones**, areas in which it is illegal to leave an unattended parked car. It is also illegal to take **photographs** of police barracks and army installations.

SEXUAL HARASSMENT, PREJUDICE, AND RACISM

For women Ireland is wonderfully relaxing: the outlandish sexism of Irish society manifests itself in a male courtesy that can range from the genuine and delightful to the downright insufferable, but you are unlikely to experience any really threatening behavior. Most uncomfortable situations can be defused by a straightforward, firm response.

This said, don't believe the general view that *nothing* can happen to you. Talk to men and they will tell you that serious sexual assaults never happen; talk to women and you'll realize they do. It is worth remembering that outside the cities, communities are very small, and local women you see hitching alone do so in safety because they know and are known by just about everybody on the road. Foreign travelers don't have that added security and, though very unlikely, you could be

unlucky. In the case of serious assault, if possible contact a rape crisis center before going to the police (telephone numbers are given in chapter listings). Attacks are rare and, though well-meaning, the Garda have little experience of handling distressed women.

Blacks and **gays** have a less easy time of it. The Republic of Ireland, and, to an extent, the rural North, are fiercely conservative, shamefully intolerant of minority groups. If you are black you may well experience a peculiarly naive brand of ignorant racism. Open comment on the color of a person's skin isn't uncommon outside the major cities, especially in the remote west, where people simply aren't used to seeing blacks.

The gay community is both the biggest and least visible minority in Ireland. Although nominally part of the UK, Northern Ireland was excluded from the 1967 Act that legalised homosexuality for consenting adults in Britain. This led one individual to take his case to the European Court of Human Rights in 1982, which brought the legal status of gays in Northern Ireland into line with the rest of the UK. In the Republic, homosexuality is still illegal, denying over 250,000 Irish citizens the most basic rights to a full emotional and social life. Encouraged by the Northern Irish gay community's success, activists are hopeful that similar legislation for the Republic is not far off. Meanwhile, intolerance is not just a product of the legislators—daily bigotry is rife and public displays of affection are out of the question.

DIRECTORY

BAGGAGE In the North, because of the security situation, there are no left luggage facilities, and you should never leave your bags unattended. In the Republic, most big city bus and train stations will have lockers or a luggage consignment.

BRING Most things you really need you'll be able to buy. Remember, though, to take warm clothes and rain gear; a flashlight is useful for exploring dingy churches and archaeological sites, as is a compass if you plan to do any serious walking; a sheet sleeping bag is pretty essential if you're using a lot of hostels; and film is relatively expensive in the Republic.

CONTRACEPTIVES Throughout Ireland anyone over 18 can buy condoms at pharmacies (though in the Republic, where legal contraception was only recently introduced, you may still find places which don't sell them—or don't approve); the pill is available on prescription only.

DEPARTURE TAX A £5 departure tax is payable on leaving the Republic—it's normally paid when you buy your plane or boat ticket.

ELECTRICITY In the Republic, electricity is 220V AC, in the North 240V AC. Plugs everywhere are British-style three square pins (just occasionally you may still find old round ones).

EMERGENCIES For police or ambulance ☎999 throughout Ireland.

KIDS Large families are still the norm in most of Ireland, and consequently it's relatively easy to travel with kids. Baby supplies are sold everywhere, and children are (generally) welcome at B&Bs, in pubs, and almost anywhere else you're likely to go.

LAUNDROMATS You'll find laundromats only in the bigger towns and on large trailer-parks/campgrounds; hostels, though, will often have a washing machine for residents' use, and at many B&Bs they'll do your washing for you. Elsewhere it's worth buying a tube of *Travel Wash*—designed to be used in hotel washbasins—which makes a lot less mess than powder.

TAMPONS Widely available at pharmacies throughout Ireland, but expensive.

TAX In the North, Value Added Tax (VAT) at 15 percent will be added to all your bills; in the Republic VAT rates vary for different goods—up to a hefty 23 percent. If you're buying a lot of souvenirs to take home, you can claim this back. Either have the shop send the goods out of the country for you (in which case no tax is paid), or ask for a special VAT receipt when you buy, take this to customs on your way out of the country, and send the receipt they give you back to the shop for your refund (less commission).

TOILETS Public toilets are reasonably common in the big towns, and generally acceptably clean, if no more. Or you can pop into the local pub, and have a drink while you're there. The Gaelic labels to look out for are *Fir* (Men) and *Mna* (Women).

TIME Irish time, both in the North and in the Republic, is five to eight hours ahead of the contiguous USA. Daylight savings is observed from the end of March through the end of October.

PART TWO

THE

GUIDE

CHAPTER ONE

DUBLIN AND AROUND

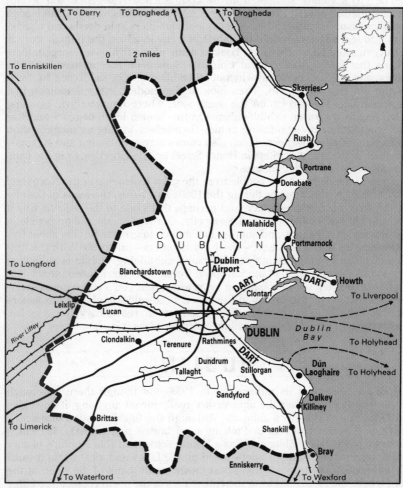

Dublin, however much its inhabitants may complain about the city's provincialism, is emphatically Ireland's capital, a splendidly monumental city clustered on the banks of the River Liffey. Approaching by sea, you'll have an opportunity to appreciate the magnificent physical setting before you're plunged into the reality of the urban sprawl; with the fine sweep of Dublin Bay, and the Wicklow Mountains providing an exhilarating backdrop to the south. The moment of actual arrival is generally less dramatic—the first thing you're likely to see is the less exciting suburbs, whether you're coming from the harbors of Dún Laoghaire or Dublin Port to the east, or from the airport to the north.

The city's vitality springs from its contradictions: elegance and wealth against glaring poverty, youthful energy against bleak economics and leaden traditionalism. In pubs and cafés, eloquent Dubliners spin deeds and characters into legends, woven into the fabric of a city in which the human story is clearly marked on every street. Look at some of the flyblown Georgian tenements that still remain around Connolly Station on the north side of the Liffey, and you'll understand why not all Dubliners were sad to see so much of the old city torn down. Then look at the modern office buildings that replaced Georgian streets on the south side, where humane civic planning gave way to corporate exhibitionism. On the human level, beggars and bag ladies walk the streets, refusing to hide themselves, in another manifestation of Dubliners' assertiveness, which also comes across in buying and selling—whether in the street markets in Henry Street or The Liberties, or in the flamboyant malls now springing up.

Despite the decanting of people from the grim tenements of the North and South Sides to the suburbs during the 1960s and 1970s, the focus of the city is still very much in the center, and perhaps that's one of the reasons why it feels so vibrant. Dublin is also a *young* city. Of roughly one million people in the immediate city area, and another half million in greater Dublin, about half are under 25, and many more—the baby boomers—under 35. With the drift of population from the country to the capital continuing, Dublin is bulging at the seams. Membership of the European Community has infused money into Dublin, and you'll see new building everywhere, but you'll also witness inner-city deprivation as bad as any in Europe. It's the collision of all these factors that makes Dublin the contradictory, pulsating, reactionary, progressive, cosmopolitan, parochial, aggravating, energetic place it is.

DUBLIN

DUBLIN celebrated its millennium in 1988, and though there was much argument as to whether the anniversary really meant anything, it does give an indication of the city's antiquity. Although the first indication of a settlement beside the Liffey is in Ptolemy's celebrated map of AD 140, which shows a place called Eblana, it's as a Viking settlement that Dublin's history really begins. The Viking raiders sailed up the Liffey and, destroying a small Celtic township, set up a trading post on the south bank of the river, at the ford where the royal road from the Hill of Tara in the north crossed the Liffey on its way to Wicklow. The Vikings adopted the Irish name, **Dubh Linn** or Dark Pool, for their settlement, which soon amalgamated with another Celtic settlement, **Baile Átha Cliath** (town of the hurdles, pronounced Ballya-aw-kleea, and still the Gaelic name for Dublin), on the north bank.

The next wave of invaders were the **Anglo-Normans**, whose involvement in Ireland began in the twelfth century with the support of the opportunistic Strongbow and a band of Welsh knights and soldiers of the beleaguered king, Dermot McMurrough. Henry II, concerned that Strongbow and his Welsh adventurers were becoming too powerful, set up a court at Dublin, thereby establishing the city as the center of British influence in Ireland and setting the precedent for the annual social and political Season, which was to shape Dublin's role and character for the next seven centuries.

Because most of the early city was built of wood, only the two cathedrals, part of the Castle, and one or two churches have survived from before the seventeenth century. The fabric of the city, in both plan and buildings, dates essentially from the **Georgian period**. By this time, soldiers who had been rewarded with confiscated land had begun to derive income from their new estates, had replaced the original fortified houses with something more fashionable, and wished to participate in the country's growing economic and political life, which was centered on Dublin. Their town houses (along with those of the growing business and professional classes), and the grandeur of the public buildings erected during this period, embodied the new confidence of the British ruling class: a group that was, however, starting to regard itself not as British, but as specifically Anglo-Irish.

In the second half of the eighteenth century the wealth of this Anglo-Irish class was reflected in a rich cultural life—Handel's *Messiah*, for instance, was first performed in Ireland, and the legacy of furniture, silverware, and architecture, though much diminished, speaks for itself. Their growing political freedom was to culminate in the **parliament** of 1782 in which Henry Grattan made a famous Declaration of Rights, modeled on the recent American example, which came very close to declaring Irish (by which he meant Protestant Anglo-Irish) independence. It was a highly limited and precarious enterprise, and it was to collapse very soon, with the abortive uprisings of 1798 and the Act of Union, which followed in 1801.

The **Act of Union** may have shorn Dublin of its independent political power, but the city remained the center of British administration in the shape of the Vice Regent, and the Seasons which formed the basis of the social and political life of the Anglo-Irish continued to revolve around the Vice-Regal Lodge in Phoenix Park. Along with the rest of Ireland, Dublin entered a long economic decline; but it was also the focus of much of the agitation that eventually led to independence. In 1829 the Catholic lawyer (and Kerryman) **Daniel O'Connell** secured an important advance by achieving limited Catholic emancipation, allowing Catholics to play some part in the administration and politics of their capital city and, in a signal victory, was elected Lord Mayor of Dublin. Dublin was also the center of the **Gaelic League**, which, founded by Douglas Hyde in 1893, encouraged the formation of an Irish national consciousness through efforts to restore the native language and culture. This paved the way for the Celtic literary revival under W. B. Yeats and Lady Gregory and the establishment of the Abbey Theatre in 1904.

Poverty and violence were the other side of the political coin, and the early years of the **twentieth century** saw the struggle for the establishment of

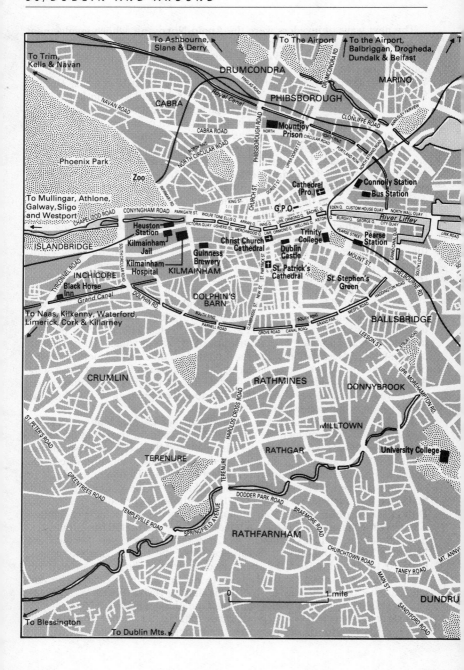

To Ashbourne,
Slane & Derry

To The Airport

To the Airport,
Balbriggan, Drogheda,
Dundalk & Belfast

To Trim,
Kells & Navan

DRUMCONDRA

MARINO

PHIBSBOROUGH

CABRA

NAVAN ROAD

Royal Canal

CLONLIFFE ROAD

CABRA ROAD

Mountjoy
Prison

NORTH CIRCULAR ROAD

Phoenix Park

Zoo

Cathedral
(Pro.)

Connolly Station

Bus Station

To Mullingar, Athlone,
Galway, Sligo
and Westport

CONYNGHAM ROAD

PARKGATE ST.

G.P.O.

Custom House Quay

River Liffey

North Wall Quay

CHAPELIZOD ROAD

Heuston
Station

WOLFE TONE

ELLIS Q.

ARRAN Q.

INNS Q.

LWR. ORMOND Q.

BURGH Q.

ASTON

City Quay

ISLANDBRIDGE

Kilmainham
Jail

VICTORIA QUAY

USHERS ISL.

MERCHANDS Q.

WELLING Q.

Trinity
College

Pearse
Station

LINK ROAD

Kilmainham
Hospital

Christ Church
Cathedral

Dublin
Castle

KILMAINHAM

Guinness
Brewery

St. Patrick's
Cathedral

St. Stephen's
Green

INCHICORE

Black Horse
Inn

DOLPHIN'S
BARN

MOUNT ST.

SHELBOURNE RD.

TYRCONNEL ROAD

Grand Canal

DOLPHIN RD.

SOUTH RING

PARNELL ROAD

GROVE ROAD

CANAL ROAD

GRAND PAR.

BALLSBRIDGE

To Naas, Kilkenny, Waterford,
Limerick, Cork & Killarney

CLANBRASSIL ST.

SOUTH RING

LEESON ST.

CRUMLIN

RATHMINES

DONNYBROOK

ST. PETER'S ROAD

HAROLDS CROSS ROAD

MILLTOWN

UPR. MOREHAMPTON RD.

University College

GREENTREES ROAD

TERENURE

RATHGAR

TERENURE

DODDER PARK ROAD

BRAEMORE ROAD

TEMPLEVILLE ROAD

SPRINGFIELD AVENUE

RATHFARNHAM

CHURCHTOWN ROAD

MAIN ST.

TANEY ROAD

MT. ANN

0   1 mile

DUNDRU

To Blessington

SANDFORD ROAD

To Dublin Mts.

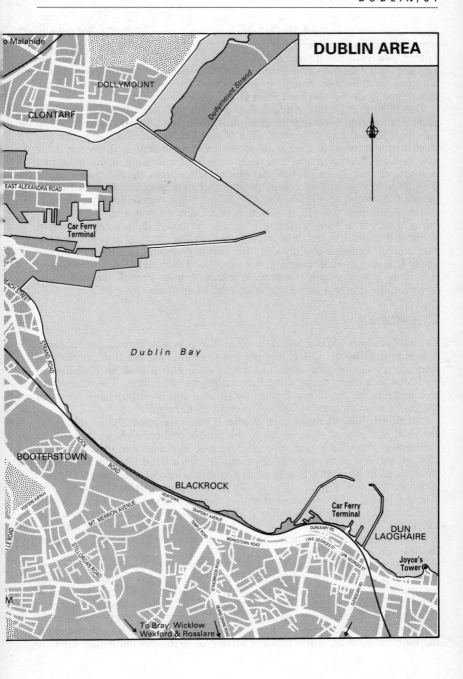

DUBLIN AREA

o Malahide

DOLLYMOUNT

CLONTARF

Dollymount Strand

EAST ALEXANDRA ROAD

Car Ferry
Terminal

TOLLINK

BEACH STREET

STRAND ROAD

Dublin Bay

BOOTERSTOWN

ROCK ROAD

FOSTERS AVENUE

'LE ROAD

BLACKROCK

NEWTOWN

SEAPOINT AVENUE

MT. MERRION AVENUE

TERRE ROAD

STILLORGAN ROAD

MONKSTOWN ROAD

STRADBROOK ROAD

DEANS GRANGE ROAD

Car Ferry
Terminal

DUNLEARY RD

LWR. GEORGES ST

UPR. GEORGES ST

GLENAGRY RD

DUN
LAOGHAIRE

Joyce's
Tower

M

To Bray, Wicklow
Wexford & Rosslare

trade unionism in Ireland. In 1913 this came to a head in the Great Lockout, when forcibly unemployed workers and their families died of hunger and cold. Open violence hit the streets during Easter Week of **1916** in the uprising that was the main event in the long battle for Irish independence. The main battles were fought in and around the center of Dublin, and the insurgents made the **General Post Office** their headquarters.

The history of Dublin **since independence** has been the history of the capital of a young nation endeavoring to leave behind its colonial past. It's to this, as well as the appalling condition of many of the old tenements, that the destruction of much of the Georgian city can be attributed. Today the inner city remains fractured and decaying, despite corporation plans to attract investment and to build housing there rather than in the inadequately planned suburban projects developments that were seen as the answer to the problem between the 1950s and the 1970s. High rise building in the city center is the one evil of city planning that Dublin has managed to avoid—when the Central Bank in Dame Street, for instance, deliberately exceeded its height limit, the builders were forced to take twenty feet off the top (although it remains slightly over the statutory limit), and the city center really has only one tall building, the repulsive Liberty Hall, headquarters of the Irish Transport and General Workers' Union. For all its sufferings, however, the center remains very much the focus of the city.

Orientation

Central Dublin is not big, and it's easy to find your way around. One obvious axis is formed by the Liffey, running from west to east and dividing the city into two regions of very distinct character—the **North and South Sides**—each of which has a strong allegiance among its inhabitants. The other main axis is the north–south one formed by Grafton and Westmoreland streets in the south, running into O'Connell Street north of the river.

The **South Side** includes most of what is left of Georgian Dublin (although the earliest Georgian squares are to the north), and certainly all that is best preserved: Fitzwilliam and Merrion squares, Harcourt Street and Trinity College, as well as the upscale shopping district around Grafton Street, and the famous St Stephen's Green, central Dublin's largest open space. Farther west are the few significant relics of pre-Georgian Dublin: Dublin Castle (started in 1205, but remodeled in the eighteenth century), Christchurch (1172), and St Patrick's Cathedral (1190). West again, you pass through The Liberties, full of bargain shops and bustle, to the gem-like seventeenth-century Kilmainham Hospital, recently restored and, near by, the grim bastion of Kilmainham Jail.

On the north side of **the Liffey** is the beginning of the huge expanse of **Phoenix Park**, Dublin's major open space and pleasure ground. Working eastwards back along the river, you come to St Michan's Church, set back a little from the quays; the Four Courts, one of the grandest of Georgian Dublin's public buildings; and then back to the rough north–south axis, O'Connell Street, now full of shops and fast-food outlets but scene of some of the bitterest fighting in the Easter Uprising of 1916. The immediate area, in terms of landmarks, is dominated by Liberty Hall and, a little farther west, the monumental Custom House, another of the grand monuments of the Georgian period.

Arrivals and Departures

Buses from out of town, the airport included, will drop you at or close by the Central Bus Station, or **Busárus**. Right by the river, this is dead central for almost anywhere in the city. Coming in from the **airport**, six miles north of the center, you can take the official airport bus for £2.50, or a scheduled city bus, #41, will do the same job for 90p. Either takes around half an hour to reach the bus station. If you arrive **by boat**, you'll come in at one of two harbors: **Dún Laoghaire** (pronounced *"Lear-ey"*; for *Sealink* services), six miles out, is on the efficient DART (*Dublin Area Rapid Transport*) city train network, which will whisk you into town in about twenty minutes; **Dublin Port** (*B&I*), nearer in, is served by local bus #53.

Leaving Dublin, the #41 bus to the **airport** sets off from Eden Quay (not all of them go into the airport compound, so check with the driver), or there's a service that goes around to all the major hotels collecting airport passengers (check times with *Dublin Buses*—see number below). For the **ferries**, take the DART service to Dún Laoghaire; buses to Dublin Port leave from Eden Quay.

Buses to all parts of the country (**Bus Éireann**) leave from the Busárus or the streets immediately around (Eden Quay/Abbey Street/Talbot Street); ☎01-746301 for information. Officially approved **private buses** are generally cheaper: ask to see the bus information file at the tourist office or make enquiries at *Funtrek*, 32 Bachelor's Walk by O'Connell Bridge (☎01-733633/733244). Unofficial buses may be cheaper still; they leave from various points around the city, especially on Friday and Sunday evenings. Check the *Evening Press* for advertisements—weekend buses generally need advance reservations.

Trains to the limited parts of Ireland served by the *Irish Rail* system leave from **Heuston Station** on the South Side (Cork, Waterford, Limerick, Killarney, Tralee, Athlone, Galway, Westport, Ballina, Claremorris) and **Connolly Station** on the North Side (Belfast, Derry, Portadown, Dundalk, Sligo, Arklow, Wexford, Rosslare Harbour). **Mainline commuter trains** serving coastal towns north and south of Dublin call at Connolly, Tara Street, and Pearse Street stations. For *Irish Rail* information call ☎01-787777.

Local Transport

It's customary to say that the way to get to know Dublin is to **walk**. It's true that the city's size makes this a theoretical possibility, but equally true that walking the city streets can quickly become a tiring slog. Luckily the city has an extensive, and reasonably priced, **local bus** network that makes it easy to hop on a bus whenever you need to. Buses start running between 6 and 6:30am, and the last city center buses leave town at 11:30pm, so if you're planning a day out it's worth checking what time the last bus leaves to bring you back. Fares average out at about 90p, so it may be worth investing in some kind of pass. A one-day bus-only pass costs £2.20; a bus and rail pass (including DART) £3; a four-day version of the latter (explorer ticket) is a still better value at £7; a weekly bus-only pass costs £8.80. Finding your way around the bus system may prove more of a problem, as there's no indication at the stops of where the buses go. Either ask a bus inspector—there usually seems to be one around, dispensing directions—or invest in a bus timetable (50p from newsstands), which includes a Dublin bus map. Or you can do what most locals seem to, pop into the nearest newsstand when you're lost, look up the route, and put the book back on the shelf.

The other useful city transportation service is the **DART**, the *Dublin Area Rapid Transport* system, which links Howth to the north of the city with Bray to the south, via such places as Sandycove, where you'll find the James Joyce Martello Tower. DART trains are quick, efficient, and easy to use, and the stretch that runs along Dublin Bay from Dalkey to Killiney, in particular, gives you such an amazing view that it's worth taking the train just to see it. It's not expensive—single fares range from 40p to 90p—but if you're considering taking more than one or two trips, it's worth buying a Day Rambler ticket for £2:50. The DART runs from 6:55am to 11:30pm.

Although, if you're lucky, you may be able to flag one down, **taxis** in Dublin don't generally cruise the streets. Instead they wait at stands in central locations, such as outside the *Shelbourne Hotel* on St Stephen's Green, or close to *Jury's Hotel* in Ballsbridge. They are not, on the whole, a good value—as an indication, the twenty-minute ride from the airport is likely to cost you around £12.

Information

The obvious first stop for information is Dublin's main **tourist information office** at 14 Upper O'Connell Street (Mon–Fri 9am–5pm; ☎01-747733): other branches are at Dublin Airport (☎01-376387), and the port at Dún Laoghaire (☎01-806984). The main office is always incredibly busy, but it's big, has much of the most frequently needed information posted on the walls, and has a vast collection of literature and maps (not all of it free). There's a room booking service, which costs 50p for accommodation in Dublin and £1.50 for anywhere else. Since the staff aren't allowed to make recommendations all you're paying for is a phone call: if you're planning to stay in bed-and-breakfasts or hotels most of the time—and you find you need more information than we supply—you can buy one of their accommodation guides and do the calling yourself.

More practical, and in many ways more useful, is the **USIT** office at 7 Anglesea Place, off Dame Street (Mon–Fri 9am–5:30pm, Sat 10am–1pm; ☎01-778117). USIT not only books bed-and-breakfasts during the summer, but also has its own hostel and a travel agency offering student discounts on ferries and flights. Come here for *Travelsave* stamps, *ISIC* cards, and information on everything that's going on in Dublin.

For **listings** of Dublin events, the best source is the fortnightly magazine *In Dublin*, which you can pick up from any newsstand for £1. An inferior alternative is the *Dublin Event Guide*, free from the tourist office.

Accommodation

As you'd expect, Dublin has plenty of accommodation in all price ranges, from hostels to five-star hotels, so finding somewhere to stay really isn't a problem. **Bed-and-breakfast** places abound, with the cheapest dives clustered around Connolly Station on the North Side. In the south there are more salubrious—and more expensive—guesthouses in the Ballsbridge area, generally regarded as a suburb but still within easy walking distance of the center.

Hotels are generally expensive, and often no more comfortable than good guesthouses, but if you're traveling out of season it's worth checking reductions, which can be considerable—the tourist office in O'Connell Street will have a list. At the top end, the *Shelbourne* on St Stephen's Green is widely acknowledged to be Dublin's best hotel, with the *Gresham* in O'Connell Street running a close second.

Hostels

The Irish Youth Hostel Association, **An Óige**, runs a hostel in Dublin at its national headquarters, at 39 Mountjoy Square, Dublin 1 (☎01-301766; open all year). You have to be a member of *An Óige* or the *International Youth Hostel Federation* to use it. A supplementary hostel, *Scóil Lórcain*, opens for July and August at Eaton Square, Monkstown, four miles from the center (☎01-801948; bus #7, #7A or #8, or DART to Seapoint). There's a **YWCA** hostel just out of town at Radcliff Hall, St John's Road, Sandymount (☎01-694521).

Less institutional than these are the **independent hostels**. *Isaac's*, otherwise known as the *Dublin Tourist Hotel*, is just five minutes' walk from O'Connell Street at 2–5 Frenchman's Lane, Dublin 1 (☎01-749321/363877; £3:50, blankets 25p, sheets 75p). It offers a mix of accommodation, from basic dormitory bunks to single and double rooms, plus a good, cheap restaurant with plenty of choice for vegetarians, music some evenings, and jazz on Sundays.

The *Young Traveler* (☎01-971772; £7:50 including continental breakfast), just north of Parnell Square in St Mary's Place, offers more luxurious and sociable accommodation in small, four-bed rooms in what used to be a school run by the Christian Brothers. It also has a restaurant and washing machine.

Cardijn House, at 15 Talbot Street, above Tiffany's Shoe Shop, (☎01-741720; £4 including breakfast; sleeping bag and sheet rental £1) closes from 10am to 5pm, although the coffee bar stays open.

A little farther out, fifteen minutes' walk from the center, the *North Strand Hostel*, 49 North Strand Road, Dublin 3 (☎01-364716; £4 plus £1 key deposit; sheets and sleeping bags available; closed for Christmas period), offers small rooms rather than dormitories, an open fire, and a bicycle lock-up. Also some way out is *Dúnsinea House*, Ashtown, Dublin 15 (☎01-383252; £5; Bus #37, #38 or #39 from Abbey Street to the *Halfway House* pub nearby), open all year.

The *USIT Hostel* at Kinlay House, 7 Anglesea Street, off Dame Street (☎01-778117), is rather more expensive at £6 per person for four-bedded rooms, £15 for a bed in a twin-bedded room, though these prices do include breakfast.

In the summer holiday, **students** in possession of an *ISIC* card can also stay at *Trinity Hall*, Dartry Road, Rathmines (☎01-971772; mid-June to Sept; £9.50).

Camping

There are several **campgrounds** around Dublin, but none particularly close in. On the North Side, a few miles beyond Swords, *Donabate* (☎01-450038; bus #33B from Eden Quay; £4 per tent) is a fairly basic site with only limited space for tents, so call in advance. There are bigger campgrounds at Ballybrack village: *Cromlech*, a relatively luxurious trailer and camping site, is three miles south of Dún Laoghaire, close to the pretty seaside village of Dalkey, on the DART line (☎01-826882/824783; £4 per tent, 50p per person; mid-April to mid-Sept; bus #46 from Dublin or #46A from Dún Laoghaire); *Shankill* (☎01-820011; Easter to mid-September; £3–4 per tent, 50p per person, more in summer), a few miles away, is close to the DART stop at Shankill, or take bus #45, #45A, #46, or #84.

Guesthouses and Bed-and-Breakfast

Staying in the center of town may be convenient, but it's rarely luxurious or cheap—all the better **B&B**s are in the suburbs. Given the relatively small scale of the city and the excellent public transit, the latter option is definitely the better.

If you're determined to find something **central**, start from the tourist office and head north towards Mountjoy Square. Most of these are pretty seedy (the hostels offer a better deal), but you could try *Leitrim House*, 34 Blessington Street (☎01-308728), a good value at £7.50; or the *Avondale Guest House*, 40 Lower Gardiner Street (☎01-745200), more expensive at £14 for a single room (£10–11 per person sharing), but including a good breakfast.

If you want a little more comfort, you're better off out of the center. Directly south, but still within walking distance, is **Ballsbridge**—on bus routes #5, #6, #6A, or #7. *Mrs O'Donoghue's* big Victorian house at 41 Northumberland Road (☎01-681105) is expensive at £16, but comfortable and friendly, with lots of non-tourist guests. About the cheapest you'll find here is *Miss V. McNamara's* at 73 Anglesea Road (☎01-689032), at £12.

Farther out again is **Sandymount**—buses #1, #2, #3, or #6—where you can stay near the sea; it's also handy for the ferry. *Mrs E. Trehy's*, 110 Ringsend Park (☎01-689850), is the cheapest, at £9 plus 75p for a shower.

Northwest of the center, Glasnevin, Phibsboro, and Cabra on the northern fringes of **Phoenix Park** are reasonable places to stay, and here you won't feel too far away from the action. *Mrs M. Lambert's* is little over two miles from the center at 8 Ballymun Road (☎01-376125); she charges £10 a night for a single room, with showers 50p extra. Mrs M. Cummins' *Renwell House*, 33 Finglas Road, Harts Corner (☎01-302061) also charges £10. Mrs E. Delahunty's *Marymount*, 137 New Cabra Road (☎01-303024) charges £11 a night.

Northeast, towards **Drumcondra** and **Clontarf**, you're into suburbia again, but you'll be close to the sea. Here rates are generally reasonable, with lots of places to choose from, particularly along the Clontarf Road, which runs right by the seafront. You could try *Paul and Carmel Geoghegan*, at 125 Clontarf Road (☎01-333196), close to Dublin Bay and on the #30 bus route; or Mrs C. Stefanazzi's *The Boulevard*, 8 Clontarf Road (☎01-339524). If you stay in Drumcondra, a little farther inland, you'll be handy for the exquisite Marino Casino, but little else. Rates are reasonable, though; cheapest seems to be *Mrs C. Kehoe*, 13 St Patricks Road, off Whitworth Road (☎01-306934), at £9.50.

The City

It's difficult to say exactly where the center of Dublin is. Visitors will generally locate it south of the Liffey, around Grafton Street, the main pedestrianized shopping street, which links St Stephen's Green with Trinity College. Dubliners, on the other hand, more often shop in the maze of streets that lead off from O'Connell Street, north of the river; and the fact that almost all Dublin's movie theaters, plus two of its most important theaters, the Gate and the Abbey, are on the North Side, also implies that that's where downtown Dublin really is. However, the majority of the city's historic monuments, including its ancient center, are south of the river; and College Green, for the sake of argument, is as good a place as any to start.

College Green and Trinity College

In some ways the topography of Dublin has stayed remarkably constant since the city was founded, when the Vikings sited their *Haugen* or *Thengmote*, the central meeting place and burial ground, on what is now **College Green**. Formerly known as Hoggen Green, it remained the center of administrative power in Ireland until the Act of Union.

Although Trinity College is the most famous landmark, the massive **Bank of Ireland**, which faces it obliquely across the busy traffic interchange, has played an even more central role in the history of Anglo-Irish ascendancy. When originally begun in 1729 by Sir Edward Lovett Pearce, it was envisioned as a suitably grand setting for the parliament of a nation—for that is how the Anglo-Irish were coming to regard themselves. Their efforts to achieve self-government culminated in the famous Grattan parliament of 1782 in which Henry Grattan—whose gesturing statue stands outside on College Green—uttered the celebrated phrase, "Ireland is now a nation." The Protestant, Anglo-Irish parliament endorsed the country's independence unanimously.

However, this rebellious spirit was short-lived; with the passing of the Act of Union Ireland lost both its independence as a nation and its parliament (which acquiesced to the extent of voting itself obediently out of existence).

With its original function gone, the building was sold to the Bank of Ireland for £40,000 in 1803. Though not exactly geared for tour-bus parties, the bank does admit sightseers during normal banking hours (Mon–Fri 10am–12:30pm and 1:30–5pm). Its interior is magnificently old-fashioned—you are shown around by ushers in costumes seemingly unchanged since the nineteenth century, and in winter, coal fires glow in the entrance hall's massive grates. In the atmospheric former House of Lords, with its coffered ceiling and eighteenth-century Waterford glass chandelier, you can see the mace from the old House of Commons.

In comparison to the mighty facade of the Bank, the modest portico of **Trinity College** seems almost domestic in scale. Founded in 1591 by Queen Elizabeth I, it played a major role in the development of an Anglo-Irish tradition, with leading families often sending their sons to be educated here rather than in England. The statues outside represent Edmund Burke and Oliver Goldsmith, two of Trinity's most famous graduates. The philosopher and statesman Burke (1729–97) adopted an interesting position, simultaneously defending Ireland's independence and insisting on its role as an integral part of the British empire; Goldsmith (1728–94) was a noted wit and poet. Other illustrious alumni include Jonathan Swift (1667–1745) and Wolfe Tone (1763–98), as well as Bram Stoker (1847–1912) and J. M. Synge (1871–1909), these last two the authors of, respectively, *Dracula* and *Playboy of the Western World*, and the playwright Samuel Beckett (born 1906).

Until recently, Trinity's Anglo-Irish connections gave it a strong Protestant bias. At its foundation, the college offered free education to Catholics who were prepared to change their religion, and right up to 1966—long after the rule on religion had been dropped by the college itself—Catholics had to get a special dispensation to study at Trinity, or risk excommunication. Nowadays, roughly seventy percent of the student population is Catholic, and Trinity is just one of Dublin's two universities. The other, University College Dublin, is based near Stillorgan in the suburb of Belfield, and forms part of the National University of Ireland.

Simply as an architectural set piece, Trinity takes some beating. It served, somewhat bizarrely, as an English university in the film *Educating Rita*—understandable, perhaps, given that it looks the way a great university should. Its stern gray college buildings are ranged around cobbled quadrangles in a grander version of the arrangement at Oxford and Cambridge (the cobbles apparently have to be relaid every seven years as the land, reclaimed from the sea, subsides). Just inside the entrance, the **Chapel** is reflected on the right by the **Theatre** or examination hall, whose elegant, stuccoed interior is sometimes used for concerts (check the notice boards in the main entrance). Both were designed by Sir William Chambers, a Scottish neoclassical architect who never visited Ireland. Beyond the chapel on the left is the **Dining Hall**, also used for exams, built by the German architect Richard Cassels in 1743. The bell tower, or **Campanile**, in the middle of the square was put up in 1853 and is believed to mark the site of the priory, which long predated the university. A startling element of color is introduced by the red brick of the **Rubrics**, student accommodation dating from 1712, and one of Trinity's oldest surviving buildings.

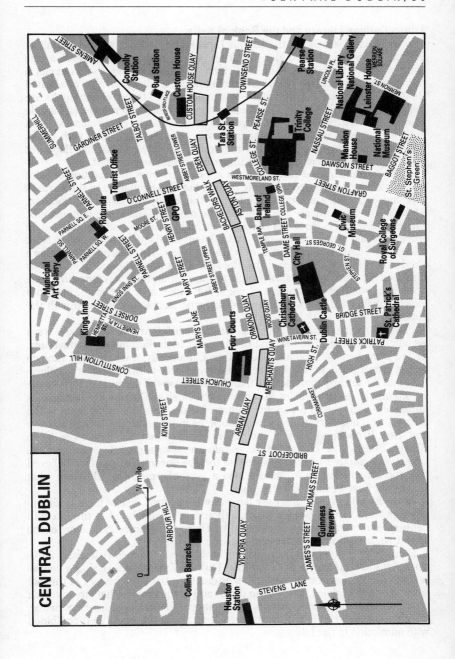

CENTRAL DUBLIN

0   ¼ mile

AMIENS STREET
Connolly Station
Bus Station
Custom House
CUSTOM HOUSE QUAY
GEORGES QUAY
TALBOT STREET
Tara St. Station
TOWNSEND STREET
PEARSE ST.
Pearse Station
LINCOLN PL.
National Library
National Gallery
MERRION SQUARE
Leinster House
MERRION ST.
SUMMERHILL
GARDINER STREET
EDEN QUAY
ABBEY STREET LOWER
COLLEGE ST.
Trinity College
NASSAU STREET
Mansion House
DAWSON STREET
National Museum
BAGGOT STREET
St. Stephen's Green
PARNELL STREET
Tourist Office
O'CONNELL STREET
WESTMORELAND ST.
Bank of Ireland
GRAFTON STREET
PARNELL SQ. E.
PARNELL SQ.
Rotunda
MOORE ST.
HENRY STREET
GPO
BACHELORS WALK
ASTON QUAY
TEMPLE BAR
DAME STREET
GT. GEORGES ST.
Civic Museum
Royal College of Surgeons
PARNELL SQ. W.
PARNELL STREET
MARY STREET
ABBEY STREET UPPER
City Hall
STEPHEN ST.
Municipal Art Gallery
KINGS INNS ST.
DORSET STREET
Kings Inns
HENRIETTA ST.
MARYS LANE
Four Courts
ORMOND QUAY
WOOD QUAY
WINETAVERN ST.
Christchurch Cathedral
Dublin Castle
BRIDGE STREET
St. Patrick's Cathedral
PATRICK STREET
HIGH ST.
CORNMARKET
CONSTITUTION HILL
CHURCH STREET
MERCHANT'S QUAY
KING STREET
ARRAN QUAY
BRIDGEFOOT ST.
ARBOUR HILL
VICTORIA QUAY
THOMAS STREET
JAMES'S STREET
Guinness Brewery
Collins Barracks
Heuston Station
STEVENS LANE

Trinity College Library and the Book of Kells

The other early survivor is the famous **Library** (Mon–Fri 9:30am–4:45pm, Sat 9:30am–12:45pm; £1.75, under 18s free), which is meant to receive a free copy of every book published in Britain and Ireland and also contains a famous collection of priceless Irish manuscripts, above all the celebrated Book of Kells. Some 200,000 of the total collection of three million books are held here in the old Library. The rest is stored off site, where over half a mile of new shelving is needed every year to accommodate new volumes. It's a long—209 feet in all—tall, aristocratic room, flooded with light, with books housed on two stories of shelves. The library originally had just one floor, but in 1859 the roof was raised and the upper bookcases were added.

Trinity's **illuminated manuscripts** are derived from the tradition of Saint Columba, which embraced not only Ireland but also Scotland and the north of England and had a strong influence on the European monastic tradition. There's still some debate over whether the most famous of the manuscripts, the eighth-century **Book of Kells**, was really copied and illuminated in Ireland at all; the location may have been Scotland—maybe Iona, Saint Columba's first Scottish port of call—or even Lindisfarne in northern England. Totalling 680 pages, the Book of Kells was rebound in the 1950s into four separate volumes, of which two are on show at any one time, one open at a completely illuminated page, the other at a text page, itself not exactly unadorned, with patterns and fantastic animals intertwined with the capitals.

Famous as the Book of Kells is, the **Book of Durrow** is in many ways equally interesting. It is the first of the great Irish illuminated manuscripts, dating from between 650 and 680, and has, unusually, a whole page (known as the carpet page, for obvious reasons) given over to ornament. It's noticeable in all these early manuscripts that the depictions of the human form make no attempt at realism—Saint Matthew in the Book of Durrow, for instance, is apparently wrapped in a poncho, with no hands. The important thing is the pattern, which is derived from metalwork, as in the amazing Ardagh Chalice and Tara Brooch, which you can see in the National Museum close by in Kildare Street. The characteristic spirals are always slightly asymmetrical, (apparently another trick to ensure that the eye doesn't tire), and it's believed that the ornamentation in general had a symbolic meaning, although what that might have been is still unknown.

At the far end of the library are two early Irish harps, one of them traditionally known as **Brian Boru's harp**, although it's been dated to the fifteenth century, some four centuries after Boru. There's also an original copy of the 1916 **Proclamation of Independence**.

From 1989, Trinity has been making a bid to entice more visitors by introducing a multi-media show called **The Dublin Experience**. Using a combination of archive and new material, it attempts to trace the history of the city from the earliest times, and will no doubt add to the crowds that already flock here to see the library's manuscripts. Tickets for The Dublin Experience, which shows every hour from 10am to 5pm, are £2.75, or £4.25 if combined with admission to the Library.

The old parts of Trinity, although they're all very much in use, tend to have the look of an architectural showpiece. For contact with **student life**, it's best to head for the New Library and the arts and social sciences block, an award-winning piece of Sixties concrete brutalism by the side entrance in Nassau Street. There's a theater and coffee bar here and plenty of information, in term-time, on what's going on. The **Douglas Hyde Gallery of Modern Art**, housed in the same complex, is one of the city's few experimental art venues and always worth checking out.

South to Saint Stephen's Green

The streets that surround pedestrianized Grafton Street frame Dublin's quality shopping area. Boasting no less than two shopping malls—the converted Georgian **Powerscourt Town House**, and an extraordinary new confection on the corner of St Stephen's Green exhibiting a confusion of cultural references that have been variously described as French, Indian, Renaissance, and Georgian—it's a totally different Dublin from that which you'll find on the North Side: chic, sophisticated and expensive.

Grafton Street

Grafton Street itself has long since lost any sense of history in the rush to commercialism, but it's a pleasant enough place to while away some time. As well as simply wandering in and out of its retail palaces—Dublin's two leading department stores, *Switzers* and the more old-fashioned and expensive *Brown Thomas*, are here, and *Powerscourt Town House* is set back a little on Clarendon Street—you can take in the street life. Since its pedestrianization, Grafton Street has become the center of what street theater Dublin offers, and this is one of the few places where you'll find street musicians and clowns entertaining passers-by.

The unmissable stop on Grafton Street is **Bewley's coffee house**. In its dark wood and marble-tabled interior, *Bewley's* serves all-day tea, coffee, and food ranging from meals to cakes and sticky buns, along with the best potato soup in the universe. It's an extraordinary atmosphere and an unbeatable value—a great place to sit and watch people, read a book, or write your novel (no one will try to hurry you, even if you've only bought a cup of tea). A testament to the vigor of the café tradition in Dublin, *Bewley's* is a place where everyone goes, and you'll see a range of people from students and old ladies to high-powered businessmen. There are two other central branches of *Bewley's*, each with a slightly different character, in Westmoreland Street (wonderful Art Nouveau fireplaces) and South Great George's Street; all are open Monday to Saturday, 7:30am to 6pm.

The Grafton Street *Bewley's* has a small **museum** on the top floor tracing the history of this Dublin institution. Founded in the 1840s by the Quaker Bewley family, it has been a meeting place for all levels of Dublin society ever since. Becoming a workers' co-operative in 1971, it almost folded in 1986 and provoked a national crisis in which the government stepped in to offer help before a buyer was eventually found.

Dawson Street

Dawson Street is altogether quieter than Grafton Street, and home of some of Dublin's better bookshops (see "Listings") as well as a number of august institutions. Chief among these is the **Mansion House**, a really delightful Queen Anne building of 1710 weighed down by heavy Victorian wrought iron. This has been the official residence of the Lord Mayor since 1715 and was also where the *Dáil Éireann*, or Irish parliament, met in 1919 to ratify the Declaration of Independence. The Mansion House isn't generally open to the public, but in any case there's not a great deal to be seen inside.

Next door, the decorous red-brick house containing the **Royal Irish Academy** is also closed to the public. One of the great learned institutions of Europe, it publishes books of Irish interest and has a weighty collection of Irish manuscripts. Next door again, **St Anne's** (Church of Ireland) church has an amazingly ornate Italianate facade which is a real surprise when you catch sight of it along Anne Street. Inside, behind the altar, are wooden shelves that were originally designed to take loaves of bread for distribution among the poor of the parish as the result of a 1720s bequest. On Thursday lunchtimes St Anne's hosts a series of recitals and other cultural activities—check *In Dublin* for details.

Kildare Street

Kildare Street is the really monumental section of the Grafton, Dawson, Kildare trio, and it also marks the point where what's left of the Georgian city gets going. The most imposing building is undoubtedly **Leinster House**, built in 1745 as the Duke of Leinster's town house. It now houses the *Dáil Éireann*, or House of Representatives, and the *Seanad Éireann*, or Senate (open, when parliament isn't in session, Tues–Sat 10am–5pm, Sun 2–5pm). The **Dáil** (pronounced "Doil") has 166 representatives—*Teachtái Dála*, usually shortened to TDs—elected by direct proportional vote, representing 41 constituencies. The Senate is composed on a vocational basis, with six members elected by the universities and eleven nominated by the *Taoiseach* (pronounced "Tee-shuck"), or Prime Minister. General elections take place at least every five years; presidential elections, which are also direct, are held every seven years.

The fashionable area of Dublin when the Duke of Leinster built his house was north of the river, and there were those who mocked him for building a town house in the south on what was then a green field site. The Kildare Street facade, facing the town, is built to *look* like a town house; the other side, looking out on to what is now Merrion Square, looks like a country house.

Whether or not the massive twin rotundas, housing the entrances of the National Library on the left and the National Museum on the right, do anything to complement the Georgian elegance of Leinster House is debatable; they were added in 1890. The **National Library** (Mon–Thurs 10am–9pm, Fri 10am–5pm, Sat 10am–1pm; free) is, however, worth visiting for its associations alone: it seems that every major Irish writer from Joyce onwards used it at some time, and the Reading Room is also the scene of the great literary debate in *Ulysses*. The Library has a good collection of first editions and works of Irish writers, including Swift, Goldsmith, Yeats, Shaw, Joyce, and Beckett. It's also often used for temporary exhibitions on Irish books and authors.

The **National Museum** (Tues–Sat 10am–5pm, Sun 9am–5pm) is the place to go to see the treasures of ancient Ireland. If you've arrived in Dublin after traveling elsewhere in Ireland, names like the Tara Brooch and the Ardagh Chalice will probably speak for themselves; it's sometimes irritating that *all* the major finds seem to have been taken to Dublin. Entrance to the museum is free, but there's a charge to get into the Treasury, housing all the real goodies.

The **Ardagh Chalice**, the **Tara Brooch**, both eighth-century, the so-called **St Patrick's Bell**, and the **Cross of Cong**, twelfth-century, are among the earliest exhibits in the Treasury. The Tara Brooch is regarded as perhaps the greatest piece of Irish metalwork, and it's thought that the patterns of manuscript illuminations such as the Book of Kells, which you can see in Trinity College Library, may be derived from this rich craft tradition. Remarkably, the Tara Brooch is decorated both on the front and the back, where the intricate filigree work could be seen only by the wearer, something that it's thought may have had ritual significance—the brooch is displayed above a mirror so that you can see both sides.

One of the more recent finds is the **Derrynaflan hoard**, a testament to the Irish enthusiasm for metal-detecting. This collection of eighth- and ninth-century silver objects was discovered in February 1980 in County Tipperary by amateur treasure-hunters using a metal detector that one of them had got for Christmas.

To discover more about the Viking tradition, go around the corner into Merrion Row (past the *Shelbourne Hotel*) for the **National Museum Annexe**, which exhibits the results of digs at the Christchurch Place, Winetavern, and Woodquay sites, around Christchurch, carried out between 1962 and 1981. The complexity of the culture is on show in such artifacts as eleventh-century combs and carrying cases carved from bones and antlers, scales for weighing precious metals together with accurate lead weights, and iron swords.

Right at the top of Kildare Street, at the point where it intersects with Nassau Street, the fussy, Venetian-inspired red-brick building on the corner used to house one of the major institutions of Anglo-Irish Dublin, the **Kildare Street Club**.

Saint Stephen's Green

Walk to the bottom of any of these streets and you'll emerge on the north side of **St Stephen's Green**, focus of central Dublin's city planning. It's an oddly decorous open space, neat and tidy with little bandstands and pergolas, laid out as a public park in 1880 by Lord Ardilaun (Sir Arthur Edward Guinness). An open common until 1663, the final buildings surrounding it went up in the eighteenth century; unfortunately, very few of them are left, and their replacements speak eloquently of the failure of 1960s planning regulations.

The **gardens**, with their ornamental pond, can be a pleasant place to while away some time on a sunny day, but in terms of architecture, or even city life, there's not a lot to see. The statue in memory of Wolfe Tone, backed by slabs of granite, is known locally as "Tone-henge."

The north side of the square—known in the eighteenth century as the "Beaux Walk" for the dandies and glitterati who used to promenade there—is dominated by the **Shelbourne Hotel**. Fittingly, the Shelbourne—which boasts that it is "the best address in Dublin"—continues to be a focus for the upper echelons of the city's social life. It's worth bearing in mind that, as with all Irish hotels, you can wander in for a drink and something to eat in the lobby at any time of day, even if you're not staying. The Shelbourne's afternoon "teas" (from 3pm) are wonderful; but the airy, chandeliered lobby comes into its own in the early evening when it's a great place for both celebrity spotting (check the next day's social column in the *Irish Times* to see who was there) and watching the parade of young Dubliners who are there to be seen. The Shelbourne is too well bred to pass comment on jeans and trainers in the lobby, but you'll feel out of place in them if you penetrate to the excellent (but expensive) restaurant (see "Eating," below).

Linked to the east side of the Green by Hume Street is **Ely Place**, where you can see some of the best-preserved Georgian domestic buildings in Dublin and get a real feel of what the street atmosphere must once have been like. The sober exteriors conceal some extraordinary flights of fancy: no. 8, for instance, has an amazing staircase with elaborate stucco work telling the story of the labors of Hercules, but unfortunately it isn't open to the public. Not one of the town houses, in fact, has a restored interior that you can go and see, which is a real pity.

University College, Dublin's other university (besides Trinity), is now housed at a new campus at Belfield in the suburb of Donnybrook, but the original building of its predecessor, the Catholic University of Ireland, is at no. 86 on the south side of the Green. The original aim was to provide a Catholic answer to the great academic traditions of Oxford and Cambridge but, despite the appointment of John Henry Newman (who had famously converted from high-church Anglicanism) as its rector, the new university was, initially, denied official recognition in Britain. Eventually, in 1853, it was successfully established as a University College. The poet and Jesuit priest Gerard Manley Hopkins (1844–89) taught as a professor; Padraig Pearse, Eamon de Valera, and James Joyce are among its more famous graduates. Next door, University Church is an amazingly prolix Byzantine fantasy, with an interior decorated with colored marble—more familiar from the cloudburst patterns on country bungalows—quarried in Armagh, Offaly, and Kilkenny as well as at the better-known quarries of the far west, Mayo and Connemara.

Harcourt Street, leading off from the southwest corner of St Stephen's Green, is a graceful Georgian Street that has survived relatively unscathed. There's nothing much to do here (though there is a good Celtic bookshop), but it's worth strolling down a little way to admire the graceful proportions and elegant town planning.

On the west side of the Green is the **Royal College of Surgeons**, which, during the events of Easter week in 1916, was held by the Irish Citizen Army with Constance Markievicz as second-in-command. The most recent interruption to the skyline of St Stephen's Green is the shopping mall on the corner with Grafton Street, its white wrought-iron detailing intended, presumably, to echo the Georgian balconies of Merrion and Fitzwilliam squares. You can't help thinking that there's no way it will stand the test of time as well as they have.

Merrion Square and Georgian Dublin

Merrion Square, Fitzwilliam Square, and the streets immediately around them form the heart of what's left of Georgian Dublin. Representing the latest of the city's Georgian architecture—flyblown Mountjoy Square and Parnell Square, north of the river, are almost all that's left of the earlier Georgian city—their worn red-brick facades are a brilliant example of confident, relaxed urban planning. The overall layout, in terms of squares and linking streets, may be formal, but there's a huge variation of detail. Height, windows, wrought-iron balconies, ornate doorways, are all different, but the result is a graceful meeting of form and function that's immensely beguiling.

Merrion Square has the feeling of grandeur and repose of much of the Georgian area, and it comes as no surprise that it's been the home of a lot of well-known people such as Daniel O'Connell, the Wildes, and W. B. Yeats. It hasn't always been simply an area devoted to gracious living, however: during the famine years, between 1845 and 1847, the park in the center of the square was the site of soup kitchens to which the starving and the destitute flocked. Nowadays the park railings are used on Saturdays and Sundays by artists flogging their wares; the area is also a center for most of Dublin's private galleries (see "Listings").

Looking along the south side of the square, you experience one of the set pieces of Dublin's architecture: the hard outlines—pepperpot tower, Ionic columns and pediment—of **St Stephen's Church** (1825). If you want to know more about Ireland's architectural heritage, and its Georgian architecture in particular that you're interested in, call at the **Irish Architectural Archive** (Mon–Fri 10am–1pm and 2–5pm). The house is a particularly run-down one but, in the absence of a town house that's restored and open to the public, it will give you some idea of what the interiors of these elegant buildings are like.

Next to the country house facade of Leinster House is Ireland's **National Gallery** (Mon–Sat 10am–6pm, Sun 2–5pm, late opening till 9pm on Thurs; free). It's a place that has a real feeling of activity, mainly because of all the people dropping in to eat at its excellent restaurant (see "Eating and Drinking"), and as a gallery it's also a delight. The collection is not huge, though there are over 2000 paintings on show, but the intimacy of its scale gives it a particular charm. The displays include seventeenth-century French, Italian, and Spanish paintings, Dutch Masters—some good Rembrandts—English watercolorists, and French Impressionists; but it's the Irish paintings that are the real attraction.

Inevitably, the Irish section is heavy on the art of the Anglo-Irish, and in the paintings you can trace the pattern of their history from the formal portraits of the early seventeenth century to the beginnings of interest in the life of ordinary people, which is to say the native Irish. Some of these pictures seem shockingly sentimental—one, by Edwin Hayes, is a calmly beautiful depiction of an emigrant ship at sunset in Dublin Harbour. Exotica, in the shape of such subjects as Indians and Mandarins, also make their appearance, presumably through the involvement of the Anglo-Irish in British military and trading activities. Later paintings include Jack B. Yeats's walls of chaotic color.

If you've traveled around Ireland before arriving in Dublin, some of the most fascinating items have to be the gallery's **topographical paintings**. Landscape paintings of estates, commissioned by their owners, they show more than what the estates looked like: they're aspirational portraits of how their owners wanted them to be. There are amazingly evocative paintings of the estates at Lucan in County Dublin, and Ballinrobe in County Mayo—a place that, though it exudes a sense of past glory, gives no indication of the pleasure gardens depicted in these paintings.

If the Irish paintings seem to stop short at the modern period, it's because the late nineteenth and twentieth centuries are well represented in the **Municipal Art Gallery** in Parnell Square (see p.54).

Eastwards—Baggot Street and the Grand Canal

Baggot Street starts out Georgian, but the street plan is pretty soon broken by the great black metal-and-glass bulk of the Bank of Ireland building, enlivened only by a few brightly colored metal constructivist sculptures. Just afterwards, you reach the **Grand Canal**, one of Dublin's two man-made waterways: the Royal Canal runs through the north of the city.

The Grand Canal was the earlier and more successful of the two: constructed in 1772 (the Royal Canal was built in 1790), it carried passengers and freight between Dublin, the midland towns and the Shannon right up to the 1960s. You can see just how slow these epic journeys across Ireland were in timetables from the late eighteenth and early nineteenth centuries exhibited in the tiny **Civic Museum** in South William Street, off Grafton Street (Tues–Sat 10am–6pm, Sun 11am–2pm). True Dubliners, or Jackeens, are said to be those born between the canals—however, there may be a bit of leeway in interpretation. The best stretch to see the Grand Canal on its journey through Dublin city is in the south, between Leeson Street Bridge and Huband Bridge.

Just over Baggot Street Bridge, **Parson's bookshop** is a ramshackle old store worth visiting for its serious Irish-interest books and complete lack of trendiness, as well as for writer spotting. It was a haunt of Patrick Kavanagh and Brendan Behan, among others.

Farther out, you come to the respectable suburb of Ballsbridge, where you'll find some of the pleasanter guesthouses (see "Accommodation" section) as well as many of the foreign embassies and smarter hotels. The showgrounds of the **Royal Dublin Society**—the first of its kind in Europe, founded over 250 years ago to promote improvements in agriculture, stock breeding, and animal medicine—are also here. If you're in town for the Spring Show in May or, even more so, the Dublin Horse Show (usually in August, though to be held in July in 1990 only), don't pass them by.

The **Chester Beatty Library and Gallery of Oriental Art**, in Shrewsbury Road, is a collection of biblical papyruses, Persian and Turkish paintings, Korans, Chinese jade books, and Japanese and European wood-block prints, some of them going back 4500 years. It's a testament to one man's tenacity: Chester Beatty, who began his career mining in the Wild West, made his first million at forty and developed a fascination with exotic art through spending his winters in Africa to ease the symptoms of silicosis. He settled in Dublin in 1950 and bequeathed this collection to the Irish nation, along with some important paintings of the Barbizon school which are shown in the National Gallery.

West of College Green: Temple Bar

Staying south of the river, the main thoroughfare leading west from College Green is Dame Street. Immediately north, the area between the modern Central Bank and the Liffey is known as **Temple Bar**. Bought up by *CIE*, (the state transportation parent company, until recently), who wanted to build a new central bus terminal to replace the one on the other side of the river, it has suffered from a benign sort of planning blight: although the bus station idea has been abandoned, shops, studios, and offices in the area have been rented out on short leases, and the streets are full of cheap restaurants, second-hand bookshops, and bric-a-brac stores, plus the admirable Project Arts Center. The place is often compared with Covent Garden in London or Les Halles in Paris, which is pushing it a bit—there hasn't been the money that has been poured into either of those projects, and Temple Bar certainly doesn't have anything like Covent Garden's relentless commercialism—but it's still one of the liveliest and most interesting parts of town.

The **Project Arts Center** (☎01-712321), in East Sussex Street, is where you're most likely to find experimental or politically sensitive theater. They also run late-night music spots on weekends, and there's a gallery space that runs temporary exhibitions; check out what's on in *In Dublin*.

Dame Street, focus of Dublin's banking and business, rapidly leads you out of the prosperous center. Soon the city plan begins to fragment into haphazardly built housing and shops, and you begin to see the other side of Dublin life—bag ladies, drunks, and beggars. It's ironic that this part of the city, with many of Dublin's sights, also draws big tourist crowds: Dublin Castle, St Patrick's Cathedral, Christchurch, and, the other side of the area known as The Liberties, Kilmainham Hospital and Kilmainham Jail are all close by.

Dublin Castle

Dublin Castle is just a short walk along Dame Street. Outside its gates, the lime-green headquarters of the Sick and Indigent Roomkeepers Society, founded in 1790, still seems to be going strong. Once inside, you're confronted with a real mix of architectural styles: an ugly modern tax office stands to your left, an over-precise Gothic fantasy of a church of 1803 adorns the ridge straight ahead, and to your right is the worn red brick of the castle itself.

Given the castle's age—it dates from King John's first Dublin court in 1207—it's a surprise to find that in its present state it's a gracious eighteenth-century building, with only the massive stone **Record Tower** showing its age. Originally there were four such towers (the base of the Bermingham tower, to the southwest, also survives), and the castle was a real fortified building; but it later became more an administrative than a military center. As the heart of British power—it continued as the Viceroy's seat after the Act of Union (1800)—it stands as a symbol of 700 years of British influence on Ireland.

The Castle will be the site of the European Parliament on one of its peregrinations in the first half of 1990, and massive amounts of EC funds have been spent on refurbishing it in honor of the occasion (this also means that much of it will be out of bounds while the Parliament is sitting). It's good to see at least one of Dublin's Georgian buildings being restored, although there are undoubtedly other deserving cases. A new conference center is also being built on the site. During excavations for this new building, part of the original moat was found, plus the base of another tower, and when the work is complete you'll be able to see part of the old city wall and the steps that used to lead down to the Liffey. There will also be a new visitor center.

For the time being, however, visits to the Castle are all guided, and pleasantly low key. Until refurbishment is complete, you get shown round the State Apartments only, and since the building is now used by the president to entertain foreign dignitaries, there's a great deal of pomp and circumstance, and the grandeur of the furnishings takes a bit of adjusting to. All the rooms have Donegal hand-tufted carpets that mirror the eighteenth-century stuccowork, for instance; superb examples of craftsmanship but really quite revolting. The best part of the whole complex, for me, was the inner courtyard, all warm old red brick and stone facing, with a little clock tower on one side.

Directly down towards the Liffey from the Castle is **Wood Quay**, site of the Viking and Norman settlements of Dublin that have yielded amazing quantities of archaeological finds (on show in the National Museum Annexe). The excavations were never completed and there's undoubtedly more to be discovered on the site, but despite a lot of argument the corporation of Dublin was able to go ahead and put up two massive civic offices, known to everyone as "The Bunkers," destroying what may have been the most important early Viking archaeological site in Europe.

Saint Patrick's Cathedral

Werburgh Street (left as you come out of the Castle, and then left again) is home of Burdock's legendary fish and chip shop as well as **St Werburgh's Church**. Reputedly, by origin, the oldest church in Dublin, its plain exterior—peeling paint in motley shades of gray—conceals a flamboyant interior that is well worth seeing. Unfortunately, as with a lot of Dublin's Church of Ireland churches, you'd better resign yourself to the fact that it nearly always seems to be closed (this one does open by arrangement, Mon–Fri 10am–

4pm; ☎01-783710). John Field, the early nineteenth-century Irish composer and pianist who is credited with having invented the nocturne, later developed by Chopin, was baptized here.

This part of Dublin is remarkable for its strange combination of urban desolation, urban renewal—generous tax concessions are ensuring that there's plenty of new building—and the massive, over-restored gray bulks of not one, but two cathedrals. Both date originally from the twelfth century—Christchurch from 1172 and St Patrick's, designed to supersede it, from 1190. The reason that both cathedrals have survived appears to be that one (Christchurch) stood inside the city walls, the other outside.

St Patrick's Cathedral (Mon–Fri 9am–6pm, Sat 9am–4pm, Sun 10–11am and 2–3pm) is now the national cathedral of the Church of Ireland (Christchurch is also C of I; the Catholic Pro-Cathedral off O'Connell Street is a subdued building dating from the days when it was expedient for Catholic churches not to advertise their presence too strongly). Once inside, it's a much more elegant place than the tank-like gray exterior leads you to expect.

The presence of **Jonathan Swift** (1667–1745), who was dean of the cathedral from 1713 to 1745, is everywhere. Immediately to the right of the entrance are memorials to both him and Esther Johnson, the "Stella" with whom he had a passionate though apparently Platonic relationship. Swift's epitaph, which he wrote himself and which appears in simple gold lettering on a plain black slab, translates:

> *Where fierce indignation can no longer*
> *Rend the heart*
> *Go, traveler, and imitate, if you can*
> *This earnest and dedicated*
> *Champion of liberty.*

Elsewhere in the church there's a tribute from the sharp-quilled English poet Alexander Pope. The two men were good friends and used to plan sharing a home in retirement (the correspondence is an interesting one, particularly for the gentle light it casts on the often vitriolic Pope, and well worth reading):

> *Let Ireland tell how Wit upheld her cause,*
> *Her Trade supported and supplied her Laws*
> *And leave on Swift this grateful verse engraved*
> *"The rights a Court attack'd a Poet sav'd"*

The north pulpit contains Swift's writing table, chair, portrait, and death mask. Best known for his satires—*Gulliver's Travels, A Tale of a Tub*, and the truly outrageous *A Modest Proposal*, in which he suggested that the poor in Ireland could solve their problems by selling their babies to the English for food—he was also highly active in contemporary Irish politics. He died at 78, the victim of a disease, unidentified at the time, whose symptoms—giddiness and deafness—terrified him with the possibility of madness. He left money to build a hospital for the insane—**Swift's Hospital**, close to Kilmainham Hospital—which, when it opened in 1757, was one of the first psychiatric institutions in the world. When Sir William Wilde, father of Oscar, exhumed and examined Swift's skull in 1853, he diagnosed the disease to have been nothing more dangerous than a disorder of the inner ear called Meniere's Syndrome.

At the west end of the church is an old wooden door with a roughly hewn aperture, formerly the chapter door of the south transept. Anecdote claims this to have brought a new phrase into the English language when, in 1492, the feuding Earls of Kildare and Ormonde met here. Ormonde's supporters were barricaded inside the cathedral; Kildare, eager to end the struggle, cut the hole in the door and put his arm through it, inviting Ormonde to shake hands. He did, peace was restored, and the phrase "chancing your arm" was born.

There are plenty of interesting tombs and memorials in the cathedral. One of the most elaborate, at the west end of the church, is a seventeenth-century monument to the Boyle family, teeming with painted figures of family members. Robert (who, as the only son, has a niche of his own in the center of the lowest tier) went on to become a scientist who proved the important relationship between the pressure, volume, and temperature of a gas, $PV=RT$, known as Boyle's Law.

At the east end of the church a series of three Elizabethan brasses tell the plaintive stories of some of the early settlers in Ireland. There's a small, plain monument in the north transept to one Alexander McGeek, a servant of Swift, erected by the Dean in what was clearly an unusual gesture—all the other tablets are to people of property. An inscription to William Taylour interestingly reverses the usual sentiments:

As You are, so were Wee
And as Wee are, so shall You be.

Finally, near the entrance, it comes as a surprise, among all the relics of the Anglo-Irish, to find an inscription in Gaelic: to Douglas Hyde, founder of the Gaelic League, first president of Ireland, and son of a Church of Ireland clergyman.

Just outside the main entrance is a compact Georgian building, faced in brick at the front but, tactfully, in the same unrelenting gray stone as the cathedral on the side that faces the church. This is **Archbishop Marsh's Library** (Mon 2–4pm, Tues–Fri 10:30am–12:30pm and 2–4pm, Sat 10:30am–12:30pm), the first public library in Ireland, built in 1701 and given to the city by the wonderfully named Archbishop Narcissus Marsh. Inside, the tiny reading cubicles and the dark carved bookcases carrying huge leather-bound tomes—some 25,000 of them in all, most dating from the sixteenth to the eighteenth century—can hardly have changed since the library was built. The chains that once protected the books from theft are long gone, but three cages for locking readers in with rare books survive, although modern readers sit in the main office under the watchful eye of the librarian.

Christchurch

Christchurch (May–Sept Mon–Sat 9:30am–5pm; Oct–April Tues–Fri 9:30am–12:45pm and 2–5pm, Sat 9:30am–12:45pm), at the other end of Patrick Street, stands isolated by the traffic system. Like St Patrick's, Christchurch suffered at the hands of Victorian restorers, but it remains a resonant historic site. Dublin's first (wooden) cathedral was founded here by

Sitric Silkenbeard, first Christian king of the Dublin Norsemen, in 1038; that church was demolished by the Norman Richard de Clare—**Strongbow**—who built the new, stone cathedral in 1172. As such the building is a monument to the fatefulness of that first serious British incursion into Ireland. Strongbow himself is buried here (or part of him, most likely his bowels), underneath an effigy which quite possibly depicts an Earl of Drogheda. Vague though the connection is, this is one of the places where you find yourself asking how things would have gone had his ambition, and that of his Welsh knights, not led him to intervene in Irish affairs.

Close by, the augustly monumental **St Audoen's Church** was transformed into a slice of walk-in history for Dublin's millennium celebrations in 1988. Two separate shows, one dealing with Norse Dublin, the other with pre-Christian Ireland, have proved so popular that, for the time being at any rate, they continue. The **Viking Experience** (temporarily closed at time of going to press), in the crypt, is the more spectacular of the two. At £2.45 it's not cheap, but unless there's a massive line it's worth going to: there's a recon-struction of the original Viking village complete with smells and real live Vikings in the shape of actors whom you can annoy by asking awkward ques-tions. Upstairs, for another entrance fee, the pre-Christian period is dealt with in an altogether tamer audiovisual show entitled **The Flame on the Hill**.

For all its air of authenticity, the pub opposite, *Mother Redcap's*, is a modern creation amid the open spaces left by the clearance of the inner-city slums. Opposite, however, the **Tailors' Guild Hall** (1706) is the city's last surviving guildhall, with an assembly room that includes an eighteenth-century musicians' gallery where Wolfe Tone and Napper Tandy spoke to the revolutionary "Back Lane Parliament" in the run-up to the 1798 uprising. Tailors' Hall is now the headquarters of *Án Táisce* (pronounced "un tusk"), one of Ireland's few building conservation organizations. Its restoration was carried out in conjunction with the Irish Georgian Society, and the two groups are currently lobbying the government to set up an umbrella organiza-tion along the lines of the English and Scottish National Trusts to look after Ireland's architectural heritage. With the setting up of a National Heritage Committee in 1988, funded from the National Lottery, that aim came one step closer to fulfilment; there are even hopes that in the future there may be grants for the restoration of historic buildings.

The Guinness Brewery and The Liberties

Heading west along High Street you'll enter **The Liberties**, an area once outside the legal jurisdiction of the city, and settled by French Huguenot refu-gees. Not that this is anywhere apparent: The Liberties are now just a series of busy streets full of bargain- and betting-shops.

The whole area immediately to the west of Christchurch, interspersed with grim corporate housing and deserted factories, is dominated by the **Guinness brewery**—a setting out of Fritz Lang's *Metropolis*, with huge dark chimneys belching smoke, tiny figures hurrying along grimy balconies, and the smell of malt heavy on the air. For all the seediness of its surroundings, Guinness is one of Ireland's biggest commercial successes. Founded in 1759, the brewery covers 64 acres, and has the distinction of being the world's largest single beer-exporting company, exporting some 300 million pints a year. Although unfortunately you can't tour the brewery, the former **Guinness Hop Store** in Crane Street houses an exhibition center (Mon–Fri 10am–3pm) where, more importantly, you can taste, free, what is arguably the best Guinness in Dublin (arguably, because the honors traditionally went to *Mulligan's* in Poolbeg Street, which still has its supporters). The upper floors of this airy, four-story building are given over to exhibitions of contemporary art, and offer fine views over Dublin.

Kilmainham Hospital and Kilmainham Jail

Plenty of buses ply the road out to Kilmainham and its beautiful, precise Hospital, and at some point you may want to hop on one; the street scene remains dusty, decaying, and industrialized. If you get off where Bow Lane joins James's Street (a sign to the right points to Kilmainham Hospital), you'll walk past **Swift's Hospital**, now known as St Patrick's (see "Saint Patrick's Cathedral," above).

Kilmainham Hospital itself was extensively and well restored between 1980 and 1984, and the result is that Ireland's first classical building—its date is 1680—is a joy to look at. The name doesn't imply a medical institution of any kind: it was built as a home for wounded army senior citizens, like Chelsea Hospital in London or Les Invalides in Paris. The plan is simple: a colonnaded building around a central courtyard, built with cool restraint so that the sober stone arcading creates a lovely, unadorned rhythm. There's an exhibition of engravings by Dürer, Rembrandt, and Hogarth, and the National Museum's silver is on display, plus there's a gallery for changing exhibitions of contemporary art. Opening times are Tuesday to Saturday from 2pm to 5pm for the exhibition space only; guided tours of the whole building are run on Sundays between noon and 5pm; admission is free on Tuesday, £1 from Wednesday to Saturday, and £1.50 on Sunday. There's a regular series of concerts (this is the venue for the Dublin Early Music Festival in March/April; check the listings magazine *In Dublin*), and brunch on Sunday between 11:30am and 1:30pm with live music—☎01-718666 to book.

Outside, a small formal garden runs down to the Liffey, and a long, tree-lined avenue leads out to the front gates, beyond which looms the grim mass of Kilmainham Jail.

Kilmainham Jail (Sun 3–5pm and in June and July Wed 10am–noon and 2:30–4pm) has a formidable history. Built in 1792, it was just in time to hold a succession of nationalist agitators, from the United Irishmen of 1798, through Young Irelanders, Fenians, and Land Leaguers (including Parnell and Davitt) in 1883, to the leading insurgents of the Easter Uprising of 1916; Padráig Pearse and James Connolly were executed in the prison yard. Eamon de Valera, subsequently three times prime minister and later president, was the very last prisoner to be incarcerated here; he was released in July 1924. The jail has been restored by voluntary workers, and you can visit the cells and the site of the executions: there's also a rather grim museum, still being added to, on this darker side of the independence struggle.

North of the Liffey

O'Connell Street and the shopping streets leading off it represent, for most Dubliners, the center of the city. It's certainly a lively area—almost all the movie theaters, plus the Gate and Abbey theaters, as well as the central bus station and a rash of fast-food restaurants are here—but it's hardly the most beautiful part of town. You wouldn't guess it now, but it was on the North Side that the Georgian development of Dublin began. Two battered squares, named after Parnell and Mountjoy, and dozens of moldering, uncared-for tenements are the only surviving evidence.

The North Side has its points of interest culturally—the Custom House, the Four Courts (two of Georgian Dublin's most important monuments), and the ancient St Michan's Church with its weirdly preserved mummies—but to get to them you'll find yourself walking through areas of urban neglect far worse than anything on the South Side. There's street life all right, but it's hardly picturesque: an old man in a battered overcoat bending to pick up scraps of firewood from the gutter, children with white, pinched faces and skin breaking out in sores. These are the things that can make you wonder what you're doing in Dublin as a visitor; and quite how the tourist busloads can accommodate such contrasts.

O'Connell Street

O'Connell Street needs no introduction: at some time or another you're bound to find yourself here, changing buses, grabbing something to eat, or using the services of the **Irish Tourist Board** office at 14 Upper O'Connell Street (☎01-747733).

Most things of historical interest have long since been submerged under the tide of neon and plate glass, but one major exception is the **General Post Office**, which stands at the corner of Henry Street and O'Connell Street. Built in 1816, its fame stems from the fact that in 1916 it became the rebel headquarters. It was from the Post Office steps that Padráig Pearse first read the proclamation of the Irish Republic, on Easter Monday 1916. The entire building, with the exception of the facade, was destroyed in the fighting; it was later restored, and reopened in 1929. From the street you can still see the scars left by bullets: inside (Mon–Sat 8am–8pm, Sun 10:30am–6:30pm) the reconstructed marbled halls are also worth a look.

O'Connell Street is reputedly one of Europe's widest, and there's a paved stretch down the middle with a series of statues. Until 1966 one of them, directly in front of the GPO, depicted Nelson on top of a column; it was blown up by IRA sympathizers in March 1966 (you can inspect the statue's head in the Civic Museum). Millennium year saw a notoriously expensive new addition to the gallery of O'Connell Street's statues: an angular recumbent woman bathed by a fountain, quickly nicknamed "the floozie in the jacuzzi."

Beside the Post Office, Henry Street leads to **Moore Street Market**, where you'll find some of the disappearing street life that people are apt to get misty-eyed about. Truth is that the same activities continue to flourish in the less romantic settings of the **Ilac** shopping center, around the corner, or in the new mall on St Stephen's Green; but that doesn't alter the fact that Moore Street's brightly colored stalls and banter are a lot of fun.

The final statue at the top of O'Connell Street commemorates Parnell, quoting his famous words, "no man has a right to fix the boundary to the march of a nation." It's a fine irony, in fast-growing Dublin, that his statue is pointing towards the **Rotunda Maternity Hospital**, dated 1752, and the very first purpose-built maternity hospital in Europe. The barber-surgeon Dr Bartholomew Mosse funded the hospital by organizing events including fancy dress balls, recitals, and concerts—one of these was the first performance of Handel's *Messiah*, which took place on April 15, 1742. The Rotunda Room itself found use as a cinema until recently.

Parnell Square

Behind the Rotunda, the **Gate Theatre** occupies the Assembly Rooms built by Dr Mosse to finance his hospital, and behind that, bordering on Parnell Square, is all that remains of the pleasure gardens, another fund-raising venture. This little open space is now a Garden of Remembrance for all those who died in the struggle for Irish independence.

Parnell Square, originally called Rutland Square, was one of the first of Dublin's Georgian squares, and still has its plain, bright red-brick houses, broken by the gray stone mass of the **Municipal Art Gallery**. This was originally the town house of the Earl of Charlemont, built for him by the Scottish architect Sir William Chambers in 1762 and the focus of fashionable Dublin before the city center moved south of the river. Chambers was also the architect of the delightful Casino, built to embellish the aesthetic Lord Charlemont's country house a few miles away at Marino; the building of Marino House itself (now demolished) spared no expense, and is said to have crippled Lord Charlemont's estate.

In its new role as an art gallery, the house has been institutionalized to the extent that it's impossible to imagine what it was like as a private residence. Nevertheless it works well as a gallery, with plenty of good lighting and an intimate scale that complements the pictures. The gallery was set up in 1908 with funds donated by Sir Hugh Lane (nephew of Lady Gregory of Abbey Theatre fame), who died when the Lusitania was torpedoed in 1915. He left his collection—centered around the French Impressionists—to "the nation," and with Ireland's independence the problem arose of which of the two nations he might have meant. In 1960 the two governments agreed to exchange halves of the collection every five years, but in 1982 the British government put in a claim for the lot; the matter still isn't settled. All the same, it makes an interesting collection, with work from the pre-Raphaelites onwards added to by more modern Irish painters such as Jack B. Yeats and Paul Henry. There are sometimes free recitals on Sunday lunchtimes (check *In Dublin* for details), and downstairs there's a good value café/restaurant.

Heading towards Mountjoy Square, the streets are full of rotting Georgian and Victorian tenements (lots of cheap dives here—see "Accommodation").

The area also has plenty of literary associations: Belvedere College in Gardiner Row is where James Joyce went to school; Sean O'Casey wrote all his plays for the Abbey Theatre—*The Shadow of a Gunman, Juno and the Paycock, The Plough and the Stars*, and *The Silver Tassie*—at 422 North Circular Road, and Brendan Behan grew up at 14 Russell Street.

Mountjoy Square itself is Dublin's earliest Georgian square, now in an advanced state of decay. Although there are some signs of revitalization, there's little left of the elegance described by Thomas Cromwell in his *Excursions through Ireland* in 1820: "Taste and opulence have united to embellish; the streets in the vicinity are all built on a regular plan; the houses are lofty and elegant; and neither hotels, shops, nor warehouses, obtruding upon the scene, the whole possesses an air of dignified retirement—the tranquillity of ease, affluence and leisure. The inhabitants of this parish are indeed almost exclusively of the upper ranks . . ."

The King's Inns

Leaving Parnell Square at the northwest, you come to the **Black Church** in St Mary's Place, a sinister, brooding building with spiky finials next to the excellent *Young Traveler* hostel (see "Accommodation"). Legend has it that St Mary's and other similar massive Protestant churches built during the 1820s were designed so that they could be turned into defensive positions should the Catholics attack. Dublin's **Wax Museum**, if you like that sort of thing, is at the corner of Granby Row and Dorset Street.

As you walk down Dorset Street and into Bolton Street, everything speaks of urban deprivation: rubbish blowing in the gutters, broken glass, barred shop windows. **Henrietta Street**, dowdy as it's become, comes as a surprise: one of the first sites of really big houses in Dublin, it has two (nos. 9 and 10, at the far end) by Sir Edward Lovett Pearce. These adjoin the impressive **King's Inns**, designed by James Gandon, architect of the Four Courts and the Custom House, but sadly not open to the public.

St Michan's and the Four Courts

Making your way from the King's Inns to the Four Courts, you're assailed by more blighted urban landscapes. Capel Street, once one of Dublin's most fashionable addresses, shows few signs of it now—it's full of cut-price furniture stores and pawnbrokers. More streets full of rubbish and rotting vegetables from the early-morning fruit and vegetable market in Mary's Lane do nothing to prepare you for a solid example of Georgian architecture and urban planning: the **Four Courts** (Mon–Fri 9:30am–5pm), designed by James Gandon between 1786 and 1802 as the seat of the High Court of Justice of Ireland and a sort of chambers for barristers.

From the outside the Four Courts have a grim perfection. Inside, the four courts—Exchequer, Common Pleas, King's Bench, and Chancery—radiate from a circular central hall. The building was completely gutted during the civil war, but has been thoroughly restored.

St Michan's Church (Mon–Fri 10am–12:45pm and 2–4:45pm, Sat 10am–12:45pm; £1), founded in 1095, is the oldest building on the North Side (though it doesn't look it—only the tower and a few other fragments are original). The crypt's combination of dry air and constant temperature, together with methane gas secreted by rotting vegetation beneath the church, keeps corpses in a state of unnatural, mummified preservation: some of the "best" are on display, with skin, fingernails, and hair all clearly identifiable, sometimes after 300 years. St Michan's also boasts an early-eighteenth-century organ, still with its original gilding, which Handel played and admired during a visit to Dublin.

Phoenix Park

As you head west towards Phoenix Park, the street scene remains desolate. A large area is taken up by the decaying remains of *Jameson's* distillery, closed in 1972: enormous walls with weeds growing from the top, and gaping, broken windows. The **Irish Whiskey Corner** is an unexpected patch of neatness—a well-kept little courtyard leads to a whiskey museum converted from an old warehouse. There's an audiovisual show on the history and manufacture of Irish whiskey, working models of the distilling process and artifacts associated with it and, best of all, at the end of the tour you're invited to conduct a comparative tasting of five different kinds of Irish whiskey with Scotch and bourbon. Open by appointment only; ☎01-725566.

The cobbled expanse of **Smithfield** seems like an opening without a purpose unless you're there on the first Sunday of a month, when it's the scene of **horse sales**. There's nothing remotely glamorous about it, but the event does possess a certain fascination. Apparently an entirely male activity, it consists of a load of horse trailers carrying filthy ponies, and deals being struck through the ritual of spitting into the palm and clapping the hands together. Many of the buyers and sellers are travelers, the people who used to be called gypsies and who speak their own secret language, *shelta*. In fact, *shelta* has nothing to do with Romany (the most common theory is that they're originally Irish people who took to the roads at the time of the famine), but the travelers do share with gypsies an impressive knowledge of horses. After the sales you'll see ragged ponies being ridden away bareback towards grim northern suburbs such as Ballyfermot, where impromptu pony races are held.

West of Smithfield stands **Collins Barracks**, a series of imposing gray stone buildings formerly known as the Royal Barracks. Founded in 1704, their chief claim to fame is as the oldest continuously occupied purpose-built barracks in the world.

Having walked through the urban confusion of the North Side, the open spaces of **Phoenix Park**, Dublin's playground, come as a welcome relief. A series of pillars stand across the road and suddenly you're surrounded by grand clipped hedges and tended flowerbeds. The name is a corruption of the Gaelic *fionn uisge*, or clear water; the park originated as priory lands, seized after the Reformation in the seventeenth century and made into a royal deer park. The Viceroy's Lodge is here as well as a 205-foot obelisk erected in

1817 in tribute to the Duke of Wellington. Wellington was born in Dublin, but was less than proud of his roots—when reminded that he was Irish by birth, the Duke used to reply, "Being born in a stable doesn't make one a horse."

The Park was also the scene of two politically significant murders in the late spring of 1882, when two officials of the British parliament, Lord Frederick Cavendish, the chief secretary, and T. H. Burke, the under-secretary, were murdered by an obscure organization known as "The Invincibles." At first it seemed that the motivation for the crime—long standing bitterness over the landlord and tenant relationship in post-Famine Ireland—was directly connected with Parnell's on-going agitation for reform on behalf of the Irish tenancy. It seemed to Parnell that he would have to withdraw from public life due to the implication—however ill-founded—that he was connected with these murders, but his obvious sincerity in denouncing them, and the effect that the event had on British policy regarding the tenancy issue, was to make his position in Ireland stronger than ever by the end of the year.

The Phoenix Park also contains Dublin's **zoo**, where the MGM lion was bred; the old duelling grounds, or **Fifteen Acres**, now the venue for Gaelic soccer, cricket, and, occasionally, polo; and a racecourse where there's a **flea market** every Sunday from noon.

If you cross to the south bank of the Liffey on the way back to town you can see the Four Courts as they're meant to be seen, across the water, and you could also stop off at the **Brazen Head** pub, at 20 Lower Bridge Street. It has recently gone through a stint of refurbishment, but since the walls have been painted a shade that seems to have come ready coated with forty years' worth of nicotine, you're none the wiser. Reputedly the oldest bar in the city, there's been an inn here since 1198; the current building, refurbishments notwithstanding, dates from the seventeenth century. A group of United Irishmen were arrested here during the 1798 rebellion.

The elegant arching pedestrian bridge before O'Connell Bridge is known as the **Halfpenny Bridge**, for the toll which was charged until early this century.

The Custom House

It's easy enough to overlook the **Custom House**, lying in the shadow of the metal railroad viaduct that runs parallel to O'Connell Bridge, east along the river. But, as the third of the great Georgian masterpieces built by James Gandon, it's well worth seeing. It is principally Gandon's public buildings that put Dublin ahead of other great, and better-preserved, Georgian cities such as Bath and Edinburgh. The Custom House was the first of them, completed in 1791 (the Four Courts, although started in 1786, were not completed until 1802, and the King's Inns were designed in 1795). It burned for five days after it was set alight by republicans in 1921, but has been restored and now houses government offices.

The best view of the building is from the other side of Matt Talbot Bridge, from where you can admire the long, regular loggia, portico, and dome, all reflected in the muddy waters of the Liffey. This elegance conceals a story of personal ambition and dirty tricks. The building was originally planned by John Beresford, chief commissioner of revenue, and his friend Luke Gardiner. A large stone in the bed of the Liffey was preventing certain craft from reaching the old customs point, farther upstream, and this was ostensibly the argument for building a new one; but Beresford and Gardiner's prime reason for backing the scheme was that it served their own purposes to shift the commercial center of the city east from Capel Street to the area where O'Connell Street now stands. Their plans were opposed through parliamentary petitions, personal complaints, even violence, and the hostile party were delighted to discover that the site for the new building was the muddy banks of the Liffey where, they thought, it would be impossible to build foundations. Gandon, however, confounded the scheme's critics by building the foundations on a layer of pine planks, which seem to have done the job.

Eating

Dublin may not be the gastronomic capital of the world, but there's plenty of choice for both lunchtime and evening eating. Cheapest fast-food outlets are centered around **O'Connell Street**, but are generally—with one or two exceptions—pretty unpleasant. Best value for **lunchtime** eating are Dublin's many **pubs**, where you can usually get soup and sandwiches and often much more substantial, traditional meals. Central Dublin also has a lot of cafés and cheap restaurants catering to its office workers. For dinner, there's no shortage of restaurants either, some cheap, some very expensive; the cheaper, livelier places tend to be concentrated around the **Temple Bar** area, between Dame Street and the Liffey.

South Side

The area **around Grafton Street** is, as you'd expect, full of restaurants of all price ranges. At least once, you really must experience one of *Bewley's* coffee houses, three of which can be found in Grafton Street, Westmoreland Street, and South Great George's Street. All of them serve tea, coffee, and everything from a full meal to a sticky bun, as well as deservedly famous potato soup, Monday to Saturday from 7:30am to 6pm.

Lunch and Light Meals

The Colony (7 Johnson's Court, a narrow lane off Grafton Street close to *Bewley's*; ☎01-712276). An elegant self-service restaurant—oil-cloth on the tables, plenty of newspapers to read—which does salads and hot dishes (vegetarian included) at lunch and dinner. Live music Wed–Sat.

Pasta Fresca (Chatham Street; ☎01-792402). Ireland's first fresh pasta shop. Its restaurant consists of a few tables and chairs in the window, always well patronized at lunchtime, so aim to get there early. Closes at 7pm.

Captain America's (top end of Grafton Street, on the first floor on the left-hand side as you head towards St Stephen's Green; ☎01-715266; open till 1am daily).

Dublin's original American-style burger restaurant, still going strong, with plenty of loud music and Tex-Mex and vegetarian dishes as well as regular burgers. There's an offshoot, *Captain America's West*, in the Dún Laoghaire shopping center should you find yourself marooned there (☎01-804688).

Bananas (15 Upper Stephen Street). Good vegetarian dishes.

National Gallery Restaurant (Merrion Square, daytime only). Good self-service restaurant where wine is very reasonable by Dublin standards.

Kilkenny Kitchen (Nassau Street, on the first floor of the Kilkenny Design Center). Great place for lunch but always packed, so be prepared to line.

Coffee Bean/Capers (4 Nassau Street; ☎01-684626). *Coffee Bean* by day, *Capers* at night, this is above the *Runner Bean*, a vegetable shop that is doing pioneering work selling exotica such as chillies, avocados and garlic in a country of cabbage, carrots, and potatoes. Decor is Seventies ethnic, with wicker chairs and Chinese paper lampshades, which makes you expect dull but worthy wholefoods, but in fact the cooking is subtle and excellent, making good use of the vegetables downstairs, with a selection of vegetarian dishes as well as plenty of choice for serious carnivores. There's a good panorama over the wall into Trinity College.

The Buttery (Trinity College). Just inside the College gates on the left, handy for a good, cheap lunch, with a wide selection of salads.

Dinner and More Expensive Places

Trocadero (Andrew Street; ☎01-775545/792385). Looks like an obnoxiously rich sort of trattoria, but in fact is pleasant, friendly, and has excellent food. It's one of Dublin's oldest Italian restaurants, and the walls are hung with plaudits in the form of signed photographs of visiting showbiz luminaries.

Shrimps (Anne's Court, just off Anne Street; ☎01-713143/716110). Small and smart, with a good selection of fish dishes if you want a really elegant dinner.

Shay Beano (37 Stephen Street; ☎01-776384). Its reputation for good *cheap* French cuisine is not altogether deserved: the set-menu dinner is pricey, although reputedly extremely good. Rather glitzy, full of smartly dressed couples, and not the sort of place where you're likely to feel comfortable either alone or wearing jeans.

Shelbourne Hotel (St Stephen's Green; ☎01-766471). Prime location and loads of cachet. You can have a drink in the lobby even if you're not staying, and the *Aisling* restaurant (which, like the lobby, faces out on to St Stephen's Green) is excellent, though decidedly not cheap. Still, it's good value by international standards, with classily presented, French-inspired cuisine. The menu includes vegetarian dishes.

The Unicorn (off Merrion Row in an unpromising little courtyard that leads off to the right a few paces down from St Stephen's Green; ☎01-762182). Plain, no-nonsense interior and an extensive Italian menu including pasta and pizzas as well as the standard meat-and-sauce dishes. With *Doheny and Nesbitt's* pub, across Baggot Street, it forms a focus for the more intellectual side of Dublin life, frequented by journalists, economists, campaigners, and musicians.

Temple Bar and Westwards

Temple Bar, between Dame Street and the Liffey, offers a variety of cheap eating places, both lunchtime and evening. Farther west are some more fancy restaurants, and the best-known fish and chip shop in Dublin.

Fat Freddy's (Crow Street/Temple Lane; ☎01-796769). One of the best of many pizza parlors, grossly decorated but cheap and filling.

Well Fed Café (Crow Street, lunchtime only). Vegetarian place run by the Dublin Resource Center, next door to *Fat Freddy's*, and even better value.

Gallagher's Boxty House (20 Temple Bar; ☎01-772762). Traditional Irish food reinterpreted in elegant restaurant surroundings.

Rudyard's (15–16 Crown Alley; ☎01-710846). Busy restaurant and wine bar on three floors: excellent spinach pancakes at lunchtime, jazz on Saturday nights.

Bad Ass Café (9/11 Crown Alley; ☎01-712596; open seven days till late). One of the best and hippest of Dublin's many pizza joints.

Nico's (53 Dame Street; ☎01-773062). Busy, unpretentious Italian restaurant.

Caesar's (18 Dame Street; ☎01-797049). Italian, similar to the above.

Marks Brothers (7 South George Street). Legendary sandwiches and good vegetarian dishes.

Fitzer's (Camden Street, towards The Liberties; ☎01-753109). One of the city's better-known restaurants, Spanish in the evenings, less adventurous at lunch-time. You'll usually have to reserve in the evening.

The Old Dublin Restaurant (90 Francis Street; ☎01-542028). Equally cele-brated, this specializes in Russian and Scandinavian food. Again, it's best to reserve for dinner or you may find yourself spending most of the evening in the *Barley Mow* pub next door waiting for a table.

Burdock's (Werburgh Street). Fish and chip take-out that is a point of pilgrim-age for enthusiasts from all over Dublin.

North Side

O'Connell Street is full of fast-food chain restaurants—everything from *Pizzaland* and *Wimpy* to cheap Chinese and the ubiquitous kebab houses that seem to be the latest in fast food to hit Dublin. While you will never be short of somewhere to fill your stomach, places where you'll want to spend any time are few. As ever, there are plenty of pubs, which make a good alternative.

Café Kylemore (O'Connell Street at the junction with North Earl Street). A cross between *Bewley's* and a Parisian brasserie, all brass and bentwood chairs, this serves good, plain basics—chips with almost everything—and has a liquor licence.

Midday's (self-service restaurant in the Peacock Theatre, Lower Abbey Street; 10am–5pm). A pioneer of vegetarian/wholefood cooking in Dublin.

Gresham Hotel (O'Connell Street). Dublin's second-best hotel serves drinks and excellent sandwiches in the elegant lobby.

Pubs and Entertainment

What to do in the evenings is never much of a problem in Dublin, even if the answer is just to head for the nearest pub. However much some Dubliners moan about the provinciality of the city's cultural life, there's plenty to keep you amused—as long as you don't depend on nights out at the opera or classical concerts, both of which are, admittedly, in short supply.

Theater

As seems fitting for a city with Dublin's rich literary past, **theater** flourishes. Understandably the tendency is to concentrate on the Irish classics, and you're unlikely to find very much that could be described as experimental or fringe. You'll find details of all theater performances in the fortnightly listings magazine, *In Dublin*.

Abbey Theatre (Lower Abbey Street, just off O'Connell Street; ☎01-787222). The grim concrete building housing the famous *Abbey Theatre* gives little away about its illustrious past. Founded in 1904 by W. B. Yeats and Lady Gregory, the theater had its golden era in the days when writers like Yeats, J. M. Synge, and, later, Sean O'Casey, were its house playwrights. Although it's still known for its productions of older Irish plays, it does encourage younger writers. In addition to the main Abbey auditorium, the building houses the smaller *Peacock Theatre*, which sometimes has more experimental shows.

Gate Theatre (Parnell Square, next to the Rotunda; ☎01-744045/746042). Another of Dublin's literary institutions; a bare, rectangular room, it stages more modern Irish plays and can be lively and atmospheric.

Gaiety Theatre (South King Street; ☎01-771717). Dublin's oldest theater stages a mix of musical comedy, revues, the occasional opera, and, every now and then, something really worth seeing.

Olympia Theatre (Dame Street; ☎01-778962/778147). Formerly *Dan Lowry's Music Hall*, and that's exactly how it looks: raffish, down-at-heel, with an air of faded, once tinselly glamor. It now puts on (no surprises) vaudeville, comedy, ballet, and drama, sometimes packing in two completely different shows in one evening with a late-night music spot to round things off.

Project Arts Center (East Sussex Street in the Temple Bar Area; ☎01-712321). This is where you're most likely to find experimental or politically sensitive work. There's also a gallery space that runs temporary exhibitions that are well worth checking out, and occasional late-night music sessions.

Cinema

Dublin doesn't have an art film house as such, but it does have a large number of **movie theaters**—almost all of them on and around O'Connell Street—showing mainstream films that may be worth checking out. Details of all of them are in *In Dublin*.

Nightlife

Dublin nightlife is a bit of a non-starter: the best entertainment is generally in the pubs. **Nightclubs** as such are mostly pretty dire, and often directed single-mindedly at the tourist or business trade. Clubbing in Dublin is a strange business, as most clubs have tiny dance floors, wine licences only and peculiar notions of elitism, with bouncers setting themselves up as style gurus. They are all pretty similar inside. Exceptions to these rules are:

Sides (Dame Lane). Well-designed space with wine and food bar, one of the larger dance floors, and a fair variety of music—soul, disco, hi-energy—and people; fashion types, students, and gays. Sunday night is cabaret night.

Pink Elephant (South Frederick Street). Full bar coupled with a lively clientele of models, A&R men, hairdressers, and execs. If you get through the door, then it can be a lot of fun. Closed briefly in July.

Risk (off South Anne Street). Tiny, and fun crowd—but may change under new management.

Cathedral Club (top of Dame Street). Interesting space in old Synod Hall with large dance floor. Entertains get-rich-quick kids. Tuesday night is the Green Linnet Club with traditional music.

Hirschfeld (Fownes Street). Large gay club on three floors.

The Waterfront (14–19 Sir John Rogerson's Quay). Airy café and late-night wine bar. Disco downstairs. Cabaret; cover charge.

Pubs and Music

Pubs are an integral part of Dublin's social life. Guidebooks are apt to write as if there's some great mystery about them, or as if they're dangerous places where you shouldn't venture alone; neither is true, and the charm of most Dublin pubs derives from the fact that they're simple, no-nonsense places, the better ones unchanged for decades, where you can get a good pint of Guinness and the people are friendly. There are around 800 pubs in Dublin, so what follows doesn't try to be anything like a comprehensive, or even a representative, guide. Instead it's a small—and very personal—selection of Dublin pubs, with some indication of where you're likely to find **music**.

The music scene is volatile, though, so if you're after something in particular—jazz, folk, traditional—the best place to check is yet again in the listings magazine *In Dublin*. *Hot Press*, the national music paper, is also worth checking out. For traditional music, contact the traditional music society, *Comhaltas Ceóltoirí Éireann* (also known as *Cultúrlann*) at 32 Belgrave Square, Monkstown (☎01-800295). Their offices are, in any case, worth a visit almost any night for their programs of traditional music and theater.

Two general points of etiquette: pubs in Dublin tend to be fairly male preserves, but if you're a woman don't let that put you off—you're unlikely to be made to feel uncomfortable, even if you're alone. And many Dublin pubs have **snugs**, or small private rooms, which can be the coziest places to drink if there's a group of you. There's nothing exclusive about these—just go in and stake your claim if you find one empty—and drinks cost the same as in the main bar.

Neary's (Chatham Street: the "th" is pronounced as in path). *Neary's* announces its presence with a pair of arms in flowing sleeves holding lighted glass orbs. Inside the place is no less exalted in tone: plenty of bevelled glass and shiny wood, plus Liberty print curtains to demonstrate a sense of style to suit the theater people who frequent it.

McDaid's (Harry Street). Another theatrical pub very nearby, this is where Brendan Behan used to drown his talent in Guinness.

Davy Byrne's (Duke Street, off Grafton Street). An object of pilgrimage for *Ulysses* fans, since Leopold Bloom stopped in for a drink.

The Bailey (Duke Street). Also on the *Ulysses* trail: in the book it appears under its old name and identity as *Burton's*, a hotel and billiard room.

Mulligan's (Poolbeg Street). *Mulligan's* traditionally served the best Guinness in Dublin; most people now acknowledge that honor to have passed to Guinness's own visitor center, but *Mulligan's* still has its partisans, among them the *Irish Press* journalists who frequent it.

Kehoe's (South Anne Street, off Grafton Street). Wonderful "snugs" if you want to curl up in comparative privacy to sip your pint.

Ryan's (Parkgate Street, near Heuston Station on the North Side). Another pub famous for its cozy, wood-lined snugs.

Doheny and Nesbitt's (Baggot Street). Tiny, atmospheric, smoke-filled room frequented by *Irish Times* hacks.

Stag's Head (Dame Court, a tiny turning off Dame Street almost opposite the Central Bank). Hard to find but worth it when you get there: inside it's all mahogany, stained glass, and mirrors. Good pub lunches too, and friendly atmosphere.

Music Pubs

International Bar (Wicklow Street). Good music pub, mostly rock bands.

O'Donoghue's (Merrion Row). The place where the *Dubliners* began their career.

Pat Egan's Backstage Bar (East Essex Street). Another likely place for rock music.

Corbett's (Werburgh Street near The Liberties). From time to time new singing clubs are set up; one of the latest, *Songs of Struggle*, takes place here on the first Saturday of every month. It's devoted to songs about the struggle for justice and bars sexist and racist songs, thereby ruling out most of the folk repertoire.

Brazen Head (20 Lower Bridge Street). Claims to be the oldest bar in the city—there's been an inn here since 1198—and boasts traditional music every night.

The Merchant (Lower Bridge Street, opposite the *Brazen Head*). Traditional music.

Slattery's (Capel Street, North Side). Traditional music.
Hughes's (Chancery Street, North Side). Traditional music.
Wexford Inn (Wexford Street). Traditional music.
An Beal Bocht (Charlemont Street). Traditional music.
Baggot Inn (Baggot Street). Rock venue handy for the Baggot Street pubs.
Dublin Underground (Dame Street). Rock pub.

Listings

Airlines *Aer Lingus*, 20 Upper O'Connell Street and 42 Grafton Street (☎01-370011); *British Airways*, 60 Dawson Street (☎01-610666); *British Midland*, 54 Grafton Street (☎01-798733); *Capital*, Dublin Airport (☎01-774422); *Dan Air*, Dublin Airport (☎01-379900 ext 4040); *Ryanair*, 3 Dawson Street (☎01-774422).

Airport Six miles north of the city center: take bus #41A or #41C from Eden Quay, 90p; the official airport bus picks up passengers from the main hotels and takes them to the airport for £2.50, ☎01-746301 for information.

Banks Banking hours are Mon–Sat 10am–12:30pm and 1:30–5pm. Branches throughout the city center. Best exchange rates are given by banks; *Thomas Cook*, 118 Grafton Street, will also give a fair rate.

Bike rental *USIT* (58 Lower Gardiner Street; ☎01-725399/725931; Mon–Sat 9am–6pm) rent bikes for £3 per day, £18 per week, or will sell you a bike at the beginning of the summer for around £150 and guarantee to buy it back for around £90. They also do repairs. *Square Wheel Cycleworks* (Crow Street above *Well Fed Café*) is a workers' co-operative cyclists' information center.

Buses The central bus station (*Busárus*; ☎01-742941) is in Store Street, behind the Custom House. *Expressway* and provincial buses all leave from here. Private buses run from the Quays.

Car rental *Dan Dooley Rent-a-Car*, 5 Lyon House, Cathal Brugha Street (☎01-720777); *Kenning Car Rental*, 42 Westland Row (☎01-772723); *Budget*, 29 Lower Abbey Street (☎01-787814/747816).

Pharmacy *O'Connell's*, 55 Lower O'Connell Street (☎01-730427), is open till 10pm daily.

City tours *Dublin Buses* ☎01-734222, or ask at Busárus. *Dublin Buses* also run cheap tours outside Dublin, to places the regular services don't visit, so it's worth inquiring about these.

Counseling *Samaritans*, 112 Marlborough Street (☎01-727700). *Open Line Counseling Center*, 3 Belvedere Place (☎01-787160). *Well Woman's Center*, 73 Lower Leeson Street (☎01-610083). *Rape Crisis Center*, 70 Lower Leeson Street (☎01-614564/614911).

Embassies *Australia*, Fitzwilton House, Wilton Terrace (☎01-761517); *Canada*, 65 St Stephen's Green (☎01-781988); *Denmark*, 121 St Stephen's Green (☎01-756404); *France*, 36 Ailesbury Road (☎01-694777); *Netherlands*,

160 Merrion Row (☎01-693444); *Norway*, Hainault House, 69 St Stephen's Green (☎01-783133); *Sweden*, Sun Alliance House, Dawson Street (☎01-715822); *UK*, 31–33 Merrion Road (☎01-695211); *US*, 42 Elgin Road, Ballsbridge (☎01-688777).

Ferry companies *B&I*, 16 Westmoreland Street (☎01-724711); *Sealink*, 15 Westmoreland Street (☎01-808844).

Gay Switchboard *Tel-A-Friend*, 10 Fownes Street (☎01-710608; Sun–Fri 8am–10pm, Sat 3:30–6pm; Thurs women only). For gay health information try *Gay Health Action* (☎01-710895).

Hospital Jervis Street; ☎01-723355.

Laundromats Nothing very central. *Sappire*, 11 Grand Street (☎01-727362); *Powder Laundromat*, 42a South Richmond Street (☎01-782655); *Exel Laundromat*, 12 Main Street, Donnybrook (☎01- 697172).

Left luggage There are left luggage offices at the following stations: Busárus (Mon–Sat 8am–8pm, Sun 10am–6pm), Heuston (Mon–Sat 7:15am–8:35pm, Sun 8am–3pm and 5–9pm) and Connolly (Mon–Sat 7:40am–9:30pm, Sun 9:15am–1pm and 5–9pm).

Legal advice *Free Legal Advice Center*, administration office, 49 South William Street; ☎01-794239.

Lost property ☎01-721311.

Police The main metropolitan Gardai station is in Harcourt Street, just off St Stephen's Green (☎01-732222). In an emergency dial ☎999.

Post Office General Post Office, O'Connell Street (☎01-728888). Mon–Sat 8am–8pm, Sun 10:30am–6:30pm.

Shopping in Dublin centers around Grafton Street and O'Connell Street. The O'Connell Street area represents the more ordinary, high-street end of the market, with cut-price shops and chain stores. *Clery's* august department store in Upper O'Connell Street and *Eason's* bookshop at 40–42 Lower O'Connell Street (beside the GPO) are two of the highlights.

The smarter stores, and the tourist shops, are all south of the river. Pedestrianized Grafton Street contains Dublin's two swankiest department stores, *Switzer's* and the more old-fashioned and smarter *Brown Thomas*. Just off Grafton Street, the 200-year-old *Powerscourt Town House* has been converted into a covered mall, with plenty of expensive clothes shops including the *Irish Fashion Design Center*, with a changing range of stalls by young designers. Round the corner in Nassau Street is the excellent *Kilkenny Design Center*, set up by the government but now privately run, stocking high-quality Irish design. **Bookshops** are concentrated in the same area: *Fred Hanna's* at 27 Nassau Street (good second-hand stock), *Waterstone's* around the corner in Kildare Street and *Hodges Figges*, across the road. For **camping equipment**, try *The Great Outdoors* in Chatham Street, where there's a ten percent discount for students and youth hostellers.

Taxis There are taxi stands throughout central Dublin. *National Radio Cabs* can be booked on ☎01-772222, 24 hours a day.

Telephones International pay phones are available in the General Post Office.

Tourist information Dublin's main tourist information office is at 14 Upper O'Connell Street (Mon–Fri 9am–5pm; ☎01-747733). Others are at the airport (☎01-376387) and Dún Laoghaire (☎01-806984). There's a Northern Ireland Tourist Information office in *Clery's* department store on O'Connell Street (☎01-786055).

Travel Agents *USIT*, 7 Anglesea Street (☎01-778117/778112) are experts in student/youth travel; *Thomas Cook*, 118 Grafton Street (☎01-771721) offers good general services; *CIE Tours*, 35 Lower Abbey Street (☎01-300777) is the biggest internal tour operator, if you want a bus trip around Ireland.

Trains *Heuston Station* on the South Side (still sometimes known by its old name of Kingsbridge) serves the south and west; *Connolly Station* on the North Side (aka Amiens Street Station) serves the east coast and the north. Commuter trains call at Connolly, Tara Street, and Pearse Street stations. ☎01-787777 for information.

Transportation information Enquiries about provincial and Dublin buses, *Expressway*, DART, and mainline rail are handled at the information office at 59 Upper O'Connell Street, opposite the main tourist information office. (Mon–Fri 9am–5pm, Sat 9am–1pm; ☎01-787777.)

OUTSIDE DUBLIN

Even without going as far as the Wicklow Mountains, whose unlikely outlines you encounter every time you look south, there are a number of trips beyond the center which are well worth making. The DART will take you southwards to **Sandycove** and the James Joyce Tower; the pretty village of **Dalkey**, with its incongruously European atmosphere; and the magnificent views across **Dublin Bay** between Dalkey and Killiney. It will also take you up to the northern terminal, the rugged hill of **Howth** at the northern end of Dublin Bay.

Sandycove and the James Joyce Tower

Taking the DART south out of Dublin, you very quickly have the happy feeling that you're leaving the grime of the city far behind. Almost immediately, the track starts to run along the coast, past **Booterstown Marsh**, a designated bird sanctuary now threatened with a highway development, and out to **DÚN LAOGHAIRE**, where the *Sealink* car ferries come in from Britain. At this distance, Dún Laoghaire manages to retain some of its flavor as a superior kind of Victorian resort, full of wide, tree-lined avenues, promenades, and wedding-cake architecture. Its port is still the base for Irish lightships and the biggest Irish center for yachting.

SANDYCOVE's main claim to fame—the Martello Tower in which James Joyce spent a week in 1904 with his friend Oliver St John Gogarty, whom he later transformed into Buck Mulligan in *Ulysses*—is for some reason not sign-posted from the station. But it's not hard to find. Turn right down the street into what appears to be the center of this sleepy suburb, then left at the lights for the seafront. You'll see the tower, next to an extraordinary bit of 1930s modern seaside building, on your right.

The reason the **Martello Tower** has become a place of pilgrimage for Joyce fans is not so much the association with the writer's life—the 22-year-old writer spent barely a week here in August of 1904, a month before he left the country with Nora Barnacle—as the fact that it features so prominently in the opening chapter of *Ulysses*. Joyce's stay wasn't a particularly happy one: Gogarty's other guest was one Samuel Chevenix Trench who, on their sixth night, had a nightmare, grabbed a gun and let off some shots into the fire-place of the room they were all sleeping in. Gogarty then seized the gun and shot a row of saucepans that were hanging above Joyce's head, shouting, "Leave him to me!" Joyce left the following morning.

The exhibits inside the tower (April–Oct Mon–Sat 10am–1pm and 2–5pm, Sun 2–6pm; erratic the rest of the year—phone ☎01-809265, the museum, or ☎01-808571, the Dún Laoghaire tourist office, to check; admission £1.20, students 90p, children 60p) amount to little more than a collection of memor-abilia—the author's guitar, cigar case, and cane are on display—that, with one or two exceptions, offer no great insights into his life. Perhaps most inter-esting are the letters, including a plaintive note to Nora Barnacle on September 10, 1904 accusing her of "treating me as if I were simply a casual comrade in lust." But it's the atmosphere of the place that really makes it worthwhile, particularly when you climb up the narrow staircase to the open top of the tower where stately, plump Buck Mulligan performs his ablutions at the beginning of *Ulysses*.

On the seaward side of the tower is the **Forty Foot Pool**, for many years a men-only swimming hole where nude bathing was the rule. Now that women are allowed (although you seldom see them) it's strictly "togs required—by order," as the notice says. The hardier swimmers use this rocky, natural swimming pool all year round. Sandycove is also good for canoeing, wind-surfing, and water-skiing.

Dalkey and Killiney

Further south along the coast lies the little town of **DALKEY**. Immortalized, if that's the word, in Flann O'Brien's satirical *The Dalkey Archive*, Dalkey (pronounced "Dawkey") is nowadays a charming little seaside town, and nothing much besides. Its origins as a walled medieval settlement and impor-tant landing place for travelers from England are evident, though, especially in the massive **Archibold's Castle**, which dominates the main street. There are narrow lanes with fine, bourgeois residences and, back in the main street, a really excellent new and second hand bookshop, with plenty of recent review copies. John Dowland, the melancholy Elizabethan lutenist and composer, may have been born here, and George Bernard Shaw certainly lived at **Torca Cottage** on Dalkey Hill: he later claimed to be "a product of

Dalkey's outlook." When the sun is shining, Dalkey has an almost Mediterranean resort atmosphere, and it's thoroughly pleasant just to stroll about and drink it all in.

In the summer you can rent a boat to take you out to **Dalkey Island**, where you'll find a bird sanctuary, another in the series of Martello towers that were built to defend the coast from Napoleonic attack, and the ruins of the early Irish St Begnet's Church. A curious ritual involving the "King of Dalkey," complete with crown and sword, is still occasionally enacted here: originating in the eighteenth century, it started out as a student joke, but became increasingly political until it was stamped out by Lord Clare in 1797.

From Dalkey Hill a ridge leads to the public park laid out atop **KILLINEY HILL** (pronounced "Kill-eye-ney"), with terrific views of Dublin Bay and the Wicklow Mountains. The stretch south from Dalkey Head is as beautiful a piece of scenery as you'll come across anywhere. As good a way as any to see it is from the DART line (if you walk, you're restricted to the road until you round Sorrento Point, so you're probably better off taking the train to Killiney): as you come out of the Dalkey hilltop tunnel you're overwhelmed by the sweep of the bay, the blue sea on one side and on the other the weird bulk of the Sugarloaf mountain.

The entire coastline from Dún Laoghaire to Bray is good for **fishing**. Off Dalkey Island the dominant catches are conger, tope, pollock, skate, and coalfish; farther out, on the Burford and Kish banks, turbot, brill, dab, and plaice are common. Fishing from the rocks and piers at Dún Laoghaire is free, and you can rent boats at Bray, Bullock, and Coliemore harbors.

Howth

HOWTH (the name derives from the Danish *hoved*, or head, and is pronounced to rhyme with "both") lies at the northernmost point of both Dublin Bay and the DART line. You can also get here on the #31 bus. The journey out on the DART is nothing like as spectacular as the southward trip: once the industrial city ends, it gives way to suburbia and it's only when you get as far as Sutton (a much sought-after address) that you even see the sea. Arriving in Howth, turn right out of the DART station for the castle, left for the village, abbey and cliff walks.

Howth Head is a natural vantage point giving views right across Dublin Bay to the Wicklow Mountains and at times, so they claim, even as far as the distant Mountains of Mourne in the north and those of Wales across the Irish Sea. Not surprisingly, it has been a strategic military point for centuries and its history involves a long line of fearful incumbents on the lookout for raiders. The legendary copper-mining Parthalons and Firbolg were the first, later conquered by the Gaelic chieftain Criomthain, whose grave is reputedly marked by a cairn on the summit. The Gaels, in turn, were ousted by the Vikings in the eighth century, and they were overthrown by the technologically and strategically superior Normans, led by Sir Almeric Tristram. His descendants, bearing the surname St Lawrence, continue to live at Howth Castle today.

Howth itself is a day-trip destination for Dubliners, and it has the happy and bracing air of a seaside resort, even off-season. There's a harbor on the north side, close to the DART station, dating from the days when Howth, rather than Dún Laoghaire, was the main packet station for Dublin. At the jetty at the end of the West Pier you can see the footprint of mad King George IV, who landed here in 1821 instead of at Dún Laoghaire (which was expecting to rename itself Kingstown in honor of the event; he made up for it later by going home via Dún Laoghaire). It was here, in July 1914, that the Irish Volunteers succeeded in landing 900 rifles and 25,000 rounds of ammunition from Erskine Childers's yacht *Asgard*. The harbor, full of working boats, is nowadays situated alongside a marina crowded with less practical craft. You can fish from the harbor pier; and, if you're in Howth on a Thursday evening, it's worth staying to see the spectacle when the herring boats come in. (Michael Wright, on the quay, sells freshly caught fish from his shop all week.)

Opposite the harbor, the rock-encrusted island is **Ireland's Eye**, an uninhabited expanse of scrub grass and ferns sporting yet another Martello tower and the ruins of a sixth-century monastic church. It's also a bird sanctuary, and you can cross by boat to visit it in summer.

Much of the interior of Howth Head is built up, but a footpath runs all the way round the coast. There are impressive cliffs and amazing views—south past the mouth of the Liffey to the Wicklow Mountains and beyond, north to the flatlands of the Boyne. To get to the cliffs, either carry straight on along the shore road, or take the #31B bus up to the summit and cut down from there.

Howth village is a sleepy, suburban place full of steep streets and sudden views. Its one monument, on a quiet site overlooking Ireland's Eye, is the ruined **Howth abbey**, the first church founded by Sigtrygg, Norse king of Dublin, in 1042. In one of the later phases of a chequered history, it was used by smugglers for storing contraband. The abbey is kept locked, but you can get the keys from Mrs McBride at 20 Church Street, opposite: inside you'll see the fifteenth-century tomb of Christopher St Lawrence and his wife.

Just below the abbey is the **Abbey Tavern**—bare, stone-walled, with stark wood furniture, turf fires, and gas lighting. It may strain a little to achieve this air of authenticity, but it's worth visiting, especially for the music in the evenings. There's a restaurant, too, specializing in fish (best to book; ☎01-390307). The other good eating place is on the walk back to the station, opposite the harbor: *Russells Restaurant*, at 1 Harbour Road (☎01-322681/322682), does cheap lunches and more sophisticated food which is also good value. Again, it's worth booking—if both *Russells* and the *Abbey Tavern* are full, you've little choice but to go back into town.

To get to **Howth Castle**, back-track a few hundred yards along the road to Dublin and turn left. The castle itself isn't open to the public, but you pass it on the way to the *Deer Park Hotel* and there's a small transportation museum (daily 2–6pm; ☎01-475623 to check). It's an impressive building, even from the outside—a true, battlemented castle, partly ruined, partly inhabited—and one that architects from Francis Bindon to Edwin Lutyens have had a hand in restoring. The gardens are famous for their azaleas and rhododendrons in May and June.

Closer in towards the city is a seaside area even more readily accessible to Dubliners, **Dollymount Strand** or Bull Island. Designated, like Booterstown Marsh farther south, a UNESCO Biosphere Reserve (though, with the plans to build a freeway next to Booterstown, it's doubtful what protection that really affords), Dollymount Strand is a spit of low sand dunes linked to the shore by a turn-of-the-century wooden bridge. Apart from vacationing Dubliners, it's host to thousands of overwintering wildfowl and wading birds, and provides a stopping-off point for Arctic migrants. Birds are not the only interesting wildlife of Dollymount Strand: just a couple of miles from the center of Dublin, there are foxes, shrews, badgers, and rabbits, as well as a wide range of grass and plant species. You can find out more at the new interpretative center, where the causeway road meets the island.

Marino Casino and Malahide

It's well worth hopping on the #20A or #24 bus from Eden Quay to **MARINO** to visit the eighteenth-century Casino, one of the most delightful pieces of Neoclassical lightheartedness you could hope to see anywhere. The bus will let you off next to some playing fields, from where the Casino, exuberantly decorated with urns and swags of carved drapery, is clearly visible to the left.

Needless to say, the Casino (June–Sept daily 10am–7pm; out of season phone the office of public works, ☎01-613111 ext 2386, for details of tours) has nothing to do with gambling. Commissioned by Lord Charlemont (whose town house in Parnell Square is now the home of the Municipal Art Gallery), it was designed by Sir William Chambers, the leading Neoclassical architect of the day, to accompany a villa which would in turn house some of the priceless works of art he had brought home from his grand tour of Europe. Marino House was demolished long ago, but the Casino, restored in 1984, survives in perfect condition, crowded with witty and pragmatic architectural features: the urns, for example, conceal chimneys.

As you go back into town, try to sit upstairs on the left-hand side of the bus. As it turns from the Malahide Road into Fairview, you can see Marino Crescent, which was once nicknamed "Ffolliot's revenge" after a painter who built it out of spite to block the view from Marino House to the sea. Ffolliot's final twist of the knife in the flesh of the aesthetic Lord Charlemont was to make the backs of the houses, which faced Marino House, an unsightly jumble of chimneys, ill-placed windows and sheds.

If you're going on to **MALAHIDE**, the #47 bus from the Casino will take you there; if you set out from center of town, the easiest way is probably to take the suburban train service from Connolly Station. Either way, the **castle** is well worth seeing. The last Lord Talbot died in 1973, after which the family home was taken over by the state, and much of its grounds given over to playing fields. It's indicative of the complex history of the Anglo-Irish that this rich and powerful Anglo-Norman family didn't actually turn Protestant until the eighteenth century. The castle even passed out of the hands of the family for ten years during the Cromwellian wars; but they managed to get it back. In the dining room is a large picture of the Battle of the Boyne; it comes as some surprise that the Talbots fought, not for Prince William, but on the losing side. It's said that of the fourteen members of the family who sat down to breakfast in the dining room before setting out to fight, all were killed.

Unpromising as the grounds may now look, the castle itself (April–Oct Mon–Fri 10am–5pm, Sat 11am–6pm, Sun 2–6pm; Nov–March Mon–Fri 10am–5pm, Sat & Sun 2–5pm; good recorded guided tour available) is terrific. Dating in parts from 1174, when a marauding Norman, Richard Talbot, seized the lands and made it his fortress, it's been added to haphazardly over the ensuing centuries to make it look just how you think a castle ought to: turrets, Gothic windows, battlements, and all. As well as being satisfyingly picturesque, what's fascinating about Malahide Castle is that you can follow its progress from a simple defensive tower—the first room you see inside, with amazing black carved panelling, is within the original square tower—to the addition of embellishments such as battlemented walls and turrets and, later still, its transformation into a country house, all fortifications now strictly decorative, with a mock-Gothic entrance. Inside, a remarkably successful attempt has been made to show the best Irish furniture in good period settings. The interiors are truly delightful, with graceful furniture and pictures on loan from the National Portrait Gallery of Ireland. If you're in need of refreshment, there's also an excellent tea room.

Malahide village, which must once have been little more than a crossroads at the gates of the castle, has long since outgrown its estate village status. It's a delight, one of those places where there's nothing much to write about, but which for some reason is really pleasant to be in: just a few grandish houses, some more modest color-washed ones, the most spick-and-span railroad station you've ever seen, and some quiet streets sloping gently down to the sea.

travel details

Trains

From Dublin Connolly to Belfast (6 daily; 2hr 15min); from Heuston to Galway (4; 3hr); from Connolly to Sligo (3; 3hr 15min); from Heuston to Waterford (4; 2hr 30min); from Heuston to Cork (8; 3hr); from Heuston to Limerick Junction (11; 1hr 50min); from Connolly to Rosslare (3 daily; 2hr 50min).

Dublin buses

From Dublin to Derry (2; 4hr 25min); Waterford (2; 3hr 30min); Donegal (3; 5hr); Galway (2; 3hr 45min); Cork (1; 6hr 20min).

Private buses

Scores of private companies connect Dublin with the rest of the country. Routes are too numerous to detail here—we've listed the most useful under the "Travel Details" section of the relevant chapters. Major companies include *Funtrek*, 32 Bachelors Walk, O'Connell Bridge, Dublin (☎01-730852).

CHAPTER TWO

WICKLOW AND KILDARE

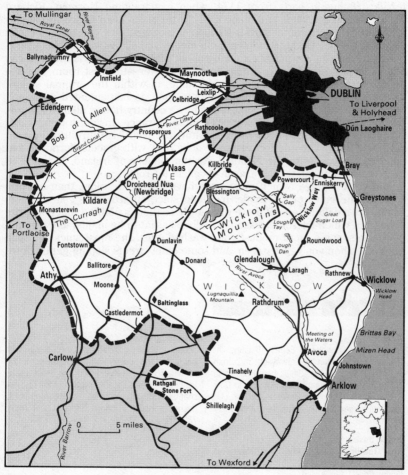

K ildare and Wicklow, both easily accessible from Dublin, provide a welcome respite from the capital's urban blight. As central counties of the Pale, each is heavily resonant with the presence of the Anglo-Irish, yet scenically they are in complete contrast to one another. **County Wicklow** has some of the wildest, most spectacular mountain scenery in Ireland, as well as some impressive monuments—the early Celtic monastery of **Glendalough** and the Neoclassical splendors of the great houses of **Russborough** and **Powerscourt** (now ruined) above all. **County Kildare**'s charms are more understated: a gently undulating landscape of farming land punctuated only by the great horse-racing plain of the **Curragh**, where the National Stud and Japanese Gardens are well worth seeing. Here, too, there are signs of the shifting patterns of settlement and land ownership—a pedimented building here, a Celtic high cross there—written into the landscape for you to read as you travel around.

Their proximity to Dublin makes **transportation** very easy in both counties. The Dublin inner city railroad network, or DART, will take you as far as the dull seaside resort of Bray on the Wicklow coast; the main line continues to the much more enticing towns of Wicklow and Arklow. The main tourist locations inland in County Wicklow are well served by buses. In County Kildare the main N7 road and the railroad line to Limerick offer ready access to most sites. The scenic beauties of Wicklow attract a lot of visitors, principally Dubliners, and the positive spin-off is that **accommodation** is no problem—there are plenty of youth hostels and cheap B&Bs. Kildare is less visited, and here you'll find yourself relying on the B&B trade.

COUNTY WICKLOW

Get on a bus in central Dublin and in half an hour or so you can be deep into **County Wicklow**, high in the mountains among gorse, heather, bracken, and benty grass, breathing in clear air with no one in sight. It's great **walking** and **cycling** country—particularly challenging for mountain bikers—with plenty of golden sandy **beaches**, too (and some rather stuffy **resort towns** closer to Dublin, best avoided). On a short trip to Ireland, you could do a lot worse than simply combine Dublin with a few days in the wilds of Wicklow. It's also a place to get to grips with two of the dominant themes of Irish history, sometimes strangely superimposed: the monastic tradition in the shape of one of its most important and charismatic sites, **Glendalough**; and that of the Anglo-Irish, at the great houses of **Russborough** and **Powerscourt**.

Wherever you go, apart from a few obvious centers like Wicklow town and Arklow, you're struck by the sparseness of population. It's the same old story as everywhere else in Ireland: first the famine, and then the gradual drift of the rural population to the towns, and Wicklow is far from being the most painful sufferer. In 1841 the population of Wicklow was 126,431; the county suffered comparatively little from the famine, which reduced it to 100,000, but steady seepage of population brought it to a low of 58,473 by 1961. Since then it has recovered to over 87,000, partly through the development of commuter towns, as first the railroad, then the suburban DART service have penetrated farther into the county.

Heading out from Dublin you could follow the coast, but a far more attractive option is to head straight for the hills, where **Enniskerry** and Powerscourt make an obvious first stop.

The Wicklow Mountains

The **Wicklow Mountains**, so clearly viewed from Dublin, are really round-topped hills ground down by the Ice Ages, with the occasional freakish shape like the Great Sugarloaf mountain, where a granite layer has arrested the weathering. Despite their relatively modest height (Lugnaquilla, the highest peak, only just tops 3000 feet), they're wild and uninhabited, with little traffic even at the main passes. Given this, and their proximity to Dublin, it's hardly surprising that the Wicklow Mountains were traditionally bandit territory, and that the last insurgents of the land agitation that spread all over Ireland following the French invasion of County Mayo in 1798 hid out here. The mountains were virtually inaccessible until after the 1798 uprisings, when the army built a road to enable them to patrol effectively. This you can still follow, from Rathfarnham in the Dublin suburbs to Aghavannagh, high in the mountains; the **Wicklow Way** partly follows the road, too.

Powerscourt House and Enniskerry

ENNISKERRY, the estate village of **Powerscourt House**, is famously pictu-resque, and there are people who travel to Ireland just to see it, and go no farther. That's just about understandable, for it is indeed picture-book pretty, with a sloping triangular "square" and plenty of day-trippers from Dublin always in attendance to admire it. But what's more interesting is that its *raison d'être* is its relationship with the adjoining great house—it was here, in the heart of the Pale, that the Anglo-Irish were at their most confident and relaxed. It's a bold statement of a theme repeated all over Ireland: big houses with adjoining tied villages. In Powerscourt's case, the estate is a sort of meta-phor for the passing of the power of the Ascendancy. An estate without a heart, Powerscourt is the shell of a house designed in 1740 by the German architect Richard Cassels (later anglicized to Castle), burned down in 1974 on the eve of a big party to celebrate the completion of an extensive program of renovation. Although the Irish Georgian Society has announced plans to restore it, the house remains a ruin, surrounded by magnificently showy gardens. Typical of the scale that Powerscourt is built on, the avenue leading up to the house is nearly a mile long—the estate itself covers some 14,000 acres.

The **gardens** (Easter to October, daily 10am–5:30pm; £2, students £1; admission to waterfall only, 70p) are essentially mid-Victorian in character, and, if you enjoy the municipal park-like formal school of gardening, well worth seeing. The Wicklow mountains to the south and east give shelter from the wind and rain, and there are some rare plants, and curiosities includ-ing a pet cemetery and the obligatory Japanese garden. The Edwardian craze for Japanese gardening had a major impact on Ireland, perhaps because the mild climate was highly suited to growing the right kind of plants. It is also visible at Russborough, close by in County Wicklow, and in its most unbri-dled and eccentric form at the National Stud not far away in County Kildare (see p.84).

The really spectacular aspect of the **landscaping** is the view across a massive 250-yard terrace to the unlikely cones of the Great and Little Sugarloaf Mountains—one of many instances in Ireland where landscape and landscaping are miraculously blended. At Powerscourt, the designer of the upper terraces was one Daniel Roberton, an all-too-human individual with a relaxed approach to his job. Roberton had himself wheeled about in a barrow, clutching a bottle of sherry; when this was exhausted his creative powers waned, and he finished work for the day. A four-mile walk (signposted) through the grounds will bring you to the **waterfall**, at 400 feet the longest drop in Ireland or Britain, and another place where the landscape seems almost too good to be true.

To get to Enniskerry and Powerscourt, take the #44 bus from the Quays in Dublin (every 25 min) or the #85 from Bray, every forty minutes.

Glencree

Enniskerry lies at the foot of **GLENCREE**, which leads up into the Wicklow mountains with good access to the Wicklow Way. There's a **youth hostel** at Knockree, halfway up the valley close to Powerscourt, but it's many degrees less prepossessing than the one right up at the head (both are *An Óige*, and it's wise to reserve in summer through the main office in Mountjoy Square in Dublin, ☎01-363111; local numbers are ☎01-867196 or 867290; £3, £2.50 for ages 16–20). **Glencree youth hostel** is a solid, pedimented stone building dating from the construction of the military road in 1798 (the barrack buildings opposite now house the **Glencree Reconciliation Center**, which attempts to promote dialogue between young people of the north and south). Both hostels are open all year round.

Glencree was once famous for its oak woods, but the small one behind the hostel was actually planted in 1988, in sad commemoration of the fact that broadleaved woodlands now cover barely one percent of the country. Farther down the valley a dense conifer plantation has been designated a place for walks, with the misleading name of **Old Boley Wood**.

Above the youth hostel, dark, sinister terrain ascends to one of the two main mountain passes, the **Sally Gap**. Close to the source of the Liffey, it has been heavily cut up by Dubliners seeking peat—another depredation inflicted upon the landscape. The most spectacular route on from here is the **military road** down from the Sally Gap to Glendalough, which runs over rough country until it joins the Glenmacnass River, an extraordinary, extended waterfall. The other road takes you past Lough Tay and Lough Dan as it winds its way down to Sraghmore.

Dramatic, inaccessible **Lough Tay**—whose scree sides plunge straight into the water—is owned by Garech de Brun, one of the Guinnesses, and the man behind *Claddagh Records*. Although **Lough Dan** has gentler woodlands, visitors are made to feel unwelcome by numerous signs warning against trespassing on private land, and barring access to the lake. Even avoiding such areas, though, there's still plenty of good, boggy walking, and some spectacular views.

Coming down to Glendalough, you go through ROUNDWOOD (one of the stops for the St Kevin's Bus Service, see below), which doesn't seem to have anything much to recommend it, although people reputedly go there for their holidays. A café here claims to be the highest café in Ireland and has a sign assuring it's been passed for food hygiene—both are no doubt true, but they rightly make no claims as to the quality of the food. Roundwood's one enticement is its good independent **hostel**, *Little Flower* (June–Sept; £3; bicycle rental available; ☎01-818145). All the same, the best bet is probably to head on down to the crossroads at Laragh, where any of the three directions lead on to more impressively lonely scenery.

The Wicklow Way

Glencree is one of the better places to pick up the **Wicklow Way**, Ireland's first officially designated long-distance walk. Following a series of sheep tracks, forest firebreaks, and bog roads, above 1600 feet for most of the way, it leads from Marlay Park in Dublin's suburbs up into the Dublin Mountains; skirts the end of Glencree; cuts across the bleak, boggy hillside below Djouce Mountain, and pushes on to Glendalough and Aghavannagh, ending up 82 miles later at CLONEGAL on the Wexford border. It's not particularly well organized—one of its chief attractions for many hikers—but the whole route can be walked comfortably in ten to twelve days.

If you want to do this, Marlay Park is accessible via the #47B or #48A bus from Dublin city center. If you're short of time, the best part to walk is probably the section between Enniskerry and Glendalough, where the path reaches its highest point at White Hill (2073 feet), from which you can get a view of the mountains of North Wales on a fine day. For this section (three days), take the #44 bus from Dublin Quays to Enniskerry, and pick up St Kevin's bus service at Glendalough.

Low as they are, the Wicklow Mountains are notoriously treacherous, and even if you're planning on spending no more than a day walking, you should make sure you have the Ordnance Survey's Wicklow Way map, plus the tourist board's information sheet on the Wicklow Way (number 30). Bad weather can close in rapidly, making the going dangerous and frightening if you're far from a road or house. All the customary warnings about mountain walking apply; if you don't have any great experience of map reading, you'd do best to follow the yellow way-marking arrows. Trail walking—and indeed the whole idea of walking for pleasure—is fairly new in Ireland; consequently, the paths are far less crowded than their counterparts in, say, Britain.

There are three *An Óige* **hostels** along the way, plus plenty of places to stay around Glendalough (see below), so accommodation shouldn't be a problem, although it may be wise to reserve in high summer. By a stroke of great imagination, two of the hostels—Glencree (see above) and Aghavannagh—are housed in the great stone barracks complexes built to serve the military road built after 1798, so you can pick up the resonances of those grim times. The middle stop is at Glenmalure, itself a forbidding, shadowy valley (see below). The youth hostel here (July–Aug; book through *An Óige*'s Dublin office, ☎01-363111), with no phone, electricity, or running water, stands at the head of the valley just above the point where the river rushes over a weir. With no other buildings in sight, it must be one of the best settings imaginable for somewhere to stay. At Aghavannagh, the hostel (open all year; ☎0402-36102) is in the massively grand and remote barracks building on a hill with views all round.

Glendalough

GLENDALOUGH—the valley of the two lakes—is one of the standard tours out of Dublin, and its popularity with tour-bus parties may persuade you to skip it. Don't. Besides being one of the most important monastic sites in Ireland, it has an amazing, quite tangible quality of peace and spirituality.

Transport to Glendalough from Dublin is easy—use the St Kevin's Bus Service (£4 one-way, £7 return), which leaves from the Royal College of Surgeons on St Stephen's Green at 11:30am every day (with a second service at 6pm Mon–Sat, 7pm Sun), and comes back at either 4:15pm or 7am; 5:30pm on Sundays. The bus passes through Bray, where you can pick up the railroad if you're heading south.

The **monastery** at Glendalough (mid-June to mid-Sept daily 10am–7pm; mid-Sept–mid-June Tues–Sat 10am–4:30pm) was founded by Saint Kevin, a member of the royal house of Leinster, during the sixth century. As a center of the Celtic church, it became famous throughout Europe for its learning, and despite being sacked by the Vikings in the ninth and tenth centuries and by the English in the fourteenth century, it was patiently restored each time, and monastic life continued tenaciously until the sixteenth century.

The **cathedral**, dating from the early ninth century, has an impressively ornamental east window, while **St Kevin's Cross** is a massive slab of granite, carved around 1150, in the Celtic form of a cross superimposed on a wheel. It may have been left unfinished, since the "halo" formed by the wheel has not been pierced. In the **round tower**, the doorway is ten feet above the ground. The traditional story, and the one that the guide will undoubtedly tell you, is that this design was adopted so that in times of trouble monks could pull up the ladder and turn the tower into an inaccessible treasury and refuge; however, more recent thinking suggests that the reason may be structural. The twelfth-century **Priest's House**, partially reconstructed 700 years later, got its name from being used as a burial place for local priests during the suppression of Catholicism. The carving above the door, so worn as to be indecipherable, possibly shows Saint Kevin between two ecclesiastical figures.

Glendalough's most famous building is **St Kevin's Church**, a solid barrel-vaulted stone oratory, also known as **St Kevin's Kitchen**. Although it may well date from Saint Kevin's time, the round-tower belfry is an eleventh-century addition, and the structure has clearly been altered many times.

All these buildings are clustered between the visitors' center and the lower lake, and you'll be shown all of them unless it's raining hard, in which case the tour gets truncated. But the real delights of Glendalough lie beyond what you get to see on the tour. As you climb above the monastery complex, landscape and architecture combine in a particularly magical way, and you could spend days walking the footpaths that criss-cross the upper valley, drinking it all in. The scenery is at its most spectacular at the secretive **upper lake**, where wooded cliffs and a waterfall plunge vertically into the water.

There are plenty more antiquities connected with the monastic life here, among the cliffs around the upper lake, many of them formerly pilgrim shrines. The site of Saint Kevin's original church, the **Temple-na-Skellig**, is on a platform approached by a flight of stone steps, accessible only by boat. **St Kevin's Bed** is a rocky ledge high up the cliff, where it's said the holy man used to sleep in an attempt to escape from the unwelcome advances of a young girl. Eventually she found his hiding place and, waking up one morning to find her beside him, he reacted with the misogyny characteristic of the early church fathers—and pushed her into the lake.

Glendalough is amply equipped to receive its many sightseers, with acres of parking space and a huge, modern **visitors' center**. This is genuinely helpful, with an excellent exhibition and a video show that sets Glendalough in the context of the monastic ruins elsewhere in Ireland; worth seeing, particularly if you're not visiting any others. The admission charge (£1; students 30p) includes the video show, exhibition, and the guided tour of the site itself. **Accommodation** is no problem either. If you want to stay right in the middle of this amazing landscape, the *Luganure* bed-and-breakfast actually overlooks the Upper Lake. There are also plenty of B&Bs between Laragh and Roundwood, although the countryside here is decidedly less attractive. Otherwise, you've a choice between the *An Óige* hostel (£3, £2.50 ages 16–20; ☎0404-5143; full of school parties in the summer holidays) and the *Mill Youth Hostel* (independent) half a mile out of Laragh, over the bridge on the right, on the Rathdrum/Wexford road. A comfortable stone building complete with craft shop and pine kitchen, it makes a good base for exploring the area.

Finally, if you need guidance on how to exploit the sporting opportunities of the area, you could check out the rock-climbing, mountaineering, canoeing, and kayaking courses offered by the *Tiglin Adventure Center* (☎0404-40169).

Glenmalure and the Glen of Imail

Northwest of Glendalough, the main road takes you over the Wicklow Gap, whence there's a tolerably tough climb up to the top of Tonelagee (2677ft). South and west, the country rises, becoming wilder and more desolate, dominated by Lugnaquilla, the highest mountain in the Wicklow range. In this direction you can head southwest along the military road towards Aghavannagh and stay in the *An Óige* hostel (see "The Wicklow Way" above), or experienced walkers and map-readers have the option of trekking to the head of Glendalough, and down into the next glen.

Either way, you'll arrive in dark and lonely **GLENMALURE**, half of which is off-limits as an army firing range. Perhaps appropriately, Glenmalure was the scene of a decisive victory by the Wicklow Irish under Fiach MacHugh O'Byrne over the English under Elizabeth I. One of the 1798 barracks, now ruined, stands at the point where the military road hits the valley. It's a symbol of decay that somehow sets the tone for the entire valley, with its enclosed, mysterious feeling and steep scree sides which scarcely afford a foothold to the heather. The road eventually peters out in a parking lot, but a track continues past a weir up to a **youth hostel** (see "The Wicklow Way" again). Past the hostel, the trail forks right for Glendalough, and left, over the Table Mountain, for the Glen of Imail.

By comparison with Glenmalure, the **Glen of Imail** is almost inviting. Again, it's dominated by the impressive head of Lugnaquilla, and likewise, half of it is reserved as an army shooting range. Altogether, it's as wild and desolate as you could wish for, though more open and lighter than Glenmalure. There's an *An Óige* **youth hostel** at KNOCKANDARRAGH.

At DERRYNAMUCK, on the southeast side of the valley, stands a cottage where Michael O'Dwyer, one of the last insurgents of 1798, took refuge when trapped by the British, and escaped because Samuel McAllister drew the enemy's fire and died in his place. Now run as a folk musuem, the cottage is unmarked on most maps, the exception being the Ordnance Survey "Kildare-Wicklow" sheet.

Russborough

The west of County Wicklow, away from the mountains, is less spectacular than the rest, and the main reason for coming here is to visit the third of Wicklow's great cultural landmarks, **Russborough House** (Easter to 31 Oct Wed, Sat, Sun 2:30–6:30pm; last admission 5:30pm) and its impressive art collection. Getting to Russborough is no problem—BLESSINGTON, the pleasant town it adjoins, is forty minutes from central Dublin on the Waterford bus.

Designed, like Powerscourt, by Richard Castle (with the assistance of Francis Bindon), Russborough is one of the jewels of the Pale. A classic Palladian structure whose central block is linked to two wings with curving arms, its design was subsequently repeated throughout Ireland, as a result of Castle's influence and its own suitability as a kind of glorified farmhouse.

In Russborough's case, it's very glorified indeed. The house was constructed for Joseph Leeson, son of a rich Dublin brewer and MP for Rathcormack in the days of the semi-independent Irish parliament: he was created Lord Russborough in 1756, and later an earl. Russborough epitomizes the great flowering of Anglo-Irish confidence before the Act of Union deprived Ireland of its parliament, much of its trade and its high society (thereafter, the rich Anglo-Irish spent much of the year in London). No expense was spared. Not only were the fashionable architects of the day employed, but the plasterers, the Francini brothers, were also of the best. The plaster ovals in the drawing room, for instance, were made to order to fit the four Joseph Vernet marine paintings that still occupy them, and the overornate plasterwork on the stairs has been described as representing the ravings of a lunatic, and an Irish lunatic at that.

Impressive though it is, the chief reason why Russborough is so firmly on the tourist trail is its **collection of paintings**. The German entrepeneur Alfred Beit (1853–1906) was a co-founder with Cecil Rhodes of the De Beer

Diamond Mining Company, and he poured the fortune he derived from that enterprise into amassing works of art. His nephew, Sir Alfred Beit, acquired Russborough in 1952, which explains why such an extraordinary collection of famous pictures is kept in this obscure corner of County Wicklow. Whatever you may feel about their irrelevance to the site, or the source of the wealth that made the acquisitions possible, there are some marvelous paintings by Goya, Murillo, Velazquez, Gainsborough, Rubens, and Frans Hals, to name but a few. Russborough has been burglarized twice: in 1974, when Bridget Rose Dugdale stole sixteen paintings to raise money for the IRA (although her booty, worth £18 million, was recovered undamaged from a farmhouse in County Cork a week later), and in May 1986. The paintings taken in the second heist are still missing and the thieves remain unknown, although early in 1989 there was a rumor that one of the paintings was up for sale in Amsterdam. Nowadays security is tight, and visitors are herded around the house in groups, with little chance to study the paintings—or anything else— in detail. You could take a second tour, but a better way to get a more leisurely look would be to visit Russborough during the **Festival of Irish Music in Great Irish Houses** in June; ☎045-65239 for information.

The lake in front of Russborough provides the house with an idiomatically eighteenth-century prospect. The impression is a false one, however—it's actually a thoroughly twentieth-century reservoir, created by damming the Liffey, which provides Dublin with twenty million gallons of water a day.

There's an *An Óige* **youth hostel** in a tranquil location on the peninsula almost opposite Russborough (open all year; book through the main office in Dublin, ☎01-363111).

Along the Coast

Unless you're heading south to County Wexford, in which case the train runs right down the coast to Wicklow town, the coastal route is probably not the best one out of Dublin—it's commuter-land for a depressingly long way.

BRAY, the first conurbation along the coast, is connected to Dublin by the DART suburban railroad, so it's very much a dormitory suburb. Originally a Victorian resort developed when the railroad was extended south of Dún Laoghaire in the 1850s, it provides a dingy welcome for the hordes of visitors from Dublin at the weekends. With a seafront full of dingy hotels, video arcades, B&Bs and fast-food shops, Bray has little charm: its chief claim to fame is that James Joyce lived here from 1889 to 1891. Perhaps the best thing to do here is to walk around Bray Head, a knob of rock pushing into the sea, where a massive cross erected to mark the holy year of 1950 serves as a reminder that you are now in Catholic Europe. There are a few secluded coves in the shadow of the Head where you can swim. It's impressive enough in an oddly genteel sort of way, but this is hardly what you come to Ireland to see, and even Wicklow town, a few miles farther on down the coast, is more dramatic and rewarding. Like most places, Bray improves if you stick with it (the tourist office in the town hall, ☎01-867128, may help persuade you of its attractions), but not much. On the whole it's better to push on down the coast—scrubby and unremarkable for the most part—through Greystones and on to Wicklow, the county town.

Wicklow

There's nothing much to **WICKLOW**, and no great reason to come, but it is the first place that wholly escapes the influence of Dublin as you go down the coast and, should you find yourself with time on your hands, it's an oddly pleasant, ramshackle town with plenty of entertainment, good, cheap places to eat, plus walking and swimming too. It has none of the presence you might expect of a county town, and comes across as a happily disorganized kind of place, full of people chatting on sidewalks and cars cheerfully parked on double yellow lines. There are solidly built little houses in bright marine pastels; B&Bs are in reasonable supply (the nearest **hostel** is the *An Óige* one at Tiglin, six miles away in Ashford, ☎0404-40259), and there's **camping** on the beach at Silver Strand, a little over two miles south of town (☎0404-67924). For **food and drink** there are plenty of pubs—try *The Boathouse* on Main Street for music—and, unusually, there's also a cheap pizza/steak restaurant, the *Pizza del Forno*, also on Main Street, which stays open until midnight, and two Chinese restaurants. You can rent **bikes** from *Harris*'s on Main Street (☎0404-67247; £4 per day, £20 per week).

Just outside town on the seaward side, a knoll encrusted with some knobbly piles of stone constitutes all that's left of **Black Castle**, one of the fortifications built by the Fitzgeralds in return for lands granted them by Strongbow after the Anglo-Norman invasion of 1169. **Wicklow Head**, unlike Bray, really is spectacular, and you can walk all the way around it (there are two tiny swimming beaches, sunny in the mornings) accompanied by exhilarating views of the open sea and, northwards, the weird silhouettes of the Great and Little Sugarloaf Mountains.

Heading south **towards Arklow** there's a string of white sand beaches. The one at **Brittas Bay**, just north of Mizen Head, is particularly good—don't be put off by the trailer park. To get to Arklow you can either take the train down the coast, or jump on the Dublin-to-Wexford bus, which will take you on a scenic detour via the heavily wooded Vale of Avoca (see below). The journey takes just under an hour, and buses leave Wicklow at 10:30am and 7pm.

Horticultural enthusiasts should also know about **Mount Usher Gardens** (mid-March to Oct Mon–Sat 10:30am–6pm, Sun 11am–6pm; £1.80, students £1:20; ☎0404-40116), a few miles inland near Ashford, where rare trees, shrubs and flowers grow in profusion in a narrow strip next to the road. For others, the gardens' main attraction may be the miniature suspension bridges where you can see engineering principles at work as they sway and bounce under your weight. Close by, up a side road, *Hunter's Hotel* is a good, old-fashioned hostelry where Parnell used to stay. It's well worth a splurge if you've money to burn, or a drink in the bar if you haven't.

Arklow

ARKLOW has all the vitality you might have expected to find in Wicklow. Built on a site sloping gently towards the sea at the mouth of the Avoca River, it has a long and prosperous history, based on fishing, shipbuilding and the export of copper ore, pyrites and even gold, mined farther up the valley. Evidence of continued riches in relatively recent times can be seen in the elegant Art Deco movie theatre at the top of the main street.

Arklow is no longer a major port, but shipbuilding continues to be a dominant factor—*Gypsy Moth IV*, Sir Francis Chichester's prize-winning transatlantic yacht, was built at John Tyrrell's yard here. So, for a grip on the past, it's worth dropping in at the **Maritime Museum** (top of the main street and turn left). A happily haphazard collection of local finds, it claims a history for Arklow going back to Ptolemy's celebrated second-century map. It also emerges that Arklow was a major center for arms-smuggling during the upheavals of 1798. The museum houses such curiosities as a whale's tooth and eardrum, and a model ship made with 10,700 matchsticks.

Accommodation in Arklow is B&B. There are plenty of pubs—an ID system operates at all of them so be prepared for trouble if you look under 18—most of which seem to have some kind of entertainment on offer, albeit slightly bizarre. Afternoon dances, demure discos, and pub quizzes all seem unnaturally popular here.

Avondale and the Vale of Avoca

Heading back up towards Glendalough via Woodenbridge—the bus from Wexford to Dublin does the journey twice a day, leaving Arklow at 8am and 1pm, and continuing through Wicklow—you pass through the **Vale of Avoca**, one of those places designated "scenic" which are a sure draw for tour-bus parties. It *is* beautiful, to be sure, once you leave the fertilizer plant behind: thickly wooded slopes on either side of the river, culminating in the **Meeting of the Waters**, the confluence of the Avonmore and Avonbeg rivers. There's an *An Óige* **hostel** here, open all year (☎0404-4259; reserve through the Dublin office, ☎01-363111).

Apart from the Meeting of the Waters, the main attraction is the handweavers at **AVOCA**, a pleasantly unassuming village on the river. The weavers are housed in a group of whitewashed buildings with steep gray roofs, where the fly-shuttle looms that caused mass unemployment when they were introduced in 1723 are presented as picturesquely traditional. You might not like Avoca's products—cloaks, kilts, and deerstalker hats in bright, heathery pinks and purples, with plenty of models for the fuller figure—but there's a good, cheap lunch room selling sandwiches, soup and cakes.

A few miles upriver towards Rathdrum is the Avondale Forest Park, where you can see Parnell's house at **AVONDALE**. The effects of the famine in Wicklow—though less severe than in other parts of the country—led Charles Stewart Parnell to start his campaign for land reform. Twelve years after his death in 1891, the first Wyndham Land Act enabled tenant farmers to use government grants to buy the land they had leased, and thus marked the beginning of the end of the long heyday of the Anglo-Irish.

COUNTY KILDARE

County Kildare, in the heart of the Pale, forms part of the hinterland of Dublin. Although it lacks the spectacle of Wicklow to the capital's south, or the extraordinary range of ancient monuments of the lush Boyne valley to the north, it has a quiet charm of its own.

The **landscape** is a calm one of rolling farmland for the most part, with open grasslands and rough pasturage, just touching the dreary stretches of the monotonous Bog of Allen in the northwest. It's ancient countryside, marked by a string of **Celtic crosses** at Moone, Old Kilcullen, and Castledermot, but you're also constantly made aware that you're in Pale country: big stone estate walls border many of the fields and Georgian proportions in the buildings are noticeable features of the landscape. More obvious attractions include the magnificent **Castletown House** with its model village at Celbridge; the **Grand Canal**, which traverses the county and has a walkable towpath; or the pin-neat **National Stud** at Kildare and its extraordinarily extravagant Japanese Garden.

Because of its proximity to Dublin, there's no problem about **transportation** in County Kildare. The main **buses** to Limerick ply up and down the N7 trunk road, with the **rail** line running close beside it for most of the way. **Accommodation** is less easy—you're reliant on B&Bs, many of them the more expensive kind, catering to business travelers rather than individual tourists.

Out from Dublin

All you see of Kildare if you're headed for the far west, as most people are, is the view from the N7, the main Dublin–Limerick road, now expressway as far as **NAAS** (pronounced *Nace*). It's an unpromising introduction to the county: a roadside sign advertises Naas as "a nice place to shop," and there's probably not a great deal more to be said. *Nás na Ríogh* (Naas of the Kings), once the center of the extensive kingdom of the Uí Dunlainge and their successors, the Uí Faelain, now seems little more than a battered concourse of shops. Its one great attraction is **Punchestown Racecourse**, whose main meeting is the three-day steeplechasing festival in late April, when the racecourse itself is greatly celebrated for its flowering gorse.

NEWBRIDGE, a nineteenth-century town which grew up around the British barracks there (now re-Gaelicized as Dróichead Núa) is similarly unmemorable, except for its traffic jams. But after Newbridge the road heads over the grassy, unfenced stretches of the Curragh, and you're into racing country proper.

Kildare and the Curragh

KILDARE town is delightful: a solid, respectable little place around a sloping triangular square, with none of that feeling of depopulation that becomes so familiar in other parts of Ireland. The town is dominated by the massive, squat Church of Ireland **cathedral of St Brigid**, who founded a religious house here in 490. The present structure dates originally from the thirteenth century, though the north transept and choir were burned to the ground in the Confederate War of 1641, and the Victorian reconstruction in 1875 is pseudo-medieval. Its **round tower**, probably twelfth-century, has a particularly elaborate doorway twelve feet up, and it's hoped that the bizarre nineteenth-century battlements that have been removed can be replaced with something more in keeping with the original style.

Accommodation in Kildare is limited to B&Bs, which are themselves a bit thin on the ground. Try Mrs O'Connell's at Fremont, Tully Road (£10; ☎045-21604); the Brontes at Emdale, Newtown Cross (£10; ☎045-22060); or contact the tourist office (summer only) which operates out of a trailer located in the parking lot on the Dublin side of town. There's the usual range of pubs plus, in the old movie house, a chi-chi steak bar that wouldn't be out of place in the metropolis; it's named after Silken Thomas, a member of the ruling Fitzgerald family, whom the growing powers of the Tudor monarchy provoked into rebellion in 1536. The uprising was unsuccessful, and a bloody massacre followed at Maynooth; later known, ironically, as "the pardon of Maynooth."

The real reason for spending time in Kildare, however, is **racing**. The Curragh is the center of the Irish racing world, with two racecourses—the Curragh itself, and Punchestown, three miles southeast of Naas—plus dozens of studs. In early morning you can see strings of slim racehorses exercising on the 6000 acres of grassland. Breeding and training them is one of Ireland's major money-makers, and much of the activity is centered on the Curragh. For an idea of the scale of the operation, *Goff's Kildare Paddocks* at KILL, which sells over half of all Irish-bred horses, has an annual turnover of around £IR20 million.

The National Stud

The best place to see the perfectionism that attends the breeding and training of these valuable pieces of horseflesh is the **National Stud**, just outside Kildare. You can easily walk out from the town, though the entrance is not the obvious one through the main gates that you pass on the road from Dublin—instead follow the signs from downtown for the Stud and the Japanese gardens. You can pay to see just the Stud, or buy a joint ticket including the Japanese gardens. This is well worth it even if you're not interested in horticulture; far more than a collection of rare plants, they're also an extraordinary legacy of Anglo-Irish eccentricity.

The National Stud itself consists of neat white buildings set in green lawns as close-cropped and well-groomed as a Derby-winner's coat—a spick-and-span monument to the greater glory and perfectability of horses. Established in 1900 by Colonel William Hall Walker, who believed that horoscopes affected horses' form, the stud enjoyed an extraordinary record of success, and in 1915 was bequeathed to the British Crown, which rewarded Walker by creating him Lord Wavertree. When transferred to the Irish state in 1943, it became the National Stud.

Colonel Hall Walker's belief in the stars is reflected in the **stallion boxes**, built in the 1960s according to his astrological principles, with lantern roofs allowing moon and stars to exert their influence on the occupants. There's a brass plaque on each door giving the stallion's name and details of his racing career. The National Stud's **museum** is an enjoyably chaotic account of the history of horses and horse-racing which contains, among other bizarre exhibits, the skeleton of the 1960s champion racehorse, Arkle. Outside is a calming Zen garden of meditation.

The Japanese Gardens

The bizarre **Japanese gardens** were laid out on drained bog (between 1906 and 1910) by Colonel Hall Walker and two Japanese gardeners. Part of the Edwardian craze for all things Japanese, they're planned to represent the "life of man." Man, emphatically, it has to be said, rather than woman. In a weirdly enumerated metaphysical joyride, you're led from birth to death via the Tunnel of Ignorance (no. 3) and the Parting of Ways (no. 6), where you're invited to choose between a life of philandering, bachelorhood, or marriage. In fact the choice is illusory: choosing marriage, you step across stepping stones to the Island of Joy and Wonder (no. 7) and meet your wife at the engagement bridge (no. 8; easily confused with the Red Bridge of Life, no. 17) and so on. Finally you pass through the Gateway to Eternity (no. 20), and it's time to go.

A Day at the Races

You don't have to know anything about horses to enjoy **a day at the races**. Irish race-going is quite unlike its English counterpart: there's none of the snobbery attached to who's who or who's allowed in the enclosure, and it's not as expensive. It's also different in that there's just as much excitement attached to steeplechasing as flat racing—steeplechasing, in fact, despite its smaller prize money, is often regarded as the better sport.

The major Irish **classic meets** are all held at the Curragh: the Airlie/Coolmore 1000 Guineas and Goffs Irish 1000 Guineas in May; the Budweiser Irish Derby in June; the Kildangan Irish Oaks in July, and the Irish St Leger in September. Punchestown is also famous for a three-day jump race meeting in late April. Details of race meetings can be found in all the daily papers or in the specialist press: *Irish Field* (published Saturday morning) and the *Racing Post* (daily). *Bord Fáilte* publishes an annual information sheet with the dates of the current year's meetings; you should also be able to get schedules from local **tourist offices**.

If you are interested in getting to the Curragh, there are **special bus and train services** scheduled to fit in with all major meetings; phone Busarus in Dublin (☎01 366111) for details.

Maynooth and Castletown House

Both Maynooth—due west of Dublin on the N6—and Celbridge (for Castletown House) are firmly on the one-day tourist-trip trail from Dublin, so you're unlikely to be on your own here. There really isn't all that much to detain you in **MAYNOOTH** (pronounced Mer-nooth, with the stress on the second syllable), pretty though it is. Its main claim to fame is its seminary, St Patrick's College, which in addition to training priests now houses two universities. For fans of Victoriana, the square is by Pubin in Gothic revival style. The ruins beside the entrance to the college are those of the thirteenth-century **Maynooth Castle**, one of the two main strongholds of the Anglo-Norman Fitzgerald family, who ruled Kildare and, effectively, most of Ireland, from the thirteenth century until the coming of the Tudor monarchs (their other castle is at Kilkea, in the south of the county). Maynooth's formal town planning is made sense of by Carton House, a Georgian gem by Richard Castle which lies at the other end of the main street. However, although its grand avenue looks promising, you can't visit the house at present (but check this; Carton has been up for sale and the situation may change).

Castletown House

Few places give a better impression of the immense scale on which the Anglo-Irish imagination was able to work than **Castletown House**, designed in 1722 for the Speaker of the Irish House of Commons, William Conolly, by the Italian Alessandro Galilei. You enter the grounds through the village of CELBRIDGE, planned to lend importance to the house itself. This exhibits the strictest classicism: the front facade, facing out over the Liffey, gives little away except for a rigidly repeated succession of windows. It's the only thing about the house that *is* restrained, though, since Castletown, from the very beginning, was built for show.

    William Conolly, who commissioned it, was a publican's son from Donegal who—like many others—owed his success to the changed conditions after the Battle of the Boyne, and made his fortune by dealing in forfeited estates. Member for Donegal in the Irish Parliament since 1692, he was a staunch supporter of the Hanoverian cause, and was unanimously elected Speaker of the Irish House of Commons in 1715. In 1717 the Ambassador at Florence noted Conolly's intention to bring to Ireland "the best architect in Europe," a move of some significance to national self-esteem. A letter to the famous metaphysician Bishop Berkeley states: "I am glad for the honor of my country that Mr Conolly has undertaken so magnificent a pile of building . . . . Since this house will be the finest Ireland ever saw, and by your description fit for a Prince, I would have it as it were the epitome of the Kingdom, and all the natural rarities she affords should have a place there." Although plans for the house were magnificent, work proceeded in a haphazard way. The cellar vaults, begun before the design of the house was finalized, still bear little relation to what's above ground; and the house interior remained unfinished—lacking, for instance, a main staircase—until the end of the long life of William's wife, who preferred building follies.

The fruits of old Mrs Conolly's imagination are most obvious in the grounds, where a **folly** closes the vista to the north, 140 feet of what appears to be a monument to chimney-sweeping, and the **Wonderful Barn** forms a focus for the view to the east. Both projects were set up to provide relief work for estate workers hard hit by the famine-ridden winter of 1739, and Mrs Conolly's sister, for one, disapproved: "My sister is building an obleix to answer a vistow from the bake of Castletown house," she wrote of the folly; "It will cost her three or four hundred pounds at least, but I believe more. I really wonder how she can dow so much and live as she duse." Incidentally, it seems that the ground on which the obelisk stands did not belong to Castletown, not that this bothered Mrs Conolly.

The **interior** decoration was the inspiration of Lady Louisa Lennox, who married into the Conolly family in 1759 at the age of fifteen. The newlyweds might have lived in London (Louisa's brother-in-law described her as wanting "to buy every house she sees"), but the fact that Louisa's elder sister, Lady Emily Kildare, had settled at Carton, close by at Maynooth, decided matters. It was Louisa who commissioned the Francini brothers to produce the extraordinary plasterwork in the halls and ordered the long gallery at the back of the house, which she considered "the most comfortable room you ever saw, and quite warm; supper at one end, the company at the other, and I am writing in one of the piers at a distance from them all." Apparently, she ordered the magnificent Murano glass chandeliers on a journey to Venice, but when they arrived they were found to clash with the room's blue, Pompeiian-style decor.

Given this personal, idiosyncratic stamp on Castletown, it seems a shame that no one lives here any more. In 1967 the house was bought by Desmond Guinness, a founder of the **Irish Georgian Society**. Established in 1958 with the aim of preserving Ireland's magnificent Georgian heritage, the society is regarded with suspicion or amusement in some quarters. It has strong Anglo-Irish leanings and shows some degree of eccentricity (the English chapter teams up with the Silver Ghost Club to cruise around the countryside in antique Rolls Royces), but it's done sterling work in, for example, providing small but vital grants that have enabled buildings to be saved. Inquiries to the *Irish Georgian Society*, Leixlip Castle, Leixlip, County Kildare (☎01-244211).

Canal Country

Monuments to eighteenth-century confidence in Irish trade, which was to be dashed by the Act of Union, the **Royal and Grand Canals** flow from Dublin through County Kildare and on into the Irish heartland. While Ireland had experienced a minor industrial revolution in the mid- to late eighteenth century, when mines, mills, workshops, and canals were created, the Act of Union precluded farther development. By walking along the **towpaths**, or cruising on the Grand Canal, you can see how industrialization affected—and failed to affect—the eighteenth-century landscape. Grand Canal cruisers are based at Tullamore in County Offaly (*Celtic Canal Cruisers*; ☎0506-21861);

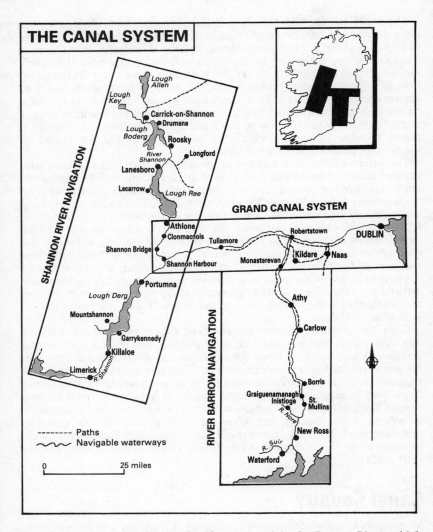

THE CANAL SYSTEM

SHANNON RIVER NAVIGATION

Lough Allen
Lough Key
Lough Boderg
Carrick-on-Shannon
Drumsna
Roosky
River Shannon
Longford
Lanesboro
Lecarrow
Lough Ree

GRAND CANAL SYSTEM

Athlone
Clonmacnois
Tullamore
Robertstown
DUBLIN
Shannon Bridge
Shannon Harbour
Monasterevan
Kildare
Naas
Portumna
Lough Derg
Mountshannon
Garrykennedy
Killaloe
Limerick
R. Shannon

RIVER BARROW NAVIGATION

Athy
Carlow
Borris
Graiguenamanagh
Inistioge
St. Mullins
R. Nore
New Ross
R. Suir
Waterford

- - - - Paths
~~~ Navigable waterways

0   25 miles

from here you can head on to the Shannon, or join the Barrow River, which meets the Grand Canal at Robertsbridge and is navigable all the way down to Waterford.

The **Grand Canal** was a truly ambitious project, running from Dublin to Monasterevin on the Kildare/Laois border, where it forks. The southern branch joins the Barrow at Athy, effectively extending the waterway as far south as Waterford; while the western branch runs up to Tullamore in County Offaly, and on to join the great natural waterway of the Shannon at

Shannonbridge. As late as 1837 the Grand Canal was carrying over 100,000 passengers a year; and it continued to be used for freight right up to 1959. The **Royal Canal** runs past Maynooth and Mullingar before joining the Shannon (many tortuous meanderings later) at Cloondara, north of Lough Rea, for access to the northwest.

Two locations are particularly evocative of canal life. **ROBERTSTOWN**, due north of Kildare, is no more than a village, yet it boasts a canal stop complete with a grand, pedimented canalside hotel (now pebble-dashed and painted bright orange). This is occasionally used for candlelight dinners and is also a center for canoe training and canal barge trips; for more information call ☎01-452655 (all year) or ☎045-60020 (May–Sept). At **MONASTEREVIN**, west of Kildare along the N7, there's a truly magnificent example of eight-eenth-century state-of-the-art technology. Here the Grand Canal crosses the Barrow on a viaduct (in eighteenth-century terms, the equivalent of a freeway overpass), with superseding technologies upstream (a railroad bridge) and downstream (the N7 Dublin–Limerick highway). Otherwise, Monasterevin follows the set pattern of an Irish Pale town: a big house, in this case **Moore Abbey** (once the home of the Irish tenor John McCormack, famous for his syrupy renditions of Irish folk songs), a church, and the town itself. This consists of a street of eighteenth-century houses on one side of the road only, their gardens sloping down to the River Barrow on the other. The houses get steadily grander going towards the canal; almost at the end of the row, *Carlow House* is a fine **bed-and-breakfast**.

South Kildare

It's a mistake to think of County Kildare as a relatively modern landscape, seeing in it only the legacies of the Anglo-Normans and Anglo-Irish. South of Naas on the Carlow road, three **high crosses** set in the green, rolling farm-land attest that settlements and cultural history here are much, much older. **OLD KILCULLEN**, off the road in a field, is the site of an early Celtic monas-tery with the remains of eighth-century crosses, and an evocative round tower damaged during the 1798 rebellion. The small village of **MOONE**, just south of Timolin, once formed a link in the chain of monasteries founded by Saint Columba, and the garden of Moone Abbey contains the ruins of a fourteenth-century Franciscan friary and a ninth-century cross. At **CASTLEDERMOT** there's more to see: two tenth-century granite high crosses, plus a bizarre twelfth-century Romanesque doorway standing by itself in front of an ugly modern church and a truncated round tower. Castledermot also has a thir-teenth-century Augustinian abbey, an early example of how the European monastic orders muscled in on the indigenous Irish church. Its substantial remains give a completely different feel to what might otherwise be merely a roadside stop; get the keys from the caretaker, who lives next door.

Kilkea Castle, the Fitzgeralds' second Kildare stronghold (after Maynooth), stands a couple of miles up the Athy road from Castledermot. It's impressive looking, though largely a sham—originally built in 1180, it was modified in the seventeenth century and most of it is a mid-nineteenth-century restoration. Recently it has been used as a luxury hotel, and a pending large-scale refurbishment looks set to take it still farther away from its roots.

Almost exactly halfway between Naas and Carlow is **BALLITORE**, an old Quaker village where the eighteenth-century Anglo-Irish political philosopher Edmund Burke was educated, and a good example of the religious toleration that it sometimes seems the British government was prepared to grant anyone but the Catholics. A museum (open afternoons) above the village library gives a vivid picture of what life was like; the industrious Quakers each plied a trade and their sober, businesslike approach made Ballitore a model village by comparison to the general squalor and poverty of surrounding places. But the dominant impression given by the copperplate handwritten letters on show is the sheer boredom of life in a place where any stranger was cause for excitement. The *Cottage Biography* of one of Ballitore's nineteenth-century residents, Mary Leadbeater (on sale at the museum) preserves more of the same stultifying atmosphere. Up towards the main road is the walled **Quaker graveyard**, whose plain, dignified tombstones seem worthy monuments to the deceased.

On the border with County Laois sits **ATHY** (emphasis on the second syllable), one of those places where a bucketful of imagination is required to envisage it as it once was; prosperity has turned a formerly handsome Georgian town with a fine main square into something much more ramshackle. A massive riverside factory sits oddly with the Georgian fanlights and a quite repulsive new church. The latter is apparently supposed to make reference to a dolmen, although the Sydney Opera House seems a stronger influence. By the riverside stands the square tower of a fifteenth-century castle built to protect the ford, nowadays a private house.

travel details

Trains
From Kildare to Dublin Heuston Stn (20 daily; 30min).

Bus Éireann
From Kildare to Dublin (15 daily; 1hr 20min).

DART
From Bray to Dublin Connolly Stn (4 daily; 25min); **Wicklow** to Dublin (4 daily; 50min); **Arklow** to Dublin (4 daily; 1hr 20min).

CHAPTER THREE

LAOIS AND OFFALY

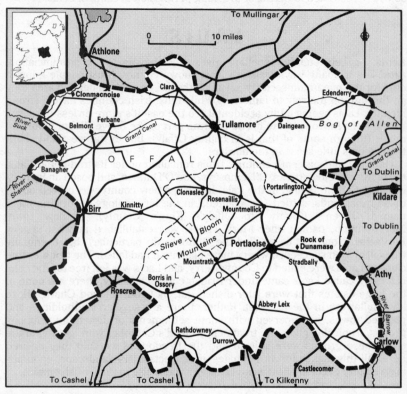

I f you've come to Ireland for the scenery, or the wild remote places, or the romance of the far west, then the central counties of **Laois** and **Offaly** probably don't hold a great deal to entice you. But this quiet and unremarkable part of the country between Dublin and the Shannon is an excellent place to get to know another Ireland, one not hyped by the tourist authorities. It's gentle, green farming land bearing the marks of a complex pattern of settlement: the Celtic church, Viking invaders, the arrival of the Anglo-Normans, and, very strongly in these twin counties, the planted settlements with which the British sought to keep their base in the Pale secure. It's a subtle, detailed landscape, which the destruction of Ireland's foreign trade by the Act of Union in 1801 ensured remained virtually untouched by the Industrial Revolution.

Transportation in Laois and Offaly is easy—the main N7 trunk road and the main railroad line to Limerick slice straight through Laois, while the industrial center of Tullamore makes an obvious transportation center, both road and rail, for Offaly. The major problem, as in much of central Ireland, is **accommodation**. There are, simply, no hostels and very few official campgrounds, so you're restricted to B&Bs, or to asking permission to camp in fields.

LAOIS

Laois, or Leix—neither spelling gives any clue as to its pronunciation, *Leash*—is in many ways Ireland's least-known county. Most people know it only for the maximum security jail at Portlaoise, or as an ill-defined area they go through on the way to Limerick. While most Irish counties have a strong identity, Laois seems oddly accidental. To the east it's more or less bordered by the river Barrow; to the north, it forms part of the Slieve Bloom mountain range (though some of that is in county Offaly); but to the west and south there seems little sense in the borders.

Until the mid-sixteenth century, Laois remained under its traditional clans, the O'Mores, FitzPatricks, O'Dempseys, and O'Dunnes, and posed an increasing threat to the British in the Pale. In 1556, a new county was carved out of these tribal lands, settled (or "planted," in the terminology of the time) and named Queen's County (to Offaly's King's County). A new town, Maryborough, named after Mary Tudor, was established at what is now Portlaoise. None of this quelled the O'Mores (in particular), but eventually transplantation succeeded where mere plantation had failed. The troublesome clans of Laois were exiled to County Kerry, and Laois was left free for the colonizers. Because Laois came under British control so early, there are none of the huge estates that were later dished out, by Cromwell and Charles II, to loyal followers in the far west. Rather, there are smaller landholdings and planned towns, interspersed with some settlements of dissenting religious groups. Ironically, given the treatment Ireland's Catholics were getting at the time, these groups were able to find the freedom of worship they desired here. All this makes for an intimate—if unspectacular—landscape, epitomizing a history of colonialism as much as anywhere else in the British empire.

Portlaoise and Around

PORTLAOISE, unremarkable except for the top security jail that leaps into the news whenever there's an argument about extradition of a prisoner to the North, is a suitably grim place. It was founded in 1547, when the O'Mores held the fortress of Dunamase to the south, as a fortification under the name of Fort Protector. In 1556 the town was planted and renamed Maryborough. Today it's seedy and depressed; the main road bypasses it entirely and, unless you arrive by train and can't avoid it, you're probably well advised to do the same. It does, however, have a **tourist office** (☎0502-21178), which may be useful for information.

What is well worth seeing, though, is the **Rock of Dunamase**, two or three miles out on the Stradbally road. An extraordinary, knobbly mound encrusted with layer upon layer of fortifications, it's a great place for gazing out, beyond the flat surrounding countryside, to the Slieve Bloom mountains to the north and the Wicklow hills in the east. There are suggestions that Dunamase was known to Ptolemy under the name of *Dunum*, and Celtic *Dun Masc* was valuable enough to be plundered by the Vikings in 845. Today, the hill is crowned by a **ruined castle** of the twelfth-century king of Leinster, Dermot MacMorrough. He it was who invited Strongbow to Ireland, and married his daughter, Aoife, to him, including Dunamase in her dowry. Explicable only in terms of the complex history of the Anglo-Normans, Dunamase eventually passed from Strongbow—Henry II's right-hand man— to the Mortimers and the O'Mores, bitter opponents of the British. It was finally blown up by Cromwell's troops in 1650. The earthworks 500 yards to the east of the fortress are still known as **Cromwell's lines**.

STRADBALLY (literally "street-town"), a few miles farther south, is notable chiefly for the **narrow-gauge railroad** at Stradbally Hall. A nineteenth-century steam locomotive, formerly used in the Guinness brewery in Dublin, runs every weekend from March to October; there's also a **traction engine museum** in the town, and a **steam engine rally** on the first weekend in August.

The South: Abbeyleix and Durrow

The south of County Laois consists of lush farmland, dotted with towns and villages. The largest of these is **ABBEYLEIX**, named after a Cistercian abbey founded here by a member of the O'More family in 1183. In one of those periodic bursts of enthusiasm that seem to be a mark of the Ascendancy, Abbeyleix was entirely remodeled by Viscount de Vesci in the eighteenth century and relocated on the coach road away from the old village to the southwest.

Unfortunately, the attractive pedimented eighteenth-century **Abbeyleix House** (designed by James Wyatt) isn't open to the public, although the gardens sometimes are. In the village, *Morrissey's Bar* is an enormous combination grocery shop and pub which probably hasn't changed in fifty years, with pew seats and a brazier, and old advertisements for beer and tobacco that seem to have been forgotten by time. It's a great place to sit and soak up the atmosphere. You can stay in a modest example of Georgian architecture at nearby BALLINAKILL. *The Glebe* is run as a B&B by Mrs Dowling (☎0502 33368; £15).

DURROW, farther south on the Kilkenny road, is yet another planned town, grouped around a green adjoining **Castle Durrow**, the first great Palladian house to be built in this area (1716). It's now a convent, but it is possible to walk up the drive and see it. The town was owned by the Duke of Ormond, who for reasons of his own had it adopted by County Kilkenny; it took an act of parliament to get it returned to what was then Queen's County in 1834.

The very **southwest** corner of County Laois is quiet farming land punctuated by small villages such as CULLAHILL, RATHDOWNEY, and ERILL. Although all you can do there is look at the neat color-washed houses, visit the local pub or shop, and ponder the changing ways of the world, just being there is delightful, and these are good places to stop over if you're cycling.

Accommodation in these parts is almost nonexistent, but Mrs Carroll does run a B&B at River House in Errill (it's best to phone ahead, ☎0505 44120; £9.60).

Slieve Bloom and North Laois

North Laois is dominated by the **Slieve Bloom Mountains** (pronounced *Schlieve Bloom*), which bring some welcome variation to this flat county. Although they scarcely reach 1200 feet—the Slieve Bloom mountaineering club is something of a standing joke with mountaineers from loftier parts of Ireland—they're ruggedly desolate enough to give a taste of real wilderness, even if you follow the **Slieve Bloom Way**. The Way, just over twenty miles in length, takes you across moorland, woods, and bog, along part of one of the old high roads to Tara and through the bed of a pre-Ice Age river valley. Along the way dense conifer plantations attempt to survive, with a little help from the taxpayer, way above the natural tree line. If your time is limited and you have a car, the best place to start is probably **Glen Barrow** or the **Forelacka valley**, where standing stones and a tumulus evince ancient human settlement just across the border in County Offaly. Otherwise, you can catch the Dublin–Portumna **bus** at Birr or Portarlington and start walking at KINNITY, a really delightful upland village that has an excellent pub.

Unfortunately, **accommodation** is limited in this neck of the woods. The pub in COOLRAIN in the Slieve Bloom foothills—good for traditional music, too—has rooms (not tourist-board approved), or, if you feel like a real treat, there's *Roundwood House* just outside MOUNTRATH, a mid-eighteenth-century Palladian mansion nowadays run as a guesthouse. Originally built by a Quaker who had made his fortune in America, it's a doll's house of a building decorated in vibrantly authentic Georgian colors, with a double-height hall boasting a Chinese Chippendale-style staircase. The tourist board says Roundwood can't call itself a hotel (too few rooms) or a grade A guesthouse (no fitted carpets or curtains—period rugs and original shutters instead) so it functions as a B&B, with prices scaled accordingly (£16 a night; £14 for dinner; ☎0502-32120).

Mountmellick, Portarlington, and Emo

Mountmellick and Portarlington are typical of the few little settlements that grew up independently of the great houses, and both were communities of outsiders. **MOUNTMELLICK**, almost encircled by the Owenmass river, was founded in the seventeenth century by Quakers, and still has a spacious eighteenth-century feel to it. You need some imagination to see the houses as the elegant buildings they must once have been, but Mountmellick in its heyday was undoubtedly both prosperous—it was famous for its embroidered white lacework—and cultured.

PORTARLINGTON was founded in 1667 by General Ruvigny, Earl of Galway, and settled by a group of Huguenot refugees, who built the elegant eighteenth-century houses with their spacious orchards and gardens, which once grew exotic fruit like peaches and apricots (particularly good examples are to be seen in Patrick Street). Some of the inscriptions on the tombstones of St Michael's Church, still known as the French Church, are in French.

One of the few really big estates in County Laois is **Emo Court**, just off N7 at NEW INN. Designed by James Gandon for Lord Arlington around 1790 (but finished, not entirely according to Gandon's plans, only in the mid-nineteenth century), it's a massive, domed building that has been impressively restored by its present owner after years of neglect when it was run as a Jesuit seminary. The enormous grounds are open afternoons from the end of March to the end of October; the house on Monday afternoons only (other times by arrangement with the owner, ☎0502-26110). If the charms of Laois's quiet landscape take hold of you, you can find out more in John Feehan's excellent topographical survey, *Laois: an environmental history*—a good example of the new breed of local history that deals with both the natural and the man-made past.

OFFALY

From the Bog of Allen in the east to Boora Bog in the west, **County Offaly** is dominated by bog and peat. A low-lying region bounded to the northwest by the meandering Shannon and its flood plain, it's only in the south that the land rises at all into the foothills of the Slieve Bloom range. The **Bog of Allen**, vast, black and desolate, has been intensively exploited for peat; and only real bog freaks will find much of interest there. **Boora Bog** is entirely different—smaller and less unremittingly flat and bare. It's the site of an archaeological find that proves that there was human life here 9000 years ago; and of **Clonmacnoise**, the greatest monastery of early Celtic Ireland.

The Bog of Allen and Tullamore

The **Bog of Allen** only really becomes overpowering after EDENDERRY, traditionally on the edge of the Pale. But even here, after miles of dark bogland, it's a distinct relief to reach somewhere with lots of people and an air of prosperity. Pushing on along the Dublin–Portumna bus route towards Tullamore, you pass through DAINGEAN, formerly Philipstown, the provincial capital in the days when Offaly was known as King's County. Both county and capital were planted in Mary Tudor's reign and named after her husband, Philip II of Spain.

ALL ABOUT BOGS

Ten thousand years ago, after the last Ice Age, the melting glaciers and ice sheets left central Ireland covered by shallow lakes. As time went by the lake and lakeside vegetation grew and died and partly decomposed, in a continuing cycle that changed these lakes to fens, and eventually into domed bogs. Ireland now has the finest range of peatlands in Europe.

At one time there were 311,000 hectares of raised bog in Ireland; by 1974 there were 65,000; and by 1985 there were just 20,000 hectares left. They continue to disappear at a rate of 3000 hectares per year. It is only recently that the Irish have awoken to the great natural importance of the boglands. Not only are they home to rare plants, from mosses to bilberries, but they provide a habitat for birds. The bog gases also act as preservatives, and the bogs of Ireland have yielded archaeological evidence of botanical and human history up to 9000 years ago in the form of pollens and plant remains, gold and silver artifacts, dug-out canoes, and human bodies.

To see a raised bog of international importance, go to **Mongan Bog** in County Offaly. Part of the Clonmacnoise Heritage Zone, it's situated on the banks of the Shannon. And if the bog bug really bites, head for the **Peatland Information Center** in Lullymore, County Kildare, where you can buy a copy of the Irish Peatland Conservation Council's *Guide to Irish Peatlands*.

Coming from either direction, the Bog of Allen to the east or Boora Bog to the west, the bright lights and solid buildings of **TULLAMORE**, astride the Grand Canal, seem welcoming. Its Victorian ambience makes the town look more English than Irish, a result of moving the capital from Philipstown to Tullamore in 1834, following decades in which the British pushed the boundaries of King's County ever farther westwards. Apart from the shops and a certain amount of nightlife, there are really only two reasons to come to Tullamore. One is **Irish Mist**, a truly delicious whiskey liqueur, samples of which might be available from the information center on Bury Quay (a little way down the Rahan road and turn right; Mon–Fri 10am–5pm).

The other reason is **Charleville Forest**, an extraordinary Georgian-Gothic mansion ("perhaps the first deliberately formed asymmetrical house in Ireland," wrote Dan Cruickshank in the excellent *Guide to the Georgian Buildings of Britain and Ireland*), built in 1779 to the designs of Francis Johnston. It has recently changed hands, and the new owner (unlike his predecessor) isn't into receiving visitors, but it's worth checking at the **tourist office** in the middle of town (by the bridge) in case this attitude has changed. In any case the estate is open, and wonderfully spooky it is too. The Gothic element is highly suggestive of a horror movie: castellated turrets, shady trees, and clinging ivy, while the house in the center of the estate, surrounded by a second wall topped by urns, is a secretive place made for diabolical activities. With its splendid old trees, leafy walks, and even a grotto, the estate has everything you could wish for. To get there, take the Birr road out of Tullamore: Charleville's gates are on the right as you leave the town— about ten minutes' walk—by the Offaly Historical Society's offices.

Durrow Abbey

Four miles north of Tullamore on N52, by some handsome wrought-iron gates to the left of the road, a signpost marks the way to the site of **Durrow Abbey**, one of the monasteries founded by the energetic Saint Colmcille (better known as Saint Columba), and the place where the *Book of Durrow*—an illuminated late seventh-century copy of the gospels, now exhibited in Trinity College Library, Dublin—was made.

A long avenue brings you to a typically Irish juxtaposition: a grand Georgian mansion next to a medieval church, which stands on the site of the monastery. A notice at the main gates gives directions to the high cross and tombstones; behind you is the formality of the avenue, ahead the well tended grounds of the house. Inside the church walls everything is different—the disused churchyard, the masonry strangled with ivy, gravestones leaning crazily on uneven ground as if the earth has opened and disgorged their contents . . . a spooky place, where Durrow's high cross and tombstones seem to represent sweet reason.

Western Offaly

Western Offaly is dominated by the bog and the Shannon, one virtually impassable, the other for centuries a means of communication; there's a huge range of ancient sites along the river. Exploring the *esker* ridges (raised paths above the bog) of this quiet, bog-and-water landscape has a certain appeal if you hit good weather. It's excellent **cycling** country, and while there's nothing specific to see much of the time, following roads that have for centuries been the only passages through the bog has a resonance of its own. The only problem is **accommodation**: for the most part you're restricted to B&Bs—and even these are few and far between—or camping in fields (ask permission first). For information on B&B availability, check with the Clonmacnoise tourist office (☎0905-74134, March–Oct).

Of the ancient sites along the Shannon, by far the most important is **CLONMACNOISE**, early Celtic Ireland's foremost monastery, in the north west of the county. Approaching from Shannonbridge, the first evidence of its whereabouts is a stone wall leaning precariously towards the Shannon. This is actually a remnant of a thirteenth-century Norman castle, built to protect the river crossing, which has leaned ever since its wooden foundations were destroyed by fire, and has nothing whatever to do with the monastery.

When you first see the monastic complex itself—a huddle of wind- and rain-swept buildings on an open plain in a bend in the Shannon—it seems hard to believe that this was a settlement of any importance. Deep in the unfashionable, untouristed center of Ireland, it's still remote enough not to receive huge numbers of visitors. Yet this was not just a monastery, but a royal city and a burial place for the kings of Connacht and Tara, including the last high king of Ireland, Rory O'Conor, buried here in 1198. As the book-shrines, croziers and other richly decorated artifacts on show in the National Museum in Dublin testify, it was also an artistic center of the highest order;

the twelfth-century *Book of the Dun Cow*, now in the Royal Irish Academy Library in Dublin, is only one of many treasures made here.

Founded by Saint Keran around 548, the monastery was largely protected by its isolation: surrounded by bog, Clonmacnoise could only be reached by boat, or along a causeway atop an *esker* known as the **Pilgrims' Causeway**. Irish, Viking, and Norman attacks it withstood, but in 1552 the English garrison at Athlone looted the monastery and left it beyond recovery. However, plenty remains: a cathedral, eight churches, two round towers, high crosses, grave slabs, and a thirteenth-century ring fort.

Seeing any significant differences between these small, gaunt, gray buildings takes a trained eye. The **cathedral**, scarcely bigger than its companions, was built in 904 by King Flann and Abbot Coman Conailleach, and rebuilt in the fourteenth century by Tomultach MacDermot; the sandstone pillars of the west doorway may have been incorporated from the earlier church. Not everything at Clonmacnoise, however, is as simple as it seems: to the right of the cathedral, **Teampull** (Temple) **Doolin** carries the elaborate coat of arms of Edmund Dowling of Clondarane, who restored the building in 1689; **Teampull Hurpan**, adjacent, was actually added in its entirety in the seventeenth century. **Teampull Kieran**, on the other side of the cathedral, is the reputed burial place of the founding saint, as well as allegedly the place where he built the first church on the site; the ruined **Teampull Kelly** is probably twelfth-century.

Of the high crosses, the early tenth-century **Great Cross**, over twelve feet high, is said to commemorate King Flann and Abbot Coman; the carvings represent the monastery's foundation and scenes from the passion story. The **South Cross**, dating from the ninth century, is decorated with flower and animal motifs.

A little farther from the main group of buildings is **O'Rourke's tower**, a round tower sixty feet high, erected just after the cathedral and blasted by lightning in 1134. On the outer boundary of the site, by the Shannon, are the **Teampull Finghin**, with another round tower dating from 1124, and the **Teampull Conor**, which was founded early in the eleventh century by Cathal O'Connor and used as a parish church from around 1790.

The **Church of the Nunnery**, away from the main enclosure, is signposted but difficult to find, and most people lose heart before they reach it. Follow the path across the site and bear left along the lane. The Church is a little farther along on the right, two lovely Romanesque arches in a field by the Shannon, exuding a feeling of peace. It's hard to imagine Clonmacnoise ever feeling crowded, but if your arrival does happen to coincide with a tourbus party, this is the place to come.

Shannonbridge, Shannon Harbour, and Banagher

From Clonmacnoise, the road to Shannonbridge skirts the Boora Bog. **SHANNONBRIDGE** has a set of traffic lights, but only because the sixteenspan bridge across the river is so narrow. Upstream, the wetlands of the Shannon open up; downstream a power station signifies the exploitation of the boglands. This is the point where Counties Offaly, Roscommon, and

Galway meet and the River Suck joins the Shannon: hence the strategically placed and massive artillery fortification dating from Napoleonic times. There's a music pub—*Killeen's Tavern*—on the main street and, should you find yourself spending a night here, a bed-and-breakfast closer to the bridge.

Farther south, **Shannon Harbour**—a few buildings and the ivy-covered *Grand Hotel*—is where the River Brosna and the Grand Canal meet the Shannon after their journey right across Ireland. As you walk down to the junction, there comes a magical point where the entire landscape seems to become water. **Clonony Castle**, a mile or two farther inland, is a ruined sixteenth-century tower house with a nineteenth-century reconstructed barn, scene of a private colonization attempt, in the seventeenth century, by an entrepreneurial German, Mathew de Renzi.

Another couple of miles downstream, **BANAGHER** is one long street sloping down to the Shannon, fortified on the Connacht side with a Martello Tower. The *Shannon Hotel* and a house farther up on the other side of the street show a local variant of classicism: pepperpot towers with elaborate doorways in which everything curves—doors, fanlights, pediments, and all. Anthony Trollope wrote his first novels while stationed in Banagher as a post office surveyor from 1841.

Birr

BIRR is a perfect example of a middling-sized town planned around a great house—in this case, Birr Castle, home of the Parsons family (Birr used to be known as Parsonstown), later elevated to the Earls of Rosse. Here, eighteenth-century urban planning has resulted in a truly delightful Georgian town, with wide, airy streets and finely detailed, fan-lit houses. Surprisingly, it's not a prissy place, but rather feels slightly seedy, down-at-heel, and full of life.

The Earls of Rosse still live at **Birr Castle**, and their house isn't open to the public. The **grounds**, however, are: laid out in the 1830s and 40s by the second Earl, they contain rare plants from all over the world as well as an enormous artificial lake and a really charming early example of a suspension bridge over the river. It's a pleasant place to while away a sunny day—the grounds are shut at lunchtime but the keepers are perfectly happy to lock you in—but much more remarkable, and Birr's real claim to fame, is the shell of the **Rosse telescope**.

In 1845 the third Earl built what was then, and remained for three-quarters of a century, the largest telescope in the world—a reflector with a diameter of 72 inches. The instrument was used by the fourth Earl (1840–1908) to make the first accurate measurement of the heat of the Moon, and to catalogue the spiral nebulae. The walls that held the telescope—at 50 feet long, it was too cumbersome to be rotated in more than one plane—are still in place, built in the same stone and battlemented style as the house; unfortunately the telescope itself has been dismantled. There's some information about the casting of the lens, no mean feat in those days, but on the whole the exhibition drastically underplays an extraordinary episode in the history of modern science.

Accommodation is the usual B&B (check with the **tourist office**, May–Oct; ☎0509-20110) or camping; if you're feeling rich or desperate, you could try *Dooley's Hotel* in Emmet Square, which is expensive but extremely pleasant. Dooley's is where the Galway Hunt acquired the nickname of the Galway Blazers after a hunt in 1809, when their over-enthusiastic celebrations resulted in the gutting of the building by fire.

Finally, a little excursion for ghostbusters. A few miles south of Clareen, as the land rises towards the Slieve Bloom mountains, the fifteenth-century **Leap Castle** fortifies the valley between Leinster and Munster. Before it was destroyed in 1922, it enjoyed the sinister reputation of being the most haunted house in Ireland, and was particularly famous for an unusual, smelly ghost, which was described both by Yeats and his contemporary Oliver St John Gogarty.

travel details

Trains
From Portlaoise to Dublin (8 daily; 1hr); Limerick Junction (13; 1hr); Cork (9; 2hr).

Bus Éireann
From Portlaoise to Dublin (6 daily; 2hr); Abbeyleix (2; 20min); Durrow (1; 30min).

Private buses
Pierce Kavanagh Coaches (☎056-31213/01-734344) serve Durrow, Abbeyleix, and Portlaoise on their daily Thurles–Dublin route.

CHAPTER FOUR

MEATH, LOUTH, WESTMEATH, AND LONGFORD

Stretching from the borders of County Dublin to the frontier with the North, and from the coast to the heart of Ireland, these four counties simultaneously epitomize green and rural Ireland and yet provide a total contrast with the west. It's a region neglected by most visitors, whose impression, if any, is one of monotonously similar countryside. Pass through at speed, as most people do, and you'll probably share that impression. But if you slow down, and target a small area for more detailed exploration, you'll discover far more. In the east there's a wealth of remains of an exceptionally long, rich history, and one or two great beaches on the coast. As you head west the interest gradually dwindles until by the time you reach **Longford** it has, frankly, died altogether. Nonetheless, the area as a whole repays exploration, and it's a very different Ireland to that you'll find in the west.

In practical terms, you'll find it easy enough to get around, with most of the sites conveniently strung along major roads well served by public transit. Accommodation is less easy, with only a handful of hostels throughout the four counties, and B&Bs only in the major centers. Still, if you base yourself strategically you'll find that a surprising amount can be seen in a short time.

Louth, the smallest of the 32 counties, stretches northwards along the coast. Here you'll find the only two towns of any real size in this chapter, **Drogheda** and **Dundalk**. Inland, hilly *drumlin* country hardens in the northeast to real mountains. Here, on the **Cooley Peninsula**, lies the most exciting part of the coast between Dublin and the border. The peninsula is also the setting of one of the richest and oldest legendary tales of Irish literature, the **Táin Bó Cualnge** (Cattle Raid of Cooley).

Until the mid-sixteenth century **Meath** (*Midhe*, middle) was combined with Westmeath, making it Ireland's fifth and most powerful province. Although it does touch the coast (with a couple of excellent beaches), this is primarily an inland county, whose exceptionally rich farmland unfurls lazily around its major river, the **Boyne**, and its tributaries. To discover the place you simply follow these waterways—above all the Boyne itself and the **Blackwater**—as

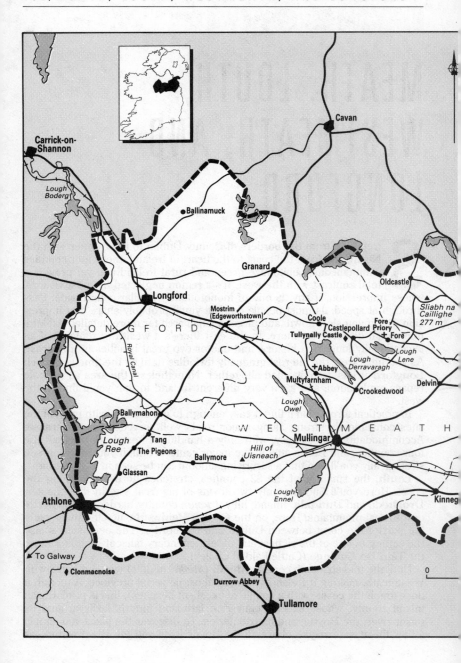

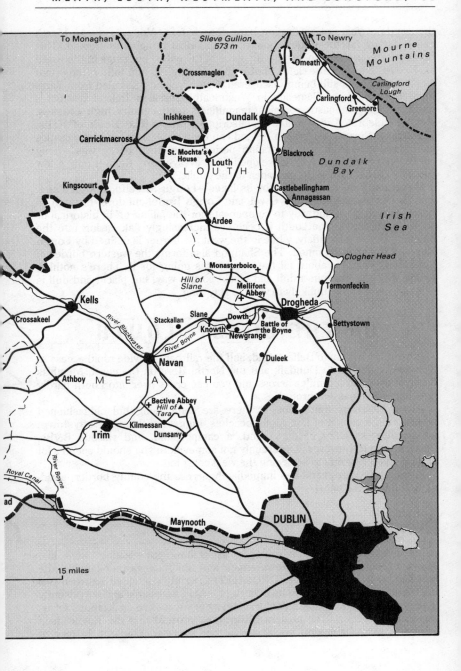

thousands of years of civilization have done before. Along its rivers, Meath can boast by far the richest bounty of historical remains in Ireland. This history starts in the Stone Age, with some of the oldest buildings in the world at **Brugh Na Boinne** and **Sliabh Na Caillighe**, and other important Neolithic remains still being discovered. Celtic Ireland was ruled from **Tara**, in Meath, and from Uisneach in Westmeath. Christian Ireland has left a wealth of early monastic remains, magnificent tenth-century **high crosses**, and the celebrated illuminated manuscript known as **The Book of Kells**. The largest Norman fortress in Ireland can be seen at **Trim**, and later castles and mansions—from the Plantation period when the county was wholly confiscated and extensively developed—are everywhere, though only a few (notably **Dunsany Castle**) are open to the public.

Westmeath is characterized by its lakes—**Lough Sheelin**, **Lough Lene**, **Lough Derravaragh**, **Lough Owel**, and **Lough Ennel** cut down through its heart—which go a long way to compensate for the falling off in historical or scenic splendor. In the south it becomes increasingly flat, easing into the bogland of northern Offaly, while in the west the border is defined by **Lough Ree** and the river Shannon. The Shannon also forms the western border of **Longford**, which is about all the county has going for it. There's nothing wrong with the place in a dull and placid sort of way, but placid and dull is what it is, and you're unlikely to want to stay long.

UP THE COAST: LOUTH

The main N1 Dublin-to-Belfast road, and the railroad, provide rapid access to **Drogheda**, and on to Dundalk and the North. Here on the coast, Meath is barely more than ten miles across and you can cross over into Louth hardly noticing you've passed through.

If you have any time, though, there are some delightful old-fashioned resorts, and a couple of fine sandy beaches. Biggest of them is **Bettystown**, where there's plenty of dark sand, a campground, and various B&Bs. Pleasant as it is, however, it's certainly not somewhere you should spend a lot of time if you're going to be seeing the west coast too.

Pressing on, Drogheda lies immediately across the county border, straddling the Boyne River.

Drogheda

Aside from its obvious advantages as a base for visiting sites like Monasterboice, Mellifont, Newgrange, and (slightly farther afield) the beaches on the Meath coast, **DROGHEDA**, tightly contained between two hills, is an enjoyable place in its own right: easily accessible and surprisingly unused to tourism. The architectural legacy of successive civilizations forms the main attraction. The ancient **Millmount mound** and the Boyne itself echo the early habitation you'll see farther upstream, but the history of

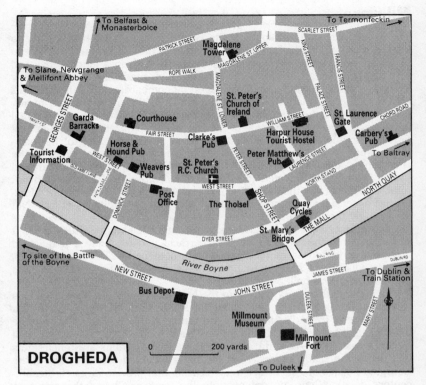

DROGHEDA

0   200 yards

Drogheda as a town really began with the **Vikings**, who arrived in AD 911 and founded a separate settlement on each bank. By bridging the ford between these two, the Danes gave the place its name—*Droichead Atha*, the Bridge of the Ford. By the fourteenth century, the walled town was one of the most important in the country, where the parliament would meet from time to time; remnants of **medieval** walls and abbeys lie like splinters throughout the town. As ever, though, most of what you see is from the **eighteenth century** or later, reflecting the sober style of the Protestant bourgeoisie (after the horrific slaughter of Drogheda's defenders and inhabitants by Cromwell).

The important surviving buildings of this age, the Tholsel, the Courthouse, and St Peter's Church, have mellowed romantically, and stand now among the **nineteenth-century** flowering of triumphal churches celebrating the relaxation of the persecuting stranglehold on Catholicism, and the riverside warehouses and huge rail viaduct that welcomed the boom years of the industrial era. More recent development, with riverside lanes and suburban housing development, has affected the flavor of the place very little—the past somehow seems stronger here than the present.

Millmount

The Meath side of town, south of the Boyne, is probably the best place to start exploring Drogheda. Atop the southern hill, **Millmount**'s Martello tower offers an excellent overview of the town, both in a literal sense and through the excellent display in the local museum sited here. The tower (key from the museum) was severely damaged by bombardment during the 1922 civil war (there's a large picture of the attack in the museum), but in any event it is the earthen mound on which it stands that gives the place its real importance. The strategic value of the site was recognized from the earliest times; in mythology the mound is the burial place of **Amergin**, the poet-warrior, one of the sons of **Mil** of the Milesians who are reckoned to be the ancestors of the Gaels. He arrived in Ireland from northern Spain around 1498 BC and later defeated the *Tuatha Dé Danann* at Tailtiu (Telltown). Another belief is that the mound houses a passage-grave. However, the tumulus has never been excavated to find out which story—if either—is true. Not surprisingly the Normans chose the same strategic eminence for their *motte* in the twelfth century, and later a castle was built, standing until 1808 when it was replaced by the tower and military barracks you see today. The quickest way up here on foot is via the narrow flight of steps by *Dina's* corner shop, directly opposite **St Mary's Bridge**. This is essentially the spot where the original bridge was built by the Danes.

The eighteenth-century houses in the barrack square now shelter various arts-and-crafts enterprises, and above all **Millmount Museum** (Tues–Sun 3–6pm), one of Ireland's finest town museums. Within a glass cabinet in the **foyer** hangs a topographical quilt (of very basic conception) showing much of Ireland's east coast—note the 2000 (or thereabouts) grains of French knots that depict the sandy shores. Next to this is a quilted cummerbund of the Georgian houses in Fair Street, very pleasing and precise in its eighteenth-century detail. When you get out into the town you'll find that the area depicted (Fair Street, along with William, Lower and Upper Magdalene streets and Rope Walk) is still rich in period buildings and architectural detail.

The **Guilds Room** follows, hung with three large drapes (the only surviving guilds' banners left in the country) celebrating the **broguemakers'**, **carpenters'** and **weavers'** trades. The broguemakers' banner—in effect an early advertisement—is particularly wonderful. It depicts Saint Patrick, who in myth rid the country of snakes, standing with his foot on a serpent: even the saint needs some protection, however, so he is sturdily shod in a pair of good Irish brogues. King Charles II also has a bit part, hiding up an oak tree to symbolize both the use of oak for tanning the leather and the security offered by a good pair of shoes (Charles escaped from Cromwell's troops in 1651 by hiding in an oak tree). The carpenters' and weavers' banners are more straightforward, the former depicting compasses and blades, the latter with shuttles clasped in leopards' mouths. In the next room there's a similar theme, with the **trade banners** of the fishermen, laborers, and bricklayers. The bricklayers' shows the **barbican at St Lawrence Gate** as their proudest achievement. This, again, is something worth seeing once you get out into the town, still standing, perfectly preserved, with two round towers flanking a portcullis entry and retaining wall. It is by far the most significant part of the town walls to have survived (part of the West Gate also exists, and a buttress and embrasure can be seen just south of the gate), and arguably the finest such survival anywhere in Ireland.

Heading down the museum stairs you come to a series of displays of a more domestic nature. Halfway down are some fourteenth-century **Chester floor tiles** found at the Magdalene tower and some pristine examples of rotary and saddle quernstones (used for grinding corn). At the foot of the staircase is a **Boyne Coracle**, a recent example of the type of circular fishing boat in use from prehistoric times right up to the middle of this century. This one has a framework of hazel twigs and a leather hide taken from a prize bull in 1943. To one side is an old photograph of the **Newgrange** monument, taken before it was restored. This is worth noting if you're planning a visit to Newgrange, especially as it shows the original position of the enscrolled kerbstone placed at the entrance to ward off trespassers. This has now been moved out of the way to avoid damage by visitors.

In the museum **basement** is a fully-equipped period kitchen, pantry, and scullery. Among the artifacts displayed are an 1860 **vacuum cleaner** (a man would wind the suction mechanism from outside the house), a tailor's **hen-and-goose irons** (clothes irons named for their various shapes and sizes) which would be heated in the fire (hence the phrase "too many irons in the fire"), a **seddle bed** (preferred by the Irish peasant because it would be next to the warmth of the dying embers and could sleep two adults lengthways and four or five children acrossways) and a vast array of other every day miscellany. On the **top floor** is a small picture gallery, and various exhibits on historical and industrial Drogheda—in general, the least exciting part of the museum. Up here, too, are rooms devoted to the Foresters and Hibernian societies, both nineteenth-century benevolent institutions set up to provide sickness benefits, burial expenses, and the like for the poor.

The Rest of Town: An Overview

Standing on the Millmount hill, you can enjoy an unimpeded **panorama** of Drogheda, with the bulk of the town climbing up the northern hill-slope opposite. From this standpoint it's clearly apparent how the tight-fitting street pattern of the medieval town gave scant breathing space for the overcrowding of succeeding centuries. The backs of the houses stagger down to the Boyne River in a colorless wash of daubed mortar, their windows staring blankly back at you. On top of the hill opposite, the fourteenth-century **Magdalene Tower** was once the belfry tower of an extensive Dominican friary, founded in 1224 by Lucas De Netterville, Archbishop of Armagh. The tower rises above a Gothic arch where the transept and nave would have met; inside, a spiral staircase reaches up into its two stories, but since it is railed off from public access it's probably seen to best advantage from a distance. In March 1394 **Richard II**, King of England, received within the priory the submission of the Ulster Chiefs; and later Thomas, Earl of Desmond, a former Lord Chief Justice, was found guilty of treason and beheaded here in 1467 (with him went his Act of Parliament for a university in Drogheda).

Lower down, the spire that leaps out from the center of town belongs to the heavily Gothic-styled **St Peter's Roman Catholic Church** (1791) on West Street, the town's main thoroughfare. It's an imposing building with a grand double flight of steps, but it's the presence of a martyr's head, on view in a tabernacle-like box that forms part of a small shrine down the left-hand aisle, that transforms the place into a center of pilgrimage. The severed head is a searing reminder of the days of religious persecution. It once belonged to **Oliver Plunkett**, Archbishop of Armagh and Primate of all Ireland in the seventeenth century when Drogheda was the traditional seat for that role. On July 1, 1681, Plunkett was executed in London for treason; as the Lord Chief Justice of England explained "the bottom of your treason was your setting up your false religion, than which there is not anything more displeasing to God." His head and mutilated members were snatched from the fire but were not brought back to Ireland until 1721, a time when the persecution had subsided somewhat. Plunkett was canonized a saint in 1975, after miracles were performed in his name in southern Italy.

East of the church, towards the docks, the back alleys and stone warehouses are relics of the short-lived Industrial Revolution and of the local brewing and milling trades. A few are being done up by a new breed of entrepreneur, but as many are empty and crumbling. The docks themselves seem mostly lifeless and deserted too, and the Boyne's funereal pace does little to enliven a depleted commercial shipping fleet where once sixty Viking ships are said to have rested at anchor. There is, however, one very bright spot down here in the form of **Mrs Carbery's pub**, as appealing as any in Ireland. This has been a local, family-run institution for over a century and in the evening or early morning (it opens at 7:30am to cater to the dockers and the men off the boats) the faint orange glow from the lanterns or fire inside makes a welcome landmark and sign of life.

Farther downstream, the **viaduct** carrying trains on the Dublin–Belfast line spans what is effectively a 200-foot-deep gorge. It's an impressive feat of nineteenth-century engineering (by John McNeill) that you can examine at closer quarters if you feel like extending your visit to Carbery's into a country stroll out along the Baltray road. Beyond the viaduct and cement plant you reach some pleasant woodland. Part of this belongs to **Beaulieu House**, a private domain that claims to have been Ireland's first unfortified mansion (1660–65), built after Cromwell's departure when the land was confiscated from Oliver Plunkett and given to Sir Henry Tichbourne, whose descendants reside there today. The house has a hipped roof in the artisan style and an almost perfectly preserved interior. Most rewarding of all is a mouth-wateringly indulgent **picture gallery** with a collection ranging from contemporary portraits of William and Mary on tall canvases by the court painter Van der Wyck to an intense collection of early twentieth-century Irish art, and much else besides. Unfortunately the house is strictly private, but the owners do open their doors to tours by the Drogheda Historical Society, so it's worth checking (at the museum) to see if your visit coincides with one of these.

Practicalities: Rooms and Food

Drogheda is a pretty easy place to find your way around. The *Bus Éireann* **bus** depot is on New Street, on the south bank of the river, and the **train** station is also on the south side, a short way east of town just off the Dublin Road. **Taxis** line up on Lawrence Street. The town is small enough not to need them for local trips, but you could arrange a lightning tour around the sights of Newgrange, Mellifont, and Monasterboice for around £20—though you'd have to be in a real hurry to want to see it all this way.

If you want to **stay**, *Harpur House Tourist Hostel* (☎041-32736) is probably your best bet, with some forty hostel beds (£4; no curfew). **B&B** is also available: *Ivy House*, a very nice Georgian home next door also offers B&B (£9.50), as does the fancier *Walker's Hotel* on West Street (£24 for a twin room).

As far as entertainment goes, check out the **pubs**, many of which are rich in character. *Carbery's* on the North Strand is probably the best known gathering place on this part of the east coast, especially for the traditional sessions on Tuesday nights (from 9pm) and Sunday lunchtimes (12:30–2:30pm). To get a seat on Sunday make sure you're there by noon. The *Horse and Hound* has a regular Friday evening "alternative" spot upstairs for blues, folk, even poets and raconteurs. A few doors down is *Weavers* (as pinched from Yeats's *The Weaver of Duleek Gate*) which is what you might call the big new saloon in town. Flash, modern, and slickly professional, they also offer some of the best snacks and food in town at very reasonable prices (three-course bar lunches at around £3–4) and a fairly frantic atmosphere. There's some kind of entertainment here most nights: rock bands on a Monday; Sixties nights or discos Wednesday, Friday and Sunday; and a piano bar during happy hour (5–7pm) on Friday and Saturday. *Clarkes*, on the corner of Fair and Peter streets, is a total contrast—quiet and old-fashioned, and popular with the local literary set. *Peter Matthews* on Lawrence Street (known locally as *MacVeigh's*) is also very popular (with a younger crowd) with lots of toffee-brown woodwork, partitions and cubicles, plus a back room for music. *Walker's Hotel* (West Street) has music Wednesday, Friday, and Sunday nights. *Branagan's* on Lower Magdalene Street is of the *Weavers* ilk (hot snacks 12:30–2:30pm and 5–11pm) but nowhere near as hip.

Just a few steps from *Weavers* on Dominick Street, *Snackmasters Restaurant* (Mon and Tues noon–3pm and 6pm–1am, Wed and Thurs noon–3pm and 6pm–3am, Fri and Sat noon–4am, Sun noon–3am) serves similar **food**, similarly good value. *Walker's Hotel* also offers a three-course lunch special at £3.95. The *Buttergate Restaurant* in Millmount Square (Tues–Sun 12:30–2:30pm, also Thurs–Sat 7–11pm; ☎041-37407) is much more expensive, but not bad value for good French cuisine. At the other end of the scale *King's Cafe* (popular with truckers), a short way out on the Collon Road, will serve up four courses for around £3.50 and a full tea for under a fiver. *La Capannina* at the bottom of Peter Street (12:30–2:30pm and 6:30pm–1:30am, closed Wed; ☎041-37022) is a good Italian restaurant.

Entertainment outside the pubs barely exists. There are two **theaters**, both amateur and neither very exciting (*Duke Theater*, Duke Street, ☎041-36122, and the *Parochial Theater*) and a couple of **movie theaters** (in the Abbey and Boyne shopping centers). There's also an occasional **disco** in Drogheda's one nightclub, *Lucianos* in the *Boyne Valley Hotel* (☎041-37737).

Mellifont and Monasterboice

Not far from Drogheda, in the south of County Louth, lie two of the great historical sites which characterize this part of the country, the monasteries of Mellifont and Monasterboice. Both are easily reached from Drogheda, and Mellifont has a very basic *An Óige* hostel which makes a good alternative base—also handy for the sites of the lower Boyne valley (covered later in this chapter)—if you're after a more peaceful place to stay.

To get to Mellifont from Drogheda (about five miles) turn off the road to Collon at MONLEEK CROSS; alternatively turn off the Slane–Collon road at the signpost. There are two **buses** a day from Drogheda (Mon–Fri 9:15am and 6:15pm, Sat 2:15pm and 6:15pm), two from Dublin via Slane (*McConnans*, 5:15pm, return 9:20am; £2.50). Monasterboice can be reached from the main N1 Dublin–Belfast road, or by continuing up the Drogheda–Collon road and following the signs to the right.

Mellifont Abbey

Mellifont was, in medieval times, one of the most important monasteries in Ireland, the motherhouse of the Cistercian movement and a building of exceptional beauty and grandeur. The ruins you see today in no way do justice to this proud past, but they're pretty impressive even so.

At its foundation in 1142—the inspiration of Saint Malachy, Archbishop of Armagh, who did much to bring the early Irish church closer to Rome—Mellifont was the first **Cistercian monastery** in Ireland. Malachy's friend Saint Bernard, then abbot of the Cistercian monastery at Clairvaux, did much to inspire the work, and sent nine of his own monks to form the basis of the new community. The abbey took fifteen years to build, and you can gauge something of its size and former glory by imagining the gargantuan pillars that must once have risen, finishing high among a riotous sprouting of arches and vaulted ceilings, from the broad stumps remaining today. For nearly 400 years Mellifont flourished, at its peak presiding over as many as 38 other Cistercian monasteries throughout the country, until in 1539 all of them were suppressed by Henry VIII.

One hundred and fifty monks fled from Mellifont, and the buildings were handed over to Sir Gerald Moore, Earl of Drogheda, who converted the place into a fortified mansion. In 1603 the last of the great Irish chieftains, **Hugh O'Neill**, was starved into submission here before eventually escaping to the continent in the Flight of the Earls. Mellifont, meanwhile, went into gradual decline. It was attacked by Cromwellian forces, and then used as William's headquarters during the Battle of the Boyne, before eventually falling so far as to be pressed into service as a pigsty in the nineteenth century. Today the remains rarely rise above shoulder height, with the striking exception of the Romanesque octagonal **lavabo**, whose basins and water jets provided washing facilities for the monks.

The rest of the ruins can be easily identified on the map provided, their ground plan almost perfectly intact. You enter through the **north transept** which originally had five chapels, three in its eastern and two in its western aisle. Two of the three on the eastern side had apsidal ends, an unusual feature for medieval Ireland, seen here presumably because of the French influence on the builders. The chancel area, or **presbytery**, has the remains of an ornate arch and a **sedilia** where the celebrants of the Mass would sit. The entire **nave** would have been paved in red and blue tiles, some inscribed with the words "Ave Maria" and others decorated with the *fleur-de-lis* emblem; the **pillars**, too, would originally have been painted in brilliant colors and topped with flowery capitals. At the river end of the nave is a **crypt**—an unusual position which in this case served to level the site on which the church was built. The **chapter house**, beyond the south transept, was once the venue for the daily meetings of the monks. It now houses a collection of medieval **glazed tiles**, moved here from around the site for safety.

Behind the Lavabo is the **south range**, where the refectory would have been, and back towards the road you'll find the **gatehouse**, the only surviving part of a high defensive wall that once completely ringed the monastic buildings. Also within the grounds are another ruined church up on the slope (converted to a Protestant place of worship in 1542) and the **youth hostel**. Whether intentionally to harmonize with the ascetic lifestyle of the monks, or simply because there are no facilities here, it's a pretty spartan place: no showers, hot water, or heating. But it's clean and enthusiastically run, and the setting is delightful, with the Mattock River gliding through gently wooded country. If you have some kind of transportation it can make a great base from which to move out to the other places of interest nearby—Monasterboice and the Brugh Na Boinne complex.

Monasterboice

Monasterboice (*Mainistir Buite* or Buite's monastery) is a tiny enclosure, but it contains two of the finest high crosses (both dating from the tenth century) and one of the best round towers left in the country. As you enter, the squat cross nearer to you is reckoned the finer of the two, and certainly its high-relief carving has worn the centuries better. It is known as **Muiredeach's Cross** after the inscription in Gaelic at the base of the stem—*Or do Muiredach i Chros*, "A prayer for Muiredach by whom this cross was made". The boldly ornate stone picture panels retell biblical stories and were designed to educate and inspire the largely illiterate populace. Some of the subjects are ambivalent and open to a certain amount of conjecture (William Wilde, father of Oscar, argued that many relate as strongly to events associated with Monasterboice as with the Bible), but most have been fairly convincingly identified.

The story begins at the bottom of the **east face** of the cross, nearest the wall, with **Eve tempting Adam** on the left and **Cain slaying Abel** on the right. Above this, **David and Goliath** share a panel with King Saul and David's son Jonathan. The next panel up shows **Moses striking the rock** with his staff to conjure water whilst the Israelites wait with parched throats, and above this, the **Wise Men** bear gifts to the Virgin Mary and baby Jesus. The centerpiece of the wheel is the scene of the **Last Judgment**, with the multitudes risen from the dead begging for entry to heaven, their hands holding one another in good will and the trumpets playing loudly. Below Christ's foot the Archangel Michael is seen driving a staff through Satan's head after weighing the balance of good and evil in one individual's favor. At the very top, saints Anthony and Paul are seen breaking bread.

The **west face** of the cross is largely devoted to the **life of Christ**. At the bottom is his arrest in the Garden of Gethsemane, with Roman soldiers and the treacherous kiss of Judas. This is followed by three figures clutching books—thought to represent the dispelling of the **doubts of Saint Thomas**. The third panel shows the **Risen Christ** returned to meet Saint Peter and Saint Paul, their faces bowed in shame at ever having doubted the truth. The hub of the wheel shows the **Crucifixion**, with soldiers below, angels above and evil humanity to the sides. This is surmounted by **Moses** descending from Mount Sinai with the Ten Commandments. The flanks of the cross are also decorated. On the **north side** are Saints Anthony and Paul again, Christ's scourging at the pillar, and the **Hand of God** (under the arm of the cross) warning mankind. On the **south side** is the Flight of the Israelites from Egypt and also possibly Pontius Pilate washing his hands. All this is capped at the top as if under the roof of the church and surrounded with abstract or uninterpreted embellishment.

The **taller cross** (the West Cross) is made up of three separate stone sections, all of them much more worn. The east face shows **David killing the lion**, then **Abraham** ready to sacrifice his son **Isaac**, with the ram which became the last-minute substitute. Above this is the worship of the **Golden Calf**, with Moses coming down from the mount to catch his people red-handed in idolatry. The panel shows their trembling for forgiveness. The other three panels, before Christ seated in Heaven at the end of the world in the center of the wheel, are hard to identify, though on the right arm of the wheel you can see the upside-down Satan being speared again by Saint Michael. The **west face** begins with the **Resurrection**, and the **Baptism of Christ** is shown on the second panel. The four three-figure panels before the wheel are once again difficult to identify, although the central figure looks a strong candidate for Christ. Once again the **Crucifixion** dominates the wheel, with Christ tied to the cross by rope; the left arm shows him being blindfolded and ridiculed while the right arm has Judas's kiss of betrayal.

Behind the West Cross stands possibly the tallest **round tower** in Ireland, 110 feet even without its conical peak. Round towers were adopted between the ninth and eleventh centuries by monks throughout the country as a defense against constant Viking attack. They needed no keystone that enemies could pull out for speedy demolition; their height created a perfect look-out post; and the entrance would be several feet from the ground, allowing a ladder to be drawn in when under attack. The only drawback, which fortunately was not the downfall of this particular tower, was that if a lighted arrow were to pierce the inner floorboards the whole column would act as a chimney, guaranteeing a blazing inferno. Sadly you can't actually go into the tower, which has been closed for safety reasons.

Finally within the enclosure are two thirteenth-century **churches**, the north and the south church. They probably had no real connection with the monastic settlement, which had almost certainly ceased to function by then, and there's little of great interest within their ruined walls.

North to Dundalk

The main reason to head northwards into County Louth, apart from reaching the border, is to get to the mountains of the **Cooley Peninsula**. You have three routes to choose from. The main Drogheda-to-Belfast road, the N1, is the fastest, speeding directly towards the border and passing **Monasterboice** early on, but with little other reason to stop. An alternative inland route to take is to head towards COLLON, taking in **Mellifont Abbey**, and from there continue to Ardee and Louth town (for **St Mochta's House**) and ultimately on to Dundalk or into County Monaghan. Both these routes give excellent, unhindered cross-country views of County Louth, especially of the *drumlins* rising inland towards counties Cavan and Monaghan.

The third option, to take the bay road out of Drogheda and **follow the coast** north, is the most scenic, and the one to choose if you want to dawdle along the way or if you're cycling. In the early stages, there's little point detouring into BALTRAY; instead, continue straight ahead for **TERMONFECKIN**, a placid country village lying in a wooded dip half a mile from the shore. The village has a small tower-house **castle** and a tenth-century **High Cross** in the graveyard of St Feckin's Church. The castle (keys from Patrick Duff in the bungalow across the cul-de-sac) dates basically from the fifteenth and sixteenth centuries and has as its most unusual feature a corbeled roof— notably less well-constructed than the 4000-years-older one at Newgrange. You can get good **food** here at *The Triple House* restaurant, whose Italian/ French menu offers five courses for £9 before 7:30pm, £14 thereafter (four-course Sunday lunch £7.50 from 12:30 to 2:30pm, otherwise open 6:30–9:30pm except Monday; ☎041-22616). If you're neither hungry nor in a hurry to push ahead, then stroll into the reception area anyhow to see three highly individual computer-print collages by the Irish artist Robert Balagh—*The Ambidextrous Paradigm*, *The Global Embrace*, and *The Plough and the Stars*.

CLOGHERHEAD is a far busier place, a bustling vacation village for the Irish, with plenty of bars aimed squarely at the holiday clientele—their briny names, *The Lobster Inn* for example, give the game away. From here the road to **PORT ORIEL** takes you to **Clogher Head** (one mile) and a tiny fishing harbor tucked hard into the coast's rockface—good mackerel fishing off the pier in summer. It's only beyond here, as you approach **ANNAGASSAN**, that the signposts designating the scenic route begin to earn their keep, with the mountains of Cooley and Mourne, one range south of the border, the other north, spectacularly silhouetted against the sky. It's an enthrallingly unimpeded view of the best that lies ahead in counties Louth and Down. *The Glyde Inn* in Annagassan has food (of sorts) and is a nice reclusive spot to take time out for "a small drop of medicine." There's little else to see around the village, although local archaeological explorations are provoking controversy as they lay bare what is claimed to have been the first permanent Norse settlement in Ireland, predating even Dublin. Continuing northwards across the humpbacked stone bridge, you've a watercolorist's idyll of rowing boats laid out along the bulging ramparts of the canalized river as it meets the sea.

Only a couple of miles farther on, you'll rejoin the N1 at **CASTLE-BELLINGHAM**. Despite the main Dublin–Belfast road blundering right through the middle, Castlebellingham remains one of the prettiest villages around (albeit in a consciously "olde-worlde" way). It's a strange clash of ancient and modern, from which you can take refuge down by the mill, now converted into a restaurant. This has a turning gable-end water wheel and a run of several man-made weirs up the back through woodland alongside a sugary, castellated hotel (good two-course bar lunches £3; *Castle Special* four-course dinner £7.50): contrived, but pretty nevertheless. Moving northward again the next significant turning off the N1 (right) takes you to **BLACKROCK** and later allows you to bypass most of Dundalk. Blackrock itself (the *Claremount Arms* has good Saturday night traditional sessions involving the uileann pipes) is an over-stretched ribbon of Victorian villas along a mudflat beach. It does, though, offer a handsomely crystalline view across **Dundalk Bay** and onto the Cooley Peninsula, by now looming close.

Ardee and Inland

The inland route is far less traveled, with less to see along it. Without transportation of your own you'll have difficulty getting anywhere, unless you're prepared for some very leisurely hitching. Nonetheless it has its rewards, mostly in just this lack of traffic or population—a rural tranquillity unrivaled even in the west. Almost exactly halfway between Drogheda and Dundalk, **ARDEE** (*Baile Atha Fhirdhia* or Ferdia's Ford) recalls the tragic legendary duel between *Cúchulain* the defender of Ulster and his foster-brother *Ferdia*, a battle brought about through the trickery of Medb, Queen of Connacht*.

> Ferdia: *"Attack then if we must.*
> *Before sunset and nightfall*
> *I'll fight you at Bairche*
> *in bloody battle.*
> *Men of Ulster will cry out:*
> *"Death has seized you!"*
> *The terrible sight*
> *will pierce you through."*

---

*Although Medb (pronounced *Maeve*) is always referred to as queen, she was more likely a goddess of Tara. The duel is only one episode of Europe's earliest vernacular epic, the *Táin Bó Cuailnge* or Cattle Raid of Cooley, but makes a glorious thirty-eight pages of reading in Thomas Kinsella's translation, *The Tain*, published in Ireland by the Dolmen Press and well worth getting hold of.

Cúchulainn: *"You have reached your doom,*
your hour is come
My sword will slash
and not softly.
When we meet you will fall
at a hero's hands.
Never again
will you lead men."

These taunting jibes laid down the gauntlet for their fight to the death, in which eventually Ferdia was fatally wounded by the *gae bolga*, a weapon summoned from the *Tuatha Dé Danann*, God Lug, by Cúchulainn during the fight in the stream. Ardee is named after the ford where this great battle was fought.

Today, Ardee reeks far more strongly of the Plantation era, with fortified buildings along the main street and a memorial **statue** to a landlord erected by his thankful tenants in 1861. The sixteenth-century **castle** on the main street (key in the house on the right) is now used as a courthouse, and inside bears no intimation of its original purpose. It stands here mainly because the town was at the northern edge of the Pale, and from here the Anglo-Irish made forays into Ulster, or were themselves periodically forced onto the defensive.

An interesting short diversion from Ardee takes you to the so-called **Jumping Church** at KILDEMOCK. To get there head east from the junction at the southern end of Ardee's main street and turn right after about quarter of a mile—the small, ruined church lies another mile down this road. It gets its name from its end wall having shifted three feet from its foundations, which, according to local lore, it did to exclude the grave of an excommunicated person. Less romantic accounts tell of a severe storm taking place in 1715 at around the time the wall jumped, but either way it's a remarkable sight, with the wall shorn clear of its foundations yet still standing (albeit at a 35-degree angle). In the graveyard are simple, foot-high stone markers, some of the earliest graveslabs for the poor.

Ardee is a major road junction, and moving on you could head northeast to Dundalk, northwest to Carrickmacross, or west to Kells. If you want to go on heading north, however, a more interesting route is along the minor roads to **LOUTH village**; keep on the left fork at the northern end of Ardee and take an immediate right towards TALLANSTOWN, where you'll need to turn right again for Louth. It's not much in itself (and certainly doesn't seem to deserve sharing a name with the county) but it does have one thing well worth seeing in **St Mochta's Church**—turn left towards Carrickmacross and immediately right onto the Inniskeen road.

According to legend the church was built in a night to give shelter to its founder, **Saint Mochta**, who died in 534. Originally part of a monastery, and dating probably from the late twelfth century, it has a high, vaulted roof, beautifully crafted, reached by a constricted stairway. In its early years it was plundered many times; these days they obviously feel safer, since the church is left open to any passing visitor. The fifteenth-century **Louth Abbey** is accessible through the graveyard back up the road, from where, if you look west, you'll notice a *motte* on the nearby hill.

Dundalk

DUNDALK you should avoid. It's a true border town in the Wild West tradition—dead when not deadly. Starting life in legendary prehistory as a fort guarding a gap in the mountains to the north (*Dún Dealgan*, the Fortress of Dealga), it became in turn a Celtic, Norse, Anglo-Norman, Jacobean, and finally Williamite stronghold. This hard tradition seems still to hang over the town, and it never seems a place where you—or for that matter the locals—can feel fully at ease.

Having said that, there are, as ever, some good **pubs**. *Mark's Bar* on Crowe Street is a sawdust-on-flagstone hide-out where the men have what looks like designer stubble but which here is probably for real: there are good traditional sessions every Thursday, Friday, and Saturday. *McManus's* pub near the library in Seatown is self-described "simply a great pub"—there are old-fashioned compartments to drink in, excellent value soup and sandwiches, folk music on Sunday nights, and more bluesy stuff on Monday. *McArdles* on Anne Street hosts *Ceolteorí* every Thursday night, or if rock is more your taste try the *Tara* on Park Street.

As far as sights go, the outstanding one is the nineteenth-century Neoclassical **Courthouse**, whose open Doric portico leads into an airy, classically proportioned interior. In the plaza outside, the Guardian Angel or motherland statue is unequivocally dedicated to "the martyrs in the cause of liberty who fought and died in the struggle against English Tyranny and foreign rule in Ireland"—a far cry from the monument of gratitude in Ardee. **St Patrick's Catholic Church** in Francis Street is also worth a look while you're here; its cornucopia of embellished towers, turrets and crenellated walls is a reasonably successful imitation of King's College Chapel, Cambridge. Inside are some rich mosaics using gold pieces in abundance to depict biblical stories.

Eating well and cheaply is not a Dundalk specialty, but there are plenty of fast-food places around the center of town which will do if you're starving. Slightly better fare can be had at the *Michael Rice Pub* on Clanbrassil Street (opposite the *Café de Paris*) or, more upscale, at *Caspars* on the corner opposite the courthouse (lunch £8, 12:30–2:30pm; dinner £15, 6–9:30pm; local bands play Wed, Thurs, Fri & Sun 9pm). **Bikes** can be rented at the *Cycle Center*, opposite the shopping complex (£3 per day; £15 per week; 9am–6pm, open till 9pm Thurs & Fri; ☎042-37159). The regional **tourist information office**, which also hosts touring art exhibitions, is opposite the courthouse.

Towards the Border: Faughert

From Dundalk, **the border** lies just eight miles on up the N1, and Newry only five miles beyond that. Just a couple of miles out of Dundalk, though, is the turnoff for the Cooley peninsula. Opposite, a lesser road leads a short distance inland to **FAUGHERT**. A small place of little modern interest, Faughert nevertheless has several interesting associations worth mentioning. **Cúchulainn** was born on the plain of Muirthemne which stretches away towards Armagh in the north, and in the legendary account he was sent a false offer of peace by Medb asking him to meet her at Faughert. Instead, fourteen of Medb's most skillful followers awaited him: fourteen javelins were hurled at him simultaneously but Cúchulainn guarded himself so that his skin, and even his armor, was untouched. Then he turned on them and killed every one of the "Fourteen at Focherd."

Faughert is also said to be the birthplace of **Saint Brigid**, Patroness of Ireland, whose three-armed cross of rushes is so common on the walls of rural Irish households. In the local churchyard you can see her holy well and pillar-stone, as well as the grave of **Edward Bruce**, who was defeated here in 1318 after being sent to Ireland by his brother (Robert the Bruce) to divert the English away from the Anglo-Scottish border. There is a stone nearby which in legend was used to decapitate him.

The Cooley Peninsula

You come to **Cooley** for the raw beauty of its mountains, to walk, and to experience a life where the twentieth century intrudes only rarely. Indeed, when you get up among the bare hilltops the peninsula's links with legend seem at least as strong as its grip on modern reality. For above all this is country associated with the **Táin Bó Cuailgne**, and in the mountains many of the episodes of the great epic were played out. Its plot (set around the first century AD) concerns the Brown Bull of Cooley (*Donn Cuailgne*) which is coveted by Medb, Queen of Connacht, in her envy of her husband Ailill's White Bull (*Finnbenach*). In their efforts to capture the bull, Medb and Ailill, who come from the west, effectively declare war on the east in general, and Ulster in particular. All the men of Ulster—save one, Cúchulainn—are struck by a curse which immobilizes them through most of the tale, leaving our hero to face the might of Medb's troops alone. The action consists largely of his (often gory) feats, but the text is also rich in topography and place names, many of them still clearly identifiable.

A single road runs around the peninsula, leaving the N1 to trace the southern slopes of the Cooley mountains and then cutting across country to Grenore and Carlingford on the north shore. It is here, facing the Mountains of Mourne across **Carlingford Lough**, that the most beautiful scenes lie, with forested slopes plunging steeply toward the Lough. The southern slopes are gentler and lazier, making a far more sedate progress to the water's edge. Among the more extraordinary sights looking north over Carlingford Lough are the patrolling British Army helicopters. Look at the map and you'll see what seems a fairly random dotted line dividing the water in two; look up and you'll see it traced out with uncanny precision in the air above you.

Before you reach any of this, however, only about a mile down the peninsula road, there's a short detour well worth taking. From the back of the *Ballymascanlon Hotel*, a footpath leads to the **Proleek Dolmen**, whose massive capstone balances with far more elegance than its 46 tons ought to allow. If you see smaller stones on top they're recent additions, flung there by visitors who hope to have a wish granted. On the path just before the dolmen, a Bronze-Age wedge-shaped **gallery-grave** can be seen: both of these monuments may become harder to visit if, as local rumor has it, they are incorporated into holes five and six of a new golf course.

Omeath and Carlingford: Bases for Hill Walking

Aside from being the more scenic, the peninsula's north shore is also the best place to base yourself for hill-walking, and the easiest for finding food and a bed. In **OMEATH**, right up towards the border, there's an *An Óige* **hostel**, a few meters off the main road behind the *Ranch Pub and Restaurant*. The youth hostel has two separate houses, one for lounging and eating, the other divided into dormitories with some basic washing facilities (no hot water or heating as yet). As ever you can't officially check in before 5pm, but the sitting area is always open to you to drop off your stuff and shelter, if it's raining. At Omeath the Lough has narrowed dramatically, so that the sedate towns of WARRENPOINT and ROSTREVOR on the Mourne Mountain slopes across the border seem within arm's reach. In summer there's a handy passenger **ferry service**, which also takes bikes, between Omeath and Warrenpoint (July and Aug only, Mon–Sat 1–5pm, Sun 1–7pm; £1 return; 5min). Staying in the Republic, you can rent **jaunting cars** (a two-wheeled, one-horse car) for short trips out of town; they run mostly to the open-air **stations of the cross** at the Rosminian Fathers' School down the road.

As a village, Omeath, with its widely scattered dwellings, is far from typical of the east coast—it was until recent years the last remaining *Gaeltacht* village of any significance in this part of the country. Around the crossroads which mark the center of town are grouped a few **grocery stores** and **pubs**, the only facilities apart from the hostel that the place offers. One of Ireland's best young flautists, Des Wilkinson, lives in Omeath, so look out for his regular Friday-night sessions in one or other of the pubs. *Davey's Lounge*, a few miles up the road towards the border, is another pub worth checking out.

CARLINGFORD, a fishing village five miles or so back down the Lough, makes a considerable contrast to Omeath, both for its neatly ordered network of cramped, terraced streets at the foot of Sliabh Foye Mountain, and in its development as an expensive resort. The latter has been remarkably successful, and the place (which was the 1988 Tidy Towns winner) retains real charm as well as some excellent places to eat and drink. There's an **oyster festival** here around the middle of August and—one of the less brilliant ideas to encourage tourists—a **leprechaun hunt** for a prize of £500 (£10 entry fee) on Easter Monday.

Carlingford is also an historic place. Saint Patrick is said to have landed here briefly on his way to introduce Christianity to Ireland (he finally ended his journey farther north, in County Down) and the settlement is ancient enough to have been raided by the Vikings. But the oldest visible remain is the D-shaped ruin of **King John's castle**, down by the main road on the water's edge. King John is said to have visited in 1210, and the Anglo-Norman castle, guarding the entrance to the lough, may be even older than that. It has its counterpart across the lough at Greencastle. The village in general retains a distinctly medieval feel, and there are a couple of solid fifteenth-century buildings: the **mint**, in a narrow street off the square, is a fortified town house with an impressive gate tower; **Taaffe's Castle**, which stood on the shore when it was built but is now some way from it, is impressively crenellated and fortified but sadly not open to the public. The best and safest **beaches** in the area are just down the coast, at GRENORE.

Jordans combination pub-bistro, in the first street above the main road, parallel to it, is probably the best of the places to **eat and drink** in Carlingford. They may try a little too hard—the menu includes such exotica as Louisiana alligator and Annalong (County Down) quail—but the food, especially the fish, is good and excellent value (dinner £10; gourmet dinner £14.50; lunch £3.50–5; open year-round 12:30–2:30pm and 7–10:30pm; you'll need to reserve, weekends especially, on ☎042-73223). There's a small room at the back of the pub which sometimes acts as a pre-dinner theater. *O'Hare's* (aka *PJ's*), on the corner near the Mint, is an old grocery store and bar, and the most entertaining place to drink—its publican has a considerable local reputation as a raconteur of tall tales. They also serve pub grub, and oysters in season, which here seems to mean most of the year. The *Village Hotel*, nearby in the Market Square, serves more substantial food (four-course lunch £8, 12:45–2:15pm; Innkeeper's special £10, 6:30–8pm). *Ghan House*, a fine Georgian mansion down near the crab-clawed pier, is yet another place where you can get a meal and a drop to drink. The best place to **stay** in Carlingford is *Viewpoint*, whose modern, motel-like flatlets enjoy good views from a little way up the hill (B&B £23 for two; ☎042-73149).

Legendary Walks

You can walk almost anywhere in the mountains behind Carlingford and Omeath, and once you're up there the heather-tufted ground on top offers some of the most beautiful hill-walking imaginable, stained with episodes from the *Táin Bó Culainge*. It's at its best in the afternoon, with the light bringing out the colors of the Mourne Mountains across the water—in the morning the sun tends to get in your eyes. The road up behind the youth hostel in Omeath offers the best approach, switchbacking its way into the hills with the climb ever increasing the drama of the fjord below. At about 1200 feet there's a parking lot where a map table marks out the major sights and there's a long spiel on the formation of the lough: a valley gouged out by a glacier which was flooded at the end of the Ice Age.

With a little imagination, it's not hard to translate the gaps, boulders, and fording points of rivers up here into the scenes of Cúchulainn's epic battles. And some of the places are clearly identified. From **Trumpet Hill** (*Ochaine*) he slew a hundred men of Medb's army with his sling on three successive nights as they rested in a plain to the west. This forced Ailill, fearing that his entire force would be destroyed, to offer up champions in single combat. Between Ochainne and the sea Cúchulainn slew the first of these warriors, **Nadcranntail**, by letting his spear fly high into the air so that it dropped down onto Nadcranntail's skull and pinned him to the ground. Then he sprang onto the rim of Nadcranntail's shield and struck his head off and then struck again through the neck right down to the navel so that he fell in four sections to the ground.

From **Slievenaglogh** (*Sliab Cuinciu*) Cúchulainn swore to hurl a sling stone at Medb's head—no easy task as she never moved without her army in front holding a barrel-shaped shelter of shields over their heads. Then one of Medb's bondmaids, Lochu, went to fetch water and, thinking it was Medb herself, he loosed two stones, killing her on the plain in the place known as

Réid Locha, Lochu's level ground. In fact, when he had the chance, Cúchulainn couldn't bring himself to kill Medb. During the final battle a deliberately salacious episode occurs when Medb suddenly gets a gush of blood that makes her need to urinate. Fergus, her chief warrior and lover, is furious at her bad timing and takes his place in the army of shields raised to protect her while she relieves herself, creating three great channels known as *Fual Medba*, Medb's foul place. Finding her in this delicate position, Cúchulainn was too honorable to kill her from behind (though he seemed happy enough to kill everyone else whenever and wherever he could).

Fual Medba is not clearly identified, but you can find the scene of an earlier episode, the **Black Cauldron** (*Dubchoire*), where Medb divides her armies to search for the bull, which has last been seen here—it's a recess north of the Glenngat valley (the valley above Ballymackellet). When the spoils are brought back and the cattle have to be driven over the mountain at the source of the Big River (the river Cronn), Fergus decides that they will have to cut a gap in the hills to get the cattle. This is the *Bernas Bo Ulad*, today known as **Windy Gap**. It's also the point in the story where Fergus and Medb hang back behind the army to make love, and where Ailill, aware of their trysts, sent a spy to take Fergus's sword, thus acquiring proof of his unguarded weakness and the basis of a phallic joke which recurs throughout the story.

Windy Gap is also the setting of a far later tale, the tragic legend behind the **Long Woman's Grave**, marked by a pile of stones at the roadside. The story concerns two sons at their father's deathbed: the elder promised to give his younger brother a fair share of the estate, saying he would take him up to a high place in the mountains and give him all he could see. He kept his word, but the place where they stood was Windy Gap, where if you look around you see nothing but the immediate hills rising on all sides. The younger son instead became a trader, and on one trip wooed a Spanish beauty to whom he gave the same promise, tempting her hand in marriage. When he brought her home and took her up to the Windy Gap to show her his estate she dropped dead on the spot from shock. Thus the Long Woman's Grave for the tall Spanish beauty is explained.

INLAND: MEATH AND THE RIVER BOYNE

The river Boyne has a name resonant of Irish history, for it was on its banks that one of the battles which shaped the nation's destiny was fought. As you travel up the river, however, this is not what most occupies your attention. For in the early stages, following the N51 to Navan, is the area known as the **Brugh Na Bóinne** complex, with some of Europe's finest prehistoric remains. The whole Boyne valley, in fact, has been heavily populated from the earliest times, and traces of virtually every period of Irish history can be found here.

Oldgrange: The Battle of the Boyne

For all the significance attached to it now—there are big Protestant celebrations in the North on July 12—the **Battle of the Boyne** was just one skirmish, and arguably not the decisive one, in the "War of the Kings." It took place at OLDGRANGE, less than five miles from Drogheda, on July 1, 1690 (the change of date came with the switch to the Gregorian calendar in the eighteenth century). The deposed James II, retreating southwards, took up defensive positions on the south bank of the river, with some 25,000 men (including 7000 well-equipped French troops, but largely Irish irregulars) holding the last major line of defense on the road to Dublin. William's forces—around 36,000—occupied a rise on the north bank from where they forced a crossing of the river and put their enemies to flight. In terms of losses, the battle was a minor one—some 1500 Jacobites and 500 of William's men—and James's forces were to regroup and fight on for another year. But in political terms it was highly significant and can legitimately be seen as a turning point. In the complexities of European struggle, the Protestant William was supported by the pope and the Catholic king of Spain, both fearful of the burgeoning power of James's ally, the French King Louis XIV. Although the victory on the battlefield was small, the news gave heart to William's supporters in Europe while making Louis fearful of extending further aid to the Jacobite cause. At the same time, it gave William breathing space to establish his control back home: in the long run, Protestant ascendancy was assured.

The location of the battlefield is directly opposite the turn off from the N51 to TULLYALLEN. Here a stepped path leads to a viewing point on the site occupied by William's troops before the battle. It's only a slight elevation, but it nevertheless commands a broad swath of the valley and it's not too hard to conjure up a picture of the armies battling it out in front of you. A panoramic plan marks out the various positions of the opposing forces.

Brugh Na Bóinne

The area known as **Brugh Na Bóinne** comprises a group of forty or so related sites of prehistoric monuments caught within a curve of the river between Tullyallen and Slane. The three most important of them, Dowth, Knowth, and Newgrange, are what is known as **passage-graves**—high round mounds raised over stone burial chambers. They predate the pyramids by several centuries, and although there's no comparison in terms of size or architecture, there are certain parallels. Just as the fertility of the Nile helped create the great Egyptian culture, so the Boyne River and its drainage have been proved to have had some of the richest soil in Europe (and considerably higher temperatures than today) around 3000 BC. On the banks flourished what seems to have been the most advanced Neolithic civilization in Europe. Physically, the tombs' size and solidity are what impress most. Beyond the massive, bare stones there's not much to be seen, but there's plenty of scope to try and disentangle the various theories about these structures, to work out who built them, from where they came, and where they went.

Dowth

Dowth is the first of the great sites if you're heading upstream, reached by taking the first left off the N51 after the battlesite, a minor road which trails the north bank of the river. Just before you reach the cairn you'll see the tower of **Dowth Castle** on the left, adjoining a rambling red-brick Victorian mansion, now converted into a Buddhist center. John Boyle O'Reilly, a Fenian patriot transported to Australia, who later became editor and part-owner of the *Boston Pilot*, was born in the castle in 1844. At the back of the neighboring ruined church there's a monument to him that forms the heart of a small **commemorative festival** every year on the Sunday closest to August 10.

The **Dowth mound** itself—a little under fifty feet high and just over 200 feet in diameter—is not currently open to visitors, as a new entrance is being planned. However, if the archaeologists are on site you can usually go up and examine the exterior of the mound. The signs of earlier excavations and of outright pillaging (in the nineteenth century, some of the stones were removed for road-making) are immediately apparent, having left a crater in the top of the mound and a large chunk burrowed out of the side. Around 100 **kerbstones**, perhaps half of which can be seen today, originally marked the edge of the tumulus. Inside are two **passage-tombs** and an early Christian chamber. The passages are similar in construction to those at Newgrange (see below) as is the decoration of the standing stones which form the walls of the passage, and the ten-foot-high corbeled roof. One distinction between the two sites, however, are the **sill stones** placed across the passage floor and at the entrance to the chamber.

The name Dowth derives from the Irish for "darkness," and the main chamber faces west to the setting sun (the minor chamber looks southwest, directly towards Newgrange). In myth, the site was built when the Druid Bresal, attempting to build a tower that would reach heaven, contracted all the men of Erin for a single day. His sister worked a spell so that the sun would not set until the mound was built, but the two then committed incest, destroying the magic and causing the sun to set; thereafter the sister declared "Dubad (darkness) shall be the name of that place forever." Today, as the sun sets on the winter solstice, its rays enter the tomb (at about 3pm), lighting up the tall stone slab at the back and then moving across to illuminate a recess in which is a decorated stone precisely angled to catch this moment, before finally sinking below the horizon.

Newgrange

The second of the tombs, **Newgrange** (June–Sept daily 10am–7pm; mid-March to May daily 10am–1pm and 2–5pm; Oct to mid-March Tues–Sat 10am–4:30pm, Sun 2–4pm; £1.50), is far more visited, so much so in fact that long lines can build up at peak times. To get there follow the road directly away from Dowth and take a left at the T-junction. You're led around the monument in a guided tour about 25 minutes long (the closing times above are the *end* of the last tour), and if you want to avoid a long wait and a large group you should try not to come between noon and 4pm or especially on Sunday during the holidays. One or two of the most popular dates are booked up months in advance, above all the winter solstice when you've no chance at all of getting in to see the phenomenon described below (it is effectively reserved for local dignitaries). You may be lucky, though, if you come a couple of days before or after the solstice, when the effect is almost as good—cloud cover permitting. To book ahead write to The Director, Office of Public Works, National Parks and Monuments Branch, 51 St Stephen's Green, Dublin 2, or contact the Newgrange office itself.

The **Newgrange tumulus** has an average diameter of around 338 feet and it's some thirty feet high at its center point. It has been so completely restored that at first sight it reminds you of a grounded Fifties sci-fi flying saucer. But once you get over the initial shock, the sparklingly new appearance of it all serves only to heighten the wonder. The quartzite retaining wall is glisteningly white, and gives some hint (not revealed at other sites where everything is gray and moss-covered) of the power this particular stone must have had for the builders. The nearest natural source is in the Wicklow Mountains, south of Dublin. You'll notice that the wall is bossed with small, round granite stones, the purpose of which no one knows. Speculation is not helped by the fact that they are probably not in their original positions: during the most extensive of the renovations (1962–75) the original photographs were lost and their placement was therefore a matter of educated guess. Other non-original features worth noting are that the front and most ornate kerbstone was originally placed by the entrance tunnel (it was moved to prevent damage by visitors); that the entrance tunnel itself was closed by a standing slab; and that the concave wall at the entrance is designed to accommodate 100,000-odd tourists each year—originally the wall would have continued directly up to the sides of the spirally decorated kerbstone. It is also believed that an obelisk once stood at the top of the mound, to mark it out from afar.

The outer ring of **standing stones**, of which only twelve uprights now remain, was a feature unique among passage-grave tombs, and it may have been the addition of a later civilization. None of the standing stones is decorated, and many show signs of being eroded by water, which suggests that they may have been hauled up here from the river. There is an inner ring of 97 **kerbstones** all placed on their sides and touching each other, engineered one supposes as a support to the layers of sod, loose stones, shale, and boulder clay (20,000 tons of it) that were laid over the chambers.

Perhaps the most important feature of Newgrange—again unique—is the **roof-box** several feet in from the tunnel mouth. This contains a slit through which, at the **winter solstice**, the light of the rising sun begins to penetrate as soon as its full disc appears above the horizon. The rays edge their way slowly up the passage tunnel, and, narrowed into a single shaft by purposefully jutting side slabs, eventually find the back of the cruciform chamber. In minutes the chamber becomes radiant with a glow of orange light which fades as suddenly as it has blazed. The sun actually rises at about 8:20am above a hill known as the Red Mountain: it reaches the chamber a couple of minutes before 9am, and by 9:15 the whole thing is over. The guided tour includes a "recreation" of the phenomenon which involves a flash of orange electric light: if you prefer to rely on your imagination, then keep your eyes shut through this performance.

The rest you'll be effectively guided through on the tour. The entry passage, about three feet wide, leads into the **central chamber** where the finest of the work is. Its corbeled roof creates a space some twenty feet high, and on the stones everywhere are carved superbly intricate decorations, apparently abstract but perhaps (see below) with some more precise meaning. On the way out, beware of the last roof-slab—on which most tall people will graze their heads even after this warning. At the entrance to the site there's a **museum and interpretative center** where aspects of Newgrange and other nearby prehistoric sites are more fully explored.

The name Newgrange derives from "new granary," simply because that was its function at one stage in its history. This hardly seems an adequate description for one of the most important Stone-Age sites in Europe, however, and an alternative derivation ("the Cave of Gráinne") is considerably more satisfying, if less accurate. The site has many **associations with myth**. First among these concern the *Tuatha Dé Danann*, the first Irish gods who descended from the sky and inhabited the land before the Celts. Dagda (the Irish Zeus, chief of the gods) gained possession of the mound by making love to Boand (the white cow goddess who later knowingly drowned herself at the source of the Boyne so as to invest the river with her divinity), first tricking her husband Elcmar by sending him on an errand for a day which took him nine months. From their union **Oengus** was born and called *ac ind Oc* (The Youthful Son). In ancient literature Newgrange is *Brugh Mac ind Oc*, the Brugh of Oengus. Oengus also appears later in the **Fenian Cycle** as the succorer of Diarmuid and Gráinne, carrying the fatally wounded body of Diarmuid to Newgrange "to put aerial life into him so that he will talk to me every day." Other legends make the local mounds the burial tombs of the kings of Tara; radiocarbon dating (to the third millennium BC) however disproves this fairly convincingly.

What does emerge is just how little concrete information there is on the people who created Newgrange. Perhaps the most convincing of the more off-beat **theories** regarding the meaning of the monuments is that of the American Martin Brennan in his book *Stars and Stones* (Thames and Hudson, 1983). He claims that the scrollwork, lozenges, and lines on the stones, which most archaeologists see as abstract decoration, perhaps with religious significance, are in fact all part of a single incredibly involved **astronomical chart** which includes not only Newgrange itself, but the rest of the Brugh Na Bóinne complex and even sites as far-flung as Loughcrew (see p.133), and those in the Curlew Mountains in south Sligo. In his book he claims that the scrollwork all relates to a calibration system based on the diameter of the earth. Brennan insists that the Newgrange monument is not only the largest but also the oldest such system in the world, predating and far outranking in sophistication the instruments of the Greek astronomers. It is not a theory you are likely to find espoused by your guide, but it does have its convincing aspects. In the end, though, you have to ask why, if they were so sophisticated, is this the only evidence that survives?

Knowth

To reach **Knowth**, carry on west from Newgrange, take a sharp right and then left at the next junction, whereupon you'll see a makeshift wooden **watchtower** overlooking the site. For now this tower is as far as you'll get, for although excavations have been going on here since 1962, the finds are so great and complicated that it will be a few years yet before anything will be open to the public. This is still worth doing if you have the time—although out of season the protective covering of black plastic sheeting makes it resemble more a piece of Christo's wrapped art than a Neolithic burial site. The discoveries at Knowth have already surpassed what was excavated at Newgrange, perhaps because the place lay undisturbed until modern times, and consequently archaeologists have been able to explore far more methodically than they have elsewhere.

Several periods of occupation by different civilizations have been identified, from the original Neolithic passage-tombs (3000–2000 BC), through occupation by the **Beaker** people (2000–1800 BC; so called because of a distinctive beaker left with each of their dead), a late **Celtic** settlement in the early centuries AD, early **Christian** occupation (eighth to twelfth centuries) and finally **Norman** usage (twelfth and thirteenth centuries) that brought an extensive settlement and a glut of *souterrains* (underground passages and chambers), some bored into the Neolithic mound itself. The main passage-tomb is about twice the size of that at Newgrange—with a tunnel over 100 feet long leading to the central chamber—and even more richly decorated. At Knowth there is also, so far uniquely, a second, smaller passage-tomb within the main tumulus, and up to twenty **satellite tumuli.** Both main tombs are aligned east–west. In construction the mound is basically the same as Newgrange, with a cruciform chamber, high corbeled roof and richly decorated stones, but here there is also evidence of settlement around the mound. Probably the two were created by two distinct communities of the same culture: a supposition backed by carbon dating that places the Knowth mound some 500 years earlier than Newgrange. At Knowth alone about 250 decorated stones have been found—over half of all known Irish passage-grave art.

South of the Boyne: Donore and Duleek

Across the other side of the Boyne River at this point are two secondary diversions, Donore and Duleek. Unfortunately you can't simply pop across, as there's no river crossing between Drogheda and Slane, but either is easily reached from Drogheda itself, or they're a minor diversion if you're heading up the N2 from Dublin towards Slane. **DONORE**'s chief interest, apart from having been James's base at the time of the Battle of the Boyne, lies in its **ten-pound castle.** In 1429 Henry VI promised a grant of £10 to every one of his subjects who, in the next ten years, built a castle twenty feet long, sixteen feet wide and forty feet high within the counties of Meath, Louth, Kildare, and Dublin, the area known as the **Pale.** The three-story castle here is built almost exactly to these measurements, though unfortunately it seems to be permanently locked up.

DULEEK (*An Damh Liag*, the stone church) is an historic little place of considerably more interest. The south-of-the-Boyne equivalent of Kells, it was founded by Saint Patrick who settled Saint Cianán here to build the first stone church in Ireland and found a monastic settlement; it was also an early bishopric. Much later, the Jacobite forces withdrew to Duleek after the Battle of the Boyne and spent the night here, while James himself fled to Dublin and then on to France. The ruined **abbey** you see today was probably founded in the twelfth century, and was abandoned after Henry VIII's dissolution of the monasteries; there are some fine tombs in the roofless building, and nearby a squat, tenth-century **high cross**. In the town square is a **wayside cross** of a different nature, erected by Dame Dowdall in 1601 as a memorial to one of her husbands—one of the finest examples of a type of cross that crops up all over the place.

If you want to **stay** in this area there's good, reasonably priced accommodation and home-produced food at the historic house of *Annesbrook*, a short way out of town (follow the signs; B&B £12.50, dinner £10.50; May–Sept; contact Mrs Kate McElveen, ☎041-23293). William Thackeray in his *Irish Sketchbook* (1842) wrote uninspiringly about Annesbrook, but its most striking asset, the Ionic pedimented portico, has an interesting tale attached. The stately entrance is said to have been hastily affixed onto the box-shaped house when its owner was told to expect a visit from George IV, the first king to arrive from England after the departure of William and James. The portico was felt a necessary addition to bring the house up to the standards expected by royalty.

Slane

Continuing on the north side of the river, Slane is still less than nine miles from Drogheda, straight down the N51. If you're coming from Knowth, continue straight ahead and you'll emerge on the main road once again. A short way east of this junction, *The Tourists' Bar* is a handy stopover for tea and snacks; a short way west, just a mile out of Slane, you'll pass the **Francis Ledwidge Museum** (irregular guided tours in summer, Sat–Thurs, otherwise get the key from the small printing firm farther down the road on the left-hand side). This stone-built laborer's cottage was the birthplace, in 1887, of the local poet Francis Ledwidge, who died on a battlefield in Flanders on July 31, 1917. Ledwidge was untypically pastoral for an Irish poet, and perhaps for this reason comparatively little known; there's none of the pain of Catholic Ireland that you'd find in, say, Heaney. His poems were instead written on the small scale, and the museum reflects this: a modest, almost spartan, house with the poetry daintily hung in miniature picture frames. The verse lines inscribed on a stone plaque outside the cottage were written when Ledwidge heard of the death of his Irish poet friend **Thomas MacDonagh**, who was executed by the British for his involvement with the Easter Rising of 1916: it's an echo of MacDonagh's own poetic translation of Cathal Buidhe's *Mac Giolla Ghunna* (The Yellow Bittern).

He shall not hear the bittern cry
In the wild sky, where he is lain,
Nor voices of the sweeter birds
Above the wailing of the rain

There's a fine parallel to this in the modern poet Seamus Heaney's *In Memoriam Francis Ledwidge*:

I think of you in your Tommy's uniform,
A haunted Catholic face, pallid and brave,
Ghosting the trenches with a bloom of hawthorn
Or silence cored from a Boyne passage-grave.

SLANE itself, set on a steep hillside running down to the Boyne, is a beautiful little place which packs a surprising amount of interest. The scene is set at the village center, where four three-story, eighteenth-century houses stand at the four corners of a crossroads, each virtually identical (with arched entrance courtyards to the side) and composed of a lovely, rough-cut, gray limestone. There's a good yarn about these, concerning the four sister spinsters said to have built them, which may be recounted to you locally. It's not true, but you can't help feeling it ought to be.

Down by the river, the Georgian theme is continued in the fine **Mill** (1766), across the road from which stands a large Gothic gate to Slane Castle, whose lands stretch out westward along the river. There's a **Transportation Museum** (daily June–Sept) on the river bank as well, with around fifty cars on display.

Slane Castle, although it has a nightclub and expensive restaurant, is not generally open to the public. Approximately once a year, however, it does open its gates to half of young Ireland for massive, open-air rock concerts promoted by the entrepreneurial Lord Henry Mountcharles. There are also guided tours (mid-March to Oct, Sun only 2–6pm; £1.60, students £1; ☎041-24207 for information) of a small number of the more interesting rooms—including one used by U2 in the recording of *The Joshua Tree*. On Friday and Saturday nights the tiny castle **nightclub** opens up in the basement (£5; 10:30pm–2:30am; arrive early to get in). On a more traditional level, the castle is the seat of the **Conyngham Family**, a classically proportioned mass of mock battlements and turrets with a neo-Gothic library. It contains a substantial art collection and many mementoes of King George IV, who is said to have spent the last years of his life involved in a heady liaison with the Marchioness Conyngham; some claim that this relationship accounts for the exceptionally fast, straight road between Slane and Dublin. Farther out in the castle grounds, and again not for public consumption beyond a glimpse from the river towpath, is **St Erc's Hermitage**.

Walking north from the crossroads, uphill, you can climb to the top of the **Hill of Slane**, where **Saint Patrick** lit his Paschal Fire in AD 433, announcing the arrival of Christianity. This was in direct defiance of Laoghaire, High King of Tara, who had ordered no fire-making until Tara's own hillside was set alight. Fortunately for Saint Patrick, Laoghaire was promptly converted, welcoming the new religion throughout the country. Near the top, the ruined **Friary Church** (1512) and separate college building are worth investigating.

The church has a well-preserved **tower**, with a very narrow and steep flight of sixty-odd steps: if you make it up you're rewarded with a broad panorama of the eastern counties, though Slane itself is all but hidden from view. In the graveyard there is a very unusual early Christian tomb with gable-shaped end-slabs. This is supposed to be the final resting place of **Saint Erc**, Patrick's greatest friend and servant whom he made Bishop of Slane. The **college** was built to house the four priests, four lay-brothers, and four choristers there to serve the church; assorted pieces of carved stonework can be found if you potter around its ruins.

Eating and Sleeping in Slane

If you're looking for somewhere to **stay** in Slane, the best option is probably a newly converted Georgian house by the canal walk, tucked in behind the mill, which offers both B&B and basic hostel-type accommodation. The **restaurant** at Slane castle is extremely good but also very pricey; *Bartles*, in one of the historic houses at the crossroads is also relatively expensive. You'll find cheaper eats at the *Conyngham Arms Hotel* (pub lunches and evening meals) or at the *Roadhouse restaurant* a few miles from Slane out on the Dublin Road (going south take the right turn just before *McKeever's Esso Garage*). There's a good **swimming** spot on the river below the weir, but check first with locals as the river currents can be strong in places.

Upstream to Navan

In its course upstream to Navan the **Boyne** runs past the grounds of several great houses. You can't visit any of them, but if you follow the river—a distance of some eight miles from Slane to Navan—you get a real sense of an all-but-vanished world. The old towpath switches sides from time to time, with no obvious means of crossing: the solution to this apparent mystery is that the horse would step onto the barge and be poled across to the other side. It is just about possible to walk all the way if you're prepared to stomp out your own path some of the time, but it's a great deal easier to walk as far as you can from this end, then travel to Navan by road and do the same from the other end. After Slane Castle itself, on the opposite side of the river, comes **Beauparc House**, the mid-eighteenth-century home of Lord Mountcharles (B&B available if you can spare £150 a night).

A little farther on you pass the remains of **Dunmoe Castle** (signposted off the N51, but accessible from there only by a nightmarish potholed lane) high on the northern bank. All that remains are two sides of a four-story castle which was square in shape with large rounded turrets at the four corners. Inside you can still see parts of the vaulted ceilings of the lower stories. Better than the crumbling structure, though, are the views it commands: in the river a diagonally dividing weir breaks the water into opposing stretches of rapids and of calm, while on the opposite bank there's a delightful red-brick mansion with a stretch of garden steps, worthy of Versailles, breaking through the wooded thickets to reach the river. Finally, shortly before Navan and right by the side of the main road, you pass the **Domhnach Mor** (Great Church), site of a superbly preserved round tower above whose arched doorway is carved a relief figure of Christ.

Navan

At **NAVAN** the **Blackwater River** meets the Boyne. It's historic crossroads and also a modern one: the N3 comes up from Dublin to follow the course of the Blackwater on into County Cavan, the route to Kells and to the Loughcrew Mountains in the northwestern corner of Meath; the N51 arrives from Drogheda to continue into Westmeath, its interest diminishing rapidly as you go; and to the south you can continue to follow the Boyne, along minor roads, to Bective Abbey, Tara, and Trim. Although it leads to a lot of places, Navan itself offers little to detain you. There's a tourist information office housed in the local *Bank of Ireland*, but it never seems to be open. You'll find a good cheap **lunch** at *Bon Appetit*, centrally placed in the Market Square at the corner of Ludlow Street, and there's a nice quiet **pub** nearby, the *Bermingham Bar* opposite the movie theater on Ludlow Street. *Peter Kavanagh's* on Trimgate Street is another good, old-fashioned pub, or there are **traditional music** sessions every Wednesday in the *Lantern*, Watergate Street.

One local sight worth going out of your way for is **Athlumney Castle**— about a mile's walk from the center of town, over the bridge then first right following the signs. Just as you come up to the ruin, veer right into **Loreto Convent** (once the castle's outbuildings) where you can pick up the keys. In the convent grounds you should immediately spot the twelfth-century *motte* (now surrounded by a ring of trees) that would have had a *Bretesche*, or wooden tower, built on it. This was purely defensive, and the owner would actually have lived closer to the river. The castle you see now is a fifteenth-century tower house to which a Jacobean manor house was added in the early seventeenth century. The Tower House has four floors in excellent condition, the first of which has a secret chamber down the stairs in the wall. The last occupant of the mansion was Sir Lancelot Dowdall, a Catholic who on hearing of the defeat of James II decided to set his home alight rather than see it fall into the hands of William's army. According to the story, he stood and watched it burn before heading into permanent exile. The interior shows large gaping fireplaces and a horseshoe stone-oven on the bottom floor which would have been the area of the kitchens (the heat from which would rise to warm up the living quarters above). It once had a gabled roof within which the servants were housed and it still has many impressive mullioned windows left as well as a magnificent oriel window overlooking the modern road.

If you head back to the bridge you can take the steps down to the **ramparts** and then follow the canalside all the way to STACKALLEN, although a certain amount of building work may disrupt your way to begin with.

The Blackwater: Kells and Northeast Meath

Following the Blackwater upstream from Navan, Kells is the obvious place to make for, ten miles up the N3 Dublin–Cavan road. En route, you'll pass the site of the **Tailteann games*** (on the hill above Teltown House), a little over

---

*Old Irish literature not untypically begs to differ, and describes the place rather as a pagan cemetery named after the goddess *Tailtiu*.

halfway. Here games and ancient assemblies sacred to the god **Lugh** took place in the first days of August (the Gaelic for the month of August is *Lughnasa*). As late as the twelfth century the games were still being recorded, and right up to the eighteenth century a smaller celebration took place, in which locals rode their horses across the river for the benefit of the sacred qualities of its waters. Christianity eventually put paid to most of the rituals, but there is still talk of what was known as the **Teltown marriages**, where young couples would join hands through a hole in a wooden door, live together for a year and a day, and then be free to part if they so wished. Today only a very few earthworks remain, and certainly if you have visited Tara, or intend doing so, there's little to be gained in stopping here.

Kells

KELLS itself (*Ceanannus Mór*) is a place of history and monastical antiquities—several high crosses, an eleventh-century oratory, a round tower, and an ancient square bell tower—but it is most famous for what is not here, the magnificent illuminated manuscript known as the **Book of Kells**, now housed in Trinity College, Dublin. The monastery was founded by **Saint Columba** in the sixth century, and from about 807 it became the leading Columban monastery in Ireland, when the monks from the original foundation on Iona fled here from repeated Viking raids. It is probable that the Book of Kells was actually made on Iona, and that they brought it with them when they moved. The new home was little safer than the original one, and was attacked time and again by Danes and later the Normans; in the twelfth century the monastic order's headquarters moved on to Derry, and by the time of the Dissolution there was little left to abolish. So most of what you actually see is eighteenth-century or later, and although the town's layout still etches out the concentric ridges of the early monastery's plan it's a surprisingly characterless place. Nonetheless, the little that survives is well worth making the effort to see.

When you arrive, head for the spire of the **bell tower** that stands within the grounds of the modern Catholic church where most of the relics are to be seen. In the church itself (if it's not open the key can be got from the gate-lodge outside working hours, otherwise search for the priest) there is a facsimile copy of the Book of Kells, and up in the gallery you'll find a small exhibition of blown-up photos of some of its pages. The **Round Tower** in the churchyard is known to have been here before 1076, for in that year Murchadh Mac Flainn, who was claiming the High Kingship, was murdered within the tower. It's a little under 100 feet high, with five windows near the top, and missing only its roof.

Near the tower is the **South High Cross**, the best and probably the oldest of the crosses in Kells, carved as ever with scenes from the Bible. Here you'll see, on the south face, Adam and Eve and Cain and Abel; then the Three Children in the Fiery Furnace; then Daniel in the Lions' Den. On the left arm of the wheel Abraham is about to sacrifice Isaac, and on the right are saints Paul and Anthony in the desert; at the top is David with his harp and the Miracle of the Loaves and Fishes. There are two other complete crosses in the churchyard, and the stem of a fourth (behind the church back-entrance door) with the inscription *Oroit do Artgal*, A Prayer for Artgal. This again has several identifiable panels. The near side shows the Baptism of Christ, the Marriage Feast at Cana, David with his harp again, the Presentation in the Temple, and others too worn to make out. On the other side are a self-conscious Adam and Eve (again), Noah's Ark, and others hard to identify with any accuracy. There are also sculptured stones embedded in the walls of the bell tower.

Saint Columba's Oratory can be found just outside the churchyard walls at the north end—coming out of the main gates take a sharp left uphill, but first obtain the keys from the chocolate-brown house just after the stop sign. It's a beautifully preserved building—thick-walled and high-roofed—and peculiarly in character with the row of nineteenth-century workers' houses alongside which it stands. In outer appearance it is not unlike St Kevin's Kitchen at Glendalough. A modern entrance has been broken in at ground level, when originally the door would have been about eight feet off the ground in the west wall (reached, for security, by a removable ladder); you can still see the intended way in around to the left from where you enter now. Inside is a space about 23 by 21 feet, where you emerge into a vaulted room that would have once had two levels (with the present ground floor as a basement). Above were three tiny attic rooms, reached now by a metal ladder, which were probably where the residents slept and also a hideout in times of trouble.

In the central **Market Square** there's another fine **high cross**, discolored by traffic fumes, said to have been placed here by Jonathan Swift. In 1798 it served as the gallows from which local rebels were hanged. Yet again, it is liberally festooned with fine stone carving. The base shows horsemen and animals in a battle scene; on the west face are the Adoration of the Magi, the Marriage at Cana and the Miracle of the Loaves and Fishes, all surrounding the Crucifixion in the center of the wheel; on the east are Christ in the tomb, Goliath, Adam and Eve, and Cain and Abel, with Daniel in the Lions' Den occupying center stage.

Staying in Kells

If you want to stay, the **tourist information** office, opposite the *Bank of Ireland* on the Dublin Road, is the best place to start for information; if they're shut try Mrs Anna Sweeney's **B&B** (☎046-41510; £9) next to the *Headfort Arms* hotel at the beginning of the Dublin Road. **Buses** pick up outside *O'Rourke's* lounge in Castle Street. You'll get very tasty **food** during the day at *Robins*, a café/lunch room at the bottom end of Market Street (closes 6pm), but in the evenings there's not much choice outside the pubs. *R O'Loughlin's* on Farrell Street serves good snacks, but otherwise good **pubs** are surprisingly scarce too. One that's definitely worth a visit, however, is the *Inishfree* on Church Street (running along the bottom of the church plot) which has Irish ballads and old-time music on Friday, Saturday, and Sunday nights at 9pm. The song *The Isle of Inishfree* was actually written there by Deek Farley, the former owner who was also once superintendent at Dublin Castle.

The Castlekeeran Crosses

From Kells the N3 follows the Blackwater northwest into County Cavan. A considerably more interesting route takes the Oldcastle road (the one that passes alongside the round tower) towards the Loughcrew Cairns (*Sliabh na Caillighe*). Only a mile out of Kells a very worthwhile short detour takes you up a winding road to the right that leads, after about another mile, to the **Castlekeeran Crosses**. Entry is signposted through the yard of a creamy-orange farmhouse and across a field which will take you into the old monastery enclosure. Hardly anything of the monastery that was known as **Diseart Chiarain**, the Hermitage of Ciaran, has survived, although you can pick out a partially earth-covered arch. The high crosses here, three of them plus a fourth in the middle of the river, are older than those at Monasterboice and Kells and far simpler. But their greatest charm lies in the fact that you'll probably be quite alone as you contemplate their history. The only decoration on the crosses are some simple fringing patterns and protruberances in the "armpits" and tops and wheel centers. The story of the cross in the river Blackwater tells how Saint Columba was caught red-handed by Saint Ciaran as he carried the cross off to his own monastery. In his shame he dropped the cross where he stood and fled back to Kells.

There is also an **Early Christian grave slab** in the graveyard, and a very good example of an **ogham stone**. Ogham was an early Irish script which was widely used from around the fourth to the seventh century AD, after which it was very gradually replaced by Latin script. Even at the height of its popularity ogham co-existed with Latin writing: it was used primarily on stones and monuments such as this, while Latin script was found in manuscripts. It is thought that the script was once used for secret communication, part of a signaling or gesture system for magical or cryptic purposes. It can be found in parts of Devon, Wales, and Scotland (presumably through Irish colonization). As late as the nineteenth century some isolated peasant communities still used ogham script if they needed to write anything down—it had the advantage that no one from outside would be able to interpret it. On stones like this, the edge is used to help define the characters. Five strokes above the line give you five letters; five below another five letters. Five strokes that cross the line make five more letters and five oblique strokes five more: to these a few less obvious symbols are added to make up the alphabet. The inscription here apparently reads *covagni maqi mucoi luguni*, but although the letters can be made out nobody seems to know what these words actually mean.

Sliabh Na Gaillighe

Sliabh na Gaillighe, the Mountain of the Sorceress (910 feet), is the highest part of the **Loughcrew Mountains**, whose two-mile east–west extent virtually cuts off the furthest tip of County Meath. From the top there's a wonderfully disparate view, with the Cavan lakelands in one direction and the undulating flow of earthy Meath in the other, blending in the far distance into the mountains of Wicklow and Slieve Bloom. Three major groupings of

Neolithic cairns were constructed on these summits, no doubt chosen to be seen from afar. The first of them (coming from the east) is known as the **Patrickstown Cairns** and has been so thoroughly despoiled, largely for building material in the nineteenth century, that no significant trace remains. The other two summits have one major cairn each: **Cairn T on Carnbane East** and **Cairn L on Carnbane West**. Each of these has a handful of satellite mounds, though these represent only a fraction of what must once have been here. The sites are not easy to get to—you'll need transportation and still face a hefty walk at the end—but they are well worth the effort. Little known as they are, the Loughcrew Cairns are almost as impressive as the Newgrange mounds (certainly when you take into account the sheer number) and you'll almost certainly be free to explore them entirely alone, and with as much time as you want. Bring a torch if you want to appreciate what lies inside.

The Oldcastle road runs beneath the northern flank of the mountains, and about four-and-a-half miles before Oldcastle you'll see a broken signpost pointing off to the left, to *Sliabh na Gaillighe*. Follow this road for a mile and then take the right (signposted) that clearly heads towards the hill complex. In the first bungalow on the right you will be able to get the loan of **keys** from Basil Balfe (buy a leaflet map off him for 20p, and to be sure of finding someone in—or if you want to be there for sunrise—phone ahead to arrange to pick up the keys, ☎049-41256). These open the iron grilles on the few major cairns on top of the hills; the minor ones have either been deroofed or are left open.

Half a mile up the road—a steep climb—you'll come to a small clearing where a stile leads into a field: this path heads to the **Carnbane West** grouping. On your way across you'll notice **Cairn M** off to your left on a high peak—except for its astronomical involvement with Cairn L this hasn't much of interest, and it's not really worth the hike. **Cairn L**, with its wide ring of kerbstones, should be obvious to you immediately. It was most recently explored by Martin Brennan (in 1980; his theories about Newgrange have already been mentioned) after years of relative neglect by archaeologists. It is his astronomical theories which are in part set out below; they are far from being generally accepted, but in the absence of other explorations they do at least attempt to answer some of the questions about the sites.

Cairn L has an asymmetrical chamber (unique among the Loughcrew cairns) with a white **standing stone**, over six feet high, positioned at the back right. It is probable that the mound was built as a majestic housing for this one special stone. According to Brennan its function is found in the rising sun on the cross-quarter days November 8 and February 4 (the days halfway between the solstices and the equinoxes). On these days a flash of light enters the tomb from the rising sun (at about 7:40am) and catches the top of the standing stone. The lower edge of the light is formed by the shadow of Cairn M and other standing slabs in L further shape it so that the ray marks out only the standing stone. If you have a flashlight, then study the decorated slab by the basin to the left of the stone, facing away from the entrance. There are many designs carved into the various stones, but at the bottom of this one, according to Brennan, you can see a pictorial representation of this astronomical event.

Cairn H Brennan sees as a warning of the November cross-quarter day. The rising sun begins to penetrate its chamber from mid-October onward with the backstone being touched come November and then from about the third onward the sun leaves Cairn H and moves on to cairns M and L for November 8. **Cairn F**, with several examples of decorative grooves, kicks off another alignment series. The sun begins to enter in late April, ready to mark another cross-quarter day on May 6, when the rays of the setting sun center on **Cairn S**. Cairn S is also aligned for the final cross-quarter day, August 8. By August 16 they enter F again, and from there move on to **Cairn I** to warn of the autumn equinox. If Brennan's theories are correct (critics tend to claim that if you look long enough, and pick enough times and days, you can prove almost anything this way), then cairns I, T, F, and S form the longest such sequence of alignments known.

To get to **Carnbane East**, return to the hill road and continue until you reach a large parking lot where a path leads up the hill to the mounds. If you lose the path, which is vague at times, just keep climbing steeply, steering left if there's any doubt; towards the top follow the barbed wire around and enter by the gate which will put you on the threshold of Cairn T. At Carnbane East, Brennan sees three mounds functioning as solar dials. **Cairn T** deals with the spring and autumn equinoxes (March 23 and Sept 22). In its cruciform chamber is a large backstone liberally patterned with chevrons, ferns, petals, and moon and sun signs. At the spring equinox a shaped patch of light passes across a passage stone and various of the other designs to focus on the large radial sun sign in the center of this stone. On the autumn equinox the sun makes a more leisurely progress, rising at about 7:11am and striking the backstone just over half an hour later. Once again it crosses the sunwheel emblem. Of the satellite mounds, neither of which have roofs any more, **Cairn S** is said to mark the cross-quarter days on May 6 and August 8, while **Cairn U** is synchronized with Cairn L to mark November 8 and February 4. Cairn S has lots of sun emblems, while Cairn U has a variety of more unusual (and less identifiable) markings. Whatever you make of Brennan's theories in the end, he has at least opened an important new area of exploration; and in the undeniable light of Newgrange's connection with the equinox there are very few people any more who would contend that these structures were simply tombs and nothing more.

Oldcastle

OLDCASTLE is a mild-natured eighteenth-century town, built around a crossroads which no longer seems to have much significance. The clock-tower that marks the center of town stopped long ago, and that seems to just about sum up the place. It has the feel of an outpost in a long-forgotten conflict. You can eat and sleep here—there's a **B&B** out on the main road, below the cairns, a good **lunch** in the *Manor Arms Hotel* in the square, traditional music at weekends in the *Céilí House Bar*—but there's not much else to do.

In terms of interest you're better off heading on to CASTLEPOLLARD, ten miles south in County Westmeath (p.145), from where you can explore the Fore Valley, Tullynally Castle, and the sights around Lough Derravaragh.

Farther Up the Boyne: Southern Meath

The Boyne River flows into Navan from the south, and some nine miles in this direction **Trim** marks the last real glory, a medieval one this time, to stand on its banks. History and a magnificent castle aside, it's not a terribly exciting place, but it does make a good base from which to explore the southern half of the county, and in particular **Bective Abbey**, **Dunsany Castle** and the **Hill of Tara**.

Bective Abbey

Bective Abbey lies about halfway from Navan to Trim between the main road and the river. A beautiful example of medieval architecture, it is also set in flawlessly idyllic surroundings by an old bridge over the river. The abbey was once a considerable power in the land, and its abbot held a peer's seat in the English Parliament—one of only fifteen granted to the whole of the Pale. At this time the church as a whole owned as much as a third of the county of Meath. The buildings you see date from a variety of different periods, sometimes bewilderingly so, but its basics are clearly identifiable.

Of the original abbey, founded in 1146 by **Murcha O Maelechlainn**, King of Meath, nothing at all survives. In the late twelfth century the abbey, the first daughter house of Mellifont, was completely rebuilt, perhaps in time to accept the disinterred body of **Hugh de Lacy** in 1195. By 1228 it was decided that Bective should sever its ties with Mellifont and go under direct rule from Clairvaux in France. Of this second abbey you can still see the **chapter house** with central column, part of the **west range** and fragments of the cruciform **church**. In the fifteenth century this church was shortened on the west side, its aisles were removed, new south and west ranges were built inside the lines of the old cloister, and a smaller cloister erected. Both the south and west alleys of this latest cloister remain. The **tower** at the entrance over the porch is in excellent shape, and you can also see the layout of the fortified mansion that was built after the abbey's dissolution in 1543.

Trim

TRIM can boast the remains of the largest Anglo-Norman castle in Ireland, ruins of various abbeys and a host of other medieval remains. Yet it remains surprisingly little frequented, and somewhat downbeat in atmosphere. Nonetheless it's worth a visit, with plenty to see in and around the town.

The **tourist office** (June–Sept) is in a temporary hut next to the castle—in the center of town on Castle Street. Out of season phone ☎046-31845 for information and access to the castle. The same number will get you good **B&B** (£9 peak, £8 off-peak), or try *Brogans* (☎046-31237) or *Keaveneys* (☎046-31745). Fancier accommodation can be found at the *Station Hotel*, six miles or so to the east in KILMESSAN, which is almost equidistant from Tara, Bective, and Dunsany. If you're hungry, you can get excellent health-food snacks from the *Salad Bowl Delicatessen* on Market Street, or more substantial **meals** at *Badges* restaurant on Emmett Street (left off Market Street, away from the river). **Pubs** are as plentiful as ever, but one you should sample is *Marcy Regan's*, a tiny, ancient place near the Crutched Friary where Marcy herself, aged a youthful ninety-odd, can usually be found chain-smoking in the corner. Remember not to order a pint for the pub only sells bottled beer.

The obvious place to start exploring Trim is the **castle** itself, right in the center of town and approached either from the riverside walk or via the gate at the end of a modern causeway off Castle Street. Inside you're free to wander at will, but there's also a guided tour which (at only 50p) makes a handy introduction to what you'll see. The first castle on the site was a *motte*-and-bailey construction put up by **Hugh de Lacy** in 1172 after he had been granted the lordship of Meath by Henry II. Within a year this was attacked by Roderick O'Conner, King of Connacht, and destroyed. A new castle was begun in the late 1190s, too late for Hugh de Lacy who, in the meantime, had had his head severed with an axe by an Irish laborer in Durrow. It was this second attempt that eventually grew to become the finest, and largest, Anglo-Norman castle seen in Ireland.

The new castle also became known as **King John's Castle** after John spent a day or two in Trim in 1210—though in fact he didn't even lodge there—but it has stronger associations with Richard II, who incarcerated his ward Prince Henry of Lancaster (later Henry IV) here for a time. In look and feel this is very much an English medieval castle, with a 500-yard **curtain wall** enclosing some three acres, five D-shaped **towers**, various **sally gates** (small openings in the wall for surprise sorties) and, most impressive of all, a massive, square, seventy-foot-high **castle keep** with its walls running at a thickness of a solid eleven feet. The keep is named after Geoffrey de Joinville who, along with Walter de Lacy, was responsible for its construction in 1220–25. De Joinville spent many years on the Crusades (his brother Jean was the companion and biographer of Saint Louis, King of France) and finally became a monk in the Dominican "Black Friary" that he built at the northern end of Trim (which is currently undergoing excavation). One unusual, and not altogether successful, feature of the keep was the addition of a side chamber on each face (three out of four survive): an experiment not repeated elsewhere as it greatly increased the number of places that could be attacked, and hence which had to be defended. Here, though, it hardly mattered given the solidity of the outer wall. Hardly anything is left inside the keep, but you can make out the outlines of two great halls and, above these, the main bedrooms. The entrance door was in the east tower on the second floor.

Outside, the curtain wall runs around only three sides of the keep—on the fourth, the deep-running river was relied on as adequate cover. As you walk around, take in especially the **Dublin gate**, with its well preserved barbican and two drawbridges, and the impressive section of the wall between here and the river, near the end of which is an underground chamber thought to have been used as a **mint** in the fifteenth century.

On the opposite bank of the river from the keep stands **Talbot's Castle**, a beautiful, three-story fortified manor house. It was built in 1425 by the Lord Lieutenant of Ireland, Sir John Talbot, on the site of an Augustinian abbey;

remains of the earlier building are incorporated into the lower floors of the castle. Queen Elizabeth I formulated a plan to convert it into Ireland's first university, but instead it was established as a Latin school whose most famous scholar was Arthur Wesley, later (having changed his name to Wellesley) the Duke of Wellington. Wellington entered Parliament as MP for Trim and, despite his contempt for his Irish roots, was responsible as Prime Minister for passing the Act of Catholic Emancipation.

Behind Talbot's Castle rises the **Yellow Steeple**, so called because of the glint of its stone in the sunset. This is the only surviving part of **St Mary's Abbey**, and its ruined state owes more to Cromwell's attack in 1642 than the ravages of time. The abbey itself once housed **"Our Lady of Trim,"** an object of pilgrimage for the miraculous cures it performed. The wooden statue was burned in front of Commander Croot, Cromwell's general, as he lay recuperating from wounds received in the attack on Trim. An artist's impression of this lost treasure can be seen at the roadside by the junction of the Dublin Road and New Dublin Road. Near the Yellow Steeple, **Sheep Gate** is the only remaining piece of the fourteenth-century town walls.

Also on this side of the river, and easiest reached from Trim Castle by heading out of Dublin Gate, along the Dublin Road, and across the river by the sign, are the thirteenth-century ruins of **Newtown Cathedral** and its cemetery. The cathedral burned down over five hundred years ago, but its ruins preserve a surprising amount that is worth seeing, especially in the cloister. The wall also acts as a sounding board to create a natural echo that is eerily brilliant in its clarity and closeness. In the cemetery, look out for the famous tomb of the **Jealous Man and Woman**, Sir Lucas Dillon and his wife Lady Jane Bathe. Their stone effigies are in Elizabethan costume and a sword rests between them. The rusty pins you'll see left in the stone tresses are thanksgiving offerings to the rainwater caught here that is reckoned to cure warts.

Taking the next left turn off the Dublin Road will take you to the **Crutched Friary** (key from the tourist information office), yet another fine medieval ruin. This was a base of the Knights of St John of Jerusalem after the Crusades, and takes its name from the wounded Crusaders who settled here. Next to it is a gorgeous old **Norman bridge**, reckoned to be the second oldest in Ireland (*Marcy Regan's*, at the other end of the bridge, similarly claims to be the **second oldest pub** in the land!). In the 1950s the film *Captain Lightfoot* used the bridge as a location, and its star, the late Rock Hudson, is said to have spent much of his time in the pub.

Around Trim

A couple of miles south of Trim is **LARACOR**, the place where Jonathan Swift lived with Stella Johnson and where he was rector (with very little rectitude) from 1699 to 1714. No trace of him, however, remains. Two miles farther is **Dangan Castle**, the family home of the Duke of Wellington, now no more than a shell and again with little trace of its past.

Perhaps a more interesting excursion is to the Gaelic-speaking community at **RATHCAIRN**, near ATHBOY, eight miles northwest of Trim, where traditional Gaelic entertainment may well be taking place. The community was uprooted from Connemara by the Land Commission between 1935 and 1940, and replanted here in Meath as a *Gaeltacht*. The population is about 350 and increasing, a unique statistic as most Gaelic-speaking peoples in their natural habitats are rapidly decreasing in numbers. Not far away, in a field beside the Athboy–Navan road, is the **Rathmore Church and Cross** (*An Ráth Mhor Teampall agus Cros*). The church was built by the Plunkett family in the fifteenth century and is full of interesting stone carvings which are worth leaving the road to take a look at. There's an octagonal shaft from a baptismal font, a violated Norman sarcophagus in the fortified tower, a decorated altar stone, the stalk of an ancient cross and other stonework. Note the corbeled roof in the other tower, now trapped as a pigeon-cote.

Tara

TARA, the home of the High Kings of Ireland and source of so many of the great tales, looks nowadays like nothing so much as a neatly-kept nine-hole golf course, a gently undulating swath of green marked out by archaeological plaques. To recreate the palace, whose wood-and-wattle structures have entirely disappeared, leaving only scars in the earth, takes a fair degree of imagination. But it's an effort worth making, for this was a great royal residence, already thriving before the Trojan Wars and still flourishing as late as the tenth century AD. The origins of the site are lost in pre-history, but it probably originally had a religious significance, gradually growing from the base of a local priest-king to become the seat of the High Kings. Its heyday came in the years following the reign of the legendary Cormac Mac Art* in the third century AD—when five great highways converged here—and by the time of the confrontation of Saint Patrick with King Laoghaire in the fifth century, its power was already declining. The title of High King was not, on the whole, a hereditary one: rather the kings were chosen, or won power on the battlefield. So they were not necessarily local—or even permanently based here—but all evoked the spirit of Tara as the basis of their power.

In later history, there was a minor battle at the site during the 1798 revolution, and in the mid-nineteenth century **David O'Connell** held a mass meeting—said to have attracted as many as a million people (a quarter of Ireland's population today)—as part of his campaign against Union with Britain.

You'll find **the site** signposted just off the Dublin to Navan road, about 25 miles from Dublin. From the parking lot it appears as a wild meadow on a table-top hill, no more than 300ft above the surrounding countryside (just beside the parking lot is the *Banquet Hall Café*, open daily 9:30am–6/7pm).

---

*One of the more frequently recounted stories concerning Cormac is about his death. After years of heroism he died, the victim of a druid's curse, in a singularly unheroic manner, choking on a salmon bone (the salmon being the Celtic symbol of wisdom). The curse had been laid after he began proclaiming his belief in a new God who would soon be arriving in Ireland (a belief borne out by the arrival of Saint Patrick). In defiance of the king's stated wishes, his body was taken to be buried at Newgrange; when the funeral procession reached the Boyne, however, the tides came to the king's defense, and in the end his body had to be laid to rest on the south side of the river, at Ros Na Rí.

There is a plan of the site near the entrance, which will help you to identify the various mounds. Once on top of what is actually very rich pasture, the power of the setting immediately becomes clear, with endless views that take in whole counties and their napkin-wrapped fields, and a huge sky.

Teach Miodhchuarta—the Banquet Hall—is on the northern hill slope and consists of two parallel banks between which runs a long sunken corridor. Its length is about 750 feet and the breadth ninety feet. An account of it in the medieval book known as the *Dinnshenchas* reads:

> *The ruins of this house are situated thus: the lower part to the north and the higher part to the south; and walls are raised about it to the east and to the west. The northern side of it is enclosed and small; the lie of it is north and south. It is in the form of a long house, with twelve doors upon it, or fourteen, seven to the west, and seven to the east. It is said that it was here the* Feis Teamhrach *was held, which seems true; because as many men would fit in it as would form the choice part of the men of Ireland. And this was the great house of a thousand soldiers.*

The *Feis Teamhrach* was the great **Feast of Samhain** (a harvest fair if you like, but more probably Halloween) and it's easy to imagine the five ancient highways thronged with people on their way to crowd the hall for the great *Feis*—bards, athletes, poets, princes, musicians, druids. The twelfth-century *Book of Leinster* and the fifteenth-century *Book of Lecan* enumerate the various grades of society in attendance and even the particular foods appropriate to each carouser (from ribs of beef for the nobility, to pork shoulders for the musicians). Both medieval books also display ground plans and agree on the building being divided into five aisles with a central open space for scores of servants and cauldrons. Sean O'Riordain, who excavated the site in the late 1950s, surmised that the roof timbers would have rested on the two side banks and that lengths of upright support posts would have created the aisles.

Northwest of the hall is a smaller group of earthworks, the first of which is **Ráth Gráinne** (Gráinne's Fort). It is surrounded by a fosse and bank and has a low mound at its center, probably once a burial mound or maybe even a house site. From here the tragic love tale of the *Pursuit of Diarmuid and Gráinne* began its journey. Gráinne was the daughter of Cormac Mac Art, who had arranged to marry her to his aged commander-in-chief, Finn Mac Cool. Instead she fell in love with Diarmuid, one of Mac Cool's young warriors, and the two of them fled together, relentlessly pursued by Finn Mac Cool. Their various hiding places lie strewn throughout Ireland, marking practically every geological oddity in the country. Further west lie the **Claoin-Fhearta**, or Sloping Trenches, created, according to the legend, when Cormac Mac Art as a youth in disguise corrected the judgements of the then-king, Lugaid MacCon. (Mac Art was also something of an Irish Solomon figure.) The consequence of his justice was that half the house where the false judgements had been given slipped down the hill, creating the sloping trenches. The southern part of the trenches witnessed the murder of the princesses of Tara, some thirty of them in a massacre whose total casualties were said to have been 3000, by Dúnlaing, King of Leinster, in AD 222.

South of the Banquet Hall lies the main group of mounds, and first of all the **Rath of the Synods**. This is so called because of the various church synods said to have been held here by Saints Patrick, Brendan, Ruadhan and

Adamnan, although little archaeological evidence has been found relating to this function. Two gold torques (flat strips of gold soldered and twisted together rope-like into a necklace) were found here in 1810. Much of the ruin, however, which appears to have originally been a ring-fort defended by three concentric banks, has been destroyed over the years—partly by the graveyard which encroaches on it, but more especially by a group called the "British Israelites" who earlier this century rooted around trying to find the Ark of the Covenant. More serious archaeologists have discovered four stages in the rath's construction; in the center was a flat-topped mound known locally as the **King's Chair**. There were timber palisades on the banks, and in the middle a house where five burned bodies were found, along with Roman artifacts which suggest trading links between Tara and the Romans in Britain or Gaul.

The **Mound of the Hostages** (*Dumha na nGiall*) is the most prominent of the mounds and also the most ancient. It contained a passage-grave to which entrance is now barred, though you can look in to see the markings on the upright slab at the threshold. About forty Bronze Age cremated burials were found inside, many in large urns which were then inverted over the remains. Eating vessels and knives were found with them, and an elaborate necklace of amber, jet, bronze, and faience around the neck of a fifteen-year-old boy, the only body not cremated. A wealth of goods from the passage-grave culture (carbon-dated 2000 BC) were also discovered, making it the most comprehensive list rescued from any tumulus in Ireland. The mound, once again, is associated with Cormac Mac Art: here he is said to have imprisoned hostages taken from Connacht, who subsequently died within the chamber.

The **Ráth na Ríogh** (Royal Enclosure), immediately to the south, is a large area surrounded by a bank and ditch, within which are two earthworks, the **Forradh** (Royal Seat), and **Teach Cormaic** (Cormac's House). Both, though they're not contemporary, are typical ring-forts, with a central raised area for a rectangular house—Cormac's has two protective fosses and banks, the Royal Seat only one. In the center of Cormac's House are a grotesque, lichen-scabbed **statue of Saint Patrick**, entirely inappropriate to the site, and the **Lia Fáil** (Stone of Destiny), a standing stone moved from elsewhere on the site and reerected here in memory of those who died in 1798. It is marked with a cross and the letters RIP. According to one tradition this stone was the original Jacob's Pillow, brought to Ireland by the Milesians from the Island of Fal. It is also said to be the stone used in the inauguration of the High Kings, and would roar three times to signify its approval of the coronation.

The final remaining Rath on the site is named after High King Laoghaire, who made the historic meeting with Patrick when he lit his challenging fire on the Hill of Slane.

Dunsany

Dunsany Castle is only a few miles south of Tara, just outside the village of DUNSANY. If you want to visit you'll need to arrange it beforehand, either with the tourist office in Trim (which will know about forthcoming planned tours) or well in advance at any other tourist office. This is still a private residence, owned by the Plunkett family (under the title Lord Dunsany) who have lived here since the sixteenth century. The Lord Dunsany who died in 1957 established an unlikely dual reputation as an author; he wrote witty sketches of London club-land, and also bizarre dream-fantasy tales that influenced such American writers as H.P. Lovecraft. It's worth going to the trouble of arranging a visit, for this is one of the finest, most thriving examples of an Irish castle you're likely to see, and packed with a wealth of art.

The castle was originally built in the twelfth century by Hugh de Lacy, another of his fortresses defending the Anglo-Norman possessions around Dublin. It has been much altered and added to since, but it's still a magnificent building, with grounds to match. Among the family relics kept here—and quite apart from the superb private art collection, and the furniture, that you'll see on the tour—are the ring and other reminders of Patrick Sarsfield, second-in-command of the Jacobite forces in Ireland and successful defender of Limerick for over a year, and possessions and a portrait of Saint Oliver Plunkett, who was hanged in London for treason (his offense: being Catholic). The Dunsanys, in fact, seem to have made a habit of being on the wrong side in Ireland's conflicts, and it's remarkable that they have held on here so long.

Neighboring **Kilkeen Castle** belonged to another branch of the Plunkett family (when the estate was divided, the boundaries were supposedly set by a race; the wives of the inheritors ran from their castles, and the border was set where they met) and during the long years of Catholic suppression it was kept in trust for them by the (converted) Protestant Dunsanys.

In the grounds of Dunsany castle there's a fifteenth-century **church**, built by and for the family on the site of a still older one—again, you'll need permission to visit. There are some fine family tombs in here and, above all, a beautiful carved fifteenth-century font, with representations of the Twelve Apostles and the Crucifixion.

WESTMEATH AND LONGFORD

As you head west, leaving the Boyne Valley behind, historical interest diminishes rapidly. The attraction of Westmeath lies mainly in its lakes, although in the northeast, around **Castlepollard**, there is an area which deserves more exploration. **Athlone**, in the far west, is an important meeting of the ways near the very heart of Ireland, and a center for cruising on the Shannon, but again it preserves little interest in itself. Longford, if you visit at all, you'll see only briefly as you pass through on your way to the northwest coast.

The main route into the counties is the N4, which follows the Royal Canal, and the border of counties Meath and Kildare, out from Dublin to **Mullingar** and then **Longford Town**. As the road enters Westmeath the N6 turns off, to cut across the south of the county to Athlone. If you're coming from Meath, roads from Navan and from Kells converge at DELVIN, to run on together towards Mullingar. Or if you're up by Oldcastle in northwestern Meath, you can cut directly across the border to the most interesting part of Westmeath, the Fore Valley and Castlepollard.

Cooksborough

Heading for Mullingar, though, the only thing that might tempt you to stop on any of the roads is **COOKSBOROUGH**, a hamlet of a few houses strung together about eight miles from Mullingar on the Delvin Road. What you're looking for is a tomb in the shape of a beehive in the graveyard. Neither Cooksborough nor the tomb is signposted but you can find it by looking out for the sign to the *Bee Hive Nite Club*: about thirty yards past this, in the direction of Delvin, enter by an old gate and cross the field to a church and graveyard smothered in bramble, weed and grass. The tomb, which looks like a stone missile poking out of its silo, is that of **Adolphus Cooke** and his nurse Mary Kelly. A famous local eccentric, Cooke was convinced that he would be reincarnated as a bee and he was making sure he was prepared for the event. During his life he was similarly convinced that one of the turkeys scratching around in his yard was his father reincarnated. He also had the windows of his house made into the shape of spoon-backed chairs, in order to reflect the furniture within. There's more information on Adolphus Cooke in the Market Hall Museum in Mullingar.

Mullingar

MULLINGAR, the chief town of Westmeath, is a raucous, wheeling-and-dealing provincial capital that pretty much sums up the things you don't come to Ireland for. The center of a rich cattle-rearing area, its inhabitants are rural but the speed and noise of everything is continually wound up by its being a big trading center on a short leash from Dublin. The first ever **Fleadh Cheoil** (Festival of Music) was held in Mullingar in the late 1960s, but it fell so far short of local expectations that the town has never asked for it back. In short, you're unlikely to fall in love at first sight with Mullingar, but with perseverance you should be able to find a few positive moments before moving on—and there are a couple of good museums.

The first of these, on the corner of the main street at the turnoff to Tullamore, is the **Market Hall Museum** (May–Sept Mon–Sat 11:30am–1pm and 2–5pm; 50p). Run by local enthusiasts, it doesn't have any one item of outstanding interest (and if it had, it would no doubt be whisked off to the Dublin Museum), but it does have a modest charm in the peculiar wealth of local items on display. There's also the usual quota of Iron Age implements, quernstones and weaponry, along with a thumbnail history of the celebrated local eccentric, Adolphus Cooke (see above).

A second museum is attached to Mullingar's **Cathedral**, an uninspiring Neoclassical structure whose tapering twin towers (which look like melting candles) you'll be able to spot in the south of town. Inside, behind the side altars of St Patrick and St Anne, are two well-known mosaics by the Russian artist Boris Anrep. To get into the **Ecclesiastical Museum**—whose contents include many wooden penal crosses and the vestments of Saint Oliver Plunkett—ask for the key at the parochial house, on the right.

Best of all, however, is the **Military Museum** at the Columb Barracks; going south, turn right after the bridge over the canal, then swing left and it's 200 easily walkable yards up on the left. The collection is currently being rehoused in the **Old Guard Room** (daily 9am–4:30pm; ☎044-48391; free) and has a surprisingly broad range of interest. There's all the weaponry you'd expect, of course, with plenty of World War I and II firearms, and uniforms and flags from all over the world. But more intriguing are the sections devoted to the **old IRA**, with various local bands' uniforms and the tunic of Dan Hogan, Chief of Staff after 1929, who was shot by the FBI in 1941. There's also the uniform of Giles Vandeleur whose role in World War II was portrayed by Michael Caine in the film *A Bridge Too Far* and a pistol said to be that of **Michael Collins**, who was Chief of Staff throughout the War of Independence and the Civil War—though it's well-known that Collins rarely carried a weapon.

More miscellaneous items on display include long, canoe-like boats of bog-blackened oak which were dredged up from the surrounding lakelands. These were first thought to be of Viking origin, but carbon dating has placed them well into the first millennium AD. Similar boats are still being dredged up today, especially in Lough Derravaragh, but are as quickly being wrapped up again in peat and resunk in the middle of the lake. One of the stranger curios is the **military cycling handbook** that was in use until at least 1964. The book instructs the young cadet as to where to put his left foot and where his right and, with even more disciplinary stringency, orders him not to twist the handlebars without the officer's permission. All of this is arranged (or not arranged) amid a fair degree of chaos, though there's usually someone to show you around and attempt to make sense of it all.

If you want to **stay** in Mullingar, there's a good **B&B**, *Hilltop* (☎044-48958), a mile or so out on the Delvin road, or you can **camp** at the *Lough Ennel Holiday Village* (£3.50 per person and tent; ☎044-48101), three miles out on the Tullamore Road. Good **food** is served in the *Greville Arms* on the main street, where a wax effigy of Joyce stands in the foyer (somewhere in *Stephen Hero* he makes mention of Mullingar).

Southern Westmeath: Lough Ennel and Belvedere House

South of Mullingar there's just one significant attraction, **Lough Ennel**. With its low-lying, rushy shoreline it's not an especially dramatic expanse of water, but is an easy place to go swimming, boating or fishing, especially if you base yourself at the campground, immediately outside Mullingar. If you do stay here, it's well worth making the short trip to **Belvedere House and Gardens** (April–Sept Mon–Fri noon–8pm, Sat and Sun noon–6:30pm; Oct–March Mon–Thurs noon–6pm; £1), also off the Tullamore road just before the turning to the campground. You're not meant to cut across the fields from the campground—the way lies across private land—but it does save a lot of walking.

The house was built by **Lord Belfield**, the first earl of Belvedere, in 1740, and conceived by him as a fishing villa. Much of Belfield's life seems to have been spent feuding with his younger brothers, George and Arthur. In 1736 he married a sixteen-year-old bride, Mary Molesworth, daughter of the third Viscount Molesworth. Within a few years of building Belvedere House he accused her of having an affair with Arthur, and virtually imprisoned her for thirty-one years at another of his houses. She was eventually released by her son on his father's death in 1774, still protesting her innocence. Meanwhile Arthur had fled to Yorkshire but when he returned to Ireland in 1759 the earl sued him for adultery and Arthur, unable to pay, spent the rest of his life in jail. An argument with his other brother was responsible for one of the first sights you'll come across in the gardens south of the house, the **Jealous Wall**. This folly is said to be Ireland's largest purpose-built ruin, and was built to block the view of Tudenham House, where George lived, from the earl's own home. Considerable expense went into the construction, including the employment of an Italian architect to design the authentic-looking Gothic facade.

The interior of the **house** is still in the early stages of renovation, a process which shortage of funds looks certain to make a long one. However, the **rococo plasterwork** of the drawing and dining room ceilings is well worth ducking inside to snatch a look at for a few moments, as is the curved balustrade staircase in the entrance recess. Otherwise, the **gardens** are the main attraction. In front of the house three terraces run down to the lake's shore, and behind woodland stretches along the northeast shore of Lough Ennell. There's also the aforementioned Jealous Wall to see, and a **walled garden**, **gazebo**, **ice house**, and **stables**. In the last of these is a **coffee shop** where you can stop for refreshments.

Northeast Westmeath

A good portion of the interest of Westmeath lies in the northeast, around the Fore Valley, Lough Lene, and Lough Derravaragh. Certainly it's the most beautiful part of the county by some way. It's easily approached from Meath, from the area of Oldcastle and the Loughcrew Cairns, or from Mullingar. If you're coming this way you'll pass, on the way up, through **CROOKEDWOOD**, near the scenic lower end of Lough Derravaragh. There are two main attractions here, a **restaurant** which is far better than you would normally hope to find in such an obscure location (*Crookedwood House*; dinner Tues–Sat 7:30–10pm, Sun lunch 12:30–2:30pm; ☎0144-72165), and **St Munna's Church**. This lies a mile and a half up the road which turns off to the right by the pub; fifty yards before is a butterscotch-colored bungalow on the left belonging to Seamus O'Simon, who has the key. It's a beautifully restored (1847 and 1927) fifteenth-century tower-fortified church. From here you can spot a *motte* on the hill slope, behind which is the Georgian house whose rustic cellar contains the restaurant already mentioned.

In such flat country, the steep wooded hills which rise around the southern end of **Lough Derravaragh** stand out immediately. You'll find continually throughout Ireland that physically atmospheric places like this are the setting for ancient tales or myths, and Derravaragh is no exception. In this case the legend is that of the **Children of Lir** (*oidheadh cloinne Lir*), one of the most tragic of all Irish fables.

Lir had married the daughter of Bodb Derg, King of Connacht. Her name was Aebh and she bore him twins, Fionula and Aodh, and then two more children, Fiachra and Conn. Aebh died and Lir then married her sister, Aoife, who very quickly became jealous of Lir's love for her sister's children. She took them to Lough Derravaragh, and with the help of a druid changed them into swans, condemned to spend 300 years on Derravaragh, another 300 years on the Sea of Moyle, the waters between Ireland and Scotland, and a final 300 on Inis Glóire off Erris Head, County Mayo. In a last-minute pang of remorse she granted them some mercy, that they could have human voices and make the most beautiful music for all humans to hear. When Lir learned of what had happened, in a rage he changed Aoife into an ugly gray vulture. Meanwhile the sons of Bodb Derg, Fergus and Aed, set out to search for the Children of Lir with a host of the Tuátha Dé Danann. They eventually found them suffering on the Sea of Moyle, but were helpless to save them from the spell. Left to their destiny the children flew towards Inis Glóire, stopping on the way to search for their father's palace on the plains of Armagh, but finding that only earth mounds remained as they were now 600 years on in their own lives. At the end of the allotted span they died, finally returning to a very aged human form for their last few breaths, and were buried at the onset of the Christian era on Inis Glóire.

Castlepollard and Tullynally

Towards the northern end of Lough Derravaragh, **CASTLEPOLLARD** is the most convenient base from which to explore the whole area, handily placed right in the middle of all the attractions. It's not the most exciting of villages, but it is picturesque, with a vast triangular green surrounded by carefully tended eighteenth- and nineteenth-century dwellings. Many of the visitors are here for the fishing, and consequently there are a number of **B&Bs**, of which the *Castlepollard Arms* is probably the most attractive.

The biggest draw in the immediate vicinity is **Tullynally Castle** (35-min tours mid-July to mid-August, daily 2:30–5:30pm; £2 for castle tour, £1 entry to gardens alone; check for possible off-season tours on ☎044-61159 or 61425), whose entrance can be found a half mile from Castlepollard down the road to GRANARD (alongside the gable of the *Derravaragh Inn*). From the gatehouse a drive leads across another half-mile of rolling parkland, very English-looking, to the castle itself. The home of ten generations of the Anglo-Irish Pakenham family—the earls of Longford—it's one of the largest and most romantic of castles in Ireland, a vast conglomeration of architectural styles (largely Gothic revival) with four towers and a long stretch of battlements.

Three hundred years ago the castle was no more than a tower house set amid the ancient oakwoods which grow around Lough Derravaragh. The park was first laid out, very much along the lines you see today, in 1760 by the first earl of Longford. His wife founded the family **library** of over 8000 volumes, which will be one room on your tour. Their son returned from the French wars to greatly expand the castle to the Gothic designs of **Francis Johnston**, whose work crops up throughout Ireland. The second earl's other claim to fame is to have refused his daughter Kitty's hand in marriage to the young man later to become the Duke of Wellington—they eventually married regardless. One of Kitty's brothers, Edward, fought as Commander-in-Chief of the British Army in the War of 1812, and died leading his troops in the attack on New Orleans. His body was sent home pickled in a barrel of rum. In 1840 the third earl added another 600 feet of battlements, a servants hall for forty, and an immense **Victorian kitchen** which will also make up part of your tour. Later Pakenhams have been less militarily inclined than their forebears: one, Charles Pakenham, forsook the army in the nineteenth century to found the Irish Passionist order of monks, and the present Lord Longford is well known in Britain for his liberal writings and involvement in prison reform.

In the grounds in front of the castle, a **Garden Walk** leads to a spacious demesne on the left, and the flower garden, Sham River pond and walled gardens off to the right. Passing farther to the right, between two stone sphinxes, is the **kitchen garden**, one of the largest in the country and still resplendent with its row of Irish yews. Slightly farther afield, the most rewarding walk of all is a forest path which takes you around the perimeter of the spearhead-shaped demesne; with excellent views back onto the castle.

The Fore Valley
East of Castlepollard towards the Meath border, the **Fore Valley** is an area of exceptional natural beauty. It's easy hiking country with a wealth of small-scale interest, especially in the **Seven Wonders of Fore**. There are moves afoot to convert these into some kind of tourist trail; so far, however, there are few visitors, and the local tradition, strengthened by an early Christian legacy in stone, still seems close to the surface. The wonders are all based on ordinary things which you can find in the valley, and in this perhaps lies the lasting strength of their reputation. They are: the water that will not boil; the wood that will not burn; the monastery built on a quaking sod; the mill without a race; the miraculous emplacement of the lintel stone above the door of St Fechin's Church; the water that flows uphill; and the Anchorite's Cell in the Greville-Nugent family vault.

The village of **FORE** sits at the eastern end of the valley, and this is the best place to start, discovering the wonders as you walk west. There's a tiny ancient cross on the tiny village green, once part of a stations-of-the-cross pattern, and a couple of pubs which are worth visiting. You'll need to pop into the *Seven Wonders* anyway, to pick up the key for the Anchorite's Cell: the *Abbey* next door has seven old murals depicting the wonders, worth contemplating over a pint. There's usually plenty of ready advice in here for anyone planning to head down the valley.

On the valley plain you'll immediately spot the ruined Benedictine Priory built on reclaimed bogland (the third wonder), and en route to it you'll pass the first two. The wood that will not burn consists of a dead branch of a tree, landscaped into a viewing spot as part of the creation of the tourist trail (from the picture in the *Abbey* pub you'll remember it looking more lively than this); the idea of piercing its bark with coins is also a recent invention. The well of unboilable water is handily close by.

The **Priory** itself was founded by the De Lacys around 1200, and its remains are the most substantial reminder of the Benedictine order left in Ireland. It was fortified in the fifteenth century; the towers also served as living quarters. There's a plan in the cloister of the various periods' additions, and some subtly sensitive restoration has been undertaken so that although it's very much a ruin, there's a strong monastic feel to the walls and halls. If you intend to ascend the **tower** at the chancel end, beware that its spiral staircase seems to wind around the diameter of a dinner plate and above all that the steps finish in mid-air; it should certainly not be attempted in poor light.

On the far hillside from here, the lower of the two buildings is the tenth-century **St Fechin's church**, which marks the site of the original monastery founded in 630 by Saint Fechin himself. At one time there were over 300 monks here. Notice the rare Greek Cross on the massive lintel stone (which weighs over two tons and was only moved by the miraculous intervention of the saint, hence Wonder Five), resting on two boulder-sized jambs. Within the ruin is a very weatherbeaten font to your left, a cross slab pinned next to the wall in the chancel at the far end (the chancel was a thirteenth-century addition), and a few other stone slabs, the engravings on which are not clear. From here a ridged path takes you up to the tiny, fortified church known as the **Anchorite's Cell** (Wonder Seven), decoratively hugged by a low-lying, castellated perimeter wall. The most famous hermit to have lived here was Patrick Beaglan, who broke his neck trying to climb out of the window in 1616, thus fulfilling his vow to stay in the cell till his death. The Romanesque doorway leads into a barrel-vaulted, sandstone interior.

The water that flows uphill (Wonder Six) refers to another of Saint Fechin's miracles; and the river leaving Lough Lene up at the head of the valley does indeed appear to flow upward (presumably an optical illusion). The mill without a race (Wonder Four) is not so easy to trace.

West to Athlone—the Heart of Ireland

As you head west from Mullingar towards Athlone on the R390, you're approaching the middle of Ireland, a spot traditionally identified as the **Hill of Uisneach**. About a mile before KILLARE (ten miles or so from Mullingar) there are two signposts pointing off the road up to the hill. Follow the second, more westerly one, climb the hill steeply, veering a little to the left, and after crossing a few fields you'll come to the **Catstone** (so-called because it resembles the poise of a pouncing cat). More historically known as the *Ail na Mearainn* (the Stone of Divisions), it's a massive boulder (now fragmented a little) set into a circular indentation of the hillside. The stone was said to mark the very center **of Ireland** and the division of the five provinces of old. A farther and longer walk up the slope will bring you to the summit of a flat-topped hill, barely 250 feet above the neighboring land yet able, on a clear day, to command a view of parts of twenty of the 32 counties of Ireland.

Here, it is recorded, stood the palace of **King Tuathal Techtmar** in the second century AD, and here some claim that the High Kings of Ireland ruled for the two centuries preceding the arrival of Saint Patrick in AD 433, when the seat moved back to Tara. On the hill there are two spurs with traces of earthworks, but these are neither easy to find nor to make out if you do, so it's probably easier to accept the history without evidence. Excavations were made here in the late 1920s, but came up with surprisingly little. No pottery was found, nor any significant trace of permanent occupation. Instead there were great **beds of ashes** which suggested that the place was used for elaborate feasts and ceremonials rather than for defense or peaceful habitation. This accords with the tales of the great pagan festival of *Beltaine* (Bel's Fire), that was said to be held here in the opening days of the month of May, when vast fires were lit and cattle sacrificed. It was both a religious festival and a market, where traders from the Mediterranean would arrive with their silks and spices in exchange for Irish tools and materials. *Beltaine*, incidentally, is now the Gaelic word for the month of May.

As you continue towards Athlone, look out for the tenth-century **Twyford Cross** on a hillside to the left about four miles before you arrive. It was re-erected here after being found sunk in a bog.

Athlone

The Hill of Uisneach may be the traditional center of Ireland, but **ATHLONE** is a more convincing modern contender. Here, east meets west and north meets south at the midpoint of the Shannon River. This position is its greatest asset, with access by boat upstream to the islands and shores of **Lough Ree**, and downstream to the magnificent early Christian site of **Clonmacnoise**. Either of these trips can easily be done in an afternoon. Contact *Avon Ree* boats on the Strand (daily 2:30pm and 4pm for Lough Ree; £3; less frequently to Clonmacnoise), and *Strand Tackle Shop*, also in the Strand, for rental of rod and reel (£1.50 for the day), or ask for details of other trips at the **tourist information** office (Mon–Sat 10am–1pm and 2–6pm) at the foot of the castle in Market Square. Much good rod fishing can also be done in Athlone, just past the weir, where you will nearly always see a line of fishermen.

The Lough Ree islands to ask for are **Inchclearaun** (although this may better be approached from a more northerly point on the lake) and **Inchbofin**. Both islands, especially Inchclearaun, have churches and early Christian graveslabs. Inchclearaun (Inis Clothrand) took its name from Clothru, who was murdered by her sister Medb so that she could bed and wed Clothru's husband Ailill and rule Connacht from the island. Medb, goddess of war and fertility, is the most famous of all the legendary and historical characters and a source of continual argument as to which branch of study (legend or history) she truly belongs under. Her life was to end in the waters by the island when Clothru's son Furbaide shot a piece of cheese from his sling into Medb's forehead and struck her dead while she was bathing, thus avenging the murder of his mother.

If you plan to stay in Athlone, there's good-value **B&B** at the *Villa St John* (Roscommon Road; ☎0902-2490), or try *Bogganfin House* (Roscommon Road; ☎0902-4255) or *Cluain-Innis* (Galway Road; ☎0902-4202). Your best bet for reasonable and **cheap eating** is the *Gate Restaurant* on Northgate Street (open from breakfast till 9:30pm), and there's a Chinese restaurant a little farther down that serves good-value lunches and is open very late. On Lloyd's Lane, leading off Church Street down to the Strand, is a takeout kebab place, and there's good lunchtime bar food at the *Anchor Bar*. This apart, the best

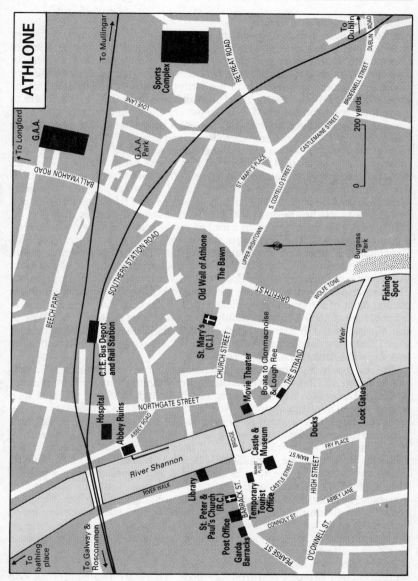

ATHLONE

To Mullingar →

↑ To Longford
To Dublin ↑

BALLYMAHON ROAD

DUBLIN ROAD

BRIDESWELL STREET

Sports Complex

RETREAT ROAD

G.A.A.

LOVE LANE

CASTLEMAINE STREET

G.A.A. Park

ST. MARY'S PLACE

S. COSTELLO STREET

200 yards

0

SOUTHERN STATION ROAD

Old Wall of Athlone

The Bawn

UPPER IRISHTOWN

Burgess Park

BEECH PARK

St. Mary's (C.I.)

GRIFFITH ST.

WOLFE TONE

Fishing Spot

C.I.E. Bus Depot and Rail Station

CHURCH STREET

Movie Theater

Boats to Clonmacnoise & Lough Ree

THE STRAND

Weir

Hospital

NORTHGATE STREET

Abbey Ruins

ABBEY ROAD

Docks

Lock Gates

River Shannon

BRIDGE

Castle & Museum

MARKET PLACE

MAIN ST.

FRY PLACE

RIVER WALK

Library

BARRACK ST.

CASTLE STREET

HIGH STREET

ABBEY LANE

St. Peter & Paul's Church (R.C.)

Temporary Tourist Office

CONNOLY ST.

O'CONNELL ST.

To bathing place ←

Post Office

Garda Barracks

PEARSE ST.

To Galway & Roscommon ↕

pub is probably *Sean's Bar*, tucked in behind the castle and easily identified by its four Ionic columns. It has popular **traditional music** sessions on Tuesdays (pipes and violin), Thursdays (violins) and Sundays. You'll find both the **post office** and a **laundromat** on Pearse Street.

Athlone in Legend and History

Not surprisingly, perhaps, given its position, Athlone has quite a history attached, and at least one important legend. The name *Ath Luain*, the **Ford of Luan**, came from (or may perhaps have inspired) the **Snám Dá Én** (Swim of Two Birds), a tale that tells of Estiu, wife of Nár. She had a lover called Buide who used to come and visit her in the form of a bird with his foster-brother Luan. The magic of their song lulled all around to sleep, allowing the lovers to enjoy their trysts undisturbed. Nár, however, questioned a druid about the coming of the birds and on learning the secret he set out for the place on the Shannon (near Clonmacnoise) where Buide and Luan could be found and shot both of them with one cast of his sling. Buide was killed instantly, but Luan managed to fly as far north as the ford that marks Athlone today, where he dropped dead from the sky. An alternative derivation of the name comes from the *Tain*, which describes how the remains of the white bull (*Finnbennach*) were deposited throughout the countryside as he died. His loins were left at a place that came to be known as *Ath Luain*, the Ford of the Loins.

In straight historical terms, this ford of the Shannon has always been strategically important. The first castle was erected in 1129 by Toirrdelbach Ua Conchobair, King of Connacht, and replaced in 1210 by the **Norman castle** which, in essence, still stands today. It saw action many times, above all in the seventeenth century in the Cromwellian Wars and the Jacobite invasion. The former put a swift end to the predominantly Catholic nature of the town, placing most of the land and political power in the hands of Protestants. The latter battles of 1690–91 saw probably the most vicious fighting in the **War of the Kings**, as the Williamites captured first the Leinster part of town and, after 12,000 cannonballs had reduced much of it to rubble, the Connacht side. In some ways Athlone has still to recover.

The few really distinguished old buildings that survive (the castle apart) can be found off Church Street in the **Court Devenish** area. Finest of them is **Court Devenish House**, a seventeenth-century Jacobean mansion now resting ruined in private grounds. Nearby the ruins of the **Abbey** (also seventeenth-century) offer perhaps the most peaceful spot in town. There's an intriguing corridor of tombstones leading off the Abbey Road into its graveyard.

The one place really worth visiting, if only briefly, is the **museum** in the castle by Market Square (June–Sept 11:30am–1pm and 3–6pm; 50p), housed in the two stories of the circular **keep**. On the upper story is a section devoted to **Folk History**, a treasure trove of rustic implements used in threshing, seeding, rope-making, harnessing, milking, and the like. There's a beautiful article on milking, telling how a few squirts were always dropped first on the grass for the fairies and at the end the sign of the cross made on the teat to bless its consumption. You'll also come across a pair of pony boots that were used when rolling the lawn, to prevent any hoof marks.

Downstairs is a more regular collection on local history, and the ever-present Stone-, Bronze-, and Iron-Age finds. There are two **Sheila na Gig** sculptures, nude female figures generally represented face on with their legs splayed and hands placed behind the thighs, the fingers opening the vulva. The sculptures were thought to be either the symbol of a fertility cult or used to ward off the evil eye, though quite how they managed the latter is not explained. Most appear in the walls (usually near the main entrance door) of castles, and occasionally churches, built between 1200 and 1600. To a lesser extent they are also found in round towers and on standing stones, bridges etc. They are also known in other parts of the British Isles, and even France, but the majority of them by far are in Ireland.

On a quite different level there's an old 78-rpm **gramophone** on which you can request your choice of the recordings of **John McCormick**. McCormick (1884–1945) was a native of Athlone and arguably one of the best lyric tenors the world has ever heard. The gramophone was McCormick's own, traveling all over the world with him so that he could use it to test out the quality of his new releases. He is said to have been born in the Bawn area, the old market area up behind Devenish Gate Street, and in 1928 he was rewarded for his work for Catholic charities by being made a count of the Papal Court. The one song that even the youngest generations in Ireland are able to associate with his voice is his *Panis Angelicus*—the record may be among the pile. Before you leave, look out for an early Christian grave slab with carvings as beautifully ornate as any high cross that you're likely to have seen.

North into Longford

The N55 rushes north from Athlone into **Goldsmith Country**, so called after its geographical associations with the works of the eighteenth-century poet, playwright and novelist, Oliver Goldsmith. It's pretty enough countryside, gently rolling and ready-made for cycling through landscaped villages and along aromatic hedge-lined lanes that run off the N55 down to various small boating points on Lough Ree (Killinure, Kileenmore, Muckanagh). But it helps to keep Goldsmith's verse in mind if you really want to appreciate it. **GLASSAN** village—"the village of the roses" or "sweet auburn" of Goldsmith's *The Deserted Village*—is untypical with its orderly layout of creamy-gray pebbledash cottages, but has a good village inn and restaurant. **TUBERCLARE**, a mile up the road, offers one of the better panoramic views towards the east of the county. A little farther (exactly eight miles from Ballymahon) is the site of the "never failing brook, the busy mill," nowadays no more than a bubbling rivulet, but still easy to identify. The original mill-stone is now said to be the lintel-stone at the *Three Jolly Pigeons* pub, a quarter of a mile up the road, where the school once stood.

Goldsmith Country seeps into **County Longford** through Ballymahon (where his mother lived) and across to PALLAS (near Abbeyshrule) where he was born. **BALLYMAHON** is a pretty dull village, but it's probably the best place to stay to explore this part of northern Lough Ree and Goldsmith country. There's **B&B** at the *Guest House* on the main street (£13 double, £7 single, dinner £6.50); you can rent a bike very cheaply (£2 per day) at the cycle shop near the bridge; and there's even something which describes itself as a nightclub.

On the road from rather dull NEWTOWNCASHEL to BARLEY HARBOUR on Lough Ree you'll pass the workshop of the bogwood sculptor Michael Casey, whose raw material is timber many thousands of years old. The wood is dug out of the bog and left for a few years to dry out. On the road from Newtowncashel to Lanesborough stands *Rakish Paddy's Pub*, worth a visit above all on a Tuesday night for its traditional session; look in for a drink anytime, though, and you can see the three superb modern metal sculptures (by John Mahan) of a seated fiddler, boy and girl dancers, and a wooden flute player obviously playing the well-known reel called "Rakish Paddy".

LANESBOROUGH itself, at the head of Lough Ree, is another place to stop off for the boating or fishing (the last bungalow before the bridge has three rowing boats for rent, £2 per hour, £6 per day, and a motor boat) but for no other reason.

Inland, County Longford doesn't improve, and as far as tourism goes the county is a desert. Still, you might enjoy trying to prove us wrong. Along with large parts of southern Sligo and Leitrim, Longford has been hard hit by very recent emigration, leaving even the grandest-looking houses and mansions deserted by the roadsides. However, if yours is an endlessly indulgent holiday and you have transportation of your own, then there are a few things you can catch on your way through.

Chief of these is **Carrigglas Manor** (June 2–Sept 10 Mon, Tues, and Fri noon–5pm, until 6pm in Aug, 40-min tours on the half-hour beginning 1:30pm; Sun 2–6pm, tours 2:30, 3:30 and 4:30pm; £1.50; B&B available at an indulgent £40, dinner £17.50). Situated just three miles out of LONGFORD on the Ballinalee road, it's the seat of the descendants of the the Huguenot Lefroys. As you go up the avenue, the stables with their classically pedimented and rusticated archways (designed by James Gandon of O'Connell Bridge and Dublin Custom House repute) are on the left. They now house a **costume museum** and tea-room. The yard and buildings are being restored at the moment but you're free to wander around it and the parkland, between the hours listed above. The costumes in the museum date mainly from the mid-eighteenth century, and were found moldering in trunks left behind at the castle. The castle's architecture is perhaps best described as Tudor-Gothic Revival, and extremely handsome it is too. It was built in 1837 by Chief Justice Thomas Lefroy, possibly the model for Darcy in *Pride and Prejudice*, as at one stage he enjoyed a romantic liaison with Jane Austen.

The **tour** of the building is directed by the present Lefroys who are attempting to restore the place to its former majesty. It should take in the dining room, with its set of 1825 Waterford glasses and original ironstone china; the drawing room with its Dutch furniture, one cabinet of which contains an original tea and breakfast set of 1799; a fastidiously well-stocked library; and family portraiture on virtually every wall. All this is explained and expanded on in detail by the present occupier.

Continuing on this same road you'll reach **GRANARD**, about fifteen miles from Longford. A famous **harp festival**, originating in 1784, took place here and was revived in 1981. Nowadays it spreads over the second weekend of August, starting on the Friday afternoon with competitions, street entertainment, *seisiuns* and *ceilidhs*. Lessons on the harp can be arranged on the spot and usually start on the Friday morning. Two **campgrounds** are set up for visitors, or you can stay (bed only) at *Finton Floods* on Market Street (behind the library). The biggest Norman **motte** in Ireland is sited at Granard, with yet another statue of Saint Patrick on top. The site is said to date back to AD 5, and to Cairbre, eldest son of Niall of the Nine Hostages.

Finally, it's worth noting a couple of Longford's other literary connections, centered on MOSTRIM or **EDGEWORTHSTOWN**. It takes the latter name from Maria Edgeworth, one of 22 children of a local luminary, who in her day was an extremely famous author (*Castle Rackrent* is perhaps her best-known work) and said to have influenced both Sir Walter Scott and Turgenev. The family vault can be seen in the graveyard of St John's church, on the road out to Mullingar, and Oscar Wilde's sister Isola is also buried here. One of his most touching poems, *Requiescat*, was written in her memory:

> *Tread lightly, she is near*
> *Under the snow,*
> *Speak gently, she can hear*
> *The daisies grow.*
>
> *All her bright golden hair*
> *Tarnished with rust,*
> *She that was young and fair*
> *fallen to dust.*
>
> *Lily-like, white as snow,*
> *She hardly knew*
> *She was a woman, so*
> *Sweetly she grew.*
>
> *Coffin-board, heavy stone,*
> *Lie on her breast,*
> *I vex my heart alone,*
> *She is at rest.*
>
> *Peace, peace, she cannot hear*
> *Lyre or sonnet,*
> *All my life's buried here,*
> *Heap earth upon it.*

travel details

Trains
From Athlone to Westport (3 daily; 2hr); Galway (1hr 10min); Dublin Heuston Stn (8 daily; 1hr 45min).
From Mullingar to Sligo (4 daily; 2hr); Dublin Connolly (4 daily; 1hr 25min).
From Longford to Sligo (3 daily; 1hr 20min); Dublin Connolly (4 daily; 2hr 10min).

Bus Éireann
From Athlone to Dublin (6 daily; 2hr 45min);
From Mullingar to Dublin (2 daily; 1hr 30min);
From Longford to Dublin (3 daily; 2hr 10min).

Private Buses
North Galway Club. Galway–Dublin service calls at Athlone. See Galway chapter "Travel Details".
Funtrek. Sligo–Dublin bus calls at Longford. See Sligo chapter "Travel Details"

CHAPTER FIVE

WEXFORD, CARLOW, AND KILKENNY

I f you are in the southeast at all, the chances are you've come to Ireland via Rosslare; it's not the most obvious of areas to visit, especially if this is your first time in the country, having none of the wild wastes of rock, bog, and water, nor the accompanying abandoned cottages of famine, eviction, and emigration that are so appealing to current romantic tastes. It is, after all, Ireland's sunniest and driest corner. However, what the region does have to offer—whether you're spending a couple of days passing through, or if you simply haven't the time for more distant wanderings—is worth savoring. On the whole the region's attractions are frustratingly lightly scattered, but its medieval and Anglo-Norman history is richly concentrated in the ancient city of **Kilkenny**—the region's only (understandably) heavily touristed town— and the surrounding lush countryside shelters some powerful medieval ruins. **Wexford** town's conviviality makes up for its disappointingly scant traces of a rigorous Viking and Norman past; **Carlow** town, sadly, doesn't. While the extreme east is dull and low-lying, and the Blackstairs Mountains open and empty, overall the southeast is characterized by a quality of rich cultivation, as much to do with its history as its natural fertility.

The settled, developed character of the region owes much to its **history** of invasion, settlement, and trade. The Vikings wreaked havoc, but they also built the port of Wexford, which developed steadily, all the while assimilating ideas and peoples from overseas, ensuring the continual cultural influence of Europe. The exchange of mercenaries from Wales, for instance, was common throughout the medieval period and, after Henry II had consolidated Anglo-Norman victories, Strongbow settled fellow Welshmen in the region: a dialect descended from these people known as "yola" survived in the far southeast of County Wexford right into the nineteenth century.

But it was the power of the English that was to have by far the greatest influence on the character of this region. The towns of Wexford, Carlow, and Kilkenny still bear the marks of their Anglo-Norman past, in city walls and ruined castles, and the well-tended farmland of rich, surrounding countryside similarly reflects centuries of English settlement. The Anglo-Norman take-over of the southeast was swift and would have been total were it not for the fiercely Gaelic enclave of Counties Carlow and Wexford. There the MacMurrough Kavanaghs became the scourge of the English in Ireland, and

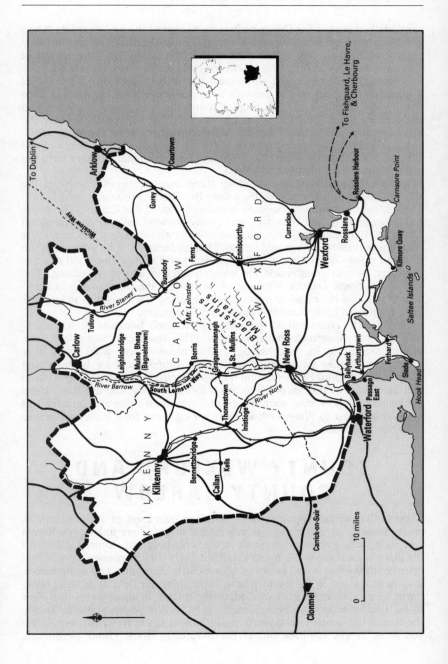

continually thwarted the Crown's attempts to control the entire region. It was Art MacMurrough who defeated Richard II in battles that lost him not only control of Ireland, but his English throne too. Only after the arrival of Cromwell was the power of the MacMurroughs broken once and for all.

Colonization was pursued vigorously: the proximity of the Pale (and of England itself) meaning the Crown's influence was always far stronger here than in the remote west. The English found the area easier to control and administer, and during the growing unrest of the eighteenth century the region remained relatively tranquil. Surprisingly then, by far the most significant uprisings of the Insurrection of 1798 took place in counties Wexford and Carlow. For nationalists the bloodshed and heroics of that summer form the region's most feted history and legend.

Inland the southeast is shaped by three majestic rivers: the Nore, the Barrow, and the Slaney, and by the empty Blackstairs Mountains, which form a rough natural boundary between counties Wexford and Carlow. The rivers roll through rich, lush pastures and pretty wooded valleys, past medieval Christian ruins and the little towns and villages whose history belongs to the trade these waterways brought inland. This landscape is at its prettiest in the hills and valleys of the Nore and Barrow, just north of New Ross, and south of Kilkenny: perfect countryside for leisurely cycling and easy walking. The signposted *South Leinster Way* meanders through the heart of this countryside to some of the choicest spots, before heading northeast to the less intimate country of Carlow and the Blackstairs Mountains.

Head for the **coast** and, to the east, superb sandy **beaches** stretch practically the entire length of County Wexford. While the south coast is less suitable for swimming, its sand banks, shallow lagoons, and silted rivers offer great opportunities for **wildlife** enthusiasts: prime spots for birdwatching include the Wexford Slobs (around the town itself); the lakes of Lady's Island and Tacumshane; the Saltees Islands off Kilmore Quay; and the Hook Head peninsula. This low-lying southern coastal region also provides an excellent quick route west to Waterford, as there's a car ferry from Ballyhack across Waterford Harbour.

COUNTY WEXFORD AND COUNTY CARLOW

Though the ancient Viking town of **Wexford** bills itself as a tourist center, you're unlikely to spend more than a couple of days here unless you have a car. Sadly, little evidence remains of the town's long and stormy history and the place is most enjoyable for its small but lively cultural scene. The wildfowl reserves of the North and South Slobs are easily accessible, and some marvelous beaches are to be found nearby, stretching the length of the county north to the popular resort of **Courtown**. Inland, historic towns like **New Ross**, **Enniscorthy**, and **Ferns** merit a call if you're passing nearby. To see the best of the **south coast**, you'll need a bicycle at the very least, certainly if you want to get anything out of the intriguing **Hook Head peninsula**, isolated and still largely unspoiled. **County Carlow** features less on most people's itineraries, for the good reason that there's little to attract a stop. The *South Leinster Way* trudges at its most lonesome and desolate through the **Blackstairs Mountains**; the county is at its prettiest along the River Barrow, for much of its length the boundary between Carlow and Kilkenny. **Carlow** itself, situated on the Dublin to Kilkenny train route, barely warrants attention.

Wexford Town

Apart from its narrow, quirky lanes (a Viking legacy) **WEXFORD** town retains few traces of its past, and only the quays suggest that it was once an important trading center. The harbor, in business from the ninth century, has now silted up, and Wexford has lost its trade once and for all to its old rival Waterford. That's not to say, though, that the town's history stopped with the fall of the Vikings. Settled by the Normans in the twelfth century, it became an English garrison town, brutally taken by Cromwell in 1649, who had fifteen hundred Wexford citizens put to death. In the 1798 Insurrection the town saw brave rebel fighting against the English Crown (and a mainly Protestant yeomanry), which was fearful that the port might be used as a landing place by the French. The rising lasted longer in Wexford than in most places but the rebels were finally put down and the Crown was quick to exact retribution. Wexford, though, plays down its contribution to Republicanism and has emerged as a positive, forward-looking place, proud of its ethnic and religious mix. It's internationally famous for its prestigious **Opera Festival**, while a more mainstream draw are the town's estimated 93 **bars**, reason enough to give Wexford at least a night.

If you're **arriving** by *Bus Éireann* or by train, you'll be dropped at the **train station**, at the north end of the quays and just past the bridge over the estuary—which, if you crossed, would take you out of town to the campground (see below), the wildfowl reserve (see below), and the beaches of the county's east coast. The *Ardcavan Coach Company*'s **buses** to and from Dublin stop at The Crescent (see "Travel Details"). The **tourist office** is down by the quays (May–Sept Mon–Sat 9am–6pm; Oct–April Mon–Fri 9am–5:15pm; ☎053-23111). And if you want to rent a **bicycle**, try *Hayes*, 108 South Main Street (☎053-22462), or *The Bike Shop*, 9 Selskar Street (☎053-22514).

The Town

Set on the south side of the broad, featureless Slaney estuary, Wexford town sits behind its **quays**, which drag on relentlessly. The only relief is **The Crescent** where a statue of John Barry, a local who founded the U.S. Navy during the Revolutionary War, strides against the buffetting wind, cloak billowing. Parallel to the quays runs Wexford's lengthy Main Street, a narrow and winding route that gives some idea of the medieval town's layout. But once you've seen it there is little else left to explore. This is Wexford's problem: it's touted as a city proud of its history, but even the site of its most bloody and violent event—the **Bull Ring**, where Cromwell massacred all but 400 of the population—is a barely distinguishable interruption. Only a monument to the fighting of 1798 draws your attention.

A lane up behind *Macken's* liquor store, on the Bull Ring, leads to the Cornmarket and the parallel streets of the small center. The massive **Westgate**, built around 1300, is the sole survivor of the medieval walled city's five gates. Nearby, too, are the remains of **Selskar Abbey**, wrecked by Cromwell, where Henry II spent an entire Lent in penitence for the murder of Thomas à Becket in Canterbury cathedral. As indications of what has been lost, both the gate and the abbey add to the general air of disappointment. As far as the town goes, that's about it, though you might like to check out the modern Gothic churches of The Immaculate Conception and The Assumption. They are identical in design and, as if to hammer home the shortage of imagination, their foundation stones were both laid on the same day in 1851.

Practicalities: Sleeping, Eating, Drinking, and Culture

Wexford has a handful of **B&Bs** right in the town. Mrs Tobin's *St John's*, 11 Lower John Street (☎053-23753; £10), is very friendly. Along Westgate are Mrs Allen's at *Westmount* (☎053-22167; £9.50), and Mrs O'Rourke's at *Westgate House* (☎053-24428; £9:50). There are others along North Main Street, and some bars along Commercial Quay also offer cheaper B&B accommodation, such as *The Wavecrest* at no. 17 (☎053-22849; £7.50). Bear in mind that rooms are at a premium during the Opera Festival (see below).

You can **camp** at the expensive municipal site, immediately over the bridge from Commercial Quay (☎053-24378; Easter to mid-Sept; £6 per tent per night)—and there's a swimming pool next to the campground. The nearest **hostel** is at Rosslare (see below); a day round-trip ticket by bus or train costs around £3.

Food, Drink, and Pub Entertainment

There's no shortage of places to get a decent **meal** and some of the best cheap eating is to be found in pubs and bars. The more notable places are picked out below, along with some specialist restaurants.

Simon's Place, 37 South Main Street, is a bar doing excellent meals throughout the day, including Sunday, for around £3. *The Wren's Nest*, Custom House Quay, also offers reliable, reasonably priced pub grub, while *Tim's Tavern*, 51 South Main Street, specializes in seafood and serves hot lunches at midday (Mon–Sat) and, between July and October, dinners in the evening, up to 8:30pm. Away from the bars, for seafood try the *Old Granary Restaurant*, Westgate, which offers lunches from around £5, and more expensive eating in the evening, or *The Bohemian Girl*, North Main Street, which also serves steaks. For pizza and pasta, try *Robertino's*, 19 South Main Street (open Mon–Sat 7:30pm–1am, Sun 6pm–1am). *The Pancake House*, Henrietta Street, is open from 8:30am for breakfasts, and serves lunch and dinner (from £4) while *Kelly's Deli*, 80 South Main Street, is a largely vegetarian café offering snacks and extravagant gateaux.

Alongside all of this the town has a vast selection of plain-drinking **pubs and bars**, many of which feature **live music** on one or more days of the week. Start your explorations at one of the following places. *The Thomas Moore Tavern*, Cornmarket, is known for being a music pub, although sessions here are sporadic, and *The Wave Crest*, Commercial Quay, also has occasional nights of traditional music. More reliably, *The Tower Bar*, North Main Street, has live music on Wednesday and Sunday. You can find ballad sessions at *Mooney's*, 12 Commercial Quay, every Friday night, and also in *The Talbot Hotel* bar every Friday and Saturday. If you're looking for jazz, try *White's Hotel*, George's Street, on Sunday, also the venue for discos and pop bands on Friday and Saturday.

Opera and Theater

The annual **Opera Festival** in October is well worth catching, usually featuring rarely performed works by renowned composers; information on ticket availability and programs from the tourist office. The festival attracts a range of other performers too, and you'll find traditional music, blues, and jazz in the bars, along with poetry readings and exhibitions. Even out of festival time Wexford has a lively cultural life, largely generated by a couple of **theaters**—*The Proteus Theatre*, Larkins Lane, South Main Street (☎053-22141), and *The Theatre Royal* in the High Street (☎053-22240/22144)—and *The Wexford Arts Centre* (☎053-23764), in Cornmarket, housed in an eighteenth-century market house and town hall. This last venue has a healthy turnover of traveling modern exhibitions, and occasionally hosts performance artists, dance groups, and music.

Around Wexford Town

Within a few miles of the town there are enough attractions for you to consider staying around. Some, like the **wildfowl reserves** at the endearingly named North and South Slobs are of specialist interest. Others, though, could claim anyone's time—not least the excellent **sandy beaches** as near as Curracloe five miles to the north, and also to the south at **Rosslare**, a possible point of arrival in Ireland.

Birdwatching in the North and South Slobs

The mud flats sheltered behind the sea walls of the Slaney estuary, known as the **North and South Slobs**, are home to the *Wexford Wildfowl Reserve*. The Slobs are the main wintering grounds for Greenland white-fronted geese, Bewick's swans, pintails, and blacktailed godwits; you can also see spotted redshanks, gulls, and terns. At the reserve there's a wildfowl collection, a research station, hides, lookout towers, and identification charts—for further information contact Alyn Walsh, *Wexford Wildfowl Reserve*, North Slobs (☎053-23129).

To reach the North Slobs you take the Dublin road out of Wexford over the bridge, and it's signposted on the right after about two miles; for the South Slobs take the Rosslare road out of Wexford for two miles, turn left at the *Farmer's Kitchen* pub, and take the second turn on the left.

Ferrycarrig and Johnstown Castle

Just two and a half miles inland from Wexford, the **Irish National Heritage Park** at FERRYCARRIG (summer daily 9am–7pm; winter daily 10am–4pm; £1.50, students 50p) plots 9000 years of social change through full-scale models of settlements, homesteads, and burial places from the Stone Age through to Norman times. It's a great place to clarify your knowledge of ancient history, and helps make sense of the numerous archaeological remains that are littered throughout the country. The park is also being developed as a nature reserve, and the environment has been carefully nurtured to provide the appropriate settings. It works well, so that as you walk through the Mesolithic campground, the shaggy lichen-covering on the hazel trees, the mud, and the reeds all help evoke a primeval bog; while the Viking shipyard nestles convincingly on the estuary's banks. Public transit **access** is by once-daily *Bus Éireann* bus from Wexford train station, or by train.

Four miles southwest of Wexford, off the Rosslare road, is the **Irish Agricultural Museum** (June–Aug Mon–Fri 9am–5pm, weekends 2–5pm; May and Sept–Oct same hours except closed 12:30–1:30pm; Nov–April closed Mon–Fri 12:30–1:30pm and all weekend; £1.25), set in the gardens of **Johnstown Castle**, a Gothic Revival castellated mansion. The museum, signposted *Research Center*, has good, clear displays on all aspects of rural life: domestic objects, farming machinery, carts and carriages, reconstructed workshops, and a lot on dairy farming. In addition, the grounds are darkly wooded with mounds of rhododendrons, ornamental lakes, hot houses, and walled gardens—all very well maintained.

The Beaches

The southeast gets more sunshine than any other part of Ireland, and as the entire coast of the county to the north of Wexford town is made up of safe and sandy **beaches**, the region is a popular spot in summer for families and caravanners.

From **CURRACLOE**, five miles northeast of town, superb, sandy dunes stretch away into the far distance, and though the surrounding little villages are overloaded in July and August, the sands themselves aren't. If you want to stay in the area, *O'Gorman's Caravan and Camping Park* (April–Sept; ☎053-37110/37221) costs £4 in high season for hikers and cyclists, £3 in low season. Camping on the dunes is discouraged. If you're not mobile, then you'll have to rely on the *Bus Éireann* **buses** from Wexford to Curracloe, which run only on Monday and Saturday.

Rosslare Harbour

The other chief seaside resort in the county is **ROSSLARE**, roughly six miles southeast of Wexford. There's a huge sandy beach and, five miles southeast, **Rosslare Harbour** which serves ferries from Cherbourg (France) and Fishguard (South Wales). At Rosslare Harbour there's a **tourist office** (April–Sept; ☎053-33232) open for all incoming sailings, and an *An Óige* **hostel** in Goulding Street (☎053-33399; grade A), clearly signposted up the hill from the harbor. This, too, stays open for whatever time the boat comes in; and there's a supermarket nearby.

Moving on from Rosslare Harbour is fairly straightforward. Trains from the pier for Wexford and Dublin leave twice daily and for Waterford twice daily from Monday to Saturday. To get to Dublin, the daily private bus operated by *Ardcavan Coach Company* is more economical; it's also an easy hitch.

ROSSLARE: TRAVEL INFORMATION

Irish Rail trains; ☎053-22522.

Sealink British Ferries; ☎053-33115.

Irish Continental Line; ☎053-33158.

B & I Ferries; ☎053-33311.

Ardcavan Coach Company; ☎053-22561.

Around County Wexford

Once out of Wexford town's environs, County Wexford splits into three main regions. To the **north**, Enniscorthy and Ferns have smatterings of historical interest, while the best of this coast's resorts is Courtown. In the **west** New Ross offers river trips that give you a different view of the county. Along the **south** coast, low-lying, flat land makes cycling easy. There are more sandy beaches here, and two scenic spots in particular are worth taking in— Kilmore Quay and the attractive Hook Head peninsula, both targets for birdwatchers.

Enniscorthy, Ferns, and Courtown

Fourteen miles north of Wexford, at the likeable market town of **ENNISCORTHY**, is the **County Museum** (June–Oct daily 10am–6pm; Nov and Feb–May Mon–Fri 2–5:30pm; Dec and Jan Sun only 2–5:30pm; 80p). Focussing on the events of 1798 and 1916, the museum is housed in the Norman castle that dominates Enniscorthy, overlooking the Slaney. Across the river, covered in mustard and yellow gorse, lies **Vinegar Hill**, the site of the rebels' main encampment during the 1798 Insurrection—and the scene of their final slaughter by English forces. If you're around in summer, Enniscorthy has an enjoyable Strawberry Fair, usually held the first or second week in July.

The higher countryside to the north and west of Enniscorthy is quite bald and spartan. This side of the Blackstairs Mountains yields little in the way of sights, though if you're heading north, **FERNS**—seven miles from Enniscorthy—would make a good lunch stop. One-time seat of the kings of Leinster, it's now a little scrap of a village, top-heavy with historic remains. An abbey was founded here in the sixth century, remains of which are in **St**

Edan's churchyard and the adjacent field. Most impressive, though, are the ruins of the thirteenth-century **castle**, with its pair of towers—which you can climb—and two curtain walls. The *Buttle Arms* in the village does daily set meals except on Sunday.

Quite the nicest family resort hereabouts is **COURTOWN**, about 25 miles north of Wexford and smack in the middle of another excellent, long stretch of sand. If you want to stay over, there's a new independent **hostel**, *Anchorage Hostel*, at Poulshone, Courtown Harbour (☎055-25335; beds £4, private rooms £5), open all year, with a shop nearby and the beach just five minutes' walk away. Three-and-a-half miles inland is **GOREY**, connected by train with Enniscorthy and Wexford, and a good base for some gentle ambling. Head for **Tara Hill**, four miles northeast of town, where there are pleasant walks and fine views of this otherwise flat coast; more information, if you need it, from Gorey's **tourist office** (July and Aug Mon–Sat 10am–6pm; ☎055-21248).

New Ross to Tintern Abbey

First impressions of **NEW ROSS**, 21 miles west of Wexford, are not encouraging: a glamorless old port of grubby wharf buildings and lackluster shops. However, the place isn't without character, thanks mostly to the river, which provides New Ross with its livelihood and gives access to the heart of the Wexford and Kilkenny countryside. From the town, the *Galley Cruizing Restaurant* runs **river trips** up the Barrow and Nore, as far as St Mullins and Inistioge (see "County Kilkenny," below), and along the Suir to Waterford. Lunch (£10), afternoon tea (£4) or dinner (£14) is part of the package, cruises operating from mid-May to the end of September; advance booking is advisable (☎051-21723, after 7pm ☎051-73752). Walkers could use the cruise as a leisurely, scenic route west to Waterford and, out of peak season, cyclists might ask to be taken along, too.

Should you find yourself with time to spare in New Ross, it's worth climbing the steep back alleys to the top of town for views over the river and hills. Any remaining time can be spent at **St Mary's Church**, alongside which are the ruins of New Ross's thirteenth-century **abbey**, with graceful early English windows, and some carved, medieval tombstones in the chancel. New Ross has a **tourist office** (July and Aug Mon–Sat 10am–6pm; ☎051-21857), while *Bus Éireann* **buses** to local towns and the Hook peninsula leave from the quays, outside *Ryans Bar*. For more independence, it's possible to **rent dinghies** from the *New Ross Sailing Club*; and **bike rent** is available from E. Prendergast, 22 The Quay (☎051-21600).

Five miles south of New Ross, the **arboretum** called the *J. F. Kennedy Memorial Park* (May–Aug 10am–8pm; April–Sept 10am–6:30pm; Oct–March 10am–5pm) contains a collection of around 5000 species of trees and shrubs. Kennedy's great-grandfather was born in DUNGANSTOWN, close by, so the place is often frequented by Americans in search of presidential roots. If you're mobile then the road south of here leads to Dunbrody Abbey (see below), just five miles away, and on to the Hook Head peninsula.

Dunbrody and Tintern abbeys

There's a fair amount of interest in a couple of places close by, easily seen before tackling the peninsula itself, as long as you have your own transportation. At the widening of the Barrow estuary stands the magnificent ruin of **Dunbrody Abbey**. A thirteenth-century Cistercian foundation, it was altered in the sixteenth century after the Dissolution of the Monasteries, when the large central tower and adjacent buildings were added.

To the east, near the muddy Bannow Bay, is **Tintern Abbey**, built in 1200 by William Marshall, Earl of Pembroke. Another fine Cistercian edifice, it owes its existence in this unprepossessing spot to a vow made by the earl after he was caught in a storm off the south coast. Praying that he might be saved, he promised to build an abbey wherever his boat came ashore. The presbytery is based on that of the foundation's more famous namesake in Wales.

The South Coast: to Kilmore Quay and the Hook Head Peninsula

In the southeast corner of Ireland the sea has made inroads into an otherwise flat region, forming small lakes at **TACUMSHANE** (popular with windsurfers) and **LADY'S ISLAND**, both venues for bird enthusiasts. Lady's Island itself sits mid-lagoon at the end of a causeway, and has been a place of religious devotion for centuries: an annual pilgrimage is still made here on August 15. On the island are the remains of an Augustinian priory and a Norman castle, both built in the thirteenth century—but the spirit of the place has been destroyed by a large, modern church building that has been tacked onto the side. There are few amenities for travelers in the area, but the *Lobster Pot* bar and restaurant at **CARNE** is a great exception, serving delicious seafood meals.

Kilmore Quay and the Saltee Islands

KILMORE QUAY comes as a real surprise after the largely dull countryside that precedes it. A small, unspoiled fishing and vacation village of thatched cottages and whitewashed walls, it's prettily situated around a stone harbor wall, looking out at the nearby Saltee Islands. There is a fine sandy beach, and you can **camp** among the dunes. Kilmore Quay hosts a **seafood festival**, usually in the second week of July—check the dates with Wexford tourist office. A fine excuse to eat plenty of seafood (whatever your budget), the festival includes a trawler race around the Saltees in which anyone can take part—just pay around £2 to one of the fishermen involved. The village has a handful of nice **bars**, like *The Wooden House* which has traditional music several nights a week during the summer, while the *Hotel Saltees* holds discos on the weekend.

Kilmore Quay is also point of departure for visiting the uninhabited **Saltee Islands**, one of Ireland's most important bird sanctuaries, especially for cormorants, shags, gannets, kittiwakes, and auks. In the nesting period of late spring and early summer, there are thousands of them; by the end of July they've all left—so time your trip carefully. Boat trips for groups are available during the summer; inquiries to Willie Bates, who lives opposite the church (☎053-29644).

The Hook Head Peninsula

It's at the **Hook Head peninsula**, which forms the eastern side of Waterford Harbour, that the coastline begins to undulate and the scenery becomes more attractive. **ARTHURSTOWN** has a tiny sandy spot you can swim from, a nice pub that serves seafood snacks, a post office, a shop and an *An Óige* **hostel** (closed Oct–April; no phone; grade C) at nos. 1, 2 and 4, the Coastguard Station. Just a mile to the north is the village of **BALLYHACK** which has a useful year-round **car ferry** service running regularly across the harbor to PASSAGE EAST in County Waterford. The crossing takes just ten minutes (see the *Waterford* chapter for details). If you've got time to kill before you cross then **Ballyhack castle** is worth a look, a fine five-storey, sixteenth-century tower house. Ballyhack village also boasts a very good seafood **restaurant**, the *Neptune Restaurant* (☎051-89284).

Unfortunately, the pretty, wooded coastline from Ballyhack, south, down the peninsula, to **DUNCANNON** is privately owned and you can't walk along it. Duncannon itself is a resort town, pleasant enough, and with a rocky coast to the south that protects its big, sandy beach. There are minimal facilities here, though: a couple of bars do ordinary sandwiches and burgers, and the *Fort Conan Hotel* is the only place to get a more substantial meal. If you're going to **stay**, try the *Hook Trekking Center* (☎051-89166), one mile from Duncannon on the Hook Road, which does B&B for £8. (The pony trekking itself only operates in June, July and August; £6 an hour, with reduced B&B rates for riders.) Back in Duncannon, there is a trailer camp, but better if you're **camping** is to sleep amidst the dunes, or ask to use a local field. From Duncannon, you can walk wherever you like southwards. To get down to the very end of the peninsula, cycling rather than hitching is the way to do it, as there's hardly any traffic. Little sandy bays lie concealed behind low cliffs, and there are lovely views across to the broad and beautiful Waterford coastline. Although the Hook promotes itself as a tourist area, the caravans and kids mostly keep to the areas around Duncannon and FETHARD, to the east, and there are plenty of isolated spots to be found. There's a particularly fine, sandy beach at **Booley Strand**, two miles south of Duncannon.

Six miles from Duncannon is the hotel of **Loftus Hall**, sitting at the end of a long drive behind an ostentatious gateway. It's said that it was built for a princess whom the owner was to bring home as his bride, and that the princess never arrived. There's something quite eerie about all this decorative splendour in such a desolate spot: the grandiose Italian staircase, for instance, is made up of 49 different shades of wood, and cost the monumental sum of £5000 in 1822. From Easter to September bar food is available all day at the hotel; Saturday and Sunday evenings there's a local group or cabaret performance; and Sunday afternoon sees **jazz** sessions.

At the peninsula's tip the shoreline is rockier, the limestone rich with fossils. Flat and desolate, the land just slips away into the sea, the extremity marked by a **lighthouse**—said to be the oldest in Europe, it was first built in the twelfth century. There are tours of the lighthouse, by arrangement (contact Mrs M.J. Wilson; ☎051-97179); or ask the keeper in charge if you can look around. This part of Hook Head is favored by ornithologists who come to watch the bird migrations, and if you're lucky you can sometimes spot seals. Crashing spray and blow-holes make it a dangerous and dramatic place in a storm—and you certainly shouldn't swim here at any time. You can **camp** near the lighthouse, though be careful not to pitch your tent by the blow-holes on the other side of the lane. The nearest **shop** is three and a half miles away at the *Texaco* station at the Fethard/Duncannon junction (Sun and Tues 10am–1pm; other days 10am–6pm, closed 1–2pm).

Tucked away on the east flank of the peninsula is the evocatively crumbling harbor of **SLADE**. There's not even a pub or a shop, you just go there to look at the place. Fishing boats cluster around its quays and slipways, stacked lobster pots lean against a fifteenth-century castellated castle. Slade is quite simply beautiful: all the stone a nutty brown color, rich, rusty and warm.

Carlow

Northwest of Wexford, tiny **County Carlow** doesn't have the appeal of its close neighbors. Much of the terrain is unenticing farming land, and the few small towns don't have a historical pull—though the county capital does sport a ruined Norman castle. The most attractive areas of the county—along the River Barrow and in the Blackstairs Mountains—are covered in the "County Kilkenny" section, being more approachable from outside the county.

Carlow Town

For centuries, the town of **CARLOW** was an Anglo-Norman stronghold at the edge of an otherwise fiercely Gaelic county. As such, it has a bloody history, the most terrible battle coming during the Insurrection of 1798 when over 600 rebels were slaughtered. Today, there's nothing to suggest its former frontier status, the small, busy town distinguished only by a fine, classical courthouse with a portico modeled on the Parthenon. Even the remains of the once proud Norman **castle** now lie neglected within the grounds of *Corcoran & Co*; if you want to poke around, ask at the factory. Otherwise, there's plenty on local military, religious and folk history in the **museum**, housed in the town hall (May–Sept daily 11am–5:30pm).

County Carlow's most impressive sight is two miles out of town on the R726 road: **Browneshill dolmen** is enormous, possibly the largest in Europe; you'll have to ask the farmer for permission to view it.

You might be stopping in Carlow town to take advantage of *St Anthony's* independent **hostel** in Pembroke Road (June–Sept; ☎0503-31390; £4). This aside, Carlow tries hard to put you off staying. Even the town's favorite young person's **bar**—*Tully's* in Tullow Street, with jazz and blues at the weekend— shuts at 6pm every day except Saturday. There are other bars around, though, like *The Phoenix* in Castle Hill Street, a homey old place with bands and ballads from time to time. If you need to **eat**, *Tully's* serves light meals (Mon–Sat); *Finnegan's* pub offers homemade pies and salads (daily till 7pm); while *Brockett's Restaurant*, 143 Tullow Street (Mon–Wed 10am–6pm, Thurs–Sat 10am–10pm), has a tasty range of home cooking and some vegetarian dishes.

You can get more local information from Carlow's **tourist office** (July and Aug Mon–Sat 10am–6pm; ☎0503-31554). There's a **train** link north to Kildare and Dublin, south to Kilkenny, Thomastown, and Waterford. If you want to get around under your own steam, **bike rental** is available from *A. E. Coleman* in Dublin Street (☎0503-31273).

COUNTY KILKENNY

County Kilkenny offers the finest of the southeast's countryside. It's rich farmland, and becomes most intensely pretty around the confluence of two magnificent rivers, the Nore and the Barrow, just to the north of New Ross. Medieval ruins are spattered all over the county, but they reach their richest concentration in ancient **Kilkenny** city—a really bustling, quaint favorite. The delightful surroundings make it almost essential to rent a bike and explore the river valleys and their medieval ruins, most notably **Kells Priory** and **Jerpoint Abbey**. The **cycling** is easy: off the main roads there's little traffic, and the minor roads that stay close to the rivers are especially scenic. Alternatively, the heart of this rich, historical farmland can be crossed **on foot**. As they head south, the Nore and Barrow rivers flow through gentle valleys of mixed woodland: the **South Leinster Way** provides unstrenuous walking, passing through handsome riverside villages—**Inistioge**, **Graiguenamanagh**, and nearby **Borris** and **St Mullins**—before heading north towards the Blackstairs Mountains. Immediate access from Kilkenny is by local bus or by taking the train as far as Thomastown and walking. Or you could see this region from the **cruises** that operate from the river port of New Ross (see p.162).

Kilkenny

KILKENNY is Ireland's finest medieval city, its setting superb: above the broad sweep of the River Nore sits the castle, while a pretty, humpbacked stone bridge leads up into narrow, cheerful streets laced with carefully maintained buildings. Kilkenny's earliest settlement was a monastery founded by Saint Canice in the sixth century, but all that remains from those days is the Round Tower that stands alongside the Cathedral. The layout of Kilkenny today owes much to its medieval history. Following continual skirmishes between local clans, the arrival of the **Normans** in 1169 saw the building of a fort by Strongbow on the site of today's castle. His son-in-law, William Marshall, consolidated Norman power in Kilkenny, maintaining the fortified city and keeping the indigenous Irish in an area of less substantial housing beyond its walls—of which only the name "Irishtown" remains. In 1391 the

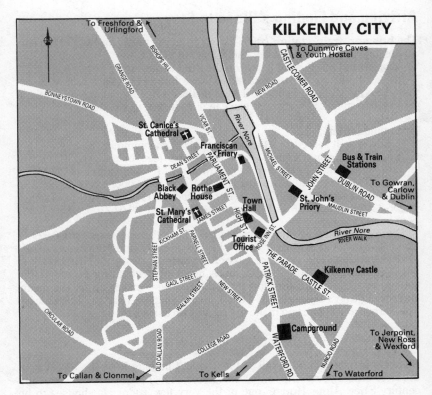

Butler family acquired Kilkenny castle, and this ensured the city's loyalty to the English Crown.

In the mid-seventeenth century, Kilkenny became virtually the capital of Ireland, with the founding of a parliament in 1641 known as the **Confederation of Kilkenny** (see "Historical Framework" in *Contexts*). This was an attempt to unite resistance to the English persecution of Catholicism, and although powerful for a while, its effectiveness had greatly diminished by the time Cromwell arrived—in his usual destructive fashion—in 1650. Kilkenny never recovered its former prosperity and importance. The disgrace of the Butler family in 1715, coupled with English attacks upon the rights of Catholics through the Penal Laws, saw the city decline still further.

Enough medieval buildings remain to attest to Kilkenny's former importance, and in a place brimming with civic pride, there's been a tasteful push towards making the town a major tourist attraction. Kilkenny is sometimes known as "the marble city" because of the limestone quarried locally, which when polished develops a deep black shine. Echoing this, the town's bar and shop signs all gleam with black and brown lacquer, the names cut in deeply bevelled, stout gold lettering.

Arriving and Finding a Place to Stay

The **bus and train station** (☎056-22024) is on the north road out of the city, at the top of St John's Street: note that in Gaelic the city is called *Cill Chainnigh*, and this is what it says on the front of buses.

It's worth visiting the **tourist office**, Rose Inn Street (May–Aug Mon–Sat 9am–1pm and 2–6pm; Sept–April Mon–Fri 9am–12:45pm and 2–5:15pm, Sat 10am–1pm; ☎056-21755), where you can pick up free maps of the city.

Accommodation

Kilkenny is well served by **B&Bs**, although in the summer the city can get crowded and during festival week in August (see below) you'll need to reserve in advance. In the center of town try: Mrs Dempsey's at 26 James Street (☎056-21954; £10); Mrs Foxall's, *St Mary's*, next door (☎056-22091; £9); or one of several along the Waterford Road—Mrs Flannery's at *Ashleigh* (☎056-22809; £9.50) or Mrs Flanagan's at *Burwood* (☎056-62266; £9.50; June–Sept only).

There's **camping** at Mrs Murphy's, 25 Upper Patrick Street (☎056-62973; £2 per person per night), a basic site but friendly and with an excellent central location. The *An Óige* **hostel**, *Foulksrath Castle*, JENKINSTOWN (☎056-67674; grade B), is eight miles north of town along N77, but the setting—a sixteenth-century fort in lush meadows—makes up for the inconvenience. *Buggy's* buses (☎056-41264) to the junction near the hostel leave The Parade at 5:30pm, and make the return trip at 8:25am.

The City

Kilkenny is focused on the hill and its castle. Climbing Rose Inn Street from the river brings you to the tourist office (see above) housed in the sixteenth-century **Shee Alms House**, one of the very few Tudor almshouses to be found in Ireland. (A walking tour leaves from here four times a day, costing £2.) At the top of Mary Inn Street to the left is the broad stretch known as **The Parade**, which leads up to the castle. Formerly used for military and civic ceremonies, in summer it now serves as a coach park. To the right, the High Street soon becomes **Parliament Street**, the main thoroughfare busy with people. Crooked and intriguing, little medieval slips and alleyways duck off it, while there's more substantial interest in the eighteenth-century **Tholsel**, with its stone pillars and arches. This was once the center of the city's financial dealings, and now is used as the town hall.

Of all the surviving buildings from the prosperous Tudor commercial period, **Rothe House** on Parliament Street is the finest. Home to the Kilkenny Archaeological Society **museum** (April–Oct Mon–Sat 10:30am–12:30pm and 3–5pm; rest of year Sat and Sun 3–5pm; 85p, students 50p), it's worth visiting for the internal structure alone, rather than the contents. Built in 1594, it's a unique example of an Irish Tudor merchant's home, comprising three separate houses linked by interconnecting courtyards.

It's the **castle**, though, that defines Kilkenny, an imposing building standing high and square over the river (June–Sept daily 10am–7pm; rest of the year Tues–Sat 10am–12:30pm and 2–5pm, Sun 2–5pm; £1, kids and students 30p; free guided tours on the hour till 4pm, 6pm in July and Aug). It was from here that the Confederate Parliament governed Ireland from 1642 to 1648, but although parts of the medieval building remain, the overall appearance of the castle owes much to nineteenth-century restoration. Whereas the furnishings and paintings suggest a civilized wealth and domesticity, the scale and grandeur of the rooms, with their deeply recessed windows and robust fireplaces, signify a much cruder political power. The biggest surprise is the flimsy wooden hammer-beam roof of the **picture gallery**, covered with folksy, pre-Raphaelite decoration—plenty of gold and burnt umber plant life smudging its way across the ceiling. Also within the castle is the **Butler Gallery**, housing an exhibition of modern art and with free art video screenings on Sunday. You can take a break in the **tearoom** (May–Oct only), once the castle's kitchen, and you may want to drop in here at other times too— you don't have to pay the castle entrance fee to visit either the Butler Gallery or the tearoom. While you're around, you might as well drop into the eighteenth-century stables, opposite the castle, which have been converted into the *Kilkenny Design Workshops*, an outlet for locally produced craft goods, expensively geared towards the tourist market.

The other must in Kilkenny is the magnificent **St Canice's Cathedral** (daily 9am–1pm and 2–6pm). Built in the thirteenth century, the purity and unity of its architecture lends it a grandeur beyond its real size. Rich in carvings, it has an exemplary selection of sixteenth-century monuments, many in black Kilkenny marble, the most striking being effigies of the Butler family. The **round tower** (50p, students 20p) next to the church is all that remains of the early monastic settlement reputedly founded by Saint Canice in the sixth century: there are superb views from the top—ask anyone working in the church or churchyard for access.

Kilkenny is littered with the remains of other medieval churches. The **Black Abbey**, founded by Dominicans in 1225, has been carefully restored and contains some unusual carvings and sepulchral slabs. On the other side of town, **St John's Priory** has only a roofless chancel, a fine seven-light window and a medieval tomb. Thirteenth-century **St Francis's Abbey** stands in ruins by the river.

Eating, Drinking, and Music

There's plenty of good choices for **food**, from pubs to restaurants. *Flannery's Hotel*, John Street, is perhaps the most popular place to eat in Kilkenny (open midday Mon–Sat), serving lunches from £3, evening meals £4–8. *Shems*, John Street, serves good basic lunches for around £3.50, as does *Daniel Bolland* in Kiernan's Street. For basic home cooking, large helpings and excellent value, try *The Kourt Kitchens* in the High Street (open Mon–Sat till 9pm, 7pm on Sun). For lighter meals, try vegetarian quiches and salads in *The Kilkenny Center*, in the old stables opposite the castle (open Mon–Sat 10am–5pm, Sun 11am–4:15pm). The tearoom in Kilkenny Castle (see above) is worth a visit for the setting and the cakes; while *Mike's*, High Street (upstairs in the shopping arcade), is worth bearing in mind for good value snacks and basic meals, despite the unappealing location, and is open daily from 9am to 6pm, Thursday, Friday and Saturday till 7:30pm, later in summer.

Bars are as alluring in Kilkenny as anywhere in Ireland, and you won't be hard pushed to find music here either, though it will be a matter of luck as to what you get.

The Kilford Arms, John Street. Regular ballad sessions (no cover charge) and bands followed by a disco (£3 entrance) on Thursday, Friday, Saturday, and Sunday. *Hendersons* bar, St Mary's Lane, features bands on a Friday and Saturday; entrance from £1. *Flannery's Hotel*, John's Bridge, has regular jazz sessions in the bar at lunchtime on Sunday, and Thursday evenings. If you are looking for a disco, try the *Club House Hotel*, Patrick Street, or the *Hotel Kilkenny*, College Road, on weekends. For the occasional big name bands, the places to look out for are the *Newpark Hotel*, Castlecomer Road; and the *Springhill Court Hotel*—pick up a copy of the weekly *Kilkenny People* for what's on information, and watch for posters.

The Arts

Other **entertainment** is fairly easy to come by in summer; *The Kilkenny People*, published on Thursday, lists what's on in the city and the surrounding villages. One event to try and coincide with would be the **Arts Week** festival, held in the last week in August. The emphasis is on classical music, but alongside this are literary readings, art exhibitions, and jazz and folk sessions. All in all, worth catching, though you'll need to reserve accommodation in advance.

Listings

Bank *Allied Irish Bank*, 3 High Street.

Bike rental *J. J. Wall*, Maudlin Street (☎056-21236); £4 per day, £20 per week, £30 deposit.

Bookshops For Irish-interest books, maps and guides, try *O.K. House*, High Street. Other shops include *Cody Books*, Kieran Street, and *The Book Center*, in the High Street.

Pharmacy *Michael O'Connell*, High Street.

Laundromat 124 Walkin Street (Mon–Sat 7:30am–6:30pm).

Police ☎056-22222.

Post Office High Street (Mon–Sat 9am–5:30pm, Wed opens 9:30am).

Swimming Pool Michael Street (10am–11pm).

Travel Agent *Mannings Travel*, High Street (☎056-22950).

Near Kilkenny: The Dunmore Caves

The tourist office will doubtless direct you to the **Dunmore Caves** (Oct–March Sat and Sun 10:30am–4:30pm; April to mid-June Tues–Sat 10am–5pm, Sun 2–5pm; mid-June to Sept daily 10am–7pm; £1, kids and senior citizens 30p), situated seven miles north of Kilkenny on an isolated limestone outcrop of the Castlecomer plateau. In 1967 Viking coins and the skeletons of 44 women and children were found among the stalactites and stalagmites. It's supposed that the Vikings attacked the native Irish, and the women and children were put in the caves for protection. The plan obviously failed, but the fact that the skeletons showed no broken bones suggests that the victims starved to death, or got lost, or that the Vikings tried to smoke them out. To reach the caves, rent a bike in Kilkenny, hitch out on the Castlecomer Road past the train station, or take *Buggy's* coach from The Parade at 12:30pm, returning at 3:40pm.

The Nore and Barrow Rivers

These fine rivers have long been of importance to the southeast, flowing magnificently through the rich countryside. Formerly they were its arteries, bringing prosperity to the heart of the region: the Nore brought trade to medieval Kilkenny, the Barrow to Carlow. Today they are treasured for their considerable beauty, and are a real treat for fishermen. The surrounding countryside is as pretty as you'll find anywhere, perfectly enjoyed by bike, or on foot—the South Leinster Way dips down into some of the choicest spots. Plan a leisurely route, and you can meander your way through picturesque little ancient villages, and take in some exceptional medieval ruins.

The Nore

The **Nore valley** is deservedly renowned for its beauty, the river rolling through lush countryside, past old villages and some engaging ruins. It is perhaps at its finest as it broadens to the south of Kilkenny, and along the tributary Kings River, eight miles from the city, sits medieval **KELLS**. Set amid lush pastureland, the tiny village is an unexpected sight. Its broad bridge is majestically out of scale; an ancient stone watermill stands on the river bank; and the encompassing deep hollow is flecked with mallows, marsh marigolds, docks, and irises. Nearby, the magnificent ruin of **Kells Priory**—founded in 1193—sits like a perfect scale model of a medieval walled city, a clean iron-gray against the surrounding green fields. The ruins consist of a complete curtain wall with square towers and fortified gatehouse, and the remnants of the fourteenth- and fifteenth-century church—one of the most impressive medieval sites in Ireland.

Signposted from Kells, two miles south, are **Kilkree Round Tower**—just one of the many round towers scattered around this part of the country—and the nearby **High Cross**, decorated with much-eroded Biblical carvings. Alternatively, if you take the Stonyford road out of Kells you'll reach placid **Jerpoint Abbey** (May to mid-June Tues–Sat 10am–1pm and 2–5pm, Sun 2–5pm; mid-June to mid-Sept daily 10am–6pm; 60p, kids 25p), which follows a typical Cistercian-Gothic layout, built square around an elegant, cloistered garden. The abbey is built of warm, oat-colored stone and is generally visited for its tombs and twelfth-century carvings—especially the animated figures in the cloister.

Thomastown and Inistioge

A mile north of Jerpoint is **THOMASTOWN**, formerly a medieval walled town of some importance, it's now simply a picturesque country town on the Kilkenny–Waterford train line. Minimal ruins of the walls, a castle, and a thirteenth-century church (with some weathered effigies) remain, and in the Catholic church you'll find the high altar from Jerpoint. If you want to stop over in Thomastown, *Bridge Brook Arms* (☎056-24152) does **B&B** for £10—and has live traditional music on a Monday. The *Waterford Travel Club* private Waterford–Dublin bus picks up at *Dunnes* shop (see "Travel Details"). If you're heading north from here, it's worth calling in at the ruined church at Kilfane (three miles away), which has the fourteenth-century Cantwell Effigy, an impressive piece of stone carving of a knight in full armor.

INISTIOGE, a few miles to the southeast of Thomastown, boasts a tree-lined square besides a fine stone bridge. The village is dotted with crumbling stonework, and little eighteenth- and nineteenth-century houses climb the steep lane that twists away from its center. The grounds of the local estate, *Woodstock*, are open to the public, for a stroll overlooking the neighboring countryside, but the house itself was burned down in 1922 after it had been occupied by the Black and Tans. There's no pub grub available in the village, just one expensive restaurant, though the greengrocer on the square will provide you with tea and sandwiches. You're not allowed to **camp** on the land by the river—ask at *The Three Stars* to use their field.

The Barrow

Northeast from Inistioge, the **South Leinster Way** footpath heads to the little market town of **GRAIGUENAMANAGH**, a gorgeous spot beside the **River Barrow**, with herons fishing in the rushing weir. The town's great age is indicated by the central **Duiske Abbey**, which dominates Graiguenamanagh. Founded in 1204, it was the largest Cistercian abbey in Ireland, and although much has been altered and added outside (including a nineteenth-century clock tower and pebble-dashed walls), the thirteenth-century interior has been lovingly preserved. Besides some original *fleur de lys* tiling and a fine effigy of a knight in chainmail, most impressive is the superb Romanesque processional doorway—heavily decorated, it's one of the best to survive the Reformation (you will find it through a door to the right of the organ). In the churchyard, near the steps outside the south transept, there are a couple of ninth-century stone crosses; and a sixth-century font from Ullard stands outside the north wall of the chancel.

If you're walking the South Leinster Way Graiguenamanagh is a good base, as there's an *An Óige* **hostel** in Graiguenamanagh Vocational School (July and Aug only; ☎0503-24177). *O'Shea's* pub nearby doubles as a grocery shop, while *The Anchor Bar* serves sandwiches and hot snacks in summer (Mon–Sat all day, Sun noon–2pm). There are a handful of good **bars**: *The Anglers Rest* has traditional music every Thursday; and *The Globe* has more mainstream music on Saturday and Sunday, and also on Thursday during the summer.

St Mullins

Five miles south down the towpath, **ST MULLINS** is tucked away from the river, among wooded hills, with the open heights of the Blackstairs Mountains beyond. A stroll through the village takes you to the scant remains of the monastery, founded in AD 696 by Saint Moling, Bishop of Ferns and Glendalough, and alongside them in the churchyard are the base of a round tower and a very worn stone cross. Down beside the stream, at the back of the ruins, a path leads to St Moling's Well, while near the center of the village stands a defensive earthwork, looking like a sturdy pudding just shaken from its bowl. You might want a break here, too: there's a **restaurant and café** down by the river, and *Blanchfield's* **pub** does soup and sandwiches (all day Easter–Sept). You can **camp** on the village green; the nearest shop is at GLYNN, one and a half miles away.

Borris—and Mount Leinster

Following the South Leinster Way north from Graiguenamanagh, along the Barrow, leads to the tiny roadside town of **BORRIS**, just over the border in County Carlow, but most accessible along the valley. It's not much of an attraction in itself, but as good a place as any to stop overnight in the area. You can **camp** on the disused railroad line, getting your fuel and provisions from *O'Shea's* bar and shop. Mrs Susan Breen in Church Street (☎0503-73231) does **B&B**. *Kiernan's* gas station (☎0503-73211) is open for cheap **bike rental** (Mon–Sat until 9pm; £2:50 a day, £14 a week).

Considering its size, there's a lot going on in Borris. Between *The Green Drake Inn*, *The White House Inn*, and *The Step House*, you'll be able to track down some live music most nights. And you're well off for **food** as well; good lunches and dinners in all of the above, particularly *The Step House Bistro* (daily noon to midnight; set dinners from £4), whose fare is home-baked, wholesome, and often vegetarian.

East of Borris, the South Leinster Way leaves the the intimate landscape of the valleys, crossing the open farmland of south Carlow and eventually skirting the bleak height of **Mount Leinster**. The way finally descends to the lonely cluster of houses that is KILDAVIN, six miles or so from Mount Leinster on the main Carlow–Enniscorthy road.

travel details

Trains
From Kilkenny to Carlow (4 daily; 30min); Dublin (4; 1hr 40min).
From Wexford to Dublin (3; 2hr 30min); Rosslare Pier (3; 30min).
From Rosslare Harbour to Dublin (2 daily; 3hr 10mins).

Bus Éireann
From Wexford to Dublin (4; 3hr); Rosslare Harbour (peak seasons only 2 daily; 20min).

From Kilkenny to Dublin (3; 2–3hr).

Private buses
Pierce Kavanagh Coaches (☎056-31213/01-734344) serve Urlingford and Johnstown on their daily Thurles–Dublin route.
Waterford Travel Club (☎051-77177) serve Thomastown, Gowran, and Carlow on their daily Waterford–Dublin route.
Funtrek (☎01-730852) run a daily service **from Wexford**, The Crescent (Mon–Sat 8am, Sun

6:30pm and 8pm; also serving Arklow, Gorey, and Rosslare. **Departs Rosslare** half an hour earlier. *Ardcavan Coach Company* (☎053-22561) operate a service **from Rosslare**, outside the chapel, (Mon–Sat 7:30am, Sun 7:30pm) and **from**

Wexford, The Crescent, (Mon 6am Tues–Sat 8am, Sun 8pm) to Dublin. Returns from Dublin daily (the *Gresham Hotel*, O'Connell St, Mon–Thur and Sat 6pm; Kildare St, Fri 6pm; GPO Sun 10pm).

CHAPTER SIX

WATERFORD, TIPPERARY, AND LIMERICK

T he route from Waterford through Tipperary to Limerick is the quickest way from the southeast, and the arrival points of the ferries, to the center of western Ireland. Yet in this chapter it's the south, not the west, that has all the real appeal. Tipperary and Limerick, despite their resonant names, are far from the most attractive counties in Ireland, while Waterford, not necessarily the first place that springs to mind, can be a delight.

Waterford, whose coastline stretches west from the expanse of Waterford Harbour towards Cork, combines many of the attractions of the south. Rolling green hills spread down to a fine shore of cliffs interspersed with expansive bays and private, enclosed beaches. There's plenty of history here, both out in the county, where **Lismore** (inland) and **Ardmore** (on the coast) preserve extensive early Christian remains, and in **Waterford City** itself, which has been an important port since the Viking invasions. Nowadays the city preserves an ancient heart, but it's also a thriving modern commercial center, young and enjoyably lively to visit. Inland, rich farmland is contained by mountain ranges that offer excellent opportunities for easy, scenic walking—and occasionally for more challenging stuff. Above all there's the **Munster Way** in the northwest, by which you can cross to Tipperary. All of this is contained within a relatively small area, and if you wanted farther confirmation that Waterford combines a little of everything it even has its own tiny *Gaeltacht* area, around **Ring**.

Crossing into southern **Tipperary**, the mountains continue, and for a while there's equally attractive walking, especially in the **Knockmealdown** and **Galty** mountains, and the **Glen of Aherlow** beyond them. For the most part, though, the county consists of prosperous, contented farming country. The Tipperary **Golden Vale** enriches its residents, but the complacent farming towns have little to offer visitors. At the very heart of the county there is, however, one site of outstanding interest—the **Rock of Cashel**. A spectacular natural formation topped with Christian buildings from virtually every period, it's effectively a primer in the development of Irish ecclesiastical architecture.

At **Limerick** you've arrived in the west of Ireland, but the county still has relatively little to tempt you. **Limerick City** itself, third biggest in the Republic, looks on the map as if it ought to be good. But it isn't. Industrial

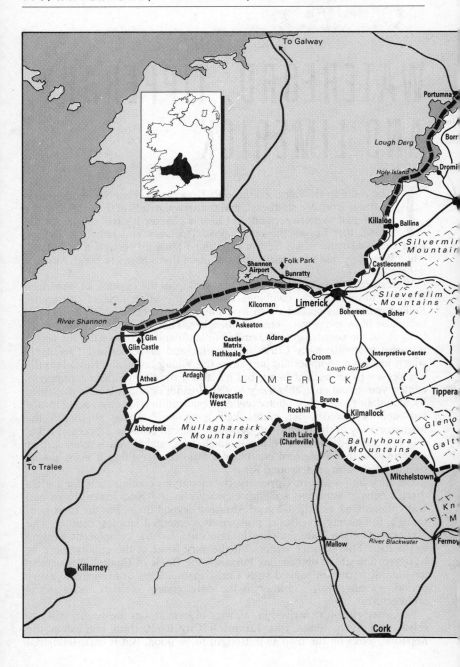

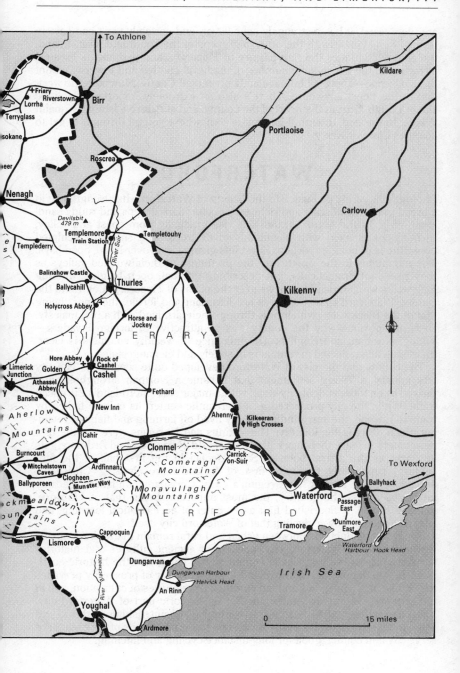

and depressed, it has a strangely sour flavor, and certainly can't compare in terms of enjoyment with the other big towns of the south and west. Inland, the county continues the rich pasture of Tipperary, and perhaps its greatest attraction is the exceptional number of medieval **castles** and towers that dot the landscape—above all immaculately preserved **Castle Matrix** in the west, one of the finest anywhere. There's also an extremely important Neolithic site at **Lough Gur**, in the heart of the county, and at **Adare** a famously quaint village. In the end, though, Limerick is somewhere you go through to get to counties Clare or Kerry.

WATERFORD

Photographs rarely do justice to the beauty of **Waterford**. Its strengths lie in a broad grandeur of scale and richness of color: dark greens and ruddy sandstone reds. In the **south**, grand hills rise gradually from coast and valley, their slopes cloaked with plantations of fir trees. The smoothly sculpted **coastline** is of bold proportions, low cliffs giving views over large, open bays. The mountains in the **north** lose the prettiness of their wooded valleys as they rise—not dramatically, but describing gradual, open heights, offering long walks with stupendous views over the plains of Tipperary. Central to the county, Waterford's **river valleys** are luxuriant and fertile, the finest being that of the Blackwater, which rolls through rich farmland with a real majesty. Here, it's obvious why the county was so attractive to foreign invaders—Viking, Norman, and English. The influence of wealthy colonists is clear, their opulence reflected in remnants of stately and elegant estates.

The county and the **city** of Waterford developed quite separately. The city was initially a Viking settlement that became a Norman stronghold, and thrived as an independent city-state, with a major share of Ireland's European trade. While the city prospered as a mercantile center, its culture linked by trade to Europe, the surrounding county lived off farming and fishing, retaining much of its Celtic identity. The Vikings and Normans were not the first newcomers to leave their mark: the area of **Old Parish** around Ardmore gets its name as the arrival point of Saint Declan in the first half of the fifth century, supposedly the very first of Ireland's proselytizing Christians, preceding Saint Patrick. The region's early Christian foundations became influential across the country, the most important being that at **Lismore**, founded in 636. It flourished first as a center of ecclesiastical learning, and later as a secular power rivaling that of Waterford city itself.

Today the distinctions between urban and rural remain marked. Alongside thriving, modern Waterford city, pockets of ancient cultures and histories survive, such as the tiny Gaelic community of **Ring**, and the historic ecclesiastical foundations of **Ardmore** and Lismore. An air of prosperity pervades the county as a whole, in farmland enriched by centuries of cultivation, and in the renewed commercial importance of the historic port of Waterford city. The coast offers sandy beaches, a handful of quaint fishing harbors, and some great seascapes. It's easily accessible too—main roads of high standard serve city and county, good for long-distance cycling and hitching.

Waterford City

WATERFORD's appearance from the river is deceptively grim: the bare and open stretch of water with its ugly gray wharves and cranes holds no suggestion of the lively city pulsating behind its dull quays. This is the commercial capital of the southeast; yet it retains buildings from Viking and Norman times, and from the eighteenth century, periods of past eminence. The web of narrow streets that grew up as the focus for commercial activity in the city's earliest days holds the modern city together in compact dynamism. While Waterford has had the modern infrastructure of an industrial, rather than a rural, center for decades, the city has developed socially and economically even within the last ten years.

Waterford is basically a modern European port wrapped around an ancient Irish city. The historic town can happily be explored in a day or so, and the nightlife warrants some sampling. One of the few buoyant commercial centers of any size in the Republic, a sign of Waterford's comparative prosperity is the number of young people the place now attracts (and sustains), in strong contrast to other parts of this country bled by emigration. Glad to be here and working, the youth have created an increasingly positive social life. Though a small city by European standards, Waterford has some excellent bars, a small but growing number of decent and imaginative places to eat, and the burgeoning youth/rock scene of an optimistic (albeit small-scale) urban environment. Alongside the city's vigorous modernity, though, there's plenty that's traditional, most obviously the place of the pub as a focal point of social activity, and the persistence of traditional music.

A farther measure of Waterford's social and economic confidence is the town's attitude towards the large numbers of "West Brits," a curiously affectionate term used to describe English people living here and a social peculiarity of the southeast. Either recently arrived, or, if remnants of the Anglo-Irish ascendancy, no longer representing a threat, they are accepted and have integrated, while keeping a separate identity.

History

The deep, navigable Suir River has been the source of the city's importance since the ninth century. Waterford has an excellent harbor; well inland, and therefore easily defended, it's also perfectly positioned for the internal trading routes of the Barrow and the Nore rivers reaching into the heart of the southeast's rich farmland. Reliable recorded history of the city starts with the **Viking** settlement founded in the mid-ninth century. The layout of the city (so similar to that other Viking town, Wexford) retains its Viking roots, the very long quays and adjacent narrow lanes forming the trading center. Waterford was the most important Viking settlement in Ireland, and its inhabitants were so feared that even the bellicose Celtic Deises had to pay them tribute—failure to pay *airgead srona* (nose money) resulted in having your nose chopped off. Reginald's Tower dates from this time, as do some of the remains of the city walls. Nearby, two well-preserved stone arches inside the

Reginald Grill Bar were in fact "sally ports" (AD 850), through which ships entered the fortified city from what is now The Mall but was then water.

The next wave of invaders to leave an imprint were the **Anglo-Normans** in the twelfth century. When the King of Leinster, Dermot MacMurrough, made his bid for the High Kingship of Ireland, he knew Waterford was strategically vital for control of the southwest. In 1170, he called on his Welsh Anglo-Norman allies to attack the city; the most important of these was the Earl of Pembroke (**Strongbow**). The city's walls and towers were formidably strong, but on the third day of attack the Normans discovered a weak point, made a breach, and flooded in, taking the city with scenes of bloodcurdling violence. Strongbow received his reward: Dermot MacMurrough's daughter Aoife's hand in marriage, and her inheritance. The marriage took place in Reginald's Tower and was the first such alliance between a Norman earl and an Irish king: a crucial and symbolic historical event.

The following year, surprised at the Welsh Norman lords' success, Henry II arrived with an awesome display of naval strength (400 ships) and gave the Waterford Normans a charter offering protection—his way of ensuring allegiance to the English crown. Subsequent English monarchs maintained this allegiance, and in 1210 King John arrived with a huge army and enlarged the city with new fortifications. The best preserved towers of the Norman walls are at Railroad Square, Castle Street, Stephen Street, and Jenkins Lane. In the thirteenth century, the city was the de facto capital of Ireland. It reaped farther royal favor through its part in running to earth two would-be usurpers threatening Henry VII; first Lambert Simnel in 1487, then Perkin Warbeck in 1497.

Waterford flourished as an important European port into the sixteenth and seventeenth centuries, trading with France, Spain, Portugal, and Newfoundland, as well as maintaining its inland trade. It was the only city in Ireland to withstand Cromwell, though his forces returned under the command of General Ireton, who took the city without the usual scenes of carnage, giving its citizens honorable terms. The city's importance in trade continued into the eighteenth century, and there's plenty of architectural evidence, both ecclesiastical and secular, of this period's prosperity. The name 'Waterford' is nowadays most famous for its **crystal**, first produced in 1783. The factory closed in 1851, but reopened in 1951, and is now one of the city's major employers.

Arriving and Finding Somewhere to Stay

Roads from the north and the east converge on the river at the **railroad and bus stations** (*Bus Éireann* information ☎051-73401); the city lies over the bridge to the south. Regular daily **trains** connect Waterford to Clonmel, Tipperary, Limerick, Wexford, Kilkenny and Dublin. *Rapid Express Club Travel*, 32 Michael Street (Mon–Sat 9:30am–6pm; ☎051-72149), operates a **bus service** to Dublin and Tranmore that's cheaper than *Bus Éireann* standard fares. Advance reservations are advisable but not essential except at weekends; you can pay on the bus. There are scheduled **flights** to London daily from **Waterford Regional Airport**, Killowen (☎051-75589). Heading east from Waterford, it's worth remebering that you can often negotiate

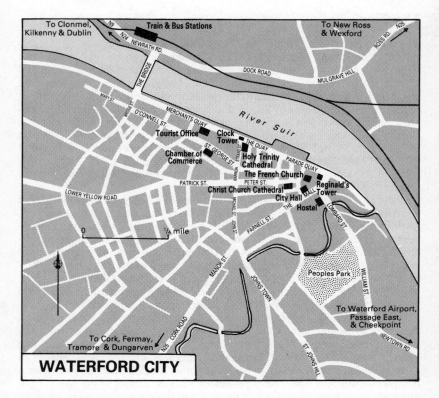

WATERFORD CITY

one-way trips to NEW ROSS on *Galley River Cruises* (☎051-21723 or 73752; around £3).

The **tourist office** (May–Sept Mon–Sat 9am–6pm; Oct–April Mon–Fri 9am–12:45pm and 2–5:15pm; ☎051-75823) is at 41 Merchants Quay, roughly midway between the bridge and the nineteenth-century clock tower. It has comprehensive lists of recommended **B&Bs**. Otherwise, you'll find these along Parnell Street, The Mall, and O'Connell Street, averaging £10 a night. The *Penrose Guest House* in Mary Street is friendly, comfy and clean, as is *O'Connell House*, O'Connell Street (☎051-74175). Others in the center of town are *Saint Thomas's B&B*, Thomas Street, off O'Connell Street (☎051-75058; £9) and *Maryland House*, The Mall (☎051-76162/75000). Similarly central (but open only March–Nov), are *Derrynane House*, 19 The Mall (☎051-75179); Mrs M Ryan's, 7 Cathedral Square (☎051-76677); and *Mayors Walk House*, 12 Mayors Walk (☎051-55427). There's one **private hostel**, in Bolton Street (☎051-79870; £3.50): turn off The Mall down Lombard Street, then take the first turn on the right. They never turn anyone away, but in low season, women traveling alone may feel uncomfortable with the level of sleazy innuendo from the proprietor. There's no **campground** within walking distance of the city.

The City

The city bustles within a nice wedge of Georgiana between the eighteenth-century shops and houses of O'Connell and George streets, which run behind the modern quays, and the decaying splendour of Parnell Street and The Mall with their fine doorways and fanlights. These converge on Reginald's Tower, and the angle the two thoroughfares describe is marked by the extensive remains of Viking and Norman city walls. The area immediately behind the quays is still the city's commercial center. Continue from Barron Strand Street through all its changes of name down to where John Street meets Parnell Street, and you find a great concentration of fast-food joints and bars. The area of lanes between The Mall and Parade Quay contain some of the city's nicest juxtapositions of medieval and eighteenth-century architecture.

Waterford's most historic building is **Reginald's Tower**, a large cylindrical Norman tower of 1003 with a concealed stairway built within its massive wall, its design similar to the Scottish *broch*. It houses the city's **museum** (Easter–Sept 11am–1pm, 2–4pm and 6–9pm, Sat 11am–1pm), which has an impressive collection of royal charters that make quite clear the central role Waterford's allegiance to the English crown played in the city's history. The collection includes the Charter Roll of Richard II (1399), a fabulous transcript of earlier charters. Wander up Bailey's New Street just behind the tower and you immediately come to Waterford's other important medieval building, the **French Church**, or Greyfriars. Founded by Franciscans in 1240, the church served as a hospital in the sixteenth century (thus escaping destruction upon the suppression of the monasteries), and from 1693 to 1815 was used as a place of worship by French Huguenot refugees, whom the city sheltered in their exile from persecution at home. It's now a solid, roofless ruin with a complete tower and fine, east triple-lancet window. Stones at the base of the outer windows have carved comic figures, and the church has some interesting carved slabs, including that of Sir Neal O'Neill, who accompanied James II in his flight from the Battle of the Boyne.

Farther up Bailey's New Street, you enter Waterford's next significant period of church-building at **Christ Church Cathedral**, Church of Ireland (May–Sept Mon–Fri 10:30am–1pm and 2–4pm, though this does vary). Built in the 1770s by John Roberts, who did much work in Waterford for both Catholics and Protestants, it's a nicely proportioned Renaissance building in soothing cream and gray, with a fine steeple and a spacious interior. It's set in an equally pleasant square, the lanes around it showing yet more classical doorways and fanlights, some fine, some derelict. The monuments inside the cathedral are worth a look, in particular that of James Rice (1469), an effigy of a corpse in an advanced state of decay, with various creatures crawling in and out of the carcass. Roberts was also responsible for **Holy Trinity Cathedral** in Barron Strand Street. Originally built in 1793, this was greatly altered during the nineteenth century to become the curving, heavy extravaganza it is today. It's a swirling exercise in decoration, hung with Waterford crystal chandeliers and striving for maximum opulence.

Christ Church apart, it's in the city's secular architecture that the best of the eighteenth century is realized. Christ Church Cathedral looks down over The Mall where the **City Hall** (1788, again by John Roberts) has a spacious entrance hall that was once used as a meeting place and merchants' exchange. It's now the council building, but if you are interested in Waterford crystal ask at the desk to see pieces from the original glassworks, including a huge chandelier. By far the finest eighteenth-century architectural detail in the city, though, is the oval staircase inside the lilac-colored **Chamber of Commerce** on George Street (open office hours). Once again the work of John Roberts (1795), it's a beautiful cantilevered staircase with fine decorative stucco work.

Georgian housing continues down O'Connell Street and into Garter Lane. On the way are Waterford's two most important **arts centers**. The *Garter Lane Arts Center* on O'Connell Street (Tues–Thurs 10am–6pm, Fri and Sat 10am–9pm; ☎051-55038 for theater and arts inquiries) has painting and sculpture exhibitions, and a good current-events notice board. *Garter Lane Two*, 51a O'Connell Street, is the home of the *Red Kettle Theatre Company*, as well as hosting traveling companies (reductions for unwaged and students). Waterford's other theater is the *Theatre Royal*, on The Mall, which stages the city's **Light Opera Festival** in October. The Regional Technical College on the main Cork road is used for classical music recitals, generally advertised in the tourist office.

Waterford Crystal Glass Factory offers free tours (Mon–Fri 10:15am–2:30pm) around its glass-cutting and blowing workshops: interesting if you've never seen it before, and a fair way to work up an appetite on a wet day, but not the "absolute must" the publicity tends to suggest. Tours take about forty minutes and must be reserved in advance; the tourist office will do this for you free of charge, or you can do it yourself on ☎051-73311. Buses to the factory leave from beside the clock tower on the quays: ask the driver to let you off at the factory.

If you want to escape the city for a while, *Galley River Cruises'* **trips to New Ross** offer a unique view of the countryside. The cruise includes either lunch, afternoon tea, or an evening meal (June–Aug, £3–7, book at tourist office or phone ☎051-21723 or 73752). Unless the cruise is very busy you can also negotiate a one-way trip to New Ross, a good way to head back to Rosslare.

Eating

There are plenty of fast-food joints down Michael Street and John Street but for more substantial fare *Poppy's Restaurant* (in the *Garter Lane Arts Center*, lunches and teas Tues–Sat 10:30am–5pm, bistro night Thurs–Sat 7–9:30pm) specializes in French and Italian provincial dishes; large helpings, lovingly prepared from £2 for lunch, £10 in the evening. *Haricot's* on O'Connell Street (Mon–Fri 10am–8pm, Sat 10am–5:45pm) is a cosy and reasonably priced healthfood restaurant catering well for vegetarians. For **pub food**, *Egans* (Broad Street; Mon–Sat noon–2:30pm) serves delicious home-made bread, soup, cooked lunches, and seafood during the summer, and hot specials daily from £3.50. The historic *Munster Bar*, on The Mall, produces generous helpings of simple dishes, freshly cooked on the premises and served at the bar

(Mon–Fri 12:30–2:30pm): it also has a restaurant upstairs (dinner around £10), almost as popular for its fine nineteenth-century oak-carved interior as for the food. **Pizza and pasta** is plentiful; *Gino's* (the Applemarket; daily noon–midnight) is cheery and serviceable with pizzas from £2.50, and home-made Italian ice cream. *Teasers*, 124 The Quays (Mon–Fri 10:30am–7pm, Thurs–Sat 10:30am–10pm), serves meals from £3.50, specializing in pastas from £5. *The Palma Grill*, Parnell House, Parnell Street, is an Italian restaurant with a pizza and pasta takeout service. *The Happy Garden*, Arundel Square, is the best **Chinese** restaurant in town; meals around £10.

Drinking and the Music Scene

Waterford has some wonderful bars, and there is a steadily growing music scene here. John Street has two of the city's favorite watering holes—*Geoff's* and *The Pulpit*, both lively, young places with a good social mix, and useful for keying into what's happening in the city. *Barrs* on Mayors Walk is also young and friendly, a good bet for women who don't want to be hassled—and the only pub we know that sells herb tea! This pub has occasional **blues/jazz** sessions on a Monday. For **traditional music** there are a few regular spots: *T.H.Doolans*, George Street; *Mullanes*, Newgate Street, a singing pub; and *The Metropole*, Bridge Street. Out of town there's *Meade's Bar* at Halfwayhouse, three miles down the road to Cheekpoint, with very good sessions on Saturdays and some Wednesdays. For **jazz**, try *The Reginald*, next to Reginald's Tower, or *The Trap* (3 The Manor, at the bottom of John Street) has soul and blues every Wednesday and Sunday night, and sometimes traditional or jazz; occasional cover charge. A good spot for local bands (rock/punk/heavy metal) is *The Mansion*, Johnstown (opposite the hospital), either free or £1.

Clubs include *Snages*, behind *Egans* pub on Broad Street (Tues–Sun £4, Sat £5), and *Stonecourt* (O'Connell Street); both with discos and expensive drinks. As everywhere, most of the hotels have discos at weekends. *The Bridge Hotel* on The Quays is a meat market, but also where big name bands play.

Finally, Waterford's music scene would not be the same without the *Freewheelers*, a local bikers club. While looking like Hell's Angels, they are in fact no *more* menacing than they look, and are more interested in their bikes than in violence. It's well worth checking out gigs organized by them—sporadic Thursday nights at *The Cleaboys*, a pub on the edge of a housing estate out of town: take a taxi, or if you have transport, follow Upper Yellow Road out of town, then on to Cleaboy Road and the pub is behind a gas station on the left. They also organize gigs out at TRAMORE, and for these they arrange buses so people don't have to drink and drive. For farther information, ask those who display *Freewheeler* posters on their premises.

Listings

Bicycles *Wright's Cycle Depot*, Henrietta Street off Parade Quay (☎051-74411), for bike repairs and parts. There is nowhere to rent bikes in the city.

Dental emergencies South Eastern Health Board (☎051-76111; Mon–Fri 9am–5pm, ask to be put through to Newgate Street Dental Clinic).

Family Planning Clinic Michael Street, above *Tokens* boutique.

Hospital Ardkeen Regional Hospital, Dunmore Road (☎051-73321); for emergencies, and dental emergencies outside of office hours.

Laundromat *Washed Ashore*, The Quays (Mon–Fri 8am–9pm, Sat 8:30am–6:30pm).

Rape Crisis Center ☎051-75248/76124/73362.

Shopping There's shopping until 9pm every Friday; the Applemarket is a general market held on Friday and Saturday. For committed junk enthusiasts, Waterford Auction Galleries (O'Connell Street; Tues–Sat) are compulsory.

Travel agents *USIT Youth and Student Travel Office*, 33 O'Connell Street (☎051-72601 or 77166; May–Sept Mon–Fri 9:30am–5:30pm, Sat 10am–1pm; rest of the year Mon–Fri 9:30am–5:30pm). *Harvey Travel Limited* (☎051-72048 or 72784) is the agent for *Slattery* and *Funtrek*.

Youth Information and Advice Center Parade Quay (Mon–Fri 9:30am–6pm, Sat 10am–5pm), is a general welfare and advice center for young Irish citizens, but can give referral advice to people in difficulties.

Around the County

It's easy to get into the heart of Waterford county's rich farmland and empty mountains from Waterford city. Fast main roads offer good hitching inland, and the *Munster Way* just north of Lismore is as good a route as any from which to enjoy the Knockmealdown Mountains. The Blackwater River valley is the county's most impressive, while that of the Nire offers more intimate scenery as it leads up from Ballymacabery (about six miles south of Clonmel, Tipperary) into the Comeragh mountains. Discovering Waterford's stunning and varied coast is slower and requires a narrower focus—it makes more sense to pick a small area, such as Ardmore, Helvick Head or Dunmore East, and explore it at a leisurely pace, than to try and see the whole coastline.

Inland: the Blackwater Valley and Lismore

Typical of the outstanding beauty of the inland county is the stretch of the **Blackwater valley** around Cappoquin, where the river makes a sharp westward turn towards County Cork, describing as it goes the southerly limit of the Knockmealdown Mountains. **CAPPOQUIN** itself is prettily situated on a wooded hillside overlooking the river. The village's B&Bs cater to a handful of fishermen at holiday times, but for all its choiceness of setting there's precious little for the visitor, and the place seems strangely neglected. The only music you'll get will be a country and western/ballad mix on Friday and Saturday at the *Sportsmans Inn*, which also has a Saturday disco and a limited range of bar food in the summertime.

Although there's nothing to detain you in the village, the surrounding countryside is lovely. Walk half a mile east, take the right fork by the statue of the Virgin, and you come to the **Glenshelane River walk**. This follows the river through its deep valley banked by pine trees and, after about three miles, brings you to **Mount Melleray**, a Cistercian monastery that welcomes visitors in search of solitude. The trail eventually opens out to more level country, affording great views of the Knockmealdowns and the Galtymore mountains of Tipperary. In all, the walk's a foretaste of the varied terrain of the major long-distance walk in this part of the country, the *Munster Way* (see below).

Set in the lovely broad plain of the Blackwater valley three miles west of Cappoquin, **LISMORE** is a gem of ecclesiastical history. Roads approach the town between the river and gentle slopes of mixed woodland—especially beautiful in spring and autumn. The setting is dominated by the hugely romantic towers and battlements of **Lismore Castle**, whose pale white-gray stone, set with mullioned windows, rises magnificently on the hill from glorious woodlands and sumptuous gardens (gardens open to the public). The castle itself is a successful mid-nineteenth-century imitation of a Tudor castle, remodeled by Joseph Paxton (designer of the Crystal Palace) around the remains of the medieval fort that originally stood here. The castle's long occupation by the Anglo-Irish aristocracy (and less permanent colonists, including Sir Walter Raleigh) explains why so much of the layout of the parkland and farmland around here is reminiscent of wealthy English shires. The whole setting is strongly evocative of Lismore's former power and glory—even though this building in fact has nothing to do with that era.

Around AD 630 Saint Carthage founded a monastic complex for both monks and nuns in Lismore, and the place flourished as a center of learning so much that in the next century, under the influence of great teachers such as Saint Colman, it became a huge university city. This growth continued into the twelfth century, despite 300 years of sporadic pillage by first Vikings, then Normans. Lismore held great political as well as religious power, and the rivalry between the sees of Lismore and Waterford, which epitomises the split histories of Waterford city and county, was finally resolved in 1363 when the two were united.

Invaders continued to attack the city, and in the late sixteenth century the medieval cathedral was almost totally destroyed by Queen Elizabeth's army. Its site is now occupied by **Saint Carthage's Church of Ireland Cathedral.** Although this was built in 1633, the overall look is elegant early-nineteenth-century neo-Gothic, the tower and ribbed spire having been added in 1827 by James Pain, and the windows of the nave reshaped at the same time. It's a lovely building, sitting in a cobbled churchyard of ancient yews and pollarded lindens. Inside is some interesting stonework, including the McGrath family tomb (1548), which has almost comic carving around the base of the stone slab. The chunky carving of a bishop holding an open book, set in the back wall, is from the tenth-century monastic settlement. In the south transept, there's some striking stained glass by Burne-Jones, the English Pre-Raphaelite.

There's not much sign of this rich history in Lismore's current economically depressed existence, but it does somehow seem to preserve a quiet reverence about itself. It does little to raise its sleepy head for visitors, and the sporadic tourist buses that pull up, briefly disgorge, and head off again, only accentuate the feeling of being left in another age.

Lismore Practicalities

If you want to stay in Lismore, you'll find **B&B** at the *Lismore Hotel* in the main street (☎058-54219; £10.50–13.50 according to season), at *Ballyrafter House* (☎058-54002; £15) or at Mrs J Power's *Beechcroft*, Deerpark Road, half a mile out of town (☎058-54273; £9.50). There's an *An Óige* **youth hostel** three miles north of Lismore (☎058-54390; grade C). For free **camping** in town go down over the bridge and to the left through the gate; there's a fabulous spot beneath the castle.

Lismore has some fascinating ancient **bars** and grocery stores, a delight to explore in themselves, though there's not much beyond this trip into the past by way of food or entertainment. Options for **eating** are pretty limited: along the main street are *Eamonn's* (hot cooked lunch Mon–Sat midday, Sun sandwiches only), *The Red House* (Mon–Sat, a great variety of pub lunches), and the *Lismore Hotel* (meals daily from £7.50, or bar snacks). If you're after **music** you might try *Rosie's West End Bar* for traditional sessions on summer weekends (she also has a snooker table), or *Eamonn's*. Failing these, you'll have to settle for the standard C&W mix at the *Lismore Hotel* on Saturday and Sunday, or the Saturday disco that's also held here.

The Munster Way

The road north from Lismore to the youth hostel is typical of this area's gorgeous river valleys, stuffed with rhododendrons, bracken, beech trees and oaks, and dripping feathery pines. Spongy mosses cover walls, and young ferns spring out of them. The hostel marks the start of the long-distance hiking path, the **Munster Way**. Immediately north of the hostel, you come to higher ground and more open spaces, scattered with sheep and fir trees. The path goes through the Knockmealdowns, round the huge peat-covered mound of Sugarloaf Hill, to a viewing spot known as **The Vee**, just five miles from the hostel. From its steep, heathery V-shaped sides there's a tremendous view of the perfectly flat vale below with its patches of fields, and the town of Cahir at the foot of the Galty Mountains. The Munster Way descends to Clonmel in County Tipperary, around seventeen miles from here, but if you don't want such a long walk you can follow the road down to CLOGHEEN and hitch to the independent **hostel** at Cahir, County Tipperary, or the **An Óige Hostel** of *Mountain Lodge*, Burncourt, Cahir (☎052-67277; grade C; closed Oct–Feb).

The Munster Way is clearly signposted all the way to, eventually, Carrick-on-Suir in Tipperary. The walk involves long distances rather than steep, dramatic inclines, and most of the way it's within a mile or so of habitation. Nevertheless solitary walkers should bear in mind that much of the route is out of sight of the lowlands, and distress signals won't be noticed. The relevant *Bord Fáilte* Information Sheet, giving route guidelines for this section of the way, is "Carrick-on-Suir–the Vee", Information Sheet No. 26J.

The Coast

Waterford's coastline offers good sandy beaches, and some breathtaking coastal walks. The open grandeur of bays like Dungarvan is offset by the intimacy of hidden fishing ports, and pockets of ancient history at Ring and Ardmore. The best of the **beaches** are at Dunmore East, Tramore, Annestown, Bunmahon, and Ardmore. Major seaside towns are connected to Waterford by regular bus services, but the choicest spots are best walked, bicycled, or slowly hitched to: using *Bus Éireann* to get to these involves a manipulation of the timetable verging on the miraculous.

Passage East and Ballyhack

Immediately east of Waterford city, at the neck of its long harbor, the pretty ferry village of **PASSAGE EAST** nestles under craggy hills, the estuary slopes aflame with wild gorse. The ferry here connects with **BALLYHACK** in County Wexford (*Passage East Car Ferry* ☎051-82488; continuous services from around 7:30am to 8pm, later in summer; average crossing time ten minutes; £1, £3 with car)—a particularly useful route east for cyclists, especially if you're making for Rosslare, or want to stay with the coast. If you get stuck in Passage East the only **B&B** lies south through the village and up the hill past the school to CROOKE (*Greenmount House*; ☎051-82165; £10). *The Farleigh Pub* in Passage East does a great range of **bar food** (Easter–Sept Mon–Sat noon–9pm, Sun noon–6pm); out of season they'll still feed you well, but with less choice. Across the water, less than a mile from Ballyhack, there's an **An Óige hostel** at ARTHURSTOWN (Grade C; May–Sept only; no phone). Ballyhack should be as pretty as her Waterford counterpart but isn't, despite the fact that the village is dominated by a fine sixteenth-century tower house. It has one miserable bar and a very good, very expensive restaurant.

Dunmore East

Farther around the Waterford coast, **DUNMORE EAST** settles snugly between small, chunky sandstone cliffs topped by masses of rambling golden gorse. The main street follows a higgledy-piggledy contour from the safe, sandy cove beside which the east village sits, towards a busy harbor full of the rippled reflections of brightly colored fishing boats, and cradled by the crooked finger of the harbor wall. From here, the ruddy sandstone cliffs make bold ribs around the coast. This is still a very active fishing harbor, but has also cashed in on its undeniable picturesqueness, with self-consciously new thatched houses sneaking in alongside the originals.

Quaint as it is, Dunmore East has become very much a playground for affluent Waterford people, and there are three large hotels to cater to them. At least this means there are plenty of facilities. You can get decent **pub food** at *The Ocean Hotel* (summer 10am–10pm; winter noon–3pm and 6–9pm; ☎051-83136), where there are singalongs most evenings in the summer, and at weekends in winter, plus discos at weekends. The conservative *Candlelight*

Inn serves bar food (noon–2:30pm and 6–9pm; ☎051-83215), and has similar entertainment. The only reasonably priced **B&B** within a mile of the village center is Mrs Butler's *Church Villa* (☎051-83390; open year round; £10). For **camping**, there's *Dunmore East Caravan and Camping Park* (☎051-83174; June–mid-Sept; £5 per unit). The **supermarket** is on Dock Road (daily 8am–7pm), and there's an Allied Irish **Bank** (Tues and Fri 10am–12:30pm and 1:30–3pm), with a Banklink machine always available. Dunmore East is the home of *Waterford Harbour Sailing Club*, where an experienced sailor might get some crewing.

West to An Rinn

Nine miles west of Dunmore East, **TRAMORE** caters to a different type of vacationer, and a different kind of bank balance. It's a busy, popular seaside resort serving families from Waterford and Cork, and has plenty of amusements, trailers, B&Bs, and a huge sandy beach. Popular *O'Shea's* is probably the liveliest bar in Tramore, with rock or blues every weekend.

DUNGARVAN is the major coastal town of County Waterford, and its setting is magnificent. There's a wonderful view over the grand, broad bay as you descend to the town, the open heights around topped by pine forests that seem to have been poured on like thick syrup. The town itself is modern, with all the amenities that go along with that, as well as a fine beach; but of more interest and charm are the small communities along the coast to the west.

AN RINN, or RING, is a pocket of Irish tradition hidden away on the modern Waterford coast. It's a tiny Gaelic-speaking community of about 800 that has somehow survived in what is otherwise one of Ireland's more developed counties, all the more remarkable given the "West Brit" flavor of much of the county's coast. The language survives healthily as do other traditions, notably music and set dancing, and Ring has its own radio station. It's quite tricky to find—signposts to An Rinn on the R674 (off the N25) are minimal—and hard to recognize when you do: like many *Gaeltacht* villages Ring consists of a community of farms and a handful of bars spread over quite a wide area, with no real center. This can be frustrating if you're not cycling, as you have to rely on hitching to and from some of the best bars. A good place to get your bearings is *Tigh an Cheoil* (☎058-46209), a bar down by the pier with traditional sessions on Thursdays, Saturdays, and Sundays throughout the year, and at other times during the summer. The owners have a field you can **camp** in, and will put you in touch with whatever's going on in the area. Other bars for **traditional music** are *Murrays*, just over a mile away at Helvick; *Mooneys*, on the way out of Ring towards Dungarvan; *The Marine Bar*, six miles west of Dungarvan on the N25; *Seanchai*; and John Paul Walsh's bar, *Old Parish*—ask locally for directions.

Ring must have some of the cheapest **B&Bs** in the country. Breda Maher's *Aisling*, Gurtnadiha, Ring (☎058-46134; open all year; £7.50), is welcoming and well run, in a fabulous spot overlooking Dungarvan Harbour, or call Liam and Breda Maher at *Helvick View*, Ring (☎058-46297; April–Sept; £7).

There's nothing specific at Ring beyond the way of life. When the tide's out, you can walk a few miles along the shoreline west of Ring around

Helvick Head. When the tide's in, a walk on this headland gives splendid views of sculpted cliffs along the coast, and of the mountains inland. Alternatively, local fishermen will take you out in their boats by arrangement.

Ardmore

ARDMORE is delightful, combining ancient history with a setting full of character. The sixth century saw the arrival here of Saint Declan, at least thirty years before Saint Patrick, and the surrounding area of **Old Parish** is so called because it's supposedly the oldest parish in Ireland. At Ardmore, a medieval **cathedral and round tower** stand on the site of the saint's original monastic foundation, commanding stunning views over Ardmore Bay. The long, low twelfth-century cathedral has massy buttresses, its stoutly rounded doors and windows confirming the proud—albeit roofless—Romanesque solidity of the building, while the slender round tower, tall and fine with a conical roof, stands alongside in poignant contrast. There are stones with early ogham inscriptions inside the cathedral, but the most exceptional carvings are in the west external wall. Romanesque arcading, originally from an earlier building, has been set here beneath the window, with boldly carved scenes showing The Weighing of Souls, The Fall of Man, The Judgement of Solomon, and The Adoration of the Magi; truly impressive, and unique in quality and design. **Saint Declan's Oratory**, supposedly his burial site, also stands in the graveyard.

The village down below consists of a pleasant row of cottages, a few pubs, a shop and a couple of excellent sandy beaches. There's a **trailer and camping** site, and in the summer the place is busy with people. Myth has it that Saint Declan arrived here from Wales, his bell and vestments magically carried by the large stone that now sits on the beach. This would explain why the boulder is of a completely different geology from the surrounding land— though the Ice Age seems a more likely, if comparatively mundane, explanation. Another improbable tale is that crawling under the stone cures rheumatism. It looks unlikely that a fit person could squirm under it, let alone an invalid. If you walk through the village to the east, up the hill and to the path past the *Cliff House Hotel*, you come to **Saint Declan's Well** and a steeply gabled **oratory**. Like many ancient wells, it's a moving spot, with fresh water springing beside three primitive stone crosses where pilgrims used to wash, and a stone chair. From here, there's a fine walk around the headland along rocky cliffs for five miles or so, as far as Whiting Bay.

TIPPERARY

Tipperary is the largest of Ireland's inland counties, and also the richest. The county's wealth comes from the central **Golden Vale**, a flat limestone plain shared with eastern Limerick that's prime beef and dairy cattle territory. This enormous stretch of farming land is abutted on most borders by crops of mountain ranges, the most beautiful of which are the **Comeragh** and **Galty**

mountains and the **Glen of Aherlow**. These are both in the south of the county, and it's this area, without doubt, that packs in the most excitement. The curling course of the Suir, Tipperary's principal river, sweeps up most of what there is to see. But for many, Tipperary's attractions hang on one site alone. The **Rock of Cashel** is the county's most dramatic feature by far, its limestone sides rising cliff-like two hundred feet above the level ground, crowned with the high walls and towers of some splendid medieval ecclesiastical architecture.

Tipperary often has a vaguely familiar ring, thanks to the World War I marching song, *It's a Long Way to Tipperary*. The county was actually picked for the song simply for the rhythmic beat of its name, which dashes the romance somewhat. Actually Tipperary isn't particularly far from anywhere in southern Ireland, and this is probably its greatest advantage: you can catch the few worthwhile sights on your way through, and still be on the south or west coast within a few hours.

Carrick-on-Suir

Tucked in Tipperary's southeast corner, at the foot of the mountain slopes of neighboring County Waterford, **CARRICK-ON-SUIR** may well be the first place you see in Tipperary. And it can be something of a letdown. It's much less pretentious than Clonmel, farther upstream (though it's trying hard to emulate its more successful neighbor), but it also has less going for it. Still, the town does possess Ireland's most beautiful **Elizabethan mansion**: similar examples abound in England but were always a rarity here. Set at the very eastern end of the main street, across the public park, the mansion was built by Thomas, Earl of Ormond ("Black Tom"), in anticipation of a visit from Queen Elizabeth I. It adjoins an earlier castle built on the banks of the Suir in 1450, and a claim that Anne Boleyn was born here is still disputed among historians. Unfortunately, the mansion has recently been closed to the public, and if you look at the frighteningly curving dip in the second storey, you'll see why—the whole brick structure looks ready to collapse. It's still worth seeing, though, if only from the outside.

Regardless of the mansion's splendors, it's as the birthplace of the champion cyclist **Sean Kelly** that the town is most proud of itself—and the tiny main square at the very west end of the main street has been renamed in his honor. **Tourist information** (summer only) can be found opposite the convent a little farther down the main street, through a barrel arch and then a rectangular arch on the right. The *Europa Grill* on the main street is a cheap place to eat. If you need to stay, there's **B&B** at *Suirmount*, Carrickbeg (☎051-40053).

Five miles north of Carrick, **AHENNY** has two beautiful high crosses in its graveyard. They're thought to be eighth-century, and are excellent examples of the transition period between the Early Christian plain shaft crosses and the highly ornate didactic crosses of Monasterboice and Kells.

Clonmel

CLONMEL, thirteen miles upstream, is far and away Tipperary's largest and most successful town. It's highly civilised, and decidedly nouveau-riche, with shopfronts sporting names like the *Mayfair Café*, *Blame James* (it's virtually a cultural tragedy to have this on Wolfe Tone Street), and a pub called *Bill Gibbs* (after the fashion designer). The bakeries, boutiques, fine delicatessens and pubs—displaying *Hofmeister* and *Budweiser* signs, rather than the familiar *Guinness* logo—that line central O'Connell Street present the overripe face of the Tipperary Golden Vale.

Nonetheless Clonmel is a beautiful place to breeze through, if only to catch sight of its preserved backstreets and quayside mills. Singular examples of period architecture include the obtuse nineteenth-century **St Mary's Roman Catholic Church**, with ziggurat tower and portico, in Irishtown, out past the imitation West Gate; the Greek-revival-styled **Wesleyan Church** on Wolfe Tone Street; the **Old St Mary's** Church of Ireland Church with its octagonal tower and tower house; what was once the eighteenth-century **Palatinate Court House** and is now the Main Guard at the eastern end of O'Connell Street; and *Hearn's Hotel* on Parnell Street, once the depot for the nineteenth-century Bianconi coaches. Bianconi came from Lombardy in Italy and set up the most successful coach business in the country, running the so-called *Bians* and using Clonmel as his principal base—for which he later became its most famous mayor. All of these are impressive from the outside; none offer much if you venture within.

There are plenty of **B&Bs** in town, including several on the Marlfield Road (*Hillcourt*, ☎052-21029; *Benuala*, ☎052-22158) and the Cahir Road (*Beentee*, ☎052-21313; *St Lomans*, ☎052-22916). The nearest **hostel** is the newly-opened *Powers The Pot* at Harneys Cross (☎052-23085; £3.50, including shower), up the slopes of the Comeragh Mountains (at 1200 feet it claims to be the highest house in the country). On the threshold of good hill-walking country, it's still not too far from the town. The owner will pick up hostelers from Clonmel in a minibus, usually connecting with the Dublin bus. To get there otherwise, follow the hostel's signpost leaving Clonmel past the *7-11* shop, over the bridge and up via the Golf Club Road (R678) for about six miles. There's a bar, home-cooked breakfasts and dinners, and a few bikes for rent. The hill can present a few problems after a night out in Clonmel, but the hostel hopes to make transportation arrangements in peak season.

There's no shortage of places to **eat** in Clonmel. The *Vale of Honey Café* on the O'Connell Mall, just off O'Connell Street, is about the cheapest in town. The *Wholefood Restaurant* on Abbey Street is a coffee and health-food shop (Mon–Sat 9am–5:30pm, lunch from 12:30pm). The *Salad Bowl*, nearby on Mitchell Street, is another good choice. For an evening meal, *Blame James* on Wolfe Tone Street (☎052-23746) is the spendthrift's answer and *La Scala*, just off Gladstone Street, has an inspiring and reasonably priced Italian menu (Tues–Sat noon–2:45pm and 5:30–10pm, Sun noon–2:30pm; five-course dinner £12). The *Wine Vaults* on Market Street is another hedonists' den. If you find yourself in need of a touch of nostalgia after all this rather untypical modernity, *Gus's Bar* on Parnell Street is a plain old-fashioned **pub**. There's **traditional music** at the *GAA Centre*, opposite the hospital on Western Road, on Mondays at 8pm; in the *Princes Bar* in Upper Irish Town on Saturday; at *O'Gorman's* pub on Thursday and Friday; and an ad hoc session in the *Railroad Bar* (*Kitty O'Donnells*) on Sunday night. This last one can be tricky to find—ask locally for directions. There are **discos** at *The Marella Hotel* and *Clonmel Arms*.

Clonmel is the capital of Irish gray**hound racing**, and you can see the sport on Monday and Thursday nights at the local stadium. The town **festival** takes place in mid-August. **Fishing** off the quay is free, otherwise you can get a day's trout licence (£3) from *The Paper Shop* next door to the **museum** (Tues–Sun 10am–6pm) on Parnell Street. The river's meant to be very good for the late run of the salmon in early September.

North via Fethard

Leaving Clonmel, you could either head southwest, to the plain between the Knockmealdown and Galty mountains (see below); or north for Cashel, in which case the route via **FETHARD** is the most rewarding. A touchingly plain place to travel through, and rarely sought out by tourists, Fethard has a number of forgotten medieval remains set at the back of the town towards the river. One of these is a ruined **Templar's Castle**, access to which is through the *Castle Inn*—contact the publican, Mr Keogh. Other remains of old friaries and Iron Age raths can be found in the surrounding land. There's also a **Folk Farm and Transport Museum** at the beginning of the Cashel Road (May–Sept Mon–Sat 10am–6pm, Sun 1:30–6pm). The one **restaurant**, halfway along the main street, couldn't be more traditional in its setting (the back room of a household, with the front room used as a shop) or cooking (plain and wholesome; four-course lunch £3.50).

Between the Knockmealdown and Galty Mountains

Of the two mountain ranges in southern Tipperary, the **Galties** make up one of the most scenic inland ranges in the country and are well worth discovering. The **Knockmealdowns** are less interesting, but offer easier hill walking. The valley between the two, which runs for about ten miles between Cahir and Mitchelstown, is not much in itself—but if you base yourself plumb in the center, you're well-placed to walk either range. The best place by far for **hikers** is the *Farmhouse* hostel (☎052-41906; double rooms only, groceries fresh from the farm; £4.50), in a small farmhouse annex just off the N8 Cahir–Mitchelstown road. It's about four miles from Cahir, up a small lane off to the left, then around two right-angle bends and by the laneside on the right. For the hitcher it's the most accessible hostel in the south Tipperary area.

Two more **hostels**, both *An Óige*, are conveniently set in the Galty mountains and the Glen of Aherlow beyond, each deliberately distanced a short day's trek from the last. The intervening terrain has its fair share of tarns, cliffs, and wooded forests. The *Mountain Lodge Hostel* (grade C; March–Sept; ☎052-67277) is a spacious Alpine-like old shooting lodge, eight miles along the Mitchelstown road from Cahir, then up a right turn, climbing for a mile by the river into the mountain. The *Ballydavid Wood House Hostel* (grade B; ☎062-54148) is in the Glen of Aherlow six miles out of Cahir. Try and arrive in daylight for this one, for although meticulously signposted, the route has enough twists and turns to get you lost.

At **ARDFINNAN**, a beautiful fourteen-arched stone bridge crosses the Suir, and a private castle stands on the overlooking hillside. Follow along the foot of the Knockmealdowns for several miles, and you'll come to CLOGHEEN, where there's the best turnoff route into the mountains, towards the terrific scenic point known as the **Vee** (see "The Munster Way"). Powerfully telescopic views over Waterford and Tipperary stretch out from beside the lough in the mountain gap, revealing how uncompromisingly flat Tipperary is, hemmed in by its opposing and distant sets of mountain ranges. You'll notice two shepherds' shelters up here, with half the back wall missing so that the shepherds could always keep an eye on the sheep on the hill behind.

Back on the main road, you'll come next to **BALLYPOREEN**, a wide-streeted crossroads turned ghost town, whose moment of glory came on June 3, 1984, when **Ronald Reagan** made a prodigal return—his great-grandfather was born here in 1810. You can read all about it and look at photos of the visit in a specially built center at the crossroads, opposite the *Ronald Reagan* pub.

The Mitchelstown Caves

The main attraction of this area, however, is the **Mitchelstown Caves**, a massive pre-Ice Age underworld that's well worth visiting. Located eight miles from Mitchelstown itself, the caves are signposted from Ballyporeen down the interlacing lanes of the valley. They are by far the most extensive and complicated cave system in Ireland (a couple of miles in all) and have remained, considering their scale, very uncommercialised. The whole underground system was discovered in 1833, when a laborer lost his crowbar down a crevice, though there are records from much earlier of one cave being used as a hiding place, most famously to shelter the Earl of Desmond after his unsuccessful rebellion in 1601.

The opening to the system is a cleft in the hill behind the house of the curator, Jackie English, whose harnessing of legend and folklore to match every calcite formation makes for an imaginative tour. Oisin, Niamh of the long golden hair, the cave of the Tir Na nÓg, the Tower of Babel, and even the Shroud of Turin are all visualized in a range of colors washed down from the minerals in the limestone above—brown from the iron oxide, blue from the copper sulphate, black from the manganese and gray from the lead and zinc. The caves were formed by the incessant action of rainwater on the rock over millions of years, and the fantastical stone formations grew out of the calcium carbonate (dissolved limestone) deposited by the dripping water, hardening as it evaporated into gigantic encrustations of stalactites and stalagmites. The temperature in the caves is around 54°F—this can feel chilly in summer, so bring a sweater. The **tours** only take in a few of the major caves, but are nonetheless worth taking—simply turn up at the caves or, if there's no one there, at Jackie English's house, any time between 10am and 6pm.

Cahir

You're unlikely to miss **CAHIR**. The town sits on a major crossroads, its rectangular-shaped central area radiating routes from each corner: to Clonmel, Cork, Cashel and Tipperary itself. Cahir's **castle** (housing a **tourist information** office in summer) is the town's one attraction, set on a rocky islet in the Suir River, beside the road to Cork. In essence the building is Anglo-Norman, dating from the thirteenth and fourteenth centuries, though the virgin appearance of the outer shell is deceptive—much of the stonework is fifteenth- and sixteenth-century, with a good deal of the brickwork going on into the eighteenth and nineteenth centuries. The Irish chieftain Conor O'Brien was the first to build a castle on the rock, but it was the Anglo-Norman Butlers, the Earls of Ormond, who made this into one of the most powerful castles in the country. The Elizabethan Earl of Essex showered the castle with artillery fire in 1599, but it had a quiet time of the Cromwellian and Williamite invasions; it receded towards ruin until rejuvenated, along with other town buildings, by the Earl of Glengall in the mid-nineteenth century. In modern times, the interior has been uniformly whitewashed, and spartanly furnished.

Entrance to the castle (May–Aug daily 10am–8pm; Sept 10am–6pm; Oct–April Tues–Sat 11am–1pm and 2–4pm, Sun 2–4pm) is along the side rampart, bringing you into the confined space of the middle ward, dominated by the three-storey thirteenth-century keep. Down to the left, you pass through a gateway topped by machicolations, musket loops to either side, where sixteenth-century invaders could have been bombarded with missiles, or boiling oil. Beyond is the much larger outer ward, and at its far end, the Swiss-style cottage built by the Earl of Glengall to live in during his extensive nineteenth-century renovations. The cottage now houses a **video theater** where a twenty-minute film enthuses rhapsodically on the antiquities of southern Tipperary.

In the the **inner ward**, two corner towers overlook the road to Cork. The larger was probably designed to be independently defensible once the keep had fallen, and dates from a mixture of periods—straight, thirteenth-century stone stairs; fifteenth to sixteenth-century stone vaulting over the ground-floor main room; and nineteenth-century renovation work in the Great Hall, whose stepped battlements reflect sixteenth-century style. The smaller, square tower at the other end of the ward and the curtain wall date from the nineteenth century, though with medieval bases. Just to the left of this second tower, steps lead to the bottom of the well tower, where the castle could safeguard its water supply during a siege. The **keep** itself consists of vaulted chambers, a portcullis and a round tower containing a prison, accessible through a trap door.

You'll notice another castellated mansion on the hill farther on along the Cork road: this was once the town prison but now offers **B&B** at much the same price as the many others around town (*Carrigeen Castle*; ☎052-41370). There's an independent **hostel** a mile south of town (*Lisakyle Hostel*; open all year; £4; camping available; ☎052-41963). Phone for a lift if you're without transportation, or leave your luggage at the owner's shop in town (*Conlans*, opposite the post office at the Dublin road exit of the main square). The hostel is basic and adequate (the *Farmhouse Hostel*, mentioned above, four miles out of town, is better). *Bus Éireann* **buses** leave from outside *Lonergan's Bar*, across from the castle; there's a timetable posted in the window.

For **food**, the coffee shop above the *Crock of Gold* giftshop, opposite the castle, provides sandwiches, scones and lunches. *Roma's Café* on the Dublin side of the square has the normal café food, and is the cheapest place in town. **Traditional music** is minimal and not of a high standard but takes place ad hoc on a Friday night at *O'Cooney's* pub on the Dublin road just before the railroad station. One of the more interesting **pubs** to pop into is *Black Toms* on the Tipperary road; sawdust floor and very macho, but animated, with ballad and rebel songs playing on the tape recorder.

Cashel

Just eleven miles north of Cahir en route to Dublin, **CASHEL** is an obvious next stop. The town has grown around, and is completely dominated by, the spectacular **Rock of Cashel**. No tour bus will bypass the site—so an early-morning or late-afternoon visit will markedly improve your first impressions. The town is not as good a base for visiting the Rock as you might hope— there are a couple of expensive hotels, but **B&Bs** are mostly on the roads in or out (one of the few central ones is *Rockville House*, the Rock; ☎062-61474), and there's no **hostel** in town. The nearest is *Boytonrath Hostel*, signposted a mile off the New Inn–Golden road, two miles from New Inn (May–Oct; bikes for rent and organic food for sale; only ten beds and quite cramped; £2.50). **Eating** in Cashel is also surprisingly limited, though there are good lunches at *Ryan's Royal Oak*, next to the post office at the southern end of town. **Tourist information** sits in the market house in the middle of the main street.

To get to the Rock from here, take the left hand route, then the first left past the Folk Village (a rather tacky reconstruction of "traditional" village life, with a newly asphalted road). You pass St Dominic's Friary (see below), and the next left takes you up the rampart to the entrance to the Hall of Vicars.

The Rock of Cashel

Approached from the north or west, the **Rock of Cashel** (April–Sept daily 9am–7:30pm; Oct–March Mon–Sat 10am–5pm, Sun 2–5pm; tours available) appears as a spectacular mirage of fairytale turrets, crenellations, and walls rising bolt upright from the vast encircling plain. It's a tour operator's dream: on one piece of freak limestone outcrop stands the most beautiful and complete Romanesque church in the country, a gargantuan medieval cathedral, a castle tower house, an eleventh-century round tower, a unique early high cross, and an exquisite fifteenth-century Hall of Vicars—medieval Irish architecture wrapped up in a morning's investigation. Two more medieval priories lie at its feet.

In legend the Rock was formed when the Devil, flying overhead with a large stone in his mouth, suddenly caught sight of Saint Patrick standing ready to form his new church on the site, and in his shock dropped the rock (in the northeast of the county, a striking gap in a mountain range is well known as the Devil's Bit). The Rock is also the place where Saint Patrick is supposed to have picked a shamrock in order to explain the doctrine of the Trinity—God the Father, Christ the Son, and the Holy Ghost as three beings of the one stem; since then the shamrock has of course become Ireland's unofficial emblem.

Approaching the Rock from Cashel town, you come first to the **Hall of the Vicars**, built in the fifteenth century to cater to eight vicar *meistersingers*, who assisted in the cathedral services but were later dispensed with due to jealousy of the power and land their privileged office entailed. The upper floor of the building is divided between the main hall, with screens and a minstrels' gallery, and what would have been the dormitories. The ground floor, a vaulted undercroft, today contains the original **Saint Patrick's Cross**, a unique type of high cross. It once stood outside, where there's now a replica. Tradition has it that the cross's huge plinth was the coronation stone of the High Kings of Munster, the most famous of whom was Brian Boru, killed in his tent by a fleeing Viking at the Battle of Clontarf. The cross is simpler than other high crosses, with a carving of Christ on one side and Saint Patrick on the other. It has an upright supporting its left arm, and is without the usual ring-wheel in the center. It may be that originally the upright and its missing counterpart represented the two thieves crucified with Jesus, and it is also possible that it was never intended as a freestanding cross in the first place, but for erection on a wall.

St Cormac's Chapel (1127–34) is the earliest and most beautiful, by far, of Ireland's surviving Romanesque churches, and the intricacies of its decoration are as spectacular as they are unique. The architecture has clear continental influences—the twin square towers, for example, were probably engineered by monks sent from Regensburg, Germany. The tympana, or panels above the grandiloquent north door (more than likely the original entrance, now leading blindly into the flank of the cathedral) and south door (today's entrance) are also rare in Irish church architecture. Above the north door is depicted a curious carved scene of a large beast ensnaring a smaller beast, itself on the point of being arrowed by a very male centaur in a Norman helmet. The north door is set in six orders of pillars, creating a tunnel-vaulted porch, which in turn is sheltered by an outer stone roof porch. Each arch is crowned with capitals, human heads, fantastic beasts, flutings, and scallops.

The small size of the chapel is particularly Irish, as are the lack of aisles and the steeply pitched stone roof—you'll find similar-looking buildings at Glendalough and Kells, though Cormac's chapel is larger than these. Inside is a nave and a chancel with a small recess in the east wall. The wall opposite you as you walk in has a tall triple arcade, in the center of which is a large round-headed window that would once have lit up the whole interior, illuminating all the painted color—of which a little remains up at the altar and just above the chancel arch. The sarcophagus at the foot of this wall, although fragmented, has an exquisite neo-Celtic design of interlacing serpents and ribbon decoration. It's said to have been the tomb of King Cormac, and certainly it's old enough (1125–50) for this to be true.

The **Cathedral** was begun only ninety years after Cormac's chapel. Although Anglo-Norman in conception, with its Gothic arches and lancet windows, it's a purely Irish-built endeavor, without help from abroad. A graceful limestone building, it features a series of tall, high-set lancet windows, and also some good examples of quatrefoil, or four-petaled, windows, especially above the lancets in the choir space. You'll notice that some of the lancets have been shortened—probably as a measure of fortification. The choir is longer than the nave and both are without aisles. The nave was shortened to make room for the castle tower, built most obviously for refuge, but also as an archiepiscopal residence. A wooden-floored hall would once have been above the nave (the corbels are still apparent), accessible from the castle tower.

The central tower, at the meeting of the transepts, is also on a grand scale, and, typically, did not appear until the fourteenth century. It's supported by four Gothic arches rising from very wide piers, their shafts sweeping beautifully into the concave bottom. Access to the tower is by winding stairs from the south transept (this may not be open to the public, so ask). Passages also ran through the nave and choir walls, supposedly for the outcasts or lepers of the community, so that they could watch the holy ceremony without being seen themselves. The transepts have shallow chapel altars with some tomb and *piscina* niches. In the north transept some panels from sixteenth-century altar-tombs survive, one with an intricately carved retinue of saints and the others more broken but just as dextrously beautiful.

The **Round Tower** is the earliest building on the rock. Its tapering features have led to suggestions that it's as early as the tenth century, though the officially accepted date is the early twelfth century. It's not a typical tower; the entrance door is eight feet above the ground, and various levels of windows guarantee viewpoints in all directions.

From the grounds of the Rock you can look down at **Hore Abbey** on the plain below, and it's an easy enough walk down, over the fields and jumping the road wall. But there's little to be gained in doing this, beyond escaping the sightseers—you can see just as well from the Rock. The thirteenth-century abbey was the last Cistercian daughter monastery of Mellifont to be built before the Reformation, and was probably built by those working on the cathedral on the Rock. Originally a Benedictine foundation, it converted after its abbot had a wild dream that his Benedictine monks were plotting to cut his head off; he expelled them and donned the Cistercian habit in 1269. There's yet another abbey ruin, **Saint Dominick's**, down the south side of the Rock in the town, but this has even less to offer in terms of things to see.

A path known as the **Bishop's Walk** leads from the Rock's rampart entrance down through the back garden of the **Palace Hotel**. The walk is officially for patrons only, but anyone planning to have a bite or a drink in the luxury hotel's basement buttery and bar can use it. The *Palace* was built in Queen Anne style by Archbishop Theophilus Bolton in 1730 as a mansion for the archbishops of Cashel (hence the Bishop's Walk to the Rock). It has a simple redbrick front and a cut stone rear. Cashel owes much thanks to this particular archbishop; it was he who saw the value of Cormac's Chapel and put his wealth into its restoration at a time when the Rock's antiquities were degenerating rapidly towards irrevocable ruin. Another legacy is the **GPA Bolton library** (Mon–Sat 9:30am–5:30pm, Sun 2:30–5:30pm; £1, students 70p; ☎062-61944), out on the road opposite the hotel and set in the grounds of the slender-spired eighteenth-century St John's Protestant Cathedral. Its manuscripts (from as early as the twelfth century), rare maps, and wealth of literary treasures were principally his bequest when he died in 1744. A selection of the books and maps are on display, changing bi-monthly, and well worth viewing.

West to Tipperary Town

Having seen the Rock of Cashel, most people head out of Tipperary for the West, and frankly this isn't a bad idea—the north of the county has little to distract you. Leaving Cashel on the N74, you come after a few miles to **GOLDEN**, where **Athassel Abbey** sits on the banks of the Suir. Once the largest medieval priory in Ireland, its ruins even today are fairly extensive—though not dramatic enough to seriously draw you off your route. The west door is the most impressive feature, and the peacefulness of the surroundings the most rewarding. The plain immediately encircling the abbey was once the site of the town; but it was razed to the ground twice during the fourteenth century—enough to obliterate it forever.

A few miles farther on, twelve miles from Cashel and less than five from the border of Limerick, **TIPPERARY** town, the county's honorary namesake, is tucked by the northern side of the Glen of Aherlow. Like many of these namesake county towns, Tipperary is much less important than it sounds. If you've already visited Clonmel, it will come as something of a shock—compared to Clonmel's yuppie prosperity, it feels out of another century altogether. The town has bold statues sculpted in granite here and there, most notably one to its literary local son, Charles J Kickham, inscribed *Poet, Novelist but Above All Patriot*.

The one spot that might tempt you to stop over briefly is an intriguing small **museum**, hidden away in the foyer of the town swimming pool, by the Cashel road exit. A tiny store of memorabilia, it exhibits photos, letters, and weaponry from the warring years of 1919–23, particularly relating to the old IRA. Tipperary was a particular hot spot during the Anglo-Irish and Civil War strife, especially through its most remembered son, **Seán Tracey**, whose battalion fired the first shots of the Anglo-Irish war (1919–21). There are letters he wrote to his family from prison, some talking about the honor the British had bestowed on him by taking the trouble to get him captured, others of a more domestic nature. A violin belonging to **Joseph Mary Plunkett** (one of the poets executed in the 1916 uprising) hangs beside revolvers, pistols, and land mines. Most striking of all, perhaps, are the photographs of the young officers shown clenching their revolvers, either posturing a rebel's stance of defiance or slightly abashed, with innocent-looking smiles. *Butler's Pantry*, a basic café near the junction of the Cahir road, offers the cheapest place to **eat** in town (£4.50 for four-course evening meal); and there are numerous **B&Bs**, especially on Emly Road.

North up the Suir

Upstream from Cashel, both the Suir itself and the attractions along its banks wane. The river passes through the larger towns of Thurles and Templemore, though its source in the Devil's Bit Mountain falls short of the major town in the northeast, Roscrea. All three centers have railroad connections.

THURLES is of very little interest in itself, but **Holy Cross Abbey** (daily 10am–1pm and 2–6pm), just four miles south, sits beside a broad reach of the Suir and is well worth a visit if you're passing by. Founded in 1180, restored significantly in the fifteenth century, and then left derelict for 400 years, the abbey was totally restored between 1971 and 1985, and is now a thriving parish church as well as a tourist attraction. You really need a chance to see photographs of the period before the restoration to appreciate its significance; these suggest that every other ruin you've seen could as easily be converted. Holy Cross always had singular importance as a center of pilgrimage, claiming to possess a splinter of the wood from the **True Cross**, Christ's cross on Calvary. The splinter relic was reckoned to have been given to Murtagh O'Brien, King of Munster, by Pope Paschal II in 1110. At the turn of the seventeenth century both O'Donnell and O'Neill, the Ulster chiefs, stopped off to revere this relic on their way to Kinsale to meet the French—no doubt hoping they'd be rewarded with a victory over Elizabeth I.

The interior of the church is fully restored, though here there's been no particular attempt at period accuracy; virtually every wall and pillar has been whitewashed, and all the pews have been varnished. The incongruities are, in a sense, inherent in the major fifteenth-century renovations that stripped the site of its medieval character and left a confused mix of revelation and awe for today. Nevertheless, it's rewarding to see the stone ribbing of the vaulted roofs and most particularly the undamaged fifteenth-century **sedilia** in the chancel area, the finest in the country. The *sedilia*, recessed stone seats for the celebrants of the Mass, are of a hard limestone shaped into cusped arches and crowned with crockets, showing decorative friezework as well as the English royal crest and the escutcheon of the earls of Ormond. In the transept to the left of the nave, you'll find one of Ireland's rare medieval frescoes, this one showing a Norman hunting scene painted in browns, reds, and greens. The exterior of the church has a startling full-length slate roof, which reaches down to the cloister pillars. There's a tourist information center, a coffee shop, and a religious goods store within the abbey complex.

If you're cycling or driving north towards Thurles you might also think of taking in **Ballynahow Castle**, a circular castle tower built by the Purcell family in the sixteenth century. To get there from Holy Cross, take the road directly opposite the Protestant church, not the Thurles route (even though the signpost says so). From Thurles itself, it's out on the Nenagh Road, right at the *Jet Petrol* station, and after another mile the castle stands next to a farmhouse where you can pick up the key (also **B&B** accommodation April–Oct; ☎0504-21297). The castle is distinguished by its circular plan; inside, entering the lowest of its five stories is like walking into an igloo, with the corbelled roof curving round almost to the floor. There are many little rooms hidden within the walls and, although undecorated and entirely bare (and quite dark), most of it is in an excellent state of preservation, and strongly atmospheric.

TEMPLEMORE is even less interesting than Thurles, but it does happen to be within easy reach of one of the more historical of listed hostels, **Cranagh Castle**, which on its own is worth a visit—though it's not particularly easy to get to. From Templemore, head first for TEMPLETUOHY, five miles away. Once there, turn right through the village and at the first bend on the other side of town head straight on, off the main road; the castle lies about a mile and a half farther on, through a narrow gap edged by two stone pillars, their rusty white gates swept back. Coming up the Thurles–Templemore road from the south, take the turnoff for LOUGHMOE (a few miles before Templemore) where you'll find the gutted ruin of a four-storied tower house. Head straight on from here for a couple of miles, then turn right towards Templetuohy; Cranagh Castle is three-quarters of a mile down on the left.

The **hostel** occupies parts of the eighteenth-century mansion house attached to the Purcell circular castle—the family lives in the basement. A wide wooden stairway overhung with Titian-hued portraits leads to the dorm rooms on the second and third floors, which are extremely spacious, with single beds and left-over period furnishing. Outside, the yard is full of the sounds of an old-fashioned farm: geese, cocks, cows, and the gallop of horses first thing in the morning. The produce here is all organic, and there's wonderful fresh milk and bread, though not at all cheap. If you're interested in the working of the farm, then ask about the courses on organic farming that are run in the peak season. It's a very relaxing place to take time out (though smokers are discouraged) and, if you're on a bike, the **Devil's Bit Mountain** is within easy reach, and worth the climb for the views.

Roscrea

ROSCREA sits on a low hillock between the Slieve Bloom Mountains to the northeast and the Devil's Bit to the southwest. It's a charming place, with streets running down the hill slopes and a certain conscious lack of worldliness. However, where the rest of Ireland has secluded river sites and spacious countryside for its abbey ruins, Roscrea has the main Dublin–Limerick road running raucously through the middle of **St Cronan's Monastery**. On one side of the road is the round tower, with a garage shed built into the side of it and the top third removed by the British in 1798. Immediately opposite, virtually on the sidewalk, is the west gable of St Cronan's church, its yellow sandstone carved out in a twelfth-century

Romanesque style reminiscent of Cormac's Chapel in Cashel. The rest of the church was demolished during the nineteenth century, and the stone used as building material elsewhere. **Saint Cronan's Cross**, just to the right of the gable, must have been a beauty once, but now it's severely weatherbeaten and hacked. Up by the center of the town is a large, sturdy-looking **Gate Tower Castle** from the thirteenth century backed by a polygonal curtain wall. An imposing eighteenth-century town house now used for office purposes stands at the center of the medieval plot. As both of these are on the Dublin–Limerick route, you'd get a reasonable view staring out of a bus window in slow traffic.

Northwest Tipperary

Once again, in comparison with the south of the county, the northwest lacks significant attractions. The remaining crumbs of interest rest on the shores of Lough Derg, not far from the sole town of any size, Nenagh. There are no hostels on this east side of the lake but there are two across the water at Killaloe and Mountshannon (see *Clare*).

NENAGH is usually jam-packed with heavy traffic trying to plough its way through. It has one singular historical remain, a colossal round castle keep (a *donjon*) with walls twenty feet thick, its five stories reaching a height of a hundred feet and topped with nineteenth-century castellations. Totally gutted within, the donjon (the final retreat tower) was originally one of three round towers which, linked by a curtain wall, formed a Norman stronghold. Founded by Theobald Walter, a cousin of Thomas à Becket, the tower was occupied by the Butlers, then captured in turn by the O'Carrols of Eile, Cromwell, went back to James II and then to and fro between Ginckel (William's chief general) and O'Carrol in the Williamite war. And there the excitement stopped until many centuries later a farmer, wanting to get rid of a nest of sparrows that were feeding on his crops, stuck some gunpowder in the walls of the donjon and blew another hole in the fortress. A few reinforced concrete steps help you to get near the top, but there's little to be seen.

Across the road from the donjon, the Nenagh **heritage center** (£1, students 50p) is set in the old jail, now a Convent of Mercy school. Housed in the octagonal Governor's House, up the driveway, the museum has a display room that houses temporary exhibitions, a mock-up of an old schoolroom with a four-foot mannequin nun (very liberal with her mascara) and a simulated old post office/bar/telephone exchange. In the basement are the usual agricultural items and a realistic but clinical-looking forge. Back at the entrance arch, the cells of the old jail have their original hefty iron cell doors, and you can also see the former exercise yard, tiny and cluttered.

There's a reasonably priced **B&B** (*Sun View*, Ciamaltha Road; ☎067-31064) quite close to the bus and railroad stations and you can get fairly good snack **food** at the *Foodhall* on the main street (Pearse Street). At the northern end of this road, the *JKC Shopping Arcade* provides more substantial lunch possibilities.

Lough Derg

Along the shores of **Lough Derg** are a number of small villages, none of them really worth making a special trip to visit (unless you're after the fishing), but which may be worth calling in at if you're cruising on the lake. The first of them is **DROMINEER**, a small and picturesque yachting harbor, with a tiny castle ruin on its pier. There's food (and drink) at the *Whiskey Still Pub* and more expensively at the *Waterside Restaurant*. **KILGARVAN** has a good antique shop next to the *Brocka-on-the-water* restaurant (Mon–Sat evenings; around £13). **TERRYGLASS**, where *Paddy's Pub* has a nice interior and bar food, offers little else besides a crafts shop in the old church.

LIMERICK

To an even greater extent than Tipperary, everyone passes though **Limerick**, and hardly anyone stays. Once here, you're tantalisingly close to the much more rewarding counties of Cork, Kerry and Clare, and frankly you're not likely to linger. Still, what interest there is lies close to the roads to Cork, Killarney, and Tralee, three main routes that run southwards from Limerick city in the northeastern corner. You should try to see at least one of two places: **Castle Matrix**, an authentic, lavishly restored and renovated tower house on the Killarney route, and **Loch Gur**, a Mesolithic to Neolithic lake and hill enclave of preternatural beauty. Both can be reached with the greatest of ease no matter what transportation you're using.

For **cyclists**, Limerick's terrain is more variable than it's usually given credit for. In its western to southwestern corner, the upland bears a likeness to barren stretches of Donegal, whereas the northern estuary stretch is indeed only a slightly bumpy flatland. The center and east bow in contour towards the eastern frontier of the Tipperary Golden Vale's rich dairy land, but not without gently rising mounds for hills, and broadish trickles for rivers. More so than any other county, the land in Limerick is dotted with an array of **tower castles**, some inhabited, but most in ruins or no more than stumps.

Historically, Limerick's most notable period arrived with the Norman strongholds, the most dominant family being the Fitzgeralds (or **Geraldines**), also known as the earls of Desmond—virtually all of Limerick's significant ruins were once this clan's power bases. They quickly became Gaelicized and ruled as independent monarchs, pulling very much away from English rule. The inevitable confrontation with Britain came to a head at the end of the sixteenth century, when the Geraldine uprising in 1571 against Elizabeth I sparked off a savage war, which brought about their downfall and destroyed in its wake much of the province of Munster.

Limerick City

Squarely on the path of all the major routes across the country, and situated pretty much at the head of the Shannon estuary, **LIMERICK** seems a logical place to make for; actually, it's a disappointment. Though it's the Republic's third city, and heavily industrialized, it somehow falls significantly short of being a metropolis (where Cork succeeds) but lacks the attractions of a typically relaxed western seaboard town (where Galway succeeds). It's also probably the most Catholic of all Irish cities, its churches seemingly crowded every minute of the day.

Like Derry in the north, Limerick also seems tainted by 300-year-old wars, carrying a stigma that it has still to shrug off. Modern unemployment and economic hard times have also left their mark. It rarely feels a terribly friendly town, and at night certain areas can feel positively intimidating. Like it or not, however, this is an important crossroads, and you're likely to end up here at some time, if only to pass straight through.

What you see now is predominantly Georgian, but nevertheless the city has three distinct historical sectors: **Englishtown**, the oldest part of the city, built on an island in the Shannon; **Irishtown**, which began to take shape in the thirteenth and fourteenth centuries; and **Newtown Perry**, the modern center and the most distinct of the three, with beautiful avenues of Georgian streets and houses—where you'll probably do most of your wanderings.

Arriving and Finding a Place to Stay

The railroad and bus stations are next door to each other on Parnell Street in Newtown Perry. There's an *An Óige* **youth hostel** not far away in Perry Square on the far side of People's Park (Grade A and strictly run; ☎061-314672); turn left from the stations to find People's Park. Most of the cheaper **B&Bs** are some way out, above all across the river on the Ennis Road where there seem to be dozens (*Parkview*, ☎061-51505; *Trelawne House*, ☎061-54063; and *Shannonville*, ☎061-53690, for example), but a few more expensive places can also be found around Newtown Perry, particularly in and around Glentworth and Henry streets—head down Davis Street directly opposite the railroads station, then right and left into Glentworth Street, which crosses first O'Connell Street (the main commercial thoroughfare) and then Henry Street farther down towards the Shannon.

The new Shannonside **tourist information office** (the Granary, Michael Street; ☎061-317522) is in a converted mill near where the river branches merge and you cross over into Englishtown; it's easiest found by following O'Connell Street north to the Custom House. You can buy **parking discs** here (20p for two hours) and at local newsstands. **Leaving** Limerick is pretty easy, with regular buses out on all the major roads and (approximately hourly) to **Shannon Airport**—Limerick is the nearest big town. Hitching out is also easy, though if you're heading for Ennis it's worth taking the #6 bus from the station to Lansdowne Bridge, saving a considerable traipse through the suburbs.

History

Limerick's history is worth spelling out. Even today, the town is only too aware of specters from its past. This lowest fording point of the Shannon was first exploited by the **Vikings**, who in the tenth century sailed up the river to *Inis Sibhton* (now Kingstown in Englishtown), an island by the eastern bank formed by a narrow bypass from the main stream now known as Abbey River.

Here they established a port, and for a hundred years war after war raged between them and the native Irish. The Vikings were frequently defeated, and were finally crushed nationally in 1014 at the Battle of Clontarf by Brian Boru, the High King of Ireland. Limerick itself was attacked soon after, and burned to the ground. Most of the Vikings didn't actually leave, but from now on they were gradually assimilated into the Gaelic population. The fate of Limerick itself didn't improve much, however, as over the next hundred years the Irish fought among themselves, burning the town to the ground again and again.

Some kind of stability was established with the arrival of the **Normans** at the end of the twelfth century. They expanded and fortified the town; King John arriving in 1210 to inaugurate King John Castle, one of his finest. High walls were built that were now to keep the Gaels out, and because of this exile the first suburb across the Abbey River began to grow into **Irishtown**. There was trouble again with the visits of Edward Bruce in the fourteenth century; but the real emasculation of the city began with the onslaught of Cromwell's forces under the command of his son-in-law, Ireton, in the late 1640s. It was concluded when the city rallied to the **Jacobite** cause in 1689.

Once James II had lost the Battle of the Boyne in 1690, most of his supporters surrendered quickly—except for the ones at Limerick. As the Williamites advanced, the Jacobite forces within Limerick castle resolved to fight it out under the command of their Irish champion **Patrick Sarsfield**, Earl of Lucan and second in overall command of the Jacobean army. Although the walls of a medieval castle had little hope of withstanding seventeenth-century artillery, Sarsfield gained time by sneaking out, with five hundred of his troops, for a surprise night attack on William's supply train. He succeeded in totally destroying the munitions, while William sat waiting for them in front of the castle walls. However, when the Williamites returned the following year, Sarsfield could finally hold out no longer, and he surrendered on October 3, 1691 to the terms of a **treaty** that's so sore an historical point that it's still stuck in the minds of most Limerick people today.

The treaty terms were divided into military and civil articles. Militarily, Jacobeans were allowed to sail to France, which most of them did, along with Sarsfield himself (he died on the battlefield at Landon, Belgium two years later). The civil agreement promised Catholics the religious and property rights they'd once had under Charles II. Within a couple of months the English reneged on this part of the treaty, and instead enforced anti-Catholic measures extreme even by Irish standards. There followed civil unrest on such a scale that the city gates were locked every night for the next sixty years. The betrayal has never been forgotten—it alone may explain the roots of today's element of Republican support in the city. The concordat was supposedly signed upon the **Treaty Stone** that rests on a plinth at the western end of Thomond Bridge. For many years, although this was used as a stepping stone for mounting horses, small pieces continued to be gouged out as souvenirs; one fragment set into a ring is known to have fetched £1000 in the USA.

It was not a promising start for the modern city, and there are those who claim that festering resentment has stunted Limerick's growth ever since.

Being also hampered with a geographical setting that gives it the Irish name *luimneach* ("a barren spot of land") has not helped. One redeeming factor has to lie in its humor; how else could its corporate motto read *An ancient city well studied in the arts of war.*

The City

The obvious place to start exploring Limerick is the oldest part, **Englishtown**, which still has the narrow curving streets of its medieval origins, if few of the buildings. Crossing Matthew Bridge, the first thing you'll see is St Mary's Cathedral. Before you go in, though, look down to the right on the embankment near the Art College, and your eye should just catch two very fine but armless torsos, metal-sculpted and set upon tall plinths facing one another some forty paces apart. This twentieth-century grotesquerie of war from within and without takes you by surprise—it's an unusually strong statement for Limerick.

St Mary's Cathedral was built at the end of the twelfth century, but only the Romanesque doorway, the nave, and parts of the transepts remain from this period. The chancel, windows, and much of the transepts date from the fifteenth century. The cathedral's unique feature is its misericords, the only set in Ireland. These are choir seats of lovely black oak with reptilian animals—cockatrice, griffins, sphinx, and wild boar—carved in bold relief. There's access up into the belfry of the castellated tower for an even better bird's-eye view of the city.

Farther into Englishtown, next to Thomond Bridge, is **King John Castle** (Mon–Sat 10am–6:30pm; 60p, students 25p; out of season, keys kept at house no. 5 across the road). Built in the early thirteenth century, it retains much of its medieval structure. It was originally a five-sided fortress with four stout round towers, but these were shortened at a much later stage to accommodate artillery positions—though one was actually replaced as a bastion in 1611. Today, the flight of entrance steps from the main road runs up to large, pointed-arch gates set between two, more slender, towers. The steps replace the drawbridge that would once have crossed a moat fed by the Shannon. In fact, the castle is probably more impressive from the outside, staring up at the cliff-like immensity of its walls, than it is from the inside, which is very bare. Ideas are afoot, however, to turn the eighteenth-century barracks houses within into some kind of tourist facility; the tourist information center can give an update. The **treaty stone** can be seen on the far side of Thomond Bridge.

Back across Matthew Bridge you're in **Irishtown**. Again little of the original building survives; much of it is now taken up by massive gray council housing. Perhaps the brightest spark here is the **Custom House**, an eighteenth-century structure of harmonious classical balance. Opposite, the **Town Hall** (Mon–Fri 9am–5pm) contains a small art gallery with portraits of local eighteenth- and nineteenth-century bigwigs and their prize animals. A little farther along, the city **museum** (Tues–Sat 10am–1pm and 2:15–5pm; free) is housed in a fine Georgian end-house in St John's Square, close to St John's Cathedral, which flaunts the tallest spire in the country. The museum is well stocked in the most traditional of ways, displaying currency as far back as the

Viking period, guild regalia, historic maps showing the old walled towns of Englishtown and Irishtown, memorabilia of the various Fenian uprisings (notably a Padraig Pearse letter from the 1916 insurrection) and various Stone, Iron, and especially Bronze Age implements. Many of the Mesolithic items (c.7000–4000 BC) were brought up from the Lough Gur area, and it's worth looking at the excavation photographs of this site before you visit it.

The most interesting museum in Limerick, however, is the **Hunt Museum** (May–Sept Mon–Fri 9:30am–5:30pm; £1, students 60p), housed in the National Institute of Higher Education (NIHE) some way from the center. To get there, head out on the Dublin Road following signs to the NIHE. After a few miles take a left turn immediately after a *Maxol* gas station for Plessay, follow the road round for another third of a mile, then turn left through the white-gated entrance to the reception at the three flag poles, and ask for the museum. This is one of the best conceived museums around, with art objects (mainly Irish antiquities but also European) of consistently high interest, beautifully presented and extensively documented. The museum owes much to the originator of the collection, John Hunt, who was also the enlightened creator of the Craggaunowen habitation project in County Clare (see p.277). Many of the objects here date from the Bronze Age; highlights include the **Antrim Cross**, one of Ireland's most important examples of ninth-century Early Christian metalwork, and thought to be a precursor of the high cross designs at Monasterboice and Kells. There's also a late Bronze Age shield, cauldron and bucket, wholly intact, and a thirteenth-century Limoges enameled casket.

Food, Drink, Music, and the Arts

By city standards, Limerick is not well-stocked with good, cheap places to eat. Reasonable lunches can be found in the cafés on O'Connell Street and around the People's Park, but in the evening you may have to content yourself with fast food and then head for the pub. Places worth trying include *Papa Gino's Pizza Parlour* on Denmark Street, a very ordinary looking eat-in/takeout, but good and inexpensive; *Luigi's* opposite the train station, a basic café/grill; and the *Speakeasy Restaurant Bar* mid-way along O'Connell Street. You'll also find home-cooked lunches and snacks in the basement of the *Belltable Arts Center* (see below).

There's **traditional music** on Monday nights at *McKnights* on Thomas Street; on Mondays (ballad singing) and Thursdays at *Denis Clearys* (bottom end of Denmark Street). Tuesday and Sunday nights there's very good traditional stuff at *Nancy Burkes*, at the top of Denmark Street; Wednesday nights at *The Shannon Arms*; Thursdays at *Costellos* on Dominic Street and the *Glentworth Hotel*, Glentworth Street. *An Chistin*, in a basement on Thomas Street, next to *Olde Tom*, is the pub for Gaelic speakers. And if all you want is a quiet drink, *Nancy Burkes* is one of the nicest pubs to drink in (on its music-free nights). Just outside the city there's also traditional music in BOTHAIR at *Pa Mc Graths* on a Wednesday night and at the *Two Mile Inn* (two miles out on the Ennis Road) on a Friday night.

Other city entertainment can be very good at the **Belltable Arts Center** (50p off all tickets for *Rough Guide* holders) on O'Connell Street; red doors under the granite arch. It usually has a summer season of Irish plays in July and August, with films on Sundays. It's also contrived some gallery space, exhibiting community and national artists (10am–8pm). The **City Gallery** (Mon–Wed and Fri 10am–1pm and 2–6pm, Thurs 2–7pm, Sat 10am–1pm; free), situated in the People's Park, emphasises international contemporary art, with a lesser focus on Irish stuff. Both the *Belltable* and the *City Gallery* are good places to make contact with the Irish arts scene, and are well worth visiting if you've more than half a day in the city. The glossy monthly *What's On* bulletin has entertainments **listings**—you can pick it up at the tourist office, or at arts outlets themselves.

The Road to Cork

Leaving Limerick city in the direction of Cork the main route is the N20, a fast, efficient but rather dull route south. If you have time to stop along the way a smaller road, the R512, has considerably more to offer—above all Lough Gur, site of a wealth of Neolithic finds and one of County Limerick's chief attractions.

Lough Gur

Seventeen miles south of Limerick city, **Lough Gur** looks as though its waters have been accidentally spilled onto the Limerick soil. It's the county's only significant lake, and comes as a rare treat in the midst of an otherwise lusterless terrain. The area around the lake has been an extremely rich source of archaeological finds—though what is visible now is often an extremely frugal sketch of what existed 5000 years ago. The lake is C-shaped, with a marshy area to the east that would complete the full circle. In the middle of this circle is a small rise known as **Knockadoon**. Knockadoon's slopes are studded with faint remains of earthworks showing ring forts and hut foundations from 3500 to 1000 BC. The length of its less secure marshy side is naturally forested and guarded at either end by two medieval tower houses, Bouchier's Castle and Black Castle. Mary Carbery's nineteenth-century book, *The Farm by Lough Gur* (Mercier Press), gives a vivid contemporary account of life by the lough—the farm still stands up the road from the Neolithic huts known as the Spectacles.

Lough Gur must have been the perfect setting for a Neolithic civilization. The lake provided fish, and the gentle hillsides produced berries, nuts, and trappings for animal hunting, as well as protection from the elements—and detection. When the lake was partly drained in the middle of the nineteenth century, and its level dropped by three yards, prehistoric artifacts were found in such quantities that stories tell of whole cartloads being hauled away. This may not be such an exaggeration; visit museums across the world today, and you'll discover some find from Lough Gur on display. The most famous discovery was a 700 BC bronze shield, perfect in its concentric rings of bosses, except for a hacking in two places by the reedcutter who discovered it. The finds here pair well with the Neolithic discoveries made in Meath; this was once a Neolithic living commune, where the *Brugh Na Boinne* site is concerned with ritual and burial. Birdlife today is abundant on the lake and, along with the grazing cattle, antlered goats, and lack of modern buildings, gives a strong intimation of the life of 5000 years ago.

How to Get There and What to See

The simplest approach to Lough Gur is to leave the R512 at Holycross. Follow the road to the northernmost section of the lake, keeping an eye out for a wedge-shaped **gallery grave**. The grave, typically, shows a long gallery space where the bodies of eight adults and four children from around 2000 BC were found. The gallery has parallel double walling of stone slabs filled in with rubble and what's called a septal slab at its back. The road then circles on round the marsh to an **Interpretive Center** (May–Sept daily 10am–1pm and 2–6pm; £1.50; ☎061-85186). Housed in replica Neolithic huts, this attempts to give some idea of what life was like for the early inhabitants. From here the chief attractions on **Knockadoon** are easily accessible on foot.

A quarter of a mile north of the Holycross turnoff, the first thing you'll have seen is a gargantuan **stone circle** close to the main road, the most substantial of the area's prehistoric remains. Possibly the grandest example in the country, it has a ring of standing stones (orthostats) marking out an almost perfect circle. A posthole was found at the center which must have held a stake, from which, with a length of cord attached, the circle could be described. Some of the stones are massive, and are bolstered within their earth sockets by smaller boulders, which were then covered. Flints, arrowheads, blades and bowls were found within the enclosure, but little has been learned about the site's exact function. A circle of this size clearly demanded a good deal of social organization and a strong sense of purpose; the obvious conclusion is that this was a great center for religious rituals, and frustratingly little else can be said.

If you're walking, an alternative approach to Knockadoon is across the stone causeway that leads from near the gallery grave to **Black Castle**. Possibly thirteenth-century, the castle is now weighed down by a swarthy camouflage of nettles, brambles, and trees. It was once quite extensive, with a high curtain wall and square towers, and acted as a principal seat for the earls of Desmond. The pathway north to Bouchier's Castle has three **Neolithic hut** site remains at various degrees up the hill slope. If you're intent on seeing them, you'll really have to rummage around among the wood thickets. A 1681 map shows the Knockadoon peninsula as an island with a drawbridge sticking out of **Bouchier's castle**. It's a typical fifteenth-century Desmond tower house of five stories; but it's still privately owned and can't yet be visited (in any case, there's a better example at Castle Matrix, later in this chapter).

Turning westward from the Black Castle towards the lakeshore in the heart of the C, you'll see various ring forts and hut traces on the bare grassy slopes. It's not much, but even this scant evidence is enough to conjure up a thriving Stone Age community on Knockadoon. Rather than continue along the bank of the lake, it's best to take this opportunity to cross back along the hilltop center, where from a point known as **M** you can get penetrating views into Kerry and Cork, with Limerick spreading towards them in a swath of low hills. **Crock** and **Bolin islands** in the lake are both *crannogs* which the mainland has now caught up with. They were built by laying down a ring of boulders, then the inner space was filled with earth and brushwood. **Garret Island** is a natural island with some stone remains of another Desmond castle.

Kilmallock

Eight miles farther down the main road from Lough Gur, **KILMALLOCK** has some good Norman remains: a tower castle, a town gate, a Dominican friary and a medieval stone mansion on the main street. **St John's Tower Castle** stands in the middle of the street and was the town citadel (you can get the key at the bungalow across the road, but there's little to see here). Turn instead down the lane opposite and you'll find a tiny **museum** (Sat and Sun 2–5pm; otherwise see C Murphy, 8 Orr Street) which won't take a minute to get through, unless you lend an ear to the home-made audiovisual history of the town. One interesting fact that crops up, and which goes a long way to explain the prestigious-looking fortifications and friary bases, is that at the end of the sixteenth century Kilmallock had a population of 2000, compared to Dublin's 5000. Kilmallock swiftly declined—its population today is only 1500.

Bruree

Three miles west of Kilmallock, **BRUREE** was the birthplace of **Eamonn De Valera**, familiarly known as the "big man" or "Dev" to a population for whom he's been the most influential political instigator since the birth of the Free State in 1922. He founded the *Fianna Fail* (Soldiers of Destiny) party in 1926, acted as premier of Ireland in 1932–48, 1951–54 and 1957–59, and assumed the honorary role of President from 1959 to 1973. This makes up a sizable chunk of the Republic's history, and his grip on the nation has left an ambivalent understanding of his worth and integrity.

De Valera was the only leader of the 1916 Easter uprising to survive. His initial death sentence was commuted to imprisonment because of his American dual nationality—he was born in New York, and at this time the British were sensitive to American neutrality in World War I. He escaped from prison in England and was unconstitutionally elected the first President of the Irish Republic in 1919; his almost miraculous survival had marked him as the man to lead Ireland out of seven hundred years of British domination. The Republic immediately declared war on Britain, and when two years of struggle forced the British to negotiate, De Valera's was the leading rebel voice against the signing of the Anglo-Irish treaty in 1921. He wanted to hold out for an all-Ireland Free State, rather than accept only 26 counties out of 32, as was laid down in the Treaty. This stance divided the Irish and provoked the Civil War of 1921–23. The one war he succeeded in keeping the Irish out of was World War II—at the end of which he had the gall to send official commiseration to the Reichstag on Hitler's death, so engrained was the bitterness of his battle with the British.

Yet, through all of this, De Valera himself was never the fighting man in the field. He was brought up just outside Bruree in a small **cottage**, which has now been turned into a modest memorial of the family's household possessions, including a bulky trunk that was used for their return from exile in New York. The cottage is signposted nearly a mile down the road to the right at the eastern end of Bruree village (key from next house on the right, 150 yards farther down the road). At the western end of Bruree village itself is the old schoolhouse, which has been turned into a **museum** (Thurs and Sun, key from house next door; 50p) stocked with memorabilia of the ex-premier and president, plus a few rural items of general interest.

The Road to Killarney

The road to Killarney is by the far the most interesting route south out of Limerick, catching the prim English beauty of thatched cottages in Adare and, much more importantly, taking in Castle Matrix, a Desmond tower house which has been brilliantly restored and gives a unique insight into life as it might have been lived in these castles.

Adare

ADARE has cultivated nearly as many antique shops as pubs. In peak season, it will more than likely be infested with tourists snapshotting the wayside cottages that sit in a neat row, their purposefully quaint deep-brown thatch hanging in low fringes. The cottages represent the nineteenth-century ideal of romanticized rusticity, as realized by the third earl of Dunraven (1812–71), landlord and master of Adare Manor and an eternal improver of circumstances for his tenants. Given that Adare is now probably regarded as the prettiest (and, it must be added, prissiest) village in Ireland, it's hard to believe that before the earl's improvements it was one of the dingiest. The cottages today feature a **tourist information** office, an antique shop and a **restaurant**, *The Mustard Seed*, whose fancy menu is matched by steep prices.

Adare Manor House, to the north of the village, is a huge, nearly obsessive assembly of castellations and turrets in limestone, built by the earl to Gothic revival designs in 1832. This castle has only recently gone into private hands as a grand hotel, cultivating the visits of very rich Americans—it costs even to walk into the grounds. The Maigue River flows by the estate a little farther up, at the head of the village, and although an exciting-looking triumvirate of **medieval buildings** beckons, a golf course steers its course next to all of them, inhibiting any snooping around you might want to do. You're meant to declare your intentions at the clubhouse (entrance a little farther up the road) but you could probably slip from ruin to ruin without being noticed. It may not be worth the effort anyhow, for the **Desmond Castle**—interesting to explore as it looks—is completely bricked up and deemed unsafe. The fifteenth-century **Friary** appears far better preserved, but it was extensively restored as late as the mid-nineteenth century. All of these are perhaps easiest viewed from the bridge.

Back in the village there are ecclesiastical sites too, starting with an **Augustinian Priory** just by the bridge. Beautifully conserved, this still serves as the local Church of Ireland, its interior as close as any to the old medieval model. The **Trinitarian Abbey**, halfway down the main street, was founded in 1230 for the Trinitarian Canons of the Order of the Redemption of Captives, and is the only house of this order in Ireland. Today, it's Adare's Catholic church, with one of its turrets at the back a deserted columbarium. If you're thinking of staying over in Adare—there are a couple of **B&Bs** in the village and plenty more in the immediate surroundings—the old courthouse on the corner of the main street next the public toilet has **traditional sessions** most evenings during the summer.

Rathkeale and Castle Matrix

About eight miles on from Adare, **RATHKEALE** was once an important Geraldine town, and the main source of interest here is their one-time stronghold, **Castle Matrix** (June–Sept Sat–Tues 1–5pm, other times by arrangement; ☎069-64284; £2, children £1). To get there, turn right at the south end of the exceptionally long main street, just after the bridge: the castle lies half a mile down the road, on the right. Castle Matrix is a fifteenth-century tower house built by the seventh earl of Desmond, and would inevitably have met with the same ruinous fate as virtually all the other 427 tower houses that once existed in Limerick, or the 2700 that once stood throughout the country, but for the brilliant restoration work of Seán O'Driscoll, an Irish-American military enthusiast. With his army expertise, he understood the design of the fortifications, and realized that measurements needed to be within an inch for the battlements on the parapets to be effective (in contrast, the ornamental battlements at somewhere like Bunratty in County Clare wouldn't last long in a fifteenth-century siege).

Tower houses flourished between the fifteenth and seventeenth centuries, especially in these southern counties. They provided a robust enough mini-fortress for the shift in the times; Anglo-Norman confidence was increasing, resulting in an expansion of settlements. The big Irish estates were being broken up due to the fall of the old Gaelic chiefs, and more towns were cropping up, with land being cultivated in hitherto uninhabited areas. Tower houses took on a uniform plan, usually of four or five floors, the top floor being the living quarters, the bottom windowless and usually used for storage. Castle Matrix has a tiny chapel recreated on its top floor and a medieval bedroom on another floor. It's stocked with exciting *objets d'art*, including a jewel-encrusted nineteenth-century Gaelic harp made by Fall of Belfast; an ebony writing bureau imported by the Southwells from China and finally donated back to Matrix some years ago, now sitting in the Oriental Room; documents referring to the "Wild Geese" (Irish officers who fled to the continent at the beginning of the seventeenth century); and the most remarkable item of all to return home—the original deed of the Southwells (the earls of Desmond), which Seán O'Driscoll accidentally came across in London's Portobello Road.

The castle derived its name from the *matres*, a Celtic sanctuary, on which it stands. The scattering of destroyed cashels and raths in the surrounding area give substance to the idea of an ancient sanctuary here. An annex of the castle offers luxury **B&B** at around £47 a night (including hot tub), and gourmet banquets are also held at the request of groups. *Rathkeale House* hotel offers food and accommodation for those living slightly less high on the hog (at about £14 a night).

Newcastle West

Between Rathkeale and Newcastle West a signpost points to **Ardagh**, the ring fort where the wonderful Ardagh Chalice was found in 1868 (it's now in the Dublin Museum); but the site here is unimpressive and it's not worth dragging yourself off the main road.

NEWCASTLE WEST should make the last, but very brief, stop on your way out of Limerick, just to look at the almost perfectly preserved **Desmond Banqueting Hall**. The hall is on the main square and very little fuss is made of it; but it's part of a scattered and hidden complex of ruined buildings—a keep, a peel tower, a bastion, and curtain wall. Even though this was once the principal seat of the Geraldines, the town hasn't harnessed its history to its advantage. The hall is in a near-perfect state of preservation, and is well ready for an inspired restoration. At present, apart from a marriage fireplace said to have been imported from Egypt, it's all bare. You can get the key from Mrs. Maureen Nash at what used to be the old gatehouse, down the driveway at the immediate right of the hall grounds.

There's another excellently preserved but entirely deserted tower house, **Glenquin Castle**, signposted left several miles off the Newcastle–Abbeyfeale road by a gas station (head for Killeady). It has very good views of the countryside, but the effort to get here is really only worthwhile if you have a car.

The Road to Tralee

The **road to Tralee**, the N69, is the least interesting of the three major routes across Limerick. It runs parallel to the Shannon estuary, but mostly through flat alluvial land, without the compensation of having the waters alongside except for the last few miles into Glin.

The first sign of interest you'll spot is **Carrigogunnell Castle**—no more than a well-worn ruin, overgrown with shrubs and trees, but with striking views across the estuary's waist. It's probably not worth leaving the main road; catch sight of it as the road passes CLARINA, from where the ruin cuts a dramatic appearance atop its rocky outcrop. The road passes a few more tower houses on the right and a Forest Park (with **camping**) on the left before reaching ASKEATON. Here, there's an Anglo-Norman **Friary** next to the Deel River, just off the main road at its second entry to Askeaton from the east. The friary was founded by the fourth earl of Desmond, Gerald the Poet, in 1389. It now seems particularly hidden away, and has one of the loveliest cloisters you'll come across and some excellent window tracery. From the dormitory above, you can pick out the towering remains of the **Castle**, penned in towards the center of the town. This is worth no more than a quick scout around (keys from Billy Casey at the house by the entrance gate); there's a large banqueting hall, very similar to the better example in Newcastle West, its vaulted ground-floor chambers remaining just within the walls. A very precarious-looking end tower (fifteenth-century) stands upon a rock in the center of what was once an island in the Deel. The castle's present decay does little to suggest its one-time Anglo-Norman prominence, when it flourished in the hands of the earls of Desmond, until their fall to the Earl of Essex during the sixteenth century.

FOYNES is a moderately busy seaport, presently occupied with plans to host a museum that will celebrate the town's past as an aviation center of flying boats. In the late 1930s and early 1940s, Foynes, as Limerick's only seaport, was the terminal for a transatlantic flying-boat service. Moving on, the afforested hillslopes that now appear mark a pleasant route along the estuary as far as **GLIN** on the Limerick-Kerry border.

travel details

Trains
From Waterford to Dublin (4 daily; 2hr 30min); Limerick (2 daily; 2hr 30min).
From Limerick two trains daily to Tipperary (1hr 30min); Cahir (1hr 50min); Clonmel (2hr 10min); Carrick-on Suir (2hr 30min).
From Limerick Junction to Dublin (4 daily; 1hr 50min).

Bus Éireann
From Waterford to Dublin (2 daily; 3hr 30min).
From Limerick to Dublin (1 daily; 6hr); Tipperary (6 daily; 50min).

Private buses
Pierce Kavanagh Coaches (☎01-734344) leave **from Dublin**, Liberty Hall on Fridays at 5:30pm for Cashel (8pm), Cahir (8:15pm), and Mitchelstown (9pm), continuing on to Cork and Bantry. A return service **from Bantry** leaves on Sundays at 3:30pm for Cork (5:15pm), Mitchelstown (6:10pm), Cahir (6:30pm), Cashel (6:45pm), and Dublin. Another service runs **from Thurles**, Liberty Square (Mon–Sat 8:45am) for Dublin, and **from Dublin**, Burger King, O'Connell St (Mon–Sat 6pm) to Thurles.
Funtrek (☎01-730852) runs daily services **from Limerick**, Roscrea, and Nenagh to Dublin, and **from Waterford** to Dublin.
Waterford Travel Club (☎051-77177) runs daily services **from Waterford**, Hanover Street, to Dublin.

CHAPTER SEVEN

CORK

Cork—Ireland's largest county—is the perfect place to ease yourself gently into the exhilarations of Ireland's west coast. **Cork City** is the south's self-proclaimed cultural capital, and manages to be simultaneously both a relaxed and a spirited place. There are no spectacular sights, but Cork has to be one of Ireland's most pleasurable and accessible of cities. Always a port, and with an island at its core, Cork nestles well inland on the estuary of the Lee River, which sustains the city with that same clear, balmy atmosphere that pervades most of the county, and in particular its coast and rivers. In the east of the county maritime history is still more richly distilled, in the small ports of **Cobh**, **Youghal**, and—most of all—**Kinsale**, all suggestive of a prosperity that Ireland could have had were it not for the systematic strangulation of its overseas trade by Britain. On the other side of this coin are the Anglo-Irish treasures: the Neoclassical perfection of **Fota House** near Cobh, and the outrageously sumptuous art treasures of **Bantry House** in the west. Both rank among the finest stately homes in Ireland.

Every county of Ireland's wild west coast has its devotees, and Cork is certainly no exception. The place elicits strong reaction from locals and visitors alike, and its rivalry with neighboring Kerry is legendary. Critics like to call it tame or mild—even genteel—since it can only occasionally match the sheer wild physicality of coasts farther north. But this quality probably has as much to do with the people, and the relative mildness of the weather, as with landscape. And west Cork is quite different.

In the main the charms of the Cork countryside are those of a gently rural backwater, but as you head west along a fabulously indented coastline of hidden bays and coves to the wild peninsulas of the extreme southwest, or through the ravine of Gougane Barra high above **Glengarriff** and **Bantry Bay**, the soft contours of a comfortable and easy prettiness slip away to reveal beauty of a more elemental kind. There's not as much of this as you might find in, say, Kerry, but in the **Cahir Mountains** careening up from Bantry Bay, the scintillating cliff scenery of **Mizen Head**, or the island-strewn **Roaring Water Bay**, teeming with birdlife, Cork has landscapes as exciting and dramatic as you'll find anywhere.

Cork City

Old **CORK CITY**—the second city of the Irish Republic—is built on an island, the two channels of the river Lee embracing it on either side, while nineteenth-century suburbs sprawl up the surrounding hills. The river gives

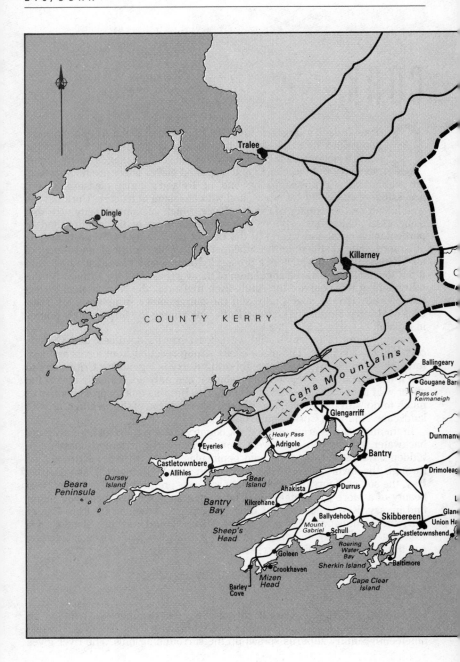

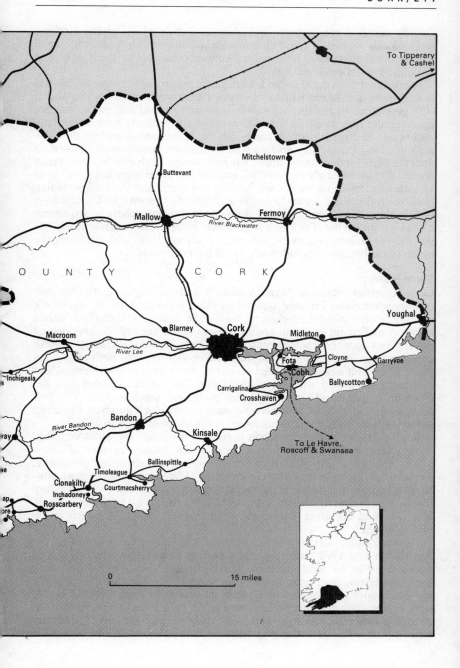

the city center a compactness and sharp definition which creates exciting tensions. It's a place of great charm, with a history of vigorous intellectual independence that makes it the natural cultural center of the South, as well as its political and commercial hub.

Approached from rural Ireland, Cork has a surprisingly cosmopolitan feel to it. Evidence of the city's history as a great mercantile center is everywhere, with gray stone quaysides, old warehouses, and elegant and quirky bridges spanning the river to either side. Many of the city's streets were at one time waterways: St Patrick's Street had quays for sailing ships, and on the side-walk in Grand Parade are capstans where merchant vessels were moored up until the eighteenth century. Important port though Cork may be, however, it doesn't feel overridingly commercial, and the Lee is certainly not the river of an industrial town. Its waters are healthy and clear, and their all-pervading presence reflects and seems to double any light, so that even on the cloudiest of days there is a balmy, translucent quality to the atmosphere which effects a calm on the visitor. Cork is a welcoming, friendly place. While it has the vibrancy to enliven and excite, the pace is always Irish, and somehow the urban island breathes enough space for all temperaments.

Some History

Cork (*Corcaigh*, meaning "marshy place") had its origins in the seventh century when **Saint Finbarr** founded an abbey and school on the site where the impressive nineteenth-century Gothic St Finbarr's Cathedral stands today. A settlement grew up around the monastic foundation, overlooking marshy swamp where the city center now stands. In 820 the **Vikings** arrived, bringing their usual violence and destruction, and wrecked both abbey and town. They built a new settlement on one of the islands in the marshes, and eventually integrated with the native Celts. The twelfth century saw the **Norman** invasion and Cork, like other ports, was taken in 1172. The new acquisition was fortified with massive stone walls, which survived Cromwell but were destroyed by Williamite forces at the **Siege of Cork** in 1690.

From this time on the city began to take on the shape recognizable today. **Expansion** saw the reclamation of marshes and the development of canals within the city, and waterborne **trade** brought increasing prosperity. Evidence of this wealth survives in the form of fine eighteenth-century bow-fronted houses, and the ostentatious nineteenth-century church architecture that decorates the city—sharp, gray, and Gothic, much of it by the Pain brothers. Traces of the great dairy trade of that period can still be seen in the Shandon area.

More recently, Cork saw much violence and suffered greatly during the Anglo-Irish and Civil wars; the city's part in **Republican** history is well documented in the local museum. The Black and Tans reigned here with particular terror, destroying much of the town by fire, and were responsible for the murder of Thomas MacCurtain, the mayor of Cork, in 1920. Cork's next mayor, Terence MacSwiney, was jailed as a Republican and died in Brixton prison after a hunger strike of 74 days. A popular hero, his hunger strike remains one of the longest achieved in the history of the IRA. One of his colleagues in Cork prison, Joseph Murphy, achieved the longest fast on record, going 76 days without food.

As part of the Republic, Cork has continued to develop—as a port, a university town, and a cultural center—and to assert its independence from Dublin.

Arrival and Accommodation

One of the joys of Cork is the fact that its scale is human; you are likely to walk when exploring most of what it has to offer. **Buses** to the suburbs and outlying towns and villages all go from the **Bus Éireann station** at Parnell Place alongside Merchant's Quay, and most of these also pick up passengers from the more central St Patrick's Street. There is a standard fare of 52p within the city. The *Bus Éireann* station also operates an expensive nationwide bus service, while the **train station** is about one mile out of downtown on the Lower Glanmire Road. *Bus Éireann* and train inquiries are taken at ☎021-504422. **Private buses** (see "Listings" and "Travel Details") operate from various central points, mostly along St Patrick's Street, and from the junction of Western Road with Mardyke Parade. If you arrive by **ferry** you'll be at RINGASKIDDY, some ten miles out, from where you can catch a #157 bus into the center. Coming in by **plane** you can easily pick up a #162 bus for the fifteen-minute journey into town. If you're **driving** remember that, as in all the major cities, a disc parking system is in operation—discs can be bought from newsagents or the tourist office.

The **tourist office** on Grand Parade (☎021-273251) will reserve rooms in **B&Bs** for around £9–10, plus 50p for a local phone call, £1.50 long distance. There's plenty of B&B accommodation along the Western Road, near the University, and along Lower Glanmire Road at the opposite end of town, near the train station. Cork's **An Óige hostel** (1–2 Redclyffe, Western Road; ☎021-543289; grade A; open all year) is a good budget place, or the *Cork Tourist Hostel* (Belgrave Place, Wellington Road, up behind MacCurtain Street; ☎021-505562; £4) is a more central alternative. There are also two **campgrounds**: *Cork City Caravan and Camping Park* is the nearest to the center of town (☎021-961866; Easter–Oct; £2.90, low season £2.50, plus 75p per person), and has a **laundromat** and **bike rental** on the site. Pick up a #14 bus from St Patrick Street or South Main Street (every 20 min) and the driver will put you down outside the site; last bus out of town runs at 11:15pm. To walk or bicycle, climb Barrack Street beside Sullivans Quay, follow it for about half a mile, then take Lough Road on the left. *Cork Caravan Park* is near the airport (☎021-961611; April–Oct; £3.50 per unit, 25p per person)—the Airport/Kinsale bus stops 600 yards from the site, or follow the signposts to Kinsale and airport, and then the signs from the airport gates.

Cork is a great city for **festivals**, the biggest of which is the **jazz festival** over the last weekend in October, but if you are planning your stay to coincide with one of them, advance booking is essential. Without it you are liable to find yourself overcharged in an inaccessible and inconvenient private home. There is usually a **Festival Accommodation Office** to cope with the crowds, but its location changes annually, so ask at the tourist office.

The City

Cork has no really spectacular sights, but it's a fine place to wander around: along the quays, through the narrow lanes, into the markets, up to Shandon. The ambience and sense of place are enjoyable in themselves, and for those with a taste for it there's plenty of nineteenth-century Gothic church architecture punctuating the river banks, and evocative remnants of a great mercantile past. Exploration on foot is rewarding—the city's medieval core is embedded in its central narrow lanes, and the meshing of its history can be felt embodied in its buildings, reflected in the constant flow of the Lee. But don't go expecting to be astounded. Enjoying Cork city is to do with tuning in to the pace and life of the place.

The **city center** is essentially the island, with its quaysides, pretty bridges, alleyways, and lanes, plus that segment to the north of the Lee that has the bustling MacCurtain Street as its central thoroughfare. The graceful wishbone arc of **St Patrick's Street**, with **Grand Parade**, forms the modern commercial heart, with a healthy smattering of the modish amenities generally associated with much larger European cities. Not that you are ever engulfed by commercialism—aggressive multinationals have not been allowed to dominate, and expensive fashion houses exist alongside modest traditional businesses. It is in such immediate contrasts that the charms of the city lie. A hundred yards from the elegant storefronts of St Patrick's Street you'll find **Coal Quay market** in Cornmarket Street—a flea market worthy of the name, well worth investigating if you are fascinated by the shabby side of a damp, rural life in its unchanged nineteenth-century setting. A minute's walk from Coal Quay Market down Paul Street brings still more variety in the environs of French Church Street and Emmet Place. **Paul Street** itself is experiencing a resurgence of commercial and artistic activity with new restaurants, artists' studios, specialist bookshops, and period clothes shops.

The eastern, downstream end of the island is the most clearly defined; many of its quays are still in use, and it's here that you most clearly get a sense of the old port city. Trips out into **Cork Harbour** are available during the summer months—ask at the tourist office. In the west the island loses definition in a predominantly residential area. Heading in this direction, though, you can follow the signs off Western Road for **Fitzgerald Park**, home of the **Cork Public Museum** (Mon–Fri 11am–1pm & 2:15–5pm, until 6pm June–Aug; admission free). Primarily a museum of Republican history, it has an excellent commentary on the part played by local characters and events in the Republican movement. There are exhibits of local archaeological and geological finds, too, and a section on the history of the dairy trade. While in the park it's worth trying the **tearooms**—a cosy atmosphere with delicious homemade cake and soups, and a useful source of information for what's on in the arts, both downtown and at the University.

North of the river Lee, **MacCurtain Street** forms the central spine of the city, and seems to act as a magnet for all the activity up here. Bristling with life among a jumble of shops, pubs, ice-cream parlors, and clubs, it provides rich ground for all sorts of food, booze, and music.

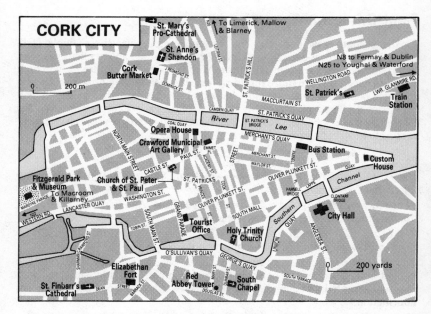

CORK CITY

St. Mary's Pro-Cathedral · To Limerick, Mallow & Blarney · St. Anne's Shandon · Cork Butter Market · N8 to Fermay & Dublin · N25 to Youghal & Waterford · WELLINGTON ROAD · St. Patrick's · LWR. GLANMIRE RD. · Train Station · 0 200 m · J. REDMOND ST · DOMINICK ST · ST. PATRICK'S HILL · LEITRIM ST · MACCURTAIN ST. · CAMDEN QUAY · ST. PATRICK'S QUAY · River Lee · COAL QUAY · ST. PATRICK'S BRIDGE · Opera House · MERCHANT'S QUAY · NORTH MAIN STREET · Crawford Municipal Art Gallery · EMMET · PAUL ST. · STREET · MERCHANT ST · MAYLOR ST · Bus Station · Custom House · PARNELL · OLIVER PLUNKETT ST. · QUAY · Channel · Fitzgerald Park & Museum · CASTLE ST. · Church of St. Peter & St. Paul · ST. PATRICKS · PRINCES · COOK · OLIVER PLUNKETT ST. · PARNELL BRIDGE · CLONTARF BRIDGE · To Macroom & Killarney · WASHINGTON ST. · MARDYKE PARADE · LANCASTER QUAY · SOUTH MAIN ST. · GRAND PARADE · SOUTH MALL · Southern · ANGLESEA ST. · City Hall · WESTERN RD · TOBIN ST. · Tourist Office · Holy Trinity Church · UNION · QUAY · O'SULLIVAN'S QUAY · GEORGE'S QUAY · SOUTH TERRACE · 0 200 yards · Elizabethan Fort · SHANDON BARRACK ST. · BARRACK ST. · DEAN STREET · St. Finbarr's Cathedral · MARY ST. · Red Abbey Tower · South Chapel · DOUGLAS ST.

On this side of the river, too, is the area of **Shandon**, a reminder of Cork's eighteenth-century status as the most important port in Europe for dairy products. To get there head up John Redmond Street, or simply aim for the giant fish atop the church tower. The most striking survival is the **Cork Butter Exchange**, stout nineteenth-century Classical buildings recently given over to select craft workshops—expensive and very much geared to the US tourist market. The old **butter market** itself sits like a generously proportioned butter tub in a cobbled square, and is currently being renovated to house the Irish National Ballet. To the rear is the pleasant Georgian church of **St Anne's Shandon** (1750), easily distinguishable from all over Cork city by its weather vane—an eleven-foot salmon. For 50p you can view the not particularly remarkable interior of St Anne's, and some old books, or for a much more worthwhile £1.50 you can climb the tower (two of its sides finished in red sandstone, two in white limestone) for excellent views, and ring the famous bells—a good stock of sheet tunes is provided.

The stark precision of nineteenth-century Gothic which is repeated time and again in the city's churches may not be to everyone's taste, but it undeniably gives the city a rhythmic architectural cohesion. Both Pugin and Pain are very much in evidence, Pugin in the brilliant Revivalist essay of the Church of **St Peter and St Paul** on Friar Matthew Quay, with its handsome lantern spire, and in St Patrick's Church on Lower Glanmire Road. Best of all is William Burges' **St Finbarr's Cathedral** (built 1867–79); obsessively detailed, its impressive French Gothic spire provides a grand silhouette on the southwesterly shoulder of the city.

Food, Drink, and Entertainment

As the second most populous city in the Republic and the nation's (self-proclaimed) cultural capital, Cork not surprisingly has an excellent range of entertainment. Pub sessions and more "sophisticated" discos are easy to find; so, less expectedly, are more highbrow cultural events. The *Cork Examiner* is the local paper with mainstream what's on information. Other places to pick up on what's happening are *The Quay Co-op*, *The Triskel Arts Centre*, *The Phoenix* and the *School of Music*—all detailed below. There's also an excellent range of cheap eating places.

Food

Bully's, 40 Paul Street (Mon–Sat noon–11:30pm, Sun 5–10pm). Wine bar serving pizzas, fresh pasta, and fish.

The Crawford Municipal Art Gallery, Emmet Place. An affordable offshoot of the famous Ballymaloe restaurant near Cloyne.

The Crawford Municipal School of Design, Sharman Crawford Street. Cheap restaurant, open during school semester only.

Fitzgerald Park Cafe, next to museum (Mon–Sat 10am–5pm). Handy for the budget hostel, a cosy and convivial place much patronized by students, with reasonably priced, homemade soups and cakes. Another good place for event information.

Halpins, Cook Street, (Mon–Sat 9am–6pm). Self-service delicatessen restaurant, serving delicious salads, seafoods, quiches, and cakes; from £3.

Harlequin Cafe, 26 Paul Street (10am–6pm). Cheap and fairly wholesome café, though not all as homemade as its appearance might suggest. A nice spot to sit and watch the world drift past, and a good place to find out about drama and arts events.

Huguenot's, French Church Street. Pricey French restaurant, excellent food.

Luciano's, MacCurtain Street. Great pizzas.

Malibu's, Perry Street (daily, 24 hours). Rather sterile, fast-food atmosphere, but worth knowing about if you feel hungry after pub closing time.

O'Brien's Ice-cream Parlour, MacCurtain Street (open until 10:50pm). Great homemade ice cream.

Pharo's, St Patrick's Street (down alleyway besides *Hobb's Menswear*, open until 6pm). Atmospheric café serving sandwiches, coffee and salads.

The Phoenix, Union Quay (Mon–Fri 11am–4pm). Pub with a vegetarian restaurant upstairs.

The Quay Co-op, 24 Sullivan's Quay (Mon & Tues 11am–6pm, Wed–Sat 11am–10:30pm). Delicious, large vegetarian meals, plus one non-vegetarian meal daily, soups, puddings and teas, all in surroundings of wonderfully faded elegance. Meals from £2.50; more expensive in the evenings.

The Triskel Arts Center, Tobin Street, off South Main Street. Quiche-and-salad type café, tasty and good value, from £2.50.

Pubs

There are plenty of good watering holes in the city, and if all you want is a drink, you won't need a guide to find somewhere. Many of them also have music, traditional or otherwise, and the following list should give some good pointers on where to find the best of this. As with any large city, though, forums and session nights change, so it's worth asking around for the best of the current action. Wherever you end up, this is not a difficult town to enjoy yourself in.

An Spailpín Fanach, Tig Taoairne Uidir 1779. Traditional Irish music nightly, bar food daily.

Applejacks, MacCurtain Street. Good jazz on Thursday.

The Donkey's Ears Bar, Union Quay. Sometimes has traditional music on Tuesday.

Gables, Douglas Street. Traditional sessions and set dancing on Thursday.

Isaac Bells, St Patrick's Quay (behind the *Metropole Hotel*). Very popular, this bar has jazz on Sunday, 5–8pm , and reggae on Monday, 8:30pm.

Loafers, 26 Douglas Street. Trendy drinking spot that attracts a young crowd.

The Lobby, Union Quay (next to the *Phoenix*). Live rock and pop bands most nights.

The Long Valley, Winthrop Street. A must purely for the eccentricities of the owner and the clientele, the place also does good substantial sandwiches.

The Metropole, MacCurtain Street. Sunday lunchtime jazz, plus jazz, ballads and folk most nights; free.

Nosey Parkers, Washington Street. Jazz Sunday morning.

The Ovens Tavern, Oliver Plunkett Street. A nice, ordinary bar with occasional set dancing.

The Phoenix, Union Quay (near the City Hall). Assorted live bands, plus traditional Irish night on Wednesday. A good place to find out what's going on generally.

Clubs

There are plenty of disco-type clubs around the city center, easy enough to stumble upon late at night. Below are some of the more interesting, again with live entertainment.

Cumnra Na Gael, Dyke Parade. An Irish Club (Gaelic spoken), with traditional sessions three nights a week. No entry charge.

De-Lacy House, 74 Oliver Plunkett Street. Busy central club; ordinary disco plus bands.

Mojo's, George's Quay. Bikers' and students' pub/club that has free music sessions: Sunday, traditional Irish; Wednesday, bluegrass; Thursday, blues; other nights, local bands and student discos. Generally no admission charge, and information posted about what's happening elsewhere.

Sir Henry's, South Main Street (£3, concessions for unemployed). Bands at weekends. Gigs start at 8pm but it's worth checking ahead what time they will finish—sometimes 11:30pm, sometimes 2am. Rock-orientated, plus punk, thrash, etc. Tuesday is film night, generally starting around 9pm, the idea being that you can watch and drink at the same time.

Art, Theater, Film, and Festivals

The latest hub of artistic activity in Cork is the **Triskel Arts Center**, found down the narrow and dingy Tobin Street, off South Main Street (☎021-272022; concessions on tickets for students and unemployed so take ID). It has changing exhibitions of contemporary art, a film theater, a continual program of performance art, poetry reading, contemporary music, and a very good health-food café. It is also an excellent source of information about what's on—Triskel will know about any theater or music going on in the city.

Other **art galleries** include the *Crawford Municipal Gallery* in Emmet Place (Mon–Fri 10am–5pm, Sat 9am–1pm), with a permanent collection of Irish and European painting and usually an interesting temporary exhibition. Nearby on Lavitt's Quay, the *Cork Arts Society* (Tues–Sat 11am–2pm & 3–6pm) is a good commercial gallery, with exhibitions of contemporary works changing every two weeks.

The **Cork Opera House** (☎021-276357) in Emmet Place offers a full program of drama, concerts both classical and popular, ballet, opera, review and variety; though very rarely anything at all out of the mainstream. A more intimate style of theater is found at **The Granary**, Glenville Place, though this has nothing like the range or number of productions. **The Everyman Theatre** is currently moving to *The Palace* in MacCurtain Street, so check with the tourist office for developments. Similarly, ask at the tourist office for what's playing at the **Ivernia Theatre** (☎021-272703) which sometimes has interesting traditional Irish entertainment. For classical concerts, look in at the **School of Music**, on Union Quay.

Cork has an extremely popular **international jazz festival** the last weekend in October. With music bursting out of every doorway, you don't need to go and see the big names to enjoy yourself if you are short of cash. It's a great time to be in the city, but advance reservation for accommodation is strongly advised. There is generally a special Festival Accommodation Office to cope with the extra crowds—its location varies, so ask locally, at one of the big halls or at the tourist office. There's also an important **film festival** in the last week of September and the first of October, with films screened at Triskel and the Opera House.

Listings

Airlines *Aer Lingus*, 30 Patrick Street (☎021-274331); *Ryanair*, 16A Worship Street (☎021-274444).

Airport Cork airport, for domestic flights only, is 5 miles along Kinsale Road; ☎ 021-313131 for flight information.

Banks Branches of the *Allied Irish* in Patrick Street, North Main Street, Bridge Street, and Western Road.

Bike Rental *Kilgrews Ltd*, 30 North Main Street (☎021-273458); *D.M.D. Cycles*, 18 Grafton Street (☎021-21529); or from the campground.

Bookshops *Waterstones*, Patrick Street; *Liam Russell*, Oliver Plunkett Street; *Quay Co-op*, Sullivan's Quay; *New Books* (Communist bookshop), French Church Street; *Collins*, Carey's Lane; *Mercier Bookshop*, 4 Bridge Street.

Buses The *Bus Éireann* station is on Parnell Place, alongside Merchant's Quay; local and intercity buses operate from here. *Bus Éireann* services cover the entire country: the main towns daily, smaller places less frequently. Check the detailed timetables for your intended route at the bus station if you're relying on getting somewhere. Phone ☎021-50442 for information. Cheaper, private buses to Dublin are operated by *Joe O'Reilly Travel* (Western Road; ☎021-270395) and *Pierce Kavanagh* (☎021-272520), and on Fri & Sun by *P.S. Travel* (55 Dame Street, Dublin; ☎01-796444)—no Cork address, but see "Travel Details" at the end of this chapter.

Camping equipment *The Tent Shop*, Rutland Street, off South Terrace, offers camping gear for sale or rent.

Car Rental *Great Island Car Rentals*, 47 MacCurtain Street (☎021-503536 or 811609).

Pharmacies *Falvey's Pharmacy*, Bridge Street; *Denis O'Leary*, 8 Grand Parade, ☎021-274563. For information on after-hours rotation service, phone ☎021-965588.

Dental Emergencies Regional Hospital ☎021-545100.

Family Planning Clinic Tuckey Street, off Grand Parade (☎021-277906); *Cura*, Paul Street, offers free pregnancy testing (☎021-501444).

Ferries to France operate from Ringaskiddy, about ten miles from Cork. *Brittany Ferries*, 42 Grand Parade (☎021-277801), sail to Roscoff; *Irish Ferries* Glanmire House, Lower Glanmire Road (☎021-504333), operate services to Cherbourg and Le Havre. *Sealink*, for Rosslare–Fishguard, are based at the tourist office (☎021-272965). *Swansea–Cork Ferries*, not currently operating, have an office at 55 Grand Parade (☎021-271166).

Gay Info ☎021-317026.

Hurley and Soccer Every Sun afternoon from Sept to June in G.A. Stadium, Blackrock.

Laundromat MacCurtain Street, next door to the *Everyman Palace Theatre*, Mon–Sat 9am–9:30pm. Also at 1 Devonsrent Street and 25 Leitrim Street.

Lesbian Line Thurs 8–10pm, ☎021-317026.

Money Exchange At the tourist office.

Public Baths Douglas Swimming Pool, Douglas Road (☎021-293073).

Quay Co-op On Sullivans Quay: a healthfood store and a secondhand and alternative book shop. The co-op is also a campaigning, educational, and social focus for gay and women's issues.

Rape Crisis Center 27a MacCurtain Street (☎021-968086), or write to P.O. Box 42, Brian Boru Street.

Taxis *Arrow Cabs* ☎021-311311; *Cara Cabs* ☎021-505722; *Express Hackney Service* ☎021-507766.

Trains The station is on Lower Glanmire Road, about a mile from downtown. ☎021-50442 for information.

Travel Agents *USIT* have two offices in Cork: at 10–11 Market Parade (☎021-270900; Mon–Fri 9:30am–5:30pm, Sat 11am–4pm) and *UCC Student Travel*, The Bootle Library, University College (Mon–Fri 9:30am–5:30pm, Sat 10am–1pm).

Tourist office Grand Parade (☎021-273251).

Women's Place and Library, c/o Quay Co-op, 24 Sullivan's Quay (☎021-317660).

Around Cork City

There are several good short trips that will get you out of Cork for the day, but back in time to take advantage of the city's nightlife. **Blarney** offers history and the scenic Lee valley; **Fota** has wild animals and eighteenth-century Classicism; and **Cobh**, seaside and water sports. It is also possible to visit **Kinsale** for the day from Cork, but allowing more time makes sense; once there you'll be reluctant to return, and probably find yourself somehow lured farther west around the coast.

Blarney

BLARNEY is an easy six miles from Cork city; buses leave the bus station every half hour. If you can manage to divorce the **castle** (Mon–Sat; May 9am–7pm; June & July 9am–8:30pm; Aug 9am–7:30pm; Sept 9am–6:30pm; Oct–April 9am–sundown. Sun; summer 9:30am–5:30pm, winter 9:30am–sundown) from the whole "Blarney phenomenon" it actually is a fine strong-hold, built in 1446 by Dermot McCarthy, king of Munster. The **Blarney Stone** has been kissed by visitors for over a hundred years, the legend being that to do so gives you the gift of eloquent and persuasive speech. The most famous story of how the legend came about tells of one McCarthy—King of Munster and Lord of Blarney—who, supposedly loyal to the colonizing Queen Elizabeth I, never actually got around to fulfilling any of the agreements between them, always sidetracking her emissaries with drinking, dancing, and sweet talk. He was said to be able to talk "the noose off his head." In her frustration the queen is said to have eventually cried out "Blarney, Blarney, what he says he does not mean. It is the usual Blarney." And so the word entered the English language.

The stone itself is a four-foot-by-one-foot limestone block set in the battlements 83 feet above the ground, so kissing it requires a head for heights. If you want to do so, you'll have to join the line in the castle keep from which you can watch everyone else (one at a time) being dangled backwards by the shins over the battlements aided by two strong men. This also gives you time to decide whether or not you really want to join in. According to a less challenging legend, the stone is half of the Stone of Scone, given to Cormac McCarthy by Robert the Bruce in gratitude for the support of 4000 men at the Battle of Bannockburn (the rest is in London, at Westminster Abbey). The views from the top of the castle are superb.

In the castle grounds **Rock Close** is a nineteenth-century folly, a rock garden supposedly built around druidic remains. Authentic or not, it is a pity that myths are such big business around here, because without the commercials these ancient yews and oaks could create a potent atmosphere. **Blarney House** (June–mid-Sept Mon–Sat noon–5:30pm), nearby, is a nineteenth-century Scottish baronial-style mansion. Inside, it's oppressively lush and Victorian, despite some fine eighteenth- and nineteenth-century satinwood furnishings and Waterford chandeliers.

The **town of Blarney** functions chiefly as a tourist service center—it is perhaps the only place in Ireland where you see not *Mná* and *Fír*, not Ladies and Gents, but "Rest Room." Naturally there are plenty of places to eat here—expensive but not impossible—and most of the pubs do bar food, which is generally the better option. One surprise is the **Blarney Woollen Mills**, one of Blarney's original industries, now doing very nicely out of the castle's visitors. It is one of the best places in Ireland for woolly bargains. Alongside is a **tourist office** (daily June–Sept 9am–7pm), and you can **rent a bike** from *McGrath Cycles* (Stoneview; ☎021-385658; £4 per day, £20 per week, £30 deposit) for some easy and scenic bicycling from Blarney up the Lee valley.

Fota and Cobh

A visit to Fota House and Wildlife Park and the pretty harbor town of Cobh can be managed in a day on a round-trip train ticket from Cork. Going by train really is the best option, taking you across the mudflats of an estuary teeming with birdlife. Both are situated on islands in the mouth of Cork harbor. **Fota Wildlife Park** (April 7–Sept 6 Mon–Sat 10am–5:15pm, Sun 11am–5:15pm; winter weekdays only; £1.90, students £1.50) is a small, pleasant park with apes, cheetahs, giraffes, and zebras (among others) all wandering about the landscaped eighteenth-century estate of Fota House.

The **house** itself (April 7–Sept 9 Mon–Sat 11am–6pm, Sun 2–6pm; Oct–March Sun & Bank Holidays 2–6pm; ☎021-812555; £2, students & unemployed £1) was originally an eighteenth-century hunting lodge, but it was enlarged in 1820. The building is one of Classical unity: Doric columns and plastered stonework outside are in complete harmony with the perfect Neoclassical interiors. More Greek columns, high decorated ceilings, and fine furnishings confirm the refined elegance of the lives led here. Fota is the perfect setting for the major collection of eighteenth- and nineteenth-century landscape paintings it houses, conveying as they do a pastoral idyll of a perfectly ordered world. On the estate is one of the most important **arboretums** in Europe, with a great variety of rare and exotic flowering shrubs and trees. The house and arboretum are currently under threat of being sold to a private company and developed as an exclusive leisure complex, so visit this exceptional house while you still have the chance.

Rejoining the train from Fota takes you out to the extremely pretty little town of **COBH**. Cobh (pronounced "Cove") is held in a quaint cup of land with steep, narrow streets climbing the hill to the Pugin Cathedral. One of the most enjoyable of these neo-Gothic monsters, it dominates the town, giving marvelous views out across the great curve of the bay to Spike Island. Thanks to its fine natural harbor, Cobh has long been an important port: it served as an assembly point for ships during the Napoleonic wars, and was a major departure point for steamers carrying emigrants to America. The first ever transatlantic steamer sailed from here in 1838, and the *Titanic* called in on her ill-fated voyage, too; a monument to the victims of the *Lusitania* disaster stands in Casement Square. The port is still used by a substantial fishing fleet. From September to February, when it is awash with fishermen, the town's character changes completely.

First and foremost, though, Cobh is a holiday resort, itself an historic function. Ireland's first yacht club was established here in 1720, and from 1830 on the town was a popular health resort, imitative of English Regency resorts like Brighton, a style reflected in its architecture. The main square is flanked by brightly-painted Victorian townhouses, and the place has a robust cheerfulness, with all the amenities of a family resort: pitch and putt, tennis, swimming, and a sandy beach. At the **International Sailing Center** on East Beach (☎021-811237) you can rent sailing dinghies (£6 per hour, £25 per day), canoes (£3–14) and windsurfing boards (£9 per afternoon)— the center also has accommodation available for long-term use. Further attractions are the **Cobh International Folk Dance Festival**, starting the second Sunday in July, and a **regatta** weekend in mid-August. You can also go **pony trekking** (*McCarthy's*, Tay Road; ☎021-811908; £3.50 per hour) or take a **trip around the harbor** (*Marine Transport Services*, Atlantic Quay; ☎021-811485).

If you want to stay, **B&B**s include *Westbourne House* (☎021-811391; £8), *Atlantic* (☎021-811489; £10) and *Ardeen* (3 Harbour Hill, ☎021-811803; £9). There's a **laundromat** behind the Clifton Bar on Midleton Street. A **private bus** service runs once a week direct to Dublin (Sunday 5pm, from the post office).

East of Cork

Beaches to the east of Cork city—with the exception of Cobh and Youghal—are unspectacular, and have nothing like the charm of the West. **BALLYCOTTON** has a little quayside, fine cliff-walks for miles to the west, and a beach half a mile away. It overlooks Ballycotton Bay and the holiday villages of SHANAGARY and GARRYVOE. **Garryvoe Beach** is very long and sandy, but beset by trailers advancing upon the shore. The east of the bay is flat and of interest only to bird watchers, its reed-infested estuary now a protected bird sanctuary. Here a river sidles along, smooth and khaki, through the mudflats to the sea.

Inland, MIDLETON is a cheery market town, and four miles to the south is the sleepy, historic village of **CLOYNE**. There is not much to see here, but it's worth a look if you're passing through this part of the country. Its interest lies in its history—what was, rather than what is. One of Ireland's earliest Christian foundations, the monastery of Saint Colman, was established here in the sixth century. In medieval times the village continued to be of religious importance with the establishment of the See of Cloyne, which extended well into County Limerick. Reminders of this era, though, are few. There's a fine tenth-century **round tower**, from whose top, 100 feet up, there are superb views (key from Cathedral house, 50p), and **St Colman's Cathedral**, a large building of warm, mottled stone originally built in 1250 but disappointingly restored in the nineteenth century. Inside, the grand and grim seventeenth-century Fitzgerald of Imokelly tomb and the alabaster tomb of George Berkley, the famous philosopher who was bishop here from 1734 to 1753, are worth a look. An Egyptian tau cross and the St Anthony's cross on the cathedral doorway are faint traces of earlier influences from the Mediterranean.

Off the Cloyne–Ballycotton road, *Ballymalloe House* (☎021-652531) is an exceptional **restaurant**, one of the most famous in Ireland; a meal here will cost you from around £20.

Youghal

YOUGHAL (pronounced "Yawl") is an ancient port at the mouth of the river Blackwater, where the counties of Cork and Waterford meet. In a small way it combines the richness of the Blackwater towns with the prettiness of Kinsale and Cobh. A picturesque holiday town, Youghal has real character, with a colorful history and some fine architecture to remember it by.

Youghal's walls were first built by the Norman settlers who established the town, but those which stand today were erected by Edward I in 1275. From medieval times the town prospered as one of Ireland's leading ports, trading with the continent—particularly France—and with England. Political disturbances and trade restrictions imposed on Irish ports by the English government meant the town's growth began to slow in the mid-sixteenth century. It fell into the hands of the earl of Desmond, and in 1579 the "rebel" earl (rebelling against Elizabeth I) sacked and burned the place. After Desmond's death, Youghal was part of the 40,000 acres granted to Walter Raleigh during the Munster Plantations, with which Elizabeth hoped to control Ireland. Raleigh, though, had little interest in Ireland, and spent most of his time composing poetry in an attempt to curry favor with the queen. In this he was abetted by Edmund Spenser, another local colonist, author of *The Faerie Queen*. Spenser proved to be capable of both great poetry and of barbarism in his dealings with the Irish; they eventually repaid him by burning down his castle Kilcolman, near Buttevant. Raleigh himself spent little time in Youghal, selling his land to Richard Boyle, the "Great" earl of Cork (and father of the scientist), who then greatly developed the town as he did all his newly acquired land.

When Cromwell reached New Ross in 1649, the English garrison at Youghal went over to the Parliamentarian side, and so the town escaped destruction. Nonetheless the importance of the port continued to diminish through the seventeenth century. Still, the decline was only relative to its former stature, and there is enough fine eighteenth-century architecture to make it clear that a small but affluent class of merchants still prospered. Today Youghal is a quiet seaside resort, and the history preserved in its buildings continues to suggest prosperity earned through centuries of vigorous commerce, and provides an insight into the privileged lives of the early colonists.

The Town

Youghal's most famous landmark is the **clock tower** which bridges the long, curvy main street: a superbly proportioned Georgian structure of warm, plum-colored stone. A century ago it was used as a prison; now it houses the town's **museum** (usually open June–Sept; currently being reorganized). Steps leading off the tower climb the steep hill through little lanes to the top of the town, where the walls and turrets of the old defenses still define the shape of the compact harbor.

The most charming buildings lie, predominantly, on the landward side of North Main Street and in the lanes that run behind it. On Main Street itself the **Red House** is a fine example of domestic architecture: built in 1710, it clearly shows the Dutch influence of the original merchant owner. Here too are seventeenth-century almshouses, built by Richard Boyle to house Protestant widows. Lanes off to the west of this end of Main Street lead to the Elizabethan **Myrtle Grove**, known as "Raleigh's House" though there's no real evidence that he ever lived there. Alongside you'll find the **Collegiate Church of St Mary's**, a large, simple, thirteenth-century building, one of the few of such age still in use in Ireland. The building has been greatly altered over the centuries, but still has interesting medieval tombs and effigies. Particularly notable are the thirteenth-century monuments in the south transept (key from Church Lodge, 2–5pm). Wrecked when the town was sacked by Desmond's men in 1579, they were later restored by Boyle, with the addition of effigies in seventeenth-century costume. Heading out of town towards Waterford, you pass the ruins of North Abbey, a thirteenth-century Dominican Priory of which little remains.

On the east side of North Main street is **Tyntes Castle**, a fifteenth-century tower house that is now sadly dilapidated (and, by the look of it, rapidly deteriorating). Edmund Spenser's widow married Robert Tynte, who lived here. Lanes off this side of the street lead to the **quayside**. Here it's all very quaint, almost too much so: warehouse buildings warm with the patina of age surround the harbor; yucca palms decorate the walk ways, and the cultivated fields of Waterford across the water look very near.

Practicalities and Entertainment

The **tourist office** (open June–Sept ☎024-92390) is in Market Square, just behind the harbor, and there are plenty of **B&Bs** along the main streets and around the quayside; two to try are Mrs P. Brooke's *Avomore House*, South Abbey (☎024-92617; £10) and Miss E. O'Brien's *Assumpta*, Devonshire Square (☎024-92134; £9; April–Oct only). To the west of town, safe and sandy **beaches** stretch for miles. There's a **laundromat** on North Main Street. A **private bus service** runs to Dublin every Sunday evening.

Every town selects which portion of its history it wishes to celebrate, and in Youghal the Raleigh connection takes first place. Thus the town celebrates music and potatoes in its **Walter Raleigh Potato Festival**, the last week in June and the first week in July. A close second is the use of the town as a location for the film of *Moby Dick*, which explains the presence of a jaunty cartoon whale on the roof of the public toilets, a thoroughly incongruous intrusion on the tastefully historic quayside. Memorabilia and photographs from the making of the film are found in the bar opposite.

During the summer months several of the bars in Youghal have regular **music** sessions—they cater to a family vacationing crowd, but there's some interesting variety nonetheless. *The Nook* on Main Street has a traditional Irish night on Wednesday, and some kind of live band, free, every night from mid-July to mid-September; Saturday and Sunday only the rest of the year. The proprietor of this bar claims Youghal is the cheapest seaside town for drink; make of this what you will—he also claims Walter Raleigh used to drink in his bar. Similarly committed to giving visitors a good time is Minnie's *The U-Tree* on Tallow Street, farther along the same stretch heading towards Waterford. There is some form of entertainment—Irish music, country and western, discos, or *ceilidhs*—on weekends all year, more often during July and August, with a cover charge of £1.50. *The Blackwater Inn* (Power's) and *The Anchor Bar* also have sessions, but Youghal has plenty of great, traditional bars too.

WEST CORK

West Cork is a place apart, its pace and character quite different from the rest of the county. The difference lies in both the land and its history, ensuring an undeniably separate identity. What it shares with the rest of Cork are the little fields that curl over and around gentle hills, and the all-permeating balmy atmosphere, but as you get sucked west, lulled by a hospitable familiarity, you gradually forget what you have left behind, happily succumbing to change. West Cork has none of the broad river valleys that serve the rest of the county, watering its pastures and nurturing towns at their crossing points. Nor does it have such fine harbors as Youghal, Cobh or Cork itself, whose flourishing overseas trade so enriched the main body of the county. Its allure is one of atmosphere, not history.

Blessed by the continual influence of the Gulf Stream, from spring onward it's warm and appealing, with a colorful clothing of vegetation to distract from the underlying paucity of the soil. Of course it rains, but in late summer hedges are stuffed with bright crimsom fuschia, and golden gorse thrives in otherwise barren places. Heading west the land becomes rockier, the life more difficult. Warm currents may take away the raw sting of ice, but winters here are hard, lashed by storms, and the landscape offers little comfort. Here poor land and the lack of safe anchorage have contributed to an historic poverty; conditions at Skibbereen during the famine years are among the most horrific recorded. Communities today are still small, and it's in this minor scale and remoteness that the charms of West Cork lie. What once meant poverty, disease, and emigration now leaves an undeveloped rural backwater for anyone lucky enough to have the time and the resources to enjoy it. West Cork has retained a slow pace that, coupled with the warm appeal of the landscape and the gentleness of the people, seems far removed from the twentieth century.

Two main styles of landscape are offered: the **mountains** that share a border with Kerry in the North, wild, yet relatively accessible; and the heavily indented **coastline** riddled with hidden sandy bays and coves, empty of people. In the southwest the country breaks up into little islands and fragments of land seemingly spat out into the ocean. Immediately north of here, three ragged peninsulas finger their way out into the Atlantic: Mizen Head, Sheeps Head, and the Beara Peninsula.

The potential of this beautiful, unspoiled, and remote countryside was first widely perceived over twenty years ago, when the area was subject to a significant social upheaval with the immigration of large numbers of Northern Europeans. "Blow-ins," as they're referred to, are people who have come to the area and have somehow managed to create for themselves an alternative lifestyle. Most of them are German, Belgian, or Dutch and came here for a number of reasons: to escape political systems they abhorred at home; to distance themselves from nuclear issues; to escape pollution, overcrowding, stress; and to key into the perceived creative energies, and the romantic mysticism, generated by the West Coast.

This influx of foreigners began in the Sixties at a time when there was plenty of money to be earned in the major cities of Western Europe, and since then there has been a process of natural selection. Those who don't make a total commitment to the lifestyle here no longer find it so easy to pop back to developed Europe, to earn swift cash with which to subsidize their romantic idyll. Consequently those who are still here are either survivors, or rich at home too. Missing the irony, many visitors consider them an intrusion, making the experience somehow less "Irish," less authentic. In fact the presence of "blow-ins" is positively beneficial to the budget traveler. While they may have originally settled with a vision of living off organic farming, craftwork, and homegrown entertainment, the harsh realities of subsistence have borne a real resourcefulness, the most useful sign of which is the recent mushrooming of **independent hostels**. Many of these are tucked away in delightfully secret places the owner has discovered and now chooses to share with visitors, and they're often worth visiting purely for the setting or the very special personal atmosphere that's been created. Another spin-off from the "blow-in" phenomenon is the high incidence of **healthfood** shops in tiny towns—welcome indeed in an area where traditional grocery shops are poor at providing anything that doesn't come in a can. Finally, West Cork has attracted a large number of people who have come here to be artists, some of whom have succeeded. A local **arts center** may be nothing more than a shed, but it can hold surprises, so look out for them. Some of the work is folksy and boring, but you can stumble across exciting stuff of refreshing originality. What adds to these centers' appeal is the deeper understanding of the land they can offer; the best work has been inspired by, and so reflects, the colors and textures of the landscape.

Travel in the West

The only way to get to know West Cork is slowly. It is possible to hitch around the main N71 road quickly to see the beautiful views unfurl, to watch one seascape replaced by another and then another by one of wild moun- tains, and for sheer scenery this *is* worth doing; but there is much more if you have the time. Slow down, change gear, and follow whatever happens to come up. Whatever your planned route, if you relax into the place, you are bound to be sidetracked into going somewhere you have never heard of, and doing things you couldn't dream of. Time can lose all meaning, and you suddenly find your holiday expand beyond recognition.

The best way to do this is either by **bike**, which can take you off the main route to discover wonderful little sandy coves cupped around a view of mossy rock stumbling into the ocean, or by leisurely **hitching**—the kind where you decide not to decide too specifically where you intend to end up, and where you plan to enjoy walking much of the way. There is something about the meandering lanes, the occasional small communities and the coaxing, balmy atmosphere of the air that lures you away from any plans you might have thought you had, and it's very easy to see how so many "blow-ins" never quite got it together to return home.

Bus Éireann serves all areas of West Cork except Sheep's Head, the north side of Mizen Head, and the Beara peninsula. Major towns are connected daily; small towns and villages off the main roads are served less frequently, so if you are relying on public transit it's worth taking details of times and days of services you are likely to want while in a major bus station. Ask about return fares—often they are as cheap as single tickets if used on certain days. Private buses also run, irregularly, on the following routes: Skibbereen–Baltimore; Bantry–Glengarriff–Castletownbere; Castletownbere–Cork; Dublin–Fermoy– Cork–Bandon–Dunmanway–Drimoleague–Bantry; and Cork–Macroom.

If you have a tent, you can **camp** almost anywhere if you ask permission first, though the Beara peninsula and the Caha mountains are very rocky. The few official campgrounds are listed in the text. You'll find **hostels** at Kinsale, Timoleague, Dunmanway, Clear Island, Glengariff, Adrigole, Castletownbere, and Allihies.

The Inland Option

Probably the most popular way to explore West Cork is to head for the near- est bit of coast, usually Kinsale, and head west, enjoying the gradual change from pretty countryside to the barren island-spattered peninsulas as you go. But a more direct route inland does have its merits, and can also be used as a shortcut to the mountains of Kerry. Unless you yearn for the sea, it's just as beautiful. The secondary roads west of Cork city run up the Lee Valley, through beautiful countryside and a number of small villages. Chief of these is **MACROOM**, a focus for tourists and music enthusiasts heading for KILLARNEY. It's on a main road, and a relatively easy hitch through the mountains. The **Boggeragh Mountains** to the north of the Lee Valley appear as high, rolling moorland, unspectacular compared with other ranges in Cork and Kerry but particularly rich in archaelogical remains: stone circles, standing stones, wedge-tombs and ring-forts. A leaflet, *Antiquities of the Boggeragh Mountains*, is available from the tourist office in Cork city—of great value in locating these sites. The Bantry road from Macroom is far quieter, passing through the dramatic glacial valley of GOUGANE BARRA and down to Bantry Bay.

Alternatively, taking the road south of Cork city to BANDON and then west to DUNMANWAY brings you to very promising country of empty hills and lakes. At Bandon there is a **campground**, signposted half a mile from the town center (April–Sept; ☎023-41232; £1 per unit, £1 per person, including showers). Dunmanway is a plain country town, but the **hostel** here is in a beautiful setting; take the post office road out of town for a couple of miles, then look out for a (poor) signpost up a hill to the right. *Shiplake House* (☎023-45750; £3.50; mid-March–mid-Nov) is a farmhouse hostel with bunks, a barrel-topped trailer for couples or families, laundry facilities, organic produce, and home-made bread, as well as free **bikes** for exploring the surrounding hills and lakes. *Bus Éireann* runs a bus from Cork to Dunmanway daily, and a bus from Dunmanway to Bantry and Glengarriff. A **private bus** serves the Dunmanway–Cork–Dublin route on weekends.

The Coast: Kinsale

KINSALE has retained much of the flavor of its rich maritime history, and in many ways has more in common with the formerly affluent ports of Youghal, Cork, and Cobh than with the impoverished and remote west, but it is an excellent place from which to begin your journey. The 18-mile road from Cork city travels through gentle rolling farmland and along the Bandon estuary. This easy, meandering coast is a favorite for fishing and bird watching; so alive with birdlife that it's rewarding even for the uninitiated. At Kinsale the harbor is broad, and cormorants and shags skim across its gentle waters. A tongue of land curls from the west into the center of the harbor, protecting the town from harsh winds, and on this promontory are the ivy-clad ruins of Jamesfort, a ruddy castle built by the English James I.

Originally a fishing town and historically a sheltered harbor of strategic importance, Kinsale now does a healthy tourist trade. Its proximity to Cork and its picturesque and historic setting have enabled it to develop along tasteful, conservative lines; there are plenty of valuable amenities, but tourism isn't allowed to run out of control. The **tourist office** (daily 10am–2pm and 4–8pm; ☎021-789522) is on Town Pier in the heart of town, next to the bus depot and movie theater: if it's not open when it's meant to be, tourist information is readily available at *Barry's* shop (open until 8pm), opposite *The Spaniards* pub in Scilly, on the eastern coast road out of town. Kinsale **An Óige hostel** (☎021-772309, open all year, reservations essential in July & Aug; grade B) is at SUMMERCOVE, two miles out of town beyond *Barry's*. As always, the tourist office can help out with **B&B** information, or try Mrs McCarthy's *Hilltop*, Sleaven Heights (☎021-772612; £10) or Mr & Mrs R. Coppard at *Ashling*, Bandon Road (☎021-774127; £9.50). As for **food**, Kinsale is a well-known gourmet center and has numerous expensive restaurants. Fortunately, it is also famous for its quantity of pubs, many of which serve delicious seafood at the bar—oysters are the local specialty. So preoccupied is Kinsale with eating that it even has a **gourmet festival** in October, crowded with the affluent well-fed.

Because Kinsale is geared to tourists, its **history** is cherished and made accessible: maps of the "Kinsale Trail" are available free from the tourist office. The town received its first royal charter from Edward III in 1434, but it was of little importance up until the **Battle of Kinsale** in 1601, a disastrous defeat for the Irish which signaled the end of the Gaelic aristocracy as a power for the English to reckon with. A Spanish fleet stood in the bay ready to support the Irish cause against Elizabethan forces, but was unable to make useful contact with O'Neill and O'Donnell attacking from the north. So the battle was lost, and although resistance to English rule continued, six years later came "the Flight of the Earls"—when the Irish nobility fled to Europe, giving up the fight for their own lands.

It was at Kinsale that, in 1689, James II landed with French support in an attempt to regain his throne, and it was also the port of his final departure from Ireland after the Battle of the Boyne. The town was an important naval base for the English crown during the seventeenth and eighteenth centuries, and the sixteenth-century tower house on Cork Street—**Desmond Castle**—became known as "The French Prison" when it was used to hold as many as 600 French prisoners during the Napoleonic war. Nearby **St Multose Church** has traces of a medieval structure, and in the church porch are the town stocks from the eighteenth century.

This history is recorded in the **museum** (9am–5pm; 20p), smack in the middle of town above the old market (1600) which has a Dutch-style facade (1704). More recent events are remembered even more closely. Within the museum is the musty old courthouse which had remained much the same from the eighteenth century up until 1915, when the inquest into the sinking of the **Lusitania** was held here and Kinsale suddenly became the focus for the world's press. The *Lusitania* was a liner traveling from New York to Liverpool when it was torpedoed by a German submarine off the Old Head of Kinsale, killing 1195 people. It remains a controversial incident: Germany claimed there was ammunition on board, the US said it contained only innocent civilians. Whatever the truth, it has been seen as a catalyst for America's decision to enter World War I. After the inquest it was decided that the courtroom should be left as a memorial. The rest of the museum is a friendly and intriguing jumble of stuff: memorabilia from the disaster; sixteenth-century royal charters and maps, local craftwork, personal effects of the eighteenth-century giant of Kinsale, and a variety of bizarre local inventions that never got any farther than the local museum.

Beyond the town's center, **Jamesfort** (1601) is fun to clamber over, but if your time is limited head instead for **Charlesfort** (1677), two miles out of town at Summercove. The outer walls of this fort, barely touched by weather or gunfire, seem pretty innocuous, but they conceal a formidable war machine. Within is an awesome system of barracks, ramparts and bastions, impressive testimony to the complexity and precision of seventeenth-century military science. The barracks were occupied until 1922, when the British left and handed the fort over to the Irish government. Today they remain largely intact, with only the barracks' missing roofs to give the place an eerily deserted feel. Free guided tours are available every hour on the hour.

Seven miles southwest of Kinsale is the tiny village of **BALLINASPITTLE**, famous in recent years for popular sightings of its miraculous moving statues. The peninsula to the south, the Old Head of Kinsale, guarantees superb cliff-walks, and at the neck of this peninsula are the remains of a fifteenth-century De Courcy castle. *Garrettstown House Holiday Park* (☎021-778156/775286; May 28–Sept 11; overnight hikers/cyclists £4 for two; gas cylinders on sale and facilities for washing clothes) is a **campground** off the main beach road from Ballinaspittle.

The Seven Heads Peninsula

The stretch of coast from Timoleague to Clonakilty is known as the **Seven Heads Peninsula**. It's a pretty, indented shoreline, good for walking and bird watching. The spruce village of **TIMOLEAGUE** sits inland on the muddy estuary of the Ardigeen River, dominated by the extensive remains of a **Fransciscan abbey** which was sacked in 1649. The much advertised **Castle Gardens** include a beautiful walled garden, but the ruins of Timoleague Castle itself are negligible, and not worth the entrance fee. Timoleague is only a small place—*O'Sullivan's* and *Pad Joe's* are good bars promising entertainment, the latter also doing **pub food**—but it does boast an excellent **independent hostel and restaurant**, *Lettercollum House* (daily; ☎023-46251; £4). This is a friendly place, worth visiting for the food alone: seafood, lamb, and vegetarian dishes, locally produced and lovingly prepared. Meals for hostelers start at around £4; those not staying at the hostel are advised to phone and reserve for the restaurant in advance. You can **rent bikes** at the hostel, which makes it a perfect point from which to explore the Seven Heads Peninsula. *Ardnavaha House Hotel* in Ballinascorthy (☎023-49135) can arrange **horse riding**.

At the broad mouth of the estuary the village of **COURTMACSHERRY** is currently being developed as a safe, quiet family resort. It's certainly tranquil—when asked what happens here one local responded "The tide comes in and the tide goes out again." That's slightly exaggerated—if you're feeling rich you can go deep-sea angling or shark-fishing (*Courtmacsherry Sea Angling Center*, ☎023-46427), horse riding can be arranged through the *Courtmacsherry Hotel* (☎023-46198), and in the evenings you may find a singalong round the piano at the *Lifeboat Inn* or *Anchor Bar*—but not outrageous. If you want to stay you can **camp** by the *Courtmacsherry Hotel* or at a site about two miles out of Timoleague on the Clonakilty road. Elsewhere around the Seven Heads Peninsula *Deasy's Bar* at RING, just east of Clonakilty, does **pub food**, while *Dunworley Cottage Restaurant* (☎023-40314), though pricey, is noted for its organic food.

The busy little village of **CLONAKILTY** has a growing reputation as a traditional music center, thanks in large part to the enthusiasm of local people. The **busking festival** for street musicians here at the end of August has really taken off—accommodation other than camping at this time needs to be reserved well in advance. **Clonakilty Festival** (June 28–July 10) includes pub talent and debating contests, and is almost immediately followed by the town's **Agricultural Show** on the second Wednesday in July. The local **pub scene** is also exceptionally lively, attracting a lot of young people. Probably the most popular place is *De Bara's* on Pearse Street, with music every night during the summer. *Shanley's* in Rossa Street frequently has jazz nights, and *Fiddlers Green*, always popular with a younger crowd, has music on Sunday evening. *O'Donovan's Hotel* puts on "Irish Nights" of singing and dancing every Thursday during July and August. The town has a couple of expensive restaurants that also do tourist menus: *The Sandlighter* serves light meals from £4.50; prices at *Súgan* start at around £6. The best **beaches** nearby are at INCHYDONEY immediately to the south; formerly an island, it's now linked to the mainland by a causeway.

There's a **tourist office** (Rossa Street; ☎023-33226; June 22–Aug 31); **bike rental** from *Healy's Bikes* (Rossa Street, also repairs) or *Tom Sheehy* (Aston Square; ☎023-33362); and plenty of **B&B**s, including Mr and Mrs T. Driscoll, *Bay View*, Old Timoleague Road (☎023-33539; £10); Mrs A. O'Driscoll, *Aisling*, Clogheen Road (☎023-33491; £9); and Mrs K. O'Neill, *Ashville*, Clarke Street (☎023-34139; £8.50). **Camping** is available at Dorothy Jennings' *Desert House* (east out of the village, turn right at the *Jet* gas pump and supermarket; April–Sept; £3), near the shore and a mere 500-metre stagger from the pubs.

West to Skibbereen

You can pick almost any spot west of Clonakilty and be sure of satisfaction— it's a beautiful coastline with a frenzy of little bays and creeks, sandy coves and tidal loughs. There are tiny lakes here and there, isolated along the shore from the main body of the sea, providing placid contrast to the furling white ocean spray. Each place—Rosscarbery, Glandore, Leap, Union Hall, and Castletownshend—has its own special charms, and at every turn there is some new delightful composition: a slither of trees, a bay, a tiny beach. If you take the main N71 you're never far from these places, with easy access by a couple of miles' walk or a short hitch. There are official **campgrounds** just off the N71 at Rosscarbery (*O'Riordan's Caravan Park*; ☎023-48216; May–Sept; £3–5 for two) and on the coast at Glandore (☎028-33280; daily; £2 per unit, £1 per person). Gas cylinders are sold at both sites.

As you journey in this direction, there are scattered historic remains to punctuate your trip. The **Drombeg Stone Circle**, on the R597 minor road between Rosscarbery and Glandore, is a fine Druidic altar dating from around 150 BC. Nearby is a **Fulacht Fiadh** of the same era: a stone trough used for cooking that would be filled with spring water and heated by throwing in hot stones from a fire. On a ridge overlooking Castletownshend is the **Knockdrum Stone Ring-Fort**, outside of which is a large rock with megalithic cup and ring marks. **CASTLETOWNSHEND** itself was the home of Edith Somerville of Somerville-and-Ross fame, authors of the "Irish R.M." stories. The graves of the two are to be found in St Barrahane's churchyard.

SKIBBEREEN, a cheerful place, smartly painted and set in a landscape of low wooded hills and pasture, is the main service and administrative center for the south of West Cork. This traditional role is still remarkably alive: on

Tuesdays and Wednesdays the cattle market still operates, drawing crowds from the surrounding country, and every Friday afternoon there's the regular country market. For travelers, it's a good place to stock up or to stop over— there are plenty of supermarkets and liquor stores, a smattering of health food shops and delis, and of course plenty of pubs. If you're after a **meal**, the *Windmill Tavern* specializes in seafood snacks from £3, and decent pub dinners are available at the *Spanish Doubloon*, *The Galleon* in Clonakilty Street, or *MacCarthy's*. *Eldon's Hotel* also serves bar snacks from £2.50 every day; *Jopplin's* (Mon–Sat 9am–6pm), upstairs in the arcade, offers home cooking from £3.50; and *The Kitchen Garden* is a healthfood and organic vegetable shop that has a cheap café attached. Although Skibbereen is not especially renowned for its pub scene, you might try the *Stable Bar*, *Annie May's* or *MacCarthy's*, all of which have occasional weekend music sessions.

The **West Cork Arts Center** on Main Street (Mon–Sat 12:30–5pm, Sun summer only) is also worth checking out. It hosts monthly exhibitions which can be first-rate, and stages occasional music and dance performances; there's a coffee shop, and a reference and slide library through which you can locate local artists. The **tourist office** (June–Sept Mon–Fri 9am–7pm, Sat 9:15am–5:30pm; Oct–May Mon–Fri 9:15am–1pm and 2:15–5:30pm; ☎028-21766), is farther along Main Street and will point you toward **B&Bs**. If this is shut you might try *Illenside*, 18 Bridge Street (☎028-21605; £8.50), or Mrs McDonald's *Glen Ilen*, Mill Road (☎028-21269;£8). You can get **Bus Éireann information** from *O'Cahalales* in Bridge Street, and rent **bikes** from *N.W. Roycroft and Son* in Ilen Street (☎028-21235, 21810 after hours; £3.50 per day, £19 per week).

Heading out of Skibbereen, Roaring Water Bay, Baltimore, and Clear Island are all easily accessible to the southwest. A slight detour will take you by way of **Lough Hyne** (pronounced "ine"), a landlocked salt lake directly south of Skibbereen, linked to the ocean only by a very slender channel down which the receding tide returns to the sea. The lough, surrounded by hillsides dripping with lush, moist greenery, is a unique phenomenon, of great interest to marine biologists. From the head of the lake steep slopes, easily climbed, rise to panoramic views: eastward along the coast to Kinsale; west across the length of the Mizen peninsula; and out across Roaring Water Bay.

Roaring Water Bay

The approach to Baltimore takes you through a landscape that is disarmingly low-key. Instead of some dramatic climax at this, the most southerly point of all Ireland, the land seems simply to be fading away: rocky terrain and scrawny vegetation accompany the windy, listless estuary, untidy with lumps of land that seem to have been tossed at random towards the sea. The whole ragged effect is as if the country is running out of substance; the landmass, already motheaten, is now fraying too. But as Roaring Water Bay and Carbery's "Hundred Islands" come into full view this tapering off is put into spectacular context: the full weight of Ireland is behind you, while ahead are dots, wracks, and scraps of islands, petering out across the great open expanse of water to Sherkin and Cape Clear.

ISLAND FERRIES

Baltimore–Sherkin Island (£2 round trip). Depart Baltimore 10:30am, noon, 2pm, 4pm, 5:30pm, 7pm, and 8:30pm; returning at 10:45am, 12:15pm, 2:15pm, 4:15pm, 5:45pm, 7:15pm, and 8:45pm.

Baltimore–Clear Island (£5 round trip). July and Aug depart Baltimore 10:30am, 2:15pm, and 7pm; returning at 9am, noon, and 6pm: June and Sept depart Baltimore 2:15pm and 7pm; returning 9am and 6pm: Oct–May depart Baltimore 2:15pm, returning

9am. Times may change on Sunday. If you stay at the youth hostel on the island, you get a £1 refund on your ferry ticket, so ask the warden to stamp it.

Clear Island–Schull In July and August only, a ferry runs from Clear Island to Schull on the Mizen peninsula, leaving around 5:30pm most days. Departures are not guaranteed, though, so you have to inquire on the island.

BALTIMORE, a delightful harbor village overlooked by a sixteenth-century O'Driscoll stronghold, is the last significant mainland settlement. Combining its traditional fishing activities with tourism in surprising harmony, it's also the departure point for ferries to Sherkin and Clear islands (see box): for most people this is the chief reason to come. During the last two weeks of July and the first two in August the yachting crowd descend en masse for the **regatta**; there are a few pricey restaurants to cater to them. At any time of year, though, you can get great seafood and steaks all day at *Casey's Cabin* (music on Sunday night in June, July & August), about a mile towards Skibbereen. *David Lyster's* bar by the harbor also serves seafood, as well as cashing checks and **changing money**. If you're staying, *Rolf's* **independent hostel** is cheerful and friendly (☎028-20289; £4; open all year but reserve ahead in July and August; organic produce on sale, light meals available; **bike rental** £3.50) or there is **bed-and-breakfast** accommodation at Mrs Brown's, the first house on the left as you head up to *Rolf's* (look for the green door; £8), and at Ann Nolan's *Fastnet House* (£9.50). As well as the scheduled *Bus Éireann*, there is a private service that operates from the harbor to Skibbereen around 10am—check the exact schedule locally.

Sherkin Island

There's really very little to **SHERKIN ISLAND**, whose hummocky mass is divided by only a narrow channel from the point beyond Baltimore. If you're after sights you'll find the extensive remains of a fifteenth-century friary, clearly visible from the mainland, and remnants of an O'Driscoll castle. O'Driscolls from all over the country still return periodically to Sherkin to select a leader of the clan, generally a good excuse for a party. Most people come here, though, for the magnificent beaches and lively pub scene with great weekend sessions. There are no rooms available on the island, but you can **camp** if you ask. The small **marine observatory** welcomes interested volunteer workers.

Clear Island

CLEAR ISLAND (*Oileán Chléire*) offers somewhat more to do, but it would be worth visiting for the ferry trip alone. There is an important ornithology station here, and on the 45-minute ride across Roaring Water Bay it's obvious that the place is paradise for wildlife enthusiasts. The bay is alive with seabirds—guillemots, cormorants, auks, and storm petrels—and with luck you may see seals and, in warm weather, basking sharks. With even more luck you might find your boat raced by a playful dolphin or two, dodging around the bows and leaping out of the ocean to crash back down right alongside the ferry.

The hilly, rocky island seems to have been pinched in the middle where two inlets, North Harbour and South Harbour, almost meet. In the south, steep and inaccessible cliffs rise from the water; the North Harbour is perfectly sheltered. Roads climb up from here through hills covered in coarse grass which seems to spread over everything; old walls, and houses long derelict. Sea pinks cling to rocky outcrops and honeysuckle clambers wherever it can. The island's high points give spectacular views back across the archipelago of Roaring Water Bay to the mainland.

The **bird observatory** at North Harbour has been here since 1959 and has complete records going back to that time. When it was set up, by an amateur group, this station was a pioneer in the constant observation of seabirds, and its work has done much for the knowledge of migratory patterns. Clear Island is one of the most important places for seabirds in Ireland, including some genuine rarities—especially plentiful are storm petrels, gulls, and cormorants. There is **hostel**-style accommodation available for ornithologists, which should be arranged in advance (through *Ruttledge House*, 8 Longford Place, Monkstown, Dublin; ☎01-804322) and is particularly busy in September and October. If you are new to bird-watching, but would like to learn more, call in and see what's happening, though be warned that midsummer is not the best season.

Clear Island is also an isolated remnant of the *Gaeltacht*, where Gaelic is still spoken by about 160 islanders. During the summer Irish youth are sent here to practice the language. The island has a **festival** of drama, music, art, and dance, *Féile Shamhna Chléire*, usually over the last few days of October. The **Heritage Centre** (June–Aug 3:30–5:30pm; £1, students 50p), a steep, well-signposted walk from North Harbour, is a tiny museum of the domestic, fishing, and seafaring history of the island. The island prides itself on being the birthplace of Saint Kieran, who supposedly preceded Saint Patrick by thirty years, but the holy well and stone that are attributed to him stand in a sadly unromantic spot by the road at North Harbour. The best of Clear Island's historic ruins is **Dún an Óir** ("Fort of Gold"), an O'Driscoll fort, impressive on a high narrow splinter of rock which is now an island at high tide—a short walk west around the coast from the bird observatory. If you want to clamber over it, ask locally about the tides and the weather. Alternatively, great views of the castle can be had from the 200-foot cliffs to the south.

The **An Óige hostel** is at South Harbour (☎028-39144, open all year, very busy Sept & Oct; grade B), where you can rent row boats from the warden. **Camping** is available by Lough Errul to the west (£1.50 per person), and there are a number of **B&Bs**: *Cluain Mara*, North Harbour (☎028-39153); Eleanor Uí Drisceoíl (☎028 39135); Helen Uí Drisceoíl (☎028-39105); and Mrs Christine Sawyer (☎028-39105). Good **pub meals** are available at any hour for around £3 at *Otters Bar*, North Harbour. If you intend staying for any length of time, bear in mind that the shop sells only canned and processed food. Bread, milk, eggs, and goats' cheese, however, are often available fresh on the island.

Mizen Head

The Mizen Head Peninsula is a beautiful, remote finger of land poking its way west, to the north of the islands. It offers great sandy beaches and superb cliff scenery, getting wilder the farther west you go. It's also an area rich in **archaeological sites**, from Bronze-Age wedge-graves contemporary with the first copper-mining of Mount Gabriel, through Iron-Age and early Christian ring-forts, down to medieval castles. A leaflet, *Antiquities of the Mizen Peninsula*, available from the tourist office in Cork city, is worth getting if you want to locate these sites. Great care should be taken at the Mizen cliffs, as the land ends abruptly and without warning.

The most spectacular of the coastal scenery is at **Mizen Head** itself— sheer, vertiginous cliffs, with an offshore lighthouse linked by a little suspension bridge. Standing at this exhilarating spot it takes little effort to imagine the great number of ships that have been wrecked in Dunlough Bay to the north. A walk around to **Three Castles Head** brings in sight the curtain wall and two turrets of an O'Mahoney stronghold, one of twelve that were built along this peninsula in the fifteenth century. The setting makes this one truly spectacular. The whole of the peninsula's wild and empty northern coast, in fact, is one of sheer cliffs and stupendous views—an impossible route for hitching, but great for those with a vehicle.

The south coast of the peninsula is more traveled, with small towns at Ballydehob, Schull, and Crookhaven, and lovely sandy **beaches**. The best of these is the long and sandy strand at BARLEYCOVE, whose rolling breakers make it a favorite with windsurfers. Nearby is the busy little resort of CROOKHAVEN, with a large **campground/trailer park** on the Goleen– Crookhaven road (May 14–Sept 10, £2); unless you want the facilities, though, there is no real need to use this—there are plenty of remote spots where you can pitch a tent for free. The only public transit along the peninsula is run by *Bus Éireann* as far as Crookhaven.

If you're looking for somewhere to stay here, you'll find more facilities back towards the main road. **BALLYDEHOB**, a town of gaily colored streets at the neck of the peninsula, was once known as the hippie capital of the West because it was said to have more "blow-ins" than locals. Heavily colonized in the Sixties, it still has traces of their influence, being a liberal place compared to others of its size, but a sleepy town nonetheless. The liveliest place these days is *Gabes' Bar*, where there's usually some kind of music and a crowd of young people to enjoy it. Other bars cater to an older crowd; *Coughlan's* on the Schull road serves up country, ballads, and dance music every Sunday, and on Wednesday too during the summer. There are a handful of places to **eat**;

Annie's Restaurant (☎028-37292) serves home made lunches and good seafood (Tues–Sat noon–2:30pm) from around £3.50 and evening meals, for which you should reserve in advance, from around £15. *The Forge Restaurant* (☎028-37312) serves midday meals, including decent vegetarian food, from around £3, evening meals from £10. *Duggans'* restaurant on Main Street (June–Sept 9am–10pm, takeout open until 12:30am; ☎028-37149) serves traditional meals at £3–7. There's a healthfood shop in Main Street, above which you'll find Kitty Kingston's **B&B** (£8); the *Ballydehob Inn* (☎028-37139; £10) is similarly friendly. Ballydehob's nearest **beach** is three miles away at Audley Cove—a pebbly cove, secluded and personal, with lovely views of the islands.

SCHULL is perhaps the most obvious place to stay on the peninsula, with **hostels**, the **ferry** for Clear Island (July & Aug 2:30pm, weather permitting), a **watersports center** that requires neither advance reservations nor a massive bank balance, and plenty of cheery amenities aimed at vacationing families and an unpretentious yachting fraternity. An attractive, seaside market town, its sheltered, bulb-shaped harbor looks out over Carbery's Hundred Islands, while to the north Mount Gabriel rises to 1339 feet, offering wonderful views. To make this walk from Schull (nine miles there and back) head up Gap Road past the convent—a clear track all the way. From the top you can continue around the north side of the mountain, to return through Rathcool and Glaun. The domes at the summit of Mount Gabriel are aircraft tracking stations. As you walk, beware of unguarded mine shafts: this rough and rocky land was heavily mined for copper in the nineteenth century, and is still dotted with Cornish-style mining chimneys.

Schull is at its liveliest during two big annual **sailing events**. The first is an international sailing festival for children, usually during the local festival week (first week in July), the second a major regatta held in Calves week (first week in August). As everywhere, festival time means **accommodation** can be difficult, and phoning ahead is advisable. If you want B&B try *Colla House* (☎028-28105), or there are a couple of **hostels**: *Kilbronogue Hostel* (☎028-28523) is signposted off the main road out of town towards Ballydehob; the *Schull Watersports Center*, The Pier (☎028-28554/28351) also has hostel accommodation at £4–5 a night, £20 a week (ring to check, as this can be group-reserved). The center organizes deep-sea-fishing trips, dinghy rent (£15 a half day), windsurfing (£5 per hour), and diving, the last for the experienced only. If you want to go **horse riding**, try the *Schull Riding Center*, Colla Road, one mile southwest of Schull (☎028-28185). **Bike rental** is available from Alan Murphy at *The Black Sheep* (☎028-28203), and mountain bikes from *Dan's Kitchen* (Cotters Yard, Main Street; £6 per day, £28 per week).

Dan's Kitchen is also one of the best cheap places to **eat**, with wholesome light meals from £1 (Easter–Oct until 8:30pm). *Adele's Coffee Shop*, also in Main Street, does excellent home made cakes, soups, salads, and fresh pasta. Good **bar food** is available at the *East End Hotel* and the *Bunratty Inn*. If you want **music** try the *Old Courtyard*, *O'Regan's*, *The Black Sheep*, *Bunratty's*, or the *East End Hotel*. There's a good second-hand **bookshop**, *Mizen Books*, in Main Street, handy for rainy afternoons; and a **bank** and **post office** (each of which have substations in Ballydehob and Goleen). *Bus Éireann* **buses** depart from *Griffins Bar*.

Sheep's Head

The peninsula north of Mizen, **Sheep's Head**, has a very ancient feel to it—barren land almost entirely devoid of people. There are only a couple of tiny villages here, and traffic is sparse—the sole weekly bus runs on Saturday—so don't try to hitch if you're going to need to return in a hurry. Nevertheless, if you have the time and the means, a tour down this sliver of old Ireland affords fabulous panoramic views over County Cork, the Beara Peninsula, and County Kerry from the top of Seefin, Sheep's Head's highest hill (1136 feet). The north coast looks down on the magnificent Bantry Bay, backed by the wild Caha Mountains.

Bantry

The beauty of **BANTRY** is its setting at the head of always-turbulent Bantry Bay, which stretches thirty miles from the town to the ocean. The deep, churning blue waters of the bay, backed by the dramatic heights of the Beara's Caha Mountains and cowering, usually, under a notoriously changeable sky, form as dramatic a backdrop as any in Ireland. The town itself sits around a long square focused at the head of the bay, with a slatey Regency Gothic church and a statue of Saint Brendan staring out to sea. In the immediate surrounds are lush wooded slopes with delightful walks and waterfalls; a safe haven, indulged between the ravages of the sea and the wilds of the rocky mountains. It's also a place of history and character—a fishing port and market town, where the traditional market is still held on the first Friday of every month.

For centuries **Bantry Bay** attracted attempts from abroad to overthrow English rule. Once inside its shelter ships were protected from attack by the rugged mountains of the peninsulas on either side. In 1689 a French fleet sailed up the bay to assist James II, but was forced to return after an indecisive battle with Williamite forces. A century later, in 1796, Wolfe Tone arrived with another French fleet, this time with revolutionary ideals, to try and overthrow the Protestant Anglo-Irish. Channel storms, however, had already reduced the fleet from 43 ships to 16 by the time it arrived, and the remaining vessels spent six days in the bay unable to land, even though, as Tone said, "we were close enough to toss a biscuit on shore." After this failure they were forced to turn back. Richard White, a local landowner, was rewarded for his loyalty to the English crown at the time of the invasion by being made Baron Bantry.

The Baron's home, **Bantry House** (daily June–Aug 9am–8pm; Sept–May 9am–6pm; ☎027-50047), nowadays provides an elegant vision of the rarefied life led by the Anglo-Irish aristocracy. Sumptuously decorated and packed with art treasures, it is well worth taking some time over. Much of the furniture is French Napoleonic, and there are tapestries and other treasures from Versailles, but what makes this house such a gem is the sheer variety of stuff that has been collected—much of it during the second earl's European wanderings in the nineteenth century. The setting is superb: ordered landscaped gardens look down over the bay, calmly asserting the harmony of the aristocratic order, unruffled by the ruggedness of the surroundings.

The other side of the past is remembered with relish by the ladies who run the **Bantry Museum**, situated behind the fire station on Wolfe Tone Square (June 14–Sept 9 Tues–Fri 3–5:30pm; ☎027-50087 or 50475). The museum is the collection of the local history society—domestic paraphernalia, old newspapers and everyday trivia of all sorts—which the curators willingly demonstrate with an entertaining blend of history and gossip. The modern **library**, at the top of Bridge Street, is also worth a look. Built in 1974, it looks at first glance like some sort of spaceship, though the design was in fact inspired by a prehistoric dolmen; as adventurous a piece of modern architecture as you'll find in the west of Ireland, it's diminishedn by a white facade that already seems thoroughly tacky. The work of local artists and craftspeople can be seen at the **Oriada Gallery** (Mon–Sat 10am–6pm, plus Sun noon–6pm June–Aug), in New Street at the back of the Bakehouse, New Street. The exhibitions here, changed monthly, are often excellent.

One final thing worth going out of your way to see, just out of town, is the fine, early-Christian **Kilnaruane Pillar Stone**. Its worn carvings depict four men rowing, an apostle, and the Cross. To find it follow the main road south out of town and take the first turning on the left past the *Westlodge Hotel*: the stone is in a field 500 yards farther on the right.

Practicalities

Finding **somewhere to stay** in Bantry should present few problems. **B&Bs** can be found on the square and along the Glengarriff Road. Ones to try include Mrs Evans, *Bay View House* (The Square; ☎027-50403; £8.50); Mrs O'Regan, *Sunville* (☎027-50175; £9); and Mrs Kramer, *The Mill* (Newtown; ☎027-50278; £8.50). If you feel like splashing out on a night or two of real luxury you can have bed and breakfast at **Bantry House** (☎027-50047), where for £23 you can sleep like an earl. The nearest official **campground** is four miles from Bantry along the Glengarriff road at *Eagle Point Caravan and Camping Park* (May 16–September 18; ☎027-50630; £2), but there are plenty of farms nearer town where you can ask to pitch your tent in a field.

Good places to **eat** are somewhat more limited. The best of them has to be *O'Connor's* famous seafood restaurant, which for many people is a reason in itself to visit Bantry. More modest fare is available at *Over the Rainbow*, a healthfood and vegetarian restaurant in Wolfe Tone Square (Tues–Sat 10am–5:30pm & 6:30–9:30pm; daytime snacks from £1.50, evening meals from £5); *The Admiral* in New Street (☎027-51350) for good French food; *Peter's Grill*, with fish dishes from £5; or *Vickery's Hotel Bar* in New Street for enterprising pub food (10am–10pm).

Regular **pubs** are plentiful as ever. The *Anchor Bar* is a convivial place to start, with a good, friendly mix of locals and visitors. For traditional **entertainment** try *Jim Crowley's* or at weekends *The Bantry Bay* for local pop bands and discos. *The Westlodge Hotel* hosts the local Sunday night disco.

Bus Éireann **buses**, connecting with Cork, Skibbereen, Glengarrif, Killarney, and the Mizen Peninsula, leave from outside *Crowley's Bar* (information inside), towards the harbor from the tourist office. Private buses run to

Cork and Dublin on weekends, and, on certain days, out to the Beara Peninsula: for details call ☎027-50062. **Bike rental** is available on Glengarriff Road, to the right just before the turning for the industrial zone (£4 per day plus £5 deposit) and from *Kramer's* (☎027-50278) and Mr P. O'Sullivan (☎027-50327). The **tourist office** (☎027-50229; June 29–Sept 3 10am–1pm and 2–6pm) is on Wolfe Tone Square, and there's a good **travel agent**, *West Cork Travel Agency* (☎027-50341), on Main Street.

Local sporting opportunities include **deep-sea fishing, sailing,** and **windsurfing** (for all of which contact John Crowley, ☎027-50030); **horse riding** at *O'Donoghue's Riding Stables*, Ardnatrush (☎027-63069); and **swimming, squash** and **pitch-and-putt golf** at the *Westlodge Hotel* (☎027-50360/50557). There's also a **regatta** in August. One local sport worth looking out for is **bowling**, a West Cork game played around Bantry on Sundays. A 28-pound iron ball is thrown along country roads, and the winner of the game is the man (it's generally only men who play) who moves the ball over a prescribed distance with the fewest throws. If you come across handfuls of grass that have been dropped along a lane at intervals, it generally means a game has been or is being played along that route—clumps of grass are used as markers.

Glengarriff and the Mountains

Heading on from Bantry you have ample choice—whichever way you travel, the scenery is magnificent. Heading **east** the road to Dunmanway and its fine independent hostel takes you through fabulous empty mountains, while the Pass of Keimaneigh farther north leads through a steep, rocky ravine up to **Gougane Barra** and a cirque lake, the source of the river Lee. An island on this lake was the site of Saint Finbarr's hermitage before he founded his monastery at Cork city downstream. The remains on the island are, however, eighteenth-century. It's an area famous for its beauty. Gougane Barra has a forest park with nature trails, but up here you can walk wherever you please.

Cradled between the Caha Mountains and Bantry Bay, **GLENGARRIFF** is an oasis of greenery. South-facing and sheltered by rugged mountains, it has a peculiarly gentle climate; oak and holly woodlands hug the shoreline while occasional palms flourish in hotel gardens. This picturesque juxtaposition has been exploited since the nineteenth century, when sensitive Victorians became alerted to the beneficial effects of the uniquely mild atmosphere in this pocket of lushness. Unfortunately, recent exploitation has resulted in a barrage of billboarding; ads for gift shops and boat trips have destroyed virtually all of the village's former character. When a tour-bus meets Glengarriff nowadays, it is difficult to say which is the victim.

It's not even possible to walk down the street without being hassled by a stage-Irish boatman trying to sell you a ticket for **Garnish Island** (March–June & Sept–Oct Mon–Sat 10am–6pm, Sun 1–6pm; July & Aug Mon–Sat 9:30am–6pm, Sun 11am–6pm). Sooner or later, you might as well give in; expensive as it is, the island trip is quite something. In 1910 the owner of Garnish conceived a plan to turn his island—then bare rock—into a floating oasis of exotic plantlife. All the topsoil had to be imported, and the resultant growth delicately nurtured for years. The end product is undeniably impressive: flowers and shrubs from all over the world flourish here, and through much of the year the place is ablaze with color, in stark contrast to the desolate mountains of the Beara a stone's throw across the water. If you decide to visit the island you can cut the cost somewhat by getting a group together to share a boat; if you're staying at the independent hostel, ask there as they sometimes have offers arranged. Be warned, however, that whatever price you fix with the boatmen for the ten-minute trip out there past basking seals, you will be charged again (£1.30, students 50p) the minute you step onto the jetty for the privilege of actually seeing the island.

Despite the commercialism, Glengarriff is also a great place to stay if you want to explore some of Cork and Kerry's most wildly beautiful countryside. You can get information on local B&B accommodation from the **tourist office** in the main street (June 22–Aug 31; ☎027-63084), or better still you can stay outside town (and away from its excesses) at *Tooreen House* **independent hostel** (☎027-63075; April–Sept; £4, private rooms £5, camping £2.50), a two-mile walk or easy hitch up the main Kenmare road. It lies on the right-hand side of the road and you should make sure that you're at the right place (look for the *Independent Hostel Association* logo, a bird flying across countryside, at the entrance) since there is a bogus hostel on the opposite side of the road, a good mile before *Tooreen House*, which should be avoided. At the real *Tooreen House* you will be able to hear a gushing mountain river plunging over rocks. Superb for walkers with maps and compasses, it is a wonderful, wild place—huge areas of barren rock with odd patches of scrawny, rough vegetation, and then the occasional seam of brilliant deciduous woods. There is a real exhilaration up here as you watch the constantly changing patterns of weather over the mountains and the bay, with squalls of rain and pools of sunlight playing games of tag across the landscape.

The Beara Peninsula

The **Beara Peninsula**, barren and remote, seems to have an energy all of its own, bounding in great ribs of rock thirty miles out into the ocean. It is a fine place for tough bicycling and tough walking, though you need to be prepared: the weather is notoriously changeable, and careful planning of routes, particularly the descent, is vital. Everywhere along the peninsula you are accompanied by fine views of the mountains and the sea, and there are occasional sandy beaches on either side. Take local advice before swimming, however, as currents can be treacherous.

In practical terms, there are enough good **hostels** to make lengthy exploration a viable proposition, but it is worth bearing in mind that a sparse population means there's little traffic of any sort—don't rely on being able to hitch back if you're in a hurry. If you're planning to **camp**, be aware that though there is no shortage of open land, a lot of it is very rocky. **Private buses—** the only public transit—connect the Beara communities with Glengarriff and Bantry four days a week, and there's also a service linking Castletownbere directly with Cork five days a week. Information on the former is available in Castletownbere at *O'Donohue's Corner House* (☎027-70007); for the Cork service contact *Super-van* (☎027-74003).

Exploring the Peninsula

The first settlement along the coast, about fifteen miles west of Glengarriff, is **ADRIGOLE**, a string of houses stretching over a couple of miles with no real center. There's a **hostel** here, in a wonderful setting on the R572 about 100 yards west past the junction for the Healy Pass, a small wooden chalet with rocky mountains to the rear and Bantry Bay below. A store and pub are nearby, and it's a perfect spot from which to do some walking. **Hungry Hill** rises to 2251 feet, a good climb rewarded by fabulous views, hidden lakes and waterfalls, while the very steep road through the **Healy Pass** leads north to LAURAGH, County Kerry, where there is an *An Óige* hostel at Glanmore Lake (☎064-8318; grade B).

Beara communities have always relied heavily on fishing, and **CASTLETOWNBERE**, the peninsula's main town, is no exception. Set on Ireland's second largest natural harbor, it's periodically awash with French or Portuguese sailors. There's a handful of cafés, well-stocked stores, a chip shop and some nice pubs to serve them. *MacCarthy's* grocery store is a bar as well, so provisions are available at all hours; *Lynch's* bar has music on weekends, and Jackie Lynch also makes sensational seafood sandwiches. Should you feel the need, there is an occasional disco at *The Wheel Inn*, one mile out of town towards Adrigole; locals will tell you if there's anything going on.

The town serves as a useful base from which to walk or cycle, or to catch a ferry for **Bere Island** which shelters the harbor; three ferries a day during July and August (☎027-75009 for information at other times). Nearby coastal walks take you to the ruins of **Dunboy Castle** and **Puxley's Castle**. The former was where an Irish and Spanish force was beseiged and overcome by the English in 1602, the latter the eerie dilapidated shell of a Victorian Gothic mansion. This was the home of the Puxley family who made their money out of copper-mining; their story, and that of the mines, was used by Daphne du Maurier in her novel *Hungry Hill*. The castle itself was burned down by the IRA in the 1920s, but its setting is idyllic: a placid inlet behind Castletownbere harbor fringed by rich woodlands, with stunning views of the wild mountains.

You can **camp** on the grounds of Puxley Castle for £2. The best regular **accommodation** is at *Beara Hostel* (☎027-70184; £4, private rooms £5, family rooms £4, camping £2.50), about two miles west of town on the road towards Allihies. The hostel is on an organic farm, so there is always produce available. **Bike rental** is available at the hostel, from D. Murphy (Bridge House; ☎027-70020), or at the *Super Valu* supermarket (£3.50 plus £5 deposit). There is a **laundromat** at West End, Castletownbere.

Moving on from Castletownbere you can head down to the remote, tiny villages at the end of the peninsula—a few houses, a store and a pub being the typical set-up. This extreme of the peninsula saw some development in the nineteenth century when copper was mined, but little remains beyond the unguarded shafts; beware of these if you're walking. Tiny **ALLIHIES**, formerly a major mining center, nowadays has simply a couple of pubs, a shop, a sandy beach, and an **An Óige hostel** (☎027-73014, April–Sept; grade B) about a mile from the village. There is also a **campground** down by the beach, and Veronica O'Callaghan's *Atlantic Seafood Restaurant*, which serves delicious food, is great value, and will make you feel like you're being well looked after.

Perhaps the quietest of the islands to be visited off West Cork is **Dursey Island**, at the very tip of the peninsula. Dursey's attractions include fabulous views, solitude, and the thrill of taking a very dubious-looking cable car across the narrow and treacherous sound. Fringed by high cliffs, you can walk up its hills for endless views westwards over the ocean, with three great lumps of rock in the foreground: the Cow, the Calf, and the Bull. For a day-trip you need to get to the very end of the R572 in the morning. The cable car has no regular schedule, but generally it's difficult getting to the island between 11am and 4pm. If you want to stop over you will need to pitch a tent—the island has just a few houses (which claim to be the most westerly habitation in Europe) and a pub.

travel details

Trains
From Cork: to Limerick Junction (8 daily; 1hr 10min); Dublin (7 daily; 2hr 30min–3hr); Tralee (2 daily; 2hr 15min).

Bus Éireann
From Cork: to Cork Airport (4 daily; 14min); Dublin (1 daily; 6hr 20min); Limerick (6 daily; 2hr).

Private buses
Funtrek (☎01-730852) runs one bus daily **from Cork**, outside *Joe O'Reilly Travel* (their Cork agent) to Cashel, Cahir, Mitchelstown, Fermoy and Dublin.
Pierce Kavanagh Coaches (☎01-734344/056-31213) operates a weekend bus departing **Friday from Dublin** (Liberty Hall) 5:30pm, calling at Cashell, Cahir, **Cork** (*Roches Stores*, Patrick Street) 10pm, Dunmanway, arrive **Bantry** 11:30pm. Departing **Sunday from Bantry** (Court house) 3:30pm, **Cork** (*Chateau Bar*, Patrick Street) 5:15pm, arrive **Dublin** (Eden Quay) 9:30pm.

O'Donohue's (☎027-70007) bus departs from **Castletownbere** (*O'Donohue's Corner House*) Thursday 7:30am for **Cork**, with the return trip from **Cork** (*Ivy League Bar*, Parnell Place) at 6pm. *O'Donohue's* **Castletownbere, Glengarriff** and **Bantry** service runs as follows:
Monday Castletownbere 7am, calling at Glengarriff 8am, arrives Bantry 8:25am. Return Bantry 11:40am, Glengarriff 12:10pm, arrives Castletownbere 1:10pm.
Tuesday, Friday and Saturday Castletownbere 10:30am, calling at Glengarriff 11:30am, arrives Bantry noon. Return Bantry 3:45pm, Glengarriff 4:15pm, arrives Castletownbere 5:15pm.
Harrington's Buses (☎027-74003) Depart **from Castletownbere** on Monday, Tuesday, Wednesday, Friday, Saturday at 8am to arrive at **Cork** 10:45am; Sunday at 5pm to arrive at Cork 7:30pm. Services depart **from Cork** (*Ivy League Bar*, Parnell Place) at 6pm on the same days, to arrive in Castletownbere at 8:30pm; Sunday departure at 8pm. The Saturday service runs only in high season.

CHAPTER EIGHT

KERRY

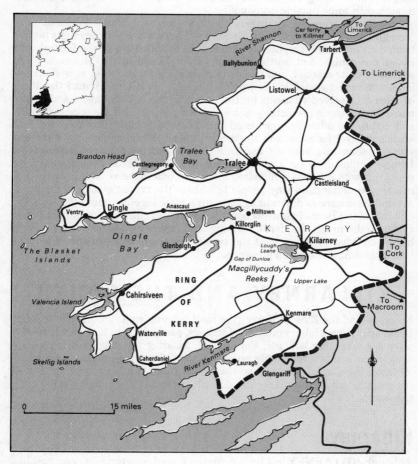

If you've come to Ireland for the scenery, mountains, sea, and the remoteness, you'll find them all in **Kerry**: miles and miles of mountain-moorland where the heather and the bracken are broken only by the occasional lake, and smooth hills whose fragrant, tussocky grass is covered with sea pinks, speedwells, thrift, and red campion, fragmenting into jagged rocks as they reach the sea. The ocean looks enormous, and you can stand in the sunshine and watch a storm coming in for miles before you have to run for cover. The only catch is that a good part of the county is very much on the tourist trail.

The plus side of Kerry's long tradition of welcoming tourists is that it's very easy country to travel in, with plenty of accommodation and food in all price ranges. And, during the summer at least, transportation is pretty good—though with some notable exceptions.

Broadly speaking, Kerry divides into four areas: the Dingle Peninsula; the Iveragh Peninsula, encircled by the Ring of Kerry, with Killarney in its hinterland; the Kenmare River, bordered to the north and south by the Iveragh and Beara peninsulas; and northern Kerry, from Tralee to the Shannon. Each section is quite distinct, and has its partisans. By far the most visited area—indeed the most visited in the whole of Ireland—is **Killarney and the Ring of Kerry**. Deservedly famous for the beauty of the adjacent lakes and mountains, this region is predictably geared up for tourism, and the principal roads and sights are often overburdened with visitors. Luckily, however, the real wilds are never far away, and whether you head for the mountains or the sea you can soon lose yourself and feel remote from modern civilization. The **Dingle** peninsula is on a smaller scale than Iveragh, but equally magical: peppered with monastic remains, it has a contemplative atmosphere that makes you understand why people talk about the mystic quality of the west. Around **Kenmare** is different again, with a tamed feeling about the scenery; one half of the Beara Peninsula actually belongs to cultivated, genteel County Cork. To the **north**, flat, fertile farming land makes for less exciting scenery, but in contrast to the rest of the county there are many signs of a long-established Anglo-Norman presence.

KILLARNEY AND THE SOUTH

Killarney and the Ring of Kerry (the road running right around the Iveragh Peninsula) attract huge numbers of visitors, particularly in high summer—be wary if you're after solitude. Fortunately, avoiding the hordes is fairly easy since mass tourism fixes only upon the most obvious attractions: Killarney, its lakes, the Gap of Dunloe, and the wholly insane notion of driving around the magnificent Ring of Kerry in a day. Steer clear of these, and you'll escape the worst.

Killarney

Although **KILLARNEY** has been commercialized to saturation point and has little in the way of architectural interest, its location amid some of the best lakeland, mountain and woodland scenery in Ireland more than compensates. The town is essentially one main street and a couple of side roads, full of souvenir shops, cafés, pubs, restaurants and B&Bs. Pony buggies and jaunting carts line up against walls while their weather-beaten owners talk visitors into extortionate trips through the surrounding country. It's all done with the charm laid on thick, true to Killarney's long tradition of profitably hosting the visiting masses ever since its discovery as a resort in the mid-eighteenth century.

The town's Gaelic name (*Cill Airne*, Church of the Sloe) doesn't imply a settlement of any great antiquity, and the Cromwellian Survey of 1654 found no town or village of that name. By 1756 a burgeoning tourist trade, soon swelled by the growing Romantic attraction to lakes and mountains, had created Killarney: "A new street with a large commodious inn was designed to be built here, for the curiosities of the neighbouring lake have of late drawn great numbers of curious travellers to visit it," said a contemporary survey. The local landowner, Lord Kenmare, quickly spotted commercial opportunities and granted free leases for new inns and houses, building four major roads to connect his creation with the outside world.

That said, the town doesn't *look* particularly planned, and the only building of any distinction is the high Gothic revival style **Cathedral**, built by Augustus Pugin in 1855. A particularly florid Victorian interpretation of medieval architecture, the cathedral inspires both respect and derision, but is worth seeing either way. During the Famine, when building work ceased for five years, the covered area served as a hospital for victims of starvation and disease.

Practical Details

Bed and breakfasts abound, although in high season the town fills up and it's worth calling the helpful **tourist office**, on the main street by the town hall (☎064-31633), to make advance reservations. The **An Óige hostel** (☎064-31240) is three miles out along the Killorglin road, at Aghadoe, but there are also four independent hostels in Killarney. Which you opt for is probably more a question of temperament than anything else. The *Four Winds Hostel* at 43 New Street (turn left outside the tourist office, left at the crossroads, and it's a few minutes' walk down on your right; ☎064-33094; accommodation for couples) is extroverted and noisy; their minibus sometimes cruises for business at the railroad station. The *Súgan Kitchen* (☎064-33104), on Lewis Road, a few minutes' walk from the station, is cosier and more relaxed, with a health-food bistro serving great food (very cheap for residents), a laundry, and traditional music. The same family also runs *Bonrower House*, near Ross Castle; reservations from the *Súgan*. The *Park Hostel* (☎064-32119) is up the hill off Cork Road, opposite the gas station. There's a **campground** at the *Fossa Caravan Park* (☎064-31497) just past the Aghadoe youth hostel west of the town. Killarney's public **laundromat** (Mon–Sat 9am–8pm) is in the little shopping mall off the High Street.

If you're passing through town en route to Dingle, you could stay instead at *Donash Lodge* in Firies, on the main Farenfore-to-Dingle L103 road (☎066-64554; May–Sept; two family/double rooms; camping possible); or *Woods Hostel* in the square at Milltown (☎066-67301; Easter–Oct; some private rooms; camping). There are also *An Óige* hostels at Conan Tuathail, three miles west of Kate Kearney's Cottage (☎066-44338) and at Loo bridge, ten miles south of town (☎064-53002).

Places to **eat and drink** are so thick on the ground that it seems pointless to list them. Nevertheless, cheap dinners are available at *Sceilig*, on High

Street; *Brian Mac's*, on the same road, is good for lunch, as is *A Taste of Ireland* on College Street. Evening **entertainment** is everywhere as you walk along the streets; the widely publicized "traditional" Irish music can seem pretty spurious when you are surrounded by busloads of other tourists, but it sounds great in places like *Jimmy O'Brien's* (near the Priory), the *Súgan Kitchen*, or *The Laurels* (for Ireland's other folk tradition, country and western). *Tattler Jack's* is an ordinary pub with lively conversation.

Even if you're not planning to bike round the Ring of Kerry, bi**cycling** is a great way of seeing Killarney's immediate surroundings (see below), and makes good sense because **local transit** is almost non-existent. *O'Callaghan Brothers* (College Street; ☎064-31465/31175) are the local participants in the Raleigh scheme; bikes can also be rented from *O'Neill's* in Plunkett Street (☎064-31970).

In May, July, and October there's **racing** at Killarney's racecourse on Ross Road, which like any Irish race meeting is well worth a detour. The tourist office can give details of **Gaelic soccer** matches; Killarney is a top team and feelings run high. If you're heading for Killarney in the spring, check out the **Pan-Celtic Week**, a gathering of artists and film-makers from Ireland, Scotland, Wales, Cornwall, and Brittany; details from the tourist office.

Around Killarney

The real reason for coming to Killarney is without doubt the surrounding landscape. Its three spectacular **lakes**, Lough Leane (the Lower Lake), Muckross Lake (the Middle Lake) and the Upper Lake, are only the appetizer. Behind them loom **MacGillycuddy's Reeks**, which have a grandeur out of all proportion to their height; rarely exceeding 3000 feet, they're still the highest mountains in Ireland.

It was the Ice Age that formed the Killarney landscape. Glaciation has left its mark on the contorted limestone valleys of the Lower and Middle Lakes, and the nearby Devil's Punch Bowl and Horses' Glen show other signs: huge rocks smoothed to sucked-sweet shapes, and improbably teetering boulders. The lower slopes of the mountains are covered with what is often virgin forest, a joy to see in a country that has cut down almost all its trees. Almost everything seems to thrive in the local combination of high rainfall and humidity, and in the woods you'll find a rich mix of trees, dominated by oak but also with bilberry, woodrush and woodsorrel, plus mosses, liverworts and lichens, the latter sensitive organisms whose continued survival testifies to the clean air here.

As elsewhere in the west of Ireland, the Killarney area's **vegetation** includes a number of plants generally found only in quite different parts of Europe. The famous arbutus, or strawberry tree—so called from its bright red (and inedible) fruit—for example, generally grows only in Mediterranean countries and Brittany. Some saxifrages, and the greater butterwort with its fleshy purple flowers and sickly green leaf rosettes, are otherwise found only in northwest Spain and Portugal (see section on "The Burren" in the *County Clare* chapter for more on the west's strange flora).

Knockreer Estate

Oddly enough, given its origins as a tourist town, Killarney turns its back on the grand scenery to the west and south, hunching itself inward so that you'd hardly guess at the delights that await you. But the gates of the old Kenmare Estate—now known as the **Knockreer Estate**—are just across the road from the cathedral, and a short walk through the grounds takes you to the banks of **Lough Leane**. The Browne family, earls of Kenmare, were unusual among the Irish peerage in that they never renounced their Catholic faith. Given lands confiscated from the O'Donoghues during the seventeenth century, they were subject in the eighteenth century to the penal laws which decreed that every Catholic landowner had to divide his property among his male heirs. The Brownes' estate remained intact quite simply because there was only one son in each generation.

At Lough Leane, the scenery is magnificent: tall wooded hills plunge into the water, with the mountain peaks rising behind to the highest, **Carrintuohill** (3414 feet). Ireland's last wild wolf was killed here in 1700, and when the weather's bad (as it often is) there's a satisfying similarity to early Romantic engravings. The main path through the Kenmare estate leads to the restored fourteenth-century tower of **Ross Castle**, the last place in Munster to succumb to Cromwell's forces in 1652. The story is that General Ludlow, having learned of a tradition that Ross Castle would never be taken from land, brought prefabricated ships from Kenmare and sailed them up from Castlemaine, whereupon the defenders—whom nothing else had budged—immediately surrendered. Near the water you can make out copper works, last used during the Napoleonic Wars and thought to date back 4000 years.

From Ross Castle you can tour the lake in large glassed-over boats like the *bateaux-mouches* that ply the Seine in Paris, but these don't make stops, and an alternative is to get a fisherman to take you out in a little craft with an outboard motor, or rent one yourself. This way, you can land on and explore the island of **Inisfallen** (if you're navigating yourself, look for a limestone outcrop in the water; Inisfallen is the island to the left, about a mile out).

Of the thirty-odd small islands that dot Lough Leane, Inisfallen is the biggest and most enchanting, particularly if there's no one else on it (which can easily happen as you watch the *bateaux mouches* grind by). The monastery founded here in the seventh century was an important scholastic center for a thousand years. Brian Boru, the eleventh-century High King and victor over the Vikings at Clontarf in 1014, allegedly was educated here, and the twelfth-century *Annals of Inisfallen*, now in Oxford's Bodleian Library, are an important source document for early Irish history. Wandering round the island is a delight; heavily wooded, it's also scattered with monastic buildings—nothing from the original seventh-century foundation, but there's a small Romanesque church and an extremely ruined twelfth-century Augustinian priory. Eighteenth-century tourists were clearly aware of Inisfallen's charms: Lord Kenmare used to give parties for his influential friends here, and the gap in the wall of the Romanesque church is where he installed a bay window when the building was converted into a banqueting house. The picturesque ruin you see now is the result of further tinkering, around 1840.

Muckross and the Lakes

The road from Killarney to the **Muckross estate** passes through unlovely territory dominated by huge modern hotels, and though jaunting carts from the center will willingly take you out to Muckross (cars are prohibited on the Muckross estate), it's more fun to rent a bike. Take the earliest available turning right into the park, to escape the busy main road. The first place to head for is **Muckross Abbey**, not only for the ruin itself—one of the best-preserved in Ireland, part Norman, part Gothic, though sadly despoiled by Cromwell's troops—but also for its calm, contemplative location, and the fact that it, like Ross Castle, hints at something predating Killarney's tourist history. Founded as a Franciscan institution by Macarthy Mor in the mid-fifteenth century, it was suppressed by Henry VIII; the friars soon returned, but were finally driven out by Cromwell's army in 1652.

Back at the main road, signposts direct you to **Muckross House**, a solid nineteenth-century neo-Elizabethan mansion designed by the Scottish architect William Burn. The **museum** (March–June and Sept & Oct daily 9am–6pm; July & Aug daily 9am–7pm; Nov–Feb Tues–Sun 11am–5pm; £2, students 80p), while no great shakes, has a section on Kerry folk life where craftspeople (blacksmiths, weavers, potters) demonstrate their trades—but only at peak times. The excellent tea shop provides a good refuge from the rain, but the gardens—well known for their rhododendrons and azaleas—are the place to be when the weather is fine.

The estate gives access to well-trodden paths along the shores of the Middle Lake, and it's here that you can see one of Killarney's celebrated beauty spots, the **Meeting of Waters**. Actually a parting, but highly picturesque nonetheless, it has a profusion of indigenous and flowering subtropical plants—eucalyptus, magnolia, bamboo, and an arbutus, on the left of the Old Weir Bridge. Close by is the massive shoulder of Torc Mountain, shrugging off **Torc Waterfall**. There's a not-terribly-informative visitor center by the parking lot for the waterfall; but the climb up the side of the mountain is worth doing, if only for the view across to Macgillycuddy's Reeks. On a good day, the Slievemish mountains on the far side of Dingle Bay are also visible.

The **Upper Lake** is beautiful too, but still firmly on the tourist trail, with the main road running along one side up to **Ladies' View**, where the egg-sandwich brigades line up with their thermoses to admire the view—which is, in fact, truly amazing, including the Gap of Dunloe and the secretive Black Valley behind the lake.

The Gap of Dunloe

Although the **Gap of Dunloe**—a narrow defile formed by glacial overflow that cuts the mountains in two—is one of Killarney's prime tourist attractions, it's possible to find a modicum of solitude if you're willing to use your legs. Jaunting carts continually run here from Killarney's center, a fact which, as the drivers compete loudly for business, you're not likely to miss. One version of the trip, combining jaunting cars with a bus ride, sets off from the tourist office at 10:30am, transferring you to a pony and buggy for the Gap itself, before returning to town at 5:15pm. Apart from costing an astonishing £19, this entails being stuck in the traffic jam of bored ponies pulling buggies up the Gap. The other option is to walk, ignoring the offers of rides that will assail you for the first half mile or so. If you fade before the four miles are up, it's possible to bargain for a ride—the whole trip generally costs about £10 a car.

Kate Kearney's Cottage, at the foot of the road leading up to the Gap—a confusion of shops and sweating horses—is the last place for food and water before Lord Brandon's Cottage, way over the other side of the Black Valley. The best time to **walk** is late afternoon, when the jaunting carts have gone home and the light is at its most magical. The road—closed to motor traffic—winds its way up the desolate valley between high rock cliffs and waterfalls (Macgillycuddy's Reeks to your right, and the Purple Mountain, so called because in late summer it's covered in purple heather), past a chain of icy loughs and tarns, up to the top, when you find yourself in what feels like one of the remotest places in the world: the **Black Valley**.

Named after its entire population perished during the potato famine, and now inhabited by a mere handful of families, the Black Valley makes you begin to feel that you've left mass tourism behind. The fact that it was the very last valley in Ireland to get electricity is some measure of its isolation, and there are no pubs or shops. From here, you can either continue on down to the Upper Lake (Lord Brandon's Cottage, food, boat rental, and the quick way back to Killarney); or pick up the Kerry Way.

Walking the Kerry Way

The **Kerry Way** is part of a long-distance footpath that's intended to go right around the Iveragh Peninsula through Cahirciveen, Waterville, Caherdaniel, Kenmare, and Kilgarvan—a sort of walkers' Ring of Kerry. At the moment it stops short around Sneem, on the peninsula's south coast. More than most of Ireland's long-distance footpaths, it's resonant of the culture, as well as the nature, of the area, consisting largely of "green roads". Many of these are old drovers' roads, "butter roads" (along which butter was transported), or routes between Kerry's ancient Christian settlements. It's also one of the best ways of starting to explore the spectacular uplands of MacGillycuddy's Reeks.

The Kerry Way starts inauspiciously in Killarney, threads down through the Muckross estate and alongside the Upper Lake—road walking, most of it—before heading up to meet the Black Valley (see above). From the Black Valley, it heads on towards Cloghernoosh via a stony path that becomes a green road. After the footbridge over the stream running out of Curraghmore Lake, there's a stretch of bridle path, and from here on you're among the peaks, with exhilarating views of Carrintuohil to the north.

Next, the footpath follows the Lack Road, zigzagging up to a saddle point at the top, then skirting the side of Lough Acoose before reaching the Glencar valley (and the first tourist accommodation since the Black Valley). No longer traversing really high ground, the rest of the way into Glenbeigh is less exciting, although the stretch on Seefin Mountain above Caragh Lake is still spectacular.

All the usual **precautions** need to be taken seriously in a region where gales blowing in off the Atlantic can make the weather change rapidly. Bring waterproof clothing, walking boots, food, and a good map; the one-inch *Map of Killarney District*, covering most of the walk, is useful, while the half-inch *Dingle Bay Ordnance Survey Map* details most of the first leg, up to the Black Valley.

You should really arrange **accommodation** beforehand. The **An Óige hostel** in the Black Valley (☎064-32300) sells supplies at strictly limited times, and an independent hostel, *The Mountain Lodge* (☎066-60134), a little farther on in the Bridia Valley, serves meals and sleeps just eight; to have dinner you need to arrive by 7pm, the stream substitutes for showers, and you can also camp. It's roughly eight hours' walk from Killarney; hitching isn't recommended, since the nearest road seeing any traffic is eight miles from the start of the valley. Next stop is the *Climbers' Inn*, hidden among woodlands at Glencar (☎066-60101; no meals available after 6pm, but there is a store). In Glenbeigh you can stay in bed and breakfasts or in an independent hostel, *Hillside House* (☎066-68228), which has a store, showers and other facilities.

For more **information on mountaineering** in Kerry, contact the *Killarney Mountaineering Club* (☎066-61127); the Kerry Mountain Rescue Team is based at Killarney police station (☎064-31222).

The Ring of Kerry

The 110-mile **Ring of Kerry** which circles the Iveragh Peninsula can be driven around in a day, and most tourists view its spectacular scenery without ever leaving their bus or car. Consequently, anyone straying from the road or waiting until the buses knock off in the afternoon will be left to experience the long, slow twilights of the Atlantic seaboard in perfect seclusion. Part of the excitement of traveling around the Kerry coast comes from the clarity with which its physical outline stands against the vast gray expanse of the Atlantic. Every gully, bay, channel, and island is as distinct as it it is on the map, giving a powerful sense of place amid the isolation.

If you really are limited to a day's exploration of the wild coastal scenery, it could be worth heading for Dingle, the next peninsula north, instead; its intimacy of scale means you can see a lot more without having to rely upon vehicles. **Bicycling** the Ring itself takes three days (not counting any diversions), and a bike will let you get on to the largely deserted mountain roads; just be sure your machine has lots of gears. Public transit doesn't serve the entire circuit—the **buses** from Killarney only go as far as Cahirciveen (twice daily in July and August, only once daily otherwise)—but during summer, flotillas of **tour buses** ply the Ring in a counterclockwise direction. Most of them leave from opposite the tourist office, where you can get details, and for an extra charge will drop you off somewhere along the way, and pick you up the next day. **Hitching** is unreliable; while you're likely to get a lift from anyone who passes, traffic simply may not exist away from the main roads.

Killorglin to Cahirciveen

By traveling the Ring of Kerry counterclockwise, you get a gradual introduction to the wild grandeur of the coastline scenery, with the Dingle peninsula and the dim shapes of the Blasket Islands visible in the distance.

The first stop on the way out from Killarney is the pleasantly unexceptional hillside town of KILLORGLIN, whose main claim to fame is the **Puck Fair**, held over three days in mid-August—a fairly bacchanalian affair with a wild goat captured and enthroned, plenty of dancing and drinking, plus a cattle, sheep, and horse fair.

Next comes GLENBEIGH, where almost everything is devoted to tourism; despite plenty of B&Bs and the *Hillside House Hostel* (☎066-68228), the town illustrates the disadvantages of sticking rigidly to the Ring. However, there are wonderful views all along the coastline and across to Dingle, and by taking the road up past **Lough Caragh**, you'll find some of Kerry's best mountain scenery, full of deep silences and the magical slanting light of the west. The lack of trees that contributes to the feeling of austerity was not an original feature of the landscape; Sir William Petty, Cromwell's surveyor-general, had an iron mine at Blackstones, and felled the forests to fuel a smelter. Alternatively, you could climb up to the three small lakes of Coomnacronia, Coomasglaslaw, and Coomsaharn (good trout fishing, but check the license situation before you cast your line).

Cahirciveen

At **Kells Bay** the road veers inland for Cahirciveen, giving you an opportunity to take a detour. Any of the turnoffs right will lead eventually to the sea, past bright fuschia hedges, with little or no traffic. "One wonders, in this place, why anyone is left in Dublin, or London, or Paris, when it would be better one would think, to live in a tent, or a hut, with this magnificent sea and sky, and to breathe this wonderful air, which is like wine in one's teeth," wrote J. M. Synge of the Kerry landscape; here for the first time you begin to understand how the Ring inspires such hyperbole.

CAHIRCIVEEN (pronounced "Caher-shivveen," stress on the last syllable) is a long, narrow street of a town and the main shopping center for the western part of the peninsula, devoting cheerfully to the tourist trade in summer. A laid-back, unremarkable place, it has more relaxed attitudes to shopping hours than anywhere else on the peninsula, lending it an odd southern flavor, and there are plenty of friendly bars.

Beyond Cahirciveen, the road sweeps inland again towards Waterville, giving you an opportunity to explore the lanes that lead out to Valentia Island and the peninsula's end. The **vacation cottages** which abound here tend to get filled up, so if you want to be sure of a place you'll need to reserve early in the year—they're administered by the Irish Tourist Board (see *Basics* for details)—but you can check availability on the spot with the Cahirciveen **tourist office** (☎066-21288). Staying here, the slow life works its spell; you can buy fish direct from the boats at Reenard Point, where the ferry for Valentia Island departs.

Valentia Island

VALENTIA, an island now linked to the mainland by bridge, is Europe's most westerly harbor, and standing at Bray Head on the island's tip, there's nothing but ocean between you and Newfoundland, 1900 miles away. Valentia's significance is out of all proportion to its size; the first ever transatlantic telegraph cable was laid from here in 1857—though permanent contact wasn't established until 1866—and for years it had better communications with New York than with Dublin.

In contrast to the endless vistas west, the island itself is small, and consequently every scrap of land has been cultivated, forming a rolling patchwork of fields stitched with dry slate walls. Valentia's position in the Gulf Stream gives it a mild, balmy climate, and the abundance of fuschias grown by the inhabitants in local hedgerows enhances its domesticated atmosphere. It's a homey, tame place to stay, though from July onward the peace is disturbed by tourists.

Access is by **ferry** from Reenard to Knightstown (ask at Cahirciveen post office for details; this runs only when the weather permits), or via the Maurice O'Neill Bridge, at the south end of the island, thirteen miles from the main coast road, and a difficult hitch. Once on the island there's no public transit at all. **Accommodation** is at a premium during the summer season, when B&Bs in Knightstown and Portmagee raise their prices to around £14; the **An Óige hostel** has space for forty at Cottages 1–5 of the Coastguard Station, but for members only, and services are spartan. The independent hostel on the harbor front is never short of space, but damp and unfriendly; midway between the bridge and Knightstown there's another independent, *Ring Lyne Hostel* (☎066-6103).

KNIGHTSTOWN is the focal village on the island and, facing Cahirciveen across the Portmagee Channel, affords fine panoramic views of the Kerry mountains. A pretty harbor front with sprucely painted fishermen's cottages is dominated by the Victorian *Royal and Pier Hotel*; now damply dilapidated and something of a white elephant, it's currently being run as an independent hostel (see above). Tolerating rather than encouraging tourists, Knightstown is deeply old-fashioned, and if there are more than three in your group, you could feel something of an intrusion. About a thousand houses cluster around a slate church hidden within a dark rookery. The main street has a few well-stocked shops, a post office offering a good selection of Irish literature and free maps of the island, and a couple of bars. Uninspiring by day, these come to life after 10pm several nights a week, when locals playing accordions and pipes accompany rigorous Gaelic dancing, the faces of the participants (average age sixty-plus) showing serious concentration in this wild pastime.

From Knightstown, take the Kilmore road down towards the lighthouse, where there's a fine view of Valentia's empty harbor, the Beginis Islands, and tiny **Church Island**. This mere rock supports the ruins of an eighth-century cell, once inhabited by a solitary monk—a soulmate of the brotherhood on the nearby Skellig Islands—whose only company was the sea birds. On a clear day you can also make out the sheer cliffs of the Blasket Islands beyond the Dingle Peninsula to the north.

Continuing west, the foreshore is an imposing clutter of megalithic slabs hurled together by the waves, with deep, limpid pools left by the winter storms. A couple of miles farther on, a wonderful swimming cove combines intimacy with the grandiose, sheltered by lush, deciduous woods, with the whole of Kerry as its scenic backdrop. This appears to be part of the grounds of **Glanleam House** (former seat of the local magnate, the Knight of Kerry), attached to which are incongruously exotic gardens, but it's actually a public beach.

The fervor with which locals urge you to visit the **Grotto** is misplaced. A gaping slate cavern, it boasts a crude, municipal-baths-blue statue of the Virgin (erected 1954) perched 200 feet up, amidst monotonously dripping icy water. Nevertheless, this is the highest point on the island, and a good walk for a clear day. But more exciting by far is the cliff scenery to the northwest, some of the most spectacular of the Kerry coast.

The Skellig Islands

From Valentia you get a tantalizing view across a broad strip of sea to the **Skellig Islands**, apparently no more than two massive rocks. Little Skellig is a bird sanctuary, and landing isn't permitted, but you can visit Great Skellig, or Skellig Michael as it's also called, and climb up to the ancient monastic site at the summit. To get there, inquire at local shops in Reenard, Knightstown, and Portmagee about **boat trips**; these are expensive at around £10 but, if the weather's good, make a fascinating and dramatic voyage. Once at sea, boats are followed by wheeling seagulls and, if you're lucky, puffins too. Oddly staid little birds that look like miniature flying businessmen, they come from the nature reserve of Puffin Island, farther north. You'll also pass the huge, jagged arch of rock that forms **Little Skellig**, where some of the 18,000 gannets with six-foot wingspans career overhead, or make headlong dives into the sea for fish.

Skellig Michael looms sheer from the ocean, a gargantuan slaty mass with no visible route to the summit. From the tiny landing stage, however, you can see steps cut into the cliff face, formerly a treacherous monks' path. Nowadays there's also a road leading to Christ's Saddle, the only patch of green on this inhospitable island. From here, a path leads on to the arched stone remains of **St Finian's Abbey** (AD 560). Among the ruins are six complete beehive cells—dry-stone huts that have survived centuries of foul weather. The island is dedicated to Saint Michael, guardian against the powers of darkness, and patron of high places. Contrasted with Valentia, it's a wild, cruel place and an awesome sanctuary of devotion, even if the monks didn't remain here all year to feel the violence of the elements.

On to Waterville

The stretch of coast between Valentia and Waterville is wild and almost deserted, apart from a scattering of farms and fishing villages. Sweet-smelling, tussocky grass dotted with wild flowers is raked by Atlantic winds, ending in abrupt cliffs or sandy beaches—a beguiling landscape where you can wander for days. The **An Óige hostel** (☎0667-9229) in **BALLIN-SKELLIGS** makes a good base and sells supplies. Monks from the Skellig islands retreated to **Ballinskelligs Abbey** in the thirteenth century, while the town itself, largely Gaelic-speaking, is the focus of the Kerry *Gaeltacht*, and in the summer it's busy with schoolchildren and students learning Gaelic.

WATERVILLE may be touristy, but it does it with a lot of grace. Popular as a Victorian and Edwardian resort and sport-fishing center, it still has an air of consequence that sits oddly with the wild Atlantic views. Its few bars and hotels aside, the town is chiefly notable as the best base on the Ring for exploring the coast and the mountainous country inland. The **hostel** at *Waterville Leisure Centre* (☎667-4400) can supply information about **surfing**, **mountaineering**, and **riding** in the vicinity.

Waterville and Ballinskelligs Bay form the setting for one of the more wayward Irish **legends**. When the Biblical Flood was imminent, so the story goes, Noah's son Bith and his daughter Cessair found that there was no room for them in the Ark. So they and their retinue set sail for Ireland which, Cessair was advised, was uninhabited, plus free of monsters, reptiles and sin, and would therefore escape the flood. However, although 49 women survived to land along with Cessair in 2958 BC, only two men besides Bith made it. The three men divided the women between them, but when Bith and Ladra, the pilot, died, Fintan, the last man, was overwhelmed, and, to his eternal shame, ran away; upon which Cessair, who loved him, died of sorrow.

From Waterville it's a long haul by bike or on foot up to the **Coomakista Pass**, but the effort is well worth it for the breathtaking views over the mouth of the Kenmare river, all grays and blues, the three rocks called the Bull, the Cow, and the Calf, and beyond them the Beara Peninsula—most spectacular when the weather's good; when it rains you can see the squalls being driven in across the ocean. However, you can't hope to avoid lots of other tourists here.

Derrynane to Kenmare

Tucked away on a little promontory of its own between the Ring of Kerry and the sea is **DERRYNANE** (pronounced "Derrynaan"), home of the family of Daniel O'Connell, the Catholic lawyer and politician who negotiated limited Catholic emancipation in 1829. Aside from his house, Derrynane itself is a pleasant place, with wide, flat sand beaches and two miles of dunes, good swimming, and rocks glistening black with delicious mussels. Although fun in the daytime, like everywhere along this western seaboard it's most atmospheric at sunset, when the long twilight lingers; the Gaels believed that sunset and sunrise were points of transition (like stiles and gates) where it was possible to slip from the "real" world into the faerie one, and here you can see their point.

The **O'Connell House** (May–Sept Mon–Sat 9am–6pm, Sun 11am–7pm; Oct–April Tues–Sun 1–5pm; £1, students 35p) remodeled by Daniel O'Connell himself, is absolutely simple—a square slate tower and roughly elegant rooms with the slanting sea-light a constant presence. The

O'Connells were an old Gaelic family who'd made their money trading and smuggling; the west of Ireland had a long tradition of trade with Europe in wine, spices, and silks. Daniel O'Connell's uncle bequeathed him a fortune, giving him the financial independence necessary to devote himself to politics. Discrimination against Catholics was widespread, and closely experienced by Daniel: another uncle was shot dead because he would not give up his fine horse, as the law demanded of Catholics.

The immediate area has plenty of ancient forts and standing stones. On the way to CASTLECOVE, there's a sign on the left for **Staigue Fort**, two and a half miles up a rough lane, a very well-preserved ring fort, possibly created as early as 1000 BC. The nearest **hostel** (with another fort 300 yards away) is *Carrigbeg* at CAHIRDANIEL, just outside Derrynane Park on a bend in the road overlooking the sea; their breakfast of muesli and brown bread is a welcome relief from the ubiquitous bacon and eggs (☎0667-5229; April–Oct). As the road winds onwards towards Sneem, there's good swimming, particularly at **White Strand**, past hedgerows blossoming with both fuschia and hydrangea.

SNEEM (pronounced "Shneem") is spectacularly set against the mountains, dominated by the 2245-foot Knockmoyle, but the village has lost something by selling out to tourism. Winner of the Tidy Towns Competition of 1988, Sneem's houses are painted in different colors—reputedly so that drunken residents can find their way home—and their picture-book prettiness juxtaposed against tourist shops and cafés has a touch of the surreal. Good local fishing is advertised by the salmon-shaped weathercock on the Protestant church.

The approach to Kenmare along the estuary is unexciting, seemingly more in character with the Beara Peninsula opposite than with wild Iveragh, and you'll have a more scenic journey back to Killarney if you take the mountain road direct from Sneem. The two routes join up again at the spectacular **Moll's Gap**, north of Kenmare.

Kenmare and the Beara Peninsula

With its unlikely stores—delicatessens, designer boutiques, and arty second-hand clothes shops—**KENMARE** feels like a foreign enclave, and you're more likely to hear British or German accents here than Irish. Neatly organized on an X-plan (laid out by the first marquess of Lansdowne in 1775), the town is pleasantly cosmopolitan; besides the resident foreigners, it's the natural crossing-over point for everyone traveling up from Cork.

Kenmare was founded by **Sir William Petty**, Cromwell's surveyor-general, to serve a mine works beside the Finnihy River. Petty was extremely active in (and benefited greatly from) the dealings in confiscated properties that went on after the Cromwellian wars. Many soldiers were paid by the impecunious government in land, but not all of them wanted to settle in Ireland, and so sold to dealers—such as Petty. His acquisition of land all over Ireland, including roughly a quarter of Kerry, was surely helped by his commission to survey the country on behalf of the government, when he investigated two-thirds of the Irish counties in the amazingly short period of fifteen months. Petty's other achievements were no less remarkable: a professor of medicine at Oxford at 27, he was also a professor of music and founder member of the Royal Society in London; an early statistician, economist, and demographer; and politically astute enough to get yet more land and a knighthood out of Charles II, even though he had earlier served Cromwell faithfully. In Kerry he laid the foundations of the mining and smelting industries, encouraged fishing, and founded the enormous **Lansdowne estate**, which once surrounded the town; many buildings still remain today.

Evidence of much more ancient settlement is the 15-monolith **stone circle** just outside the center of town on the banks of the river; go up by the right of the market house that faces the park, past some Lansdowne estate houses. Walk up the lane at the cul-de-sac sign, and a few yards after it meets another lane coming in from the left you'll find the circle, behind a high ditch.

Kenmare has two independent **hostels**: the rather off-puttingly clinical *Fáilte* in Henry Street (☎064-41083), and the ramshackle, disorganized *Kenmare Private Hostel* (☎064-41260). There are also plenty of **bed and breakfasts**, both in and just outside town; check vacancies at the **tourist office** on Main Street (☎064-41233). As for **food**, *The Pantry*, at 30 Henry Street, has a stock of health-foods, plus organic vegetables and a wonderful range of unpasteurized cheeses; the *Dunboy Cafe*, at no. 16 opposite, lets you taste them in more comfort. *An Leath Phingin*, 35 Main Street (☎064-41559), in an old house with stone walls, wooden tables, and a turf fire (burning even in June), is an excellent—though not cheap—Italian-Irish restaurant, with good seafood, and plenty of choice for vegetarians. Kenmare's famous *Park Hotel* at the top of the main streets is also worth investigating, if only for a drink, despite the intimidating number of BMWs and Mercedes parked in the driveway. Further west at Lauragh is an **An Óige hostel** (☎064-8318).

The Beara Peninsula

Cross the river from Kenmare and you're on the **Beara Peninsula**, which Kerry shares with Cork. Beara has its followers, but after the wildness of the rest of Kerry, it can at first seem over-lush and polite, with more of the flavor of Cork. Even along the Kenmare River, though, the scenery is attractive enough and curiously, once you actually cross into County Cork, the Beara becomes far wilder (see p.246).

Turn right after the bridge, and the road runs through heavily wooded country alongside the Kenmare estuary, with a signpost to the left for **Inchiquin Lake** a few miles later. Following this, you soon quit the luxuriant vegetation as the bumpy road ascends rapidly to the lake, giving exhilarating views of the countryside left behind. A waterfall tumbles down from a second lake, and on the far side of Inchiquin Lake is **Uragh Wood**, one of the last surviving remnants of the ancient sessile-oak groves that once covered most of Ireland. The entire valley is packed with plants: large-flowered butterwort covers the meadows in spring, and you can find Irish spurge, saxifrage, arbutus, and other flora specific to the southwest. At the lake itself, the surrounding hills seem to act as some kind of intensifier focused on a tiny **stone circle** by the side of the water—bringing to mind the theory that these prehistoric monuments indicate earth forces. There's salmon, sea trout and brown trout **fishing** in both lakes, but, as always, check the license situation before you start.

Following the main road for LAURAGH, you're still in the enormous estate once owned by Petty. The gardens at **Derreen House**, for a long time one of the Irish residences of Petty's descendant the Marquess of Lansdowne, are open to the public, and stocked with plants which clearly luxuriate in the mild sea climate, including such exotica as tree ferns and bamboo, plus rhododendrons and camellias. Yet despite its magnificence, it doesn't compare with the wild and windswept grassy uplands. Head westward from Lauragh, and you're soon over the border into Cork; south, the road climbs spectacularly above Glanmore Lough to Healy Pass—again, the county border—giving amazing views in both directions.

DINGLE AND THE NORTH

In common with the rest of the far west, particularly the Gaelic-speaking areas, the **Dingle Peninsula** has almost fallen victim to its own romance. Its remoteness and beauty, the hard life and poverty and (above all in the *Gaeltacht* areas) the language have all lent fuel to easy romanticizing, creating the modern mythologized picture of the west. In Dingle's case, the myth is strengthened by its location on the extreme western seaboard of Europe, its numerous early Christian remains, the wealth of Gaelic literature created on the now uninhabited Blasket Islands—and the fact that *Ryan's Daughter* was filmed here. Concern about the peninsula's reputation for fey otherworldliness is such that the local paper has found it necessary to assure Irish visitors that there are actually real night spots here.

All the same, a great nightlife is not the reason to visit this region. True, there are plenty of pubs in **Dingle town**—a small place reputed to have 52 of them—and lots of traditional music, perhaps even a *ceilidh*. The town's been fortunate in only realizing its tourist potential in the past few years; while Killarney is stuck with its tacky souvenir shops and pubs, Dingle has done an altogether more elegant job, mixing traditional places and new seafood restaurants.

But Dingle really scores with its landscape and antiquities. The former is spectacular, dominated by 2627-foot Stradbally Mountain, while west of Dingle town lies a Gaelic-speaking region, strongly resonant of its history. Outside the Aran Islands, Dingle probably has the greatest concentration of Celtic monastic (and older) ruins. On a fine day it can be exhilarating, with views out as far as the monastic settlement on Great Skellig, off the Iveragh Peninsula; but it's still more exciting in the rain, when cloud hovers over the land and you find yourself in a white mist through which the dim shapes of oratories and beehive huts loom mysteriously.

Heading for Dingle: Milltown and Inch

Though most of the peninsula's delights are to the west of Dingle town, there are a few notable stopping points on the way, especially if you're **bicycling** from Killarney. There's a magnificent ride taking the right fork at Aghadoe (where the youth hostel is); for the entire stretch up to Milltown, the very minor road offers wonderful views of the almost unreal-looking McGillycuddy's Reeks to your left. At MILLTOWN, if you're exhausted already, there's an independent **hostel** in the Square (*Woods Hostel*; ☎066-67301; Easter–Oct; camping also possible). Otherwise, push on past Castlemaine Harbour and set out along the straight road beside the peninsula's edge, a seemingly endless ride if you're biking against the wind.

At **INCH** there's a break in the shoreline where a long, narrow sand-bar pushes out into Dingle Bay. Good bucket-and-spade territory when the weather's fine, its shifting dunes seem once to have been a place of Iron Age settlement. Inch also provides somewhere to stay before Dingle: high above the bay at Inch Heights, the *Natural Living and Healing Center* (☎066-58189; phone ahead), a B&B, serves macrobiotic, vegan and vegetarian food. Anne Hyland, who also owns the restaurant in Annascaul, runs classes in relaxation, yoga, art, and shiatsu. Soon the road turns inland for ANASCAUL where *Anne's Kitchen*'s good vegetarian and vegan food is worth stopping for. If you're not in a hurry to press on to Dingle, climb up to **Anascaul Lake**, in extraordinary boulder-scattered surroundings on the slopes of Stradbally Mountain.

Dingle Town

Getting to **DINGLE** is easy. The **bus** leaves from outside Killarney's railroad station at 10:35am every day, and there's a more frequent service from Tralee. Once you're here, there's not a huge amount to see, but Dingle town's a peculiarly pleasant place to stay, devoted to fishing and tourism, and certainly makes the best base for exploring the peninsula. Though crammed with pubs, little restaurants, and B&Bs, the town somehow never feels too crowded, and even if you don't like the way the place has geared itself up for tourism, you'll be glad when the weather's bad—which it often is—that there are plenty of places to hole up.

Essentially just a few streets by the side of **Dingle Bay**, Dingle has a hugely impressive natural harbor where the boats come in and where **Fungi the dolphin** likes to play. Half-tame, Fungi is one of Dingle's main tourist attractions. It may sound silly, but there are people who talk of their meetings with this solitary maritime mammal in the terms of a religious conversion, and others travel hundreds of miles just to meet him (inquire at the tourist office about boats).

The solidity of the town's color-washed houses suggests this was a place of some consequence, and Dingle was indeed Kerry's leading port in the fourteenth and fifteenth centuries. It later became a center for smuggling, and at one stage during the eighteenth century (when the revenue from smuggling

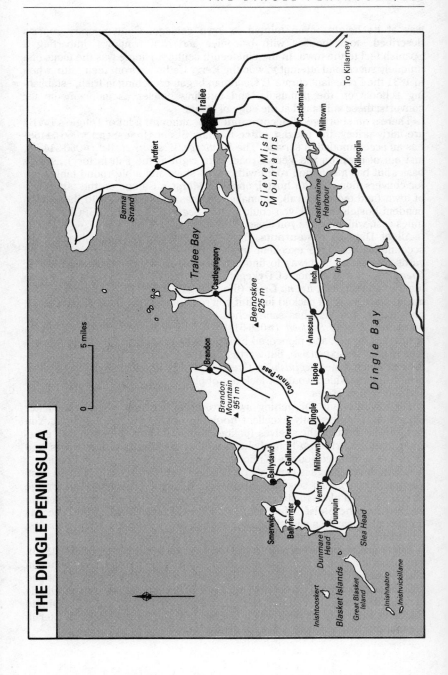

THE DINGLE PENINSULA

To Killarney

Tralee

Castlemaine

Milltown

Ardfert

Killorglin

Slieve Mish Mountains

Banna Strand

Tralee Bay

Castlemaine Harbour

Castlegregory

Inch

Inch

Beenoskee 825 m ▲

Anascaul

Brandon

Dingle Bay

Connor Pass

Lispole

Brandon Mountain 951 m ▲

Dingle

5 miles

0

Ballydavid

+ Gallarus Oratory

Smerwick

Milltown

Ballyferriter

Ventry

Dunquin

Dunmore Head

Slea Head

Inishtooskert

Blasket Islands

Great Blasket Island

Inishnabro

Inishvickillane

was at its height) even minted its own coinage. Contemporary reports described stone houses with balconies and oval windows, imparting a Spanish feel to the town. In the nineteenth century, Dingle was the focus of a uniquely successful attempt to woo the Kerry Catholics from their faith, when in 1831 the Protestant curate T. Goodman began preaching in Irish, establishing schools on the peninsula, and building houses as inducements for converts; these still stand at the edge of town.

There's no shortage of **accommodation**, although a lot of Dingle's B&Bs are fairly pricey; the **tourist office** in Main Street (June–Sept; ☎066-51188) has an accommodation service. The *Westlodge/Westgate Hostel* (☎066-51476), just out of town on the Ventry road (turn right at the fish factory), is very basic, but has a common room with a coal stove and a big round table built for conversation. *Lovett's* hostel, opposite Moran's Garage on the other side of town (and more central), is smaller and has no phone. If both these independent hostels are full, you could try the *Seacrest Hostel* in LISPOLE, a few miles east, which brings you close to the cliffs and beach.

All of Dingle's **restaurants**, from the cheapest to decidedly expense-account places, serve excellent fresh seafood, landed just a few hundred yards away. The best way to find them is just to wander around and look; *Greaney's*, on the corner of Dykegate and Strand Street, does good cheap lunches and dinners. *Eri na Grine* (the Rising Sun) on Lower Main Street is a useful place to get a packed lunch if you're going to spend the day bicycling or walking, and also has sandwiches and tasty vegetarian meals. Moving upmarket, *Doyle's Seafood* (☎066-51174) in John Street is the best-known restaurant locally, and pioneered haute cuisine in Dingle. The often miraculous dishes are expensive, but worth it, in the evenings; there's cheaper bar-food at lunch time. *Beginish*, in Green Street, is an elegant pink-and-green establishment which wouldn't look out of place in any city center, with good seafood at high prices.

For daytime, and for getting away from bad weather, there's no better place than Dingle's truly excellent **bookshop-café**, *An Cafe Liteártha*. You can browse through the shelves (politics and local interest sections are especially good), scarf down home-baked goods and soups, read the papers, and listen to the mingled sounds of rain and conversation in Gaelic and English.

Life in the evenings is centered on Dingle's **pubs**, with many of them hosting traditional music sessions on any given night. *O'Flaherty's* on Bridge Street is a good place to start, with music most nights, or advice on where to find it somewhere else. *Mrs Nelligan's Pub* on Lower Main Street also has traditional music, in a slightly staider setting, or try *Murphys* or the *Star Inn*, on Strand Street, for Friday- or Saturday-night revels with dancing.

Bikes are available for rent from *Moriarty's* on Main Street (☎066-51316), which participates in the Raleigh Rent-A-Bike scheme and has mountain bikes—useful on the punishing Conor Pass. *Paddy's* in Dykegate Street and *O'Sullivan's* in Strand Street also rent out bikes. Special **events** in Dingle include the mid-July cultural festival, **Ducas An Daingean**; the **Dingle Races** in early August (well worth seeing); and the **Dingle Regatta** later in the month. See the tourist office for details.

West of Dingle

Unlike some *Gaeltacht* areas, the Gaelic-speaking area west of Dingle doesn't blow its own trumpet, and it's probably best not to expect too much of a linguistic experience. You may never hear a word of Gaelic spoken, and any written Gaelic is more likely to come from the stalwart Sixties relics who've established pottery kilns and tea shops in the remotest parts of the peninsula than from native Gaelic speakers. But all around you, written into the wild landscape, are the relics of the **ancient Gaelic culture**. Ring-forts, beehive huts, oratories, and stone crosses are more prevalent here than almost anywhere else in Ireland; the vigor of the Christian culture that set out from here to evangelize and educate the rest of Europe is almost palpable*.

Cycling around Dingle, you can put your bike in a ditch and take off up the mountainside to explore local beehive huts; arm yourself with proper rain gear, and bad weather ceases to be a problem. **Public transit** in the west of the peninsula amounts to a bus from Dingle to Dunquin on Tuesday and Saturday at 9am and 5pm, with an extra service to Slea Head at 1pm in July and August.

Towards Slea Head

The next town after Dingle is VENTRY, once the main port of the peninsula, and another fine natural harbor. Beyond it looms the enormous, gnarled shoulder of Mount Eagle, dropping almost sheer to the sea with only a precarious ledge for the road. It's in these inhospitable surroundings on the stretch out to Slea Head that the main concentration of ancient monuments can be found. What follows here can only be an introduction to the major sites; the minor ones alone could take weeks to explore. A good local map (the half-inch ordnance survey one will do) is essential, while several excellent guides to the peninsula exist for real enthusiasts (available at *An Cafe Liteártha* in Dingle town).

First off there's the spectacular **Dun Beag**, a scramble down from the road towards the ocean about four miles out from Ventry (just after the road goes through a double fuschia hedge). A promontory fort, its defenses include four earthen rings, with an underground escape route, or souterrain, by the main entrance. It's a magical location, overlooking the open sea and the

---

*This culture is vividly brought to life in Penguin's *A Celtic Miscellany*, a collection of epigrams, nature poems, satires, and love poems translated into virile Gaelic idiom rather than the traditionally romantic Celtic twilight mode. "Pleasant to me is the glittering of the sun today upon these margins, because it flickers so," some ninth-century scribe noted in the margin of an illuminated manuscript; "Whether morning, whether evening, whether by land or by sea, though I know I shall die, alas, I know not when," runs a more somber epigram, also of the ninth century; and a tiny example of the nature poetry of the same time goes, "Winter has come with scarcity, lakes have flooded their sides, frost crumbles the leaves, the merry wave begins to mutter." *An Cafe Liteártha* has copies.

Iveragh Peninsula, its dramatic suitability to the setting only increased by the fact that some of the building has fallen off into the sea.

Becutesyn Dun Beag and Slea Head the hillside above the road is studded with stone beehive huts, cave dwellings, souterrains, forts, churches, standing stones, and crosses—over 500 of them in all. The beehive huts can be deceptive—they were being built and used for storing farm tools and produce until the late nineteenth century, so not all of them are as old as they look. But once you're standing among genuinely ancient buildings like the **Fahan group** (signposted, with a 50p admission charge) and looking south over a landscape that's remained essentially unchanged for centuries, the Iveragh Peninsula and (if they're not hidden by clouds) the two Skellig islands in the distance, you get a strong sense of past lives, with their unimaginable hopes and aspirations.

The Blasket Islands

At **Slea Head** the view opens up to include the desolate, splintered masses of the **Blasket Islands** (*Na Blascaodai*), uninhabited since 1953. The weather in Blasket Sound can be treacherous—two of the Armada's ships were shattered to matchwood when they came yawing around the cape in September 1588—but inhospitable as they seem, the islands were once the home of thriving communities. The astonishing body of **Gaelic literature** that emerged from these tiny islands (Maurice O'Sullivan's *Twenty Years A-Growing*, Peig Sayers's *Peig*, and Tomas O'Crohan's *Island Cross-Talk*) gives a vivid picture of the life of the islanders which, although remote, was anything but unsophisticated. Ironically, these literary works describe life among people who could neither read nor write, but their oral tradition emerges as far from primitive.

In the summer boats bound for **Great Blasket** (*An Blascaod Moór*) leave the pier just south of Dunquin every hour between 11am and 5pm (May–Sept in good weather; ☎066-56146 or 56280; around £6 return). Whether or not you choose to overnight, Great Blasket's delights are simple ones: sitting on the beaches and staring out to sea, tramping the many footpaths that crisscross the island, or trying to spot a seal. If you're staying, the island offers an amazing view of the sun sinking into the ocean, and echoes the words of The Pogues' emigration song, "Thousands Are Sailing": ". . . this island that is silent now, but the ghosts still haunt the waves. . . ."

The comfortable **hostel** (☎066-56146) only sleeps ten, so it's best to telephone in advance. Bed and breakfast accommodation and free **camping** are also available, but there's no store on the island, so you need to bring supplies. At the café (noon–5pm), overnighters can order good, cheap vegetarian dinners.

If the Blasket hostel is full, there's an *An Óige* one on the mainland a little farther on at DUNQUIN, with plenty of beds (☎066-56121), or a B&B in the local *Kruger's Pub*, where you may also come across some live music. The best place for daytime eating is the *Dunquin Pottery Cafe* (10am–8pm), although the pottery is not as beautiful as at Louis MacNulty's studio, on the other side of Dunquin.

Ballyferriter and Ballydavid

A couple of miles farther around the headland, largely Irish-speaking **BALLYFERRITER** can be bleak out of season, but in summer there are several cafés, plus a **heritage center** (10:30am–6pm; £1, students 50p). The little northward lanes will lead you to impressive 500-foot hilltop walling at Sybil Head, and the Three Sisters rock (with the Norman ruins of Castle Sybil, built within an older promontory fort); or to Smerwick Harbour and **Dún án Óir**. In September 1580 at Dún án Óir (the golden fort), a band of Italians, Spanish, English, and Irish tried to invade Britain, backed by papal funds and rallying to support Catholic Ireland against Protestant England. However, the English won and massacred the rebels—men, women, and children—as a warning to others; the poet Edmund Spenser participated in the indiscriminate slaughter.

At the other end of Smerwick Harbour lies BALLYDAVID, backed by the mass of Brandon Mountain and within easy reach of the cliffs at Ballydavid Head. There's a women's **hostel** here, run by Mary Begley in the back of *Begley's Bar*. **Brandon Creek**, just east of Ballydavid Head, is one of a number of contenders for Saint Brendan's sixth-century departure point, when he sailed off to discover the "Islands of Paradise" in the "Western Ocean" and, arguably, America.

Riasc, the Gallarus Oratory and Kilmakedar

Back to Ballyferriter, and a short way out of the village—keep left on the main road, turn right over the bridge by a gas pump, then right again—is the monastic site of **Riasc**. Recent excavation has revealed walls and foundations a few feet high, and the ruins evoke the early Christian monastery, dating from the tenth century.

The single most impressive early Christian monument on the Dingle peninsula, however, is the **Gallarus oratory**, a little farther east. It's the most perfectly preserved of around twenty such oratories in Ireland, and looks almost too good to be true, though apparently it hasn't undergone any great restoration programs. It can't be dated with any great certainty, but it's thought to have been built between the ninth and twelfth centuries (although Christian architectural activity dates from the late sixth or early seventh century, it wasn't until the ninth century that churches began to be built of stone rather than wood), and to represent a transition between the round beehive huts elsewhere on the peninsula and the later rectangular churches. The problem with this construction (and the reason why so many similar buildings have collapsed) is that the long sides tend to cave in—if you look carefully at the Gallarus oratory, you can see it's beginning to happen here too.

The next architectural stage can be seen a mile to the north in the rectangular church at **Kilmakedar**. Its nave dates from the mid-twelfth century, and the corbeled stone roof was a direct improvement on the structure at Gallarus. The site marks the beginning of the **Saint's Road**, dedicated to Saint Brendan, patron saint of Kerry, which leads to the top of Brandon Mountain—the route taken by pilgrims to Saint Brendan's shrine. If you want to follow this tough but historically resonant route up the mountainside, it's marked on the half-inch ordnance survey map. Alternatively, there's a marked route from the west beginning between Cloghane and Brandon.

Dingle's Interior

The **interior** of the Dingle Peninsula is dominated by two mountains, Brandon Mountain and Stradbally Mountain, separated by the steep **Conor Pass**. This mountainous terrain is excellent walking country: not only are there countless relics of the Celtic church (and earlier) to explore, but the area is dotted by a series of lakes that give the tussocky landscape some focus. There's an independent **hostel** at the foot of the pass on the northern side, the *Conor Pass Hostel* in Stradbally (☎066-39179; open all year), from where it's also an easy journey to the good sandy beaches and swimming at Stradbally and Castlegregory.

Tralee

The main reason for being in **TRALEE** is that the train brings you here on your way to the rest of Kerry. It's a tacky, flyblown commercial town with nothing much to recommend it except the way out: four buses a day go down the Dingle Peninsula daily except Sunday (when there's one).

Tralee is a point of embarkation rather than somewhere to stay, and the helpful **tourist office** (☎066-21288) is in the lobby of *Siamsa Tire Theatre* in Godfrey Place. If you do find yourself having to overnight, there are two **hostels** (as well as innumerable B&Bs): *Pitlochry* (☎066-23174), a mile out of town at 31 Lisdara, just around the corner from a sports complex where you can swim, play tennis, and so on, and *Droumtacker* (☎066-25209), off the Listowel Road, another mile farther out.

You can rent **bikes** in Tralee (though if you're headed for Dingle, it's a tough ride over the Conor Pass) from *J. Caball Himself*, Staughtons Row (☎066-21654), *Tralee Gas Supplies*, Strand Street (which also stocks mountain bikes, which may be useful; ☎066-22018); or *Vincent O'Gorman* in Ballydavid (☎066-55162). All these are part of the Raleigh Rent-A-Bike scheme.

Finding a cheap place to **eat** in Tralee isn't a problem—the town is full of them, though mostly pretty depressing. *Ruth's Wholefood Restaurant* is a daytime-only operation, with fresh spring water from the owner's farm-well supplied free. Another vegetarian restaurant, also daytime only, is *Bratts* in The Square. Plenty of pubs, too: try *Kirby's Broque Inn* in Rock Street for jazz and traditional music, or *Crosty's*, in Castle Street. The **Folk Theatre of Ireland** has its home at the *Siamsa Tire Theatre*, though performances don't draw the same crowds as the **Rose of Tralee International Festival**. Held in the last week of August, with much accompanying merriment, this is a beauty contest in which foreign women who can demonstrate some credible Irish connection compete for the dubious honor of being Rose of Tralee. For those who are interested, details are available from the Festival Office in Lower Castle Street (☎066-21322).

Sights around Tralee

More worthy of your time than anything in Tralee itself is the ruined thirteenth-century cathedral at **ARDFERT**, five miles to the northwest. In a landscape littered with ruined ring-forts, castles and churches, Ardfert was the site of a monastery founded by Saint Brendan in the seventh century, and which later became the center of the Anglo-Norman church in Kerry. There's also a Franciscan friary and two smaller, fifteenth-century churches.

It's also worth taking the road out to **Banna Strand** for the spectacular view over Tralee Bay, and its association with Sir Roger Casement, to whom there's a monument. In April 1916, on the eve of the Easter Uprising, Casement was captured by local police as he attempted to land at Banna Strand from a German submarine (see "Murlough Bay" in *Antrim* for more details). Tried and executed for high treason in the same year, his body was returned from England to Ireland in 1965 to be reinterred with full military honors. If you're driving, you can carry on round the cliffs of Kerry Head for more great vistas—south over Tralee Bay, north across the mouth of the Shannon.

North Kerry

This coastal road aside, North Kerry is unexciting, undulating farmland rolling up to the Shannon. The main road from Tralee heads up through **LISTOWEL**, a workaday Irish town that does, however, have a degree of literary distinction. In June it hosts a week-long festival of writers' workshops and meetings; Brian MacMahon, a local schoolteacher, is a strong proponent of the rigorous Irish short story tradition (for examples, try *The Sound of Hooves*, a recent volume of Kerry stories available locally). From Listowel the main road continues to TARBERT on the Shannon estuary, and from there trails the river inland (through County Limerick) towards Limerick and Shannon Airport. Immediately north of Tarbert, the **car-ferry** across the estuary (every hour on the half-hour, 7:30am–9:30pm, 20min; every half hour at peak times) provides a useful short cut into County Clare; there's no other river crossing west of Limerick.

Turning aside at Listowel, **BALLYBUNNION** lies about ten miles away on the coast at the mouth of the Shannon. It does have a kind of charm—it's the kind of sleepy resort that most people remember with a mixture of affection and horror from childhood vacations, and there are good sandy beaches—but unless you're beguiled by nostalgia you're unlikely to want to stay long. Two golf courses, and caves to explore under the cliffs, provide something to occupy you if you do. In summer, you'll save a long walk past the "No Vacancy" signs by checking out accommodation possibilities at the tourist office which operates out of a mobile trailer; check at the local post office for details of its whereabouts. They also have tourist information here.

If getting to Limerick in a hurry is your main preoccupation, the faster route runs inland via Newcastle West. On this road CASTLEISLAND offers stores, and places to stop for a drink or a bite to eat, but no reason to delay more than this.

travel details

Trains

From Killarney to Tralee (4 daily; 35min); Cork (2; 1hr 45min); Dublin (2; 3hr).

Bus Éireann

From Killarney to Shannon Airport (summer only 1 daily; 3hr 10min); Tralee (2; 35min).

From Tralee to Limerick (3 daily; 2hr 20min); Cork (1; 2hr 30min).

Private buses

Funtrek (☎01-730852) runs one bus daily, two on Fri and Sun, **from Tralee**, outside the Brandon Hotel, to Adare, Newcastlewest, Listowel, Killarney, and Dublin.

CHAPTER NINE

CLARE

P hysically, **County Clare** is clearly defined, with Galway Bay and the Shannon estuary to the north and south, its eastern boundary the massive Lough Derg, and the Atlantic to the west. Strangely, the county is sometimes glossed over by visitors as simply land between the magnificent scenery of Kerry and Galway. It's true that it doesn't have the scenic splendor of either of these and, for many, the north of the county is too bleak to be attractive. Nonetheless, Clare has a subtle flavor that, once tasted, can be addictive.

Clare is known as the "banner county," for its courageous political history, particularly in the fight for the Catholic Emancipation; and the "singing county" for its strong musical traditions, which are still very much alive, and constitute a major reason for coming here. Both titles—the strong and the gentle—suggest something of the character of the place, and are echoed in the contrasts of the landscape.

The **Burren** heights in the north are stark and barren, while **Ennis**, the county's capital, is surrounded by low, rolling farmland. Fabulous cliff scenery stretches for miles around Clare's southern extreme at **Loop Head**, and is spectacularly sheer at the **Cliffs of Moher**, farther north. In between are sandy beaches and small seaside towns and villages. In the east, **Lough Derg** offers panoramic views across to the mountains of Tipperary from the slopes of the Slieve Bernagh and Slieve Aughtie mountains, and the opportunity for watersports.

This varied countryside holds plenty of specialist interest. The Burren is a major attraction for geology and botany enthusiasts, and is also rich in ringforts, dolmens, and cairns in the north. The legacy of later communities is found throughout the county, in the thickly sprinkled medieval monastic remains, and tower houses of the O'Brien and MacNamara clans.

Ennis

The Fergus River, small and fast-flowing, seems thoroughly in keeping as it runs through **ENNIS**, a bustling market town and the commercial capital of County Clare. In the town's historic center, **Ennis Abbey** is the finest monument (guide/information service mid-June to mid-Sept 10am–6pm; at other times ask at the Friary in Francis Street; 60p). Founded by the O'Briens, kings of Thomond, as a Franciscan friary in 1242, most of the building dates from the fourteenth century. In parts it is striking: the nave has graceful

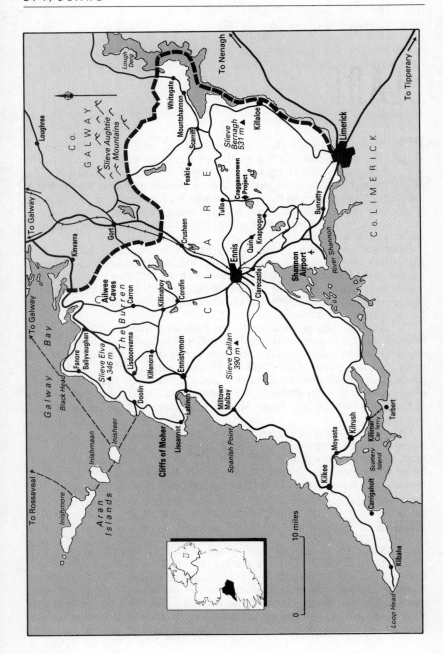

lancet windows and there is much good medieval sculpture, in particular the fifteenth-century MacMahon tomb (now incorporated in the Creagh Tomb) which has fine alabaster carvings of the Passion. Six hundred years ago Ennis Abbey had 350 monks and over 600 pupils and was considered the finest educational institution for the clergy and upper classes.

Today, as capital of the unyielding "banner county," Ennis is proud of its more recent nationalist history. A classical monument of **Daniel O'Connell** solidly dominates the old narrow streets that meet in **O'Connell Square**. In 1828 County Clare returned O'Connell to Westminster by such a huge majority that he had to be allowed to take his seat, despite the fact that he was a Catholic, which should have barred him at the time. He went on to gain the passing of the Catholic Emancipation Act. It was in Ennis, too, that **Parnell** made his famous speech advocating the boycott in the land agitations of the late nineteenth century. **De Valera** was Teach Daíl (member of Parliament) for the county from 1917 to 1959 (and Taoiseach for much of that time) and is remembered in a memorial outside the classical courthouse, and in the **de Valera Library Museum** on Harmony Row (Mon, Wed, Thurs 11am–5:30pm; Tues and Fri 11am–8pm; free), which houses a small collection of seventeenth-century Flemish paintings, and changing exhibitions of modern Irish artists.

The town's status demands that it has a **cathedral**, and this nineteenth-century building with a sharp spire stands icy and gray at the far end of O'Connell Street, at odds with this friendly town. From the main O'Connell and High Streets run ancient narrow lanes leading to the **old market place**, where a Saturday produce and livestock market is held.

Music

While you can easily see Ennis in an afternoon (there are no towns of any size in the county), it is worth staying longer for the traditional music. *Cois na hAbhna*, less than half a mile out on Gort Road (☎065-34158), is a center for local traditional music enthusiasts, and throughout the summer they have *Oiche Cheili* and *Seisiun* evenings—both evenings of song and dance, though the latter is a more structured entertainment (July & Aug, Sat & Thurs; June & Sept, Thurs only; 9pm; £3). These sessions also move around the county, so it's worth watching out elsewhere—tourist offices in the county have "What's On" information.

Ennis itself is musically alive, and for such a small town there are plenty of **bars** with traditional, jazz, and rock sessions. For **jazz**, a regular, popular spot is *The Old Ground Hotel* (O'Connell Street) on a Sunday lunchtime and evening, and occasional Saturday evenings, or *Patrick's Bar*, which also has traditional folk music. Other good **folk** bars include *Brogan's* (Wed–Fri) and *Brandon's*, both on O'Connell Street. The latter also has **rock and pop** bands, as do *The Banner Arms*, Market Square (Sat–Mon), *The West County Inn*, *Dilingers* (Wed–Fri) and, one mile out on the Tulla Road, *Auburn Inn* (Wed–Fri). Obviously the crowd depends on the band, and it's really a matter of luck, but Ennis is so small you are unlikely to be hunting for long. For **discos** try *The Lifford Arms*, New Bridge Road, and *Queens Hotel*, Abbey Street. There is also a **movie theater** on Station Road.

Getting There, Sleeping, and Eating

There are direct bus connections between Ennis and **Shannon Airport** (same-day arrival and departure inquiries, office hours, ☎061-61666; reservations ☎061-45556) thirteen miles away in the south of the county and the major airport on the west coast, with flights to Dublin, UK, Europe, and the USA. Ennis is on the Limerick–Athenry **train** line; note that trains to Dublin only go twice a week, on Tuesday and Thursday; change at Limerick. **Bus Éireann** run a service direct to Dublin on weekdays only, as well as a regular service to Limerick (6 buses per day); see "Travel Details" for information.

There are plenty of **B&Bs** in the town center, or you can reserve them through the **tourist office** which is half a mile out on the Limerick road (May & June, Sept & Oct, Mon–Fri 9:30am–6:30pm, Sat 9:30am–1:30pm; July–Aug daily 9am–7:30pm; Jan–April Mon–Fri 9:30am–1pm and 2–5:30pm). Good possibilities include *Derrynane House* (O'Connell Square; ☎065-28464), *Woodquay House* (Woodquay, off Parnell Street; ☎065-28320) and *Ardlea House* (Clare Road; ☎065-20256). The cheapest place to stay in Ennis is *Walnut House* hostel (☎065-28956; B&B £8; double rooms from £5; bikes for rent; laundry facilities) which is just over the traffic lights at the cathedral end of O'Connell Street; Mr Fitzgerald will greet you with a warmth and friendliness that transcends the lack of sophistication. The other place in town to **rent bikes** is at *Michael Tierney*, 17 Abbey Street (☎065-29433; £4 a day, £20 a week). There's a **laundromat** on Lower Market Street (Mon–Sat 9am–6pm).

For budget daytime **meals**, plenty of pubs serve decent food; but if lunchtime pubbing puts too much strain on your wallet, you have the choice of a couple of snack-and-salad bars in Parnell Street: *The Miller's Rest* and *Maison Neuve* (Mon–Sat 8am–6pm). *Lady Dee's* restaurant, up an alley off Abbey Street, serves cooked dinners from £3 and stays open until 9pm, including Sunday. The *O'Connell Bar Restaurant* serves meals from £5 until 6pm (closed Sun). Other reliable late servers are *The Golden Mountain* Chinese takeout and restaurant on O'Connell St, from £4, and a chip shop in Lower Market Street, open until midnight.

If you intend to visit a number of the region's **museums and castles**, it may be worth getting a *Shannon Explorer Ticket* (£5.50, students £3, available from tourist offices), which cuts entrance fees.

Around Ennis

Ennis sits in a low-lying strip of land that runs from a deep inlet of the Shannon River right up to South Galway. To the east of the town are lush fields edged by white-gray walls and clumps of wild flowers: pinks, purples and yellows of willow herb and ragwort, the strong white horns of bindweed, and even the occasional orchid. Farther east, the land breaks into little lakes and rivers before becoming gently hilly to meet the Slieve Bernagh mountains. This gentle farmland makes for easy bicycling, and your trip can be punctuated by village pubs, and plenty of church ruins and castles.

A favorite among these is **Quin Abbey**, the area's best-preserved Franciscan friary, founded in 1433. The main church building is graceful, its slender tower rising clear over the high, open archway between chancel and nave, and making a distinct outline against the green of the surrounding pastures. Climb up a floor to the first story, and you can look down on the abbey's complete cloister that has not only the usual arches, but also slim buttresses. For all the uplifting beauty of the tower, the abbey seems to be built on a human scale, to function as a place in which to live and worship rather than to impress and dominate.

On the other hand, the massy walls of **Knappogue Castle** emanate an awesome sense of power. Leave Quin and continue two miles south on the L31 to reach this huge sixteenth-century tower house (☎061-71103; May–mid-Oct daily 9:30am–5pm; £1.90, students £1.15). It was originally built by the Macnamaras, but they lost it to Cromwell, who then used it as his HQ—thereby, no doubt, saving it from the major damage he inflicted elsewhere. At the Restoration the Macnamaras managed to regain ownership of the castle, and hung on to it until 1800. It's been beautifully restored, and inside are boldly carved sixteenth-century oak fireplaces and stout oak furniture. At odds with the overall flavor of Knappogue, the nineteenth-century domestic additions are furnished as if eighteenth-century rooms, beautifully appointed with Irish Chippendale furniture and Waterford crystal. The main body of the castle is used for medieval banquets.

The second left turning, two miles south of Knappogue, brings you to the **Craggaunowen Project**, tucked on the edge of a reedy lake under a wooded hillside (April–Oct daily 10am–6pm; £2.25, students £1.30). This is based around another fortified tower house, the ground floor of which houses a collection of sixteenth-century European wood carvings. The project itself aims to recreate a sense of Ireland's ancient history, with reconstructions of earlier forms of homes and farmsteads; a ring-fort and a *crannog*, for example. Young workers experiment with old craft techniques, using replicas of wooden lathes, kilns, and the like, and double up as guides if asked. The most adventurous and certainly the most famous of the working replicas here is Tim Severin's *Brendan*, a leather-hulled boat in which he and four crew successfully sailed across the Atlantic in 1976, to prove that the legend of Saint Brendan could be true. Saint Brendan's story—he was supposedly the first man to discover America—is recorded in a ninth-century manuscript, and the design of the *Brendan* is based on its descriptions, along with the features of *curraghs* still used off Ireland's west coast. The result is a remarkable vessel of oak-tanned oxhides stretched over an ash-wood frame. Craggaunowen is also the home of an actual Iron Age road, excavated at Corlea Bog, County Longford. Made of large oak planks placed across runners of birch or alder, it must have formed part of an important route across difficult bog.

For refreshment, there's also a nice **tea shop** here, which serves delicious homemade cakes.

Eight miles beyond Craggaunowen, the village of **CRATLOE** is renowned for its oak-wooded hills overlooking the Shannon and Fergus estuaries, and is a particularly lovely spot for walking.

Bunratty

The N18 Limerick–Ennis road, very handy for tour buses, passes the extremely touristy **BUNRATTY**. **Bunratty Castle** stands on what was once an island on the north banks of the Shannon. The Vikings of Limerick recognized the site's strategic importance for protecting trade, and so they fortified it—you can still see the moat. The first castle here was built by Normans but they lost control and, in 1460, the Macnamaras built the castle that stands today. The exceptionally fine rectangular keep has been perfectly restored and now houses a large collection of furniture, tapestries, paintings, and ornate carvings from all over Europe, spanning the fourteenth to the seventeenth century. In the castle grounds, the **Bunratty Folk Park** is a complete reconstruction of a nineteenth-century village. In rural Ireland this hardly seems necessary, though you can watch people engaged in traditional crafts (☎061-361511; Castle and Folk Park 9:30am–5pm, the Folk Park remains open until 7pm in July and Aug; adults £3.10, students £1.60). The nearby *Durty Nellies* is a favorite tourist bar, regularly overrun by tour-bus parties.

North: Dysert O'Dea and Corofin

Alternative routes from Ennis take you north through low-lying country fretted with rush-bordered lakes. Seven miles north is **Dysert O'Dea**: take the Ennistymon road out of Ennis, after two miles take the right fork for Corofin, and it's up a road to the left. Dysert O'Dea is the site of the ancient monastic foundation of Saint Tola (d. 737), and was the scene of an important battle in 1318 when the O'Briens defeated the de Clares of Bunratty, thus stopping the Anglo-Norman takeover of Clare. There are remains of a Romanesque church (twelfth–thirteenth-century) with a richly carved south doorway and grotesque carvings of animal heads and human faces. Nearby is the base of a round tower and the twelfth-century *White Cross of Tola*, with carvings of Christ and a bishop in high relief, Daniel in the lion's den, and other intricate patterning. The **O'Dea Castle** nearby is a museum and archaeology center (May–Sept daily 10am–7pm; £1.50).

COROFIN lies at the heart of the abundance of little lakes that wriggle their way north of here, their banks dotted with ruined O'Brien strongholds. The area offers good fishing and tranquil cycling, disturbed only by the wind scything its way through squeaky bullrushes, reeds, and yellow-water irises. Here the **Clare Heritage Center** (☎065-27955; March–Oct daily 10am–6pm, other times by appointment) portrays the traumatic period of Irish history between 1800 and 1860, and fills in the horrors that the Bunratty Folk Park omits: famine, disease, emigration, the issue of land tenure. The center also has a genealogy service for those with origins in the county.

Lough Derg

The west bank of **Lough Derg** is a seam of beautiful countryside set between bald, boggy mountains and the great expanse of the lake. It forms the county's eastern boundary and, isolated by the empty heights of the Slieve Bernagh and the Slieve Aughtie mountains, has a different character from the rest of Clare. The waterway's wealth of fish and bird life, and the quaint villages on either shore, have long made Lough Derg popular with a wealthy Lough-cruising set, whose exclusive brand of tourism means villages are fairly conservative and well-kept. The hunting, shooting, and fishing set are well catered for, and tend to dominate the character of local pubs; but there are also pockets renowned for their traditional music sessions, attracting predominantly local crowds.

The main road north varies the scene, at times clinging to the lakeshore, at others gaining higher ground and panoramic views over the lough, its islands, and the mountains of Tipperary. It connects Portumna, County Galway, at the head of the Lough, with Killaloe at its southerly tip (both historic, pictureque towns), and laces together a handful of choice little villages.

How To Go and Where To Stay

Access to the area is via Limerick or Portumna. *Bus Éireann* runs at least one **bus** daily from Limerick to Killaloe, Tuamgraney, Scarriff and into the hills to Feakle. For timetable information phone Limerick ☎061-42433. *P.S.Travel* has a **coach** which connects Birdhill (three miles south of Killaloe) with Dublin, Ennis and Limerick daily. Journeys along the shore north of Scarriff involve **hitching** or **cycling**, though this isn't such a good idea in the Slieve Bernagh and Slieve Aughtie mountains to the west. Here roads are empty, making hitching impossible, and deceptively steep and unsheltered, making cycling tough. You can **rent bikes** from Michael McCarthy (Hotel Road, Killaloe; ☎061-46983) and from *Guerins* (Mountshannon) for £3 a day, £18 a week.

The area has been opened up to the budget traveler by two new **independent hostels**. *Lough Derg Hostel*, Killaloe (☎061-76466; late March–Oct; £3.50) has 36 beds, three family rooms, and laundry facilities. For the *Lakeside Watersport Hostel*, Mountshannon (☎061-27225), take the road north out of Mountshannon and it's the first turning off to the right. The hostel is open all year, costs £3.50, and has family rooms. Camping costs £3 per tent plus 50p per person. The hostel is a great place for **watersports**; there is no need to reserve in advance, and it's all very reasonably priced, with canoe or windsurf rent at £2 per hour, rowing boat £4 a day, sailing boat £10 per day, motor boat £10 per day, and waterskiing £20 per hour. There's a **campground** at Killaloe (☎061-76329; May 6–Sept 18; £5.50 high season, £4.50 overnight, plus 40p per person).

Killaloe

The great mass of Lough Derg channels into the Shannon below **KILLALOE** for the final stretch of this great river's journey to the sea. The town's an ancient crossing point, and an old stone bridge still spans the waters. The old part of Killaloe focuses around **St Flannan's Cathedral**, and the narrow lanes that run up the steep slopes to the west suggest the town's ancient origins. The Cathedral itself is a plain thirteenth-century building, impressive in its solid simplicity, with a low square tower, and straight, strong buttresses. Just inside the entrance is a heavily decorated Romanesque doorway from an earlier church, and alongside it the huge **Thorgrim Stone**, unique in its ogham and runic inscriptions (ogham is a form of the Latin alphabet associated with early Christianity, the runic forms are Scandinavian in origin)—it's probably the memorial of a Viking convert. In the churchyard the stout, solid Romanesque **St Flannan's Oratory** dates from the twelfth century, and is complete with barrel-vaulted roof. Just over a mile north of town on the western shore of Lough Derg, **Beal Boru** is an earthen fort and possibly the site of Brian Boru's palace "Kincora," which was either here or in Killaloe itself.

Killaloe's a great spot for watersports, and popular with Lough cruisers and day-trippers from Limerick; even so there are only a handful of places to **eat**. On the east side *Morgan's Lounge* does pub grub at any time during the summer months. Also on this side of the bridge, *Patsy's* takeout food is open until late daily, throughout the year. The *Lakeside Hotel* serves snacks and sandwiches at any time—if you can't afford their restaurant it's uninspiring, but a haven of warmth and convenience. Nearby, upmarket *Peter's Restaurant* specializes in seafood; open in the evenings. Across the bridge, up the hill opposite the Cathedral, *Morrissey's Piano Bar* serves food from noon, Monday to Saturday.

Killaloe is not the best spot for **music**, but you can be lucky: *Sean Achaoí* in Bridge Street (west of bridge) sometimes has traditional sessions and ballads at weekends; *The Anchor Inn* has a mixture of music—pop, traditional, ballads—on Saturday and Sunday, and an Irish Night on Wednesday with set dancing. Over the bridge in County Tipperary, *Morgan's Lounge* works hard to cater to the Limerick crowd with a mixture of folk and rock on Saturday, Sunday, and a couple of nights during the week in summer. Finally, the *Lakeside Hotel* has ballad and folk sessions on Saturday.

The West Bank

The villages along the scenic road north are all very small. Wealthy tourists into hunting, shooting, and fishing tend to stay in fancy hotels, and amenities for other visitors are sparse—even campgrounds here cost above the average rate.

The best spot to stay, Killaloe and Portumna aside, is **MOUNT-SHANNON**. It's amongst the prettiest of the villages and has a couple of cosy combo pub/grocery shops with music in the summer, a restaurant, and a hostel (see "How to Go and Where to Stay" above). You can **rent bikes** and buy *Camping Gaz* at *Guerins* grocery shop (daily until 7pm), and there's a safe swimming area at the lakeshore. From Mountshannon, too, you can take a boat to **Holy Island**, which had a monastic settlement from the seventh to the thirteenth century; ruins from this period are still there.

North of Mountshannon, the beauty of the scenery fades as the main road leaves the lakeshore, and the mountains to the west become less dramatic.

Near WHITEGATE, *McDermotts* bar is renowned for its Sunday-night traditional sessions, although the place is currently changing hands. **WILLIAMSGATE** is tiny, and dominated by its handful of bars. *Kate and Paddy's* is a friendly place catering to the hurling and hunting crowd, and offering traditional food—Irish stew, bacon and cabbage—at any time, plus occasional country and western or traditional sessions.

South of Mountshannon, **SCARRIFF** is a little farming town set high in rough, open country overlooking the lough. It's a handy place to pick up provisions, and the *Clare Lakelands Hotel* serves very good seafood and hot lunches daily from £3.50. The hotel bar has music three or four nights a week from Easter to September, a mixture of country and western and traditional, plus discos on Saturday and Sunday. *O'Beirne's Cafe* also does good seafood and salads. *The Merriman Inn* serves midday pub lunches, and has traditional music in the summer. There's a *Bank of Ireland* here, open until 5pm on Mondays, and the *Allied Irish Bank* opens at *Melody's Pub* on Monday and Thursday (10am–12:30pm, 1:30–3pm). There's a **drycleaners and laundry** at *Hogan's*, Feakle Street (Mon–Sat until 6pm, closing at 1pm on Wed). In nearby TUAMGRANEY, little more than a hamlet, *Hassett's Lounge* regularly has a variety of entertainers.

Clare's South Coast

The south coast of the county has glorious sandy beaches, stunning cliff scenery, and a couple of popular family holiday resorts. Inland doesn't look so promising. Southwest from Ennis the country flattens out and becomes scrubby and barren: bog, marsh, the odd clump of cotton grass here, the occasional lump of thistles there, with only sporadic pockets of cultivated land. The bald flank of Slievecallan is to the north, and the outline of the Kerry hills to the south across the Shannon.

Kilrush and Scattery Island

At present, the best reason to stop in Kilrush is for a trip across the broad Shannon estuary to **SCATTERY ISLAND**—before it gets spruced up for mass consumption. Scattery was last inhabited in the late 1970s and as you land the quay before you is dotted with overgrown, derelict cottages. Walking up the lanes, spongy with moss and bracken, you disturb the burrows the island is now riddled with, and rabbits pop out madly all over the place. Saint Senan founded a **monastery** here in the sixth century, and at one time there were seven monastic settlements. The community suffered greatly from Viking raids, but there are still several church remains dating from between the ninth and the fifteenth century.

Wherever you wander on Scattery, you get the feeling of stepping back into a timeless past, a mythical world protected by its isolation in the Shannon estuary. But Scattery's most impressive feature has to be the **round tower**, perfect in form, the stone made a warm mustardy yellow by the lichen that covers it. Unusually for a round tower, the doorway here is at ground level. **Access** to the island is by small boat from CAPPA, adjacent to Kilrush. There is no regular schedule so you need either to phone and arrange this in advance (☎061-51327), or to ask the tourist office to phone for you. Your trip is dependent on tides and the readiness of the boatman, but persevere—it's worth it.

At the moment **KILRUSH** itself boasts regular, traditional **Horse Fairs** in March, June, October, and November, but the character of the place is soon to change radically. The construction of a yachting marina marks the main thrust of the town's bid for the upscale tourist trade, and in the **market square**, a statue of the Maid of Éireann (commemorating the Manchester Martyrs) looks resolutely down the broad main street to the quayside where it's all going to happen. Off to the right in Toler Street, the spacious **Saint Senan's Catholic church** is worth looking in for the Harry Clarke stained glass windows. Local businesses, hotels, B&Bs and pubs are preparing for big changes, and behind the traditional facades, rooms are being assiduously upgraded. All this means that you can currently get high-quality accommodation and **food** at reasonable prices. Particularly good seafood is available daily in *Kelly's Bar*, Henry Street, from £3, and in the evenings there's an *à la carte* restaurant upstairs. *The Haven* in Henry Street also has good bar snacks. *Ryan's Deli*, Henry Street, does homemade pizzas, burgers, and tacos, Monday to Saturday, 10am to 6pm.

The **tourist office** in the main square (Mon–Fri 10am–1pm and 2–6:30pm, Sat 10am–1pm) will reserve **accommodation**. Mrs M. O'Mahony's *Ferry Lodge*, Cappa Road (☎065-51291; cross the river at the bottom of the main street), is both friendly and palatial at around £9. Similarly hospitable is Mrs M. Daly's *St Martins*, Shannon Heights, Kilkee Road (☎065-51198). For **camping**, *Aylevarroo Caravan and Camping Park* (☎065-51102, May 14–Sept 4; £4/£5) is less than two miles from Kilrush on the N67 Killimer Road. As for **banks**, *Allied Irish Bank* and *Bank of Ireland* are both in Frances Street. **Bus Éireann information** for **buses** to Ennis and around the coast throughout the year, and to Galway and Cork during the summer, is available from *Crotty's* in the square. Two private bus companies provide cheap travel to Dublin and Limerick.

If you're **cycling or driving on to Kerry**, you can cut out many miles and the mental congestion of Limerick city by heading for KILLIMER, five miles from Kilrush, and taking the **car ferry** to TARBET (☎065-51060; April–Sept weekdays 7am–9pm, Sun 9am–9pm; Oct–March weekdays 7am–7pm, Sun 10am–7pm. Outward sailings leave on the hour, return sailings from Tarbet depart on the half hour; £6 single car, £8.50 round trip, £2 cycles).

Kilkee

KILKEE is a small, busy seaside holiday town with all the amenities you'd expect: cheap cafés, restaurants, amusements, and nightlife. Popular with the bucket-and-spade brigade, the town comes as a healthy piece of normality if the off-beat romanticism of the west coast has become too much. There's a magnificent beach, a crescent of golden sand set in dramatic cliff scenery. The beach's westerly tip meets an apron of laminated rock strata known as the Duggerna Rocks, which protects it from the ravages of the Atlantic. Here, when the tide is out, deep, clear tide pools form, full of colorful marine life.

The area is a favorite for scuba diving and snorkeling, but even without equipment, exploration is rewarding. There are exhilarating walks for miles along the cliffs both to the north and, more spectacularly, to the south around **Loop Head**, where you can walk for sixteen miles along the cliff's edge past stack rocks, blowholes (where the sea spouts up through crevices in the rock), and the natural Bridges of Ross. The other good way to see this peninsula is by **bike**; you can rent them at *P.T.Keller's* and at *Williams Pharmacy*, Circular Road (☎065-56041).

In the little church at **MONEEN**, near KILBAHA at the tip of the peninsula, is the nineteenth-century curiosity known as *The Little Arc*. In Penal times Catholics were forced to be both ingenious and secret in the practicing of their faith. Here they were not allowed to worship on land, and so built a little hut on wheels which was kept on the beach and wheeled down below the high-water mark between tides, beyond the legal grasp of the local Protestant landowner. The priest would then say mass in it while the people stood around on the beach.

There is no shortage of **guesthouses and B&Bs** in Kilkee, though it's worth remembering that this is a popular resort and can be packed out in August. Addresses are available from the **tourist office** in O'Connell Street (☎065-56112; summer only). *Kincora*, O'Connell Street (☎065-56107; £10) is a very friendly B&B. In the same street, Mrs M. Hickie, *Bay View* (☎065-56058; £9) also does B&B. The west end of Kilkee has accommodation too at Mrs Enright's, *Aran House* (☎065-56170), and at Mrs Haugh's, *Dunearn House* (☎065-56152), both at £10. Pitching tents is discouraged on the open land towards Loop Head, which would be very exposed to gales, but there are two **campgrounds** in town: for *Cunninghams Caravan and Camping Park* (☎061-51666; open Easter weekend and May 14–Sept 17; £4 per tent plus £1 per person) turn left approaching town from Kilrush, go through the roundabout, and turn left at the Victoria Hotel. There is a second, fairly unattractive site just up the Kilrush road from the main square.

Bus Éireann services link Kilkee with Ennis and other coastal towns. Cheap private buses to Dublin and Limerick leave from the square, opposite *Kincora* guesthouse.

There are plenty of bars and cafés to **eat** at during the summer. If you want to spend over £15 on a meal anywhere in the county, try *Manuel's Seafood Restaurant*, Corballwy, Kilkee (☎065-56211), one mile north of town. Booking is advisable as it's extremely popular, and with good reason: the atmosphere is zany and congenial, the food ambrosial. For **banks**, the *Bank of Ireland* and the *A.I.B.* are on O'Curry Street. As for **sports**, squash courts are available in the *Thomond Hotel*, billiards and snooker at *The Olympia*, and pitch-and-putt or golf can be played at the west end. **Strand Races**, exciting informal horse races, are held on the beach, usually on the last weekend in August.

Heading North

The coastline north of Kilkee is one of fine cliffs and sandy beaches, though not all of them are accessible. **MILTOWN MALBAY**, eighteen miles north of Kilkee, is a Victorian resort, strangely situated inland. The place comes alive for the *Willie Clancy Summer School* held here (usually the first week in July), when the town becomes packed with traditional music enthusiasts from all over the world. Two and a half miles away is **SPANISH POINT**, so called because it was here that survivors from wrecked Armada ships swam ashore, only to be executed by the High Sheriff of Clare. It's a holiday spot for nuns, and appropriately enough there's a very quiet **campground**, *Lahiff's Caravan and Camping Park* (☎065-84006; April–Sept; £4.50), as well as an excellent sandy swimming beach. To the east of Spanish Point is Slieve Callan, and if you cross it on the R474, after four miles you come to KNOCKNALASSA, where there is a wedge-shaped gallery grave to the right, known as *Diarmuid and Grainne's Bed* (after the Gaelic version of the Tristan and Isolde story).

LEHINCH is a busy family holiday resort with a broad sandy beach, ideal for surfing. The town pitches itself to a conservative market, its two golf courses hosting major golf competitions in July and August (Lehinch Golf Club ☎065-81003). Lehinch's Entertainment Centre (☎065-81108) has a movie theater, heated pool, discos, bingo and, every Tuesday, a **ceilidh**. While there's plenty of good music, both country and traditional, to be had in the bars, the place lacks charm; there's no historic center, and it's very much a seasonal town that shuts down in winter. If you do stay, there's **camping** at *Lehinch Camping and Caravan Park* (☎065-81424), which has a **laundromat** (Thurs & Sat 9:30am–6:30pm, and every day in June, July, & Aug), and **bike rental** (£4 a day). There's **pony-trekking** three miles away at Ballingaddy (☎065-71385). The **tourist office** is in the middle of the main street (June–Aug daily 10am–1pm and 2–6:30pm).

Towards the Burren: Liscannor and Ennistymon

If you've come this far north, you're probably on your way to, or coming from, the Burren region; if so, the best stopover spots are at ENNISTYMON or **LISCANNOR**.

Liscannor has a couple of nice bars, a campground, supermarket, post office, and two **hostels**. *The Village Hostel*, Liscannor (☎065-81385; year round; £3.50) is right next to the bars. *The Old Hostel*, Dereen, Liscannor (April–Sept; £3), is less than two miles farther west up the L54. The sandy stretches towards Lehinch from Liscannor, towards the mouth of the river, are unsafe due to quicksand.

ENNISTYMON, just over two miles inland from Lehinch, is by contrast an old market town (Tuesday is market day) with low shop-fronts, a pretty nineteenth-century Gothic church, and some great old bars tucked away in the most unlikely of places. The town has a life, albeit a leisurely one, regardless of tourism, and its people enjoy **traditional music** and ballads in the **bars**

year-round: try *Phil's Bar*, Main Street; *O'Malley's*, Parliament Street; or *The Falls Hotel* at weekends. The setting is surprisingly green; duck down behind the *Archway Bar* and the **Cascades Walk** takes you alongside the Cullenagh River as it rushes over slabs of rock through the heart of the little town, with its slate-gray houses and wooded banks. Lodged at the side of these falls is a rudimentary hydroelectric power station housed in a shed, providing electricity for the Falls Hotel—a resourceful piece of alternative technology. Ennistymon's **old church** is an eighteenth-century roofless ruin on a hill above the town, from where you can see the blue river snaking its way out of the woods and beyond to the sea at Liscannor.

For **accommodation**, *The White House Hostel* (£3.50) is on the Main Street, up behind *Phil's Bar*. The Christian Brothers will let you **camp** in their grounds at the top of Parliament Street; **tourist information** is available at *Kam Knitwear* (March–Nov 9am–6pm; ☎065-71387). **Cheap buses** depart from the square for Ennis, Limerick, and Dublin.

The Burren

Bleak and gray, **the Burren** can come as a shock to anyone associating Ireland with all things green. It's an extraordinary landscape of stark rock, fading lower green fields, and above all the sky and the ocean. Its cliffs and terraces lurch toward the sea like huge steps of wind-pocked pumice. Bone white in sunshine, in the rain it becomes darkened and metallic, the cliffs and canyons blurred by mists. A harsh place, barely capable of sustaining human habitation, it was well summed up in the words of Cromwell's surveyor Ludlow: ". . . savage land, yielding neither water enough to drown a man, nor a tree to hang him, nor soil enough to bury." There are no sweet rolling fields here, but stick with it and its fascination begins to emerge—cruel and barren as it is, there's a raw beauty about the place, and an exceptional combination of light, rock, and water.

Geology and History

The Burren (*Boireann* or rocky land) is a huge plateau of limestone and shale that covers 100 square miles of northwest Clare, a highland shaped by a series of cliffs, terraces, and expanses of limestone sidewalk, with little to punctuate the view. The only visible **river** is the Caher at Fanore since the Burren's waterways are largely underground: rainwater seeps through the highly porous rock and gouges away many underground potholes, caves, and tunnels. The only **lakes** are peculiar to this landscape; known as *turloughs*, they are hollows which become lakes only after heavy rainfall when the underground systems fill up, and vanish after a few dry days. All this gives the Burren an austerity of almost mythical dimensions, suggesting ancient privations. The sidewalking that stretches before you is a floor of gray rock, split by long parallel grooves known as grykes. The panorama is bleak, but close up, wild flowers burst from the grooves in specks and splashes of brilliant color.

A botanist's delight and enigma, the Burren supports an astounding variety of **flora**—arctic, alpine and Mediterranean plants grow alongside each other. The best time to see the flowers is late spring, when the strong blue, five-petalled spring gentians flourish. Here too are mountain avens, various saxifrages, and maidenhair fern. Later in summer the magenta bloody cranesbill and a fantastic variety of elsewhere-rare orchids bloom: bee orchids, fly orchids, and the lesser butterfly. More common flowers look stunning by sheer force of quantity: bright yellow birdsfoot trefoil and hoary rockrose, plus milkwort. Nobody knows exactly how these plants came to be here, nor why they remain. It has been suggested that some of the Mediterranean flowers have been here since Ireland had a far hotter climate, but how they survived is a source of speculation; it may be the peculiar conditions of moist warm air coming in from the sea, the Gulf Stream ensuring a mild, frostless climate, and very effective drainage through the porous limestone. It's also thought that the bare rock absorbs heat all summer and actually stores it, so that the Burren land is appreciably warmer in wintertime than areas of a different geology. There's more on the Burren's geology in the **Burren Display Center** in Kilfenora—see entry at the end of the chapter. Obviously flowers must not be picked.

In recent centuries the Burren has supported a sparse population, living, like most of the west of Ireland, in harsh poverty. It was to this land, west of the Shannon, that Cromwell drove the dispossessed Irish Catholics after his campaign of terror. Few could survive for long in such country. The area's lack of appeal to centuries of speculators and colonizers greedy to cream the fat off Ireland's lusher pastures has meant that evidence of many of the Burren's earlier inhabitants has remained. The place buzzes with the prehistoric and historic past, having over sixty Stone Age (3000–2000 BC) burial monuments, the most common types being wedge-shaped tombs, cairns, and dolmens; over 400 Iron Age ring-forts (500 BC–AD 500), which were defensive dwellings; and numerous Christian churches, monasteries, round towers, and high crosses.

How To Go and Where To Stay

The best way to get to know the Burren is slowly. The presence of some very good independent and budget hostels coupled with plenty of warm pubs in which to soak up the atmosphere of the "singing county" makes this a feasible and attractive proposition. There are **hostels** at Kinvarra, Fanore, Doolin, Lisdoonvarna, Ennistymon, and Liscannor, details of which are given in the text, as are **campgrounds**, since, on all this rock, it can be difficult finding ground on which to camp.

You can get to the area by taking a **Bus Éireann** connection from stations at Galway or Ennis. There is a direct bus service from Limerick and Galway to Doolin. Travel to the Burren from Dublin by train is less direct, the nearest stations being Gort or Crusheen, approximately ten miles to the east. Two **private bus** companies serve Ennistymon, in the south of the Burren: *West Clare Travel Club* and *P.S. Travel*. **Bikes** can be carried for an extra £5 on the *P.S. Travel* coaches, but must be booked at the same time as your seat. **Bike** rent is available at *Byrne & Sons*, Ennis Rd, Miltown Malbay (☎065-84079/ 84111); *Lynch & Howard*, Kilfenora, (☎065-84079); and in Ballyvaughan, down by the harbor (☎065-77059, also **bike repairs**). The following hostels also rent bikes: *Doolin Hostel*, Doolin; *Aille River Hostel*, Doolin; *The Bridge Hostel*, Fanore; *Doorus An Óige Hostel*, Doorus; and *Johnston's Hostel*, Kinvarra.

Seeing the Burren

To see the Burren's archaeological and ecclesiastical sites, go by car or bike; to get to know its landscape and flowers, go on foot. For either of these, Tim Robinson's excellent **map** *The Burren* (£3.50, available in tourist offices, good bookshops, or directly from him at Roundstone, County Galway; postage 75p) is usefully detailed and will make finding sites easy. There are two routes north–south across the Burren that are of particular **archaeological interest**; these run from Bell Harbour to Killinaboy and from Ballyvaughan to Leamaneh. If you're doing a lot of **walking**, a compass is a good idea as there's a shortage of easy landmarks. You're allowed to walk more or less where you want; a good start might be the fairly relaxed nine-mile **guided walk** (May–Sept 10:30am–4:30pm; £3–4; ☎065-20885 eves; departs Mon, Ballyvaughan Square; Tues and Fri, Doolin *White Hostel* and Ballynalacken Castle; Wed, Fanore Church; Thurs, Bell Harbour Post Office. Departures from Doolin are at 10am).

Kilfenora Caving and Outdoor Centre (☎065-71422), at KILSHANNY, near Kilfenora, is the place for **outdoor pursuits**; caving, gorge-walking and mountaineering cost £10 a trip, ponytrekking £6 per hour. Experienced **cavers** can rent equipment from *The Bridge Hostel*, Fanore.

South Galway Bay

Approaching the Burren from Galway brings you to some of the best spots: tiny villages on the northerly edge, little settlements between glinting inlets and the eerie white Burren hills—Kinvarra, Doorus, Aughinish, Bell Harbour, New Quay, Ballyvaughan. These offer magical views across the wide expanse of Galway Bay, where changes in the broad sky are reflected in the bay's surface, and the shimmering silver-and-turquoise light bounces off the white-gray Burren rock.

Kinvarra

Set in the southeasterly inlet of Galway Bay, **KINVARRA** is a fishing village with a stone quayside so pretty it's almost cutesy; water laps the shore while swans drift to the side of Dunguaire Castle. This quaintness has been recognized, and for such a small place there are disproportionate amenities: a smattering of coffee shops, an expensive restaurant, a supermarket, and some good bars. None of these set the little village off-balance, though, and the only environmental aberration is a bizarre development of modern thatched two-story houses with Victorian gas lamps, worth noting as a lesson in bad proportion and absurd detail. **Accommodation** is provided by the cheerful, independent *Johnston's Hostel* (☎091-37164, May–Sept; £3.50, camping £2.50, bike rental £3) and there's enough variety in the area to warrant a reasonable stay between the rigors of Burren-walking and Galway city-life. The informative *Kinvarra: A Ramblers Map and Guide* by Anne Korff and Jeff O'Connell is worth getting if you intend to explore the immediate countryside; available in local shops and at Dunguaire Castle.

Dunguaire Castle (☎091-37108; mid-April–Sept daily 9:30am–5pm; £1.60, students 90p) was built in 1520 and is a well-restored tower house, one of several used by Shannon Development for medieval banquets. These "castles" were in fact fortified houses, very much a fashion for wealthy landowners from 1450 to 1650, and found in their greatest concentration in East Clare, East Limerick, and South Galway. If you've not yet been in one, this is a particularly good example, as the guide has both a vigorous grasp of local history and the political sense of the old building. Kinvara has a **festival**, *Cruinniú na mBád*, on the last weekend in August, with the racing of Galway's traditional fishing vessels—the Galway Hookers—singing, and dancing.

Doorus

This whole area is associated with the poetry of the **literary revival group** of Yeats, Lady Gregory, AE and Douglas Hyde, and it was in what is now the **An Óige hostel** in **DOORUS** (☎091-37173) that the idea of a national theater was first discussed—later to become the Abbey Theatre in Dublin. The hostel was then the home of Count Floribund de Basterot, who entertained and encouraged the group (and also the likes of Guy de Maupassant and Paul Bourget). Given the political implications of the Irish literary revival, it's perhaps ironic that Count Floribund's cash came from French estates which his fleeing aristocratic ancestors had somehow hung on to, despite the Revolution.

Doorus itself is a small peninsula which, until the eighteenth century, was still an island. The gentle waters to the south are pleasant, tidal backwaters that strongly contrast with the wide sweep of beach to the north, which is stony but safe for swimming and surfing—there's a lifeguard on duty in summer. The beach of Parkmore, to the northeast, however, is dangerous. The **village** has only a pub and a shop, but there are **sessions** in *The Travellers Inn* most Sunday nights. You can **camp** at the hostel (☎091-37173) or down by the beach. Here, through the hostel warden, you can **rent bikes** (£3 a day) and *curraghs*, or go pony-trekking, and occasionally cabin cruiser trips around Galway Bay are available for seal-spotting, though they're pricey. Along this coast mussels are free for the picking—ask a local for the good spots.

West to Ballyvaughan and Fanore

You can walk the wriggling coastline from Doorus down to Aughinish or back to Kinvara, or cycle out to the Martello tower at Finvara and around the inlet of Muckinish Bay. All along this North Clare coast, where the Burren borders Galway Bay, short stretches of well-tended farmland reach from the foot of the hills to the shoreline, and water glints through gaps in the high stone walls. To the south, the Burren slopes off and dissolves in subtle half tones, while way over Galway Bay the muted cobalt mountains of Connemara are hazy in the distance. There's a wealth of birdlife along these shores: cormorants, guillemots, terns, herons, grebes, fulmers, mallards, teals, and swans.

BELL HARBOUR (*Beulaclugga*) is at the southern tip of Muckinish Bay. If you take the Carran road from here you'll soon see the mile-long road to the placid **Corcomroe Abbey** signposted on your left. A twelfth-century Cistercian foundation of considerable remains, it's beautifully set in a secluded valley. Similarly situated between Galway Bay and the Burren, **BALLYVAUGHAN** is an attractive village with a quay of neat gray blocks. Its significance as a trading center has dwindled into tourism, but it makes a calm haven from which to explore the Burren hills. It has a cluster of shops, an expensive restaurant, and a Rent-an-Irish-cottage scheme (reserve, well in advance, through *Bord Fáilte*). **Free camping** is possible down by the shore just beyond *Monk's* bar, which does good seafood and has **music** on Fridays and Saturdays throughout the year, and on other nights during the summer. The *Ballyvaughan Inn* offers standard home-cooked dinners from £5, plus music; and the *GAA* (*Gaelic Athletic Association*) club also occasionally has good sessions. **Bike rental and repairs** are down by the harbor (☎065-77059, June–Sept, £5 a day, £25 for 7 days). *Clare Coast Charter*, which operates expensive **deep-sea fishing trips**, are also based here (June–Sept ☎065-77014; off-season ☎065-21131).

From Ballyvaughan, there's a difficult choice between two alluring roads. If you follow the scenic coast road to Black Head, you can stop at the cosy independent *Bridge Hostel* at **FANORE** (☎065-76134, April–Oct; £3.50). The hostel offers **bike rental** and **caving**, but only has eighteen beds, so in July and August it's best to phone ahead. Alternatively, take the N67 south to the Ailwee Caves or Corkscrew Hill (see below). Both routes take you through some stunning scenery.

Into the Hills

The Aillwee Caves (daily: mid-July–mid-Aug 10am–8pm; early or late summer 10am–7pm; winter 10am–5pm; £2.30, £2 students; ☎065-77036) are two million years old, and the tour takes you through caverns of stalagmites and stalactites. It's very well lit, the tunnels are extensive, and there are spectacular rock formations. However, these caves are privately owned, massively promoted, and the tour is very fast; the experience does not induce the wonder it should.

Leaving the Aillwee Caves, if you rejoin the R480 and follow it south, you pass (to the left) Gleninsheen and Poulabrone **Megalithic tombs** after two and four miles respectively. The former is a wedge-shaped tomb a short walk from the road; the latter is the most famous of the Burren's portal dolmens, dating from 2500 BC. Just over half a mile farther on, on the right, is **Caher Connell**, a fairly well-preserved ring-fort. The surrounding uplands are in fact littered with such remains, this area having a particularly high concentration of them. The road goes on to Leamaneh Castle (see "Inland," below). The other north–south route particularly good for archaeological remains is the **Bell Harbour–Killinaboy road**, which, if you pass through TURLOUGH and take the left fork after passing through CARRON (both tiny), brings you to a limestone valley with several ring-forts, the most impressive of which is **Caher Commaun**, a ninth-century triple cliff-fort to the east of the road. Back on the road heading south there are many gallery graves before you descend to KILLINABOY.

Taking the Corkscrew Hill route from Ballyvaughan brings you to the popular spa town of **LISDOONVARNA**. The spring waters here contain magnesia, iodine, and iron, and reputedly have therapeutic qualities. The town's principal sulphur spring is in the *Spa Wells Health Centre*, which has pump house, sauna, baths and massage rooms. Traditionally, the place is famous for its month-long **matchmaking festival**, much loved by the writers of glossy magazine articles. This nowadays begins the first weekend of September, with blues and traditional folk sessions in the bars. The more recent music festival, over the first weekend in August, is largely devoted to country music. There are plenty of B&Bs in the town and a **hostel**, *Kincora* (£3.50), right in the center. There's a **tourist office** here too (June–Aug; ☎065-74062).

Doolin and the Cliffs of Moher

The village of **DOOLIN**, marked as *Fisherstreet* on some maps, has become *the* music mecca of the "singing county," and in fact of Ireland's West; by the time you get here, you'll no doubt have already met a good few traditional music enthusiasts on their way from across Northern Europe. Without the music, Doolin would be a forlorn and desolate place, lodged beside a treacherous sandy beach at the tail end of the coast that climaxes with the Cliffs of Moher. Bold shelves of limestone sidewalk step into the sea by the pier, from which a **ferry** now runs to **Inisheer**, the smallest of the Aran Islands (June–Aug, 10 trips daily 9am–8pm; April and Sept daily but less frequent; in winter, on demand; £10 return).

Music may be its *raison d'être*, but the village is now ruthlessly geared to providing **accommodation**, with over 100 hostel beds and a campground, for as many visitors as it is possible to squeeze into the place's three pubs. There is *The Rainbow Hostel* (☎065-74415; year round; £3.50, camping £2, fishing tackle and food available); *Aille River Hostel* (£3.50; bike rental, fishing tackle and food available); and *Doolin Hostel*, (☎065-74006; £4; laundry and drying room, bureau de change, bike rental). The **campground** is by the pier (☎065-74127; open Easter and May–Sept; £1 plus £1 per person). Despite their number, hostels do get packed in August, so phoning ahead is a good idea (if they're full, try the ones in Liscannor and Ennistymon, a handy five and eight miles away respectively—see earlier in this chapter). Whatever day of the week you arrive in the summer, traditional music will be playing in the bars—though while the music will be fine, the "pub experience" might pall, as you can find yourself sitting amidst an audience rapt in reverential silence, awed at just being there.

Around four miles south of Doolin, the **Cliffs of Moher** are Clare's most famous tourist spot. At their highest they tower 660ft above the Atlantic. Standing on the headlands that jut over the sheer, ravaged cliffs with their great bands of shale and sandstone, you can feel the huge destructive power of the waves. At points the battering of the water has left jagged stack rocks standing, continually lashed by white spume. Erosion is constant: during a storm five years ago a section of the cliff fell, taking its picnic table with it. The cliffs have to be seen, but be prepared for the oppressively commercial **visitors center**, where readily-changed money and travelers' checks are quickly spent on expensive food and souvenirs. Be prepared too for the professional Irish "characters," ready to sell you any baloney you're willing to buy, and the swarms of tourists newly armed with piercing tin whistles. Do see the cliffs, though—you can soon walk away from the crowds in either direction. The cliffs actually stretch for five miles, from Hag's Head, just west of Liscannor, to a point beyond **O'Brien's Tower**—a superfluous viewing point with telescope.

Inland

On the southern edge of the Burren is the tiny village of **KILFENORA** with its much publicized **Burren Display Center** (☎065-88030; mid-Mar–Oct daily 9:30am–5pm and until 7pm in July & Aug; £1.60, students £1.30). The center clearly explains the basic geography and geology of the Burren (in English, French and German) with the aid of a landscape model and a film. Most people find the presentation helpful, though some consider it no more than an expensive geography lesson. At any rate, the center has a very good **tea room**.

Next door is **Kilfenora Cathedral**, certainly worth a visit for its high crosses. The finest of these is the twelfth-century *Doorty Cross*, showing three bishops and what is probably Christ's entry into Jerusalem, with beautiful Celtic patterning. In the churchyard are remains of two other twelfth-century high crosses: one near the northwest corner, one opposite the church door. Wander through the gateway behind the church to see a fourth cross, with a decorated crucifixion, in the field to the west. The cathedral, built in 1190 and altered in the fifteenth century, has a roofless chancel with a finely carved triple-light east window and two effigies of bishops, possibly fourteenth-century.

The road east of Kilfenora passes **Leamaneh Castle**, a fifteenth-century O'Brien stronghold, adjoining which is a four-story building with mullioned and transomed windows (circa 1640). Of interest in **KILLINABOY** is a ruined eleventh–fourteenth-century church with a *Sheila na gig* over the doorway: a carving of a naked woman with grotesquely exaggerated sexual attributes (*sheila* is the Gaelic equivalent of Julia, *gig* means breast) which was probably some kind of fertility idol. They're more usually found above castle doorways, and it may be that its siting here was intended as a warning against the sins of the flesh. From Killinaboy the road continues to Corofin (p.278).

travel details

Trains
From Ennis: to Dublin (via Limerick); only 2 per week (Tues & Thurs 7.45am; 2hr 50min).

Bus Éireann
From Ennis: to Limerick (6 daily; 45min); Cork (3; 3hr); Shannon Airport (14; 45min).

Private Buses
Bill O'Mahony Coaches, **from Ennis**: to Dublin (4 on Friday, 3 on Sunday; 3hr 40min).

CHAPTER TEN

GALWAY, MAYO, AND ROSCOMMON

Galway, Mayo, and Roscommon mark a distinct change in the west of Ireland scene. Coming from the south, **County Galway** may at first seem a continuation of what has gone before in Clare and Kerry. And Galway city is in some ways the west coast town par excellence—an exceptionally enjoyable, free-spirited sort of place, and a gathering point for young travelers. But once you get beyond the city things start to change. The landscape is dramatically harsher and far less populous, and there are fewer visitors too.

Lough Corrib, which splits Galway in two, delineates another dramatic split in the landscape of the county, this time between east and west, inland and coast. To the east of the lake lies tame, fertile land which people have farmed for centuries, while to the west lies **Connemara**, a magnificently wild terrain of wind, rock, and water. The **Aran Islands**, in the mouth of Galway bay, resemble Connemara both in their elemental beauty and in their culture; the Galway *Gaeltacht* comprises the islands, Iar-Chonnact, and some scattered communities in north Connemara and Joyce Country. Again, **Galway City** straddles the divide. A bridging point both physically and culturally, it's a fishing port, an historic city, and now the focus of an energetic social and artistic scene.

If you continue up the coast you'll enter **Mayo**, where the landscape softens somewhat but is still relatively free of tourists. The pilgrimage center of **Knock** and the attractions of historic towns like **Westport** aside, it's the coast which is once again the main draw. Physically it's as exciting and rugged as any in the Republic, and far less exploited, though the downside of this is that facilities for travelers are relatively thin on the ground. An exception is **Achill**, the largest Irish offshore island, which provides both some of the most spectacular cliffs and some practical necessities for travellers, as it's a moderately popular holiday resort. **Roscommon** is entirely landlocked, and less visited still. In a sense this is understandable, as there are few real excitements, and the land is for the most part flat and low-lying. Nevertheless the fine detail of this landscape, scattered with small lakes and large houses, has a slow charm. There are places that merit a look as you pass through, and in the extreme north, around **Lough Key**, there's some very attractive scenery indeed.

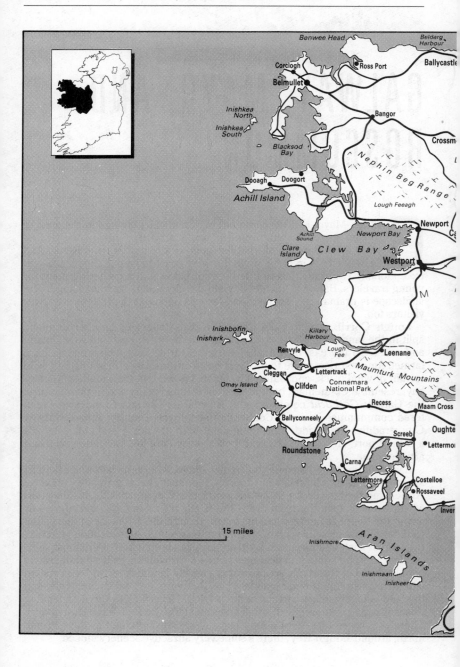

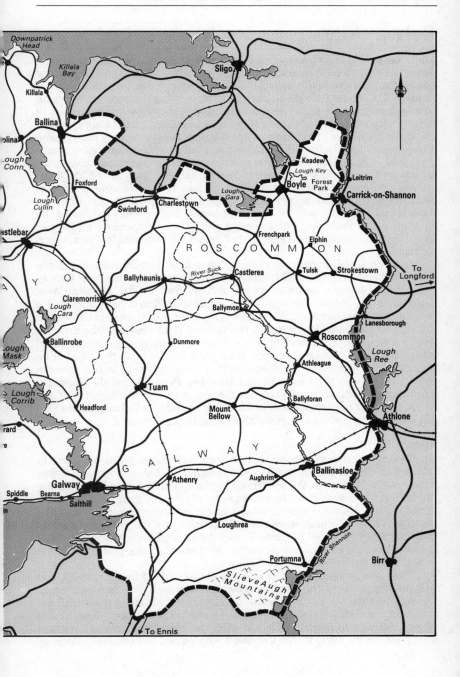

Galway City

The city of **GALWAY**, folk capital of the west, has a vibrancy and surly hedonism that make it unique. People come here with energies primed for enjoyment—the drink, the music, the "crack"—and it can be a difficult place to leave. University College Galway guarantees a high proportion of young people during school semester, maintained in summer by the attractions of the city's festivals. This youthful energy is an important part of Galway's identity, quite distinctive in a country plagued by emigration. Galway has become a playground for disaffected Dubliners, and folksy young Europeans return each year with an almost religious devotion. The city commands a vigorous loyalty: try badmouthing the place, and you're liable to find yourself in a fight.

Again in contrast to other Irish cities, Galway is experiencing a surge of economic growth, and is currently Europe's fastest-growing city. Constant renovation is in progress in the small and crowded city center, and during the summer it has the energy of a boom town, with an expanding number of shops and restaurants to cater to the surge of fashionable visitors and students.

Prosperity allows a vigorous independence from Dublin, reflected in the artistic dynamism of the city. It's a focus for the traditional music of Galway and Clare—Galway's status as an old fishing town on the mythical West Coast adding a certain potency—while the *Druid Theatre* has stimulated a new interest in theater here. At no time is the energy of Galway more evident than during its **festivals**, especially the **Galway Arts Festival** (the first two weeks in August), when practitioners of theater, music, poetry, and the visual arts create a rich cultural jamboree. It's a great time to be in the city, but be prepared for a squeeze on accommodation. The last weekend in July sees the place buzzing with the **International Busking Festival**, and the **Westend Traditional Festival** takes place on the last weekend in August. For the locals, the most important event in the social calendar is **Galway Races** (the last week in July), when accommodation is again at a premium.

History

Galway originated as a crossing point on the Corrib River, giving an access to Connemara denied farther north by the Lough. It was seized by the Norman family of De Burgos in the thirteenth century, and developed as a strong Anglo-Norman colony, ruled by an oligarchy of fourteen families. They maintained control despite continual attacks by the bellicose Connacht clans, the most ferocious of whom were the O'Flahertys. To the O'Flaherty motto "Fortuna Favet Fortibus" (Fortune Favors the Strong), the citizens of Galway responded with a plea inscribed over the long-vanished city gates: "From the fury of the O'Flahertys, good Lord deliver us."

Galway was granted a charter and city status in 1484 by Richard III, and was proudly loyal to the English crown for the next two hundred years. During this time the city prospered, developing a flourishing trade with the continent, especially Spain. However, its loyalty to the monarch ensured that when Cromwellian forces arrived in 1652 the place was besieged without mercy for ninety days. It was Cromwell who coined the originally derisory term "the fourteen tribes of Galway"; this didn't worry the Irish, who returned the disdain by proudly adopting the name as a title. The city went into a decline from the mid-seventeenth century onwards, and only recently started to revive.

The history of the **CLADDAGH**, a fishing village that existed long before Galway was founded alongside it, is quite distinct from that of the city proper. An Irish-speaking village of thatched cottages, the Claddagh was fiercely independent, having its own laws, customs, and chief, and it has always remained a proud, close-knit community. Boat-building skills are still passed down through generations, though of course this work is on the decline, and the old vessels known as Galway Hookers are now used more by boating enthusiasts and for transporting turf to the Aran Islands than for fishing. It is from here that the famous **Claddagh ring** originates, worn by Irish people all over the world. It shows two hands clasping a heart surmounted by a crown and represents love, friendship, and respect. It's worn with the heart pointing towards the fingertip when betrothed, the other way when married.

Arriving and Finding a Place to Stay

Ryanair has regular **flights** between Luton and Galway (£54 single off-peak); reservations in Galway from the **tourist office** in Eyre Square (☎091-65205). There are four direct **trains** from Dublin Heuston Station on weekdays and two on Sundays, while others connect with trains at Athlone. *Spot Fares* are available on certain trains, by far the cheapest at £10 for a day round-trip, and *Irish Rail* frequently has special round-trip fare offers. For train inquiries from Galway phone ☎091-62131, 62132, or 62141.

Bus Éireann runs one **bus** from Dublin daily; again there's a range of special fares, a one-way costing as little as £6 (inquiries ☎091-62141). *North Galway Club* (inquiries and reservations ☎093-55416) runs a similarly priced **bus** between the two cities; booking a day in advance is advisable especially for Friday travel (see "Travel Details"). The *USIT* travel agency on the university campus (Mon–Fri 10am–5pm; ☎091-24601) is the best agent for youth and student travel. Alternatively, *Corrib Travel*, in the center of town in Cathedral Building, Lower Abbeygate Street (☎091-63879/68318), deals with *Slattery's*, *Supabus*, *Eurotrain*, student flights, and youth fares, and offers a £9 one-way fare to Dublin airport.

Accommodation

There are plenty of **hostels** in and around Galway, but they get very full during festival time and throughout August—phone ahead or arrive early. There are two downtown: *Arch View Hostel*, Dominick Street (open all year; ☎091-66661; £3.50), and *Corrib Villa*, 4 Waterside (☎091-62892; £3.50). The *Mary Ryan Hostel*, 4 Beechmount Avenue, Highfield Park (☎091-23303), a twenty-minute walk from the center, includes breakfast and a shower for £3.90—walk via Taylors Hill Road, or take a #2 bus from Eyre Square to Taylors Hill Convent, from where there's a footpath to Highfield Park. Farther out is the *Galway Tourist Hostel*, Gentian Hill, Knocknacarra, Salthill (open all year; ☎091-25176; £3.50); take a Salthill bus from Eyre Square.

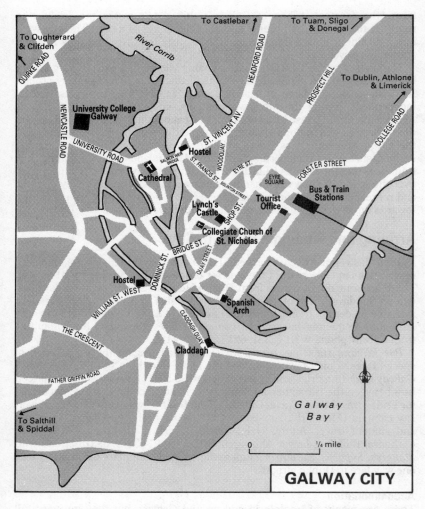

GALWAY CITY

There's no shortage of **B&Bs** in the city center either, with several in Prospect Hill: Seamus O'Flaherty's B&B is at no. 34 (☎091-66302; £8/£10); Joan O'Sullivan's at no. 46 (☎091-66324; £10); and Brigid Quilter's at no. 58 (☎091-61073; £9). The R864 Salthill Road also has plenty, though it's a little farther out. You can **camp** downtown for free on the grass down by the Spanish Arch, or for £2 you can pitch in the garden of *Glenavon* B&B, to the west of the city in Upper Salthill, near *O'Connors Bar*. Otherwise there are campgrounds at *Ballyloughane Caravan Park* on Dublin Road (April–Sept; £5 per unit; ☎091-55338), and several in Salthill, the pleasantest being *Hunter's*

Silver Strand Caravan and Camping Park, about four miles west on the coast road (March 27–Oct 2; £4.80 per unit, 20p per person; ☎091-92452 or 92040).

Orientation

Arriving in Galway you are bound to pass **Eyre Square**, also known as the J.F. Kennedy Memorial Park. The **Bus Éireann station** is off the south end of the square, as is the **tourist information office** on the opposite corner; it's also the departure point for the cheap private buses. This small park, set in the middle of a traffic interchange, is one of the points to which people gravitate, the other being the Shop and Quay Street area. It's used as a performance space during festivals, and outdoor sessions can start up here at any time, the relaxed atmosphere lending itself to improvisation. Visually, though, the place is a mess. A sentimental statue of the writer Padraic O'Conaire, a seventeenth-century doorway, a couple of cannons from the Crimean war and a clutter of disused flagpoles all detract from what should form the focus of the square: Eammon O'Donnell's splendid sculpture, whose arcs of rusted metal and gushing white fountains evoke the sails of the Galway Hookers, and recall the city's maritime history.

Galway's center is defined by the River Corrib. Issuing from the Lough, it thunders under Salmon Weir Bridge and wraps itself round the full body of the city, meeting the lively **Shop and Quay Street** areas at Wolfe Tone Bridge, where it flows into the bay. Such is the social pull of Shop and Quay streets that many visitors never make it beyond the bridge, and see the river as the city's boundary. This is a big mistake, as over the bridge is the Claddagh, and a few miles west of that is **Salthill**, Galway's commercial seaside town. The Claddagh now appears as a small area of 1930s municipal housing, but it's worth getting to know for some of its excellent bars and cheap eats. From here you can wander beside the pleasant walkways of river and canals, watching salmon hatchlings make their way upstream and cormorants dive for eels, while gawky herons splash through watery suburban backgardens. At the harbor, a walk out around the stone pier places the city in its impressive setting, with a level coastline stretching to the west and the eerie Burren hills washed and etched in half tones across the bay.

The City

The prosperity of maritime Galway and its sense of civic dignity were expressed in the distinctive town houses of the merchant class, remnants of which are scattered around the city in the form of finely carved doorways, windows, and stone slabs bearing armorial carving. The **Browne doorway** in Eyre Square is one such monument, a bay window and doorway with the coats of arms of the Browne and Lynch families, dated 1627. Just about the finest medieval town house in Ireland is **Lynch's Castle** in Shop Street, now housing the *Allied Irish Bank*. The Lynches were Galway's most prominent family for three hundred years. A local story relates that in 1493 James Lynch Fitzstephen, mayor of the town, found his own son guilty of the jealous murder of a Spanish visitor, and such was the popularity of the lad that no one in the town would take on the job as hangman—so the boy's father did it himself. Dating from the fifteenth century, the house has a smooth stone facade decorated with carved panels, medieval gargoyles, and a lion devouring another animal. Step inside for a detailed history of the building and its heraldry, and to view two pieces of Galway silver: a seventeenth-century sword and an eighteenth-century mace. In Market Street, outside Saint Nicholas's Collegiate Church, is the similarly styled **Lynch's Window**. In Bowling Green, a lane just off Market Street, is a gift shop which was formerly the home of **Nora Barnacle**, wife of James Joyce.

Down by the harbor stands the **Spanish Arch**; more evocative in name than in reality, it's a sixteenth-century structure that was used to protect galleons unloading wine and rum. Behind it is a fine piece of medieval walling, and next door is housed the uninspiring **Galway Museum** (May–Sept Mon–Fri 10:30am–5pm), where the only things of real interest are the old photographs of the Claddagh. Far more promising is the development of the **Spanish Arch Gallery and Print Workshop** nearby, which promotes printmaking through monthly exhibitions. It holds an annual national exhibition that runs concurrently with the Galway Arts Festival.

The city has two churches of interest: the **Collegiate Church of Saint Nicholas** and the **Cathedral of Our Lady Assumed into Heaven and Saint Nicholas**. The first is the largest medieval church in Ireland, having been built in 1320 and enlarged in the next two centuries. Dedicated to Saint Nicholas of Myra, patron saint of sailors, it's decorated with finely chiseled carvings and gargoyles, akin to the style of Lynch's Castle. The cathedral, in hideous contrast, was commissioned about twenty years ago by the then bishop of Galway, Michael (pronounced Me-hile) Brown—hence its nickname, "The Taj Michael". It sits on the banks of the river like a huge toad, its copper dome seeping green slime down the formica-bright limestone walls. Inside the horrors continue in a senseless jumble of stone, mahogany, and Connemara marble. It's so remarkably awful that it demands attention, and viewed from a long distance its sheer bulk does achieve a grandeur of sorts.

On the road behind the cathedral is the more restrained **University College Galway**, a mock-Tudor imitation of an Oxbridge college, which was opened in 1849 at a time when the majority of people in Connacht were starving. The university has the dubious distinction of having conferred an honorary degree on Ronald Reagan. More importantly, it is now UNESCO's base for an archive of spoken material in all Celtic languages, and summer courses for foreign students are held annually in July and August.

If a restful trip on the water appeals, at nearby Woodquay you can either rent a rowing boat (May–Sept) or take the Lough Corrib river cruise (1pm, 3pm, and 4:30pm; £4), which goes five miles up the river through flat countryside punctuated by derelict castles, out into the open expanse of the lake.

Salthill and the Beaches

Beyond the Claddagh is **SALTHILL**, Galway's seaside resort, complete with amusement arcades, discos, seasonal cafés, and a fairground. Salthill's **tourist office** is on the front (July & Aug daily 9am–7pm; June & Sept Mon–Sat 9am–6pm; ☎091-63081). The huge **Leisureland** amusement complex is used as a forum for big gigs, and also has a swimming pool (summer daily 10am–9:30pm). **Lower Salthill** has a long promenade with a series of unspectacular but safe and sandy beaches. Even on a hot summer's day it's never so busy as to be oppressive, and its great asset is the view over a glittering expanse of water to the Burren. West of here, **Upper Salthill** is a mess of a suburb that sits around its golf course, despoiled by huge billboards and trailer parks.

Probably the nicest of the sandy beaches immediately west of Galway city is the small one at **White Strand**, nestling beneath a grassy headland about three miles out of the center. Here, in a small inlet backed by a copse, is also the pleasantest **campground**, the *Silver Strand Caravan Park*. The nearest pub to this site is *The Twelve Bens*, just over a mile west. Galway's other special beach is **Ballyloughrun**, east of the city; this too has a campground alongside, and can be reached by taking the public footpath along by the railroad line, or by either the Renmore or the Merlyn Park bus from the station.

Food and Entertainment

If the "crack" has eluded you so far, this is where you're going to find it. The bars are the social lungs of this town, and even the most abstemious travelers are going to find themselves sucked in. You are guaranteed to find music somewhere—probably in a bar—and similarly there's absolutely no problem finding places to eat.

Eating

Finding tasty, filling food is easy in Galway, and relatively cheap. *McDonagh's Seafood Bar* on Quay Street is a must for seafood; stop in for a thick and creamy seafood chowder for £1.50, or stay for a full meal—nobody minds what you order, you just get the feeling that someone actually wants to feed you. *Food For Thought*, Lower Abbeygate Street, and also in the back of the tourist office, serves very cheap health food and vegetarian **snacks** and light meals. The *Hungry Grass*, Cross Street, is a wholesome café with healthy sandwiches. The best breakfast in town for under £2 is to be had at *The Happy Spud*, Abbeygate Street.

The cheapest health food meal in Galway is served at **midday** at the *Peadar O'Donnell Unemployed Centre*, Dominick Street. Visitors are welcome since custom in the café helps fund the center and its various campaigns. Also good value around midday is **pub food**, from £1.50 and up: try *The Quays*, *Naughtons*, and *MacSwiggen's*, all in Eyre Street.

Finding food in the **evenings** isn't as problematic as it can be elsewhere in Ireland. *L'Hermine*, Upper Abbey Street (Mon–Sat 8:30am–9pm; ☎091-68539), a crêperie run by French staff, serves delicious crêpes, *tartes* and coffee. The popular *Sev'nth Heaven*, Quay Street (Mon–Sat noon–9:30pm, Sun 1–6pm; ☎091-63838), has pizzas, quiches, and vegetarian food at lunchtime and pasta in the evening. *Nora Crub*, Shop Street (Mon–Sat 9am–9pm), offers vegetarian dishes, seafood and steaks. Pizzas, tacos, and ribs are dished up at *The Brasserie*, Middle Street (Mon–Sat noon–9pm; ☎091-61610). For **takeouts** there's *Conlon's* fish and chips, nice but pricey, or *The Kebab House*, 4 Dominick Street (daily noon–3am), with delicious, sizable helpings.

Drinking and the Music Scene

To experience Galway city you have to frequent one of the lively **bars** with which the place teems. **Traditional music** is performed in many of them; some of it will be depressingly overamplified, but you can hit a great session on any day of the week and at almost any time of the day during the summer months. The bars of Shop and Quay Streets are especially good possibilities, and *The Quays Bar* is currently *the* place to drink for locals and visitors alike; equally popular is *Naughton's* (*Tigh Neachtain*) across the street. *MacSwiggin's* in Eyre Street and *O'Connell's* in Eyre Square are good tradi- tional-style bars, while around the corner in Forster Street *An Pucan* has musicians on a regular basis. On the other side of town, *The Crane Bar* in Sea Road is renowned for its traditional sessions, and *Mick Taylor's* in Dominick Street is a friendly, relaxed place with a vaguely left-wing clientele.

Arus na nGael, Dominick Street (☎091-55479), is an Irish-speaking club devoted to traditional music and dance, run and frequented by Gaelic enthu- siasts. Admission is usually free, though during the summer it has special programs costing £3 (£2.50 hostelers). Outside the city, *O'Connell's* in Salthill also has a name for traditional music (June–Sept Mon–Thurs, plus singalongs at weekends).

Jazz sessions are a feature of Sunday mornings at *The King's Head*, Shop Street, *The Cellar Bar*, Eglington Street, and *The Great Southern*, Eyre Square.

Galway has its fair share of **discos**, with not a lot to choose between them. *Misty's* in Eyre Square, and *Bentley's* and *Zachs* on Prospect Hill are pubs until midnight when they transform; if you're in before 11pm you won't pay an admission charge. Otherwise there's *Central Park*, Upper Abbeygate Street, Thursday to Sunday. If you are staying in Salthill, there's *CJ's*, next door to *O'Connell's*, *The Oasis* (cheapest at £2), or *The Warwick Hotel* at weekends.

During school semester, the *Warwick* is the forum for student union gigs, with details of what's on available at the university. Other than this there aren't really any steady **rock venues**, except maybe *Cloggs*, off Dominick Street, which is active in promoting local bands and has something on most nights.

The Arts

Galway is experiencing a real growth in artistic activity. It's the home of the versatile *Druid Theatre Company* (☎091-68617; tickets £6, students £5), in Chapel Lane, off Shop Street; a relatively young company, it produces six new plays a year—many of them new Irish works—and undertakes extensive tours. If you're lucky enough to be in Galway city when they're on, reserve a ticket in advance, as they play to packed audiences. Galway's Irish-language theater is *Taibhdhearc* in Middle Street (☎091-62024/63600). The *Galway Arts Center*, Nun's Island (☎091-65886), is used as a performance space for dance, theater, and music, as well as having a lively program of visual arts exhibi- tions. It's also a good place to find out what is going on in the arts locally.

Inside the old quad of the university campus is a gallery which has occa- sional art and photographic exhibitions. The city's **movie theaters** are the *Town Hall Cinema*, Courthouse Square, and the *Claddagh Palace*, Lower Salthill.

Listings

Bike rental Ballalley Lane, off Eyre Square/Williamsgate Street (June–Sept daily 9am–6pm; £4 daily, £17.50 weekly; ☎091-66219). Also available in Queen Street, behind the tourist office (☎091-65763), and at 2 Atlantic Terrace, Salthill (£3.50 daily, £17.50 weekly; ☎091-55978).

Bookshops *The Pedlar Bookshop*, Quay Street, has a secondhand and new Irish section, also maps. *Hawkins House* bookshop, Churchyard Lane, includes comprehensive feminist and Irish-language sections.

Camping equipment *Great Outdoors*, Eglington Street (☎091-62869).

Health Galway Regional Hospital, Newcastle, Galway (☎091-24222); STD Clinic (☎091-64000); Family Planning Clinic, 16 Merchants Road (☎091-62992; Mon–Wed 10am–4pm, Thurs 10am–9pm, Fri 10am–5pm, Sat 11am–5pm; pregnancy testing £5; contraceptives on sale); *Abortion Helpline* (Tues 7–9pm; ☎091-67511).

Help and advice *The Peadar O'Donnell Unemployed Centre*, 19 Upper Dominick Street (☎091-66801/61412), a resource and campaign center for the unemployed, is also the focus for a broad cross-section of social campaigns and feminist groups; it runs a women's drop-in center Friday 8–10pm. *Galway Rape Crisis Center*, 15a Mary Street (☎091-64983).

Horseback-riding *Clonboo Riding School*, Clonboo Cross, Corrundulla (near Annaghdown; ☎091-91362).

Laundromats *The Laundromat*, Sea Road (Mon–Sat 9am–6pm); *Laundrex*, Old Malte Arcade, High Street (Mon–Sat 8:30am–6pm); *Laundromat*, 153 Upper Salthill (summer Mon–Sat 9am–9pm, Sun noon–6pm; winter Mon–Sat 9am–7pm).

Lesbian and gay information *Lesbian Line* (Wed 8–10pm; ☎091-24810).

Library Galway County Library, Hynes Building, St Augustine Street.

Luggage consignment Ballalley Lane bike rent (see above) for 50p, or at the station for 80p.

Police, Mill Street (☎091-63161).

Windsurfing At Ballyloughane; £8 a session (☎091-55612).

THE ARAN ISLANDS

The **Aran Islands—Inishmore, Inishmaan**, and **Inisheer**—lying thirty miles out across the mouth of Galway Bay, have exerted a fascination over visitors for decades. Their geology creates one of the most distinctive landscapes in Ireland, the limestone sidewalks giving the islands a stark character akin to the Burren of County Clare. This spectacular setting contains a wealth of pre-Christian and early Christian remains, and some of the finest archaeological sites in Europe. And it's not only works in stone that have survived out here: the islands are Gaelic-speaking, and up until the early part of this century a primitive way of life persisted, a result of the isolation enforced by the Atlantic.

History

The Aran Islands abound with evidence of their early inhabitants: the earliest ring-forts possibly date from the Iron Age, the majority from the early historic period. The next group of people to figure are the Christians, who came here to study at the foundation of Saint Enda in the fifth century and went on to found Iona, Clonmacnoise, and Kilmacduagh. However, the earliest ecclesiastical remains date from the eighth century.

As Galway's trade grew, so the strategic importance of the islands increased, and in medieval times control of them was disputed between the O'Flaherties of Connaught and the O'Briens of Munster, the latter generally maintaining the upper hand. In 1565 Queen Elizabeth resolved the dispute by granting the islands to an Englishman on condition he keep soldiers there to guarantee the Crown's interests. In the mid-seventeenth century the islands lost their political usefulness; the Cromwellian soldiers garrisoned there simply transferred to the new regime after the Restoration and became absorbed into the islands' traditional way of life.

After the decline of English interest and influence, the islands fell into poverty, aggravated in the nineteenth century by rack-renting. That rents should be levied on this barren rock suggests a cruel avarice, and not surprisingly, Aranmen were active in the Land League agitations; acts of defiance included walking the landlord's cattle blindfolded over the Dun Aengus cliff edge. Despite this link with the general political movement on the mainland and the islands' use as a refuge for Nationalists during the war of independence, it is their isolation that has allowed the continuation of a unique, ancient culture. Ironically, this very isolation has been a source of interest for outsiders in the twentieth century.

With the burgeoning fascination for all things Gaelic from the 1890s onwards, the Aran Islands, along with the Blaskets, became the subject of great sociological and linguistic inquiry, the most famous of their literary visitors being J.M. Synge. His writings brought the islands to the attention of other intellectuals involved in the **Gaelic Revival**, and the notion of a surviving community of pure Gaels provided fuel for the Nationalist movement. In fact this notion was misconceived. The distinct physical type found on Aran—dark skin, large brow, and Roman nose—is the legacy of the Cromwellian soldiers who were left on the islands.

In 1934 Robert Flaherty made his classic documentary *Man of Aran*, which recorded the ancient and disappearing culture he found here. (The film can be seen during the summer in Halla Ronain, Kilronan, at 3:30pm and 7:30pm; £2.) While the folklore and traditions recorded in the film are obviously on the decline, much remains. Some of the women of Inishmaan still wear the bright red patterned shawls; the men occasionally wear the traditional gray-blue tweed sleeveless suits. *Curraghs*—light wood-framed boats covered formerly with hide, now with tar-coated canvas—are still used for fishing, and for getting ashore on the smaller islands when the ferry can't pull in. I even witnessed, as in the film, a man fishing with a simple line off the edge of a 200-foot cliff. Fishing is still very much a way of life on Inishmaan, while tourism is the major earner on Inishmore and Inisheer. This means that though their purpose will change, knowledge of these customs will not vanish, and tourism may even help ensure the language survives, as Gaelic provides the islanders with a curtain of privacy against the visitors.

TRANSPORT TO THE ISLANDS

Several ferry companies operate between Galway and the Aran Islands, but they are rivals and won't let you mix your journeys between services on one ticket. A return to any of the islands costs in the region of £12, and it's usually possible to buy tickets on the boat. With any of these ferry services it's a good idea to check on the times of return journeys with the skipper, since weather conditions can mean alterations.

Inter Island Boat Services (☎099-61266 or 61115, evenings ☎091-83322) leaves SPIDDAL (11 miles west of Galway, 7.5 miles east of Inverin Hostel) for all three islands at 10am daily from Easter to the end of September; phone for schedule at other times. The ticket office is at the pier at Spiddal, though advance reservations are not usually necessary.

Aran Ferries Teo (☎091-68903, evenings ☎091-92447 or 95036) operate from the tourist office, Galway (daily March–Nov, weekends Dec–Feb), departing Rossaveal for Inishmore at 10:30am, 1:30pm, and 6:30pm; a connecting bus to Rossaveal leaves the tourist office one hour before the boat departs, costing £4 one-way, £5 round-trip .

Bus Éireann operate services direct from Galway to Kilronan, Inishmore (May 31– Sept 10), with connections to the two smaller islands on Tuesdays and Sundays— but the journey takes two and a half hours, as opposed to 45 minutes by the other routes. Tickets from Galway station (☎091-62141, 62132 or 63081); sailings usually 10am, but variable. A **fly/sail** scheme is available, one journey by air, one by sea, if the outward journey commences from Galway. Round-trip tickets for £30 must be reserved before date of travel at *Irish Rail* or *Aer Arann*. *CIE* also runs an island service via Rossaveal, departing Galway bus station at 9:15am.

From Doolin (County Clare) ten ferries leave daily between June and August; there's one daily from April to the end of September, and an occasional service in winter. It costs £10 round trip.

You can also **fly** to the islands. *Aer Arann* operates from Carnmore Airport, five miles east of Galway. (A minibus leaves the tourist office 45min before each flight.) Tickets can be reserved at the tourist office from Monday to Saturday, and on Sunday by phoning the airport (☎091-55437, 55480 or 55448). The Apex fare (£35 round trip) must be booked seven days in advance although the return date can be left open; £45 includes a round-trip air fare plus one night's B&B; the student fare is £25 return, as is the standby. Island airport numbers are: Inishmore ☎099-61109 or 61131; Inishmaan ☎099-73007 or 73002; Inisheer ☎099-75014.

Getting There

You're at the mercy of the weather here; unless you can afford to fly, be aware of the possibility of getting cut off from the mainland if the weather breaks. Inisheer and Inishmaan are particularly vulnerable, their piers being impossible to get to or from when the wind is high.

It is possible to do a **day trip** from Galway or Doolin (County Clare) to any of the islands, but you really need two full days to see the main sites of

Inishmore alone. Staying over on Inishmaan is the only way to experience its bewitching silence, and though Inisheer is so small that a day trip from Doolin is feasible, an overnight stay gives a priceless dimension to a visit—a taste of the islands' elemental forces. Though they are always considered as a group, each of the islands has its own distinct flavor and pleasures.

Provisions on the islands are slightly more expensive than on the mainland, and on Inishmaan are pretty basic. It's particularly difficult to get hold of vegetables as islanders grow their own with no surplus for sale, and you cannot buy *Camping Gaz* bottles on any of the islands.

The most detailed **map** of the islands is produced by Tim Robinson of Roundstone, available on Inishmore and at bookshops and tourist offices in the Galway and Clare area. In fact the Aran Islands are quite easy to explore and the map isn't essential for finding the major sites. It is, however, of great value to those interested in the detailed archaeology of the place and in Gaelic place names.

Inishmore

Although there's some truth behind the snobbery that denigrates **Inishmore** as the most tourist-oriented and least "authentic" of the Aran Islands, its wealth of dramatic ancient sites overrides such considerations. And though there does tend to be a sudden rush of camera-wielding visitors with the arrival of the midday ferry, Inishmore is big enough to absorb them quickly.

It's a long strip of an island, a great tilted plateau of limestone, with a scattering of villages along the sheltered northerly coast. The land slants up to the southern edge, where tremendous cliffs ripple along the entire length of the island. Walking anywhere on this high southern side, you can see the geological affinity with the Burren of County Clare, and visualize the time when these islands were part of a barrier enclosing what is now Galway Bay. As far as the eye can see is a tremendous patterning of stone, some of it the bare formation of the land (the sills of gray rock split in bold diagonal grooves), some the form of dry-stone walls that might be contemporary, or might be pre-Christian. The textures blur so that it's impossible to make sense of planes and distances, the only certainties being the stark outline of the cliffs' edge and the constant pounding of the waves below. Across the water in contrast are the Connemara mountains, colored pink and golden and slatey blue in the evening sun. Up the bay is Galway, now an insignificant speck, and around to the southeast, appearing as just a silvery ridge, are the Cliffs of Moher.

Practical Information

The best way to **get around** Inishmore is by a combination of cycling and walking. *Aran* **bicycle rent** is at Frenchman's beach, Kilronan, where the ferry docks (£3 per day, £17 for seven days); *Costello's Bike Rental* (May-Sept; £2.50, £3.50 per day) is opposite the *American Bar* farther up the lane. Bear in mind that in high season all bikes often vanish with the arrival of the ferry at noon. **Pony buggies** will take you on a circle tour for about £20 per group of four, or there's a **minibus** tour of the island that leaves Kilronan around 12:30pm (£4). If you have limited time you can take the public minibus up the island through the villages that stretch over seven miles to the west—MAINISTIR, EOCHAILL, KILMURVEY, EOGHANACHT, and BUN GABHLA—and walk back from any point. The bus leaves Kilronan grocery shop, up behind the hostel, every two hours between 9am and 5pm (£2 oneway). The village of KILLEANY, a mile and a half to the south of Kilronan, has to be either walked or cycled to.

The cheapest **place to stay** is the *Aran Islands Hostel*, Kilronan (April–Sept; £3.75; ☎099-61255). B&Bs can be booked through the **tourist office**, next door to the hostel kitchen, across the lane from the hostel itself (June–Aug Tues–Sun 11:30am–7pm; ☎099-61263). Mrs Gill, *Ard Einne*, Killeany (☎099-61126), and Mrs M. Dennis, *The Cliff House*, Kilronan (☎099-61286), are open all year, both charging around £10, and in the summer there are others. **Camping** is only possible down by the idyllic beach at Kilmurvey, a lovely sweep of white sand looking out over to the Connemara mountain range, but anywhere else is either bare rock or a treasured piece of cultivatable land. Should you stumble across a likely spot, finding its owner and asking permission is essential.

The island's main **grocery shop** is in the lane behind the hostel. There is also a shop at Kilmurvey, one at the corner before you go down to the beehive hut at Clochan na Carriage, and one just west of Eognacht (half a mile and 1.5 miles west of Kilmurvey respectively). Kilronan has a **post office**, with a public phone outside, and the *Bank of Ireland* opens here Wednesday only (10:15am–12:30pm and 1:30–3pm). A **money exchange service** operates from *Carraig Donn*, a craft shop selling hand-knitted Aran sweaters by the pier at Kilronan, open seven days a week from April to October.

The Island

Inishmore's villages are strung along the main road that runs the length of the northern shore, the hub of activity being **KILRONAN**, where the ferry lands. The island has some great sandy **beaches**: the one at KILMURVEY (four miles west of Kilronan) is safe and sheltered, with fabulous views of the Connemara mountains, or you could take the main road to its eastern extreme and then walk north to get to the safe beaches from Carraig na gCailleach, through Carra na Loinge, down to Poll an Ghabhna. Tucked closer to KILLEANY (around two miles to the south of Kilronan), near the airstrip, is Tra na Ladies, which looks nice, but where you can get caught by tides or sinking sand. You can **walk** just about anywhere so long as it doesn't look like someone's garden, but be careful when walking anywhere on the south of the island in poor visibility, as the cliffs are sheer and sudden.

The Forts

The most spectacular of Aran's prehistoric sites is Inishmore's fort of **Dun Aengus** (signposted from Kilmurvey, three-quarters of a mile), a massive semicircular ring-fort of three concentric enclosures lodged on the edge of cliffs that plunge 300 feet into the Atlantic. The inner citadel is a twenty-foot-high, eighteen-foot-wide solid construction of precise blocks of gray stone, their symmetry echoing the almost geometric regularity of the land's natural limestone paving and the bands of rock that form the cliffs. Standing on the ramparts you can see clearly the chevaux-de-frise outside the middle wall, a field bristling with lurching rocks like jagged teeth, designed to slow down any attack.

The place is tremendously evocative, and it's easy to understand how superstitions have survived on the islands long after their disappearance on the mainland. Visible west of the cliffs of Inishmore under certain meteorological conditions is the outline of what looks like a mountainous island. It's a mirage, a mythical island called **Hy Brasil** that features in ancient Aran stories as the island of the blessed, visited by saints and heroes. Until the sixteenth century Hy Brasil was actually marked on maps.

Dun Eoghanachta is a huge drum of a fort, a perfect circle of stone settled in a lonely field with the Connemara mountains a scenic backdrop. Its walls are sixteen feet thick, and inner steps give access to the parapets. Inside are the foundations of the ancient dry-stone huts known as *clochans*. It's accessible by tiny lanes from Dun Aengus if you've a detailed map; otherwise retrace your steps to Kilmurvey and follow the road west for just over a mile, where it's (poorly) signposted off to the left.

Dun Ducathair (the black fort) is especially worth visiting for its dramatic location. It's a promontory fort, and what remains is a massive stone wall straddling an ever-shrinking headland precariously placed between cliffs. The eastern gateway fell into the sea early in the last century, leaving the entrance a perilous twelve inches from the sheer drop. Inside are the curved remains of four *clochans*. It's about a two-mile walk from Kilronan—head south out of the village for about three-quarters of a mile, take a turning on the right just before a tiny electricity generating station, and follow the lane to the cliffs. Once at the cliff edge you can see the fort on the second promontory to your left.

The dating of these forts is tricky: Dun Aengus and Dun Ducathair are probably from the first century BC, whereas Dun Eoghanachta and **Dun Eochla** (just south of Eochaill) could have been constructed at any time between the first and seventh centuries AD, or possibly earlier. The massive buttresses of Dun Eochla are nineteenth-century additions, but the forts have generally been kept in exceptional condition.

Church Sites and Clochans

From the fifth century onwards Aran became a center of monastic learning, the most important of the hermitical settlements being that of Saint Enda (Eanna). At **the seven churches**, just east of EOGHANACHT, there are ancient slabs commemorating seven Romans who died here, testifying to the far-reaching influence of Aran's monastic teaching. The site is in fact that of two churches and several domestic buildings, dating from the eighth to the thirteenth centuries. Here Saint Brendan's grave is adorned by an early cross with interlaced patterns and, on the west side, part of a Crucifixion carving. There are also parts of three high crosses, possibly eleventh-century, and in the southeast corner of the graveyard, alongside the slabs of the Romans, lie several ninth-century slabs incised with crosses and inscriptions.

The most interesting of the ecclesiastical sites on Inishmore is **Teampall Chiarain**. Take the low road from MAINISTIR and follow the lane parallel to the shoreline, and you'll come to it, a simple twelfth-century church on an old monastic site. Alongside is **Saint Kieran's Well**, a long, U-shaped spring backed by huge blocks of plant-covered stone. It's very pagan-looking—such wells often held sacred significance in pre-Christian times, and were sanctified in name with the arrival of Christianity. Similarly, some of the tall stones that stand around the site look pre-Christian even though they have crosses inscribed on them. The one by the east gable has a hole in it that may have held part of a sundial, and nowadays people sometimes pass handkerchiefs through it for luck.

Teampall Bheanain, on the hill behind KILLEANY, is a pre-Romanesque oratory of around the sixth or seventh century, dedicated to Saint Benen. It's distinguished by its very steep gable ends, and by its unique north–south orientation. In all probability it used to form part of the great early monastic site that existed at Killeany.

The finest of Aran's *clochans* is **Clochan na carraige**, just north of Kilmurvey. This nineteen-foot-long drystone hut has a corbeled roof whose arrangement is probably an early Christian design. There are fifty lesser examples of such huts on Inishmore.

Food, Drink, and Entertainment

Not surprisingly, seafood is the great specialty on the island. *Dun Aonghasa*, Kilronan (Easter–June and Sept–Halloween daily noon–9pm; June–Sept daily 10am–10pm), has probably the most varied menu, and is good value for anything from light snacks up to full meals. *Dormer House*, behind the hostel, is a friendly B&B that also feeds non-residents; it's all home cooking and a full meal will cost around £10. *An Tsean Cheibh*, Kilronan (April 7–Sept; ☎099-61228; midday meals from £4, evenings from £6), specializes in seafood. Kilronan also has a chip shop, open daily in summer until 10pm, and later if there is a *ceilidh* on. An outfit offering what it describes as "vaguely vegetarian food"—cheap and wholesome—operates from the hostel kitchen but availability is subject to the temperament of the proprietor.

You can punctuate your bicycling or walking with tea and snacks at *Man of Aran Cottages* in Kilmurvey (June–Aug)—used as a set in the film—or at *Johnston Hernon's Guest House*, situated at the foot of the path to Dun Aengus from Kilmurvey (May–Sept).

If you want an early night at the hostel, forget it; the **pub** downstairs is extremely noisy. It's convivial enough, but it's still a good idea to wander away from here to sample some of the island's other bars: *The American Bar, Joe Watty's* farther west, *John Dirrane's* at the top of the road as it slopes down to the beach at Kilmurvey, or *Tigh Fitz* bar in Killeany. In addition to this there are **ceilidhs** in Kilronan parish hall (June–Sept Tues–Sun; occasionally in winter; £2, students £1.50). They're obviously for the tourists, but good fun nonetheless.

Inishmaan

Coming from Inishmore you are immediately struck by how much greener **Inishmaan** is. Brambles and ferns shoot from walls, and bindweed clings to the limestone terraces. Here the stone walls are a warm brown and seem to almost glow with yellow moss. They're remarkably high—up to six feet—and form a stone maze that checkers off tiny fields of lush grass and clover. Yet despite this lushness, the island feels dour and desolate. Farming here is at subsistence level; farm buildings and cottages are grubby and dull, and soggy thatches sag over low doorways. The only sudden splashes of color are from tiny cultivated gardens—the bright reds, pinks, and oranges of geraniums, gladioli, and carnations.

The island is shaped something like an oyster shell. It rises in distinct levels from the soft dunes of the north, through stages of flat naked rock, up to minuscule green pastures, then again up a craggy band of limestone (along which sit the main villages of the island), eventually leveling out on higher ground to meet the crinkled blowhole-pitted southerly edge. Inishmaan is the least visited, least touched by tourism of the three islands, though it has had visitors since the turn of the century. J.M. Synge stayed here for four summers from 1898, recording the life and language of the people. His play *Riders to the Sea* is set here, and his book *The Aran Islands* provides a fascinating insight into the way of life he found. "Synge's Chair," a sheltered place on the westerly cliffs overlooking St Gregory's Sound, was his favorite contemplative spot. Traces of the ethnic culture he discovered remain. Some of the women still wear the traditionally brightly colored shawls; Gaelic is the main language, though English is understood; and the islanders get on with what they've always done: farming and fishing. There's no hostility to visitors, but tourism isn't the islanders' concern. If you want to be impressed or entertained, you'll have to look elsewhere.

Forts and Churches

One of the most impressive of the Aran forts is Inishmaan's **Dun Conchuir**, loosely dated between the first and seventh centuries AD. Its massive oval wall is almost intact, and commands great views of the island, being built on the side of a limestone valley. (In myth, Conchuir was the brother of Aengus of the Firbolg.) To the east, the smaller **Dun Fearbhai** stands above the village of BAILE AN MHOTHAIR and looks out over the little eighth-century **Cill Cheannannach** by the shore. In this context the interior of the island's modern church, just below Dun Conchuir, comes as a shock: garish stylized windows of virulent turquoise and purple from the workshop of Harry Clarke. Stepping outside, the old magic reasserts itself, with the island's ancient graves and wells.

Eating, Sleeping, and Other Practicalities

Inishmaan's indifference to tourism means that amenities for visitors are minimal. The **shop** in the main street of the central village has limited provisions: canned foods, bread, and milk. *Padraig O'Conghaile's* **pub** is a haven of luxury in such a setting: warm and friendly, and excellent snacks are available at any time, with music sessions on weekends. There are few other going commercial concerns on the island: a seasonal café below Dun Conchuir, and an expensive Aran knitwear shop, which also houses the **Inishmaan Museum**, a fascinating photographic archive of island history, all documented in Gaelic. **B&Bs** are cheaper than on the mainland (around £7), though if you have an evening meal it generally nearly doubles the price. If you want to reserve ahead, the only one you can phone is Mrs A. Faherty (☎099-73012); if you arrive on spec, ask at the pub. Farmers will let you **camp** if you ask them—all land belongs to somebody here. There is no pharmacy or doctor on the island, and **emergencies** are dealt with by a nurse who serves all three islands (☎099-75006). A **public phone** is situated outside the post office, and the *Bank of Ireland* operates on the first Tuesday of every month.

Inisheer

Inisheer, at just under two miles across, is the smallest of the Aran Islands. Tourism has a key role here; Inisheer doesn't have the archaeological wealth of Inishmore, or the wild solitude of Inishmaan, but the introduction of regular day-trip ferry services from Doolin promises a constant, if small, flow of visitors. This new service also now makes for a handy route from County Clare to Connemara. Of course tourism threatens the very stuff of its attraction—the purity of ethnic traditions and a romantic isolation—but for the moment Inisheer retains its old character, and for some it's a favorite place.

A great plug of rock dominates the island, its rough, pale gray stone dripping with greenery. At the top the fifteenth-century **O'Brien's castle** stands inside an ancient ring-fort. Set around it are low fields, a small community of pubs and houses, and windswept sand dunes. Half buried in sand just south of the beach is the ancient **church of Saint Kevin**; still in use in the last century, it is now used only to commemorate him as the patron saint of the island every June 14.

The **tourist information office** (June–Aug daily 11am–7pm), in a hut by the pier, will give you a map and a list of **B&Bs**, which all cost around £8. The *Co-op* (☎099-75008) will also do this for you, and will make advance reservations by phone in high season—the first weekend in August and Pentecost weekend are usually booked up well ahead. Up behind the post office there's a cosy **hostel** with eight beds (open all year; £3.50); for advance reservations write to Rory Donohue, The Hostel, Inisheer. Inquiries (not reservations) are taken at the post office (☎099-75001). The only **camping** is on the official site (£2 per tent, 50p per person, showers 50p). The island's main **festival** is its *curragh* racing and sports day, normally held on the second Sunday in August.

There are only two places to get a cooked **meal** on Inisheer: *Radharc na Mara* (June–Aug, until 8pm) serves snacks or meals from £3, and the *Ostan Inis Oirr* (Hotel Inisheer; June to mid-Sept; ☎099-75020) does bar food and meals for non-residents, from 9am to 9pm, with evening meals from £7.50. Both the hotel bar and *Tigh Ruairi* bar have **music** any time of the week during the summer. There is no bank on the island, but you can **change currency** (though not traveler's checks) in the shop.

CONNEMARA

Dominated by two mountain ranges, **Connemara** is exceptionally beautiful. The **Twelve Bens** and **Maam Turks** glower over vast open areas of bog wilderness, while to the southwest the land breaks up into myriad tiny islands linked by causeways, slipping out into the ocean. The whole area has superb beaches, huge sweeps of opalescent white sand washed by clear blue water. Chance upon good weather here and you feel you've hit paradise; even on the hottest of days the beaches are never crowded.

This is country you visit for its scenery rather than its history. There is little evidence of medieval power in west Galway, either ecclesiastical or secular, beyond a few castles along the shore of Lough Corrib, and the occasional one farther west. The great exception is the profusion of monastic remains dotted over the little islands off the west coast. Mainland settlements up until the nineteenth century were scattered, and the area has always been sparsely populated, due to the poverty of the land. There's never been much to attract marauders or colonizers, and any incursions have involved a battle against the terrain as much as against the people. It's easy to see how such a land would remain under the control of clans like the O'Flahertys for centuries, while gentler landscapes bowed to the pressure of foreign rule. In the famine years the area suffered some of the worst of the misery, and a thinly peopled land was depopulated further as people chose to escape starvation by emigration, despite its dangers and uncertainties.

Continued economic deprivation and isolation have meant that an ancient rural way of life has continued for far longer here, so Connemara is still Irish-speaking, the largest of the *Gaeltacht* areas. A *Gaeltacht* summer school is held in **Spiddal**, and **Casla** (Costelloe) is the home of the new *Radio na Gaeltachta*. English is spoken too, however, and the only difficulty for the visitor is that the signs on the roads, and on some buses, are often in Gaelic.

For all its beauty, the dramatic mountain landscape of west Galway is surprisingly undeveloped in terms of tourism, owing in part to the infamous Irish weather and in part to the fact that walking has not been the popular recreation in Ireland that it is in other, more urbanized European countries. If you're in search of solitude, you won't have to go far to find it.

Transport, Accommodation, and Other Practicalities

Bus Éireann services link all villages on major routes between Galway, Oughterard, Roundstone, Clifden, and Cong. They are reliable, although infrequent, with often only one daily. Timetables can be picked up in Galway bus station. Connections from Clifden to Westport only operate on Thursday.

As everywhere, there are two cheap ways to stay: camp or hostel. You can **camp** more or less anywhere, but bear in mind that a lot of the area is bog and therefore very wet. Away from towns and villages, you may have trouble getting water; very irritating when in the middle of a bog! *Camping Gaz* bottles or canisters are also rare in the region, so stock up in Galway city if you're *Gaz*-dependent. If you do run short, try *Keogh's* in Oughterard or *The Twelve Bens*, High Street, Clifden. *Bord Fáilte* -approved campgrounds are listed in the text.

HOSTELS IN CONNEMARA

If you're hosteling in August and at festival times it's advisable to phone and reserve ahead; in this part of the country there aren't B&Bs at every turn to fall back on.

Indreabhan (Inverin) *An Óige* hostel (☎091-93154; grade A) on the coast road seventeen miles west of Galway; shop nearby.

Carna Hostel *Budget Hostel* (☎095-32240; open all year; £3.50).

Binn Leitri (Ben Lettery) *An Óige* hostel, Ballinafad (☎095-34636; grade A); shop in hostel, bike rental available.

Clifden Hostel, Beach Road, Clifden (☎092-46089; £3.50); and *Leo's Hostel*, White House, Beach Road, Clifden

(☎095-21429; dorms £4, private rooms £4.50, camping £2)—very friendly, with coal fires.

Killary Harbour *An Óige* hostel, Rosroe, Renvyle (☎095-43417; grade B); very friendly, shop in hostel, drying room, family rooms or dorms.

Cong Hostel *An Óige* hostel, Lisloughrey, Quay Road, Cong, County Mayo (☎092-46089; grade A); clothes washing and drying facilities, money changing, store, and bike rental.

If you intend to go **walking** bear in mind that the mountains here are potentially **dangerous**. There is no organized mountain rescue service such as you get in European countries that are more developed for mountain sports. The Ordnance Survey 1:126,720 maps are based on surveying done in 1837 and are inaccurate, especially above the 1000-foot contour. If you are doing any serious walking it is worth getting either the *Connemara Map and Guide Booklet* (£6.50), or *The Mountains of Connemara* (£5.50), a map and guide to eighteen walks, including The Western Way. Both are produced by *Folding Landscapes* of Roundstone, Connemara, County Galway, and can be obtained in tourist offices in the west of Ireland, or by mail (add 75p p&p). **Bike rental** is available at Clifden, Galway, at hostels already mentioned and from Gerard Coyne in Tullycross (☎095-4).

Most of Connemara's more beautiful **beaches** are safe for swimming, including Clifden, Lettergesh, Dog's Bay, Gurteen Bay, Renvyle, Ardmore, Mannin Bay, Aillebrack, Omey, Letterfrack, and Spiddal. It is, however, a very varied coast, so if in doubt, ask about safety locally.

Finally, being the *Gaeltacht*, signposts are often in Gaelic, as are names on buses; see the box on the next page for a list. Variations in the Gaelic spellings are common—sometimes the "An" is omitted.

Iar-Chonnact

Draw a triangle between Maam Cross, Rossaveal, and Galway and you've defined the area known as **Iar-Chonnact**, an open and bleak moorland of bog. Occasional white-splotched boulders lie naked on the peat that stretches to the skyline; any grass that survives is coarse and wind-bitten, and, except for small pockets of forestation, the bog has no trees. It's difficult, wet walking country, but numerous lanes and *bohreens* lead to tiny loughs set in the granite hollows of the hills—good for fishing for brown trout, sea trout, or salmon.

The Rossaveal to Oughterard Road

The moorland reaches its highest point near Lough Lettercraffoe on the **Rossaveal to Oughterard road**, giving fine views down onto **Lough Corrib**, whose intricate green and wooded shores are a vivid foil to the barren west. This is the road to take if you're heading for the dramatic walking country of the mountains and plan to base yourself at Clifden. It makes the easiest hitch and most pleasant bike ride from Galway, avoiding the boring strip development down to Spiddal, and taking you instead along the shore of island-flecked Lough Corrib, past crumbling ruins.

These include the main sixteenth-century O'Flaherty fortress of **Aughnanure Castle**. A six-story tower standing on a rock island surrounded by a fast-flowing stream, Aughnanure was one of the strongest fortresses in the country at the time of Cromwell's blockade of Galway (1652–54). Now restored, it is open to the public (June–Sept 10am–6pm; otherwise key with caretaker). **OUGHTERARD** itself is a small town serving fishing-based tourism, from where you can rent boats out onto the lough. Approached from the east, Oughterard can beguile you into thinking that Connemara is going to be a populated, thriving, developed place, but arriving from the west it seems a lush, green oasis, the beech trees that line the banks of the river sumptuous and luxuriant after the barren wilds of the bog.

The main N59 road then takes you through the hamlets of RECESS, where all you will find is *Joyce's* bar and shop, and MAAM CROSS, where there's a craft shop, gas station, and a pub which serves **food** all day. Close in under the rugged peaks of the Twelve Bens is **Ballynahinch**, a castle which was once the home of the land-owning Martin family, now a hotel with a bar open to non-residents. On Ballynahinch lake are the remains of an old O'Flaherty castle, known as "Martin's Prison" due to the use it was put to by Ballynahinch's most famous son, Dick Martin—aka **Humanity Dick** (1754–1834). The story behind the name is that Richard Martin, originally dubbed "Hairtrigger Dick" because of his dueling prowess, spent his adult life campaigning for animal rights, and any tenant he caught causing suffering to animals was thrown into jail in the castle. Dick was known to have fought

GAELIC/ENGLISH PLACE NAMES

An Caiseal	Cashel	*Casla*	Costelloe
An Cheathru Rua	Carraroe	*Cill Chiarain*	Kilkieran
An Clochan	Clifden	*Cloch na Ron*	Roundstone
An Cloigeann	Cleggan	*Eanach a Chuain*	Annaghdown
An Fhairche	Clonbur	*Leitir Meallain*	Lettermullen
An Spideal	Spiddal	*Leitir Moir*	Lettermore
An Teach Doite / X Mam	Maam Cross	*Mionlach*	Menlo
An Tulach	Tully	*Na Forbacha*	Furbo
Baile Conaola	Ballyconneely	*Sraith Salach*	Recess
Baile na hInse	Ballynahinch	*Srib*	Screeb

duels on behalf of threatened animals, and when asked why he did so replied: "Sir, an ox cannot hold a pistol." More constructively, he pushed various acts through parliament protecting farm animals from maltreatment, and was instrumental in founding the RSPCA.

West Around The Coast

The **coast road** is the alternative route west from Galway, passing through the *Gaeltacht* villages of Barna and Spiddal. The *Spiddal Craft Centre* is a collection of workshops showing high-quality sculpture, ceramics, weaving, and jewelry, open all year. Beyond ROSSAVEAL (where you can get boats for the Aran Islands) the land breaks up into little chains of low-lying islands, linked to one another by natural causeways. These islets, more gentle than the main body of Connemara, make a perfect place to get lost in—meandering around the inlets and gullies you experience a happy disorientation .

The beach at CARRAROE (*An Cheathru Rua*) is a strand made up of tiny fragments of coraline seaweed. Near ROSMUCK, a speck of a hamlet, is the cottage of the republican and poet **Padraig Pearse**, who was executed after signing the 1916 proclamation. The cottage where he wrote plays in both English and Irish is open to the public. At CARNA you can wander out onto Mweenish Island and look out to Saint MacDara's Island, where the remains of a monastery still stand. Such was the former reverence for the saint that fishermen would dip their sails three times when passing the island. A three-day festival, *Feile Mhic Dara*, is still held during July in Carna.

The only settlement of any size in the area is **ROUNDSTONE**, a fishing village at the foot of the Errisbeg mountain. Curving its back to the Atlantic, the quaint stone harbor looks across its sheltered waters to the magnificent Twelve Bens of Connemara. Fishing is the main source of income, along with an unobtrusive tourism that makes the most of the unique prettiness of the setting and the glorious beach at Gurteen Bay. A huge sweep of white sand with lucid blue water, this is really very seductive. There's a **campground** here, the *Gurteen Caravan Site* (☎095-35882), a mile and a half west of Roundstone; it also has a laundromat. An Industrial Development Authority complex is discreetly tucked away to the west of the village, where you can wander around the various studios and see traditional instruments being made (flutes, goatskin *bodhrans*, whistles, and harps), visit pottery workshops and call in on *Folding Landscapes*—the people who produce the maps.

As far as **food and drink** go, Roundstone has a couple of expensive restaurants, some tea shops, and a handful of nice bars with music on weekends. There's particularly good pub grub at *O'Dowd's Bar*, and also in their *Seafood Restaurant* (Easter–Sept noon–10pm; ☎095-35809). Other popular bars are *Connolly's*, *Keanes Hilltop Bar*, and *Vaughan's Lounge* in the *Roundstone House Hotel*. You can **rent bikes** from *Michael Ferron's* shop (£3 a day, £18 a week). To go **pony-trekking** contact James de Courcey, Errisbeg, Roundstone (☎095-35803), who takes treks on beaches or in the mountains for between £5 and £7 per hour. There are several places for **bed and breakfast**—try Paraic and Carmel Faherty, *Connolly's Bar* (☎095-35863; £9.50), Patricia Keane, *Heather Glen* (☎095-35837; £9.50), or Mrs C. Lowry, *St Joseph's* (☎095-35865; £10).

It's an easy couple of hours' walk from Roundstone up to the top of **Errisbeg**—follow the fuchsia-flooded lane up the side of *O'Dowd's* bar and then the track ahead. The views are panoramic: the frilly coast of isthmuses and islets runs out to the south, while the plain of bog to the north is vast and open, punctuated only by the irregular glinting surfaces of dozens of little lakes, like sinister jellied eyes on the stark face of the landscape. It's through this wilderness that the **bog road** runs, the source of such superstition that some local people will not travel along it at night. Around the turn of the century, two old women who lived in the road's only dwelling robbed and murdered a traveler who'd taken refuge with them, and the road is considered to be haunted. From Errisbeg the view across the bog to the Connemara mountain ranges is tremendous. To the west, long beaches of white sand scoop their way north—Gurteen, Dog's Bay, Ballyconneely, Bunowen and the coral strand of Mannin Bay—each echoing the beauty of the last.

Clifden

Because of the dramatic grandeur of the Connemara mountains and the romantic pull of Galway, you expect **CLIFDEN**—known as the capital of Connemara—to be something special. In fact it's a very small place with only two significant streets. Its great asset is its position, perched high above the deep sides of the boulder-strewn estuary of the Owenglin River. The circling jumble of the Twelve Bens provides a magnificent scenic backdrop, and the broad streets seem consciously to open out, to take in the fresh air of the mountains and the Atlantic. Gimlet spires of matching nineteenth-century churches pierce the sky, giving Clifden a sharp, distinctive skyline.

Clifden seems to be trying hard to cultivate the cosmopolitan atmosphere of Galway. Lots of European tourists come here, but, aiming to serve all tastes, the town ends up catering to few. Bars have loud disco music blaring out onto the streets—exactly the kind of thing most Gaelophile Europeans have come to get away from. It attracts a fair number of young Dubliners too, revving up the life of this otherwise quiet, rural town. The place is at its most interesting when it's busy being Irish—during the annual **Connemara Pony Show**, for example, on the third Thursday in August (entrance around £2). This is for the sale and judging of Connemara ponies: tough, hardy animals, well suited to a harsh bog-and-mountain existence, yet renowned for their docile temperament. Clifden also has a community festival in the last week of September.

Practical Information

Despite its limitations, Clifden makes a good base if you're hosteling or camping. *Bus Éireann* **buses** leave from Market Street, with three buses to Galway daily in the summer, and one a day for the rest of the year. *M.M. Lee Travel*, Market Street (☎095-21188), is an agent for *Supabus*, who run coaches to England. The **tourist office** is on Market Street (June Mon–Sat 10am–6pm; July and Aug Mon–Sat 9am–6pm; ☎095-21163).

There's plenty of **B&B accommodation** in the center of Clifden, though they can be very busy in July and August. *Corrib House*, Main Street (☎095-21346), is the cheapest in town at £7.50, and very friendly. Others, all around £10, are: Mrs M. King, *Kingstown House*, Bridge Street (☎095-21470); Mrs K. Morris, *Ben View House*, Bridge Street (☎095-21256); and John and Barbara Lydon, *Benbawn House*, Westport Road (☎095-21462). For Clifden's **hostels**, see the box on p.313.

There are plenty of places for **bike rental**: the B&B next door to the tourist office rents them out during the summer at £3.50 a day, £20 a week, as do *John Mannion*, Railroad View (☎095-21160), *Flanagan's*, and *Joyce's Garage*, both on Market Street. Clifden's **laundromat** is in Main Square. **Pony-trekking** is organized at *Errislannan Manor* (☎095-21134; closed Sun; £10 per hour), about a mile beyond the Alcock and Brown Memorial, south of Clifden on the L102. Alternatively, try *Goulane Stables*, a mile and a half along the Galway road.

As for **food and drink**, there's no problem getting provisions in Clifden, and plenty of places do good bar food. *Mannion's* is plain, but one of the nicest bars for the drink, music, and food; the *Marconi Bar*, Main Street, serves light meals from £3–4; *An Spailpin Fanac* has bar meals in the same price range. *My Teashop* on Main Street is good for salads and snacks, while the *Corrib House Restaurant* opposite offers a seafood menu from £8 and does good cheap pizzas in its adjoining café. For evening meals at £10 and upwards, try *O'Grady's Seafood Restaurant*, Main Street, or *Doris's Restaurant*, Market Street. For good sandwiches, cappuccinos, and homemade ice cream, try *Kelly's Coffee House*, off Main Square; *The Coffee Shop*, Market Street, has expensive but delicious coffee and cakes.

Around Clifden

Clifden offers easy access to some beautiful scenery. To get to the **Twelve Bens** you will need to cycle, hitch, or skillfully manipulate the bus service. For more spontaneous walking, take the westward **coast road** out of Clifden (past the hostels) to a fine, sandy beach and a path that follows the shore of Clifden Bay. The shell of a nineteenth-century Gothic castellated mansion that you pass on the way was the home of John D'Arcy, who founded the town. Running north from beside the hostels, the **sky road** takes you to more desolate countryside and the long thin inlet of Streamstown Bay. Stick to the road and you'll eventually come down to the little village of CLADDAGHADUFF, where at low tide you can walk across to **Omey Island**. There are excellent beaches here, used for pony races during August. In the bay three miles north is the little village of CLEGGAN, and the ferry for the island of **Inishbofin** (see below).

To the immediate south of Clifden there's equally pleasant country. A fourteen-foot airplane wing carved in limestone sticks out of the bog four miles from Clifden on the **Ballyconneely road**, as a melodramatic memorial to the landing of Alcock and Brown at the end of their pioneering non-stop transatlantic flight in June 1919. Beyond this is the coral strand of Mannin Bay, excellent for swimming, as is that at Doonlonghan.

Inishbofin

The island of **Inishbofin** is a mellow, balmy place, quite different from the mainland. It's more fertile, its sandy beaches are sheltered, and there's a general softness to its contours. The only jagged features are the cliffs to the west (the "stags"), a fine vantage point for viewing seals basking on the shore. Even the high heathery moorland soon gently descends to the placid Lough Boffin, rimmed with rustling water iris and bullrushes. The lough is the scene of the island's most durable myth, a story that explains how it got its name. Several versions of the tale exist, but the basic elements are constant. For eons the island lay shrouded in mist under the spell of an enchantment, but one day two lost fishermen came upon it and lit a fire on the shore, thus breaking the spell. As the mist cleared they saw an old woman driving a white cow along the strand. She hit it with a stick, and was instantly turned to rock. Taking her for a witch, the men hit her and they too immediately turned to rock (*Inis Bo Finn* means "Island of the White Cow"). The only white cow you'll see on the island today (and on postcards) was born on the morning of a local girl's wedding, and given to her as a marriage gift by her father, so perpetuating the romantic association.

The known history of the island starts in the seventh century, when Saint Colman arrived here from Iona after a quarrel with Rome over the method of calculating the date of Easter. No remains exist of the monastery he founded, but ruins of a thirteenth-century church stand on the original site in a sheltered vale beside the lake in the east. Later the island was taken over by the O'Flaherties, and then Grace O'Malley is supposed to have fortified the place for her fleet. Coming into the island's long protected harbor you'll see the remains of a sixteenth-century castle, low on the hummocky terrain. It was taken and strengthened yet further by Cromwell, who used Inishbofin—and other west coast islands—as a kind of concentration camp for clerics. The most chilling reminder of his barbarity is the rock visible in the harbor at low tide. Known as the **"bishop's rock"**, it was here that Cromwell chained one unfortunate ecclesiastic, then let his troops watch the tide come slowly in and drown him.

Getting There, Eating, and Sleeping

You can visit Inishbofin on a day trip from Clifden, even without a car. Take the 8am bus to **CLEGGAN** (summer Tues and Fri; rest of the year Tues only), which returns at around 7:30pm—but check with the driver. **Ferry** tickets are available from *King's Grocery*, Cleggan, or on board the *Dun Aengus* (sailings late May to late Sept at 11:30am, returning 5pm; late June to late Aug extra sailing at 1:30pm; £6 return; further information ☎095-45806/ 44642). A less reliable service is run through *Malachy*, The Pier Bar, Cleggan (☎095-44663; departing 11am, returning 6:30pm), a company that also arranges deep-sea fishing trips.

There are two hotels on the island, both of which have **restaurants** open to non-residents. A midday meal in *Day's Hotel* will cost you around £5, evenings a lot more. If you are on a slim budget then take advantage of their excellent bar food, available all day. *Miko's* **pub** is very friendly and has **music**

sessions any time of the week during the summer season, and at weekends in winter. If you want to reserve **B&B** (around £14) in advance, write to Lena Schofield, Horse Shoe Bay, Inishbofin, County Galway; to rent a cottage contact Frances Concannon, Post Office, Inishbofin. There is an island shop, with the usual limitations on supplies—in particular, no *Camping Gaz*. There is no bank, but *Miko's* pub will change traveler's checks.

You can **camp** on any of the open common land. A particularly good spot is at the east end of the island at Rusheen beach, from where you're treated to the glorious sight of the Connemara mountains lurching into the sea. The only places that are dangerous for swimming are at Tra Geall, just beneath Doonmore, opposite the island of Inishark in the west.

The Connemara National Park

The **Connemara National Park** typifies the scenic splendor of west Galway. Its chief functions are to promote the area's natural beauty and conserve this area of bog, heath, and granite mountains. The park includes part of the famous **Twelve Bens** range—Benbaun, Bencullagh, Benbrack, and Muckanaght—all of which are for experienced walkers only. Less threatening are the spectacular Polldark River gorge and Glanmore valley, and the multi-faceted granite Diamond Hill.

The park's **visitors' center** (April–Sept daily 10am–6:30pm; ☎095-41054), near Letterfrack, is a good source of information on the fauna, flora and geology of the area. It's also the focus for the bogland conservation work that's going on hereabouts, and the herbarium here is worth looking at if you're interested in botany. The staff can suggest safe hiking routes of varying length and difficulty, and you can leave details of your own route and intended time of return—an invaluable service in this potentially hazardous landscape. The center has free kitchen facilities available for walkers and an indoor "picnic" area. In July and August a botanist leads a guided walk of about two-and-a-half hours, currently leaving at 10:30am on Monday, Wednesday and Friday, though it's wise to phone and check this schedule. As well as offering facilities to outsiders, the center is doing much to raise local awareness of the value of the area as a tourist amenity—particularly important in view of the current threat of gold-mining in the area.

LETTERFRACK itself is an orderly nineteenth-century Quaker village in a rugged setting. The village is tiny, but there's good food, and occasionally music, at *Veldon's* and *The Bard's Den*. There's also a post office, phone, shop, and money exchange. Two miles east of here, the towers of **Kylemore Abbey** sit in a rhododendron-filled hollow against lush deciduous slopes. Its white castellated outline, perfectly reflected in the reed-punctured lake, has made it the subject of many a postcard, but Kylemore is in fact a phony Tudor building created by a nineteenth-century Liverpool shipping magnate. A girls' boarding school now occupies the house; visitors are welcome to its restaurant and pottery showrooms, but otherwise the interior is private. You can, however, walk through the woods to see the medieval-style Victorian church, with its interior of Connemara marble.

Alternatively, a detour around the Renvyle Peninsula off the N59, north-west of Letterfrack, takes you through **TULLYCROSS**. A Rent-an-Irish-Cottage scheme operates in the village, the cottages fully incorporated into the main street with the intent of helping visitors mix in with the local social life. The effect is pretty suburban—rather like a set for a Gaelic series of *Neighbors*. Nearby **Renvyle House** is of immense interest in Irish literary and political history. At one time it was visited by the great Edwardian comic twosome Somerville and Ross, authors of *Stories of an Irish R.M.*, but the house's most famous owner was Oliver St John Gogarty, the distinguished surgeon, writer and wit. An associate of the Gaelic League, he attended the literary evenings of Yeats, Moore, and AE, and is immortalized as "stately plump Buck Mulligan" in Joyce's *Ulysses*. Renvyle is now a hotel (☎095-43511/43444), also offering facilities such as horse-riding, windsurfing, and a swimming pool to non-residents. About a mile west of the hotel is a ruined O'Flaherty **castle**, superbly overlooking the sea. The coast road to the east offers magnificent scenery, a great route for the **hostel** at Killary Harbour if you are cycling, and some fine sandy beaches.

Inland, the N59 route to Killary Harbour is faster and similarly beautiful. The lightly wooded shore around Ballinakill Harbour provides a brief luxuriant interlude before the landscape of wild bog and granite reasserts itself with ever increasing austerity. The **An Óige hostel** (☎095-43417), where Wittgenstein finished writing his *Philosophical Investigations* in 1948, has a deeply ponderous setting at the mouth of Ireland's only fjord, a cold dark tongue of water which cuts eight miles into the barren mountains. The hostel is five miles of extremely difficult hitching off the N59, so be prepared to walk. There's a shop at the hostel open evenings—otherwise you have to go to LETTERGESH shop and post office. From the hostel walk south, past the adventure center (see below); take the right turn before the crest of the hill, and keep on for about one and a quarter miles; the shop is the first big house on the left, with a phonebooth outside. A *Bank of Ireland* van operates from here at 1pm on Thursdays. There are good sandy beaches in the vicinity.

The *Little Killary Adventure Centre*, Salruck, Renvyle (☎095-43411), runs courses in mountain walking, climbing, sailing, canoeing, windsurfing, archery, and orientation. Courses start from £50 for a weekend, £170 a week, and are generally reserved well in advance, though it is often possible to join a course for part of a week or weekend.

MAYO

Seen by many as simply a passage between scenic Galway and literary Yeats country, Mayo is little visited—though it's difficult to see why. Like Galway to the south and Sligo to the north, it has a landscape of high sea cliffs, lonely mountains, and bright fuschia hedges; in the wild, remote boggy area to the northwest are the vestiges of a *Gaeltacht*; and on Lough Conn there's some of the best fishing in Ireland. Yet, with the exception of the Georgian town of **Westport** and **Achill Island**, the biggest of the Irish offshore islands and a traditional Irish holiday resort, Mayo is off the west-of-Ireland tourist trail.

This is all the more incomprehensible since the railroad will take you right out to Westport, on the coast, and the opening of the new international airport at **Knock** has made the northwest more accessible than ever before. Mayo is eventually bound to become busier, but for the moment it remains wonderfully empty.

The Barony of Murrisk—and Clare Island

Unless you're flying into Knock (see p.329), you'll probably enter Mayo by road from Galway, via the spectacular scenery of **Killary Harbour**, part of the lobe of land between the Galway border and Westport that's known as the **Barony of Murrisk**. This is country as rugged and remote as anything you'll find in the west, and two ranges of hills, the Mweelrea Mountains and the Sheefry Hills, provide terrain for energetic walking, mountaineering, riding, fishing, and canoeing.

Delphi and Louisburgh

The road due north from Killary threads along a narrow valley which opens up, briefly, for a lough-fishery with the unlikely name of **DELPHI** (in the local pronunciation, "Delph-eye"). The story behind the name involves the first marquess of Sligo, whose seat, misleadingly, was at Westport. The flamboyant marquess, a friend of Lord Byron, was caught in the sway of romantic Hellenism, and in 1811 set sail for Greece to search for antiquities. He swam with Byron off Piraeus, and rode with him overland to Corinth; but when he got to Delphi, he suffered a bout of homesickness, finding that it reminded him of nothing so much as his fishery at home in County Mayo. After numerous adventures, and some pillaging of ancient sites, the marquess returned home to reminisce. Nowadays, there's an **adventure center** (☎095-42208) at Delphi, offering supervised instruction in windsurfing, mountaineering, canoeing and so on. **Pony trekking** is based at the *Drumindoo Stud* (☎098-66195).

North of Delphi, the road runs alongside sombre Doo Lough, also known as the Black Lake, and over desolate moorland before reaching **LOUISBURGH**. Pronounced "Lewis-burg," this is one of the few instances where a town this side of the Atlantic has been named after one on the other: it was renamed after Henry Browne, uncle of the first marquess of Sligo, had taken part in the capture of Louisburgh, Nova Scotia, in 1758. Louisburgh is essentially little more than a crossroads, but its planned buildings give it an incongruous air of importance, and it's a pleasant enough place to stay. The **Granuaile Interpretive Centre** is currently being set up here, providing a lot of useful information both about the historical resonances of the scenery and on local flora and fauna; Granuaile is the Irish name for Grace O'Malley, the fierce pirate-queen of Clare Island (see below).

Louisburgh makes a good base for exploring the sandy **beaches** that run along the north coast as far as Murrisk Abbey, as it has some good kitchenette-studio accommodation (details from ☎098-66260) and a reasonably priced hotel, *Durcan's*, in Chapel Street (☎098-66140; around £12). Just outside Louisburgh, at Old Head (on the Westport Road), there's a **campground** with showers and laundromat (☎098-66021). Another good beach is the Silver Strand, claimed grandiosely in the local tourist leaflets to be second only to Florida's Key West. You can reach it by turning southwest at the crossroads just outside Louisburgh on the Killary road; it has a couple of **B&Bs**.

Clare Island

Follow the road from Louisburgh west along the strand to the land's tip, and you reach **Roonagh Quay**, where a boat leaves twice a day for **Clare Island**. The crossing takes 25 minutes, with boats leaving morning and evening; check times with the tourist office in Westport (☎098-25711) or with the *Bay View Hotel* on the island (☎098-26307). Although it's tiny—only fifteen or so square miles—Clare Island rises to a height of 1522 feet in a massive shoulder of land that dominates everything around. There's not much here besides the hills, some ruins, and some unfrequented sandy beaches, but there's plenty of walking, and you can go pony-trekking, or water-ski, windsurf, or fish.

Clare Island is famed as the stronghold of **Grace O'Malley**, or *Granuaile ni Mhaille* (c:1530–1600), the fearless and none-too-scrupulous pirate. The daughter of Owen O'Malley, chief of the western islands, she made herself queen of the Clew Bay area when he died, and earned her place in Irish legend by being one of the few Irish chiefs to stand up to Elizabeth I, insisting on being treated as her regal equal when they met in London in 1575. Constantly mentioned in sixteenth-century dispatches, her exploits included dissolving her marriage to her second husband, Sir Richard Burke of Mayo, by slamming the castle door in his face and stealing all his castles. Her own castle is at the eastern end of the island and she—or a close relative—is buried in a tomb on the north side of the ruined thirteenth-century Cistercian abbey halfway along the south coast of the island.

You can stay overnight on Clare Island, at the *Bay View Hotel*, which isn't too expensive (around £15 a night) and also organizes local watersports.

Croagh Patrick

The land between Louisburgh and Westport is dominated by the strange, perfectly conical silhouette of **Croagh Patrick**, which at 2513 feet is by far the highest mountain in the immediate area. The sandy beaches of the shore peter out at Bertra Strand, just short of MURRISK and the ruins of **Murrisk Abbey**, a house of Austin friars set up on the shore of Clew Bay by the O'Malley family in 1457.

Looking out over the hummocky islets of the bay, the abbey is the best starting point if you want to climb the mountain. On the landward side, a little saint's head carved in the wall peers glumly up the slope—it's a tough climb. Still, there's a surprise when you get to the top; the summit isn't conical, as it looks from the bottom, but forms a flat plateau, with a little chapel and a breathtaking view: on a good day you can see right from the Twelve Bens in the south to the mountains of Achill Island in the north, the Nephin Beg east of the island, and on to the Slieve League in Donegal.

In 441 **Saint Patrick** spent the forty days of Lent on the mountain in prayer and fasting, and it's from here that he is supposed to have sent the reptiles of Ireland crawling to their doom. Just to the south of the summit is the **precipice of Lugnanarrib**, where Saint Patrick stood, ringing his bell, then repeatedly hurling it over the edge, each time taking with it a stream of toads, snakes, and other creepy-crawlies. Luckily he didn't have to go down to the bottom to get his bell back—helpful spirits did the job for him. There's a pilgrimage to the top of Croagh Patrick, which some people do in bare feet, every year on the last Sunday in July.

Westport

Set in a picturesque eighteenth-century landscape on the shores of Clew Bay, **WESTPORT** is a comfortable, relaxed town, still recognizably Georgian, with a leafy mall, octagonal square, a canalized river, and one of Ireland's great stately homes, Westport House.

The town was planned by the architect James Wyatt, and its formal layout comes as quite a surprise in the midst of the west. In its heyday Westport was very prosperous, fattened by the trade in linen, and cotton cloth, and yarn. In 1817 the monthly sales of linen were worth £3000, and of yarn £1000, figures that were quite staggering at the time. However, like many places throughout Ireland, Westport was hit hard by the Act of Union of 1801. Though local landowners like the first marquess of Sligo (the one who swam with Byron) supported the Act in the belief that it would be of economic benefit, the reverse was in fact true: Irish hand looms were no competition for the new spinning jennies in Britain's industrial towns, the national linen and cotton industries declined, and Westport's economy was ruined. Mass unemployment forced a choice between reverting to subsistence farming, or starting a new life in America.

Its quiet Georgian beauties apart, the reason Westport is on the tourist trail nowadays is **Westport House** (open every afternoon April–Oct), a mile or so out of town towards Clew Bay. Beautifully designed in 1730 by the ubiquitous Richard Castle, with later additions by Thomas Ivory and James Wyatt, this was one of the first Irish houses opened to the public—and unfortunately it's adept at any and every way of making money. There's a zoo park in the grounds, horse-drawn trailers for rent, while the dungeons (which belong to an earlier house) have everything from a trace-your-ancestor service to a machine that claims to tell you whether or not you're sexy. On the plus side, though, the dungeons also contain a fairly useful secondhand bookshop, and the house and location are wonderful if you can ignore the commerce. Inside the house there's a *Holy Family* by Rubens, a violin which used to belong to J. M. Synge, and, on the first floor, a room with lovely Chinese wallpaper dating from 1780. A lot of the mahogany in the house was brought back from Jamaica by the first marquess, who was instrumental in freeing slaves during his time as governor there.

On the walls of the staircase, a series of paintings of local views by James Arthur O'Connor, commissioned by the second marquess in 1818 and 1819, show an idyllic nineteenth-century landscape: bustling activity as sailing boats are unloaded at Westport Quay, an overweeningly romantic version of the dramatic scenery at Delphi. This was wishful thinking—Westport in the 1810s was already overshadowed by the changes in the relationship with England, and by 1825 was finished as an industrial center.

Practicalities

For **accommodation** you've got a choice between two independent **hostels**. If you've had enough of Georgian elegance, there's the rough, stone-built *Granary*, past *Ryan's Hotel* on Quay Road, just before the road forks (April–Oct; ☎098-25903). Or, a mile and a half out of town on the Louisburgh road, there's a sort of svelte Georgian bungalow overlooking Clew Bay, *Summerville* (mid-March–mid-Oct; ☎098-25948). There are plenty of **B&Bs** around too—check at the **tourist office** (in the Mall; ☎098-25711) for availability. Most of the **pubs** in Westport have music of one sort or another; there's a good health-food **restaurant** on Bridge Street (up from the Octagon), which is also an excellent information center, and another good place to eat, *Quay Cottage* (☎098-26412), which serves enormous salmon salads and plenty of vegetarian food, at the entrance to Westport House

Biycling from Westport is rewarding, if strenuous—there are hills in almost all directions except towards Newport. Bike rental is from *J. P. Breheny & Sons*, Castlebar Street (☎098-25020). **Horseback-riding**, which will let you get off the road, is available half a mile out of town on the Castlebar road at the *Drummindoo Equitation Center* (☎098-25616).

North to Newport

The road north out of Westport, bordered by bright fuschia hedges, follows the shore of Clew Bay to **NEWPORT**. A neat, trim little town unashamedly devoted to tourism, Newport's main boast is that one of Grace Kelly's ancestors once lived here. It's also a center for **deep-sea fishing**; if you go into the swanky *Newport House Hotel* (around £36 a night) in the evenings you'll see massive sea trout—caught by guests earlier in the day—laid out for less energetic people to admire.

You may well be tempted to hurry on to Achill or the wild Erris peninsula, but Newport is a serviceable base for both the sea and the Nephin Beg mountains. If you do stay, the *Skerdagh Outdoor Center*, three miles out of Newport on the L137, functions as a **hostel** and also arranges bicycle rental, rock climbing, orientation, hill-walking and canoeing (June–Aug, but group reservations taken at other times; ☎098-41500) There's kitchenette-studio **accommodation** at Loch Morchan at Kilbride, just outside Newport (☎098-41221), or if you want to drink in the comfortably urban atmosphere of Newport itself, try the *Black Oak Inn* on Medlicott Street (☎098-41249; £8.50). For **horseback-riding and pony-trekking** the contact is ☎098-36126; permits for fishing are issued at the *Newport House Hotel*. **Tourist information** is available from the stand at *Darac Crafts* in the Main Street (☎098-41116).

Achill Island

More than with most places in the west, you need good weather for Achill. Although it's the part of County Mayo most developed for tourism, this means no more than a few hotels, bed and breakfasts, and hostels, and if it rains there's simply nothing to do but pack up and head for Westport or Sligo. Given good weather, though, Achill can be magical. Its sandy beaches never seem overcrowded, although they attract plenty of (mostly Irish) tourists in high summer. Inland, the bogland and mountains are dotted with ancient relics—standing stones, stone circles, and dolmens. The largest of the Irish offshore islands, Achill was Irish-speaking until very recently. Tourism here seems to have had an almost entirely beneficial effect; before its arrival, islanders subsisted to a very great extent on money sent home by emigrant relatives.

Walking is the best way to get to know Achill, although the island can be fairly strenuous going. **Slievemore**, the island's highest mountain at 2205 feet, is a massive pile of quartzite and mica. At its foot, on the seaward side, are the **Seal Caves**, burrowing way back under the mountain; you can visit them by boat from DUGORT. On Slievemore's southern slopes stands a dolmen with a stone circle at each end, and a booley village of huts formerly used during summer pasturing—a reminder of a much newer, but equally outdated, transhumant way of life. Close to Dugort, some ruined buildings and scattered gravestones are all that's left of a village known simply as **The Settlement**. It was founded in 1834 by a Protestant vicar, the Reverend E. Nangle, who bought up sixty percent of the island and built schools and a printing press in an ultimately unsuccessful effort to evangelize the islanders.

Continuing counterclockwise you come to **Croghaun**, a whisker lower than Slievemore at 2195 feet, whose seaward side boasts what are claimed to be Europe's highest cliffs. On its eastern side is **Corrymore Lodge**, where the notorious land agent Captain Boycott once lived (see p.330). The best approach to the summit is via Lough Acorrymore, above Corrymore Lodge; from the top you're treated to a magnificent view of the Belmullet peninsula and the scattered islands, while mountains rise spectacularly in the southeast.

On the south side of the island is KEEL, with its two-mile sandy beach, at the east end of which are the fantastic **Cathedral Rocks**, eroded into a series of caves and pillars by the wind and water. They are backed by the **Minaun**, at 1532 feet another mountain worth climbing for the view. Close to the southern tip of the island is **Kildownet Castle**, a stronghold used by the pirate queen Grace O'Malley.

There are two independent **hostels** on Achill, both open all day—useful if you hit bad weather. The *Wayfarer Hostel* is right on the strand at Keel (March–Oct; ☎098-43266); the *Valley House*, closer to Achill Sound, has a bar (April–Nov; ☎098-47204). For more comfort, *McDowell's Hotel* at Dugort does good **B&B** (April–Sept; ☎098-472051; £12) and excellent food, including vegetarian. There are regular B&Bs scattered about the island; *McDowell's* is a center for locals, with frequent traditional music sessions. The *Boley House* at Keel (☎098-43147) is a **restaurant** in a small, stone-built cottage with turf fires—again vegetarian food is available but it's popular, so reserve in advance. There's a **tourist office** at Achill Sound, but it's often closed.

The Belmullet Peninsula and Bangor Erris

The **Belmullet peninsula**, a flat slab of land that seems tacked onto the mainland almost as an afterthought, is the one part of Mayo where some Gaelic is still spoken. It's sparsely populated, but its houses tend to be scattered evenly rather than grouped into villages, in the way that's characteristic of the west of Ireland, and you're hardly ever out of sight of habitation. The seaward side of the peninsula is raked by Atlantic winds to such an extent that almost no vegetation can survive. Landward, overlooking Blacksod Bay, is much more sheltered and has some beaches, notably at **Elly Bay**. To the east and north the land rises, though the cliffs are not hugely spectacular. There's an impressive castle at **Doonamo Point**, its wall cutting off the neck of the peninsula and enclosing three *clochans* and a circular fort.

BELMULLET itself is a functional little village, its streets perpetually mired with mud from the bogs. The surrounding district of Bangor Erris as a whole is bleak; there are people who fall in love with its uncompromising lack of comforts, but it can also make you understand why a lot of Irish people have mixed feelings about conservationist enthusiasm for the black bog—you can't grow anything on it, it's dirty, and it's horrible to live in.

For **accommodation** on the peninsula, there's *Kilcommon Lodge* at PULLATHOMAS (open all year; ☎097-84629), an independent hostel that also does bed and breakfast and meals; or if you need more comfort try the *Western Sands Hotel* in Belmullet itself (☎097-81906; £10).

Off the peninsula, the coastline is wonderfully dramatic, with some terrific walking country. **Benwee Head** is a massive cliff of almost 820 feet, with great views of the Donegal cliffs to the northeast and the **Stags of Broadhaven**, a series of seven 300-foot rocks which stand a mile and a half off the coast. Farther east, near PORTURLIN, the waves have carved the rocks into weird, contorted shapes, including the **Arches**, a thirty-foot opening in the cliff which the brave—or foolhardy—attempt to row through in good weather at low tide.

Inland, the moors of the Barony of Erris, in contrast to the Mullet peninsula, really are deserted. At BELDERRIG an excavation of a Stone-Age settlement is in progress, but there's little to see as yet. East again, a detached rock with a fort on it at **Downpatrick Head** has some blowholes which send up tall plumes of water in rough weather.

Killala and Around

KILLALA is a must, both for the magnificent local scenery and for its historical connections. Scene of one of the most significant events in Irish history—the unsuccessful French invasion organized by Wolfe Tone in 1798—it's a pleasantly run down seaside town, so small it's difficult to believe it's a bishopric, with lovely wild sea coasts and some good roads for bicycling. And there's the added attraction of a new **An Óige hostel** in an old, stone house near the center of town (☎096-32172; grade A). **B&Bs** are scarce—this is not tourist country—but you could try Mrs Carey's *Rathona House* (☎096-32035; £9), four miles out of town, or Mrs Caplice's *Avondale*, Pier Road (☎096-32229; £9.50).

The French Invasion

On August 22, 1798, three warships flying British colors anchored at Kilcummin, near Killala. The Protestant Bishop Stock, relieved that they were apparently English and not the rumored French invasion fleet, sent his two sons and the port surveyor to pay their respects. They were immediately taken prisoner; the invasion had begun. After a brief resistance, Killala succumbed to the French, and at sunset that evening a French soldier climbed to the top of the Bishop's Palace and replaced the British flag with a green flag with a harp in the center, bearing the words *Erin go Bragh* (Ireland for Ever).

Wolfe Tone, the inspirational leader of the United Irishmen, had been working since his exile from Ireland in 1794 to secure foreign aid for his planned insurrection against the British. However, by the time the first French expedition (of 1100 men under General Humbert) reached Killala, rebellion had already been all but crushed. Not only was there a military mismatch between the French professional soldiers and the few poorly armed Irish novices who joined them, but there were ideological clashes, too. The French had expected that liberation from British rule would appeal to Catholics and Protestants alike, and were farther confused to find the Irish volunteers greeting them in the name of the Blessed Virgin and apparently having no idea of the significance of the French Revolution.

The rest of the story is sadly predictable. With some heroic fighting, the Franco-Irish army took Killala, Ballina, and Castlebar, but on September 8, near the village of Ballinamuck in County Longford, seriously depleted in both numbers and weapons, it was defeated by the united armies of Lord Cornwallis and General Lake. The French were taken prisoners of war and returned to France; the Irish rebels were hanged.

A month later, sailing with another French force from Brest, Wolfe Tone was himself captured—along with the French fleet—off the coast of Donegal. He was subsequently court-martialled and condemned to death. Despite his insistence that he should be treated with military respect and therefore shot, he was sentenced to hang. Before the sentence could be carried out, he cut his throat with a penknife in his cell. He came to personify the tradition of revolutionary violence in the cause of an independent Ireland.

The events of 1798 led directly to the Act of Union with Britain three years later, while the land agitation that spread throughout the country laid the foundations for land reform, Catholic emancipation, and, eventually, the long process that led to Irish independence.

(Most local newsvendors sell Bishop Stock's *Narrative* of the events of 1798—a surprisingly sympathetic account of the uprising.)

Inland to Lough Conn

The road from Killala to Ballina quickly leaves the drama of the northern coast and runs through flat farm country. It's remarkable only for two abbeys on the Moy estuary, **Moyne** and **Rosserk**, both of them founded in the fifteenth century. Rosserk, with a tower at the water's edge, is the bigger and more poetic of the two, but both have good cloisters.

There's nothing very much to recommend the busy town of **BALLINA,** except as a place to stock up on provisions and information. *Keehane's* in Arran Street is a reasonable bookshop, and the West-of-Ireland **cycling club** is based at *American House* in Francis Street (☎096-21350)—it also has cheapish accommodation (£12 a night), and you may find they're more interested in getting you to stay than in giving information.

Lough Conn is a magnet for anyone who likes fishing, though at the moment it's impossible to say what the situation will be with regard to fishing licenses. During the rod licenses campaign of 1988, however, when most of the lakes in the west were closed, Lough Conn remained open, so it's worth checking out even if the trouble continues. East of Lough Conn the country is flat and generally unexciting, but westward the Nephin Beg range of mountains has impressive walking country.

On the shores of Lough Conn, south of CROSSMOLINA, **Enniscoe House** is a Georgian mansion now run as farmhouse accommodation. As such it isn't cheap (£37 a night), but the owner, Susan Kellett, is putting together a heritage center and is happy to show visitors around the house, as long as they phone first (☎096-31112). Enniscoe is a good example of easygoing Georgian attitudes to architecture: originally built in the mid-eighteenth century as a three-story house, it was extended in the 1790s (and damaged in 1798 when the French army marched down the back avenue) to include a grand facade overlooking Lough Conn. The result inside is two completely different structures whose floor levels and room sizes don't correspond at all.

Accommodation is in the plentiful bed and breakfasts around the lake, or at one of two independent **hostels**—*Cooltra Lodge* in PONTOON, between Lough Conn and Lough Cullen (late June–Sept), or *Gannons Hostel* in the pretty town of FOXFORD, three miles away. There's a comfortably run-down hotel, the *Dolphin* (☎096-31270; £9), in relaxed, raffish CROSSMOLINA.

Castlebar and Around

CASTLEBAR, although it's the county town of Mayo, is a bit of a disappointment, especially compared with the airily planned spaces of Westport. The tree-bordered town green is quite pretty, but otherwise it's a dullish place. Historically, it's notable for a Franco-Irish victory in 1798, known as the Castlebar Races, at which General Humbert's army routed a stronger force commanded by General Lake.

Seven miles south of Castlebar on the Ballinrobe road is **Ballintubber Abbey.** Founded in 1216 for Austin friars by Cathal O'Connor, King of Connaught, it's an important site and ought to be atmospheric. Sadly that's not the case. It's been grossly over-restored, and around the church the Stations of the Cross form a kind of ghastly theme park in stone, including representations of an empty tomb, an inexplicable dolmen, and some human figures whose overall impression is obscurely pornographic.

Becutesyn Castlebar and Foxford, at **STRADE,** is the **Michael Davitt Museum,** which preserves a number of mementoes, and documents the activities of the Land League in which Davitt played a major part.

Knock

Ever since an apparition of the Virgin Mary, accompanied by Saint Joseph and Saint John, was seen on the gable of the parish church of **KNOCK** in 1879, it has been a place of pilgrimage. As a passer-by in Ireland, it's surprisingly easy to forget the all-pervasive influence of the Catholic church, but at Knock you're brought face to face with it. Whatever you may believe about the possible veracity of the apparitions, Knock rates for Catholics, along with Lourdes in France and Fatima in Portugal, as one of the leading modern miraculous confirmations of their faith. A massive and ugly church with a capacity of 20,000 was opened in 1976, the pope visited the shrine in 1979, and in 1986 a new international airport was opened at nearby **CHARLESTOWN**.

When Monsignor Horan, the local cardinal, first hatched the plan for the new **airport** it seemed a crazy and profligate idea, and there were years of bitter controversy over this apparent waste of public funds. In fact it has proved remarkably successful, and as well as bringing in pilgrims to see the shrine, the airport has had the effect of opening up the northwest of Ireland for travelers—to the extent that Mayo is in reach of London for weekend breaks, and house prices in the county are soaring as wealthy inhabitants of southeast England buy their second homes. The Lourdes-to-Knock run is also used by fishermen from the southwest of France to reach the lake fisheries of the west of Ireland.

The airport (situated three miles from Charlestown at the junction of the N17 and N5) is open from 9am to 6pm daily, serving many UK airports including Luton, Stansted, and Coventry. An *Aer Lingus* shuttle service to Dublin connects with major international flights. For further information on accommodation in the Knock area as well as flight schedules, telephone the Knock Regional Development Company (☎094-67222).

As a town, Knock is nothing much to look at. The scene of the apparitions has been glassed in to form a chapel, and pilgrims can be seen there praying at all hours. Other than that, and the religious kitsch shops, it's not a place to hang around, unless you've just flown in and need a place to stay. If this is the case, there's no problem finding something. There's a pretty luxurious hotel, the *Belmont* (☎094-88122; £18), and numerous **B&Bs**: try Mrs Carney's *Burren* (Kiltimagh Road; ☎094-88362; £10), or *Mervue*, overlooking the shrine (☎094-88127; also £10).

Cong and Around

CONG lies between Lough Mask and Lough Corrib at the point where the dramatically mountainous country to the west gives way to the flat and fertile farmland that makes up the east of County Mayo. A picture-book pretty village that caters to plenty of tourists, it's also the site of the ruined **Cong Abbey**, which was founded in 1128 for the Augustinians by Turlough O'Connor, King of Ireland (though it's probably built on a seventh-century monastic site). The doorways represent the transition between the quite different styles of Romanesque and Gothic. The cloisters look just a little bit too good to be true; they were partially rebuilt in 1860. At its height, Cong Abbey had a population of some 3000, and the practicalities of feeding such multitudes can be glimpsed in the remains of the refectory and kitchen by the river, where a fishing house over the water contains a fish trap beneath the floor. The *Cross of Cong*, a twelfth-century ornamented Celtic cross originally made in County Roscommon for the abbey, gives an indication of the wealth and status of the foundation—it's now on show at the National Museum in Dublin.

From the abbey there's a pleasant wander through woods down to the river. Cong's big house is **Ashford Castle**, at the point where the river meets Lough Corrib, now converted into a luxury hotel. Although its history goes back to the thirteenth century, what you see is essentially a castellated Victorian reconstruction.

Just north of Cong on the Ballinrobe road is one of those mysterious monuments that abound in Ireland. On the right-hand side of the asphalt stands a massive stone-stepped pyramid, with an inscription, almost indecipherable, including the name George Browne and some worn Roman numerals, dating it somewhere in the eighteenth century. The Brownes are the family who occupy Westport House, but the reason for the pyramid remains obscure.

In the 1840s attempts were made, as a famine relief project, to dig a canal between Lough Corrib and Lough Mask. A river exists between the two lakes, but runs underground through porous limestone for most of its length, though you can get to it at various points, including the Pigeon Hole, a mile or so north of Cong. The behavior of the river might have been an indication of what would happen to the canal: the porosity of the rock meant that the water just drained away, and Cong is left with a dry canal, complete with locks.

Cong has an **An Óige hostel**, signposted from the center of the village (☎092-46089; Grade A), and numerous reasonable **B&Bs**. Try Mrs Connolly at *The White House* (☎092-46358; £9.50); Mrs Bourke at *Woodlands*, Caherduff, The Neale (☎092-46060; £10), half a mile out of town, or Mrs Coakley, also a short way out at *Hazel Grove*, Drumshiel (☎092-46060; £10.50). The *Rising of the Waters Inn* (☎092-46316/46008) has rooms for around £8.50. For kitchenette-studio accommodation around Cong, contact Western Regional Tourism on ☎091-63081.

Loughmask House (not open to the public), on the shores of Lough Mask a couple of miles due north of Cong, was the home of the notorious **Charles Boycott**, a retired captain of the British army and land agent to Lord Erne. His behavior toward the tenant farmers during the Land League unrest of the 1880s made him one of the victims of Parnell's "moral Coventry" policy, subsequently known as "boycotting." As Parnell himself put it in an outdoor meeting in Ennis in 1880:

> *You must show what you think of him on the roadside when you meet him, you must show him in the streets of the town, you must show him at the shop counter . . . even in the house of worship, by leaving him severely alone, by putting him into a sort of moral Coventry, by isolating him from the rest of his kind as if he were a leper of old, you must show him your detestation of the crime he has committed.*

EAST GALWAY

East Galway cannot rival the spectacular landscapes of west Galway or County Clare, nor their romantic isolation. Nonetheless, to hurry through east Galway without seeing what the place does have to offer would be a mistake. A lot of the land here is low-lying and easily cultivable, which made it attractive to earlier settlers. They've left not only a network of roads and villages, but also a wealth of historic remains, particularly medieval monastic sites. The east of the county has nothing like the strong ethnic culture of the west, but towards the south the musical traditions of County Clare wash over the county boundaries and form an important part of the region's culture. And while the landscape is never exciting, some of it is very pleasant, notably the lakesides of **Lough Derg** at **Portumna**, and the delightful southern shore of Galway Bay, which becomes particularly special where the heights of the Burren of County Clare become a part of the scene.

Transportation and Accommodation

In contrast to Connemara, transportation in east Galway is easy. The Galway to Dublin **trains** call at Athenry and Ballinasloe, and there are *Bus Éireann* services to surrounding towns (For bus and train information phone Athenry ☎091-44020 or Ballinasloe ☎0905-42105). *North Galway Club* runs a Dublin-to-Galway bus that picks up in Tuam, Athlone, Ballinasloe, Loughrea, Craughwell and Oranmore. **Hitching** is relatively easy too, since the area is well served by busy main roads. **Bike rental** is available from *P. Clarke & Sons*, Dunlo Street, Ballinasloe (☎0905-42417) and Tony Cunningham, Dominick Street, Portumna (☎0905-41070).

There are independent **hostels** at Aughrim, near Ballinasloe, and at Kinvarra, and an **An Óige hostel** at Doorus. There are plenty of **B&Bs** around Tuam, Athenry, and Ballinasloe. **Tourist offices** at Tuam (July and Aug; ☎093-24463) and Ballinasloe (July and Aug; ☎0905-42131) can give information on accommodation around the region.

East of Lough Corrib

The east shore of Lough Corrib provides a gentle route between County Mayo and Galway city, less dramatic than the Connemara roads. The lake shore and the many rivers are popular with fishermen, and visitors with no taste for field sports have a number of medieval ruins to admire.

Two miles north of Headford is **Ross Errilly** (or "Ross Abbey"), the biggest and best-preserved Franciscan abbey in Ireland. It was originally founded in the mid-fourteenth century, but the bulk of the buildings belong to the fifteenth—the Franciscan Order's greatest period of expansion. The church buildings themselves are impressive enough, with a battlemented slender tower (typical of Franciscan abbeys) and well-preserved windows, and there's a wonderful tiny cloister; but it's the adjacent domestic buildings and the picture they give of the everyday life of the Order that are perhaps the most interesting. Stand in the cloister with your back to the church and ahead to the right is the refectory, with the reader's window-side desk up in the far northeast corner. Straight ahead is a second cloister (this one without arcading), and behind that the bakehouse. To the northwest of this second courtyard lies the kitchen, where you can see a water-tank used for holding fish, and an oven which reaches into the little mill-room to the rear.

Five miles south of HEADFORD, a detour off the main road leads you right down to the Lough shore and the ruined Franciscan friary of **Annaghdown**— far less impressive than Ross Errilly—and a nearby Norman castle. It was at the friary, after all his voyaging and preaching, that Saint Brendan finally died, nursed by his sister, who was head of Annaghdown nunnery. The road loops back to rejoin the main Galway road.

Northeast County Galway is served chiefly by the small market town of **TUAM**. There's little here to detain you, but should you wish to sniff out the scant remnants of the town's former importance, have a look inside the Church of Ireland Cathedral on Galway Road. It's primarily a nineteenth-century building, but a magnificent Romanesque arch, showing strong signs of Scandinavian influence, and the accompanying east window, have survived from a twelfth-century chancel. The shaft of an ornamented high cross is set in the wall near the west door. It's a great shame that so little remains of medieval Tuam. A monastery was founded here in the sixth century by Saint Iarlath, a disciple of Saint Enda of Inishmore, and in the medieval period Tuam became not only an archdiocesal see, but also the power center of the O'Conors of Connaught. The high cross in the town square also dates from the twelfth century. It's highly decorated but actually a bit of a patchwork, as the head and the shaft don't really belong together. Should you need to stop over in Tuam, there's no shortage of **B&Bs**: try Mrs Clarke, *Chessington House*, Ballygaddy Road (☎093-24584; £9) or Mrs O'Connors, *Kilmore House*, Kilmore, Galway Road (☎093-28118; £10), half a mile out of town.

Still more medieval ruins are dotted roundabout: if you're heading through Dunmore in the northeast of the county, there's **Dunmore Abbey**, an Augustinian priory of 1425, and just to the west of the town a Norman castle built by the de Berminghams. Alternatively, seven miles south of Tuam off the N63 Galway–Roscommon road, **Knockmoy Abbey** is a Cistercian foundation of 1190—though the central tower is probably a fifteenth-century addition. The most remarkable feature of the abbey is on the north wall of the chancel, where you'll see one of Ireland's few medieval **frescoes**. Extremely faint (only the black outlines are original colors) it depicts the legend of the Three Dead Kings and the Three Live Kings. Under the dead kings an inscription reads "We have been as you are, you shall be as we are"; the live kings are out hawking. Underneath this is a picture of Christ holding his hand up in blessing, and a barely visible angel with scales.

Chances are you'll see **ATHENRY**, if at all, from a train. The place is more renowned for the song *The Fields of Athenry*—which you're unlikely to have got this far without hearing—than as a tourist center. Still, if you've time to kill between connections, it's worth darting out of the station to take a look at its remains of Anglo-Norman power—so much a feature of east Galway and so conspicuously absent in the west of the county. The town was founded by the de Berminghams, and large portions of its Norman town walls have survived, along with a tower-gate, five flanking towers, and a market cross. On the edge of town stands a bold thirteenth-century **castle**, again built by the de Berminghams, its stout, three-story keep still impressively intact (Mon–Fri 8am–5pm). If you're looking for **bed and breakfast** try Miss Gardener's, Old Church Street (☎091-44464; £9) or Mrs O'Connor's, Swan Gate (☎091-44681; £9).

Ballinasloe and Around

The county's eastern boundary is one of water: Lough Derg, the Shannon, and the River Suck. The tourist-geared villages are again catering mainly for the fishing fraternity, but there is enough of historic interest to warrant leisurely exploration. **BALLINASLOE** is the main town in east Galway. It's been important as a crossing point on the Suck since 1124 when Turlough O'Conor, King of Connaught, built a castle here, though the remains that can be seen today date from the fourteenth century. You're only really likely to be here if you've come for the famous **horse fair**, which starts on the first weekend in October and lasts for eight days. The largest of the ancient fairs left in the country, drawing horse dealers from all over Ireland and England, it gives a fascinating glimpse of a slowly dying way of life. The bartering is very much a game, though a serious one. Generally, both parties know the value of the beast in question, but enjoy the bartering ritual anyway, with its possibilities of outdoing an opponent. The logic seems to be that if a man isn't up to the bartering, he doesn't deserve the right price for the animal. This system of exchange is threatened by EC regulations which insist that animals be sold by weight, a sorry demise for an ancient tradition.

If you intend to visit the fair, you'll have to reserve accommodation well in advance. For **B&B** in the town itself try Mrs Molloy, *Ashling*, Old Mount Pleasant Avenue (☎0905-42457), or there's Mrs N. Mulqueen, *Adare*, Dublin Road (☎0905-43282), and Mrs Burton, *Woodlands*, Dublin Road (☎0905-43123), half a mile out—they all charge around £9.

Tiny **AUGHRIM**, to the northwest of Ballinasloe, makes a good base from which to explore some of the ecclesiastical remains of the area. *Hynes* hostel is attached to the local pub, which has music at weekends during the summer (☎0905-73734; open all year; £3.50; camping £2). The hostel has only twelve beds, so it's worth phoning ahead in July and August; during the horse fair it's booked up way in advance. In 1691 Aughrim was the scene of a key battle of the Williamite War, in which the Irish and French forces were defeated; a small **museum** in the local primary school has finds connected with the battle.

Four miles to the northwest are the very beautiful remains of **Kilconnell Friary**, a Franciscan foundation built near the site of the sixth-century church of Saint Conall, which gives the place its name. The friary held out successfully against Cromwellian attack in 1651. The ruins are extensive, with additions to the early-fourteenth-century building showing that there was increased monastic activity here in the later Middle Ages. There's a very pretty arcaded cloister, and in the north wall of the nave are two splendid canopied wall-tombs.

The countryside to the south of Ballinasloe makes a dull setting for two fine pieces of ecclesiastical architecture, well worth taking in if you're staying at Aughrim, or heading south towards Portumna and Lough Derg. The first is **Clontuskert Abbey**, five miles south of the town. From the road it looks impressive in this open countryside, like some iron-gray battleship adrift on the flat and muddy approaches to the Suck. The church is the only sizable remnant of the abbey complex, with a Perpendicular west door of 1471, carved with figures of the saints. Nine miles farther south is **Clonfert Cathedral**, on the site where a Benedictine monastery was founded around 560 by Saint Brendan. In subsequent centuries the monastery was pillaged, but towards the end of the twelfth century the church was rebuilt, and dedicated to Saint Brendan. There's a superb Romanesque doorway made up of six arches, each a perfect semicircle, and richly carved with heavily stylized plants and animals. The capitals are Romanesque cubes carved with crazy, bold animal heads. The bishop's palace beyond the cathedral—now in ruins as a result of an accidental fire—was the home of British fascist Sir Oswald Mosley after his release from prison in 1949.

Portumna

PORTUMNA, on the north shore of Lough Derg, is a traditional market town and Shannon crossing point, happy to be cashing in on the exclusive tourism that drifts its way on the Lough cruisers, yet still retaining a friendly and unpretentious character. Close to the shore is **Portumna Priory**, for the most part a fifteenth-century Dominican building, though its delicately arched cloisters are built around the remains of a much earlier Cistercian foundation. The national monument status of nearby **Portumna Castle** is something of a local joke. It's a fine early-seventeenth-century mansion with Jacobean gables, something of a rarity in Ireland, and in a state of extreme dilapidation. Clearly it will not be open to the public for some years, but nobody minds if you take a look via the fields to the rear. The castle's estate is a wildlife sanctuary with a large herd of fallow deer and Japanese sika deer.

Portumna really has more in common with the other little towns on the luscious scenic strip that lines Lough Derg, catering to the more conservative tourism of the Lough cruisers. There's a **tourist office** here during the summer months and several good **B&Bs** in the center. It's easy **camping** country too—just ask a farmer—and in the summer there are **public showers** down by the lough jetty. Swimming is safe here on the lake but not on the river. There are two very friendly places to **eat**, both in the main street: *Peter's Restaurant*, a fast-food place that will rustle up whatever you like, and *Clonwyn House*, which does traditional cooked meals any day any time.

Although small, Portumna has an astounding 21 **pubs**, and there's no shortage of ballad sessions, but no traditional music, unless you catch one of *Clonwyn House*'s Sunday-night *ceilidhs*, when the old folk come in to do their set dancing. Friday and Saturday nights the place has discos and pop music.

The *Bank of Ireland* is on Clonfert Avenue, open until 5pm on Wednesday, and the post office is in Abbey Street. There's also a **laundromat** here—*Frank's* in Brendan Street.

Loughrea and Southern Galway

LOUGHREA is similar to Portumna in that it's a lakeside market town, but it's smaller and doesn't have the beauty of Lough Derg for its setting. In the thirteenth century Richard de Burgo founded a **Carmelite Monastery** here, which still stands in an excellent state of preservation next to the abbey. The town has a late-nineteenth-century **Cathedral**, the interior of which demonstrates the development of the modern Dublin School of Stained Glass—an acquired taste. Much earlier religious art is on display next door in the **Loughrea Museum** (Mon–Fri 9:30am–4:30pm, Sun 3–5pm; at other times ask at the church for the key). This small museum includes episcopal vestments and carved crucifixes from the seventeenth century; beautifully simple silver and gold chalices from as early as 1500; penal crosses; and a few rare wood carvings from the twelfth and thirteenth centuries. The Kilcorban *Virgin and Child* is the earliest of only three such carvings that have been found in Ireland.

In a field two miles to the north of Loughrea, near BULLAUN, stands the **Turoe Stone**. It's a superb, rounded pillar-stone, decorated with the bold swirls of Celtic La Tène art, a style found more typically in Brittany. This one is the finest in Ireland, and dates from the third or second century BC. It's probably a phallic fertility stone, used in pagan rituals.

The countryside of the southwest of the county around the southern shores of Galway Bay is among Galway's prettiest areas, and was greatly loved by Yeats, Lady Gregory, and others associated with the Gaelic League. Two miles to the north of GORT lies **Coole Park**, the old demesne of the house of Lady Gregory, much visited by Yeats, and the subject of some of his most famous poetry. All that remains of the house itself are some crumbling walls and a stable yard, but the grounds and the lake are now a particularly beautiful forest park. Its **autograph tree**, bearing the graffiti of George Bernard Shaw, Sean O'Casey, Augustus John, and others, has been incarcerated in railings and barbed wire to stop the less famous getting in on the act. A mile and a half northeast of Coole is **Thoor Ballylee**, signposted off the N18. This is a sixteenth-century tower house which Yeats bought in 1917, renovated, and made his home for the next ten years. It's now open to the public (May–Oct daily 10am–6pm), and has rare and first editions of his works.

Four miles south from Gort, just off the Corofin road, are the remains of **Kilmacduagh**, a monastic settlement founded by Saint Colman Mac Duagh around 632. The sheer quantity of buildings—dating from the eleventh to the thirteenth centuries—is more impressive than any particular architectural detail: a cathedral, four churches, the "Glebe House", and a round tower 115 feet high, all on one site. And the setting, against the shimmering, distant Burren slopes, lends something magical to the ancient, gray stone.

The main road to Galway is a busy one and passes through the villages of Galway's "**oyster country**"—KILCOLGAN, CLARINBRIDGE and ORANMORE—bringing it plenty of visitors, particularly during the **Oyster Festival** over the second weekend in September. The most famous of the oyster pubs are *Paddy Burke's Oyster Tavern* at Clarinbridge and *Moran's of the Weir* at Kilcolgan. Two miles south of Kilcolgan off the KINVARRA road stands **Drumacoo Church**, a fine stone building of about 1200, with a Regency Gothic chapel of iron alongside, rusting and derelict.

The villages of DOORUS, AUGHINISH, and KINVARRA, on the south shore of Galway Bay, are all dealt with in the section on "The Burren," in *County Clare*, as you're more likely to visit them from Clare than from Galway .

ROSCOMMON

Roscommon has the unjust reputation of being the most boring county in Ireland. A long sliver of land running from south to north, it's the only county in Connaught without any seacoast, though it is bounded for almost its entire western border by the upper reaches of the Shannon. Although most of the county is either bog or good grassland pasture, on the Sligo and Leitrim border the Curlew mountains rise high and wild. Chances are you'll be approaching the county from the south, which is not its best aspect; the most worthwhile places are Boyle, in the far north, and Strokestown in the east, approached from Longford.

Roscommon and Castlerea

There's nothing much to **ROSCOMMON** town, pretty much in the middle of the county, but it's an oddly pleasant place to spend time in and soak up the atmosphere. Its solid tone is set by heavy stone buildings such as the *Bank of Ireland*, once the courthouse, and the **county jail**, which now houses a collection of shops and has a toothed top that gives the town a characteristic silhouette identifiable for miles around. The jail was the scene of all public hangings in the county, and used to have a female hangman called Lady Betty, whose own sentence for murder had been suspended on condition that she did her gruesome job for free.

Roscommon boasts two impressive ruins. On the Boyle road out of town, the enormous and well-preserved **Roscommon Castle** was built by the Normans in 1269, burned down by the Irish four years later, and rebuilt in 1280. Remodeling clearly continued for some time—there are some incongruously refined windows among the massive walls. The other ruin, in the lower part of the town, is the **priory**. Roscommon actually takes its name from a Celtic saint, Saint Coman, who was the first bishop here, and under whom the see became well known as a seat of learning, having close ties with the more famous abbey at Clonmacnoise in County Offaly. The priory ruin, however, is Dominican, dating from 1253. Amazingly enough, despite the religious persecution that followed the Reformation and the Plantations, the

Dominicans managed to hang on well into the nineteenth century, the last two incumbents, parish priests of Fuerty and Athleague, dying in 1830 and 1872 respectively.

Accommodation around Roscommon is not exactly plentiful. The *Royal Hotel*, right in the center, is one of those fine, upstanding inns that still exist in rural Irish towns: good fun, plenty of locals in the bar, comfortable, but not especially cheap at around £20 a night. Otherwise, you've a sprinkling of B&Bs to choose among. These include Mrs O'Grady's *The Villa* (Galway Road; ☎0903-26048; £9.50), Mrs Campbell's *Westway* (Galway Road; ☎0903-26927; £9), or, a mile out on the Sligo road, Mrs Dolan's *Munsboro House* (☎0903-26375; £10).

Castlerea

CASTLEREA in the west, Roscommon's third most important town after Roscommon and Boyle, is an unprepossessing place, and the only real reason for going there is to visit **Clonalis House**, just outside the town to the west. Clonalis is the ancestral home of the clan O'Conor, which claims to be Europe's oldest family, dating back to one Feredach the Just in AD 75. The house is a Victorian pile, stuffed with mementoes and archival material, including the harp of the seventeenth-century blind musician Turlough O'Carolan.

Strokestown

In the east of the county, on the N5 from Longford, **STROKESTOWN** is a gem of a planned town whose reason for existence is **Strokestown House**, once the heart of the second biggest estate in Roscommon after Rockingham. The enormously wide main street—reputedly the result of an ambition on the part of an early owner to have the widest street in Europe—ends abruptly in a castellated wall with three Gothic arches, behind which lies Strokestown House.

It's a graceful Georgian residence designed by Richard Castle on a plan—a central block with two side wings linked by curved arms—whose adaptability as a sort of glorified farmhouse ensures that it turns up again and again throughout Ireland. Sold by the family of the original owners to the local car mechanic in 1979, the house has never gone through an auction and as a consequence retains everything from furniture to early papers. A lot of restoration work has already been done, and there are ambitious plans for a museum on the Famine, plus a restaurant and the conversion of one of the yards into a kind of time-share arrangement, with gyms and tennis courts to finance it all.

The house is already open to the public (May–Sept, Wed–Sun; noon–5pm) and makes a good place to get to grips with the Anglo-Irish tradition. Its story is a fairly typical one. Originally a massive 27,000 acres, the estate was granted to one Nicholas Mahon in reward for his support of the Stuarts during the English Civil War. The original house, finished around 1696, was fortified but not particularly grand; only one room of it survives, the stillroom in the cellar, which has just been restored by the Irish Georgian Society. As the family became richer and more secure, it made more grandiose additions, and the current house dates essentially from the 1730s, with some early-nineteenth-century alterations. One of its really extraordinary features is a gallery that runs the length of the kitchen, allowing the lady of the house to watch what was happening there without having to venture in; on Monday mornings she would drop the week's menu down from the gallery.

Strokestown's owners included one particularly nasty piece of work, Major Denis Mahon, who is believed to have been one of the first landowners to charter less-than-seaworthy vessels (the notorious "**coffin ships**") to take evicted tenants to America during the Famine. Whether or not the ships he rented actually arrived at their destination isn't known, but his activities were reported and censured in contemporary newspapers both in Ireland and abroad. In 1847 he was shot dead on his own estate.

Meanwhile, one of the house's charms is that it's not stuck in a Georgian time warp like many of the grand houses you can visit, but is clearly a home that's been well lived in for hundreds of years. To give a measure of the interconnectedness of Anglo-Irish society even in comparatively recent times, the lady who sold the house to the mechanic, the redoubtable Mrs Olive Hales Pakenham Mahon, married the heir to the Rockingham estate in 1914, thus uniting the two biggest estates in Roscommon, though the land empire set up by this dynastic marriage crumbled very soon afterwards. Also in the house, in one of the upstairs bedrooms, is a painting of horses and sheaves of corn by Woodbrook's Phoebe Kirkwood.

The best **place to stay** in Strokestown is the *Strokestown Arms* (☎078-33302; £12, £10 out of season), just outside the gates of the house. If it's full, they should be able to give you details of B&Bs in the vicinity.

Boyle

It's disparagingly said that County Roscommon doesn't have any towns. It does, and **BOYLE** is one of them. Although it isn't a place marked out by particular charm or beauty, there's enough here to keep you entertained for at least a one-night stopover. Boyle grew up around the greatest estate in County Roscommon, **Rockingham**, and although the estate was disbanded long ago and the house—in what is now the Lough Key park—burned down in 1957, the town is still marked by their ghostly presence. The main street, for instance, was planned as an avenue to lead up to the house.

In Boyle itself the most charismatic building is the **Cistercian monastery**, consecrated in 1220 and one of the early results of the arrival of foreign monastic orders in Ireland during the medieval pan-European upsurge in spiritual life. In 1142 a group of monks sent to Ireland by the founder of the Cistercians, Saint Bernard of Clairvaux, at the instigation of Saint Malachy, established the great abbey of Mellifont in County Louth. Clonmacnoise, the important Celtic monastery on the banks of the Shannon in County Offaly, was quickly abandoned, and within twenty years monks from Mellifont had settled at a site beside the Boyle River here at Mainistir na Buaille.

The monastery is small and compact, in very pale stone, well enough preserved to let you see how the monks must have lived. You still go in through the gatehouse, and there's a wonderful church with Gothic arches down one side of the nave, Romanesque down the other. Keys are obtainable from **Abbey House**, next to the monastery. This is also a guesthouse and, wedged between the rushing river and the abbey, is one of the best **places to stay** in Boyle (☎079-62385; open all year).

Lough Key Forest Park and Woodbrook

The road out of Boyle towards the **Lough Key forest park**, part of the old Rockingham estate, leads through the gate of the grounds, itself a Gothic fancy, and past a castellated lodge. The park has been thoroughly and relentlessly amenitized, with a terrible wood-and-glass restaurant at the side of the lake, and a massive asphalt parking lot on the former site of the great house. Yet the stable block, church, icehouse, and temple—the graces of an eighteenth-century estate—give an impression of what it must have been like; with boats for rent and plenty of ring forts to explore, it's a pleasant enough place to spend a sunny day.

A little farther out of Boyle on the Carrick-on-Shannon road, **Woodbrook** is another old Anglo-Irish house. It's not open to the public, and the reason for mentioning it is that it's the subject of a remarkable book, *Woodbrook*, written by an Englishman, David Thompson, who worked there for most of the 1930s as tutor to the Kirkwood family's two young daughters. Sometimes naive, sometimes sentimental, it's strong in its documentation of the passing of Anglo-Irish culture.

travel details

Trains
From Galway to Athenry (4 daily; 15min); Athlone (4; 1hr); Portarlington (3; 2hr); Dublin (4; 2hr 30min).
From Westport three daily to Castlebar (14min); Castlerea (1hr 10min); Roscommon (1hr 30min); Dublin (3hr 30min).

Bus Éireann
From Galway to Dublin (2 daily; 3hr 45min); Limerick (5; 2hr).

Private buses
Funtrek (☎01-730852) run one bus a day, two on Fri **from Galway**, Imperial Hotel, to Athlone, Ballinasloe, Loughrea and Dublin.
North Galway Club (☎093-55492 or 01-266888) departs **from Galway**, Kiltartan House, Forster Street daily for Dublin (Mon–Sat 8am, Fri extra buses at 11am and 6pm, Sun 6pm). Departs **from Tuam** Cathedral daily for Dublin (same hours as above). Departs **from Dublin**, Ormond Quay, for Galway (Mon–Sat 3pm, extra bus Mon 1:15pm, Sun 10:30pm) and Tuam (Mon–Sat 6pm, extra buses Fri 5:15pm and 10pm, Sun 10:30pm). There are summer connections to Dublin Airport.
Feda O'Donnell Coaches (☎075-48114) depart **from Galway** Cathedral (except Sun evening departures, which leave from Eyre Square) daily for Letterkenny, Co Donegal, serving many towns along the way including Knock, Sligo, and Donegal town, and continuing on to Gweedore (dept Galway Mon–Thurs 4pm, Fri 5:30pm, Sat 10am, Sun 8pm). Depart **from Letterkenny** Mon–Thurs 9am, Fri 10:30am and 4:30pm and Sun 3:30pm).

CHAPTER ELEVEN

SLIGO AND LEITRIM

C ounties Sligo and Leitrim pair up well, offering a distinctively luscious and gentle scenery that contrasts with the wilder streaks of Donegal and Mayo, yet is as far removed from the dullness of Longford and Cavan to its east. **Leitrim**, one of most neglected counties in the country, is an area of lakelets and low mounds, and presents a singularly withdrawn face to the outside world. **Sligo**, phenomenally underrated, is the more enticing of the two, having the beautiful mountains of **Benbulben** and **Knocknarea**, and the enchanting **Gill** and **Glencar** loughs. Much of the terrain is gently undulating farming land, allowing long cross-country views to the higher outcrops in the county's far corners: the **Ox Mountains** to the west, the **Bricklieve Mountains** to the south and the **Dartry** range to the north. And at **Streedagh** and **Mulaghmore** you'll find some of the country's finest beaches.

Sligo is rich in historical terms as well. Especially interesting are the extensive Neolithic cemetery at **Carrowmore**, to the west of Sligo town, and the large prehistoric village at **Carrowkeel**, on top of the Bricklieve Mountains. The wealth and variety of legends covering its terrain has no rival, and its modern literary associations are no less strong, as this landscape and its culture nurtured the greatest of Irish poets, **W. B. Yeats**. His poetry is saturated with the atmosphere of Sligo, and his presence still makes itself felt at places such as the island of **Innisfree** on Lough Gill and **Lissadell House**.

Sligo Town

SLIGO, with a population of about 18,000, is, after Derry, the biggest town in the northwest of Ireland and a real focal point for the surrounding area. The first recorded mention of Sligo dates from AD 807 when the town was sacked by the Vikings, and by the thirteenth century it had become the gateway between Connacht and Ulster, with a castle (since destroyed) on what is now Castle Street. The Middle Ages were a period of sporadic violence, most notably between the Anglo-Norman Maurice Fitzgerald and the O'Connells. Thanks to its strong defenses, Sligo was the last of the western garrisons to surrender to Williamite forces after the Battle of the Boyne.

The town suffered greatly during the Famine, when its population was reduced by a third through death and emigration, but by the end of the last century things had picked up to the extent that it was described in guidebooks as "a progressive and busy centre." The upswing has continued to the present day, and in summer the streets are always crowded with visitors—but if you have a chance to look at the photos of old Sligo hanging in the

Allied Irish Bank on Stephen Street, you'll realize how remarkably constant the appearance of the town has been. The tightly packed and narrow back-streets make it feel a little like Latin Quarter Paris, with grocery stores and bars on the street corners open late into the evening. Apart from the Dominican abbey there's not much left in the way of sites that recall the town's long history, but the old-fashioned market-town atmosphere and the equally atmospheric old pubs make it an ideal base for exploring the surrounding countryside and sights.

The Town

The thirteenth-century **Dominican Abbey** has had a checkered history, having been destroyed a couple of times by both accident and design since its foundation. Its life as a religious foundation came to an'end in 1641, when the whole town was sacked. These days the abbey makes a good place to have a picnic since its walls still stand and the chancel and high altar, with fine carvings, are in a good state of preservation. If the abbey is locked you can get the key from the caretaker, Mr A. McGuinn at 6 Charlotte Street, although you won't be missing much if you just take a look through the gates.

The **Municipal Art Gallery** (Tues and Fri 10:30am–12:30pm), housed in the County Library on Stephen Street, possesses a lot of paintings and pencil drawings by Jack Yeats, brother of the poet. His work has a strong local flavor, and his later efforts like *The Graveyard Wall* and *The Sea and the Lighthouse*—are especially potent evocations of the life and atmosphere of the area. If you're going to be heading north into Donegal, look out for *Early Morning in Donegal Lough* by Paul Henry, which will give you a taste of things to come. Also worth more than a passing glance are the paintings by George Russell, better known as AE, the mystical poet and contemporary of W. B. Yeats.

In the same compound as the library but situated just by the entrance gate are the **Sligo County Museum** and **Yeats Memorial Museum** (daily 10:30am–12:30pm and 2:30–4:30pm), which basically comprise two rooms. The more unusual items in the local history section are a sequence of excellent nineteenth-century sketches of the monastic ruins on Inishmurray, and a double-weight hundred-year-old firkin of bog butter. Memorabilia in the Yeats museum include photographs and commentary of his funeral, lots of letters and photos of the man himself, and the Nobel Prize medal awarded him in 1923. Before you rush out, read a bit of the long article on Michael Coleman, one of Ireland's most famous fiddle players; Fritz Kreisler, the greatest of classical violin players, wrote at the beginning of the century that even he could not attempt the kind of music Michael Coleman played, even if he practiced for a thousand years.

Just down the road, at Douglas Hyde Bridge, the **Yeats Memorial Building** is the headquarters of the *Yeats Society* and host to the *Yeats International Summer School*. Inaugurated about thirty years ago, the gathering has become something of an academic institution, attracting scholars from all over the world.

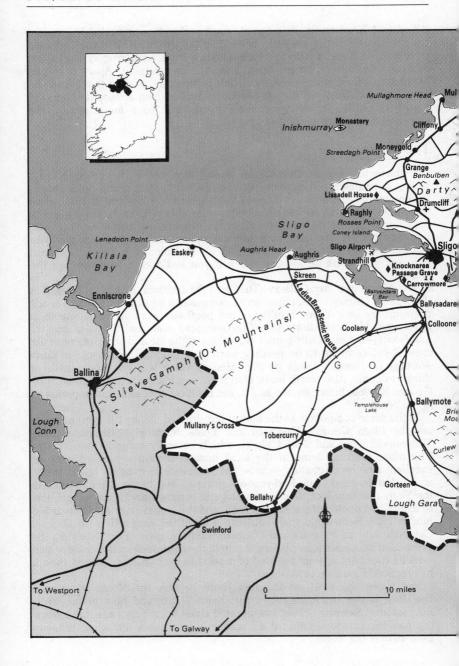

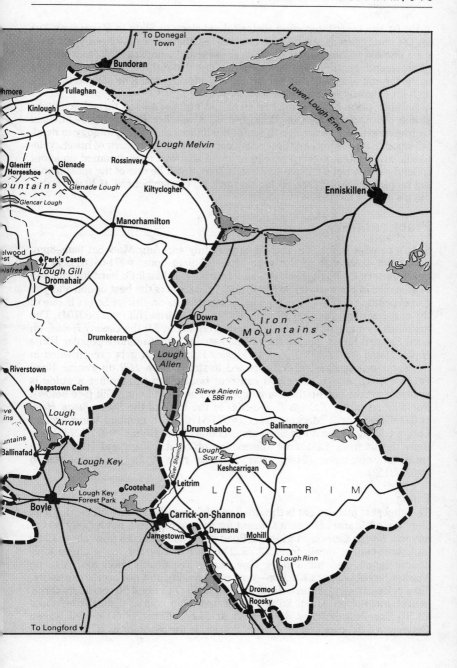

By far the most interesting historical set-piece in Sligo is *Hargadon's Pub* on O'Connell Street. An exclusively male establishment until ten years ago, it's a fine old talking-pub, with dark recesses and compartments, and shelves of nineteenth-century earthenware stout-jugs. Note the little swivel windows at the far end of the serving bar, where the whiskey could be slipped through with little fuss by either drinker or landlord.

Another place of great interest is an old butcher's shop turned sculpture studio, *Michael Quirke's* on Wine Street. A butcher for 27 years, Michael Quirke began nine years ago to sculpt the figures of Irish mythology in dead-fall-wood. Every feature of these small carvings bears the mark of his encyclopaedic knowledge of every legend or myth that was ever dreamed up about Ireland—if you get a chance to listen to him, it will be one of the most inspiring moments of your stay. So far his work isn't too expensive (£30 upwards), but it's getting increasingly popular.

Practicalities

Sligo's **tourist office**, on Temple Street (July and Aug Mon–Sat 9am–8pm, Sun 10am–2pm; rest of the year Mon–Fri 9am–5pm; ☎071-61201), is the headquarters for Sligo, Donegal, and Leitrim, but has little hard information to give out. In Sligo town itself **bed and breakfast** is the best option and you can expect to pay £9–10 per person: *Bridge Houses* on Bridge Street is one of the cheaper ones. Another B&B is *Aisling*, on Cairns Hill (☎071-60704). The town has a couple of **hostels** with beds from about £4: the *County Hostel,* on Lord Edward Street, beside the railroad station, and the more popular *White House Hostel* (☎071-22030) on Markievicz Road, which gets overcrowded in the summer. Another recently-opened hostel is *Eden Hill* on Pearse Road (☎071-43204). At the latter you can rent **boats**, and in summer a guide is available to take you up the Garavogue River and into Lough Gill (see below). For bike rental try *Raleigh Rent-a-Bike* at the back of the *Silver Swan Hotel* (☎071-67560), or 3 Market Street (☎071-5170). For minibus tours around Lough Gill and other north Sligo areas contact John Houze (☎071-42747); the tours depart from the tourist information office at 9:30am and 1:30pm from June to September (£4–5). *Bus Éireann* runs from the train station (☎071-2152).

Eating

The cheapest place to **eat** is the small snack bar at the welfare office, down an alleyway off Market Street; it's meant for the unemployed, but happily serves anyone. *Forte's Café* on Markievicz Road does main courses from about £1.90 and three-course meals from £2.75. The *Ritz Restaurant* has a cheap four-course lunch, and the *Village Café* serves reasonable food too. Also on Market Street is *Kate's Kitchen*—very good quality and not overly expensive. Up a price category, *Beezies Dining Salon* at 45 O'Connell Street, offers three-course meals from about £6 and individual main course dishes from about £3.50. Excellent lunches are served at *The Cellars*, 30 O'Connell Street; *Cosgrove's*, a delicatessen on Market Square, is the place for picnic food.

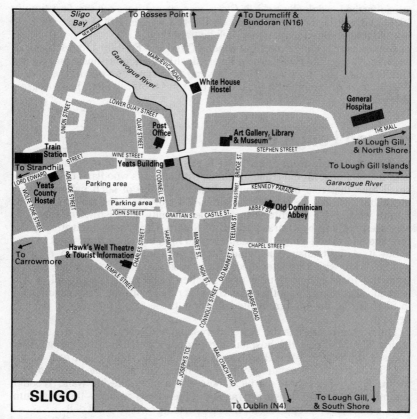

SLIGO

Pubs and Entertainment

When it comes to **pubs**, Sligo does well. *Hargadon's Pub* (see above) is one of the best, with several compartments where you can sit and drink and talk. *Hennigan's Pub,* Wine Street, has pop/rock once a week, usually Thursday, and mainly traditional stuff on Sunday. *McGlynn's* on Market Street is a cosy and usually crowded bar, with folk/traditional music almost nightly in summer (Tues, Fri and Sat during the rest of the year); sometimes it gets a bit too reverential though, and the folk music probably wouldn't satisfy the purists. *Comhalta's* has sessions on Wednesdays in the *Silver Swan Hotel*, Hyde Bridge, a forum for other types of music most other nights. The cognoscenti should head for the *Trades Club*, on Castle Street; from 9:45pm every Tuesday the best sessions you'll find in Sligo take place here, sometimes with a brilliant young violinist and, from time to time, Lord Templemore on spoons—arrive early to ensure getting in. (The entrance is an ordinary house door and is easy to miss.) The *Fleadh Cheoil* traditional music festival, originally held in Clare, was staged here for the first time in 1989, and will be held here again on the last weekend of August 1990. Be warned that accommodation may well be tight then.

Xanadu's on Teeling Street has **discos** (Wed and Fri–Sun 11pm-1:30am; £4 including food). *The Blue Lagoon*, Riverside, has traditional music on Monday and Tuesday and discos on Thursday and Saturday. For **plays**, the *Hawk's Well Theatre* on Temple Street (below the tourist office) often has a reasonable program.

Around Lough Gill

A pleasant day-trip from Sligo Town is the 24-mile circuit of **Lough Gill**, a lake that's almost Mediterranean in feel, with luscious woodland covering the small hills that rise off its winding banks. A place of such natural beauty inevitably features in legend: Lough Gill's story tells of a warrior called Romra who had a daughter named Gille ("beauty" in Irish). One day Gille was seen bathing by Omra, a friend of Romra. Omra was captivated by the girl, and she wasn't altogether indifferent to him, but when Romra got to hear about it, a fight ensued in which Omra was killed and Romra received wounds from which he later died. Grief-stricken, Gille drowned herself, and from the tears of her doubly grief-stricken nursemaid Lough Gill(e) was formed. According to another tale, the silver bell from the Dominican abbey in Sligo lies at the bottom of the lake; only those free from sin can hear its pealing.

The northern shore is the more interesting, and reached from the town by taking The Mall past the hospital, turning onto the L16 at the garage, until you see signposts for the **Hazelwood** estate on the right. A left turn off the road leading into the estate grounds will bring you after half a mile to **Half Moon Bay**, where there's a picnic site and a nice lakeside walk. Wooden sculptures by various artists are ranged in the woods around—the most stunning is a set piece of chariot and horses, set in its own artificial dell.

Back on the L16, there's nothing to stop for until you near the Leitrim end of the lake, when the road begins to skirt the shore on its approach to **Parke's Castle**, a romantic-looking seventeenth-century fortress positioned only ten yards from the water (June–Sept 10am–6pm; £1). Look out for the narrow passage that runs under the wall to carry *curraghs* onto the lake, and for the small sweathouse (a kind of turkish bath), whose therapeutic steam was intended to be followed by a freezing dip in the lake.

Rounding the eastern side of Lough Gill, in County Leitrim, provides the most enjoyable contact with the lake until a steep road runs up to the left towards Manorhamilton (see below), with the main road veering away from the lake and on to the village of DROMAHAIR. At the entrance to the village a signpost points out a path to **Creevylea Abbey**, a Franciscan friary founded in 1508. Now mostly ruined, it still has some fine sculptures in the cloister arcade; look out for Saint Francis with the stigmata, and another of him preaching to the birds from a pulpit. Until a few years ago the place was used for burials, and some of the tombstones date from as recently as the 1970s.

The return journey to Sligo is frustratingly remote from the lake, and the sole diversion—to **Innisfree**—is really only for avid enthusiasts of Yeats' poetry.

> *And I shall have some peace there, for peace comes dropping slow,*
> *Dropping from the veils of the morning to where the cricket sings;*
> *There midnight's all a glimmer, and noon a purple glow,*
> *And evening full of the linnet's wings.*

"The Lake Isle of Innisfree"

The shore opposite the island is a good three miles from the main road; should you want to go over, a small boat is available on most summer days. The south road back into Sligo passes **Cairns Hill Forest Park**. From the parking lot a path leads to a cairn on top of Cairns Hill, with a view across to a second cairn on the peak of Belvoir Hill. These are reckoned to be the tombs of Romra and Omra, though another legend makes them out to be the breasts of a monstrous hag, with Lough Gill as her navel.

North of Sligo Town

Leaving Sligo along the coast to the north, almost immediately there's the possibility of a short detour to **Rosses Point** (bus #286 from Sligo), via the promontory that forms the north side of Sligo Bay. It's a perfect picture-postcard scene, with the streaks of Coney and Oyster islands guarding the entrance to the bay, and the distinctive beauty of Knocknarea standing behind. A sea marker called the "Metal Man" marks the deepest part of the channel for Sligo-bound boats; placed there in 1822, it was called by Yeats the "Rosses Point man who never told a lie." The tip of the headland, **Deadman's Point** (now an upper-crust recreation center), took its name from a sailor who was buried at sea here with a loaf of bread thoughtfully provided by his comrades—they weren't sure whether he was really dead but wanted to despatch him quickly so they could make port before the tide changed. For food, head to *Austie's Sea Food Bar*, in the village at Rosses Point.

Drumcliff, Benbulben, and Glencar Lough

Sticking to the main N15 road out of Sligo you'll bypass this small peninsula, to reach water again at **DRUMCLIFF** (bus #290 or #291), an early monastic site probably better known as the last resting place of W. B. Yeats. His grave is in the grounds of an austere nineteenth-century Protestant church, within sight of the nearby Benbulben, as the poet wished. You could easily miss the simple gravestone bearing the epitaph from Yeats's last poem:

> *Cast a cold eye*
> *On life, on death.*
> *Horseman, pass by!*

In 575 Saint Columba founded a monastery here, and you can still see the remants of a round tower on the left of the roadside and a tenth-century high cross—the only one in the county—on the right. The east face of the cross has carvings of Adam and Eve, Cain killing Abel, and Daniel in the Lion's Den; the west face shows scenes from the New Testament, including the Presentation in the Temple and the Crucifixion. Local excavations have turned up a wealth of Iron- and Bronze-Age remains too.

At 1730 feet, **Benbulben** is one of the most dramatic mountains in the country, and its profile changes constantly as you round it. According to the Finn Mac Cumaill legend it was here that Diarmuid was killed by the wild boar, its bristles puncturing his heel—his one vulnerable point. Access to its slopes is easy, but avoid it after dark as there are a lot of dangerous clefts into which the unsuspecting walker can all too easily plunge. There are **hostel** facilities at the *Yeats Tavern* (☎071-63117) in Drumcliff, about a hundred yards past the church. It's part of the roadside pub, and although handy for drinks and basic eating, you won't want to spend more than one night there. There's also a B&B at *Castletown House* (☎071-63204).

Just to the east of Drumcliff, but best reached from the T17 road to Manorhamilton, is **Glencar Lough** (bus #125 or #283 from Sligo), set into the back of Benbulben. Follow the road around the northern edge of the lake passing the recently reopened barite mine sheds on the left, until you see the "Waterfall" signpost. From the nearby parking lot a path leads up to the waterfall itself, which at nearly fifty feet high is worth going out of your way for, particularly after heavy rain. There are more waterfalls, visible from the road, in the upper reaches of the valley, although none is quite as romantic as this one. For an even better mountain walk continue along the road to the eastern end of the lake, where a track rises steeply northward to the **Swiss valley**, a deep rift in the mountain crowned with silver fir.

Cooldrumman and Lissadell House

Beyond Drumcliff, the first left turn off the main road (signposted "Lissadell") runs to CARNEY village, to the north of which is an area known as **Cooldrumman**, where the **Battle of the Book** took place. This battle followed the refusal of Saint Columba to hand over a psalms book copied from the original owned by Saint Finian of Moville, in defiance of the High King, who ruled that just as a calf belongs to its cow so every copy belongs to the owner of the book from which it is made. Columba won the battle at a cost of 3000 lives; repenting the bloodshed he had caused, he then went into exile on the island of Iona.

In Carney a signpost to the left indicates the way to **Lissadell House** (May–Sept Mon–Sat 2–5:15pm; last tour at 4:30pm; bus #290 or #291 from Sligo), a nineteenth-century stately home whose popularity is mainly due to its Yeatsian associations. This was the home of the Gore-Booth family, who produced several generations of artists, travelers, and fighters for Irish freedom. During the Famine Sir Robert Gore-Booth mortgaged the place to feed the local people and doled out rations from the hall. His granddaughters Eva Gore-Booth and Connie Markievicz were friends of Yeats (his "In Memory of Eva Gore-Booth and Con Markiewicz" is displayed at the gate) and took part in the 1916 rising. Connie was condemned to death by the British for her participation, but was pardoned and went on to become the first British female MP and then Minister of Labor in the Dail's first cabinet. The house is full of relics of the colorful lives of its inhabitants, with odd touches like the dining room's full-length mural portraits of family members and retainers, painted by Count Casimir Markievicz (Connie's husband).

The area around Lissadell has some nice walks and reputedly the warmest patch of sea on the Sligo coast. Also worth seeking out is *Ellen's Pub*, whose cottage-home atmosphere draws people from miles around. *Ceilidhs* are sometimes held in the back room, and on Friday, Saturday, and Sunday from June through September musicians gather here to belt out tunes on fiddles, accordions, and banjos. There's a relaxed attitude to the licensing laws here, so relaxed in fact that the pub was closed down for a while in 1986. To find it, follow the road past the turning for the Lissadell estate, bear right away from Maugherow church, turn left at the pub/grocery store at the crossroads and then take the second right—it's another mile straight ahead. Hitching is possible, because everyone knows where you're trying to get to if you're anywhere in the area.

Raghly Point to Mullaghmore

To the west of Lissadell is RAGHLY, a small harbor with a forlorn pier and raised beach from where there are good views of the bay and surrounding mountains. On the way there you'll pass **Ardtermon Castle** (closed to the public), the seventeenth-century fortified manor house once occupied by Francis Gore-Booth, an ancestor of the Lissadell House Gore-Booths. Ten years ago the place was more or less a ruin, but since then it's been well restored by its German industrialist owner.

Next stop along the coast is sandy **Streedagh Strand** (7 buses daily from Sligo), most easily accessible by taking the main road to Grange (see below) and following the signposts from there, as roads on the Raghly peninsula are hard to disentangle. A substantial German expatriate colony in this area has earned it the nickname of "Little Bavaria," and the prices of some of the chalets at Streedagh Strand itself (up to £50,000) have provoked a degree of chagrin from the locals. The beach is a fantastic stretch of sand, superb for long walks or horseback-riding by the waves (there are several stables in the district), and when the tide is at its lowest you can walk around to the caves at the southern end to do some fossil-collecting. At the very north end of the beach is *Carrig na Spainneach* (Spaniards' Rock), where three ships of the Spanish Armada foundered. Nearby are numerous anonymous burial stones, said to mark the mass graves of some 1100 sailors who either drowned or were butchered by the British.

At GRANGE itself there's not much of worth apart from an old boys' bar off to the right, over the bridge, and a small museum in the local school on the main road (open summer only). However, if you venture inland (past the pub) you'll get a changing perspective of Benbulben as you approach the "Gleniff Horseshoe", a scenic road that runs along a glen on the flank of the Dartry range, and gives easy access to the top of Benbulben.

At **MONEYGOLD**, a short way beyond Grange, there's excellent accommodation at the *Organic Farm and Hostel* (☎071-63337; B&B £8), where you can also try organically produced cheeses and sample local fish and shellfish. The hostel organizes very cheap bike rental and horseback-riding on Streedagh Strand; you can also help work on the small farm for a week or more and earn yourself free food and accommodation. **CLIFFONY**, a couple of miles farther toward Bundoran, is remarkable for the **Creevykeel Court- Tomb** (just past the village by the roadside), one of the most extensive Neolithic sites in the country, comprising two roofless tombs within a stone court.

Mullaghmore headland is the most attractive of all the promontories north of Sligo town. A left turn at the Cliffony crossroads takes you onto it, past **Classiebawn Castle** (closed to the public), a Disneylandish construction built by Lord Palmerston; it became the home of Lord Mountbatten shortly before he was killed by the IRA in 1979, when his boat was blown up in the bay. (A road graffito in the vicinity—*Blessed are those who hunger to death*—attests to hard-core Republican support hereabouts.) **MULLAGHMORE** is a dainty place with a peaceful, skiff-filled harbor and a very good beach. If you're spending some time here, there's good walking along the rocky shelves of Mullaghmore Head, at the end of the village, where the ocean waves crash constantly within feet of you. Alternatively, you could explore the area on horseback: mounts can be rented from the stables on the crest of the hill. If you're wondering what all the nuns are doing in Mullaghmore, it's because the village has a convent vacation retreat at which they can relax after the rigors of their parishes. Non-ecclesiastical travelers can camp in the sand dunes as long as they're inconspicuous, and the *Beach Hotel* offers B&B and good food. *Lomax Boats* rents out fishing boats (£80 per 8-hr day; maximum 6 persons; rods £4 per day), and can arrange trips to Inishmurray in summer (see below). For a quiet pint try *Annie's Bar*, and you may get a basic bite to eat in the *Pier Bar*.

The island of **Inishmurray**, lying about four miles off the shore, has been deserted since the 1950s, but the trip out to it is more than worthwhile, for its ruined sixth-century monastery, its church, and its early Christian gravestones, some of the best-preserved in the country. In addition to *Lomax Boats*, trips are run by Mr Christy Herrity, *Carns*, Moneygold (☎071-63365; £75 for maximum group of 10), and Mr Mulligan, *Dun Ard*, Mullaghmore (☎071-67126). The crossing takes 75 minutes, and you can spend several hours on the island.

West of Sligo Town

Taking the route directly west out of Sligo town—the Strandhill Road—you'll be heading in the direction of Knocknarea Mountain. A right off this road runs down to Sligo Bay, where concrete markers delineate a low-tide crossing to Coney Island. More excitingly, a left turn eventually takes you into a fieldscape studded with over sixty megalithic tombs, the **Carrowmore Megalithic Cemetery**. Though half the stones have disappeared, this is still the second largest such site in Europe after Carnac in Brittany. It's an intoxicating meander alongside the dolmens, stone circles, and cairns, under the eye of the big mother cairn of them all *Medb's Cairn*, on top of

Knocknarea. The easiest ascent of the mountain is along the path that meets the road skirting its southern flank (the western slopes are too difficult). The sixty-foot cairn on the summit is said to be the tomb of Queen Medb of Connaught, but as she was killed elsewhere it's unlikely that she's buried here; experts reckon that the 40,000 tons of rock were put here by Neolithic farmers—but it has yet to be excavated to find out why.

Towards the end of the headland, at **STRANDHILL** (bus #285 from Sligo), there's a large, wild beach along which the sea sweeps massive boulders in winter. Sligo airport is close by, and it's a thrilling sight to see the small *Aer Lingus* planes coming in over the top of *Medb's Cairn*. At the end of the airstrip stands the tenth-century **Killaspugbone Church** (access across the beach), where Saint Patrick allegedly tripped on the threshold and lost a tooth. A beautiful casket in which the sacred tooth was enshrined—the *Fiacal Padraig*—is now in the National Museum in Dublin, but the whereabouts of the tooth is a mystery. The old Strandhill village was sited here until the drifting sand forced the villagers to move a few centuries ago. In Strandhill village look out for *Dolly's Cottage*; sessions take place there some evenings, and during the day it's a kind of folk museum (July and Aug daily 3–5pm).

Ballysadare to Enniscrone

The main road westward from Sligo, flanked by the northern foothills of the Ox Mountains and the innocuous coastline of northwest County Sligo, is scarcely an enthralling route, yet a few things crop up on the way to north Mayo that are worth a mention. If bicycling, take the road running parallel to and nearer the coast. **BALLYSADARE**, situated at the head of a beautiful bay with striking views back to Knocknarea and Benbulben, has the remnants of a seventh-century monastery and a pre-Romanesque church, neither worth stopping for. *The Thatch Pub*, at the very southern end of town, is an old-fashioned pub where you should be able to hear a traditional tune or two (Thurs all year, plus open sessions Tues in summer).

Just after SKREEN, is the turn off for the Ladies Brae Scenic Route, one of only two trails across the vast **Ox Mountains** (*sliabh ghamh*, stony mountain) into south Sligo. Following the course of a tumbling stream between forests of fir, the road ends not far from COOLANY. Much of the Ox range consists of unexciting heathery slopes and flat, boggy upland, but the second route across the mountains—starting with a left turn off the road just before Easky (see below)—takes you up through the gorgeous setting of **Easky Lough** and then down a dramatic descent of the southwestern face of the range into the area surrounding Tobercurry (again see below).

Originally a monastic settlement, **EASKY** was a vital link in the anti-Napoleon coastal defensive chain, as its two nearby martello towers attest. These days the place is acquiring a bit of a reputation as a surfers' paradise, which means increasing numbers of tourists. At the mouth of the salmon-rich Easky River are the ruins of the fifteenth-century **Rosalee Castle**, which many of the locals are convinced is cursed (key from a Mrs Mary Morrissey, above *Clerk's* shop). A few years back it was all set to be renovated with government money, and a committee was set up to steer the village into a new tourist-fed prosperity. Suddenly the chairman of the committee dropped dead, then the secretary drowned, and finally, before the project was hastily disbanded, the treasurer choked on a steakbone and was rushed to hospital. Maybe this is why the village signs read *GOD BLESS YOU* as you leave. The only **pub** of any singularity is *Sheila Sullivan's*, a talking pub for the old fellas.

ENNISCRONE, on the east side of Killala Bay and the western boundary of County Sligo, is a popular seaside resort for the Irish, with trailer parks hidden away in the sand dunes, plus the traditional golfing amenities. There's a sweeping three-mile crescent of sandy beach, with ten Victorian bath-houses, built to exploit the health-giving properties of seaweed and hot sea-water.

One other thing you can't fail to notice in Enniscrone is a powerful metal sculpture of a black pig in someone's front yard on the main street (the myth-ical Black Pig was chased across Donegal Bay and came ashore at Enniscrone). It supposedly was commissioned by the council, then appropri-ated by the house's owner when the unprepossessing result was rejected. The local **tourist office** is on Main Street (☎0967-36202).

South of Sligo

The single worthwhile sight in the village of **COLLOONEY**, five miles south of Sligo along the N4 (bus #247, #267, #275 or #285 from Sligo), is the **Teeling Monument** at the northern entrance to the village, built to commemorate Bartholomew Teeling, hero of the Battle of Carricknagat. The battle, which was fought nearby, occurred during the rebellion of 1798, when a combined Franco-Irish force—on its way to Ballinamuck in County Longford—was held up by a single strategically placed English gun. Teeling charged up the hill and shot the gunner dead, turning the tide of the engagement. After their defeat at Ballinamuck the French were treated as prisoners of war, but 500 Irish troops were massacred. Irish-born Teeling, who was an officer in the French army, was later hanged in Dublin. The monument links Teeling and his fallen comrades with subsequent generations of Irish freedom fighters .

The more appealing route south from here, to Lough Arrow, involves a turn off the N4 at **DRUMFIN**, along the road that goes through the geriatric village of **RIVERSTOWN**. Several miles on, standing by the roadside behind a modern bungalow, is **Heapstown Cairn**, a Neolithic passage-tomb as large as *Medb's Cairn* and traditionally the last resting place of Ailil, brother of King Niall of Tara. A lot of the cairn-stones have been plundered for building material, but even in its diminished state the cairn remains impressive, best appreciated by climbing it and taking in the view from the top. What's most fascinating about the view is the perfect central position the cairn takes in relation to the surrounding circle of hills, some with cairns on their peaks.

One option from here is to go down the eastern shore of **Lough Arrow**, whose blue waters are set with ringlets of isles. When the sun is shining there are few spots to beat it, especially if you can take a rowboat onto the tranquil lake—keep your eye out for boats lying by the banks and then ask at a nearby house. The road round the southern edge of the lake goes through BALLINAFAD, at the back door of the Bricklieve Mountains. The road into Balinafad from the Curlew Mountains of Roscommon gives the most stupendous view in the whole of Sligo, right up to Benbulben—it's worth backtracking up the hill to get it. **Ballinafad castle** (left off the road at the top of the village) is a sixteenth-century building remarkable only because its huge circular towers and squat walls are of a thirteenth-century design.

Carrowkeel and Keshcorran

The other and more interesting route southward from the Heapstown cairn takes you along the top of Lough Allen to meet the N4. Cross at CASTLEBALDWIN and climb the road leading up behind *McDermot's Pub* for the Bronze-Age **Carrowkeel Cemetery**—be warned that it's a long and fairly arduous walk, but the panorama on the way is marvelous. Comprising fourteen cairns, a few dolmens, and some fifty-odd pieces of stone foundations, the site is the most important cairn colony west of Sliabh Na Caillighe in northwest Meath. To get there follow the ascending road for a few kilometers, turn left as signposted, follow the track around the hill's flank, through the gateway, take the next left around the side of the opposite slope and the cairns will be marked forty yards up through the heather.

Also of interest in the area are the caves on the hill of **Keshcorran**, which you can get to by rejoining the main road across the mountains, then turning left down the hill, taking every descending turning until you reach a major road where the pub *The Traveler's Rest* stands. Take a right here towards KESH and after the *Foxes Pub* and grocery store a fingerpost points right—after a couple of hundred yards you'll spot a line of caves cut into the forehead of the mountain. The caves have no depth at all, but the feeling of isolation is immense at this spot. It was here that the baby Cormac Mac Airt, later to be the greatest of all the High Kings who ruled at Tara, was reared by wolves.

Ballymote

If, instead of taking the Lough Arrow route from Collooney, you follow the N17 southwest, you could make a diversion along the L11 to the small market town of **BALLYMOTE**. Its fourteenth-century castle, built by Richard de Burgo (the "Red" Earl of Ulster), was once the strongest in Connaught, but has associations with major defeats—it was O'Donnell's before he lost at the Battle of Kinsale, and it was James II's possession before he lost at the Boyne. The village sports a couple of nice old bars: *Sally's*, towards the east end of town, which has a dark wooden interior for serious drinking (music Sat & Sun); and *Hayden's* on the main southern street (occasional open sessions). For **accommodation contact** John Perry at *The Corran Restaurant*. He will arrange B&B (£8–9) or just a bed at the standard hostel price (☎071-83372); the restaurant is the best place to eat, and the proprietor acts as local information service.

The most stylish B&B in the vicinity is at **Templehouse** mansion, three miles from here on the shores of the lake. Founded by the Knights Templar and expanded in 1560, this is one of the grandest and oldest Anglo-Irish houses ever built in Ireland, on a 950-acre estate with 97 rooms, five of which are for B&B guests (B&B £25, dinner £18, April–Dec; ☎071-83329). To get there take the left fork off the Collooney end of town; it's near the N17 to Tobercurry.

Tobercurry

The district around **TOBERCURRY**—and south Sligo in general—has a reputation for traditional music: Michael Coleman, the greatest of Irish fiddle players, came from here, and it's also where The Chieftains had their roots. Today the town and the surrounding area is economically very depressed, with boarded-up houses a common sight, and scenically it's not too exciting either. Tobercurry town is a busy little market center, usually devoid of visitors. The **tourist information** is based in *Killoran's Traditional Restaurant*, where you can eat well and cheaply—don't miss out on the famous fresh salmon from the Moy River. The restaurant also has a dance floor at the back, where it holds boisterous Irish evenings (June–Sept Thurs 9:30am–12:30pm). In the second week of July the town has a **music week**, featuring short courses in music and Irish dancing. For **accommodation**, Anne Killoran can arrange free camping or a bed at the standard hostel rate. *Carrick's* fishing and sporting tackle shop, a few doors down from *Killoran's*, rents out rods, and at the *Lough Talt Inn*, several miles up the Ballina road, boats can be rented for trout fishing on the adjacent lake.

The L133 runs down to **GURTEEN**, once a thriving center for traditional music, now a place with something of the scent of a ghost town. Yet some of the finest musicians in the country still live up in the hills, and from time to time they might come down to strike up a tune. *Teach Murray* has a session on Mondays, and the *Roisín Dubh* has spontaneous music making.

Lough Gara, tucked away in the southernmost pocket of the county, is not as appealing as the map suggests it might be, having a very undramatic surrounding shoreline. **Moygara Castle**, signposted near the lake, is similarly anticlimactic, with just one of its original four towers left intact.

County Leitrim

The **Leitrim** scenery is more distinctive than it's normally given credit for, but the county has no places of historical interest, and is not an area that will detain you for long. It stretches fifty miles from County Longford to its slim two-mile coastline at **Tullaghan**, and is neatly split into a north and south section by the vast interruption of **Lough Allen**, the first lake on the River Shannon. The southern half is the more interesting, owing mainly to the presence of the **Shannon**, though the lake-peppered terrain to the east of the river also merits exploration. The northern section, around **Manorhamilton**, is a contrastingly mountainous territory; its most beautiful features—**Glencar** and **Lough Gill**—are shared with Sligo, and are best approached from there.

Carrick-on-Shannon

The small town of **CARRICK-ON-SHANNON**, beautifully positioned on a wide stretch of the Shannon just below Lough Key, makes a good base from which to bicycle round the southern loop of Leitrim or to investigate Lough Key and Lough Boderg in Roscommon. The single piece of historical interest the town has to offer is the miniscule **Costello Chapel**, at the top end of Bridge Street. Billed as the second smallest chapel in the world, it was built in 1877 by the fanatically devout businessman Edward Costello as a memorial to his wife, who died at a young age that year. The couple's lead coffins, protected by thick slabs of glass, lie in two sunken spaces on each side of the tiny, beautifully tiled aisle. Also worth a call is **Cyril Cullen's** pebble-finished Georgian house, *Summerhill* (on the road to St Patrick's Hospital), where he sells porcelain figures and his own distinctive knitwear designs—he breeds his own Jacob sheep for their wool. You may be lucky enough to get a chance to hear his 150-year-old harp made by J. Fall of Belfast, the first craftsman to take up harp-making after O'Carolan's death. There are only two such instruments in Ireland, the other being in Padraig Pearse's memorial house in Dublin. You might also be shown his marvelous collection of Bridget Gore-Booth paintings.

Practicalities

Carrick boasts one of the best hostels in the country, the *Town Clock Hostel* (☎078-20068), situated at the junction of Main and Bridge Streets. **Camping** is allowed on the river bank by the bridge, just in front of *Michael Lynch's* boat rental, and you can use the washing facilities at the *Clancy's* supermarket nearby. There are plenty of **pubs** in town. *Seán's Plaice* (sic) has a very jovial atmosphere with noisy singalongs on a Sunday morning, and is good for food too. *Burke's Bar*, just a few doors up from *Seán's*, has traditional music on Thursday nights. If you're looking for a place where silence is golden, then try *Armstrong's* next door to the Costello Chapel. *The County Hotel* has traditional music sessions every Friday during July and August, although you have to pay a £3 cover charge. *The Anchorage Bar*, near the bottom of Bridge Street, is the place where the youngsters hang out (music Oct–March on Sun, and on Wed during the rest of the year).

For **food** try *Cryan's*, at the bottom of Bridge Street, where you can get a three-course meal at a reasonable price. The *Coffee Shop*, also on Bridge Street, has very nice home-baked items and is the best place for a snack lunch. For picnic provisions, *Doherty's Bakery* on Main Street is the place to go. *The Bookshop*, across the road from *Doherty's*, has a good selection of Irish literature and general contemporary stuff.

Carrick's **tourist office** is on the Roscommon side of the river; *Michael Lynch*, on the same side but before the tourist office, has **boats** for rent (£15 per day with outboard; maximum 5 people). *White Dolphin* boats organize trips up the river leaving from the bridge on the hour (10am–5pm; £3.50 per person). Rental of **bikes** and fishing tackle is available at *Geraghty's* on Main Street.

South of Carrick

As with most of Leitrim, there's little of substantial interest in the area south of Carrick, but if you're passing through there's a couple of places where you could at least slow down a bit. The village of **JAMESTOWN**, on the main Longford road, is a regal plantation settlement—the main road passes through a gate in the old estate walls. The Georgian mansions and the wooded river banks create the aristocratic feel of a bygone age. Excavations in the summer of 1989 at nearby **DRUMSNA**, another riverside village, have unearthed huge stretches of a Stone-Age wall, one of the oldest artificial structures in the world. It's been estimated that it would take a labor force of 30,000 men ten years to build its full length. *Taylor's Lounge*, right by the bridge, does bed and breakfast. A plaque on the wall records that Anthony Trollope began his novel *The MacDermots of Ballycloran* here in 1848; the MacDermots were great Catholic landowners during the eighteenth century, but were then ruined by the Penal Laws.

DROMOD is the home village of one of the most extraordinary characters in Leitrim, a Kerryman called **James McCarran**, whose chaotic antique shop is almost as intriguing as the stories he tells. If he tries to sell you a saddle from the Battle of Hastings, think twice before shelling out. **ROOSKY**, a mile or so down the road, has just one attraction—*The Crow's Inn*, which has sessions on Thursday nights, with uilleann pipes and dancing—and even that is on the Roscommon side of the river.

To the east of these villages is **MOHILL**, reached by turning off the main road at Drumsna or Dromod. A sculpture on the main street commemorates its most famous son—**Turlough O'Carolan**, the blind eighteenth-century harpist and composer (he wrote "The Star-Spangled Banner," believe it or not). The last of the court bards, he lived by traveling around the chieftains' households playing his new compositions. He was also reputed to have been as great with the whiskey bottle as he was on the harp; it's said that on his deathbed he asked for a cup of the stuff, and finding that he hadn't the strength to drink it, touched the cup with his lip, saying that two old friends shouldn't part without a kiss. The **Lough Rinn Estate** near Mohill, recently opened to the public, is a large expanse of woodland with a carefully nurtured conglomeration of unusual plants, shrubs, and trees. The mansion house is open for guided tours (11am, 11:30am, noon, 2pm, 3:30pm, 4pm, and 4:30pm), but there isn't much to really see. *Fitzpatrick's* pub is more entertaining, with sessions on Tuesday night.

North of Carrick

A couple of miles north of Carrick (#277 bus) is the county's namesake, **LEITRIM** village. It's a tiny one-street place with a lovely canal-side setting—best appreciated from the pub on the bank. Though its name translates as "the back of the old cow's ass," **DRUMSHANBO** (four miles north from Leitrim) would make a decent alternative base from which to see south Leitrim. It sits at the southern tip of Lough Allen, noted for having the best pike fishing in Europe. Every June the village holds a festival of music and dance—details from the **tourist office,** based at Mrs Mooney's **B&B** on the corner of the High Street and the Carrick road. You can **camp** for free in a field a little way down the Carrick road, near the heated swimming pool complex (Irish dancing in the *Teach Cheoil* Mon night in summer; music on other summer evenings). The vacation cottages on the opposite side of the lake from the pool have a good restaurant that's a bit less expensive than the high-quality *Highbank House* on the High Street. For cheaper eating there's a café out the Manorhamilton end of town. The pea-green, thatched *McManus* bar on the High Street has a music session every Thursday evening, but a much more interesting bar to drink in is *Conway's*, at the head of the Manorhamilton road. There are a couple of **buses** a day in the direction of Dublin, usually at 8am and 6pm (☎078-31174). **Bike rental** is available from the garage on Convent Street, going out in the Dowra direction, or from *McGrath's Cycle Shop*, opposite the tourist office. **Rowboats** can be rented from Mrs McGuire, who lives in the large house to the side of the vacation homes.

Neither bank of Lough Allen is particularly attractive, but the eastern route along the bottom of **Slieve Anierin** is the better bet, taking you up to the county border at DOWRA. Just before the village there's a rewarding climb up into the Iron Mountains (take right turn off by *John Ryan's* pub/grocery store on side of the road); a very rugged track for much of the way, it twists and turns to follow the course of the river that cuts between the rock faces.

To Ballinamore

The best move from Drumshanbo is to take the Ballinamore road into the array of lakes that attracts most of Leitrim's tourism. This route makes a pleasant trip by bike, as many of the lanes skirt the shores as they wind between the hills. Two of these hills have legendary names—**Sheemore** and **Sheebeag** (the "hill of the big fairies" and the "hill of the little fairies"; there's a well-known Irish set-dance by the same name). As with all such enchanted hills, this pair are supposed to open up on *Samain* (Hallowe'en), when their gods and goddesses roam the land.

Sheemore is a couple of miles before KESHCARRIGAN on the south side of Lough Scur; unfortunately it's not signposted, so you might have to question a few of the locals for directions. Topped by a cairn and a St Patrick's Cross, the hill commands the best view across Leitrim; the cairn is believed locally to be Finn Mac Cumaill's grave. On your way again along the south of Lough Scur you'll pass a dolmen by the roadside before reaching **Sheebeag**, which has a gorse-covered cairn but is less exciting than its bigger brother. To get there follow the road straight on rather than turning left into Keshcarrigan, and take a sharp right up the hill and continue for a mile or so.

There's nothing much doing in Keshcarrigan apart from some traditional music every Friday night in *McKeown's* bar. FENAGH has a few more bars, plus the ruins of a monastery and two churches founded in the seventh century by Saint Caillain. The key for the ruins is kept at the *Kealadaville* **B&B**, a hundred yards up the Mohill road.

It's not far from here to **BALLINAMORE**, which has a heritage and folk museum in the library building halfway down its main street. Highlight of the dull collection seems to be the "authentic detachable shirt collar worn by executed 1916 patriot Seán MacDiarmada"—and if you don't believe it there's a photograph of the man to prove it. For drinking and listening to a bit of music, try *Reynold's* on a Thursday night. *Caroline's Restaurant*, at the bottom of the main street, is a nice place to eat.

North Leitrim

Focal point of the mountainous area north of Lough Allen is **MANORHAMILTON**, lying in the saddle of five valleys. Manorhamilton was founded on top of a strategic plateau by Sir Frederick Hamilton, a Scots colonist, during the seventeenth century; his castle was destroyed in the 1650s, but the ruins can still be visited. Today it's a handsome crossroads town, but with little happening to drag you all the way up there.

However, the road over to **KILTYCLOGHER** makes quite an exhilarating scenic drive, but although the village is trim and pretty there's nothing that should detain you after you've seen the **Seán MacDiarmada** statue. He was born here, and executed in Dublin in 1916 for his part in the uprising. The route on up from here to Kinlough runs along the eight-mile western shore of **Lough Melvin**, whose only remotely picturesque spot is the paltry ruins of **McClancy's Castle**, standing on an islet a few yards from the northern end of the lake. It was here that the eight survivors from the three Spanish galleons wrecked off Streedagh Point finally found refuge.

KINLOUGH, near the tip of the lake, is a wholly undisturbed village, and has a surprisingly interesting little folk museum at the Manorhamilton end. Part of the museum is the old *McCurran's Bar* (key from the grocery store across the road), where a half-bottle of Guinness stands fermenting on the wooden bar counter, and a poteen still shaped like a diving bell stands by the wall. There's another more conventional room to the museum, with folk and historical knickknacks crammed into every available space; a newspaper cutting shows De Valera on his way to the Dail for the first session of the new Irish Free State.

TULLAGHAN, a few miles away, is a dreary resort on a dreary strip of coast.

travel details

Trains
From Sligo 3 daily to Collooney (10min); Ballymote (3; 20min); Boyle (3; 40min); Carrick-on-Shannon (3; 50min); Dublin (3; 3hr 20min).

Bus Éireann
From Sligo to Belfast (1 daily; 6hr); Galway (3 daily; 3–5hr).

Private Buses
Funtrek (☎01-730852) operates daily services **from Sligo**'s Wine St parking lot to Carrick-on-Shannon and Dublin.

CHAPTER TWELVE

MONAGHAN AND CAVAN

Fishermen apart, nobody comes to Monaghan or Cavan for a holiday. That's not to say there isn't some very enjoyable countryside—there's plenty—but it just doesn't compete with the grandeur of Sligo and Donegal, nor the expansive beauty of Fermanagh. These counties sit side by side as if one is a physical imprint of the other—Monaghan all small hills, Cavan all small lakes. County Monaghan is renowned for being *drumlin* country—rashes of rounded hills that diminish as you head west into Cavan where the land breaks up into a crazy pattern of tiny lakes. Both landscapes have their charms, both their practical difficulties. If you're walking or cycling in either county, a compass can be very useful—the terrain isn't inaccessible or dangerous, but there's such a network of winding, crisscrossed roads that you can very easily get lost. In Monaghan the *drumlins* all look similar, while the myriad lakes of Cavan enforce constant twists and turns. Bicyclists should also be aware that a lot of the minor roads are appallingly riddled with potholes, and dodging them slows you down considerably.

With County Donegal, Monaghan and Cavan share the peculiar identity of being historically part of **Ulster*** yet nowadays included in the Republic. Donegal's coastline links it with the West, but Monaghan and Cavan are far more involved with and affected by the North. The **border** counties of course shelter a lot of Republican activity for purely geographical reasons, but there's also a strong affinity between Cavan and Monaghan people (Protestant and Catholic) and their Ulster neighbors; until Partition, they shared a culture and a history. Cavan and Monaghan communities are intermittantly touched by the North's violence, and appreciate that they don't have to live it every day. Republicanism just south of the border can appear stronger than in the North; the aims here are clear, and people are not worn down by daily facing the realities of the conflict. It's no more appropriate to assert your opinions on Irish politics here than in the North—at the very least people find it intrusive. It's also advisable to steer clear of the border itself, which can be quite tricky; it twists and turns, and signposting is rarely better than minimal.

Although the border has sharpened political and social definitions, there is a sense in which it also shelters both of these counties. You'll probably be struck by the old-fashioned feel of the countryside; while slow, rural ways are as prevalent in other Irish counties, the sharp contrast with the industrializa-

---

*Confusingly, the name Ulster has come to be used to describe Northern Ireland. In fact, the ancient province of Ulster consisted of nine counties; at Partition, Monaghan, Cavan, and Donegal were severed from the six counties which now form the North.

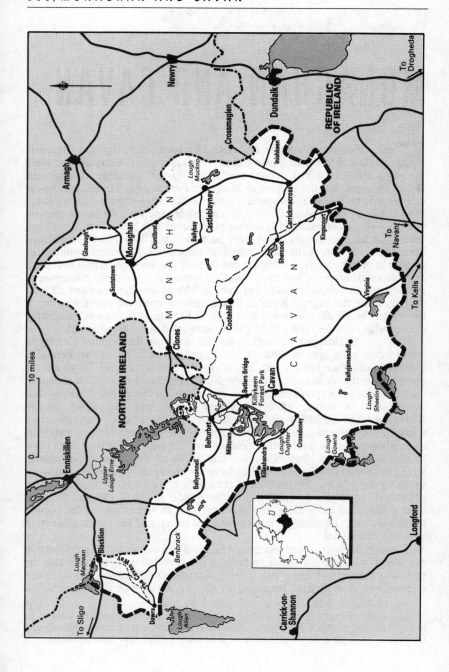

tion and British development over the border makes them more striking here. Uncertainty about the future and the possibility of violence has slowed development, leaving an unhurried rural ordinariness that constitutes much of these counties' appeal. They are not gaily painted for tourists, nor visibly quaint, and there's a dour Scottish severity in many of the villages, particularly in Monaghan—clear evidence of the Ulster Planters. But as you explore you'll find both counties have real charm, understated and quiet.

COUNTY CAVAN

There's little of historical interest left in **County Cavan**, and what interest there is often lies in the landscape itself. In former times the region was even more water-riddled, boggy, and forested than it is today. This complex of lake and bog was extremely difficult for foreign invaders to penetrate and control, and also made the land less desirable. Only the most durable relics have survived. There are plenty of **court cairn tombs** in the region, evidence of Neolithic peoples from as early as 6000 years ago, but they're hard to find unless you know what you're looking for. Similarly invisible are the lakes' *crannogs*—manmade islands built as early as the Stone Age, but more typically developed as secure settlements from the first century AD, and now merged with back in to the general landscape, indistinguishable from natural islands. **The Celts** had their principal pagan shrine at **Magh Sleacht** near present day Ballyconnell. Several Celtic stone idols bearing bold representations of the human head have been found in the lake areas of Cavan and Fermanagh, particularly potent pagan symbols. Some of them were found in circumstances suggesting that they were deliberately hidden in recent times to deny them their power, a sign of their continuing folkloric importance. Sadly, though, none of these idols can be seen in their original setting, and most now form part of the collections of the National Museum in Dublin or the Fermanagh County Museum at Enniskillen.

When **Saint Patrick** established his seat at Armagh, he also set up a monastery at Kilnavert. Rather than crudely asserting a new dogma, the proselytizing Christians allowed pagan and folkloric traditions to continue, mingling them with the new creed. The filtering through of the new faith was fairly rapid, but more brutal invaders found the area far harder to penetrate. The network of lakes and waterways proved difficult to negotiate, and foreign invaders arrived with neither knowledge of the terrain, nor the physical means needed for conquest. The **O'Reilly** family, who dominated Cavan from the beginning of recorded history to the seventeenth century, continually blocked Anglo-Norman attempts to take control, and this explains the lack of Norman developments in the region.

Despite Elizabeth I's attempts to divide and rule by creating the **County of Cavan** (more a piece of propaganda than a sign of real political strength) and playing one Irish barony off against another, it was only after the failure of the Irish cause at the Battle of Kinsale that Cavan received the stamp of foreign invaders. Ancient Gaelic ways were crushed by the Jacobite plantation and the county was divided up between English and Scottish settlers.

Every parish was to have a Protestant church, and the new town of Virginia was built in memory of Elizabeth. As usual, the best land was given to the English and Scottish newcomers, leaving the Irish population to face poverty and the loss of religious freedom.

The rebellion of 1641 was a direct result, and **Owen Roe O'Neill**, the Ulster Confederate leader based at Cavan, played an important part, defeating the British General Munro at Benburb to the north of the county in 1646. However, O'Neill failed to follow his victory through, and the Irish Confederates were eventually defeated. After O'Neill's death in 1649, Cromwell quickly took control of Cavan and the resulting confiscation of land and property from the Irish guaranteed the Protestant domination of the county.

Until Partition Cavan's subsequent history was much in line with the rest of Ulster. In the eighteenth and nineteenth centuries the linen and woollen industries ensured a measure of economic growth, though Cavan was always one of the poorer parts of the province because of the difficulties of the land; and the Famine of 1847 brought large-scale emigration. At **Partition**, Cavan was included in the Republic, thus retaining its Irishness; but it shared the fate of Monaghan and Donegal in being torn from its historic and cultural Ulster identity.

Getting Around Cavan: Places to Stay

Cavan town is very much the transportation hub of the county, and it's here you're likely to arrive. *Bus Éireann* (☎049-31353 for information) connects Cavan town with all major towns in the Republic and the North, leaving from Farnham Street, and **private buses** run to Dublin and Donegal. As for accommodation, the only **independent hostel** in the county is in Ballyconnell (see below) but there are plenty of **B&Bs** in Cavan town, Bailieborough, Belturbet, Cootehill, Killeshandra, Kingscourt, Lough Gowna and Virginia. As everywhere, people will usually let you **camp** in their fields if you ask, but if you want the amenities of a campground there's *Lakelands Caravan and Camping Park* at SHERCOCK (☎042-69206; open May 28–Aug 27; laundry facilities; £3) in the east of the county, and *Lough Ramor Caravan Park* at VIRGINIA in the south (☎049-47447; April–Sept; £2 per unit, 25p per person).

Cavan Town and Lough Oughter

The focus of scenic interest in County Cavan is the complex of tiny lakes which riddle the north of the county. They're known collectively as **Lough Oughter**, and form part of Upper Lough Erne. The land here is so fretted with water that its very fabric seems to be disintegrating. Contours are provided by very low, unassuming hills, while the waters are edged with reeds, spindly silver birch, and alder. Everything is on a small scale; there's little grandeur to the scenery, but the landscape has a subtle attraction nonetheless. Roads making their way through the labyrinthine network of lakes are quiet and empty. It makes little sense to head for a particular point in

Lough Oughter—it's hard to tell when you've got there anyway—and the best plan is probably just to enjoy the gentle confusion.

The county is renowned for its **fishing**, and a conservative tourism is growing which neither scars the land nor disturbs the peace. Forest parks have been developed, not to encourage families to bring the kids, but to give fishermen access into the heart of the lake complex. Everywhere the stillness is profound. The nicest of the little towns serving fishing visitors are Belturbet, Virginia, and Cavan town itself. BELTURBET sits prettily on a hill besides the river Erne, an angling and boating resort, while VIRGINIA is picturesquely situated beside Lough Ramar, and adds golf to these amenities. Both are straitlaced, well-kept towns. Five miles west of Belturbet in BALLYCONNELL, the county's one **independent hostel**, the friendly *Sandville House Hostel* (☎049-26297; March–Nov; £3.50), is well-placed just off the main R200 road to West Cavan and Sligo. Housed in a converted barn alongside a large Georgian house, the hostel is not heavily used because of its remoteness, but if you do find your way here you're liable to stay longer than planned. A good stop on your way west, it also offers a retreat *from* the West if the West Coast experience gets too much. To the southeast, there's also the pretty village of BUTLERSBRIDGE, with a notoriously enjoyable bar, the *Derra Garra Inn*: touristy, but serving good food.

CAVAN town grew up around an abbey, but nothing remains of this beyond its memory and an eighteenth-century tower beside the burial place of Owen Roe O'Neill. Today it's a pretty subdued place. It has two main streets: Main Street is the principal artery for shops and bars, while Farnham Street has an older character with some very nice stone Georgian houses, a Classical courthouse of warm sandstone, and a huge Catholic cathedral built in the Forties, that surprisingly succeeds in confirming status and a sense of place without being overbearing. For **bed and breakfast**, try Mrs McMahon's *New County* (38 Farnham Road; ☎049-31694; £10); or, ten minutes' walk out of town, Mrs P. Adams' *Shandra* (Golflinks Road, Lisdaran; ☎049-31183; £10). Other useful facilities include a **laundromat** (*Supaklene Services*, on Farnham Street), a **travel agent** (*McGinnity Ltd*; 2 Coleman Road; ☎049-31811), and a **tourist office** at Farnham Street (usually open June–mid-Sept, though currently under review; ☎049-31942). You can **rent bikes** at *O'Dwyer's Cycles* in Bridge Street (☎049-32939).

Around the County

Around three miles west of Cavan on the R198 to CROSSDONEY stands the modern Protestant Cathedral of **Kilmore**. The modern structure is of little interest, but set in the wall is an impressive Romanesque doorway, removed here from a monastery that stood on Trinity Island, three miles to the west in Lough Oughter. Its deep, chunky carving is superbly intricate, and repays detailed attention. Follow the narrow road that runs north from here to the hamlet of GARTHROTTEN, and you can enter **Killykeen Forest Park**. Here **Clough Oughter** is a thirteenth-century circular tower built on a *crannog*, the best of its kind in Ireland.

Alternatively from Crossdoney, you can follow the road round the west side of Lough Oughter, through KILLESHANDRA and MILLTOWN. In contrast to the dearth of viewable history in the county as a whole, Mrs Faris's *Pighouse Collection*, a **folk museum** at Corr House, CORNAFEAN (open anytime, but phone ahead to check she's in; ☎049-37248; adults £1, kids 50p), is a massive accumulation of miscellaneous remnants of the past. To get there, take the Killeshandra road from Crossdoney, bear left at the Arva signpost, then first right—it's difficult to reach without transportation. Three huge barns are full of dusty junk, only a small part of which (the section on domestic utensils and furniture) has so far been catalogued and labeled—the rest you rummage through and interpret for yourself. There's a vast and fascinating range of stuff which includes (for example) a fine collection of embroidered eighteenth-century waistcoats, Victorian and Edwardian evening gowns, samples of old lace, and a huge collection of porcelain cheese dishes.

Further on, just south of Milltown, you'll find **Drumlane Church** and **Round Tower**. A monastery was founded here by Saint M'Aodhog in the sixth century, and Augustinians from Kells took the place over in medieval times. The church itself is plain and roofless, but its setting beside a lake, and its size in such an intimate landscape, are impressive. The earliest parts of the building are thirteenth-century, but it was substantially altered in the fifteenth century, from when the carved heads outside the doorways and windows date. The round tower is eleventh-century, and of good, clean stonework.

West Cavan

To the northwest of Milltown and Killeshandra, **West Cavan** sticks out like a handle, tracing the line of the border. It's quite different from the rest of the county: wilder and higher, with peat-covered hills, granite boulders, and mountain streams. In this bleak inhospitability it has more in common with the wilds of Donegal than the more intimate Cavan lakeland. The **Cavan Way** is a signposted walk of seventeen miles that takes you through rugged terrain from DOWRA to BLACKLION, where it meets the southwestern end of the **Ulster Way**. Small maps of the route can be picked up in tourist offices. From the heights above Blacklion there are spectacular views over Lough MacNean and the Fermanagh lakeland, to the Sligo and Leitrim mountains in the west, and on a clear day to the heights of south Donegal. Along the route **Shannonpot** is the source of Ireland's mightiest river—the Shannon—and figures heavily in Irish myth, though it's little visited. Dowra and Blacklion are tiny and remote: the former high on the young Shannon before it fills Lough Allen, the first of many lakes, the latter a border-crossing point.

There are **bed and breakfasts** in Blacklion and Dowra, both unlikely to be oversubscribed, though it's best to phone ahead and check. In Blacklion try Christina McManus's *Benbrack House* (☎072-25) or *Loughmacneann House* (☎072-22), both on Main Street; in Dowra ask at the pub.

COUNTY MONAGHAN

Monaghan's countryside is first and foremost *drumlin* country. **Drumlins** are lumpy mounds of land left by retreating glaciers at the end of the Ice Age, and the exceptional number of these small hills packed together in County Monaghan serves as a very good example of what geology textbooks call "basket-of-eggs" topography—a reference to the land's appearance from on high. The result at ground level is that the soil is poor, and the land broken up into small units which are difficult and uneconomic to farm. The *drumlins* are grass-covered, and light hedgerows stitch their way across them, marking out the fields. Initially it's a charming scene, but it soon becomes repetitive; the pathways between *drumlins* are pretty enough, but once you're round or over one small hill the next is much the same. Little lakes provide occasional relief, and are excellent for fishing, but they're nowhere near as numerous as in Cavan.

The feel of this landscape has been captured in the poetry and prose of **Patrick Kavanagh**, rated by many as Ireland's finest poet after Yeats. He was born in Inishkeen in the south of the county, and his writing evokes the poor quality of peasant life—and something too of the monotony of the rural landscape.

Particularly in the north of the county, the terrain has led to an insane crisscrossing of lanes; a compass is a good idea, as is an awareness that all available maps are unreliable. It makes for delightful walking if you're not in too much of a hurry. In these hilly areas you can wander undisturbed for miles along the labyrinth of ancient tracks and lanes—though it is advisable to try and avoid the border. If you know what to look for you can seek out the sites of court tombs, forts, and cairns from the Bronze Age. Many of them, thanks to the underdevelopment of the land, have remained virtually untouched. The best megalithic sites in the region are the Lisnadarragh wedge-tomb, **Dun Dubh**, at TIRAVERA; and the **Tullyrain triple ring-fort** near SHANTONAGH.

But most of Monaghan's towns and villages have very clear origins in the seventeenth and eighteenth centuries. The influence of Scottish planters and English colonists is obvious in the number of Planters Gothic and Presbyterian churches, in the planned towns, and in the landscaped estates developed around conveniently picturesque lakes. Stark, stern architecture reflects the character of the hardworking and hard-driving settlers who came here determined to extract prosperity from farming, and from the linen industries which they introduced. Probably the most extreme examples of such discipline are the dour, austere stone cottages of GLASLOUGH, cold and orderly in the north of the county. Like Cavan, Monaghan's cultural identity is deeply rooted in her Ulster history.

Practically speaking, while you'll have no problems finding **B&Bs** in towns like Monaghan, Carrickmacross, and Castleblayney, decent **places to eat** are surprisingly hard to come by, especially in the evening, and you may find yourself eating fast food more often than you'd like.

Monaghan Town

You're most likely to find yourself in **MONAGHAN Town** while on your way to somewhere else. There's little here for the tourist, but the actual fabric of the place is quite interesting as you pass through. Monaghan town epitomizes what makes this county very definitely Ulster, and yet quite distinct from Cavan. The planning of seventeenth-century settlers, the prosperity of the eighteenth-century linen industry (largely the achievement of Scots Presbyterians), and the subsequent wealth and status of the town in the following century are all very much in evidence.

Three central squares are linked by a chain of lanes, a layout not, in fact, altogether typical of Plantation towns. At the center is the **Diamond**—the name given to all these Ulster "squares"—in the middle of which stands a grandiose Victorian drinking fountain, the kind of memorial strongly reminiscent of any nineteenth-century industrial British city, yet strangely out of place in rural Ireland. When it was placed here, the earlier seventeenth-century Scottish settlers cross, with its multifaceted sundial, was shifted to **Old Cross Square**, where it still stands. Alongside the Diamond is **Church Square**. Here a Classical courthouse, a solid Victorian bank and hotel, and a very pretty Regency Gothic church, large and spacious, stand together, conferring a strong sense of civic dignity. The town's importance for British imperialists is quite clear, and a large obelisk commemorates a colonel killed in the Crimean War. Everything about the place suggests a conscious attempt at permanency, its buildings placed with a view to posterity; even the rounded corners of the most mundane buildings and their boldly arched entries—both features unique to Monaghan—suggest strength and pride.

Beyond Church Square, at the top of Market Street, is a pretty, arched **Market House** built in 1792. A solid, graceful building of well-cut limestone, with finely detailed decoration of carved oak leaves and oak apples, this houses the **tourist office** (☎047-81122; usually June–Sept, though currently under review). In the opposite direction, Dublin Street leads down to Old Cross Square. At no. 10 stands the birthplace of Monaghan's most famous son, **Charles Gavan Duffy**—a nationalist who was instrumental in the founding of the Irish Tenant League. He was also the co-founder, along with Thomas Davis, of *The Nation*, a paper which was to disseminate politically sensitive ideas. Beyond, high on a hill out of town, **St Macartan's Catholic Church** commands views over the whole town and surrounding countryside. It's a Gothic Revival building of hard gray sandstone, completed in 1892; the spire is very high, and the interior, complete with an impressive hammer-beam roof, is spacious. As you stand on the steps looking out over the surrounding land you get a real feeling of its era—it's a most successful nineteenth-century statement of religious liberation and pride.

As well as being a busy commercial and administrative center, Monaghan looks after the county's vigorous and sometimes violent history at the award-winning **Monaghan County Museum** (Hill Street; Tues–Sat 11am–1pm and 2–5pm; free). This has a permanent collection of archaeological material, prehistoric antiquities, examples of traditional local crafts, domestic utensils, and paintings, prints and watercolors from the late eighteenth century to the present day. Recent acquisitions include textiles and banners, but the museum is most proud of the **Cross of Clogher**, a processional cross dating from around 1400. Contemporary art exhibitions are also held here. The **Heritage Centre** (Broad Road; Mon, Tues, Thurs and Fri 10am–noon and 2–4pm; Sat and Sun 2–4pm; £1) tells the story of the religious order of Saint Louis, with an intelligent display meticulously put together by one of the sisters; you're guided through it with a cassette recording.

Monaghan Practicalities

Bus Éireann (☎047-81621) link Monagahan with all major towns in the Republic and with Armagh, Belfast, Derry, Omagh and Strabane in the North. **Private buses** connect with Dublin (*P. J. McConnon*; ☎047-82020). For longer distance transportation, *O'Hanrahan Travel* (59 Dublin Street, ☎047-81832/81133) is the local agent for *Eurotrain*, *Slatteries*, and *Supabus*. The *Sinn Fein Advice Centre* on Dublin Street has an extensive collection of **Nationalist literature and music**—though its opening hours seem wildly erratic.

Decent **B&Bs** include *Ashleigh House* (37 Dublin Street; ☎047-81227; £9), *The Cedars* (Clones Road; ☎047-82783; closed Dec; £10), and *Swan Lake Hotel* (North Road; ☎047-81179; £12.30); there's no **campground**, but you should be able to find somewhere to pitch a tent if you ask at a farm out of town. None of the **places to eat** are particularly inspiring. The *Swan Lake Hotel* serves bar lunches daily (from £2.50) as does *The Courthouse Bar* in Church Square. The *Coffee Shop Restaurant* offers chicken, burgers and chips (Mon–Sat 9am–8:15pm, Sun 5–7:30pm) while the fast food at *Tommies Restaurant* (7 Glaslough Street; noon–3:30pm) includes steaks, roasts, grills, pizza and curry, to eat in or take out. *Genoa Restaurant and Ice-Cream Parlour* (61 Dublin St; Mon–Thurs until 8:30pm; Fri–Sun until 12:30am) has similar fare.

As far as **entertainment** goes, there's little beyond occasional music in bars. In Dublin Street *The Shamrock Bar* is rock- and pop-oriented, while *McKenna's* has local rock bands on Wednesday, country, folk, and ballads at weekends. There are a couple of local theater groups who are very active; if your visit happens to coincide with a local production it's well worth going to see them. In July there's also a fiddler's festival—**The Oriel Festival**.

The Rest of the County

Unless you're heading for the North, there are two main routes out of Monaghan: west to Clones, or south to Carrickmacross, the county's second town. On the latter route you'll pass first through **CASTLEBLANEY**, whose two proud broad streets hinge upon a fine Georgian courthouse at what was once the market square. Castleblaney was built by English colonists to serve the needs of a large estate, beautifully situated beside Monaghan's largest lake, **Lake Mucknor**, and this is still the town's finest asset. When the English picked their spot they knew what they were doing: it's a particularly attractive demesne of mixed woodlands and gentle slopes beside placid waters. The estate is now a forest park, with clearly signposted walks around beautiful grounds. *Lough Muckno Caravan and Camping Park* is a thoughtfully concealed **campground** amid the trees (May 1–Sept 11; £4 per unit, small tents £2.50; laundry facilities, showers, bottled gas, take-out foods; ☎042-45031) that attracts families and fishermen in search of peace and quiet. **B&Bs** include Mrs Fleming's *Lochbeg* (Corracloughan, just outside town; ☎042-40664; £9.50) and Mrs Coogan's *Hazelwood House* (Annahale, Dundalk Road; ☎042-46009; April–Oct; £9). For **food** there's *Joan's Pantry* (Mon–Fri), a delicatessen and café serving light, wholesome lunches, or a Chinese restaurant (upstairs over *Ronnie's* lounge bar; daily 5–11pm).

Carrickmacross

CARRICKMACROSS itself is the county's second most important town, boosted in the nineteenth century by a prosperous lace-making industry. The town has one broad main street; a Planters Gothic church stands at one end, a large Georgian house at the other. In between lies a bustling array of pubs, shops and Georgian houses. Just outside the town, landscaped parkland of sumptuous oaks and beeches surround **Lough Fea**. Farther out, some three miles down the Kingscourt Road, is the **Dún a Rí Forest Park** with more good wooded walks. There are plenty of **B&Bs** near the middle of Carrickmacross, up the Derry Road past the Texaco filling station: try Mrs Hanratty's *Cloughvalley House* (☎042-61246; £8.50); Mrs Martin's *Nocdale* (9 Ard Rois Avenue, Cloughvalley; ☎042-61608; £8.50); or the *Shirley Arms* (Main Street; ☎042-61209; £12.50). *M&S* **laundromat** is on Main Street (9am–6pm, Sat 9am–7pm, closed Sun and Wed).

Inishkeen

INISHKEEN, to the east of Carrickmacross, is the birthplace of **Patrick Kavanagh**, which is not in itself any very good reason to visit. There's a small plaque bearing some of his verse in the village and the house he lived in is well signposted—but you can't go in and it's an entirely uninteresting building. In a more distant past Inishkeen was the site of a sixth-century monastic center; scant remains of the abbey and a round tower survive. The **Folk Museum** (May–Sept Sun 3–6pm) deals with local history, folklife and the old Great Northern Railroad. For **entertainment**, Daniel McNello's *Kavanagh Hide Out* has country music sessions every weekend.

Clones

In quite the other direction from Monaghan, in the west of the county, **CLONES** (pronounced "Clo-nez") is a busy, friendly market town barely half a mile from the border. Situated on top of a hill, its streets give a good perspective over the surrounding countryside. The town as it appears today dates from 1601, when the English took it over and started to develop it. It's very obviously an Ulster town, with large Presbyterian and Methodist churches to rival the usual Catholic and Church of Ireland offerings. The solemn and impressive **St Tiernach's church** (Church of Ireland) gives out onto the fine Diamond, and there is some evidence of eighteenth-century prosperity in the town's handful of Georgian houses. There are also traces of

Clones' earlier identity, the most impressive being the weathered, deeply-carved **High Cross** which stands on the Diamond. Depicted on it are Adam and Eve, the sacrifice of Abraham, Daniel in the Lion's Den and, on the north side, the Adoration of the Magi, the Miracle of Cana, and the Miracle of the Loaves and Fishes. Though worn, there's still a strong impression of the richness of the carving. In the sixth century Saint Tiernach founded a monastery at Clones. It became an Augustinian **abbey** in the twelfth century, and the tumbled down traces of this can be seen in Abbey Street, along with those of a round tower. Just on the edge of town is an ancient *rath* (an enclosure used as a dwelling) of three concentric earthworks.

Nowadays, the town's chief claim to fame is as the home of **Barry McGuigan**, the former world-champion boxer. His supporters club is the *Diamond Hotel*, which also happens to be one of the best places for **bar food** in the county (Mon–Sat lunchtime and evening). There's excellent food too at the *Lennard Arms Hotel* (daily, anytime; it's also on the Diamond) which offers **B&B** from around £11; *Creighton's* in Fermanagh Street is the other option if you're looking for somewhere to stay (☎047-51284; £15).

travel details

Bus Éireann
From Cavan: to Belfast (2 daily; 3hr–4hr 40min) Dublin (3 daily; 2hr).
From Monaghan: to Belfast (3 daily; 1hr 40min) Dublin (6 daily; 2hr 15min).

Private buses
Funtrek (☎01-730852) runs a daily service **from Cavan**'s Main Street to Dublin.

Wharton's Bus (☎049-37114) runs a daily service **from Cavan**, outside the *Lakeland Hotel* (Mon–Sat 8am, Sun 7pm) for Dublin. Departs **from Dublin**, opposite the gates of the Rotunda Maternity Hospital, Parnell Square, for Cavan (Mon–Sat 5:45pm). Extra buses in both directions on Friday.

CHAPTER THIRTEEN

DONEGAL

Not many people would disagree with the assertion that **County Donegal** has the richest scenery in the whole country. Second only in size to Cork, it has a spectacular 200-mile coastline, an intoxicating run of headlands, promontories, and peninsulas that rises at **Slieve League** to the highest cliffs in Europe. Inland is a terrain of glens, rivers, and bogland hills, of which best-known parts are the **Glencolumbcille** Peninsula and around **Ardara** and **Glenties** in the southern part of the county. Well served with a string of hostels, the Glencolumbcille area attracts more visitors than any other, yet the landscape of northern Donegal is, if anything, even more satisfying, especially the **Rosguill** and **Inishowen** peninsulas, and the interior region sometimes called the **Donegal Highlands**—around **Errigal** Mountain, **Lough Beagh**, and **Lake Gartan**. Other noteworthy areas are the **Rosses** and **Bloody Foreland**, which are reminiscent of the more barren stretches of Connemara and make up the strongest *Gaeltacht* districts in the county. The only piece of Donegal not worth spending some time in is the eastern half of the county, which shares more low-lying fertile ground with Counties Derry and Tyrone.

The county's original name was *Tír Conaill*, which translates as "the land of Conal," one of the twelve sons of Niall of the Nine Hostages. Subsequent to the "**Flight of the Earls**" in the early seventeenth century the British changed the name to that of their main garrison *Dún na nGall*, "the fort of the foreigner," which has a certain irony, because Donegal always eluded the grip of British power, mainly due to its wild and untillable terrain. In 1923, at the time of the partition, the Protestant leader **Carson** let it remain with the Republic, reasoning that its Catholic population would probably have voted the county and with it the whole of the North back into the Republic at a later stage. Hence the peculiarity of its being the most northerly piece of the island, yet belonging to the South, to which it's attached by just a thread of land.

Bundoran and the Road to Donegal Town

BUNDORAN (*bun dobhráin*, mouth of the Doran River) is one of Ireland's liveliest seaside resorts, busy day and night with mainly Northern Irish vacationers and courting couples strolling around the amusement arcades, souvenir shops, and pubs. The town center is concentrated into a mile of main street with the tiny river and bridge separating the lifeless western part of town (known as the West End) from the Catholic East End with its pubs, B&Bs, eating places, and golf course. As an introduction to the county of

Donegal it's entirely misrepresentative, and unless you really want to seek out a boisterous vacation atmosphere Bundoran is probably best viewed from the window of a bus.

If you do stop, the chief attraction is a lovely, golden-sand beach known as **Tullan Strand**, a bracing stroll along the coastal promenade away from the northern end of the town beach. The walk takes in rock formations known as the **Fairy Bridge** and the **Puffing Hole**, with the Atlantic thundering below and appetizing views across to the much more rewarding Glencolumbcille Peninsula. Along with the beach at Rossnowlagh, Tullan Strand is reckoned among the most exciting surfing spots in the world, which also makes them some of the most dangerous for swimming.

Bundoran Practicalities

The cheapest **place to stay** in Bundoran is the basic *Homefield Holiday Hostel* (☎072-41288; £3.50; large kitchen, lounge and washing machine); to get there take a right turn at the church just before the bridge in the West End. **B&Bs** are plentiful along the main street—try for example *Atlantic View* (West End; ☎072-41403) or *Kieran House* (East End; ☎072-41345). For **eating** the *Deverish Restaurant* (north side of main street) has a varied and reasonably priced variety of dishes, or the *Angler's Restaurant* offers a three-course meal for less than £5. More upmarket but still not overly expensive is the *Fitzgerald Hotel* (just after the bridge) with a tourist menu at £7.50. Most **pubs** in Bundoran are pretty ordinary, and permanently crowded with vacationers in season. *O'Neills* (on the left side past the bridge) is the exception: loud in its Republican sympathies with a jukebox playing only rebel songs and a bar-counter full of Republican literature for sale. **Bicycles** can be rented in *Michael Goodwin's* shop in the West End.

Ballyshannon

BALLYSHANNON, four miles on at the mouth of the River Erne, more genuinely marks the beginning of County Donegal, though it too is quickly passed through by most tourists who are eager for the scenic splendour farther north. In fact it deserves a quick look, and at the time of the **Music Festival** (first weekend in August, a legal holiday) you shouldn't miss it on any account. This is one of the most popular festivals of traditional music in Ireland, with a mix of the biggest names and unknown talents: if you want a room you'll need to reserve in advance, although if you turn up unannounced a floor will always be found for yourself and your sleeping bag.

The town stands a few hundred yards upstream from a ford, at the point where the river's fresh water begins to mix with that of the ocean. All the interest lies up the steep, northern slope, and is easily combined in a single, straightforward stroll. The main arteries here form a wishbone, and halfway up the left-hand branch, just left off the road and past an overbearing Masonic Lodge, is the graveyard where the poet **William Allingham** (1824–89) lies; his grave is a white marble slab by the left side of St Anne's church. Allingham was born in Ballyshannon and, like T. S. Eliot, began work in a

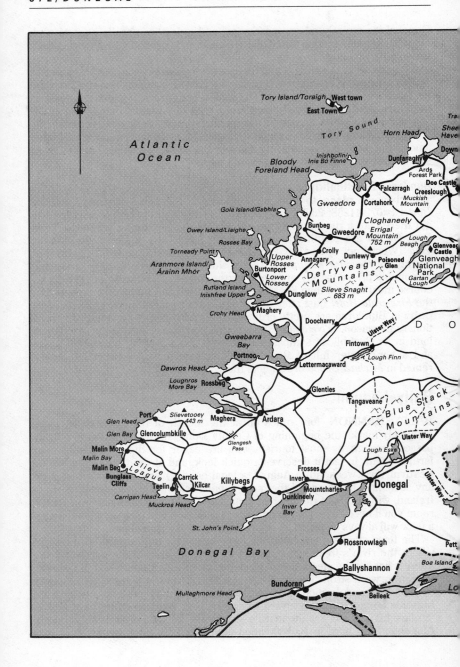

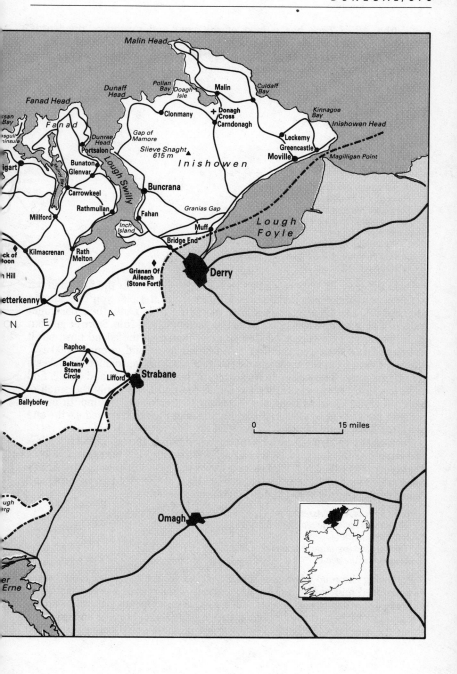

Malin Head

Dunaff
Head
Pollan
Bay
Doagh
Isle
Malin
Culdaff
Bay

Fanad Head

Clonmany
Donagh
Cross
Carndonagh

Kinnagoe
Bay
Inishowen Head

Gap of
Mamore

Leckemy

Greencastle

Fanad

Dunree
Head
Portsalon

Slieve Snaght
615 m

Inishowen

Moville

Magilligan Point

Bunaton
Glenvar

Carrowkeel

Buncrana

igart

Rathmullan

Fahan

Granias Gap

Lough
Foyle

Millford

Inch
Island

Muff

Kilmacrenan
Rath
Melton

Bridge End

ck of
oon
Hill

Grianan Of
Aileach
(Stone Fort)

Derry

etterkenny

N E G A L

Raphoe

Beltany
Stone
Circle

Lifford

Strabane

Ballybofey

0   15 miles

ugh
erg

Omagh

er
Erne

bank (the *Allied Irish* has a bust of the poet and preserves the words scratched by him on a windowpane). He later become a poet of national significance—his verse, although usually very light in tenor, is uniquely sonorous in its descriptive lilts and rhythms:

Up the airy mountain
Down the rushy glen,
We dare not go a'hunting
For fear of little men
Wee folk, good folk,
Trooping all together,
Green Jacket, red cap,
And white owl's feather

By the craggy hillside,
Through the mosses bare,
They have planted thorn trees
For the pleasure here and there;
Is any man so daring
To dig one up in spite,
he shall find the thornies set
In his bed at night.

From the graveyard there's a fine view looking down over the town and out to the surrounding hills north and south. Down at the pier you can see the backs of the tall, old warehouses lined along the river bank, their basement walls dripping with seaweed, and also the ancient isle of **Inis Saimer** just out in the river. There's only a wooden summer-house on the island now, but it claims to have sheltered the first colonization in Ireland, around 3500 BC, offering safety from the ferocious beasts that would have roamed the forests across the way. The water here seems to teem with fish and you'll find anglers still trying to catch them well into the night, with only the smell of bakery behind them as company. Looking farther out to the mouth of the estuary, the view also takes in the white dunes of FINNER, nowadays the site of a large Irish Army camp.

Back on the road, a left turn by the thatched pub at the top of the hill takes you out along the Rossnowlagh road, where a second left turn (marked by a fingerpost sign, "Fishing") takes you down to the scant remains of **Abbey Assaroe**. Founded by the Cistercians in 1184, it's pretty barren now, and Allingham's hundred-year-old description remains apt:

Grey, gray is Abbey Asseroe.
The carven stones lie scattered in
briar and nettlebed
The only feet are those that come
at burial of the dead.

Following the road down past the abbey and around to the left, you'll come to a restored mill beside a lively little stream. This makes a pretty picture of millrace and rotating cog wheels, but there's a less obvious natural beauty to be found if you pass through the log gate next to the old bridge and go on up along the stream's left bank. Within a few minutes you'll come across two man-made **caves**. One is a small grotto known as the Catsby; the other (now around 30 yards deep) is said to have once reached all the way under the abbey and run for two miles towards Rossnowlagh. The grotto was once a popular site for Penal Masses that had to be held secretively during the enforcement of the Penal Laws during the eighteenth century—and you'll find in the Rossnowlagh museum the carved stone known as the Monk's Head that once sat above the entrance.

Back in the mill area, head back up the hill for a few yards and watch out on the left for a little track, beginning with a stone stile beside a bungalow, that runs down to the shore of the bay. Saint Patrick is said to have once stepped ashore here, and today there are several rusted metal crosses perched on small stony outcrops and a tree covered in tattered ribbon mementos. It goes without saying that there's a natural well that sprung up at the spot where the saint's foot touched the shore; you'll find it down by the furthest cross. Bless yourself with its water three times and your prayer for a cure will be answered.

Ballyshannon Practicalities

There are plenty of **B&Bs** in and around Ballyshannon, most of them on or easily visible from the main road. The two cheapest **places to stay** are a small kitchen-equipped hostel-chalet opposite *The Thatch Pub* on Bishop Street (£4 per person, 2 single beds and 1 sofa bed, no sheets supplied; call at *La Verna* next door for the key), and at *Duffy's Hostel* on the Donegal Road, on the corner with Cluainbarron Road (☎072-51535; £4; some bikes for rent). **Restaurants** lie mainly on the right-hand road, where there are several reasonably priced options, or for a bit more style try *Danby House*, a few hundred yards out the Rossnowlagh road.

As well as its August music **festival**, Ballyshannon has a number of other festivities worth looking out for. There's a **drama festival** of mainly Irish plays in early June; the **Allingham Festival For Writers** over a weekend at the beginning of October; and traditional **harvest fair** celebrations around the middle of September, a rural affair with crowds from the surrounding countryside. The rest of the time you can fill your evenings at the *Abbey* **movie theater**, at the north end of town by the Donegal road (every night except Friday, when there's bingo); there are Monday-night Irish **dance classes** in the Market yard if you want to learn a few steps; and Gaelic soccer every other Sunday. At nearby BALINTRA there's horse-racing in the open fields. The best **pub** in town is *Sean Og's*, with **traditional music** every Wednesday night and rock on Saturday. The **bus** depot is down at the bridge: six departures a day to Bundoran, three to Derry, four to Donegal, one or more to Rossnowlagh, and a couple a day to Sligo and Dublin.

Rossnowlagh

ROSSNOWLAGH (translates as "the heavenly cove"), on the coast a short detour off the main Donegal road, has a magnificent long stretch of beach raked by Atlantic surf and, to the south, good cliffs for walks. There's a waterskiing, surfing, and canoeing club beside the *Sand House Hotel*, but unfortunately it's private, although one of the many surfing buffs will probably be able to help you out with equipment or at least advise where else to get your hands on it. The **Franciscan Friary** nearby has a captivating one-room museum (daily 10am–6pm) crammed with Stone-Age flints, Bronze-Age dagger blades, penal crosses, pistols, and other local miscellany. This includes a lovely set of uillean pipes with green felt bag and very handsome regulators, a fiddle that belonged to the great piper Turlough MacSuibhne, and a seventeenth-century Flemish painting on glass (*The Christ of Pity*) used as a devotion plate. A mile north of Rossnowlagh towards BALLINTRA (itself an unappealing place) lies **Glasbolie Fort**, a huge earthen rampart twenty feet high and nearly 900 feet round. It's said to have been the burial place of a sixth-century High King of Ireland.

Donegal Town

DONEGAL TOWN has surprisingly little to offer. It's not even the county capital (which is Letterkenny) and the lasting impression is one of traffic jammed around the busy (triangular) **Diamond** at the center, the old market place. Just about the only thing to see in town is the well-preserved shell of **Donegal Castle** (c.1610; Tírchonaill St. by the Diamond and overlooking the River Eask), a fine example of Jacobean architecture. Built by Sir Basil Brooke in the early seventeenth century, it combines strong defense with domestic grace—note the mullions, arches, gables, and no fewer than fourteen fireplaces, over the grandest of which are carved the escutcheons of Brooke and his wife's family, the Leicesters. The castle tower on the right (topped by Brooke with a Barbizan turret) as you enter was originally a stronghold of the O'Donnells, who ruled Donegal between the thirteenth and sixteenth centuries before fleeing to Spain around 1600. It was then transformed by Brooke (also responsible for the design of the town) who added the mansion to the left where the kitchens and bakery would have been found on the ground floor, with living quarters on the floor above.

On the Diamond stands an obelisk commemorating the compilers of the famed **Annals of the Four Masters**. The *Annals* were put together in an abbey on the coast close to Bundoran and testify to years of research which collected all known Irish documents into a history of the land beginning in 2958 BC and ending at the time of writing, AD 1616. The first entry dates back forty years before the biblical Flood, and relates to a visit of Noah's granddaughter to Ireland.

Down at the quay a French anchor is displayed, probably dating from the time when French troops were being ferried across to aid Wolfe Tone's rebellion in 1798. On the left bank of the River Eske not far from here stand the few ruined remains of **Donegal Friary**, while on the opposite bank a woodland path known as the **Lovers Walk** runs out alongside the bay with a nice view onto its many sandy islets and stony shoreline. The only real reason to stay long in Donegal town, though, is to explore the surrounding countryside, especially in the direction of the **Blue Stack Mountains** which rise at the northern end of **Lough Eske** (see next page).

Practicalities

One advantage of staying here is that you've plenty of choice. There are literally dozens of **B&Bs** scattered around the town, but many of them are very small, so to avoid a lot of walking it's simplest to call at the **tourist office** on the Quay (Mon–Sat 10am–1pm and 2–6pm; ☎073-21148; also does money exchange). A couple of the larger ones to try if you arrive outside working hours are *Arranmore House* (Coast Road; ☎073-21242) and *Windermere* (Quay Street; ☎073-21323). There are also two **hostels**, the independent *Peter Feely's* (Bridge End; ☎073-22030; £4; cramped and often crowded, but jovial atmosphere) and the *An Óige Ball Hill Hostel*, about three miles out in a former coastguard station on the north side of Donegal Bay (Grade A; ☎073-21174). Again this tends to be busy, but it's right on the shore (swimming is safer at a second beach twenty minutes' walk away), you can **camp**, and you can rent horses nearby (contact Anne Carney, on the Ball Hill road; £6 an hour; pony-trekking for beginners).

Eating places are plentiful: there's excellent fast food at *Southern Dixie* opposite the tourist office (11:30am–1:30pm, until 3am on Fri and Sat); *Talk of the Town* (on the Derry road opposite the cathedral) has very good-value lunch specials; the *Atlantic Cafe* (town end of Derry road) is also good for a substantial cheap meal; or for something light and very cheap try *McGrory's Snack Bar* (Castle St.), handy if you're waiting for a bus. The *Foodland Supermarket* (by which the buses congregate on the Diamond) has a great selection of cheeses, meat, and fruit—the last such stock you'll probably find in the county. As for **pubs**, they're as ubiquitous as ever, although none seem to offer much in the way of music. The *Old Castle Bar*, next to the castle, is fine for a quiet drink. The *Abbey Hotel* in the Diamond is the only contender for entertainment, with a **disco** and dance on Sunday night (10:30pm–2am; £4; sometimes on Friday too in the summer), and **Irish nights** (not for the purist) from Monday to Wednesday in July and August. In LAGHY, three miles south on the Sligo road, *Carlin's* pub has old-time dancing on Tuesday, and Irish nights in summer.

Buses stop outside the *Foodland* on the Diamond, with the timetables in the office behind the newsvendor (where luggage can also be left). The *Apollo Laundromat* (Mon–Sat 9am–6pm) is on Upper Main Street just past the cathedral. **Bikes** and **fishing tackle** can be rented from *O'Doherty's* (☎073-21119; Main St.), which is also a useful stop for supplementary information about the region. The owner is very knowledgeable and also has photocopied local maps for sale (10p) marking out all the interesting sights in the surrounding countryside and also the best fishing spots in the south Donegal area; **fishing permits** are also issued here.

If you're after souvenirs, or simply a way to fill a wet afternoon, then it might be worth heading out to the **Craft Village**, three-quarters of a mile from town on the Sligo road. Based here is a small group of young craft businesses, some of whose work is worth a look.

Inland from Donegal: Lough Derg, Lough Eske, and the Blue Stack Mountains

Southeast of Donegal town, the corner of the county tucked into a fold in the border is replete with little lakes well stocked for fishing. The largest of these, **Lough Derg** (the red lake), is the most often visited; in the middle of this lake is a rocky islet known as **Station Island**. The island has long served Europe as one of the most demanding focuses of pilgrimage and retreat for those Catholic believers who feel in the need of rigor and solitude to recharge their faith. Today it still thrives in this role (especially June to August) and the island cannot be visited for any other reason—though some casual travelers and non-believers do get some sort of stimulation out of undergoing this ancient ceremony, lasting a minimum of three days. Participants go without sleep or food (bar black tea and toast) and walk bare foot over rocks, praying at selected points. (There is one comparatively luxurious dispensation where you're allowed to boil the water of the lake and sweeten it with sugar if you're so pushed to do so.) In the Northern Irish poet Seamus Heaney's book, *Station Island*, a number of poems deal with the mystique surrounding this ritual. To get there you have to approach by the L84 from PETTIGO or a #115/289 bus from Ballyshannon should drop you nearby.

Lough Eske

Lough Eske (whose name means the Lake of the Fish) lies less than five miles upriver from Donegal, with the Blue Stack Mountains rising behind. It's no longer a particularly great fishing spot, though it is known as a place to catch char, a nine-inch-long species of the salmon family. They lurk in the depths at the center of the lake, moving out to the shallower edges around late October where they can easily be caught using worms. The sandy banks of the River Eske are also known for oysters—some of which are reputed to contain pearls.

The best way to get to this area of soft beauty, especially if you're bicycling, is to take the minor road which runs north of the river (from the town turn off Killybeg's road a little way above the hostel), though you can also take the main Derry road (the N15) and turn off by the B&B *Naomh Aengus*. Either route will bring you to a forgotten and forested estate at the southern end of the lake with the ruins of one of the Brooke family's old fortified houses (1751) at its center. The estate is now owned by the Forestry Commission but is relaxed about visits from the public. Circling the lake clockwise from here, you'll pass the western gate of the estate and then a farmyard; a hundred yards or so farther on look out for a gap in the hedge on the left where you'll find hidden a massive cauldron nearly six feet high and six feet in diameter. This is a **Famine Pot**, manufactured in Britain and shipped over by English landlords. It would be filled with Indian meal (a substitute corn-based porridge) and placed in a field where local people would come during the Famine and fill their own smaller pots to take home.

The Blue Stacks

Carrying on up the western road shore you'll reach the point where the river flows in at the lough's northern tip. Nearby a dirt road runs off to the left to take you into the **Blue Stack Mountains**. At the top of the pathway that leads on from the track, there's a very fine waterfall from where, if you want to continue, the **Ulster Way** leads by Lough Belshade (*bél seád*, the lake with the jewel mouth). If you're intending to tramp around the mountain range it's best to keep to the folds of the hills, for there are many marshy patches on lower ground; be prepared for patches of mist to descend during bad weather. If you're only making a day-trek of it then the photocopied maps from *O'Doherty's* are good enough for bringing you back safely if you lose your sense of direction; there's hardly any danger in the area apart from that of being caught by the descending mist. For longer and more intense trekking inquire at *O'Clery's Bookshop* in town about Ordnance Survey maps of the area.

Towards Glencolumbcille

The most appealing route on from Donegal town is the one which follows the north shore of the bay all the way out to Glencolumbcille, near the point. The first turning off this road will lead you down to **Holmes beach** and *Ball Hill* hostel. **MOUNTCHARLES**, the first place of any size on the main road, has little to offer beyond the atmospheric *Cellar Club* in the basement of the *Seamount Hotel*. There's good jazz and sometimes folk here every Thursday (£1.50, which includes food)—well worth an evening. **FROSSES**, a mile or so inland off the road between Mountcharles and Inver, is a pleasant, tiny village that has traditional music every second Saturday of the month in *Frosses Hall* (open session; listen out for the singer Rita Gallagher; begins 9pm; £1). The cemetery here has the graves of two of Ireland's famous literary figures: the novelist Seamus MacManus and his wife, the very underrated poet Eithne Carberry.

The tiny hamlet of **INVER** and its small strand, just a few hundred yards off the road, is worthwhile scenically and also to have a drink (or hear traditional music on Wed, Fri and Sun) in the *Rising Sun* pub. Inside, this has a ceiling in the shape of the hull of a boat, and stone shelves for the spirit bottles; it's also the birthplace of Thomas Nesbitt, inventor of the harpoon gun. At **DUNKINEELY** another less worthwhile detour from the main road takes you down a long, narrow promontory to **St John's Point**, where a crumbling castle stands at the tip. As you head out, there are great views over Donegal Bay, especially back towards the narrow entry of Killybegs Bay, with **Rotton Island** at its mouth. A little farther on from Dunkineely, approaching **BRUCKLESS**, you'll spot a magical little lagoon staked out with with poles for raising clams. Look out for a "handknit" sign at the top of a track that will lead you down to a dwelling where you can buy oysters (about £4 a dozen) and mussels (£1 a kilo). On the other side of the lagoon you can see an eighteenth-century Georgian house, which now offers stylish and not too expensive **B&B** (*Bruckless House*; ☎073-37071).

Killybegs

Shortly beyond Bruckless the road runs away from the bay, and there's a right turn which cuts off the peninsula, heading directly for Ardara. If you stick to the coast road, however, you'll round Killybegs Bay and arrive in the most successful fishing port in the country, **KILLYBEGS**, where tons of top-quality stuff are hauled onto the quaysides daily. This marks the halfway point to Glencolumbcille, and also the point where the scenic interest changes dramatically for the better. The mile-long approach road around the bay is idyllic and the town itself is perched on a slope, its gleaming white-washed buildings huddled around cramped narrow streets.

In summer the place is abuzz with traffic, mostly heading down to the quay, where you can purchase the fish in the early evening. A huge **deep-sea fishing festival** takes place here during the first three weeks in August. Picturesque though Killybegs is, it isn't exactly overflowing with interest, and most of the pubs are aimed squarely at working fishermen; the only entertainment is a dull closed session on Wednesday in the *Lone Star* pub, and sessions Thursday to Sunday 10pm to 1am at *Hughies*, both on the road out to Kilcar.

If you're staying in the town it's worth calling at the church at the top of the hill for a glimpse of the **McSweeney tombstone**, covered in Celtic carving. The cross standing on the hillock nearby is an ugly specimen that stands to remind one of ugly times, the penal days. As for **accommodation**, B&Bs are plentiful, or you could try the excellent *Hollybush Hostel*, one mile before Killybegs on the main road (☎073-31118; £3.50). The adjoining pub—favored by local farmers and fishermen—has open sessions every Sunday and sometimes Friday and Saturday during the summer. The hostel owner also rents out bicycles and fishing tackle, and can arrange boat rental for sea-fishing (£80 per day, all tackle supplied; up to 10 people per boat). *McGeehan's* **buses** leave the Pier Bar for Ardara and Dublin at 8:10am and for Glencolumbcille at 10:25pm.

Carrick, Teelin, and the Slieve League

The road on to **KILCAR** divides just after the *Blue Haven Restaurant* (old-time Irish evening on Thurs), a few miles out of Killybegs, and once again it's best to follow the coast, with fine views all the way. In Kilcar itself look out for *Piper's Restaurant Pub* which has a *comhaltas* every Wednesday and occasionally other cultural entertainments. *McGeehan's* **buses** leave outside *John Joe's* bar at 7:50am for Dublin via Killybegs and Ardara, and for Glencolumbcille at 10:50pm.

Between Kilcar and **CARRICK**, a little over a mile away, you'll come upon one of the jolliest independent hostels in the country—*Derrylahan Hostel* (☎073-38079; £3.50; camping available). This is an ideal base for exploring the elementally beautiful countryside around Carrick, especially Teelin Bay and the awesome **Slieve League cliffs** to the west. In Carrick itself the *Slieve League* **pub** is a must, its shelves piled with the largest variety of whiskies you'll ever come across—*Middleton, Redbreast, Chinese, Hewitt's* triple-distilled single Scottish lowland malt, *Glenfiddich*, etc—served by a loquacious

Pioneer (the name given to a religious abstainer from drink), Paddy Carr. The **traditional music festival** that the pub organizes over the last weekend in October is one of the more popular and successful in the region.

The road to **TEELIN** (*tigh linn*, house of the flowing tide) follows the west bank of the River Owenee, whose rapids and pools are good for fishing. The village is Gaelic-speaking and rich in folklore, which has been recorded over the last half-century by Seán O'hEochaidh, Donegal's great folklorist. The best pub in town is the *Rusty Mackerel*, at the entrance to the strip of village buildings—it's easily recognised by its garish color and mural painting of one of its old fisherman regulars.

There are two routes up to the ridge of **Slieve League** (*sliabh leic*, mountain of flagstones): a less-used back way (follow the homemade fingerpost pointing to *Baile Mór* just before you come into Teelin) and the road route that follows the signs out of the village to BUNGLASS (*bunglas*, the end of the green) which turns out to be exactly what it says, the end of the grass a thousand feet above a sheer drop. Both routes are walkable and very enjoyable: the former looking up continually at the ridge known as the "One Man's Path", on which walkers seem the size of pins, and the frontal approach swinging you up and around in the most spectacular way to one of the most thrilling cliff scenes in the world, the **Amharc Mór** (great view). The sea moves so far below it seems like a film that has lost its soundtrack, and the 2000-foot high face of Slieve League glows with mineral deposits in tones of amber, white, and red. It is said that on a good day it is possible to see one third of Ireland from the summit.

If you want to make a full day of it, you can follow "One Man's Path" onto "Old Man's Path" (simply because it's a few inches wider) over the crest of the mountain, then bound down the heather-tufted western slope and make your way across towards the verdant headland of **MALINBEG**, where there's a paradisical, crescent-shaped strand enclosed by a tight rocky inlet. The path is accurately named. In places it's only a few feet wide, and in wet or windy weather it can be extremely hazardous. On a fine day, though, it's a spectacular—if terrifying—traverse. Malinbeg itself is a village of white bungalows, with the land around ordered into long narrow strips. Three miles offshore lies **Rathlin O'Birne island**, a place with many folklore associations: there are occasional boats across, but nothing to see beyond some early Christian stone relics and a ruined coastguard station.

Beyond Malinbeg it's relatively easy to extend your walk through MALINMORE (the large *Glenbay* hotel serves snacks) onto Glencolumbcille. The whole distance from Teelin can be comfortably completed in six hours.

Glencolumbcille

Approaching **GLENCOLUMBCILLE** (the Glen of St Columbcille) by road you cross a landscape of desolate upland moor, its oily-black turf banks stitched into patches of heather and grass, where not even sheep seem able to survive. After this, the rich, verdant beauty of the Glen (as it's invariably known) comes as a welcome shock. Less than forty years ago this area was on its last legs, a typical example of rural depopulation. Its new lease on life is owed to the former parish priest, Father James MacDyer, who introduced a series of collective enterprises—in knitting, agriculture, and tourism—that are sending goods out of the valley and bringing people (visitors and new residents) in.

Development has done nothing to diminish the natural beauty of the place however. Its central buildings are painted up in radiant colors—the village church in lavender, a whitewashed semidetached housing project for the newlyweds, one old pub in submarine yellow and another in a Mediterranean sky-blue—and for visitors there's the beautifully positioned *Dooey Hostel* above the fine shingle strand at the mouth of the valley (☎073-30130; camping). To walk there, keep on the village road as far as the Folk Village (see below) and then take a path up to the left; in wet weather the longer route, by road, may be easier.

From behind the hostel, cliff-walks steer off around the south side of the bay above a series of jagged drops. Rising from the opposite end of the valley mouth, the promontory of **Glen Head** is surmounted by a martello tower. On the way out you pass the ruins of **St Columbcille's Church**, with its "resting slab" where Saint Columba would lie down exhausted from prayer. (To clear up the confusion, Columba and Columbcille/Colmcille are the same person—the latter is the name by which he was known after his conversion, and means "the dove of the church.") North across this headland you can climb and descend again to the forgotten little cove of PORT a few miles away. Absolutely nothing happens here, though Dylan Thomas once stayed, renting a cottage for several weeks and then disappearing early one morning without paying.

Glencolumbcille village is widely known as a place of pilgrimage, a status it's held since the seventh century AD, in consequence of the time Saint Columba spent in the valley. Every June 9 at midnight the locals commence a three-hour, barefoot itinerary of the cross-inscribed slabs that stud the valley basin, finishing up with mass at 3am in the small church.

The **Folk Village** next to the beach usually has tourists tripping over one another on the strictly guided tours (Easter–Sept Mon–Sat 10am–8pm, Sun noon–3pm; £1.50). There's free access to the **National School** replica, which has a display of informative photographs and research projects, and a section on the American painter Rockwell Kent, who painted marvelous canvases of the area's landscapes. Also open at no charge is the **Sheebeen** house, where you can try a taster of seaweed wine (11 percent with a smashing bouquet) or other concoctions such as honey, fuchsia, or elderberry, and then buy a bottle—you can also pick up some whisky marmalade while you're there.

The site's tea house does cheapish food, and sells watercolors as a sideline. Another place to **eat** in the village is the *Lace House Restaurant* on the main street above the tourist office (☎073-30116), with freshly baked home-style bread and evening meals. In summer, one of the nearby pastiche vacation cottages does **B&B**; others are available for weekly rental. **Buses** for Donegal Town leave from *Biddy's Bar* at 7:30am (*McGeehan's*) and 8:25am (*Bus Éireann*), with additional *McGeehan's* services 2.50pm on Friday and 3pm Sunday.

Maghera and Ardara

Leaving Glencolumbcille you can either retrace your steps along the coast or take the road through the heart of the peninsula towards Ardara. This takes in the dramatic **Glengesh Pass** (*gleann géis*, the glen of the swans), winding down through wild but fertile valley land. Just before reaching Ardara a road to the left runs along the northern edge of the peninsula for five and a half miles to **MAGHERA**, with narrow **Loughross Beg Bay** on one side and steep mountains rising from the road on the other. A mile before Maghera you'll pass the transfixing **Essaranka Waterfall**, and Maghera itself (tea house in the village) is an entrancingly remote place, backed by an exceedingly beautiful glen and fronted by a strand that runs along to an intriguing series of caves. One of the larger caves is said to have concealed a hundred people taking refuge from Cromwell's troops; their light was spotted from across the strand and all except one (who hid on a high shelf) were massacred. Some of the caves are only accessible at low tide and you'll need a flashlight. Behind the village a tiny road runs up into the glen, a former hideout of poteen smugglers.

ARDARA is a pretty big town by Donegal standards, and also one of the best places to buy **Aran sweaters**, sometimes at half the price you'll find farther south. *Molloy's Tweed Factory* at the southern end of town is the biggest outlet, but all the stores are well stocked with hand-loomed knitwear and tweeds. It's also a great place for **pubs**, dozens of which seem to be crammed into its L-shaped main street. For a quiet drink try the ancient *P. S. MacGiola Dé* to the south or the *Corner House* bar at the corner of the L—old and poky, and very suitable for a morning bottle when buying the groceries. For a livelier time you shouldn't miss *Peter Oliver's* (music every night June–Sept; traditional dancing every Wed in hall at back; £1); the publican himself is a musician, and there are fiddles, button accordion, banjo, mandolin, and bodhrán on the wall ready to play. *Nancy's*, a cosy 200-year-old pub run by the same family for seven generations, is also good, with something happening most nights during the summer (listen out for the fiddler John Gallagher). *Laburnum House*, on the corner of the Portnoo Road, does **B&B**. A *McGeehan's* bus leaves for Dublin from outside the post office daily at 8:30am.

From Dawros Head to Crohy Head

The **Dawros Head Peninsula**, immediately north of Ardara, is a much tamer land than Glencolumbcille's, with many tiny lakes (great for fishing, get licence in Ardara) dotting a quilt of low hills. The terrain of purple heather, fields, streams, and short glens make a varied package for the enthusiastic walker. You don't get many outsiders here, but the trailer parks and campgrounds of PORTNOO and NARIN are densely populated with with Northern Irish tourists. As you approach Narin, just before the pastel-shaded Kilclooney church, look back to the right and you'll spot the **Kilclooney Dolmen**, probably the most elegant in the country. (The Narin end of the peninsula in general is rich in these remains.) The spearheaded two-and-a-half-mile-long **Narin strand** is a wonderful beach, safe for bathing, and at low tide you can walk out to **Iniskeel Island** where there are the ruins of two twelfth-century churches with some cross-inscribed slabs.

The most worthwhile sight on the peninsula is **Doon Fort**, which occupies an entire oval-shaped islet in the middle of Loch Doon. To get there take a left out of Portnoo and then left again alongside a lake where you'll see a sign up for boat rental: this leads to the farmhouse of Mr McHugh, who will row you out to the island for a small charge. The idyllic setting, rarely disturbed by visitors, makes the hassle worth it; although its walls are crumbling, this fort has been untouched for over 2000 years, and there there are only four such structures in the land). The walls stand fifteen feet high and twelve feet thick—their inner passages were used in the Fifties for storing poteen. Two other lakes nearby, **Lough Birrog** and **Lough Kiltoorish**, have ruined castles, both built by later Irish chieftains, the O'Boyles. Their stones, however, have mostly been carted away for house-building, slid across the ice when the lakes froze over.

If you want to **stay** on the peninsula, you could try *Dunmore Caravans*, in Narin (£6 single, £10 for 2, £15 for 4–6), but there's little chance of a vacancy in midsummer. *Dawros Bay Hotel*, north of Rossbeg, offers accommodation at hostel rates (☎075-45252; £4 per bed, £3.50 breakfast); it's well-placed for headland walks, but the nearest grocery store is in Portnoo.

Inland to Glenties, Fintown, and Doochery

GLENTIES is a village of Plantation grandeur (courthouse, old lodge, and highland hotel) set at the foot of two glens. It also sports the largest disco in the northwest, the *Limelight*; situated at the north end of town, it makes an eccentric contrast with the various ethnocentric names of the smaller establishments—*Paddy's Bar*, *Wee Joe's Bar* and *Paul's*. Another community attraction is a beautiful **church** designed by the contemporary Derry architect Liam McCormack, at the Ardara end of town; the vast sloping roof reaches down to six feet from the ground, and the rainwater drips off the thousand or so tiles into picturesque pools of water. The newly opened **Museum and Heritage Centre**, opposite the church in the Neoclassical courthouse (June–Sept Mon–Fri 11am–1pm and 2:30–5pm, Sat and Sun 2:30–6pm; £1), is well stocked with items from all periods, including an interesting set of pleas submitted to the courts during the Famine; there's also an Edison phonograph that'll play "It's a Long Way to Tipperary." There's good **traditional music** at the *Glen Tavern*, three miles out on the Ballybofey Road, beautifully situated by the river at the foot of the Blue Stacks; the star performer is local fiddler Vincent Campbell, who may come down if a session strikes up—otherwise there are sessions on the last Saturday of the month at 9:30pm). **Eating** out is a problem—the *Rosses Restaurant Bar* serves tea and sandwiches, and that's it. Nor is accommodation terribly handsome—**B&B** at the *Claradon*, Glen Road (☎075-51113; Easter–Oct). The town's most famous son was **Patrick MacGill** (*Children of the Dead*, *The Rat Pit*), a navvy turned author and the inspiration for a literary festival held in his honor each year in the last week of August.

The trip inland to Doochery via Fintown and then down the Gweebarra valley to the coast at LETTERMACAWARD is a fine scenic loop. **FINTOWN**, nine miles northeast of Glenties, is a ramshackle roadside place set beside a lake at the foot of towering mountains. Once again, the scene has a mythical coloring—it was here that Fergoman was attacked by wild boars, and cried out so piteously that his sister was driven to distraction and dived into the lake, where she drowned.

DOOCHERY lies five miles northwest across a route that cuts against the grain of the hills. It's desolate but delightful journeying through moorland streaked by turf banks, where bulbous knuckles of rock force the road to duck and lunge from side to side. The village itself has a few pubs and grocery store but no accommodation, which is a pity, for it would be a delightful base. Nine miles northeast, up the Gweebarra River, is the Glenveigh National Park (see below), while five miles downstream are the headlands at Lettermacaward.

The **Dooey Point headland** makes a scenically interesting little detour if you have spare time. The northern shore on Traweenagh Bay is the more gratifying, with a fine stretch of beach backed by sand dunes. Classic thatched cottages and abandoned Volkswagens are two of the main characteristics and on the southern side lies **Corr Strand**, fertile ground for mussels and clams, with a handy bar nearby.

The Crohy Head Peninsula

The southern approach to **Crohy Head** curls around the headland's central mountains, looking down onto a rocky shelf of coastline from which plumes of spray rise like geysers. As you come round the headland to the final approach up to the three-story An Óige hostel (one of the best-run in the country; ☎075-21330; April–Oct), the globular outline of **Aranmore Island** appears, close to the Rosses coast. The hillside below the road can be dangerous at points because of a remarkable landslip known as the *Tholla Brista* (broken earth), but this, and the great sea-stack known as *An Briste* (the breeches), make the headland an even more dramatic experience for the walker.

The one-pub fishing village of **MAGHERY** lies at the foot of the north side of the headland. Its most unusual feature is the tall wall that runs by the abandoned manor house at the far side of the short strand; called the *Famine Wall*, this windbreak was built by the villagers for the landlord, who devisd the task so that he could pay them a wage as famine relief. **Minibuses** run daily from Maghery to Dunglow and back, usually at 10am.

The Rosses

The **Rosses**, a vast expanse of rock-strewn land and stony soil, is one of the last strong *Gaeltacht* areas. Spotted with over 120 tiny lakes, the crumpled terrain stretches from Dunglow in the south to Crolly in the north; the coastal route between these two boundaries is infinitely more rewarding than the more direct inland route.

Upper Rosses

With its bustle of shoppers and its multitude of pubs, **DUNGLOW** is a fairly easy place to settle into quickly, but there's little other than ad hoc entertainment to make lingering worthwhile. It's at its liveliest for the midsummer **Mary of Dunglow** festival, a parochial variation on the Miss World idea that provides a good pretext for general festivities and late-night drinking. The town is also synonymous with the rejuvenating work of **Paddy the Cope**, a poor Rosses boy who in the Fifties envisioned the salvation of these poor communities through cooperative ventures; cooperative supermarkets throughout the Rosses—megastores in West Donegal terms—stand as a testament to him.

The *Tirconnaill* **bar** at the top end of the street is a genuine old-timers' bar with not a note of music interfering; the *Atlantic Bar* has rock music every Saturday and traditional on Fridays and Sundays. For **eating**, *Doherty's Restaurant* is a good low-priced grill which also has a specialty of squid Provençal for as little as £2.50. *Doherty's* **private buses** run daily in July and August, through Fintown and Letterkenny to Derry.

Passing the smoking funnels of a kelp processing factory, the coastal route heads off in the direction of **BURTONPORT**, half a mile off the main road. A settlement of a handful of houses and pubs, it's the embarkation point for Aranmore Island or, if you can find someone to take you out, for the smaller islands hereabouts. With the establishment of government buildings on **Rutland Island** in the eighteenth century this area became the first English-speaking district in the whole of Donegal. The English connection endures. Until a few years ago a colony of post-hippies known as the "Screamers" ran an organic commune on another island; their departure coincided with the arrival of three eccentric ladies from England, who live in immaculate, formal Victorian style in the white mansion at the entrance to Burtonport. Known as the "Silver Sisters", Miss Tyrrell, Miss Lucinda and their young maid are an engaging sight, doing their shopping in the village dressed in bonnets and sober black garments edged with white lace. They welcome only visitors with a serious interest in their anachronistic way of life, not the merely curious .

The village has little to say for itself, and its **pubs** now look somewhat lifeless. The *Skipper Tavern* is the only one where you might hear traditional music. For **eating**, *Kelly's Arran Bar* will probably be able to offer you a plate of mussels for a few punts, and even salmon and lobster in season. Otherwise you'll have to make do with pies or fish and chips. Mrs McGinley, down by the pier, does **B&B** (☎075-42047).

Aranmore Island

It's a twenty-five-minute journey out to **Aranmore Island**, through the straits between the nearest cluster of islands (Rutland, Inishfree, Inishcoo, and Eighter), and then across an expanse of open water to the island's main village, LEABGARROW (7 boats daily in summer; £2). There is an **An Óige** hostel here (no telephone; June–Sept). The high middle ground of bogland and lakes reaches a greater altitude than anywhere else in the Rosses, and has great views back to Burtonport. A few roads crisscross the island, the villages being ranged in true Rosses style around the rim of the eastern and southern sides—the western and northern shores are uninhabited, and perfect for walking. Intriguingly, there's no *Gardá* on Aranmore, so you see very few cars with tax discs, and might catch sight of a ten-year-old popping into the driver's seat and setting off. The **pubs** (of which there are only six or seven) also tend to stay open until the small hours—which is convenient, as there really is no other form of nightlife. The most dramatic of the several beaches is at the lighthouse end of the island, and approached by a set of steps down the side of a perpetually crumbling cliff.

Lower Rosses

The road up through the Lower Rosses to Gweedore passes through a wild and crazed terrain of granite boulders and stunted vegetation. On the coast, especially beautiful sections are along the lip of **Cruit Island Bay** (a couple of miles north of Burtonport) and the **Rannafast** headland, which rises between ANNAGARY and CROLLY. As you come down the hill into Crolly, look out for a sign pointing to **Leo's Tavern**—on most nights it has traditional music, and since Leo is the father of the family group **Clannad** and the singer Enya, you may well catch them on a home visit at famly reunion times of year. The large *Teach Phaidí Óig* pub used to be one of the great traditional music-making places, but events are nowadays far less regular. **Lough Keel**—tucked into the back of Crucknafarragh Mountain southeast—allegedly contains Ireland's feeble answer to the Loch Ness monster, glimpsed on numerous occasions over the past five years.

Inland: the Derryveagh Mountains

The central area of North Donegal rivals any of the best parts of the Donegal coastline, and if you're traveling northward from the south of the county, makes a far better destination than the Bloody Foreland. The road to get onto is the one that goes through the hamlet of Gweedore (see below), along the northern shore of Lake Nacung, and into **DUNLEWY**, where an **An Óige hostel** nestles at the foot of **Errigal Mountain**. Quite often the area is shrouded in mist, but on a clear day the beauty of Errigal is insurpassable, its silvery slopes resembling Hokusai's images of Mount Fuji. Should you venture into the one and only **bar** in Dunlewy, be careful as you enter the lounge—the dartboard hangs a couple of inches to the side of the door.

Turn off just below the church at the eastern end of Lake Nacung for the **Poisoned Glen**—the route continues over the bridge, and then you should follow the bank of the river deep into the gorge, always heading for the col up at the shoulder of the Derryveagh Mountains. It's not an easy tramp, for a lot of the ground is marshy, but it's the beginning of one of the finest wild walks imaginable. From the col the view behind is as fantastic as that in front, where the Glenveigh River flows into Lough Beagh. You're now in the **Glenveigh National Park** and may well see deer hereabouts. Going straight down the hill, head for the road, which you should then follow for a short distance before bearing onto the old disused vehicle track that will take you down the barrel of the glen. The Glenveigh River writhes its way to a tiny sandy shore at the head of the lake, where rhododendrons and tall spruces grow. Waterfalls plummet down the sheer cliff sides on the other side of the lake, and **Glenveigh Castle** (May–Oct Tues–Sun 10:30am–6:30pm) now appears above the treetops on a small rocky knoll. The drama and grandeur of this walk into the heart of the estate is far greater than that of the routine approach on the north side of the lake, beautiful as that is. The castle itself, a battlemented nineteenth-century creation swathed in flower gardens, looks best from below.

The most interesting way to get from Glenveigh Park to Gartan Lake, in the next valley east, is to follow the three-mile track across the mountain bog tops (possible to drive), which is the only track leading off the Glenveigh estate road. On weekdays between the beginning of September and the end of February you're forbidden to leave this road or any other recognized foot-path—it's the deer-hunting season, and you may get shot.

Gartan Lake and Around

The environs of **Gartan Lake** are one of the supreme beauties of the whole of Ireland. **Saint Columba** was born into a royal family here in AD 521; his father was from the house of Niall of the Nine Hostages and his mother belonged to the House of Leinster. If you walk over from Glenveigh you'll pass his birthplace—take the first road right at the first house you see at the end of the mountain track, and you'll come to a colossal cross marking the spot. Close by is a slab locally known as the "Flagstone of Loneliness", because the saint used to sleep on it, and thereby gave the flagstone the miraculous power to cure the sorrows of those who lie upon it. During the height of the emigrations, people used to come here the night before depar-ture in the hope of ridding themselves of homesickness. Archaeologically it's actually part of a Bronze-Age gallery-tomb, and has over fifty cup-marks cut into its surface. Going back to the track leading downhill will bring you a main country road, where a left turn will take you towards the remains of a little church called the **Little Oratory of St Colmcille**. It's an enchanting ruin, no larger than a modern living room, with a floor of old stone slabs now pointed by clay and grass. To the side of the tiny rough-hewn altar is the "Natal Stone", where the baby Columba first opened his eyes; to this day pregnant women visit the slab praying for a safe delivery.

Go back down the country lane in the direction you came from and follow on around to the left for **Glebe House** (Easter week and late May–early Oct Tues–Sat 11am–6:30pm and Sun 1–6:30pm; £1). Set in beautiful gardens on the northwest shore of the lake, the house is a gorgeous Regency building richly decorated inside and out, and with an art gallery in one of the outbuild-ings. The kitchen has various paintings by the "Tory Island" group of paint-ers (see p.391), most remarkably James Dixon's impression of Tory from the sea. A remarkable collection of paintings and sketches adorns other parts of the house, including international names like Kokoschka, Renoir, Braque, Picasso, and Degas. The study is decked out in original William Morris wallpaper and there are Chinese tapestries in the morning room. It's well worth buying the guidebook and taking the tour.

Moving on around the northeast of the lake in the direction of Churchill, a right turn off this road immediately after crossing the bridge will take you down to the modern **St Colmcille Heritage Centre** (Mon–Sat 10:30am– 6:30pm, Sun noon–7pm; £1.50), on the opposite shore from Glebe. The exhibition space is largely devoted to tracing Columba's life and the spread of the Celtic church throughout Europe. It's not as boring as sounds, for there are a few intriguing items—very beautiful stained glass windows of Biblical scenes by Ciaran O'Conner and Ditty Kummer, and a step-by-step illustration of vellum illumination and calligraphy. The road to the heritage center continues a little farther to the **Gartan Outdoor Pursuit Center**, where it's possible to reserve a **hostel bed** for the night (☎074-37032)—a must if you're going to have any chance to enjoy the area to the full. Continuing east from here towards Letterkenny, you ascend from the northern shore to Church Hill, with superb cross-country views as far north as the peninsulas.

The Rock of Doon and Kilmacrennan

Lying a few miles northeast of Gartan, **The Rock of Doon** and **Doon Well** are reached by taking the last right turn off the L77 just before it reaches the N56, which runs into Kilmacrennan; this will take you into a rural dead-end right next the well. Just as you approach the area of the well, the road runs along at the bottom of the large bushy outcrop that is the **Rock of Doon**. For centuries it was this spot where the O'Donnell king was crowned before a great gathering of his followers. The inauguration stone on the summit is said to bear the imprint of the first Tirconnell king, a mark into which every successor had to place his foot as his final confirmation. A bush weighed down in multicolored tassles marks the spot of the **well**—looking just as you'd imagine a school-play representation of the burning bush that confronted Moses. You're supposed to take off your shoes as you approach, and be well intentioned before taking the water. You'll probably pick up a story or two of dramatic conversion and miracles effected by the water, which is sent to Irish emigrés all over the world.

KILMACRENNAN is a sweet-looking inland village farther downstream on the Leannan River, but there's no reason to hang around there. The *Village Tavern* has reasonably priced pub grub.

Letterkenny

Ever since Derry was partitioned into the North, **LETTERKENNY** has been Donegal's major commercial center. It has an ebullient bustle about it which, in the context of its surrounding blanket of green fields, reminds one of a typical Cork town. Although it's just at the edge of Lough Swilly, there's no water in sight, and the main visual element is the file of advertising down the main street. Its only notable sight is the huge nineteenth-century cathedral, with its intricate stone-roped ceiling and gaelicized Stations of the Cross.

Letterkenny has an **independent hostel** in a terraced house at the back of Upper Main Street (☎074-21181); there's a laundromat just a couple minutes' walk down to the bypass road below). The *O'Boyce Snack Bar* offers the cheapest, fastest and most basic **food** in town; it's handy for the bus station, down by the traffic circle at the Derry side of town. In the big shopping center directly behind the bus station, the *Oasis Bar* has a variety of reasonably priced lunches; there's also a delicatessen in the center. At the top of the same street is *Steers Fast Food* which is also good value, while the slightly pricier *Rumpoles Restaurant*, at the very top of the street, has tasty meals too. The *Tin Tai Restaurant* on Lower Main Street does very cheap three-course lunch specials.

You may struggle to find a bar with Irish music—the *Cottage Bar* on the main street, just a few doors down from the **post office** has various types of music, and the *Three Ways Inn*, about a mile out the main Derry road, holds occasional *comhaltas* evenings. However, *Frank Mullen's* **record** shop (9am–6pm Mon–Sat), on the main street, has a comprehensive tape selection of all kinds of Irish music. An indication that you're approaching the North is that the *Sinn Fein* office occupies a main-street shop at the southern end of town; it has literature from the prisons and the usual socialist and Republican material. Finally, there's a **money exchange** franchise on the main street (11am–6pm).

The Gweedore and Cloghaneely Districts

The southwest edge of **Gweedore** district (named after a miniscule settlement) is marked by of Bunbeg, Middletown, and Derrybeg, their cottages sprinkled across a blanket of gorse and mountain grasses. Some buildings are gray and decaying, some are roofless or grass-covered; others are at various stages of completion. It's a dispiriting kind of landscape, and it continues like this right up the coast and around the **Bloody Foreland** to Gortahork and Falcarragh in the Cloghaneely district.

BUNBEG, it must be said, has a gorgeous little harbor packed with smallish trawlers—it's half a mile from the village along an enchanting rollicky road. In summer you can negotiate a boat trip from the pier to offshore islands such as Inishinny, Inishmaine, Inishirrer, Umfin, Inishfree, Owey, and Gola, which was reluctantly abandoned but to which the fishermen often return. The **beach** farther up the coast is approached by taking any track left from the road running north out of the village. The most popular bar in Bunbeg is *Teach Niúdaí Beag*, once a great spot for traditional music but now quieter than it used to be. You can **eat** extremely well at *Mooney's Restaurant* (5-course dinner £12); *Micky Gallagher's* has cheap bar grub, while *Sergeant Pepper's* is a good place for kebabs and pizzas. The *Ostan Gweedore* holds **discos** (Wed, Fri, and Sun; £2.50), and has country and western music on Wednesday.

At GLASSACH, a few miles after Derrybeg, the road abruptly ascends onto the Bloody Foreland, a grim, stony, almost barren zone, crisscrossed with stone walls. The road turns eastwards at KNOCKFOLA, hugging the side of the mountain, with the bogland and its hard-worked turfbanks stretching below towards the Atlantic. At **MINLARACH** (*mín lathrach*, the gentle spot) you should be able to spot the distinctive shape of Tory Island far out to sea. A road runs down to the pier, from where you can pick up a boat to take you out to the island; Bunbeg and Dunfanaghy are other possible departure points. In the dead of winter a trip is virtually impossible, and at any time of the year you must always be prepared to be stranded for anything up to a fortnight if the weather takes a sudden turn for the worse. Minlarach has a few pubs and a grocery store, handy if you're waiting for a boat.

Tory Island

With its ruggedly indented shores pounded day and night by the ocean, **Tory Island**, though only eight miles from the mainland, is notorious for its inaccessibility. The island is completely treeless and, it's claimed, ratless too—thanks to the intervention of Saint Columba, who arrived here in AD 500. There's no hotel or guesthouse on Tory—you simply bring a sleeping bag and inquire about a floor to sleep on. It has two villages, West Town and East Town; the former possesses the church, school, and post office, and two of the island's three shops. There's no pub, but the community hall is pressed into service for drinking and music.

In the winter nothing could equal the austerity and harshness of this place, and most of the island's one hundred or so inhabitants go onto the mainland to pass the worst months. An idiosyncratic brand of Gaelic is their first language, and it's indicative of their independence that they refer to the winter migration as "taking a visit over to Ireland." Fishing is still the staple trade, but some of the men supplement this a little through **painting**, a circumstance which originated in a chance encounter between the English painter Derek Hill and one of the fishermen, **James Dixon**, in 1968. Dixon (now dead) had never lifted a brush before the day he told Hill that he could do a better job of painting the Tory scenery, but he went on to become the most famous of the island's school of primitive painters. (Glebe House has a remarkable painting by him—see "Lake Gartan," above.)

It's no surprise to learn that potent legends are attached to the island. **Balor of the Evil Eye** (the Celtic god of darkness) supposedly had his residence on Tory, the remains of his castle standing on the eastern cliffs. There's also said to be a crater in the very heart of the island that none of the locals will approach after dark, for fear of incurring the god's wrath. Another superstition focuses on the **wishing stone** in the middle of the island, three circuits of which will lead to your wish being granted. It was utilized to defeat invaders by wrecking their ships—the British gunboat*Wasp*, sent to collect taxes, was caught in a sudden storm that killed all but six of its crew. The islanders have never paid tax since.

Some monastic relics from Saint Columba's time remain on Tory, the most unusual of which—and now the island's emblem—is the **Tau Cross**. Its T-cross shape is of Egyptian origin, and is one of only two such monuments in the whole of Ireland. It is now relocated and set in concrete on Camusmore Pier in West Town. There are other mutilated stone crosses and some carved stones lying around, several by the remains of the round tower.

Gortahork and Falcarragh

The first town you'll come across to the east of the Bloody Foreland is nondescript **GORTAHORK**. The *Teach Bhillie* is an old men's drinking place, while the *Irish College*—up to the right after you pass *Whorskey's* on the left—has *ceilidhs* every night throughout July and August. The bar in *MacFadden's* hotel has snack lunches and a reasonably priced Sunday carvery lunch.

FALCARRAGH is certainly a little more riveting, with more to offer by way of pubs, shops and other amenities. The local tourist committee has recently made **hostel rooms** available down at **Ballyconnel House**—take the coast road at the village crossroads, and the gate posts of the estate are beside the main road where it bears left. Set in 500 acres of woodland, the house was built in the mid-seventeenth century, once belonged to one of the great landlords of the area, Sir John Olphert, and was taken over by the State in 1923. It's planned to open a heritage center and museum here. Falcarragh beach is reached by following the same main road for a few miles—eventually the dunes will appear behind a parking lot. This is one of the more beautiful strands on this northwest coast, but a strong undertow makes it unsafe for swimming. For **eating**, *John's Café*, at the Gortahork end of town, is the best place. The *Gweedore* has **music** of varying kinds most nights in July and August, and serves lunches and evening meals.

Leaving Falcarragh, the road to Dunfanaghy opens onto a significantly milder landscape, with the green grass now beginning to outstrip the ruggedness, and the occasional reed-fringed lake with swans by the roadway.

Horn Head and Around

DUNFANAGHY, seven miles from Falcarragh, is the gateway to the Horn Head peninsula. It's an aristocratically self-conscious Plantation town, whose strongly Presbyterian atmosphere stands in amazing contrast to anything west or south of it. The measure of the place is given by the fact that its one and only memorial was raised in honor of an agent for the estates of a nineteenth-century landlord. It hasn't a single fast-food outlet or café, but instead proffers several hotels and an art gallery (mostly a monotone of soft Irish landscape impressions, supplemented by an assembly of heavily polished antique knickknacks) just on the outskirts at the west end of town. *Dan Devine's* is the liveliest and cosiest **bar**, with friendly bar staff. For **eating**, *Danny Collin's* pub offers soups and pricey but delicious seafood.

Horn Head is one of the finest headlands in the country, a 600-foot rock face scored by ledges on which perch countless guillemots, puffins, and gulls The best view of the cliffs, sea-stacks, and caves is from the water, but the cliff road is vertiginous enough in places to give you a good look down the sheer sides. To get there take the access road at the Falcarragh end of Dunfanaghy village; it descends to skirt the side of a beautiful inlet before rising steeply to go around the east side of the head. A spectacular vista of headlands opens up to the east—Rossguill, Fanad, and Inishowen—but none can match the drama of Horn Head's cliffs, their tops clad in a thin cover of purplish heather.

Moving east again, the road follows the side of Sheephaven Bay; sign-posted turnoffs run to the popular vacation spots of PORTNABLAGH and MARBLE HILL STRAND, the latter possessing one of the greatest lengths of silver sand in the country.

The Creeslough Area

The sleepy village of **CREESLOUGH** stands on a slope commanding gorgeous views across the gullet of Sheephaven Bay. Partway down its main street is one of Liam McCormack's churches, its whitewashed whorl and backsloping table-roof reflecting the thickset **Muckish Mountain** nearby. You can see the mountain from within the church—it's usually enswirled in mist, what's known locally as the Donegal *smir*. Creeslough and Falcarragh make the best launching pad for a climb up the mountain; from Creeslough follow the road out to Muckish Gap, down at the southern face, and from there the route ascends the grassy slopes to the flattened summit. There are pubs and grocery stores in the village itself, but the nightlife is dull, so it's not a place to choose for an overnight stay.

The coastal road northward onto the Rossguill peninsula offers a couple of worthwhile diversions. **Doe Castle**, to the left just before Lackagh Bridge (see below), has been superbly reconstructed. The castle's tall central keep, standing within a bawn and rock-cut fosse, was the original fortress of **McSwyney Doe** whose graveslab is now pinned to its wall. The carving on the stone is faint, but its ornateness makes it historically important; the seven-speared fleur-de-lis at the top represents the close family connections with Scotland, and other carvings show a fox, cow, dolphin, and eagle, as well as Celtic tracery. A walk around the battlements affords a view of the south-ernmost corner of the Sheephaven Bay; when the tide is out the whole peace-ful expanse looks like a desert, with only a slim channel of water gliding through the sandbanks. If the castle gate is padlocked, a key is kept in the cottage fifty yards back down the approach road.

Lackagh Bridge is an even better viewpoint, the curving silty shoreline lying downstream, and a ginger-brown picture of rushes and heather-drifting reaching deep into the hills upstream. Immediately after the bridge there's a turn off to **GLEN** (two miles), a roundabout way to Carrigart (see next section) that's worth taking for the scenery and the opportunity for a drop-in at Glen's *Old Glen Bar*. It's a low-ceilinged place, smoky, and atmospheric, with music on weekends and most other nights as well. If solitude is what you want, this is a good area to explore; apart from Glen Lough, there are several other lakelets in the district, all lying in a silent, rocky landscape.

The Rosguill Peninsula

CARRIGART is the back-door entrance to the extremely beautiful and very manageable **Rosguill Peninsula**. It's a beguiling village whose **bars** define the essence of the place; *P. Logue's*, at the west end of town, is a welcoming sort of hideaway. Also note *MacGettigan's* grocers, at the eastern end of the main street, with its old-fashioned wooden counter and shelving, and a tempting array of bottles in the window.

The route into the peninsula starts by the side of the church; follow this road for a little, then fork left, and you'll be going past the rabbit-infested dunes at the back of a fantastic and usually deserted beach. The three-mile strand runs in a scimitar's curve all the way back to the bottom of Sheephaven Bay—it's a marvelous four-hour walk to Doe Castle, though when the tide comes in you could have to do a mile or so of the journey on the inland lanes. **DOWNINGS**, at the top of the strand, is a small, sprightly holiday center used mainly by Northern Irish tourists (especially from Belfast), with trailer parks hogging the rear end of the beach and vacation chalets creeping up the hillside behind the village. The one **pub** you should be sure to head for is the *Harbour Bar*, at the far end of the village (traditional music Tues, Thurs and Sat), which usually attracts the *Gaeltacht* crowd during the summer months. The *Fleet's Inn*, at the center of the village, runs discos during the summer, when the *Beach Hotel* opposite holds nightly folk sessions, often lasting until 3am.

The main street runs on around the west side of the headland to become the panoramic *Atlantic Drive*, first passing an access road that runs down to the pier. Just before the pier is the only nourishing eating-place on the whole peninsula—the *Coffee Shop*, great for homemade everything (11am–8pm).

If, instead of taking the left fork to Downings, you go right, you're on your way to the **An Óige hostel** at Tra Na Rossen beach (see "Practicalities" below). The route goes by the *Singing Pub* (traditional music Sat), sited on a turning up to the left. Opposite this turning and down to the right is **Mevagh Church** graveyard. It has an early Christian cross and an intriguing slab into which some cup-like cavities have been carved. And there's one gravestone that cannot but bring an appreciative smile: *Pat MacBride 1910–86 Shoemaker and Philosopher.*

The hostel at first sight looks like an Alpine refuge out of *The Sound of Music*. One of the first things you should do on arrival is bolt up the hillside immediately behind—at the summit the view is stupendous. You'll see Mulroy Bay, looking as though it has leaked from a gaping wound somewhere in the land mass, and a seemingly endless length of mountain ridges behind it. Further along there's the bombastic height of Horn Head, while closer in rises the central hump of the Rossguill Peninsula, and the **Tra Na Rossen** beach serene and untouched below. The remainder of the headland back towards **Mulroy Bay** stretches only as far as a trailer park and another beach at MELMORE (not safe for swimming); the coastal rocks on the way conceal the occasional cove and cave.

Practicalities

The peninsula's **An Óige hostel** is perfectly placed at the northeastern corner of the headland, right next the Tra Na Rossen beach. The management is very friendly, there's virtually no curfew, and of course the views from the dorms are great. Fish can be bought from the fisherman who lives in the bungalow behind the hostel; a grocery van stops by every Monday around midday.

For transportation, *Patrick Gallagher's* private **bus** service leaves Letterkenny's Market Square for the peninsula at 6pm, and leaves Downings at 10:45am every morning. It's quite easy to **hitch** to the hostel, as everyone knows exactly where you're heading. For **bicycle** rental try *Charlie Coyle Cycles* (☎074-55427), based out the Creeslough road just outside Carrigart, in the bungalow next to the clump of fir trees). The only **bank** in the area is in Carrigart (Mon–Wed and Fri 11am–2pm, Thurs 11am–1pm).

The Fanad Peninsula

The **western** route into the **Fanad Peninsula** is undramatic on the whole, but it has some patches of idyllic scenery close to the Mulroy Lough and near the northwest corner, where the low-lying headland resembles the Rosses – wholly unlike the other headlands on this north part of Donegal.

MILFORD makes an uninspiring beginning to the western route; **CARROWKEEL**, a bit farther on, offers a bit more excitement, being a popular vacation spot. The *Mulroy Ballroom*, one of the few remaining Sixties show-band ballrooms, carries on the tradition with an Irish night (Wed June–Aug); it's on the Milford road out of town. Opposite is the *Rockhill Campground Park* (tents £4.60, plus 20p per person; horse trekking available), providing the only basic **accommodation** in the place. The *Village Restaurant*, out at the northern end of the village, has a high-priced but wide-ranging menu. The road north from Carrowkeel runs alongside the water's edge up to BALLYWHORISKEY, at the top of the peninsula, where the geography changes into flatland, with dwellings spread out in the *Gaeltacht* manner. A left turn at the FANAD DRIVE signpost, just outside an old gray school building, will take you through hillocky and boulder-strewn terrain to a few small beaches and a pier; from here you can return to the main road to Fanad Head (see next page). The large **Ballyhiernan Strand**, farther along towards the head, has a few trailer parks behind its grassy dunes if you're seeking a place to spend the night.

The Eastern Route

The road crawling up the **east** side of Fanad is a much more interesting route. It starts at **RATHMELTON**, a sedate and neat little village that attracts Dublin yuppies. Its main part sits on the eastern bank of the broad black flow of the Leannan River, famous for its salmon. The *House on the Brae* coffee shop sells home-baked **food** (entrance facing the river); more substantial but more expensive is *McDaid's* restaurant and wine-bar right on the junction of the quay road and the high road. For a smidgen of entertainment, the *O'Donnell Arms* puts on traditional music on a Friday night and country and western on a Saturday. If you're only passing through, *Sweeney's Tavern* is the nicest refuge for a stopover drink.

Next stop north, **RATHMULLAN**, looks pretty with its long row of seafront housing following the curve of the bay, but the beach itself is to be avoided, having two sewer pipes running down to the water's edge. In 1587

Red Hugh O'Donnell was lured into a British merchant ship here, on the pretense of a merry drink, and ended up in Dublin jail for six years; in 1609 it was the departing point for the "**Flight of the Earls**", the event that marked the end of the Gaelic nation. The view across to Fahan on the Inishowen peninsula is enticing (a small ferryboat operates in summer), but the only thing to delay your passing through is **Rathmullan Friary**, one of the better-preserved historical ruins in Donegal. The original part of it was built by Rory MacSweeney in 1508 and then presented to the Carmelites. George Bingham plundered it in 1595 and used it as a barracks, and in 1618 it was farther adapted as a castle residence by Bishop Knox. Only the chancel area continued to serve as a church until its eventual abandonment in 1814. Today you can see traces of Gothic doorways and narrow window apertures. On the way into Rathmullan there's very good **eating** to be had at the *Water's Edge Restaurant*; otherwise there's only fish and chips.

Four miles farther north, out on the Portsalon road, a signpost to the left takes you up a little track towards the tenth–century **Drumhallach Cross Slab**; it's only four and a half feet in height, but has delightful carvings of two figures sitting on the arms of the cross sucking away at their thumbs. This curiosity is linked by local folklore with Finn Mac Cumaill, who one day burned his thumb while tending to the salmon of knowledge, and immediately stuck it in his mouth—thereafter doing the same whenever he needed to be wise. The lower figures on this front face are harder to make out, but are meant to represent bishops.

Back on the main route, the road climbs to give great views across to Dunree Head and the Urris range of mountains, on the Inishowen Peninsula. Just approaching the summit of this climb, and above the patch where the oyster beds lie, is a tin-roofed cottage offering home baking—convenient for **Bunnaton Hostel** (£4 plus £1 for bedding; 2 double rooms and 2 singles), an old coastguard station half a mile away. To get there follow the path off to the right down by the clump of fir trees. There's a small store of provisions here, a couple of bikes for rent, and great walks nearby. The hostel overlooks a delicate and accessible cove with a rocky beach, and also has an equally nice view inland up the valley of **Glenvar**, which will take you across to Carrowkeel on the western side of the peninsula.

Continuing north, the road rises until you're running along the cliff-top approach to the most spectacular views on the peninsula at **Saldanha Head**. From here you're looking down onto the three-mile stretch of golden sand at Balinstocker Strand. The tiny village of **PORTSALLON**, on the other side of the strand, was once a great vacationing spot, but is now more of a ghost resort, with its grand crenellated hotel abandoned down on the front. Just in front of it, however, is *Rita's Bar*, still thriving in its Fifties decor, with wooden bar counter and shelves for sweets and bottled drinks.

To Fanad Head

Though some stretches are forested, most of the five-mile-route north from Portsallon to Fanad Head is through humpy and barren land, with clusters of granite pushing through marshy ground. By the roadside there's a **Holy Well**, decked out with a crazy collection of mementoes: beads, prayer books, plastic knife and fork, a golf tee, badges, mugs, bottles, medicine bottle, and so on. Before reaching the Head, there is one other curiosity worth taking in—the rock formation known as the **Great Arch**. Follow the signpost on the right of the road, then take the path down to the new house that has just been built, and finally cross the fields to the pebbly strand. You'll see the arch to your left, a sort of natural Arc de Triomphe with the sea crashing all around it. Only half a mile off the same main road at this point but to the left (signposted) is *Knock Donnely* B&B, just before Shannagh lake (☎074-31050); they offer evening dinner and vegetarian **meals** throughout the day. The road straight on from the B&B will lead you away from Fanad Head and over towards the western tip of the peninsula.

If you return to the main road, you'll find that it leads straight on to **Fanad Head**, which contains very little other than a lighthouse and its namesake pub. The *Lighthouse Tavern* doesn't live up to its situation, serving hot toddies out of microwave, but allegedly has wild country and western sessions (July and Aug Tues, Fri and Sun). The road from here runs on down to the low, rocky coast, where the pebble beach emits a strong hiss as each wave gets sucked back down its slope.

The Inishowen Peninsula

Rarely sought out by tourists due to a combination of its northerly location and its proximity to the "troublesome" North, the **Inishowen Peninsula** is perhaps the great overlooked treasure of the Irish landscape. It's a diverse and visually exciting terrain, where the views usually encompass the waters of the loughs or the Atlantic waves. Every aspect of the land is superb—the beaches (especially **Fahan, Tullagh,** and **Pollan**), the towering headland bluffs (**Malin, Inishowen, Dunaff,** and **Dunree**) and the central mountain range, with **Slieve Snaght** (*sliabh sneachta*, the mountain of the snows) at the center of it all. The peninsula's name derives from **Eoghán**, who was made First Lord of the island by his father Niall, the High King of Ireland. Phases of the peninsula's history before and after Eoghán have left a legacy of fine antiquities, from the **Greenan Fort** to a host of beautiful early Christian crosses (**Cloncha, Mura, Carrowmore,** and **Cooley**).

Western Inishowen

The most stimulating of all the Inishowen sights, the Greenan Fort, is a short way off the western route into the peninsula from Derry city. The turning is past BRIDGE END, on the south side of the Letterkenny–Derry road, by the Liam McCormack-designed **Burt Church**, probably the most beautiful new church in all Ireland. The seating is set concentrically, under a whitewashed ceiling that sweeps up into a vortex to allow sunlight to beam down directly upon the altar; the allusions in every detail to Neolithic sepulchral architecture (especially Newgrange) are fascinating and very atmospheric.

Greenan Fort (a mile up the hill from the church) was already 1700 years old when the Alexandrian geographer Ptolemy showed it on his map of

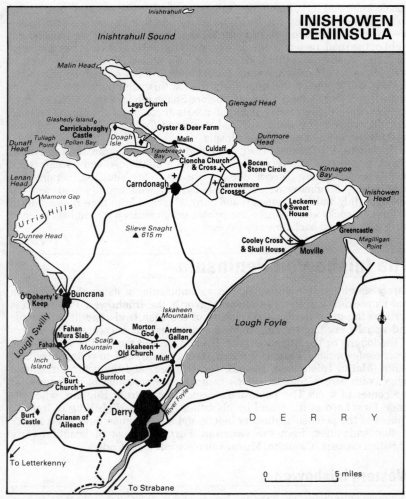

INISHOWEN PENINSULA

Inishtrahull

Inishtrahull Sound

Malin Head

Lagg Church

Glashedy Island

Glengad Head

Dunaff Head

Tullagh Point

Carrickabraghy Castle

Pollan Bay

Doagh Isle

Oyster & Deer Farm

Malin

Trawbreaga Bay

Culdaff

Dunmore Head

Kinnagoe Bay

Lenan Head

Cloncha Church & Cross

Bocan Stone Circle

Mamore Gap

Carndonagh

Carrowmore Crosses

Inishowen Head

Urris Hills

Slieve Snaght ▲ 615 m

Leckemy Sweat House

Dunree Head

Cooley Cross & Skull House

Greencastle

Magilligan Point

Moville

O'Doherty's Keep

Buncrana

Iskaheen Mountain

Lough Foyle

Lough Swilly

Fahan Mura Slab

Fahan

Scalp Mountain

Morton God

Ardmore Gallan

Inch Island

Iskaheen Old Church

Muff

Burnfoot

Burt Church

River Foyle

D E R R Y

Burt Castle

Crianan of Aileach

Derry

To Letterkenny

To Strabane

0   5 miles

Ireland in the second century, and most people today find it the most impressive of all the pagan antiquities left in the country. Thought to have been founded by the druids as a temple to the sun, it was said in the years after Christ to have been the base of various northern Irish chieftains. Here Saint Patrick supposedly preached in AD 450, and baptized Eoghán, the founder of the O'Neill clan. In the twelfth century it was sacked by Brian, the king of Thomond, in retribution for a raid on Clare, with the result that a large amount of its stone got hauled away. What you see today owes a lot to the reconstruction by a Dr Bernard in the late nineteenth century. It's enclosed by three earthen banks, but its most stunning asset is the view across the primordial jumble of mountains and hills far away to the west and the loughs to each side of Inishowen immediately to the north.

Fahan and Buncrana

To get back toward the western coast of the peninsula from here, the safest bet is to return to Bridge End and turn onto the road to **FAHAN**. The beach at Fahan is delightful, as are its monastic ruins. The first abbot was Saint Mura (one of six saints in one family), and what remains today from his time is the **St Mura Cross-Slab**, a spellbinding example of early Christian stone decoration, though it's a shame that it hasn't yet been cleansed of its lichen. There's said to be a rare Greek inscription on its side, but it's hard to locate.

The main street at **BUNCRANA**, a few miles north, is one long carnival parade of shops, each with a name saluting one or other of the local clans—Casey, McLoughlin, Hegarty, O'Doherty, Grant, McGonagle. The town gets packed out during the summer, for this is the Derry people's unrivaled seaside resort. Amusement arcades are here by the dozen, as are **B&Bs** in the Victorian backstreets towards the shore. For **eats** in the town check out the Italian cooking at *Cassidy's Coffee Shop* on the left-hand side just as you round the corner into the main street. *Dorrian's* on the main street is also a good bet for a substantial lunch. The place is crammed full of **pubs**; if you're looking for a plain and unpretentious bar try *Rodden's*, and for a more upbeat venue try *O'Flaherty's*, which often has music.

The left turn that runs down to the pier at the north end of the main street will take you onto the coastal path to **Stragill Strand**, a beautiful and isolated stretch of golden sand. There's a **campground** here, from which you can go on to reach Dunree Head by just following the track away from the beach up to the main road. The view across **Lough Swilly** at this point is extremely satisfying, with the closed-in feel of a large mountain lake.

Dunree to Doagh Isle

Perched on a headland overlooking the mouth of Lough Swilly, just past the tiny village from which it takes its name, **Dunree Fort** began life as a martello tower and was then enlarged into a fortress. It's now manned by the Irish army and has a museum of predictable military memorabilia (June–Oct Tues–Sat 10:30am–6pm, Sun noon–6pm; £1). A steepish climb going north out of the village will take you past a scattering of weather-beaten thatched cottages before you cross a small bridge close to the **Gap of Mamore** (*madhm mór*, the great mountain pass), looking like a bite taken out of the Urris Mountains. From here the road spirals steeply downwards, an ever wider and more spectacular view of the flat foreground to Dunaff Head opening up with every bend. The mile-long **Tullagh Strand**, to the east of Dunaff Head, is a safe bathing beach, with a campground and trailer park just behind it (☎077-76289 or 76138); *Marky's Tavern*, by the roadside, has music at weekends. The road from here works its way inland between the mountains to CLONMANY, a village of predominantly cream-colored row houses and a few grocery stores. The backdrop of mountains on all sides shields it from any thought of an outside world.

The popular vacation village of **BALLYLIFFEN** makes an earthy contrast, with a hotel at each end, a disco, and several **B&B**s. Try Mrs K. Grant, *Pollin House*, Carndonagh Road (☎077-76203) or Mrs McLaughlin, *The Vartry*, at the Clonmany end (☎077-76370). Its principal attraction is the beautiful **Pollan Strand**, at the northern tip of which stands the ruin of **Carrickabraghy Castle,** an O'Doherty defense built in the sixteenth century. Weathered by centuries of spray and sea-salt, the stones of the tower show colors ranging from the darkest hues through oranges and reds to golden yellows.The beach itself has wonderfully wild breakers, which make it unsafe for swimming.

The castle sits on the western side of a promontory called **Doagh Isle**, which you can drive onto by a road to the east of Ballyliffen. You shouldn't miss a trip onto it, for **Trawbreaga Bay** (*traigh brége*, the treacherous strand) on the eastern side, is an exquisite piece of coastline. The mouth of the bay is bewitching—if you walk onto the beach here you'll find the sea has fashioned the rocks into myriad shapes and colors.

Carndonagh

Just before you turn into **CARNDONAGH**, coming from the Ballyliffen direction, there's a church on the corner by the turnoff. Against the church wall is the elegantly shaped and decorated seventh-century **Donagh Cross**, with two diminutive pillar stones to its right and left. The pillar stones show figures with rather large heads, while the cross depicts evil little characters jumping out of its Celtic interlacings—all of which harks back to the pagan druidic religion. A few other decorated stones stand by the entrance. The buildings of Carndonagh town are stacked up the hillside, near the crown of which stands the all-surveying Catholic church. The town **museum** in the basement of the Wesleyan church, near the base of the hill as you come from the Ballyliffen direction (July and Aug Mon–Sat 2–4pm), has many intriguing folk items. For **accommodation** try *Teirnaleague*, left off Church Street then straight on for a mile (☎077-74471). The *Sportsman's Inn*, on the Diamond, does stews and salads, and may have traditional music on Saturday night. Carndonagh has a **folk festival** in the third week of July but it's not one of the more lively ones.

East of Carndonagh—the Ancient Sites

Not far to the east of Carndonagh are a neighboring set of historical remains—the Carrowore high crosses, the Cloncha cross, the Bocan stone circle, and the temple of Deen. To get to the **Carrowmore High Crosses** take the Moville direction out of Carndonagh for four miles, then take a right forty yards after the signposted turning for Culdaff; the two plain crosses are eighty yards up the road, one on each side. These and a few meager building-stones are all that remains of the ancient monastery of Saint Chonas. For the **Cloncha Cross and Church** get back to the Culdaff turning and follow it for a couple of miles until you see a small bungalow with a garden hedge of small firs—the site is behind it. This was once the most important monastic foundation in Inishowen, a status borne out in the beautiful designs carved on the cross's stem. Inside the church are a few more carved stones, the outstanding piece being a tenth-century tombstone.

For the other two sites, take a right here towards Moville and then a left uphill for fifty yards—the **Bocan Stone Circle** is through the first field gate on the left. Only a handful of the stones still stand, among a junkyard of fallen ones; they were all placed here at least 3000 years ago. There's a fine vista of the surrounding ring of hills, with which the stones seem deliberately aligned. On the other side of the main road from the circle is a gallery-tomb known as the **Temple of Deen** (go a little farther along towards Moville and take a right up as far as the wire barrier—you'll spot it from there only). It's nothing extra special, but it's possible that what is exposed today is only the central chamber of an immense cairn. Unfortunately, no archaeological work has yet been done on either this or the stone circle. **CULDAFF** is the nearest base for all of these places, but apart from having a quaint little pier and an ancient stone bridge there is little to entice you down there. For **accommodation** try *McGrory's Guest House, Bar & Restaurant* (☎077-79104) or *Glendaff House* (☎077-79159).

To Malin Head

Four miles north of Carndonagh is **MALIN** village, tucked picturesquely into the side of Trawbreaga Bay. A Planter settlement, with an overtly charming central green, it has only one pub, which must make it unique for its size. A little way north of Malin a signpost shows the way to **Five Fingers Strand**, across the bay from Doagh Isle—it's worth the detour for the ferocity of the breakers on the beach and the long walks on its sands. The beach recently made the headlines when a large IRA cache of arms was found buried here. Back on the main road, you'll quickly come to a left turn leading you straight to Malin Head; a more indirect route is to take a left that veers off this road and a left again at the next signpost, which brings you to the top of a hill overlooking Five Fingers Strand—one of the most captivating views of this part of the peninsula. Going downhill from here feels like a slightly less intoxicating version of the descent from the Gap of Mamore, and is decidedly more thrilling than the direct lowland road. **Malin Head**, the northern extremity of the island, might not be as stupendously extreme as other Donegal headlands, but is nevertheless excellent for windy and winding coastal walks. Look out for a large chasm in the cliffs known as Hell's Hole and the now-deserted **Inishtrahull Island** that aptly translates as "Island of Yonder Strand".

Eastern Inishowen

The route from Derry to Inishowen Head, along the Lough Foyle side of the peninsula, is the nightclubbing circuit for the youth of Derry, and you'll see cars, buses and hitchers racing down here on Friday and Saturday nights. Favorite destinations are the mock-Tudor *Tiffanys/The Ture Inn*, a few miles beyond **Muff**, *The Point Inn* at **Quigley's Point**, a few miles farther on again, and *Scamps* at **Redcastle**, several miles on again. Scores of new bungalows hog the slopes to capture their slice of the panorama.

The first few miles of the road entering this part of Inishowen belongs to the British sector of the north of Ireland; you'll approach the army checkpoint a half-mile short of the border at CULMORE POINT.

Muff and Around

The tiny village of **MUFF**, just a few minutes' drive north of the border, has the only **hostel** on the whole of the peninsula. Run by the Independent group, it's a very cosy and welcoming place (March–Oct); you get there by taking a left turn at the end of the village, just before the *Burmah* gas station. Mrs Reddin on the Main Street offers a **B&B** alternative (☎077-84031). The village is not quite as dead as it looks. *The Carman's Bar* has Irish music on a Wednesday and it's possible that*The Squealin' Pig* will do something in the way of traditional music on Friday and Sunday. The pub with the toreador and flamenco mosaic outside has country-and-western music and dancing from Friday to Sunday. For **eats** the town café has steaks and pies. *Lough Swilly* **buses** run six or more buses a day from Derry.

The countryside immediately around Muff has several interesting megalithic remains. In the **Iskaheen** district (the hostel area) there are few standing stones not far from the sparse ruins of an old abbey that marks the spot where Eoghán, son of Niall of the Nine Hostages, died of grief for his brother Conal. To get to the more impressive of the stones from the abbey go past the nearby St Patrick's Church for a quarter of a mile, by the garden packed with elves and then go up into the second field up behind the new-looking bungalow; from the stone you have the best view of the whole area.

Another nearby site worth seeking out is the **Ardmore Gallan** stone. Dating from the Bronze Age, it's a striking monumental stone standing all on its own in a farmer's field. It is heavily carved with symbolic forms, having forty small cup-dents and a large vertical valley down the middle of one face. To get to it, take a left off the Moville road about half a mile out of Muff, then up the lane at the side of the red-doored house; next follow the road straight up and finally take a right turn to the farmyard at the end—the stone is in the far side of the field in front of the yard.

Also to be recommended is the fourteen-mile trip across the mountains through **Gráinne's Gap** and on to Buncrana on the western side of the peninsula (see above). There's fantastic views back down onto the Foyle estuary from the gap, and the inland scenery is all trickling creeks, heathery boggy slopes lined with turf banks, and rocky granite outcrops.

Moville and Around

Set on a gentle hillock beside the Foyle, **MOVILLE** is a very agreeable seaside resort of the convalescent variety—one can imagine a grandfather clock ticking away in every household. It's handy for a rocky shoreline walk that you can pursue as far as Greencastle without too much difficulty (although at a few points you'll have to circumspectly walk across the bottom of a few private gardens). The village will rarely stir itself to offer anything more than even a tingle of excitement, but if you're on the lookout for somewhere to shrug off a rainy day, then try *The Prospect Bar* down by the gaudily painted Temperance Hall—which has folk-and-ballad singing (Thurs, Fri and Sat). *Rosato's*, on the Carndonagh road, is the best place for a snack and a cosy drink. For **accommodation** try the *Naomh Mhuire*, at the top end of Main Street(☎077-82091). You can rent bikes at *The Bike Shop*, halfway up the same street.

There's a few historical pieces in the district, most notably the **Cooley Cross** and **Skull House**, both signposted off to the left of the main road a quarter of a mile before Moville. Follow the turnoff up the steep hill for about a mile, always bearing right, and it's there—an ancient Celtic wheel-cross, guarding the entrance to a walled graveyard. There are very few examples of this kind of cross with the pierced ringhole in its head; the hole was once a pagan device used to clinch serious treaties, the hands of the opposing parties being joined in amity through it. The Skull House, in the graveyard, is in the form of the type of tomb usually kept for saints, and in this case it's probably that of **Saint Finian** (the one who argued with Columba), whose monastery this was. If you peep through the front hole you'll see some bones.

Greencastle to Kinnego Bay

Though its harbor is surprisingly ugly, **GREENCASTLE** has a pleasant view across to the extensive golden sands of Magiligan Strand on the British side of Lough Foyle. At dusk you'll see the area across the water begin to sparkle with lights like a ship at sea—these are the lights of the prison camp, just hidden behind the dunes. By the road to Stroove (see below) are the ruins of a fourteenth-century **Richard de Burgo** castle, built on a rocky knoll to guard the narrowest part of the lough. De Burgo saw it as the greatest castle-building enterprise in Donegal, and hoped it would be just the thing to quell the local Inishowen chieftains, the O'Donnells and the O'Dohertys. But the O'Dohertys in the end took control of the castle, until they ended up bickering among themselves and causing most of the damage seen today. It's in no great shape, with gaping holes right around its circular enclosure making it look like a large mock-up of a stone circle, though viewed from the shore it's a fairly impressive sight. Next door is **Greencastle Fort**, a fortress built in the Napoleonic era; designed as a lookout post, it unsurprisingly affords good views across the estuary. Back in the village, *The Ferryboat* bar on the seafront offers meals and **B&B** as well as drink (☎077-81021).

At **STROOVE** (pronounced "shroove") the scenery jumps into a more exciting gear, with fine clambering walks along its coastline to the lighthouse. There you'll have to return to the road to reach its small beach, from where doughtier walkers can resume the scramble as far as the cliffs of the awesome **Inishowen Head**. An easier way to the Head is to simply follow the road until it turns left, where you go straight on up the hill instead; a car can make it up the first couple of miles, but after that you run the risk of getting stuck in a rut. From the Head, it's a beautiful but tiring walk to **Kinnego Bay**. The alternate route entails going back to the main road and following it to the right turn by the thatched cottage in Stroove—this will take you over the promontory through two beautiful glens, where fields set at impossible angles line the valley sides. Approached by a precipitous descent, Kinnego is one of the most secluded sandy beaches around, tucked in between the rocky walls of headland against which the waves throw spray as delicate as lace embroidery. A diagram on a roadside plaque shows where three of the Spanish Armada ships sank just off the coast; most of the ships' wreckage discovered over the last twenty years is now on view in Derry's Foyle College. The nearest **B&B** is back in Stroove, with Mrs Gillespie (☎077-81020).

travel details

Bus Éireann
From Donegal to Dublin (3 daily; 5hr).
From Letterkenny to Dublin (3 daily; 5hr).

Private Buses
Funtrek (☎01-730852) operates a daily service
from Letterkenny to Dublin.
For connections to Galway, see that chapter's
"Travel Details."

THE NORTH

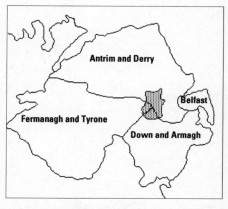

nfluenced by television reports and coverage in the less than objective press, a large portion of the North American population regards Northern Ireland as a place in which sectarian violence is the dominant factor of everyday life. It's not. There *are* ravaged streets, security checkpoints, armored patrols, and fortified army and police headquarters, but you'll encounter them only in the major pressure points: chiefly parts of **Belfast** and **Derry City**, and along the border. In the rural districts of counties **Antrim** and **Derry** you'll scarcely be aware of the "troubles", and even in **Down** and **Armagh**—whose towns feature regularly in the media as "hot spots"—it's highly unlikely that you, as a traveler, will feel in any way at risk.

Yet the caricature is more potent than the reality. Despite the fact that the North is generally as hospitable as the Republic, it's little frequented by tourists, with the exception of a few areas: the coastline of **County Derry** (including the magnificent black basalt geometry of the **Giant's Causeway**); the green **Glens of Antrim**; and the **Mourne Mountains**, to the south of Belfast. These might be the most immediately appealing landscapes, but exploring the rest can be a rewarding experience. Away from the spectacular coastline, the country settles down into rolling farmland punctuated by the planned towns of the merchant companies that were entrusted with the resettlement of this region in the seventeenth century. The inland counties of **Tyrone** and **Fermanagh** are dotted with traces of their history—archaeological sites, castles, ruined churches, raths and dolmens. Fermanagh, centered on **Lough Erne**, is a good place to head towards for watersports and fishing; scenically, Tyrone is duller, though it rises both physically and in terms of interest towards the wild and desolate **Sperrins** in the north.

Antrim and Derry

Belfast

Fermanagh and Tyrone

Down and Armagh

mirrored - by a television reports and coverage in the local that objective presss, a large portion of the North American population regards Northern Ireland as a place in which sectarian violence is the dominant factor of everyday life. This is not. There are indeed security checkpoints, armoured patrols and fortified army and police headquarters, but you'll encounter them only in the major measure points chiefly parts of Belfast and Derry City and along the border. In the rural districts of counties Antrim and Derry you'll scarcely be aware of the Troubles, and even in Down and Armagh—some towns require caution at the media as "hot spots"—it highly unlikely that you, as a traveler, will feel in any way at risk.

Yet the caricature is once potent than the reality. Despite the fact that the North is generally as hospitable as the Republic, it is little frequented by tourist, with the exception of a few areas the coastline of County Derry including the magnificent basalt promontory of the Giant's Causeway, the green Glens of Antrim, and the Mourne Mountains in the south of Ulster. These might be the most immediately appealing landscapes, but exploring the rest can be a rewarding experience. Away from the spectacular coastline the countryside dips down into rolling farmland punctuated by the planned towns of the northern counties that were urbanised with the presence of the element of the region in the seventeenth century. The inland counties of Tyrone and Fermanagh are dotted with Lakes of their Islands — archipelago of islets dotted, rained churches, stone and dolmens — Enniskillen, centred on Lough Erne, is a good place to head towards for water sports and fishing generally. Ulster is dollar, though it first both physically and in terms of interest towards the wild and desolate sporting in the north.

CHAPTER FOURTEEN

BELFAST

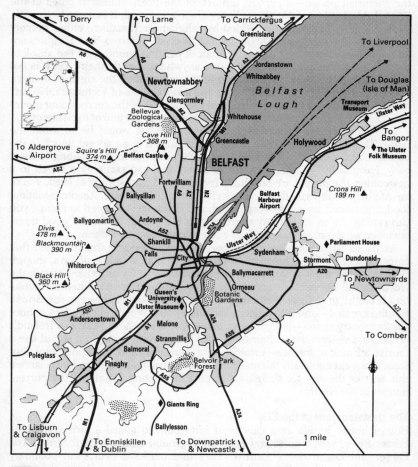

B elfast, the capital of Northern Ireland, is not somewhere you can be indifferent to. A third of the population of the North live here, and they grab more than their share of world headlines. Armored vehicles and heavily armed patrols roam the streets, and there are regular searches and checkpoints. On the other hand, the tourist authorities try to portray their city as some kind of Hibernian Rio—a farcical idea but also one to which the city's magnificent setting of mountains, pellucid skies, and the great natural harbor of Belfast Lough does lend some credence.

If you've never been, it is almost certainly not what you expect. Belfast, though it no longer has any real relationship with its lough inlet or its major river, the Lagan, is a city by water. To look at, it is a wholly English creation of the Victorian period—a parody, almost, of the great industrial cities of the English Midlands and North, and once their great rival. It is a predominantly Protestant city but also one divided by religious factionalism, either fiercely (in West Belfast) or fawningly (in the middle-class suburbs). The Troubles are all too apparent, not least in the plethora of parking pounds and the absolute prohibition on leaving a car unattended anywhere outside them. Yet it is not really a dangerous place to visit, and in the midst of all the signs of modern depression it remains a beautiful city, and a storehouse of Victoriana. No part of the city is more than a few miles from the foothills of the surrounding mountains, and in many parts the hills magically appear at the end of each street.

To visit Northern Ireland without seeing Belfast would be to avoid the issue. This is the voice of the North—pronounced in an accent which is the coarsest and loudest in the land. In purely practical terms, visiting is dead easy. Normal life continues, albeit in a way that can come as a shock to a newcomer, the people are strikingly friendly, and, statistically at least, you're as safe here as in virtually any other city of comparable size. Accommodation, food, and transit are all well-organized, and if you feel the need to escape you can rapidly get to almost anywhere else in the North, or there's good transportation on the main road and rail routes down towards Dublin.

As far as what you should see goes, it's experiencing the city itself that comes top of the list. This need not take more than a couple of days, though Belfast is also an easy base from which to visit virtually anywhere else in the North. In the city center, concentrate on the glories that the industrial revolution brought: grandiose Victorian buildings as self-satisfied as any the British Empire created—and magnificent Victorian pubs. West Belfast offers a more contemporary vision—a depressed, blue-collar area where Northern Ireland's sectarian divisions are at their most starkly apparent. It may not sound like a tourist attraction, but it's certainly an eye-opener; and the ephemeral (but sometimes exceptionally talented) art of the mural painters who have claimed this part of the city for their own gives a fascinating insight to the current temper of the North.

The Development of the City

Belfast began its life as a cluster of forts built to guard a ford across the Farset River, which nowadays runs underground beneath High Street. The Farset and Lagan rivers form a valley that marks a geological boundary between the basaltic plateau of Antrim and the slaty hills of Down; the softer red Triassic sandstones from which their courses were eroded are responsible for the bright red color of the Belfast brick that pervades the city today.

In the early days, however, Belfast was very slow to develop, and indeed its history as a city doesn't really begin until the seventeenth century. A **Norman** castle was built here in 1177 but its influence was always limited, and within a hundred years or so control over the Lagan valley had reverted firmly to the Irish, under the **O'Neills** of Clandeboye who had their strong-hold in the Castlereagh Hills. Theirs was the traditional Irish pastoral community, booleying their livestock and families between the hills and valley plain. Then, in 1604, **Sir Arthur Chichester**, a Devonshire knight whose son was to be the first earl of Donegall, was "planted" in the area by James I, and shortly afterwards the tiny settlement was granted a charter creating a corporate borough. By the restoration era of 1660 the town was still no more than 150 houses in five or six streets, and Carrickfergus at the mouth of the lough held the monopoly on trade.

By the end of the seventeenth century, however, things were looking up: French Huguenots fleeing persecution at home brought skills which rapidly improved the fortunes of the local linen industry, and by the turn of the century the population had reached about 2000. In 1708 the town was almost entirely destroyed by fire, but it was only a temporary setback; throughout the **eighteenth century** the cloth trade and shipbuilding expanded tremen-dously, and the population increased ten-fold in a hundred years. It was a city noted for its liberalism. In 1784 Protestants were overwhelming in their gene-rosity to help build a church for the Catholic population. And in 1791, three Presbyterian Ulstermen formed the society of **United Irishmen**, a gathering embracing Catholics and Protestants on the basis of common Irish nationality. Belfast was the center of this movement and thirty Presbyterian ministers in all were accused of taking part in the 1798 rebellion—six were hanged.

Despite the movement's Belfast origins, the rebellion in the North was in fact an almost complete failure, and the forces of reaction backed by the wealthy landlords quickly and ruthlessly stamped it down. Within two genera-tions most Protestants had abandoned the nationalist cause and Belfast as a sectarian town was truly born. In the **nineteenth century** Presbyterian ministers like the Reverend Henry Cooke and Hugh (Roaring) Hanna began openly to attack the Catholic church, and the sectarian divide became wider, and increasingly violent. In 1835 several people were sabred to death in Sandy Row, and sporadic outbreaks of violence have been virtually constant from that day on. Meanwhile, the nineteenth century saw vigorous commer-cial and industrial expansion. In 1888 Queen Victoria granted Belfast city status; the city fathers' gratitude to her is stamped on buildings throughout the center. By this time the population had risen to 208,000 and with the continued improvement in both the linen and shipbuilding industries, the population exceeded even that of Dublin by the end of the century.

This century has been less kind. Although Partition and the creation of Northern Ireland with Belfast as its capital inevitably boosted the city's status, decline has been fairly constant over recent years. Bombing in World War II destroyed much of the city, and in the past ten years great tracts of West Belfast have been demolished in a belated attempt to improve living condi-tions. Outside the center, this is a very modern-looking place. Today the linen industry has disappeared altogether, and shipbuilding is rapidly crumbling, but the city is struggling very hard for revitalization and billions of pounds are being poured in—from Britain and the European Community—in the hope that economic revival might bring with it some kind of more hopeful future.

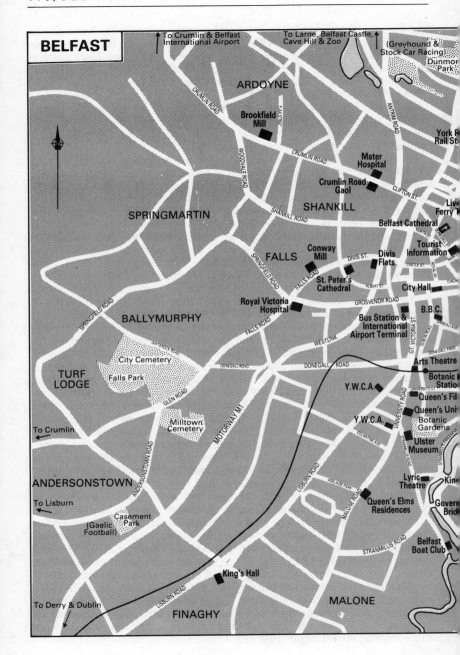

BELFAST

To Crumlin & Belfast International Airport

To Larne, Belfast Castle, Cave Hill & Zoo

(Greyhound & Stock Car Racing)
Dunmor
Park

ARDOYNE

CRUMLIN ROAD

Brookfield Mill

CRUMLIN ROAD

Mater Hospital

Crumlin Road Gaol

CLIFTON ST.

York R
Rail St

WOODVALE ROAD

SPRINGMARTIN

SHANKILL ROAD

SHANKILL

Liv
Ferry

Belfast Cathedral

FALLS

SPRINGFIELD ROAD

FALLS ROAD

Conway Mill

DIVIS ST.

Divis Flats

Tourist Information

CASTLE ST.

St. Peter's Cathedral

ALBERT ST.

City Hall

SPRINGFIELD ROAD

Royal Victoria Hospital

GROSVENOR ROAD

B.B.C.

BALLYMURPHY

FALLS ROAD

Bus Station & International Airport Terminal

WESTLINK

GT. VICTORIA ST.

DONEGALL PASS

Arts Theatre

WHITEROCK ROAD

City Cemetery

Falls Park

DONEGALL ROAD

DONEGALL ROAD

Botanic Statio

TURF LODGE

GLEN ROAD

Y.W.C.A.

UNIVERSITY ST.

Queen's Fil

Queen's Uni

Milltown Cemetery

Y.W.C.A.

UNIVERSITY ROAD

Botanic Gardens

Ulster Museum

To Crumlin

MOTORWAY M1

TIGANTILE AVE.

To Lisburn

ANDERSONSTOWN

ANDERSONSTOWN ROAD

Lyric Theatre

Kin

Casement Park
(Gaelic Football)

LISBURN ROAD

MALONE ROAD

Queen's Elms Residences

Gover
Bri

Belfast Boat Club

STRANMILLIS ROAD

To Derry & Dublin

LISBURN ROAD

King's Hall

FINAGHY

MALONE

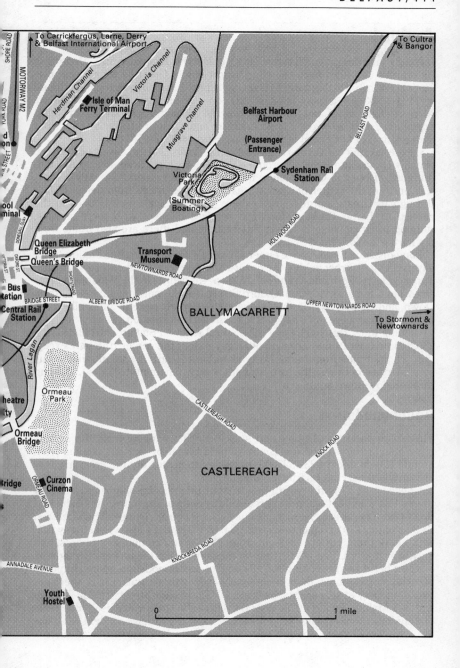

To Carrickfergus, Larne, Derry & Belfast International Airport

SHORE ROAD

YORK ROAD

MOTORWAY M2

To Cultra & Bangor

Herdman Channel

Victoria Channel

Musgrave Channel

Isle of Man Ferry Terminal

Belfast Harbour Airport

(Passenger Entrance)

BELFAST ROAD

Victoria Park

(Summer Boating)

Sydenham Rail Station

HOLYWOOD ROAD

ol minal

DONEGALL QUAY

Queen Elizabeth Bridge

Queen's Bridge

OXFORD ST

SHORT STRAND

Transport Museum

NEWTOWNARDS ROAD

Bus Station

BRIDGE STREET

Central Rail Station

ALBERT BRIDGE ROAD

BALLYMACARRETT

UPPER NEWTOWNARDS ROAD

To Stormont & Newtownards

River Lagan

Ormeau Park

CASTLEREAGH ROAD

KNOCK ROAD

heatre ity

Ormeau Bridge

CASTLEREAGH

Bridge

ORMEAU ROAD

Curzon Cinema

KNOCKBREDA ROAD

ANNADALE AVENUE

Youth Hostel

0   1 mile

Arrival

If you **fly** into Belfast you'll arrive either at **Belfast International Airport,** in Aldergrove, 19 miles from the city (airport bus to Great Victoria Street Bus Station, Mon–Sat half-hourly 6:40am–10:20pm, Sun hourly 7:15am–10:15pm; ☎08494-22888 for airport information), or less likely at **Belfast Harbour Airport,** four miles out (services only to British regional airports with *Loganair, Jersey Airways, Manx Airlines,* and *Capital Airlines*; train from Sydenham Halt to Central Station or take a taxi; ☎0232-457745).

Of the **ferries** to Northern Ireland, only *Belfast Ferries* Liverpool service actually comes into Belfast Harbour—the rest dock at Larne, twenty miles to the north. Donegall Quay, where the Liverpool ferries dock, is only a short way north of the center of town; it's easiest to take a taxi from here, or walk through to Great Georges Street where you can pick up city buses to the center. At Larne Harbour *Ulsterbus* services connect with ferry arrivals, running to Great Victoria Street Bus Station, and there are also trains from the harbor to York Road Station.

Long-distance **buses** arrive either at Great Victoria Street Bus Station (actually in Glengall Street behind the *Europa Hotel;* services to the west—Armagh, Tyrone, Derry, Fermanagh and west Down—as well as to the Republic and for airport and ferry services) or Oxford Street (for the north and east—Antrim, Down, and east Derry). Both of these are extremely central, and well served by city bus services. ☎0232-320011 for *Ulsterbus* information.

Coming in by **rail** you'll be at the Central Railroad Station (☎0232-230310/ 235282) on East Bridge Street, a little way east of the center (the only exception are the trains from Larne Harbour to York Road). A special rail-link bus service runs between the two stations every ten minutes or so, passing through downtown on the way.

Accommodation

There's no shortage of **places to stay** in Belfast, ranging from the famous city-center *Europa Hotel* (on Great Victoria Street by the bus station; from around £90 double; ☎0232-327000) to the youth hostel, but the great majority are fairly ordinary B&Bs from around £10 up.

Cheapest of all is the **youth hostel,** but price is the only reason to stay there. For a start it's almost three miles south of downtown on Saintfield Road (the A24 towards Newcastle; bus #38 or #84 from Donegall Square East; £4.50 a night, £10 non-members; ☎0232-647865) and it's also very strictly run, with an 11:15pm curfew, lock-out from 11am–5pm, compulsory chores, and only two showers. The **YWCA** (not women-only) near the university might be a better bet if you're looking for this type of accommodation, more comfortable with single rooms, though barely cheaper than a regular B&B; there are two branches, at Queen Mary's Hall, 70 Fitzwilliam Street (☎0232-240439) and 3–5 Malone Road (☎0232-668347). **Queen's University** itself also rents out student rooms during school vacation and if you have student ID these are exceptional value, though they are meant to be reserved in advance—

contact *Queen's Houses*, 14–16 Upper Crescent (☎0232-245133 ext 3740) or *Queen's Elms*, 72 Malone Road (☎0232-381608/668535). Prices are as low as £3 (bed only) for students, though for adult non-students they can be close to B&B prices.

A high proportion of the **B&Bs** are also in the university area, south of the downtown, especially on Botanic Avenue, Eglantine Avenue, and Malone Road. The **tourist office** (50 High Street; ☎0232-246609) has complete lists and can make reservations for you. Otherwise ones to try include *Botanic Lodge Guest House* (87 Botanic Avenue; ☎0232-327682), *Liserin Guest House* (17 Eglantine Avenue; ☎0232-660769), *Eglantine Guest House* (21 Eglantine Avenue; ☎0232-667585), *East Sheen House* (81 Eglantine Avenue; ☎0232-667149; one of the best), *Pearl Court House* (11 Malone Road; ☎0232-666145), *Malone Guest House* (79 Malone Road; ☎0232-669565), and *Beaumont Lodge* (237 Stranmillis Road; ☎0232-667965). If you want to pay more, *Camera House* (44 Wellington Park; ☎0232-660026) is a very luxurious B&B, much better than most hotels at £20–25 a night.

The nearest **campgrounds** to the city center are *Jordanstown Lough Shore Park*, some six miles north in Newtownabbey (Shore Road, Newtownabbey; ☎0232-868751 or 863133), basically a trailer park; and *Belvoir Forest Site*, about four miles south, for which you need a permit in advance (from the *Forest Service*, Department of Agriculture, Room 34, Dundonald House, Belfast; ☎0232-650111 ext 456).

Getting Around

Although you can walk easily enough around the center, distances to the more outlying attractions can be considerable, and many of the places to stay are also some way out. Fortunately there's an excellent city **bus** service that covers almost anywhere you're likely to go. Almost all of them set off from Donegall Square, right at downtown, or the streets immediately around, and the best way to start is to pick up the map which outlines the main services from the tourist office (you can also phone ☎0232-246485 for bus information). The fare for city-center journeys is 50p, and there's a zone system which comes into operation as you head farther out. You can pay on the bus, but you'll save time and a little money if you buy a **multi-journey** ticket in advance (£3.80 for eight journeys, from newsagents and other shops throughout the city). You push the ticket into a machine on the bus to cancel one journey each time you travel—two people can use the same ticket as long as you cancel it twice. For journeys across zones, you again have to cancel the ticket twice. *Ulsterbus* also serves the routes from the city center to Lisburn, via either the Falls and Andersonstown roads, or Lisburn Road. These leave from either the old GNR station, or the Grosvenor Road. (Phone ☎0232-320011 for details.)

Black taxis which run along set routes into West Belfast, picking up and dropping passengers anywhere along the way, can also be extremely handy, and at about 35p a journey they're also cheap. The ones which operate into the Catholic areas (all of these go up Falls Road itself) set out from the

Smithfield area of Castle Street, and some of them will be prepared to give you a tour round Catholic West Belfast for £6–7 an hour. Cabs servicing Protestant areas run from North Street, slightly farther north, and charge much the same, though they may find the idea of a tour around Protestant West Belfast a slightly strange one. Some Belfast people are reluctant to use these cabs, believing that the money raised goes into the hands of sectarian racketeers on whichever side. **Regular taxis**, based at the rank in Donegall Square and others throughout the city, charge a minimum £1.50, which rapidly starts to increase on the meter if you're going any distance.

If you're **driving** you need to be careful about where you park your car; it's made abundantly clear that you're not allowed to leave it unattended in downtown **control zones** (clearly marked with black-and-yellow signs) and it's always best to use specified parking lots. If you want to leave your car anywhere else, check with a local first, as the situation changes fairly rapidly. Just about the only place to rent a **bike** in Belfast is *Ernie Coates* on Grand Parade (☎0232-471321).

Downtown and the Sights of Belfast

Donegall Square, in the center of which stands the City Hall and from all around which buses and taxis set out for every part of the city, is very much the physical heart of Belfast. Immediately north is the main shopping and commercial area; to the south entertainment and accommodation. Most of the grand old Victorian buildings so characteristic of the city are within walking distance, especially to the north and to the east, toward the river. Farther out, **north Belfast** boasts Cave Hill, with its castle and zoo, and plenty to see on the way there. **South Belfast** has the "Golden Mile," with its pubs and entertainments, stretching out past the university, the Botanic Gardens and Ulster Museum. In the **east**, across the river beyond the great cranes of Harland & Wolff, lies suburbia, and very little of interest. Blue-collar **West Belfast**, by contrast, seems almost a separate city in its own right, divided from the rest by the four lanes of the Westlink freeway.

Around the City Hall

The **City Hall** presides over Belfast city center, a handy landmark for visitors and principal departure point for city buses. A boorish-looking building, quadrangular and squat, its once-white Portland stone is now milky-gray and its architecture unashamedly plagiaristic—turrets, saucer domes, scrolls, and pinnacle pots. In the eighty-odd years since it was built, any functional civic purpose the building has served has been secondary to its role in propagating the ethics of Presbyterian power. This is clear at the main entrance, where stands Queen Victoria, portrayed as Empress, her maternal gaze unerringly cast across the rooftops towards the Protestant Shankill area. At her feet, sculpted in bronze, are proud figures representing the city fathers' work ethic; a young scholar, his mother with spinning spool, and father with mallet and boat. More powerfully intransigent than the symbolic domineering of any

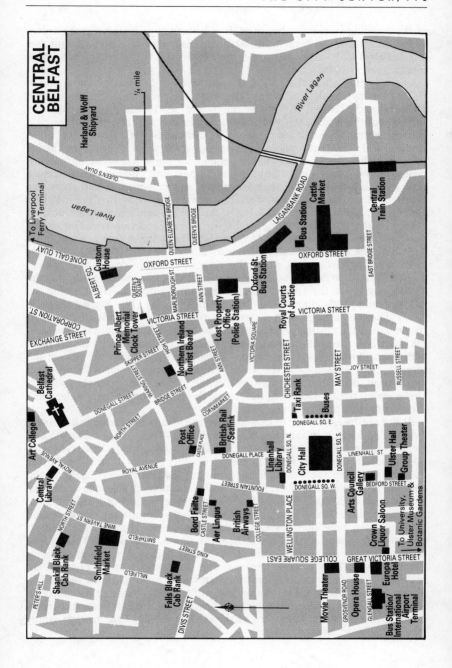

CENTRAL BELFAST

of the building's statuary, however, is a banner high up among the colonnades, embracing the main drum, which proclaims the Unionist catchphrase: "Belfast Says No"—an expression of their opposition to the Anglo-Irish agreement signed in 1984.

The City Hall offers the only real opportunity to be shown around one of Belfast's many classical buildings. There are 45-minute guided **tours** daily at 10:30am and 2:30pm (July–Sept only) and at 10:30am on Wednesday throughout the rest of the year; admission is free and access is through a security entrance at the rear (opposite Linenhall Street). Inside, the **main dome**, and an unreachable whispering gallery, are 173 feet above you—modeled on that of St Paul's in London, the dome has zodiac signs, both painted and in stained glass windows, around its rim. The marbled **entrance hall** itself is palatial, with staircase pillars and colonnades, and there are bronze and marble statues as well, two of which portray Frederick Robert Chichester, Earl of Belfast (1827–1853): the first, upright and stalwart-looking, stands on the principal landing, while the other, Frederick reclining on his deathbed, has been hauled out of the rain into the Octagon entrance porch.

Also on the principal landing is a **mural**, executed in 1951 by John Luke, celebrating Belfast's traditional industries, now mostly dead—ropemaking, shipbuilding, weaving and spinning. Oddly though, the central position in the picture is given to the Town Crier, perhaps a reference to Belfast having the oldest continuously running newspaper in the world (*The Newsletter*, since 1737). The tour also takes in the **robing room**, where the trick is to ask to try on one of the cloaks for a snapshot. The building's highlight is the **council chamber**, the walls wainscotted in hand-carved oak and its center filled with councillors' pews and a visitors' gallery (open only on the first of the month), both also in oak. It's a very civilized scene, hung with drooping portraits of British royalty and aristocracy; the seating puts the majority Unionists on the far side, with the rest of the parties on the near side, while the ever-present press sit in between.

At the northwest corner of Donegall Square stands the **Linenhall Library** (Mon–Wed and Fri 9:30am–6pm, Thurs 9:30am–8:30pm, Sat 9:30am–4pm), Belfast's oldest library, established in 1788. Irish-language and reference books occupy the first floor, fiction is on the ground floor. The library contains probably the best collection of early Belfast printed books in the country. On the second floor, its "Political Collection" is a unique accumulation of over 40,000 publications dealing with every aspect of Northern Irish political life since 1968—a range of literature that encompasses every election poster printed since then, as well as documents ranging from party political ephemera to doctoral theses sent in from all over the world. This radical approach is not a new departure for the Linenhall; one of the institution's librarians was Thomas Russell, executed in Downpatrick in 1803 for inciting rebellion in sympathy with Robert Emmett's 1798 uprising down south. The library is an independent institution and you're free to examine its collection which is indexed under both subject and author, on the first floor; free, but a donation is welcome. There are also excellent facilities for tracing family trees, if you're interested.

The Shopping Center: Cornmarket

The streets leading north off Donegall Square North take you into the **city center** proper, downtown Belfast. The grand old department stores here, in creams, pinks, and browns, have only recently been transformed into a flood of up-tempo shops. Mercifully, though, it's only the ground floors that have been converted, leaving the lofty grandeur of the floors above undisturbed. New structures, too, go up swiftly, but they at least tend to reflect the rhythm and sheer hulk of their nineteenth-century forebears. The 1970s saw many bombing blitzes on this shopping area, but in the 1980s, whether because of racketeering or a change in the bombers' hearts, the area seems to have been left alone. Little traffic is allowed inside the precinct, the whole area is cordoned off by security barriers at the major points of entry—and blocked off totally by green military railing at all other routes. That said, there's really little to discover in this area, apart from a few necessary amenities. There's also a recently opened shopping complex, The High Park Centre (just off High Street), which has a wide range of shops, a multi-story parking lot, plus a good range of cheap places where you can eat during the day.

The pedestrianized **Cornmarket**, marked by a cap-hooded bandstand painted red, is where the various cults gather; skinheads, punks, mods and drunks, though most prevalent are the religious chanteurs. This spot (or near enough) is also where Henry Joy McCracken was hanged, after leading the Antrim rebels in the ill-fated (and in the north almost farcically unsuccessful) 1798 rebellion.

From the Entries to the Docks

Nearby, along Ann Street, and off down any left or right turning, you're in among the narrow alleyways known as the **Entries**. There are some great old saloon **bars** down here, like *The Morning Star* in Pottinger's Entry, with its overlarge frosted windows and Parisian café-like curvilinear counter; *The Globe* in Joy's Entry; and *White's Tavern* in Winecellar Entry (off the High Street), the oldest pub in the city. **Crown Entry** was where the "Society of United Irishmen" was born, led by the triumvirate of Wolfe Tone, McCracken, and Samuel Nielson; Nielson printed his own newspaper in this area, the *Northern Star*, full of the French revolutionary ideals of liberty, equality, and fraternity—treasonous material which got him hounded out of town. Also in Crown Entry, Sheridan, the playwright (of *School for Scandal* fame) had his "pathetic" comic school.

Across the High Street, to the north, there used to be a similar set of Entries that ran through to Waring Street, but many of them were destroyed by bombing during World War II. Still, this end of the **High Street**, with the Farset River running underground (and invisible) below, is the oldest part of the city, and its atmosphere is still in places redolent of the eighteenth century. At the docks end of the High Street stands the **Prince Albert Memorial Clock Tower**, built between 1867 and 1869 and wilting just a little off the perpendicular. It's a strange memorial, especially as Prince Albert never had anything to do with Belfast, but it's a handy landmark. And beyond here are more of the grand old classical-style buildings that stud Belfast (see below).

Before moving on, this is a fairly good position from which to view the world's second and third largest cranes, *Goliath* and *Samson*, across the river in the Harland & Wolff **shipyard** in East Belfast. They are the city's proudest international asset; among other craft, the ill-fated *Titanic* was built here and the shipyard is nowadays said to possess the largest dry dock in the world—over 600 yards long and 100 yards wide. Unfortunately, the area is very security conscious, as its workforce has always been predominantly Protestant, and access is virtually impossible—something that sadly also cuts off a lot of the east side of the river.

In fact there's virtually no reason to cross the river into **East Belfast** at all. There are a couple of reasonably pleasant parks, but the only real lure, for transportation buffs, is the **Witham Street Gallery**, on Witham Street off Newtownards Road (Mon–Sat 10am–5pm; buses #16, #21, #22, or #24 or train to Bridge End station). This collection of carriages, cars, trams, trains, bicycles and motorbikes is part of the Ulster Folk and Transport Museum (see "Down and Armagh"), and its exhibits are rotated with the ones there. The nucleus of the exhibition is the collection of Thomas Edens Osborne, a local bicycle dealer who was an associate of John Dunlop (of tire fame); it runs from the earliest vehicles to Northern Ireland's most recent and disastrous association with the motor industry, De Lorean.

From the Albert Memorial to the Cathedral

North of the Albert Memorial are a series of grand edifices which grew out of a civic vanity similar to that invested in the designing of the City Hall. The **Customs House**, a Corinthian-style building, is laid out just behind the memorial in the shape of a letter E, designed by Charles Lanyon between 1854 and 1857. Unfortunately, it's not open to the public, leaving you unable to verify stories of fantastic art masterpieces stored in its basements—though it is known that Anthony Trollope, the nineteenth-century novelist (and not-so-well-known inventor of the pillar-mail box), once worked here as a surveyor's clerk. Another of Lanyon's designs, the **Belfast Banking Company** building (1845), is at the Donegall Street end of Waring Street. Originally an eighteenth-century Assembly Rooms, it was transformed by Lanyon into a palazzo-style remodeling of Barry's *Reform Club* in London. On the same street, you'll also stumble upon the **Ulster Bank** (1860), an indulgent Italianate building of rich yellow sandstone, fronted by a spate of fluted pillars and, up on the parapet, with decorated Grecian urns at the sides of an allegorical representation of war maidens. There's a fence of intricately wrought iron railing and a few reassembled Victorian street lamps, too, stubby but quaint.

The most monolithic of all these grand buildings, however, is the Protestant **Cathedral** of St Anne's, a neo-Romanesque basilica started in 1899. It's at the junction of Donegall Street and York Street, close to the beached buoys of the modern Art College. Despite a glorious west door it's almost wholly insignificant: were it not for the body of **Lord Edward Henry Carson**, entombed underneath the nave floor, it would be quite without interest. Carson (1854–1935) is a name that Ulster has never forgotten and it's possible to view St Anne's as nothing but a mausoleum to his memory. The bodily symbol of partition, he's seen either as the hero who saved Ulster, or the villain who sabotaged the country's independence. A Dubliner of Scots-Presbyterian background, Carson took the decision in 1910 to accept the leadership of the opposition to Home Rule, which in effect inextricably allied him to the Ulster Unionist resistance movement—an association which is about the only thing for which he is remembered. Yet his personality and integrity went far deeper than this. He abhorred religious intolerance and, behind the exterior of a zealous crusade, he sincerely believed that Ireland couldn't prosper without Britain, and only wished that a federalist answer could have involved a united Ireland. Nonetheless, this was the same man who, as a brilliant orator at the bar, and in the role he loved the most, brought about the humiliating destruction of Oscar Wilde at his trial in 1895.

As it continues north Donegall Street becomes Clifton Street, which takes its name from **Clifton House** (1771–74). Better known as the "Poor House," or the "Charitable Institute for the Aged and Infirm," it's in handsome Georgian style, of pedimented brick with an octagonal-based stone spire at its rear and symmetrically projecting wings to its sides. This is one of the simpler but more effective buildings that Belfast has to offer, yet was designed by an amateur architect and local paper merchant, Robert Joy, uncle of the hapless Henry Joy McCracken. The Institute was built at a time of much poverty and unrest, brought about by the Donegalls' eviction of tenants when their leases started running out—the very same Donegalls whose name is tagged to so many of Belfast's streets.

South Belfast: the University Area and the River

The university area inhabits part of the stretch of **South Belfast** now known as "The Golden Mile," starting at the Opera House on Great Victoria Street and reaching past the university, up into the Malone and Stranmillis roads. It's an area in which you're likely to find yourself spending much of your time, since it's littered with eating places, pubs and bars, B&Bs, and guest-houses. Dozens of restaurants have sprung up here in the last five years, the gourmet explosion said to have been triggered by the refurbishment of the grandiose, turn-of-the-century **Opera House** in 1980, which hauls in the money-spenders from the suburbs for a night's entertainment.

Among the welter of attractions on the Golden Mile is one of the greatest of Victorian **gin palaces**, the *Crown Liquor Saloon*, now a National Trust property but still open for drinking. The saloon has a glittering tiled exterior—amber, carmine, rouge, yellow, green, blue and smoke-gray—resembling a spa baths more than a serious drinking institution. The rich, High Victorian stuccowork continues inside, too: the scrolled ceiling, patterned floor and the golden-yellow and rosy-red hues led John Betjeman to describe it as his "many-colored cavern." With your drinks, grab a snug and shut the door (best to avoid the busy lunchtime and mid-evening periods); it's like sitting in a railroad-carriage compartment, with pieces of conversation creeping over from the neighboring snugs. There's no let-up in decoration in here either, with the mirrors painted, the oak paneling sporting flourishes of friezework (like the heraldic beasts guarding each snug entry) and the mounted gun-metal plates provided for striking matches. The push-button bell activates an indicator on a board above the bar, though it's just as much an experience to order at the bar from the white-aproned and black-bowtied staff. The bar counter itself is a gorgeous S-curve of tile work, with exotically carved timber dividing screens.

The **Golden Mile** itself buzzes with activity in the evening, even on a weekday if school's in session. The cheaper restaurants are at the city end of Great Victoria Street, with the more expensive ones up Stranmillis Road and in and around the skirts of the BBC on Bedford Street. There's a plethora of accommodation, too, among the grid pattern of the broad, tree-lined streets surrounding the university campus, much of it in old three-story Victorian homes. The area also has two excellent antiquarian **bookshops** on Dublin Road, Roma Ryan's *Books and Prints* and *Prospect House Books*, both pretty good for Irish material—though the prices are not giveaways by anyone's standards—and also a few secondhand bookshops, like *The Bookshop* (next to the *Belle Epoque* restaurant on Great Victoria Street) and *Bookfinders* (Mon–Sat 10am–5:30pm, Thurs until 7pm) at 47 University Road.

Before heading straight into the University Quarter, sidestep off Great Victoria Street into **Sandy Row**, which runs parallel. A strong, working-class, Protestant quarter with the tribal sidewalk-painting to prove it, it's one of the most glaring examples of Belfast's divided worlds, wildly different from the Golden Mile's cosmopolitan sophistication, yet only yards away. In Donegall Road, off to the west, are some of the murals which characterize these sectarian areas—see under "West Belfast" below. Sandy Row used to be the main road south and, although hard to believe today, it was once a picturesque ribbon of whitewashed cottages.

The University Area

Back on the Golden Mile, and just past the southern end of Sandy Row, are three churches (Moravian, Crescent, and Methodist) whose distinctive steeples frame the entrance to the **University Quarter**. It's a highly characteristic area, many of the row-houses leading up to the university buildings representing the final flowering of Georgian architecture in Belfast. The **Upper Crescent** is a magnificent curved Neoclassical block, built around 1845 but sadly neglected since, and now used mainly for office space. The **Lower Crescent**, perversely, is straight.

It's **Queen's University**, though, that's the architectural centerpiece of the area, flanked by the most satisfying example of a Georgian house-row in Belfast, **University Square**, Here the red brickwork has mostly been kept intact, with the exception of a few bay-windows put in by the Victorians. The block now houses various faculty buildings. The **Union Theological College** on College Park, which was temporarily the site of the Northern Ireland parliament until Stormont was built in 1932, closes off the vista between the terrace and the university. Not surprisingly, given its Italianate lines, this is another Lanyon design, as is the University College itself, built in 1849 as a mock-Tudor remodeling of Magdalen College, Oxford. Across the road from here is the Students' Union, a white 1960s design with its own 'No' banner, this time to student loans.

Just to the side of the Union are the **Botanic Gardens**, first opened in 1827 and deservedly the most popular of Belfast's gardens: compact, with walks well sheltered from the noise of surrounding traffic. Within the gardens is the **Palm House** (Mon–Fri 10am–5pm, Sat and Sun 2–5pm; free), a greenhouse predating the famous one at Kew Gardens in London, but very similar in style, with a white-painted framework of curvilinear ironwork and glass. It was the first of its kind in the world, another success for Lanyon who on this project worked in tandem with the Dublin iron-founder Richard Turner.

Also in the Botanic Gardens you'll find the **Ulster Museum** (Mon–Fri 10am–5pm, Sat 1–5pm, Sun 2–5pm; free; buses #69, #71, #72, #83 or #85), resited here in 1929 and expanded in 1972 with a concrete extension that matches the Portland stone surprisingly subtly. You'll need a fair bit of stamina to get through the museum, since it's a monster of a collection. Displays run from a dinosaur show, through reproductions of early Irish Christian jewelry, to the history of the post office in Ireland, waterwheels and steam engines, local archaeological finds, Irish wildlife, rocks, fossils and minerals—the list is exhaustive and exhausting. Still, everything is well explained and well laid out, and if you're keen to know about crocodiles' digestive systems or see a 35-million-year-old mackerel, then you could happily spend a full day here. (If you have the time, the museum is much more enjoyable taken in several small doses.) The various **art collections** are excellent: try the top floor for modern work by Francis Bacon or Henry Moore and, best of all (and the one thing you won't see elsewhere), the Irish artists represented—Louis le Brocquy, Paul Henry, and Belfast's own most acclaimed painter, Sir John Lavery. The museum's **Girona exhibition**, treasures from the Spanish Armada ships which foundered off the Giant's Causeway (see *Antrim and Derry*), and the museum's showpiece, can't be viewed at present. It should be permanently on display again from August 1990, when the sections on loan elsewhere have been returned and improvements to the building are complete.

Further South: the River and Giant's Ring

To go farther south from the University Quarter is to head through the glades of middle-class suburbia—an area that is singularly uninteresting. However, a ten- to fifteen-minute walk out on Stranmillis Road (the name derived from *struthan milis*, "sweet stream") will take you to the **Lagan Towpath**; follow the signs to the Lagan Meadows. The newly tarred towpath can be tramped for about eight miles to Lisburn, passing old locks and lock-houses, rapids, woodland, and marshes. The waterway opened in the late 1790s, ready to carry the newly discovered coal at Lough Neagh, but its utility declined with the advent of the railroad in 1839. Today, it's been harnessed as part of the "Ulster Way" for rambling and canoeing enthusiasts. Traveling south towards the affluent Malone area, you'll find the internationally renowned **Mary Peters Track**, part of the Malone Playing fields, which is first off Upper Malone Road. Set in what amounts to a natural amphitheater, with the Castlereagh Hills in the distance, the track, established by Olympic gold medalist Mary Peters, is one of the tracks of international standard on the European Grand Prix Athletics Circuit, so is certainly worth a visit if you're a sports enthusiast.

Less of a walk, but just as interesting, is to head a couple of miles up the river path to Shaw's Bridge, from there up a country road, following signs to Edenderry, along Ballysillan Road, and finally a right turn up Giant's Ring Road. Here, the **Giant's Ring** is a gargantuan, ceremonial burial ground or meeting place, its grassy interior the size of three soccer fields, contained by a twenty-foot-high circular earthen rim. You wouldn't be far wrong to think that its inwardly sloping wall would make an excellent speed-track circuit, for in the eighteenth century it was used for horse racing—six circuits making a two-mile race, with spectators jostling for position on the rampart's top. Most captivating of all is the huge dolmen left at the central hub of this cartwheel structure. As a single megalithic remain it is immediately more impressive than the great structures of the Irish High Kings at Tara, though here there's little information concerning its origins and usage. The ground chosen for the site, high above the surrounding lowlands (probably once marshy lake), is an impressive one; there's a powerful feeling that the great dramas and decision-making of the ancient northeast must have been played out here. If you want to do the walk in just one direction, *Ulsterbus* #22 passes below the site three times a day.

North Belfast: Cave Hill

North Belfast's attractions amount to no more than a castle and the city's **zoo**, out on Antrim Road (daily 10am–5pm; buses #2, #3, #4, #5 or #6), both conveniently next door to one another on the slopes of Cave Hill. In truth, though, it's **Cave Hill** itself that should be your real target.

Several paths lead up from the castle estate to the hill's summit—a rocky outcrop known as "Napoleon's Nose"—where there's an unsurpassable strategic overview of the whole city and lough. From here you can't help but appreciate the accuracy of the poet Craig Raine's aerial description of the city in his *Flying to Belfast*—like "a radio set with its back ripped off." Cave Hill was once awash with Iron-Age forts, for there was flint (for weapon-making) in the chalk under the basalt hill-coverings. In 1795, Wolfe Tone, Henry Joy McCracken, and other leaders of the United Irishmen stood on the top of Cave Hill and pledged "never to desist in our efforts until we have subverted the authority of England over our country and asserted our Independence."

Belfast Castle (and its wooded estate) is open to the public, recently upholstered and restored but, sadly, virtually empty of period accoutrements. It stands on the former deer park of the third marquis of Donegall, whose wish it was for the sandstone castle to be built here to the designs of Lanyon and his associates, in 1870. Consequently, the exterior is in the familiar Scottish Baronial style, inspired in part by the reconstruction of Balmoral Castle in Aberdeensrent in 1853: six-story tower, a series of crow-stepped gables, and conically peak-capped turrets. The most striking feature of all, however, is the serpentine Italianate stairway that leads down from the principal reception room to the garden-terrace below.

West Belfast

West Belfast has always been the city's blue-collar area. Here, in the eighteenth century, the flax and linen mills were established which in turn produced the relentless, gridded street pattern, lined with housing for the workers and their families. The overcrowded conditions were deplorable, and the sectarian riots of 1886—the worst of the nineteenth century—inspired the creation of two separate neighborhoods, Catholic and Protestant. In 1968 and 1969 this division was pushed to its limit when sectarian mobs and gunmen (on both sides) evicted over 8000 families from their homes in the city, mainly in West Belfast—until then the largest forced population movement in Europe since the end of World War II.

Today, however, West Belfast is no Beirut. It's as safe an urban area as any for the stranger to stroll around, and although it's principally residential, several of its districts are worth investigating. Of most interest are the partisan **mural paintings** seen in both Catholic and Protestant areas, an ephemeral art with new murals replacing old ones as the houses they're painted on are demolished. As you wander the back streets, you'll be captivated (sometimes captured) by the extraordinar friendliness of the people, an experience that's the high point of many people's stay in Belfast; you'll not come across this openness in any other part of the city, more remarkable here given the rigors of life in West Belfast.

The busy **Westlink expressway**, which effectively separates West Belfast from the rest of the city, linking Motorways 1 and 2, seems innocent enough as it sweeps across the city, but there are those who see it in a more sinister light, as part of the security process. Certainly it's handy for the police and army, restricting east–west access to a handful of main arteries. These points, overhead bridges and traffic circles, are virtual border crossings, easily sealed and easily monitored. It looks menacing too: the traffic signals are enclosed in cages, a footbridge over the freeway walled and roofed to keep missiles away from the cars passing below.

The Falls

Two routes lead into the heart of the **Falls** area: one along Grosvenor Road, the other through Divis Street. The latter is the more infamous and is also the route that carries the main injection of black taxi-cab traffic into the area. The taxis assemble in ranks at the end of Castle Street, in the Smithfield area, their routes strictly into the Catholic enclaves; a printed sign in Gaelic (the only official-looking one of its kind in Belfast) should be enough to emphasize the point for you. Rides are set at a fixed rate of around 35p and the cab leaves once it's full. The drivers, incidentally, are said to be Republican ex-prisoners.

Smithfield itself used to have a large, covered bazaar which has now been replaced by **Smithfield Retail Market**—actually a set of small shop units rather than a traditional open-air market. The area is currently undergoing large-scale redevelopment by private developers (another shopping complex on the way) and Belfast City Council also has plans to extend and improve the

Smithfield market itself. There is a reminder of the old character of the area on Winetavern Street, with several bookshops and junk antique places.

The Divis Flats and Divis Street

Crossing the Westlink via Divis Street confronts you immediately with the single most devastating symbol of disillusionment in the area—the **Divis Flats**. The flats take their name from Divis Mountain, the highest in the surrounding bowl of hills, whose name translates—poignantly—as "mountain of tears." The twin spires rising behind the flats belong to St Peter's Catholic Cathedral, a nineteenth-century Gothic design, not without its own hint of prophetic irony at having been modeled on the spires of Cologne cathedral. At the base of the flats, the moonscape sandlot is the only play area for the children. It's fringed with a necklace of curbstones, placed there by the community to keep out joyriders, who used to trek here from all over the North. The RUC—who want the curbstones removed to make their own access easier—has been accused of ignoring this "ordinary" community crime. Certainly the local tactics seem less heavy-handed than those of the police, who have shot fourteen joyriding kids in various incidents throughout the province.

The flats themselves, ugly, gray, punctured by colored cardboard and window glass, are a structural disaster; the ceilings and beams are cracked, sewage outlets blocked, the detritus flooding from one home to another, the elevators broken, the stairways unlit, asbestos visible—while unemployment in the complex exceeds eighty percent. To have begun building Divis (in the late 1960s) at a time when the rest of Europe already regarded such structures as failures was a decision of the blindest ignorance, and in 1983 the Divis community set up a "development committee," to bring about the demolition of the flats. A few of the towers have already gone and total destruction is expected in around seven or eight years—or maybe longer. The last structure to be demolished will almost certainly be **Divis Tower**, capped by a military fort of corrugated iron sheeting. Along with its sister fort, farther south next to the traffic circle at Donegall Street, this is one of the few high-rise places round here that has no problem with the lift, as supplies and personnel are flown in by helicopter. If you're keen to have a closer look at the flats, no-one will take offense: in fact, the tenants having been ignored for so long, your intrusion will probably be welcomed.

A little farther up Divis Street, on the other side of the road, is a gable wall **mural**, striking because of its pacifist content: a Madonna and Child, serenely centered in a pale blue sky and surrounded by little white clouds. Predictably, though, even this traditional theme is tampered with. Below the scene is a turbulent sea, its violent waves a bile-green, and the swaddling-clothes are finely streaked in the creases with blood-red.

Falls Road

Moving on, you enter **Falls Road** proper, which continues for a farther two miles out past Milltown Cemetery (see below) and into Andersonstown. There's a life and activity along this route the like of which you'll find nowhere else in Belfast, with the possible exception of the Shankill Road—shared taxis being flagged down, the odd collection of loitering males, an armed foot patrol edging its way along, and kids and prams being pushed through the streets. Most of the interest is concentrated in the **Lower Falls** (which is the area you've now entered), the road's left-hand side flattened and rebuilt with red-brick row-projects of four-roomed, two-story units. The right side of the road is more of a hodgepodge, taking in the bright blue swimming pools (target of an IRA bomb in 1988 that killed two Catholic civilians), the DHSS (known as "the Brew") cooped up in an awning of chicken wire, a weary-looking Victorian library, a Worshippers of Peace Convent, and farther up, on Andersonstown Road, the *Sinn Fein* Community Office and Press Center, its windows bricked up, doorways caged and monitored by video-camera. The path edging, built up with knee-high boulders, is intended to take the blast of any car bomb.

Over the road from here, a mural expresses solidarity with the African National Congress (ANC), Nelson Mandela's portrait enlarged in a semi-silhouette—though the ANC was swift in its rejection of any such support from the IRA. By now, too, you'll have noticed the blockade of iron sheeting which divides the streets. Called the **"Peace Line,"** it has the Protestant working class living directly on the other side. Down one of these streets, Conway Street (by the DHSS), stands the old Conway Mill, recently revitalized by a concerted community effort, spearheaded by community activist Father Des Wilson. Inside you can buy the wares of the few small businesses that operate out of here, or you can get a square meal and mug of tea for 50p in the small community canteen on the second floor.

Farther on you'll pass the redbrick buildings of the **Royal Victoria Hospital**, on the left as you head towards Andersonstown. Since the Troubles began, the Royal, as it's known locally, has been internationally acclaimed for its ability to cope with the consequences, though it's now as famous for its world-class medical care in all fields as it is for its strategic location.

There's little to see beyond here, although a few hundred yards farther down the Falls Road, on the left across a small rubble patch, is one of the more powerfully evocative of the Republican murals. It carries the words of Mairead Farrell: *I have always believed we had a legitimate right to take up arms and defend our country and ourselves against the British occupation.* Farrell, a prominent member of the IRA, was gunned down by an SAS team in March 1988 (along with Sean Savage and Danny McCann), in the controversial and much-publicized Gibraltar murders.

Follow the road on for another mile and it'll lead to **Milltown Cemetery**, recognizable by the army encampment there. A peaceful place, it's significant as the main Republican burial ground in Belfast—and was also the site of grenade-throwing and shooting in 1988 at the funeral of Sean Savage, one of the IRA men killed by the SAS in Gibraltar. Enter through the stone arch and you're immediately surrounded by a numbing array of Celtic and classical crosses. If you're in search of the Republican plots, continue directly on from the entrance for about a hundred yards, then veer right, heading towards a corrugated warehouse shed just outside the perimeter of the cemetery. Along the way are two plots, marked off by a low green border fence. The nearer one holds a large memorial tablet listing the Republican casualties in the various uprisings from 1798 to the present day. The far plot contains a modern granite-block sculpture, and also the graves of Bobby Sands, Mairead Farrell, Sean Savage, and others. Once you start to look, it's not difficult to spot the graves of many other victims of the Troubles, a devastatingly long list of (usually young) men and women. The M1 expressway lies below, at the bottom of the burial park: it was onto this stretch of road that Michael Stone, the Loyalist attacker, was pursued after he'd opened fire at the funeral of Sean Savage.

The Ballymurphy Murals

There's one last set of **murals** worth taking in, up behind the Falls area in the **Ballymurphy Estate**. To get there, turn right off Falls Road up Whiterock Road, passing alongside the City Cemetery wall and its slogans (*He is not your son but what if he was* and *The West has the best Vote Sinn Fein*). Once over the brow of the hill, take the next right into Ballymurphy Road, heading towards Springhill Avenue.

This whole area is in the process of being leveled to make room for new housing, but in the meantime the burned-out hulks of masonry couldn't possibly look more depressing. The only relief is in the color of the mural paintings. One carries the proclamation *Our day will come*, showing three paramilitaries with guns raised in front of the tricolor; another nearby is an astonishing contrast, depicting a peaceful, nineteenth-century scene of reaping the hay on a sunny harvest day. Turn past this last mural up towards Springfield Road and, a hundred yards or so up on the left, you'll see two of the most highly regarded gable-wall murals in Belfast.

The first is an enlarged copy of a Jim Fitzpatrick mythological piece, dazzlingly well executed by a young Belfast man, **Gerry Kelly**. Mural painting has taken on such a standing in the community that a competition is held to elect an annual winner; Kelly has been responsible for many Republican murals and this particular one was elected the winner for 1988. It shows a musclebound, helmeted warrior in athletic pose, brandishing a smoking blade in his right hand with sunrays colorfully torpedo-ing out in concentric circles from around him. It celebrates the arrival of the *Tuatha Dé Danann*, said to have been the fourth of the six legendary colonies which invaded Ireland, arriving in 1896 BC. Legend has it that they came from four cities in the northern Greek islands, where they learned their druidry and magic. The character here, Lug—best-known king of the Tuatha—is portrayed as protector of the Catholics.

The other mural here couldn't offer a more strikingly realist alternative. Painted in memory of the eight IRA men ambushed and shot by the British security forces at Loughgall in May 1987, it lists the names of the dead men alongside representations of them in black caps and combat uniform: in the background are the green Armagh hills, a fiery sky, and blue water, the usual symbolism of territorial claims. A little farther up on the right are lesser murals; a portrait of Bob Marley; a small twelve-piece set showing the demise of the Union Jack, fragment by fragment, giving rise to the Starry Plough; a humorous cartoon mural on *low profile*; and a *Free Leonard Peltier* appeal. Peltier was a North American Indian said to have been framed by the FBI—another example of the community's need to feel solidarity with other oppressed groups around the world.

The Shankill and Crumlin Roads

The Protestant areas of West Belfast receive much less attention from visitors, yet they're no less interesting—and no less deprived in terms of unrest and economic misfortune. Suffering in West Belfast operates more on a class scale than a sectarian one. For the outsider, this area is particularly rich in murals and if you want to see them, the Protestants have their own taxi-ranks, with cabs departing from the top of North Street—fares again around the 35p mark.

Crossing the Westlink into the **Shankill Road** (its name comes from *sean chill*, the old church), the graffiti begins to tell a different story; one says *The British army is welcome in Ulster*. A little way up on the left is a typical *Ulster Volunteer Force* mural, its centerpiece the outline of the six counties, without the rest of Ireland. At either side of the province stand two paramilitaries, one a 1912 Ulster Volunteer Defender in "home guard" attire, the other a contemporary Loyalist in all-black body and head gear. Accompanying them is the slogan *They fought then for the cause of Ulster. We will fight now*.

An alleyway on the right here will lead you into the Shankill projects. Almost immediately you'll find yourself in the midst of the greatest concentration of wall paintings around (there are more in Percy Place, nearby). In conception and technique, Protestant mural painting is markedly different from the Catholic tradition. Here, instead of sophisticated artwork, the execution is simple, symmetrical, and largely unsymbolic. One mural depicts a thin William of Orange on his white horse; others show flag-waving, the emotive expression of loyalism as a creed. Slogans abound—*One faith, one Crown*; *Ulster Scotland, United we stand*, and others which need no explanation, mostly executed in red, white, and blue.

Farther up Shankill Road, on the wall of a Protestant social club on the right, another mural is a seventieth-anniversary commemoration, comparing the Protestant soldiers of the Somme (1916) to the UVF prisoners of war in Long Kesh—a message to the British authorities to get their priorities in order. Eighty yards farther on again, on the left, a monochrome drawing again commemorates the UVF of 1912. It has four volunteers, with rifles firing in the course of battle, positioned around their armored vehicle—a statement that alludes to their fight being in defense of their property.

The **Crumlin Road**, too (you can easily make your way across from any point here), offers several gable walls for mural-musing. Most are faded, but there's a prominent set at Queen's Land Street, with a particularly unusual one in which shamrocks and the harp (traditional emblems of the Free State) are depicted alongside the red hand of Ulster. Others on the street depict the Star of David, possibly a statement of solidarity with Israel against the PLO and hence the IRA—the PLO/IRA link is tacitly acknowledged by all.

Heading back towards the city you'll pass an army encampment, set back from the road, with a tentacled iron-sheeting corridor and lookout post. Further down, you pass between the courthouse and the notorious Crumlin Road jail, with their underground connecting tunnel. Finally, at **Carlisle Circus**, the traffic circle with the missing statue that was once of Ian Paisley's nineteenth-century counterpart, Roaring Hanna, there's a mostly unimpressive mural chronicling the death of William McCullagh, a leading UDA man who was shot dead on the Shankill Road by the INLA in 1981 in retaliation for a spate of sectarian murders carried out by Loyalists.

Other Loyalist murals can be seen along the **Donegall Road**, west off Sandy Row. As you cross the railroad bridge approaching the Westlink you'll catch sight of a very large wall painting on the gable end of Roden Street; it can be seen clearly from Donegall Road itself. It bears the mottos *Quis Separabit* and *In memory of John McMichael*, with the abbreviated initials of four of the organizations under his command, the UFF, UDF, LPA, and DSD. McMichael was killed in December 1987 by a bomb placed under his car. As well as being a leading member of the UDA he was responsible for forming its political wing, the Ulster Loyalist Democratic Party and for formulating the UDA document "Common Sense."

Not far from the roundabout on the Westlink is a photogenic mural of King William, this time on a very indignant white horse, rearing out of the waters of the Boyne. The Protestant Donegall Road ends at this intersection, and the same road continues on the other side as the Catholic Sraid Dun Na nGall— the only road in West Belfast that the communities can really be said to share.

Food, Drink, and Entertainment

This is a big city, and it's rarely hard to find something to eat, or to keep yourself amused in the evenings, even if the latter more often than not means drinking in a pub. As a last resort, there are plenty of **takeout** and **fast-food** places downtown, many of which will still be open when the pubs close. Many of the best places to eat and drink are just south of the city center, along the Golden Mile.

Eating

If you're staying at a B&B, chances are you'll emerge in the morning full of enough fried food to keep you going all day, but if you do want **breakfast** you'll find plenty of cafés ready to dish up a good old-fashioned "Ulster Fry." At *Bonne Bouche* (Fountain Street in the center) you'll be stuffed with bacon, eggs, sausage, tomato, potato bread, soda bread, and pancake all for around £1; *Isibeals*, a burger place in High Street, is another good bet.

Heading down the **Golden Mile**, especially on Great Victoria Street itself, you've ample choice. A few to look out for include (from the top down):

Knife and Fork Grill (Wellwood Street off Great Victoria Street). A cheap and basic café, sit in or takeout.

Boyne Bridge Tavern (Sandy Row, across the road from the tobacco factory). Limited, meaty menu but good value.

The Archana (Amelia Street, behind the *Crown Liquor Saloon*). Indian restaurant, very cheap for lunch Monday to Wednesday, eat-all-you-can buffet Sunday evening.

Moghul Restaurant (Great Victoria Street). Another Indian place nearby, again with lunchtime and Sunday-night specials.

Ruby King (Great Victoria Street). Decent Chinese restaurant.

Harveys Pizzas (Great Victoria Street, noon–midnight). Popular pizza joint.

La Belle Epoque (Great Victoria Street). Fancy, expensive French restaurant.

Sloanies (Great Victoria Street; 4:30pm–12:30am). Bistro/wine bar with a pleasantly relaxed atmosphere.

The Butler Delicatessen (Dublin Road; Mon–Fri 8:30am–7pm, Sat 9am–6pm, Sun noon–7pm). A good deli where you can also sit down and eat.

Scruples (Botanic Avenue). Good-value set meals.

Chez Delbart, also known as *Frogities* (10 Bradbury Place, off Great Victoria Street; possibly worth reserving by phoning ☎0232-238020). Good food at good prices, though you often have to line up. Serves wine or bring your own bottle (there's a shop across the road) for £1 corkage.

Students' Union Cafeteria (second and third floors of the Union building, lunchtime only). Adequate and cheap.

From the above, you'll see that when you want to eat all you really have to do is wander down Great Victoria Street until you see something that takes your fancy, and in the evening it's also much the liveliest part of town. If that doesn't happen to be where you are, though, there are other possibilities. In the center one of the best places for lunch is upstairs at *Kelly's Cellars* (30 Bank Street, down the side of the *Allied Irish Bank*). There's also plenty of pub food available here: try the *Capstan Bar* (10 Ann Street); the *Bradan Bar* (83 May Street); the *Kitchen Bar* (Victoria Square); or *White's Tavern* (Winecellar Entry). In **West Belfast** there isn't a great deal of choice, but there are two of the cheapest places to eat in the city. The already-noted *Conway Mill* (Conway Street, off Falls Road) has a community center where you'll get a basic but substantial main dish and a mug of tea for 50p; while the *Mill Diner* (Crumlin Road, part of the Brookfield Mill complex; Mon–Fri 9am–3pm) has excellent value sandwiches and light meals.

Pubs

The situation with **pubs** is very much the same as with restaurants: the liveliest are on Great Victoria Street or down around the university, and if you start drinking at the *Crown* you can do a substantial pub crawl without moving more than about 100 yards from where you started.

The Crown Liquor Saloon (Great Victoria Street opposite the *Europa Hotel*). The most famous and spectacular pub in Belfast (see p.419) with a clientele that likes to think itself intellectual (there's no music). Good repertory of Ulster food—champ, colcannon, etc—and also Strangford oysters in season (£3 a dozen), usually gone by early afternoon.

Robinsons (Great Victoria Street, next door). Very packed, very trendy young crowd. The older, downstairs bar is akin to a tamer version of the *Crown* and, again, oysters and snacks.

The Brittanic Lounge (Amelia Street, above the *Crown's* side entrance). Sedate, cosy, and faintly exclusive (and more expensive than usual), this place even has a uniformed foyer attendant. Has some interesting Harland & Wolff pictures and memorabilia, including items from the *Brittanic* liner itself, the sister ship of the *Titanic*.

The Beaten Docket (Great Victoria Street, just below the *Crown*). Packed with fashion-conscious youngsters upstairs and down. Very loud music.

The Linenhall (Clarence Street, around the corner from the BBC). BBC accent-control zone. A very self-congratulatory place, yuppie and arty, but a pleasant bar—best in the evenings when they serve food and sometimes have music in the (otherwise closed) back lounge.

Cratchets (Lisburn Road at the corner of Camden Street, near the University). Another yuppie haven.

Lavery's (Bradbury Place). Snazzy outside but a regular pub within, with an ordinary, local crowd. Popular, though for no apparent reason.

Students' Union (University Road). Several bars with lots of heavy student drinking, but good-natured and cheap. You're really supposed to be a student to drink here, but no-one seems to mind.

The Eglantine Inn (Malone Road). Known to the students who pack it out as the "Egg." Very crowded, with a disco-bar upstairs.

The Botanic Inn (Malone Road opposite the "Egg"). Perhaps inevitably, known as the "Bot." Again almost entirely students, and plenty of atmosphere.

The Empire (Botanic Avenue, just up from the station). Cellar bar with a boisterous beer-hall atmosphere. Good-value food.

Maddens (Smithfield). Great, unpretentious, atmospheric pub. Lots of locals drinking in two large square rooms, one upstairs, one downstairs. Serves cheap stew and soup. Fantastic musical sessions.

Pat's Bar (Prince's Dock Road, in the north of the city by the docks, off York Road, easiest reached by taxi). Recently renovated in traditional style, with two bars (one large, one small) and open fires.

The Rotterdam (Pilot Street, also in the docks near *Pat's*). Great place with good music—see below.

The Liverpool (Donegall Quay, virtually opposite the Liverpool ferries). Small, two-roomed place with a pool table taking up one of them. But friendly and handy if you're waiting for the boat.

The Morning Star (Pottinger's Entry). Fine old-fashioned bar, busy in the day, quiet at night. Other good bars in the Entries include *The Globe* (Joy's Entry), *White's Tavern* (Winecellar Entry) and the *Kitchen Bar* (Victoria Square), which probably possesses the smallest urinal in the world.

Kelly's Cellars (30 Bank Street). Ancient interior and excellent food make this popular with tourists. Not much atmosphere though.

Music

As so often in Ireland, the best entertainment you'll find in Belfast is music in the pubs. Some of the main sessions and venues are listed below—often the same places already recommended for a simple drink—but you should look out for posters or check the listings in the *Belfast Telegraph* for up-to-date details. The tourist office also has details, updated regularly.

Kelly's Cellars (30 Bank Street). Folk music on Saturday afternoons, blues on Saturday nights.

Maddens (Smithfield). Excellent traditional sessions on Monday, Wednesday, and Saturday from around 9pm; sometimes as many as twenty musicians with music going on upstairs and downstairs at the same time.

The Linenhall (Clarence Street). Jazz on Monday, Wednesday, and Saturday nights; rock on Thursday; from 9:30pm. Cover charge £1.50.

Students' Union (University Road; officially you must show a student pass or get a Queen's student to sign you in, though pleading may work). Folk evening in the upstairs bar on Thursday (50p). Riotous atmosphere and great fun: plenty of mock *ceilidh* swinging goes on because none of them know how to do it properly.

The Liverpool (Donegall Quay). Traditional sessions on Sunday evenings and some Saturdays.

Pat's Bar (Prince's Dock Road). Sessions irregular but great when they happen.

The Rotterdam (Pilot Street). Music most nights, ranging from jazz and blues to folk and traditional.

Errigle Inn (320 Ormeau Road). Traditional sessions on Monday nights.

Limelight Ormeau Avenue, near the BBC. Basically a disco/nightclub, with cabaret on Tuesday, Friday, and Saturday, and bands on other nights of the week (£2).

Film, Theater, and Other Entertainment

When it comes to other forms of entertainment, Belfast reveals itself as little different from any British provincial city—there's not a lot going on. Again the *Belfast Telegraph* will have details of just about everything. As far as film goes there are plenty of mainstream **movie theaters** showing the usual general release stuff—big downtown ones include the four-screen *Cannon* (Great Victoria Street; ☎0232-222484) and three-screen *Curzon* (Ormeau Road; ☎0232-681373)—but the only really enterprising place is *Queens Film Theatre* (University Square Mews off Botanic Avenue; ☎0232-667687), with two screens showing slightly more esoteric stuff.

Theater is concentrated south of downtown, starting most noticeably with the grand *Opera House* on Great Victoria Street (☎0232-241919). Belfast's most prestigious venue, this has a wide-ranging program of national and international opera, ballet, and theater (both popular and serious), and is well attended. The *Arts Theatre* on Botanic Avenue (☎0232-224936) shows mostly comedy or very popular stuff; the *Lyric Theatre*, in a much more isolated position farther out on Ridgeway Street (☎0232-660081) takes on more serious drama, especially from the Irish heritage.

The **classical music** performed in the city rests mostly in the hands of the Ulster orchestra at the *Ulster Hall* on Linenhall Street (☎0232-241917; it's also used for big rock and pop concerts); you may also catch concerts—professional and amateur—at the *Whitla Hall*, Queen's University (☎0232-245133). The biggest pop and **rock gigs** are staged at *King's Hall*, Balmoral. There are a few **art galleries** to browse around if you have time on your hands. The *Arts Council Gallery* on Bedford Street exhibits mainly contemporary art (it also has a good coffee shop) as does the *Tom Caldwell Gallery*, a private basement gallery on Bradbury Place. The *Malone Gallery* (31 Malone Road) shows more experimental contemporary works and is probably the most interesting of the three. For **festivals** see the listings section below.

Listings

Airlines *British Airways* (9 Fountain Center, College Street; ☎0232-240522); *Aer Lingus* (46 Castle Street; ☎0232-245151); *British Midland* (Suite 2, Fountain Center; ☎0232-225151); *Dan Air* (☎0345-100200); *Loganair* (☎0232-247979).

Airports Two airports serve the Belfast region. *Aldergrove International Airport* (☎08494-22888) is used by all international flights and most major British airlines (including the *British Midland* and *British Airways* shuttles). Buses run every half hour to Great Victoria Street Bus Station, but if you're heading straight to Derry, or any other train station on that route, you can save time and money by taking a taxi to Antrim train station. *Belfast Harbour Airport* (☎0232-457745) has direct services with smaller operators from Blackpool, Edinburgh, Exeter, Glasgow, Luton, Liverpool, Manchester, and Teeside. Catch a train to the city center across the dual carriageway (Sydenham Halt station) or take a taxi (£4).

Banks Most of the major UK banks are allied to the following Northern Irish ones, all of which have downtown branches: *Ulster Bank Ltd* 47 Donegall Place (☎0232-320222); *Allied Irish*, 2 Royal Avenue (☎0232-246559); *Bank of Ireland*, 54 Donegall Place (☎0232-244901); *Northern Bank*, Donegall Square West (☎0232-245277); *Trustee Savings Bank* 4 Queens Square (☎0232-325599).

Bookshops *Just Books* (7 Winetavern Street) is an alternative community bookshop stocked also with magazines and political postcards; *Roma Ryan's Books and Prints* and *Prospect House Books* on Dublin Road are good for antiquarian tomes; *The Bookshop* on Great Victoria Street for general second-hand stuff; *Bookfinders* at 47 University Road; *University Bookshop* on University Road; *Waterstones* on Royal Avenue.

Buses ☎0232-246485 for city bus information, or pick up a timetable from the kiosk on Donegall Square West. Most routes operate from points around Donegall Square. Services outside Belfast are operated by *Ulsterbus* from either the Great Victoria Street Bus Station (actually in Glengall Street, behind the *Europa Hotel*; services to the west and the Republic) or Oxford Street, near the main railroad station (for the north and east). ☎0232-320011 for *Ulsterbus* information.

Car Rental *Avis*, 69 Great Victoria Street (☎0232-241414; also at Aldergrove Airport, ☎08494-22333, and Belfast Harbour Airport, ☎0232-240404); many other big names at the airports. *Bairds Rentals* on Boucher Road (☎0232-247770) is usually cheaper.

Family Planning Clinics *UPAA* 338a Lisburn Road (☎0232-667345); *LIFE* Bryson House, Bedford Street (☎0232-229241); *CURA* (☎0232-644963).

Ferries *Sealink* (Larne–Stranraer) is on Castle Lane (☎0232-327525); *P&O European Ferries* (Larne–Cairnryan) is based at Larne harbor only (☎0574-74321); *Belfast Ferries* (Belfast–Liverpool) is at 47 Donegall Quay (☎0232-326800). There's also the less well used *Isle of Man Steam Packet Company* (Belfast–Isle of Man) on Northern Road (☎0232-351009).

Festivals *Belfast International Festival at Queens* (2–3 weeks in Nov) claims to be Europe's second biggest arts festival after Edinburgh; *Belfast Folk Festival* (3 days in Sept); *Royal Ulster Academy Annual Exhibition* (Ulster Museum, 3 weeks in Oct); *Orangeman's Day* on July 12.

Hospitals Shaftesbury Square Hospital, near the University (☎0232-329808); Belfast City Hospital, Lisburn Road (☎0232-329241); Royal Victoria Hospital, Falls Road (☎0232-240503). ☎999 for emergency service.

Luggage Consignment Due to the obvious security considerations, there is, unfortunately, no official place where you can leave your luggage.

Markets The *St George's Casual Retail Market* (also known as the *Variety Market*) on May Street (Tues and Fri mornings) is the liveliest. The Friday Food and Variety market is by far the more popular with about 200 traders taking part; on Tuesday it's more of a fleamarket-type affair, selling new and secondhand clothes and a variety of junk. The *Smithfield Retail Market*, at the back of the new Castle Court development (West Street/Winetavern Street) is also pretty good. It operates from about 30 shop units and sells new and secondhand goods and clothes; plans are afoot for expanding and redeveloping this in 1990. For **antiques**, try the Saturday market at *Alexander The Grates* (Donegall Pass; open all day), which sells local bits and pieces at very reasonable prices.

Police ☎999 for emergency service. Main downtown police station is in North Queen Street.

Post Office General Post Office, Castle Place.

Tourist Information The Northern Ireland Tourist Board is on High Street (☎0232-231221). *Bord Fáilte*, for the Republic, can be found at 53 Castle Street (☎0232-327888).

Trains Nearly all trains operate from the Central Station on East Bridge Street (☎0232-230310 or 230671). Trains for Larne Harbour (and the ferries) use York Road Station (☎0232-235282). The two are connected by a shuttle-bus service. Botanic Station on Botanic Avenue is handy if you're heading north for Portstewart or Derry.

Travel Agents *USIT*, 31a Queen Street (☎0232-242562); *American Express*, 9 North Road; *Thomas Cook*, 11 Donegall Place.

Welfare *Gay Counseling Service* and *Lesbian Line* (☎0232-222023 Mon–Thurs 7:30–10pm); *Belfast Rape Crisis Center* (☎0232-249696).

travel details

Trains
From Belfast: to Lisburn (4 an hour; 15min); Portadown (2 an hour; 30min); Dundalk (5 daily; 1hr 20min); Dublin (6 daily; 2hr); Larne Harbour (2 an hour; 45min); Derry (6 daily; 2hr 20min); Colerine (8 daily; 1hr 35min).

Ulsterbuses
From Belfast: to Derry (2 daily; 1hr 30min; also 3 via Omagh, 3hr); Antrim (10; 35min); Ballymena (8; 50min); Portrush (2; 2hr); Newry (9; 1hr 10min); Monaghan (3; 2hr); Enniskillen (6; 2hr 15min); Sligo (1; 4hr); Portadown (2; 55min); Dublin, connecting with *Bus Éireann* service at Monaghan (3 daily, 4hr) or at Newry (5, 5 hr); Cork, connecting with *Bus Éireann* (1 daily, 11hr); change at Cahir for Waterford (11hr), at Roscrea for Limerick (9hr), or at Athlone for Mullingar (6hr 40min); Galway, connecting with *Bus Éireann* (2 daily, 6hr 30min) via Cavan (3hr).

CHAPTER FIFTEEN

ANTRIM AND DERRY

T

he northern coastline of counties **Antrim** and **Derry** is as spectacular as anything you'll find in Ireland; certainly it's the major reason to make your way north of Belfast. From most of the coastline, on good days, the Scottish coast is clearly visible, and much of the population, predominantly Protestant, derives originally from Scotland. Unlike other parts of the north, the region attracts lots of tourists and perhaps because of this, it's one of the parts where you'll feel most comfortable traveling—the odd red-white-and-blue curbstone and anti-Catholic graffiti apart, there's generally little evidence of the Troubles up here. The two main attractions are side by side. The nine **Glens of Antrim**, in the northeast corner, closest to Scotland—green, fertile fingers probing inland from high cliffs—are immediately followed to the west by the weird geometry of the **Giant's Causeway**. And along the way are plenty of firm, white strands and rocky heights, relatively unfrequented except for a couple of boarding-house resorts.

Thanks to the Scottish connection, the main point of arrival for the area is the decidedly unlovely port of **Larne**, which marks the Irish end of the shortest crossing from Britain. From here, the main road follows the **coast** all the way around to the attractive resorts of **Portrush** and **Portstewart**, though if you don't have a car this doesn't make getting around as easy as you'd think—buses are few and far between. Hitchhiking, though, isn't difficult. The **train**, alternatively, cuts a less interesting **inland** route through dull farming country—though you can reach either end of the coastline from Belfast, with trains both to Larne and Portstewart. But the rest of the stops on the way to **Derry** are at some fairly grim inland towns: **Antrim**, **Ballymena**, and **Coleraine**. The other inland route is the A6 road from Antrim to Derry, passing through and near some of the counties' **planters' towns**, the most impressive of which is **Moneymore**.

If transport can be a problem, then at least **accommodation** is easy, with a good sprinkling of hostels, plenty of campgrounds and unpretentious, reasonable B&Bs where you're generally assured of a friendly welcome. Indeed, the coastline represents the acceptable face of Northern Ireland, and the people are usually very keen to reassure you that life here is normal.

Larne

Arriving by sea is always impressive, but unfortunately, approaching **LARNE** this way—from Cairnryan or Stranraer—gives you no indication of what's to come. It's a plain, prim, boring town, whose graffitied walls proclaim untidily, in case you hadn't guessed already, that there's "No Popery Here."

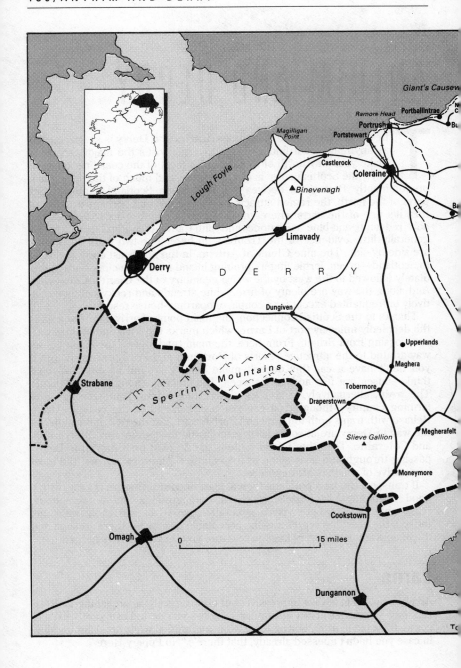

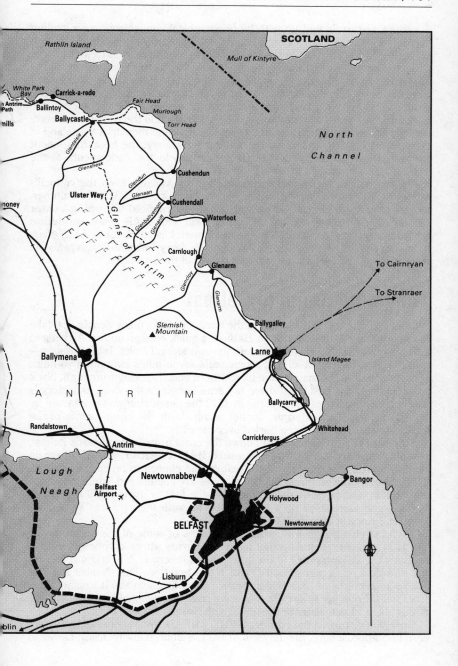

Larne's history is tied up with its geographical convenience as a landing stage. Norse pirates used Larne Lough as a base in the tenth and eleventh centuries; Edward Bruce, brother of Robert, landed here in 1315 with a force of 6000 men in his attempt to urge the Irish to overthrow the English; and in 1914 the Ulster Volunteers, opposed to the Irish Home Rule Bill, landed German arms here. History apart, though, Larne's not a place to hang around. The only real landmark is the **round tower**, at the entrance to the port, and even that's a reproduction. The other sight is the ruined, sixteenth-century **Olderfleet Castle**, which cowers among the industrial wasteland of the harbor. Frankly, unless you're waiting for a ferry, the best thing about Larne is the road out: you can either head up to the enticements of the Antrim coast, or straight in towards Belfast.

If you're stuck, then **tourist information** is available from the council's offices in Victorian Road (Mon–Fri 9am–4:45pm; ☎0574-72313); in summer, look out for the trailer in the parking lot at **Murrayfield shopping center** (Mon–Sat 10am–6pm; ☎0574-71313). Both will book B&B **accommodation** for you, which is plentiful. The nearest **hostel** is at BALLYGALLY (see below) five miles north up the A2. Incidentally, **ferry information** is available from ☎0574-74321; see *Basics* for more details of the crossings.

The Route South to Belfast

Although all the real interest lies to the north of Larne, many people first take the opportunity to head **south to Belfast**, a quick enough option. Arriving in Larne by boat you'll see, on your left, the spit of land called **Islandmagee**— not, in fact, an island at all, but a peninsula seven miles long and two miles wide, attached to the mainland at its southern end. Tapering from high, black basalt cliffs on the east coast down to Larne Lough on the west, its history is sadly representative of these parts; in 1642 the population was massacred by the garrison at Carrickfergus, farther south down the coast—some of the victims are said to have been hurled over the cliffs.

Both road (the A2) and rail run down the coast from Larne towards Belfast, cutting across the neck of the peninsula. **BALLYCARRY**, just off the main road, has the remains of the first Presbyterian church to be built in Ireland. The tradition is an enduring one: curbstones are painted red, white, and blue, and a gable-end carries a colorful mural—the first of many you'll see in this region—showing a man on a prancing horse, with the caption, "Remember William, Prince of Orange 1690."

The **church**'s graveyard contains the tombs of some of the supporters of the 1798 uprising, including that of James Burns, whose cryptic gravestone requires the following key to decipher: the numbers 1, 2, 3, and 4 represent the vowels a, e, i, and o, and 5 and 6 the letter w. There's also a grand Masonic memorial of 1831, which bears a patriotic poem about Ireland: *Erin, loved land! From age to age, Be thou more great, more famed and free*—noting, at this stage, about Ulster or the union with Britain.

Once you've turned the corner at WHITEHEAD, you're into Belfast Lough and fast approaching the city's outriders. About halfway from Larne to

Belfast, **CARRICKFERGUS** is an unremarkable, halfhearted sort of seaside town. The one real point of interest is **Carrickfergus Castle**, one of the earliest and largest of Irish castles. Built around 1180 by the Anglo-Norman invaders (and in continuous use until 1928), it reflects the defensive history of this entire region. In 1315 it underwent a year's siege before falling to the combined forces of Robert and Edward Bruce, after which it was retaken and held by the English for most of the next three centuries. In 1760 the castle was overwhelmed by a French force, and hurriedly recaptured; and in 1778 the American privateer, Paul Jones, fought a successful battle with the British vessel *HMS Drake*, America's first naval victory. The story is that Belfast citizens—most of the Protestants were sympathetic to the American Revolution—rushed out to cheer the victors. If you want a military view of the province's history of armed struggle, then the castle contains a **Cavalry Regimental Museum** (Mon–Sat 10am–6pm; Sun 2–6pm, until 4pm Oct–March; 75p), full of weapons and armor.

Otherwise, Carrickfergus claims plenty of literary associations, though not all of them are tangible: the Restoration dramatist, William Congreve, lived in the castle—his father was a soldier—until he was eight; Jonathan Swift's first sinecure was at Kilroot, just outside Carrickfergus, and it was there, between 1694 and 1696, that he wrote *Tale of a Tub*; and the poet Louis MacNeice spent his childhood in Carrickfergus. Still, none of these claims to fame are as desperately inadequate as that of the connection with the American president Andrew Jackson, whose parents emigrated from Carrickfergus in 1765. The **Andrew Jackson Center** (daily 10am–5pm; June–Aug also 6–8pm) isn't even their home, but a reconstruction of an eighteenth-century thatched cottage, with a little museum.

One reason to give Carrickfergus a little more time might be the **annual fair**, *Lughnasa*, which is tackily medieval—with wrestlers, archers, minstrels, and people dressed up as monks—but great fun nonetheless. It's held at the beginning of August; check the dates with the **tourist office** on Castle Green (June–Aug only), or at the Town Hall (☎09603-51604).

The Glens of Antrim

Northwest of Larne lie the nine **Glens of Antrim**, cutting back from the sea to wild country behind. It's a curious landscape, with enormous contrasts between the neat, seaside villages and the rough moorland above, and its well-defined topography gives first-time visitors the strange sensation that they know it well already.

Until the present coast road was blasted out of the cliffs in 1834, the Glens were extremely isolated, despite their proximity to the Scottish coast. They were also one of the last places in Northern Ireland where Irish was spoken; perhaps surprisingly, Gaelic remained widely spoken in the North far longer than in the south. **Transportation** is still a problem here. For most of the year there's no public transit at all—only school buses, which may be prepared to stop unofficially and give you a lift. The Larne–Cushendall **bus** runs six times daily (Mon–Sat), and in July and August there's a once-daily service in each direction; check times with local tourist offices. **Hitching** is generally fine, though you'll often be told the tale of a German woman student who was murdered on a ride north from Larne in 1988. One alternative means of getting about is **pony trekking**, which can be a delight in the Glens in good weather. The main center is at Ballycastle, at the northern extremity of the glen-fractured coast; see p.443.

Larne to Glenarm

Taking the road northwards out of Larne, you leave the dull suburbs behind fairly quickly, the view broadening out to take in the open sea and, beyond it, the low outline of the Scottish coast. The first place you come to is **BALLYGALLY**, with a wide, wild bay and a sandy beach embraced by hills. There's something about the sobriety of the architecture that makes it look more like Scotland, an impression heightened by the crow-stepped gables of **Ballygally Castle**, built by seventeenth-century planters. You can stop in here for a drink—it's now a hotel—although it's more impressive from the outside. If you're heading on towards the Glens, there's nothing much to keep you in Ballygally, but there is a **youth hostel** (closed in Nov and on Wed Dec–Feb; ☎0574-83355).

The southernmost of the Glens, **Glenarm**, is headed by a village of the same name, which grew up around a hunting lodge built by Randal MacDonnell after Dunluce Castle, farther up the coast, was abandoned. Glenarm became the major seat of the earls of Antrim, something that might lead you to expect that **Glenarm Castle** would be worth seeing. But major rebuildings in the eighteenth and nineteenth centuries have left it a fairly horrendous compilation of styles, an unexciting amalgam of turrets and portcullises that deny each others' impact.

GLENARM village itself, though, is a delight, and very much a taste of what's to follow, with a broad main street of color-washed buildings leading up to an imposing gateway, the old estate entrance, which now leads into the glen itself. The lower part of the glen is blighted with Forest Service conifers, but carry on and you reach National Trust land, and far better walking. There's nowhere much to **stay** in Glenarm, but should its charm beguile you, try *Margaret's Cafe* (☎057484-307) on the main street, which does a very reasonable B&B for £8.50.

Carnlough and Waterfoot

CARNLOUGH stands at the opposite side of the next bay northward, at the head of **Glencloy**—the "glen of hedges." The village's most striking feature is the sturdy, white limestone architecture; until the 1960s Carnlough's way of life was tied up with its limestone quarries. The center of the village, all built in shining, white stone, was constructed by the marquess and marchioness of Londonderry in 1854, no doubt with profits in view. Over the main road there's a solid stone bridge that once carried the railroad which brought the limestone down to the harbor; the harbor itself, with an impressive breakwater, plus the clock tower and courthouse, are also of limestone.

Cheap **B&B accommodation** is thin on the ground in Carnlough, though the **tourist office** (☎0574-85210), inside the Post Office in Harbour Road, can help. If you're **camping**, there are two small trailer parks, the *Bay View Caravan Park* (☎0574-85685) and the *Whitehill Caravan Park* (☎0574-85233), that allow tents. *Black's Pub*, also on Harbour Road, is the place to head for **music**, with sessions most nights. The solid *Londonderry Arms Hotel*, once owned by Winston Churchill, is worth a stop for a drink, too, if only to admire the bizarre collection of mementoes of the 1960s racehorse, Arkle.

From Carnlough the road skirts round a gaunt shoulder of land to **WATERFOOT**, a short strip of houses with a cheap **inn** that comes to life in the evenings. There's also a B&B at *Glen Vista*, 245 Garron Road (☎02677-71439; £7.50). Waterfoot is the scene of the *Feis na nGleann*, one of the great competitive Irish sporting and cultural festivals, held in July.

It's **Glenariff**, though, Waterfoot's glen, that is the real attraction. Wide, lush, and flat-bottomed, it's abruptly cut off by the sea, while a few miles up the glen is the *Glenariff Forest Park*, which—though it costs to enter—has a **campground** (☎026637-232; contact the head forester in advance) and a spectacular series of **waterfalls**. You could cheat, though, and see some of the waterfalls by taking the forest park road and turning left at the *Laragh Lodge* sign; stop at the restaurant.

Between Waterfoot and **Red Bay** pier, there's a series of **caves** with an odd history. The so-called "school cave" was where lessons were conducted for the children of Red Bay in the eighteenth century—a practice made necessary by the oppressive Penal Code that outlawed Catholic education. And the largest of the caves, "Nanny's Cave," forty feet long, was the home of the redoubtable distiller of illicit poteen whiskey, Ann Murray, who died, aged 100, in 1847.

Cushendall and Around

CUSHENDALL lies at the head of three of the nine Glens of Antrim, on the shores of Red Bay, and may become a busy port, if a projected ferry service between Red Bay and Scotland materializes. For the moment, however, it remains delightfully understated, its charming color-washed buildings grouped together on a spectacular shore. The red sandstone **tower** at the main crossroads was built in 1809 by one Francis Turnly, an official of the East India Company, as "a place of confinement for idlers and rioters"; there are plans to turn it into a tourist and heritage center. Meanwhile, the **tourist office** (☎02667-71415) is housed in a trailer off the Glenballyemon road, where you can check for details of **dancing and traditional music** in local pubs. *Joe McCullum's*, in Mill Street, is worth a try, sessions usually taking place on Thursday and Saturday throughout the summer.

Cushendall is probably the best base for exploring the Glens of Antrim, and accordingly it's well provided with **accommodation**. In addition to bed-and-breakfast places, there's a **youth hostel**, *Moneyvart*, on Layde Road (closed in Dec and on Tues Nov–Feb; ☎02667-71344)—leave town by Shore Street, go left at the fork, and look out for the youth hostel sign on the wall. There are also three trailer parks that allow **camping**, so you shouldn't be pushed for somewhere to stay.

Beyond Cushendall, the land rises sharply and the main road swings away from the coast, which is good news for walkers. A clifftop path, running northwards from the beach, takes you to the calm ruins of the thirteenth-century **Layde Old Church**, chief burial place of the MacDonnells. It's nothing spectacular, although if you have family roots to trace in the Glens it may be worth checking out; the tourist office staff at Cushendall have been cataloguing the gravestones and can tell you more about the people buried there.

The other trip from Cushendall is to what's known as **Ossian's Grave**, on the main road to Cushendun (see below). There's a double fake involved here: Ossian, the legendary son of Finn Mac Cumaill, was the supposed author of the Ossianic Cycle of poems, translated and popularized—and largely fabricated—by James Macpherson in the 1760s. This was to give impetus to the early Romantic movement, particularly in Germany and Scandinavia. However, the tomb doesn't actually have anything to do with Ossian as it's a Neolithic court-grave. All the same, standing in a sloping field above the valley, with views to Glendun, Glenaan, and, in the distance, Scotland, it oozes spirit—as good a place as any to reflect on the shaky origins of the first Celtic literary revival.

Beyond the grave runs **Glenaan**, one of the smallest of the glens, soon petering out as little more than a dip of red reeds and black seams of peat between two hills of heather and cotton grass.

Cushendun to Fair Head

CUSHENDUN is an architectural oddity on a windswept bay. It was once a fashionable resort, almost entirely designed, between 1912 and 1925, by the stylish architect of Portmeirion in Wales, Clough Williams-Ellis. However, it has nothing of the cutesy Italianate style that has made Portmeirion famous: built to a commission from Ronald McNeill, the first (and last) Lord Cushendun, and his Cornish wife, Maud, Cushendun's houses are of rugged, rough-cast whitewash with slate roofs—a Cornish style which clearly weathers the Atlantic storms as efficiently here as in Cornwall.

All of Cushendun is National Trust property, and it shows. It's a tiny and well-tended place where tourists—and everyone else—seem peculiarly out of place; but there's a **hotel**, a couple of guesthouses and a (municipal) trailer park that also allows **camping** (☎026674-254). If you need information, the **tourist office** (☎026674-506) is in the main street.

North of Cushendun, there's not much point in taking the main road, which runs inland, unless you have to; it traverses some impressively rough moorland, but you'll be missing some of the best of the northern coastline. Edged with fuschia and honeysuckle, the coastal road switchbacks violently above the sea to **Torr Head**, the closest point on the Irish mainland to the Mull of Kintyre in Scotland, only thirteen miles away—it's said that Protestants from this coast used to row from here to church on the Scottish mainland. You can also pick up the signposted **Ulster Way** around here, although it swings inland immediately after Cushendun, joining the coast again at Murlough Bay. Despite the spectacular views you get from the top of Carnanmore mountain, the coastal route is probably better.

That said, people will tell you that the **Ballypatrick Forest Park**, on the main road, is worth seeing. It's not, unless you're thrilled by the idea of a one-way driving route past things like fjords and even prehistoric cairns marked out like a lunch-break parcourse. **Camping** is allowed in the park, but check with the Forest Service in Belfast (☎0232-650111 ext 456) before turning up.

Murlough Bay is probably—perhaps because of the absence of a main road—the most spectacular of all the bays along the northern coast. From the rugged clifftops, the hillside curves down to the sea in a series of wild-flower meadows that soften an otherwise harsh landscape. As much as anywhere else on the Irish coastline this is a place for just spending time and drinking it all in.

The **stone cross** by the second parking lot is a memorial to **Sir Roger Casement**, an extraordinary figure who was both a successful administrator for the British and a martyr for the Nationalist cause. Following a brilliant career in the Belgian Congo and Peru, he was given a knighthood in 1911. But, believing that Britain's involvement in World War I could give Ireland the opportunity for independence it needed, he negotiated with Germany for military aid and, at the height of the fighting, arranged for a German submarine to land a shipload of arms at Banna strand on the Kerry coast. His plans were discovered, however, and he was arrested and hanged.

The last headland before Ballycastle is **Fair Head**, with massive cliffs rising to 200m all the way around, and a really spectacular view across the North Channel to the Scottish islands—Islay, the Paps of Jura and, beyond them, the Mull of Kintyre. It's easy to believe that local Protestants could row across the channel to church on Sundays, and seeing the landscape makes even more sense of the confusion of land ownership between Ireland and Scotland. Rathlin Island (see below) was hotly contested right up to the seventeenth century, while the MacDonnells owned land both here and on Kintyre. (Kintyre, incidentally, was considered dangerous enough to English interests to be settled, or "planted"—with people from elsewhere in Scotland—in the seventeenth century, just as Ireland was.) **Lough na Cranagh**, one of three lakes in the hinterland behind the cliffs, has an oval island that is actually a *crannog* or lake dwelling, with an encircling man-made parapet wall.

Ballycastle

Situated at the mouth of the two northernmost Antrim glens, Glenshesk and Glentaise, the lively market town of **BALLYCASTLE** divides the glens from the Causeway coast, and is clearly a base for touring in either direction. As such it has the air of a family resort, and is pleasant enough, particularly if you find yourself passing through at the time of the *Fleadh Amhran agus Rince*, the three-day music and dance **festival** in June, or the **Ould Lammas Fair** in late August. This last event is more than just a tourist promotion—Ireland's oldest fair, it dates from 1606 when the MacDonnells first obtained a charter, and has sheep- and pony-sales as well as the obligatory stalls and shops. You may be able to find the edible seaweed, dulse, and the tooth-breaking yellow toffee (it's so hard you break it with a hammer) called "yellow man," delicacies that feature in a sentimental song that originates in Ballycastle:

Did you treat your Mary Ann
To dulse and yellow man
At the Ould Lammas Fair in Ballycastle-O?

Ballycastle still has a solid, prosperous air about it that derives from the efforts of an enlightened mid-eighteenth-century landowner, Colonel Hugh Boyd, who developed the town as an industrial center, providing coal and iron-ore mines, a tannery, brewery, plus soap, bleach, salt and glass works. Ballycastle's prosperity, though, really depended on its coal mines; lignite was mined at Ballintoy, on the coast a few miles farther west, but that enterprise came to an abrupt end in the eighteenth century when the entire deposit caught fire, continuing to burn for several years. There's a local **museum** in the main street, which is completely useless as a historical record—just a jumble of local artifacts—but has plenty of information about local events. Just opposite is an excellent, though tiny, **second-hand bookshop**, where you can pick up cheap copies of contemporary Irish poetry.

Ballycastle proper is a couple of miles inland, linked to a little resort on the coast, from where boats leave for Rathlin Island (see below). At the seafront there's a memorial to Guglielmo Marconi, the inventor of the wireless, who in 1898 made his first successful transmission between Ballycastle and Rathlin. If you're looking for a B&B, this is the place to stay, as there's a good sandy **beach** close by.

A little way out, on the main road to Cushendall, are the ruins of **Bonamargy Friary**, founded by the dominant MacQuillan family around 1500. A number of members of the rival MacDonnell family are also buried here, including the hero of Dunluce Castle, Sorley Boy MacDonnell, and his son Randal, first Earl of Antrim. An indication of the strength of the Irish language in these parts is that the tomb of the second earl, who died in 1682, is inscribed in Gaelic as well as the usual English and Latin: the Irish inscription reads "Every seventh year a calamity befalls the Irish" and "Now that the marquis has departed, it will occur every year." The **Margy River**, on which Bonamargy Friary stands, is associated with one of the great tragic stories of Irish legend, that of the Children of Lir, whose jealous stepmother turned them into swans and forced them to spend 300 years on the Sea of Moyle (the narrow channel between Ireland and the Scottish coast).

If you're going to **stay** in Ballycastle, as well you might, the **tourist office** in Mary Street (☎02657-62024) can point you in the right direction; bed and breakfasts and guesthouses are plentiful. There's no **youth hostel** until Ballintoy (see below), but—again—there are lots of trailer parks which also take tents, including *Watertop Open Farm* (☎02657-62576) on the A2 Ballyvennaght road. There's **pony-trekking** available in Ballycastle, too, at the *Loughaveema Trekking Centre* (☎02657-62576), on the Ballyvennaght road.

Rathlin Island

Ballycastle is the departure point for rugged **Rathlin Island**, six miles and a fifty-minute boat trip offshore, and just twelve miles from the Mull of Kintyre in Scotland. In summer, **boats** go every day (and the *Rathlin Guest House* can arrange crossings; ☎02657-63917); or you can get a passage on the mail boat, which leaves at around 10:30am on Monday, Wednesday, and Friday year-round (call Rathlin Post Office; ☎02657-63907 for info). In winter, it can get too rough for the boat to make the trip; note that the mail boat doesn't always come back the same day, so it's worth making sure in advance that you can stay on the island as accommodation is strictly limited.

Rathlin is an impressive, cliff-ridden island, its vegetation stunted by salt winds, its barrenness seemingly in keeping with its stormy history. It was the first place in Ireland to be raided by the Vikings, in AD 795, and has been the scene of three bloody massacres, one by the Scots and two by the English. In 1595 the mainland MacDonnells sent their women, children, and old people to Rathlin for safety from the English, but that didn't stop the English fleet, under the earl of Essex (whose soldiers, incidentally, included Sir Francis Drake), from slaughtering the entire population; Rathlin was deserted for many years afterwards.

The island's cliffs are good bird watching country, particularly **Bull Point**, on the western tip. The foot of the cliff is riddled with caves, many of them accessible by boat only in the calmest of weather, and many also filled with detritus from wrecked ships which storms have brought to the surface. **Bruce's Cave**, on the northeast point of the island, below the lighthouse, is a cavern in the black basalt where, in 1306, so the story goes, the despondent Robert the Bruce retreated after being defeated by the English at Perth. Seeing a spider determinedly trying to spin a web persuaded him not to give up—and he went back to Scotland to defeat the English at Bannockburn. You can rent a boat to see the cave, but only in calm weather.

There's not much in the way of **accommodation** on Rathlin: just one guesthouse (*Rathlin Guest House*; ☎02657-63917) and a **campground**. Life on the island is simple and uncomplicated, but not entirely basic, so you'll also find a restaurant, a pub, and two stores. (All the electricity on the island, incidentally, comes from generators, and since there's only really one stretch of serviceable road, Rathlin residents don't have to pay road tax.)

West to the Giant's Causeway

The Ulster Way joins the coast at Ballintoy, just west of Carrick-a-rede island, but there are a couple of places between it and Ballycastle that are worth seeing. The first of these, **Kinbane Castle**, is a decaying sixteenth-century fortification on a long, white headland, built by Colla Dubh, brother of the redoubtable Sorley Boy MacDonnell. The pathway is slippery and badly eroded, but it's worth climbing up to the castle to inspect these Irish defenses against the English.

As you draw even with **Carrick-a-rede Island**, you'll see the **rope bridge**, the second biggest tourist attraction in these parts. Strung eighty feet above the sea, between the mainland and the island, the bridge leads to a commercial salmon fishery on the southeast side of Carrick-a-rede—but its main function is to scare tourists, something it does very successfully. Walking its sixty-foot length, as the bridge leaps and bucks under you, is enough to induce giggles and screams from the hardiest of people. The bridge is taken down in September, when the salmon fishing season ends, and put back up in April.

White Park Bay is a delight, a mile-and-a-half sweep of white sand with a **youth hostel** that makes a good base for exploring this stretch of coast (closed Dec; also closed Wed Nov–Feb; ☎02657-31745); you can rent bikes from the hostel. **BALLINTOY** has a dramatic harbor with a dark, rock-strewn strand contrasting oddly with the neat, pale-stone breakwater. In the summer it's lively with boats and visitors; in winter it's bleak and exposed. The little white clifftop church is a replacement of the one where local Protestants took refuge from Catholics in 1641, before being rescued by the earl of Antrim. A landlord of Ballintoy in the eighteenth century was Downing Fullerton, who founded Downing College in Cambridge; the staircase and oak paneling were removed from the castle at Ballintoy when it was demolished and taken to Cambridge. In good weather you can rent boats for fishing and trips along the coast. **Sheep Island**, the bizarre rocky column standing just offshore, is home to a colony of cormorants.

A footpath from Ballintoy leads to **PORTBRADDAN**, a hamlet that's hardly more than a few houses. The interest here is in the brightly colored bit of ecclesiastical architecture that is supposedly the smallest church in Ireland—twelve feet by six and a half. Needless to say, there are other contenders.

Dunseverick Castle

From here the coast path leads around a headland and through a spectacular hole in the rock and then, by degrees, up to the cliffs of **Benbane Head**, which is where the bizarre geometry of the Giant's Causeway really begins in earnest. The road almost meets the path at **Dunseverick Castle**, now no more than the ruins of a sixteenth-century gatehouse, but once capital of the old kingdom of Dalriada and the terminal of one of the five great roads that led from Tara. It was, naturally enough given its location, one of the main departure points for the great Irish colonization of Scotland that took place from the fifth century onwards. Dunseverick also features in one of the great Irish love stories, the ninth-century *Longas mac n-Usnig*, or "The fate of the children of Uisneach." Deirdre, the betrothed of King Conor, falls in love with his bodyguard, Noisi. Together with Noisi's two brothers—the sons of Uisneach—they flee to Scotland. Fergus, one of Conor's soldiers, believes the king has forgiven them and persuades them to return home. Landing at Dunseverick (or, some say, Ballycastle), they take the high road to Conor's court at Armagh, but the king kills the brothers and seizes Deirdre, who dashes her head against a stone and dies. And Fergus, outraged, destroys Conor's palace (though not, apparently, the king himself).

The Giant's Causeway

Ever since 1693, when the Royal Geographical Society first publicized it as one of the great wonders of the natural world, the **Giant's Causeway** has been a major tourist attraction. The highly romanticized pictures of the polygonal basalt rock formations by the Dubliner, Susanna Drury, which circulated throughout Europe, did much to popularize the Causeway; two of them are on display in the Ulster Museum in Belfast, and copies are in the visitor center at the site. Not everyone was impressed, though. William Thackeray ("I've traveled 150 miles to see *that*?") especially disliked the tourist promotion of the Causeway, claiming in 1842 that "The traveler no sooner issues from the inn by a back door which he is informed will lead him straight to the causeway, than the guides pounce upon him." And although the Causeway is probably less overtly money-making now than at almost any time since the late seventeenth century, it still attracts plenty of people. There's a massive and over-appointed visitor center (see below), and a minibus on the site rules out the necessity for any physical exertion whatsoever. But even in high season, it's easy enough to escape the crowds by taking to the cliffs.

For sheer strangeness, the Causeway can't be beaten. Made up of an estimated 37,000 black basalt columns, each a polygon—hexagons by far the most common, pentagons second, and sometimes figures with as many as ten sides—it's the result of a massive subterranean explosion some sixty million years ago, stretching from the Causeway to Rathlin and beyond, to Islay, Staffa (where it was responsible for the formation of Fingal's Cave), and Mull in Scotland. A huge mass of molten basalt was spewed out onto the surface and, as it cooled, it solidified into what are, essentially, crystals.

Simple as the process was, it's difficult, when confronted with the very regular geometry of the basalt columns, to believe that their origin is entirely natural. The Irish folk version of their creation is certainly a more appealing explanation, if a touch sentimental. It's the everyday story of a love affair between giants: the Ulster warrior, Finn Mac Cumaill, became infatuated with a giantess who lived on the island of Staffa, off the Scottish coast (where the Causeway resurfaces), and built this great highway to bring his lady-love to his side. This tale is recounted, alongside the scientific account, in the visitor center's exhibition—along with some fanciful embellishments, such as an estimate of Finn's height calculated on the basis of a large shoe-shaped stone that's known as his boot.

The best way to **approach** the Giant's Causeway is undoubtedly along the cliffs, preferably on a wet and blustery day when you're scared you'll lose your foothold along the muddy way. The waymarked **North Antrim Cliff Path**, cut into the cliffside alongside the black geometric configurations, runs all along this stretch of coast. **Public transit** to and from the Causeway is well organized in summer; an open-topped **bus** runs between Coleraine (the stop is opposite the railroad station) and Bushmills, stopping at Portstewart, Portrush, Portballintrae, and the Causeway (though you can flag it down anywhere along the way), running every couple of hours in each direction. If you're traveling by **train** from Belfast, the line ends at Portrush, from where you can either catch the above bus, or the #172; more details on ☎0265-43334.

Visiting the Causeway

The Causeway's **visitor center** is not a place to linger unless you're very cold or very wet. There's a paying exhibition that doesn't tell you a great deal, its lone interesting exhibit one of the **trams** from the tramway that used to run between the railroad station in Portrush and the Causeway. Opened in 1883, it was the first electrically powered tramway in Europe, and ran on hydroelectric power generated from the river Bush. The tramway wasn't built simply for the tourists: it was thought that the area would be developed for iron-mining, and the tram-owner, William Traill, planned to make his fortune. There was some concern over the possible dangers of using hydroelectricity, and Traill sought to allay fears by dropping his trousers and sitting on the live rail—it was only later that he admitted that he'd suffered a severe shock. The line was closed in 1949, although there are apparently plans to reopen it.

Taking the asphalted **path** from the visitor center (and dodging the mini-bus that's provided) brings you to the **Grand Causeway**, where you'll find some of the most spectacular of the blocks, and where most of the crowd lingers. If you push on, though, you'll be rewarded with relative solitude and views of some of the more impressive formations, high in the cliffs. Many of them have names invented for them by the guides who so plagued Thackeray and his contemporaries—the Organ and the Harp, for example—but at least one, **Chimney Point**, has an appearance so bizarre that it persuaded the ships of the Spanish Armada to open fire on it, believing that they were attacking Dunluce Castle, a couple of miles farther west.

Before you reach Chimney Point, **Port-na-Spania** is the place where the *Girona*, one of the many ships of the Armada to run aground around here, foundered in September 1588. The treasure she was carrying was recovered by divers in 1968, and some of the items are on show in the Ulster Museum in Belfast. Carrying on, you climb up to **Benbane Head** on a wooden stair-case and can then return to the visitor center along the tops of the cliffs.

The **boats** that ply for trade at the Causeway will show you the caves that aren't accessible from the land: Portcoon Cave, 450 feet long and 40 feet high; Leckilroy Cave, which you can't go into; and Runkerry Cave, an amazing 700 feet long and 60 feet high.

Dunluce Castle

A couple of miles west of the Causeway sits sixteenth-century **Dunluce Castle** (Tues–Sat 10am–7pm; closes at 4pm Oct–March), easily the most impressive ruin along this entire coastline. Sited on a fine headland, high above a cave, it looks as if it only needs a roof to be perfectly habitable once again. Its history is inextricably linked with that of its original owner, **Sorley Boy MacDonnell**, whose MacDonnell clan, the so-called "Lords of the Isles," ruled northeastern Ulster from Dunluce. English incursions into the area culminated in 1584 with Sir John Perrott laying siege to Dunluce, forcing Sorley Boy ("Yellow Charles" in Gaelic) to leave the castle. But as soon as Perrott departed, leaving a garrison in charge, Sorley Boy hauled his men up the cliff in baskets, later repairing the castle from the proceeds of the salvaged wreckage of the Spanish Armada ship, the *Girona*. Having made his point, Sorley Boy made his peace with the English, and his son, Randal, was made Viscount Dunluce and Earl of Antrim by James I. In 1639 Dunluce Castle paid the penalty for its precarious, if impregnable, position when the kitchen, complete with cooks and dinner, fell off during a storm. Shortly after-ward the MacDonnells moved to more comfortable lodgings at Glenarm, and Dunluce was left empty.

However, it remains an extraordinary place. The MacDonnells' Scottish connections—Sorley Boy's son continued to own land in Kintyre—show in the gatehouse's turrets and crow-step gables; the seventeenth-century Great Hall, medieval in plan but Renaissance in style, has tapering chimneys of the Scottish style; and there's a strange touch of luxury in the loggia that faces—oddly—away from the sun.

You can see the **cave** below the castle without paying to go in. Piercing right through the promontory upon which Dunluce stands, with an opening directly under the gatehouse, it's a spectacular scramble, particularly in wild weather.

The castle is just beyond **PORTBALLINTRAE**, a decorous little place with some friendly **hotels** if you wanted to stay over. The bus between Bushmills and Coleraine stops here.

Bushmills

Just a few miles inland of Portballintrae, **BUSHMILLS**'s main attraction is the **Old Bushmills Distillery**, on the outskirts of town. Whiskey has been distilled here legally since 1608, making it the world's oldest licit distillery, and it's well worth taking the free **tour** (at least twice daily Mon–Fri, except Fri pm; ☎02657-31521 to confirm place). The great claim about Bushmills whiskey is that it's distilled three times, instead of the twice that's usual in Scotland; but perhaps the biggest surprise is just how unsubtle a business the industrial manufacture of alcohol is, despite all the lore that surrounds it. Basically, you're shown around a massive factory where an extraordinary range of (mostly unpleasant) smells assails your nostrils, making it difficult to imagine that the end product is something that will delight the taste buds. All the same, at the end of the tour you're offered a tot of the hard stuff; the best bet is the unblended malt, representative of what goes on in Bushmills itself, as the grain whiskey that goes into the blend is distilled in Cork.

Accommodation in Bushmills is all in guesthouses, but if you're feeling in need of luxury try the very different *Auberge de Seneirl* (☎02657-41536; £16), discreetly signposted off the Coleraine road. It's expensive by guesthouse standards but is well equipped—swimming pool, sauna, hot tub, solarium—and has a **restaurant** which serves the best French food you're likely to find in Northern Ireland. The owners aren't keen to take guests who don't want to eat in the restaurant, but if you can put up with a slightly uptight management style (traveling alone, and not driving an expensive car, I was cross-examined aggressively before I was allowed to stay) it can be an excellent place to hole up after the rigors of walking the cliffs.

Portrush, Portstewart, and Castlerock

The coastline west of Portballintrae to **Magilligan Point** is a major vacation spot, the twin resorts of **Portrush** and **Portstewart** filled with tourists in July and August, mainly from the rest of the North. **Castlerock**, too, gets its fair share of beach-goers, but the Inishowen Peninsula, on the other side of Lough

Foyle, is now well in sight, and the beaches on the Republic side are often more exciting and less crowded. From Magilligan Point, site of a high-security prison as well as a nature reserve, the coastline—overlooked by the dramatic crag of **Binevenagh**—is flat and undramatic, some of it consisting of land reclaimed from the sea to grow flax for the eighteenth-century linen trade.

Portrush

PORTRUSH, built on the Ramore Peninsula, has sandy beaches backed by dunes running both east and west, and everything you'd expect from a seaside resort, including summer drama staged in the Town Hall and plenty of amusement arcades. To the east, towards Dunluce, the beach ends in the **White Rocks**, where the weather has carved the soft, limestone cliffs into strange shapes, the most famous of which is the so-called "Cathedral Cave," 180 feet from end to end. **Nightlife**, such as it is in Portrush, is centered on two wine bars, the *Ramore* and *Rogues*, which face each other across the harbor. The *Harbour Inn* has a more expensive (and, reputedly, extremely good) **restaurant**, while there are plenty of cheap Chinese restaurants, fish-and-chip shops and the like.

Accommodation is exclusively in B&B and boarding house establishments, most of them very friendly and welcoming. The **tourist office** (☎0265-823333) will reserve a place for you; it's in the Town Hall, and has plenty of information and maps of the Causeway Coast too.

Portstewart

Like Portrush, **PORTSTEWART** (which is actually across the county border in Derry) is full of peeling, Victorian boarding houses. Of the two, Portstewart has always had more airs and graces; the railroad station is said to have been built a mile out of town (vacationers had to make the rest of the journey by steam tram) to stop vulgar people from coming.

Out of season it's difficult to discern much difference between the two, but in terms of sheer location Portstewart wins hands down. Just west of the town is **Portstewart Strand**, a long, sand beach firm enough to drive on—which the locals delight in doing—as well as with some of the best surfing in the country. Again, a good place if you hit fine weather and feel like getting out your bucket and spade.

Accommodation possibilities are similar to those in Portrush. The Town Hall **tourist office** (☎0265-832286) can help with reservations, and there are also lots of **campgrounds** in the area—though most of them are actually fairly unattractive trailer parks that take tents. Closest are the *Golf Links Hotel Caravan Park*, 140 Dunluce Road (☎0265-823539) or the municipal *Carrick Dhu Caravan Park*, 12 Ballyreagh Road (☎0265-823712).

Castlerock and Mussenden Temple

Beyond Portstewart, the coastline rears up as great cliffs once more, before settling down into monotonous flatness beyond Magilligan Point for the run into Derry. There's a long sand beach at **CASTLEROCK** (and a heated swimming pool, too) and, at the A2 crossroads a mile south of Castlerock, **Hezlett House**—a long, low thatched building of wood cruck construction. It's a building method that's common in England, but enough of a rarity here to warrant preservation by the National Trust.

Farther west along the A2, a pair of huge, ornate Pompeiian gates on the left mark the entry to **Mussenden Temple**, a domed rotunda clinging precariously to the cliff-edge. This is almost all that is left of the great estate of Frederick Hervey (1730–1803), fourth Earl of Bristol and (Anglican) Bishop of Derry, the enthusiastic traveler after whom all the Hotel Bristols throughout Europe are named. The "Earl Bishop," as he was known, commissioned Michael Shanahan to build the temple in honor of his cousin Mrs Frideswide Mussenden, who died before it was finished. It was then used as his summer library and, with characteristic generosity and a fairly startling lack of prejudice, the Earl Bishop allowed Mass to be celebrated in the temple once a week as there was no local Catholic church. The inscription on the frieze translates, smugly, as "It is agreeable to watch, from land, someone else involved in a great struggle while winds whip up the waves out at sea."

Inland: Coleraine and Limavady

Given the attractions of the coast, it's almost impossible to see why anyone would want to visit the two towns immediately inland, though you'll pass through if you're heading for Derry city, and Donegal, by the most direct route. **COLERAINE**, designated a joint conurbation with Portrush and Portstewart, is entirely unprepossessing. There's a big, pedestrianized shopping center, anonymous and depressing, and seemingly a church on every street corner, each representing a different non-conformist tradition. It's evidence, if you want it, of the richness, in purely denominational terms, of the dissenting Protestant tradition in the north. Coleraine has a major campus of the University of Ulster, a bone of contention with the people of Derry, many of whom believe that the only reason the University didn't go there was that the authorities wanted it to be in a predominantly Protestant location. The Coleraine campus provides cheap **accommodation** in the summer vacation (☎9265-44141) if you can think of any reason at all for staying.

Just a mile south of Coleraine, on the eastern bank of the river, is **Mountsandel**, a 200-foot mound, apparently the earliest-known dwelling place in Ireland, though the recent discoveries in Boora Bog in County Offaly must give it a run for its money. The post-holes and hearths of the wooden houses that once stood here have been dated to around 7000 years BC.

LIMAVADY is a great improvement on Coleraine, though not exactly a holiday attraction either, with a broad main street that's still recognizably Georgian. Number 51 was the home of Jane Ross, who noted down the famous "Londonderry Air"—better known as "Danny Boy"—from a traveling fiddler in 1851. The **Roe Valley Country Park**, a couple of miles south of Limavady, preserves Ulster's first hydroelectric domestic power station, opened in 1896, with much of the original equipment intact, and a small weaving museum. There's also a **campground** (☎050-4762074) if the ones on the coast didn't appeal.

Derry City

At the end of the coast, immediately before the border, **DERRY** lies at the foot of Lough Foyle: a major crossroads where the coast road meets the faster, duller route direct from Belfast, and from where roads head on—west into Donegal and the Republic, south into Tyrone. Ireland's fourth largest city, and the second largest in the North, its size makes it Belfast's sister city, but it has a markedly different atmosphere, being two-thirds Catholic. Within Ireland, Derry is highly regarded both for its characteristically caustic humor—best caught in the busier bars and at the soccer matches at the Brandywell—and for its musical pedigree, having produced names as diverse as Dana, Phil Coulter, The Undertones and many less well known. This last claim to recognition is misleading, though—Derry may produce musicians, but its own music scene is largely inaccessible to outsiders.

Approached from the east in winter twilight or under a strong summer sun, the city presents a beguiling picture, with the spread of the Foyle River and the rise of the city's two hillsides, terraced with pastel-shaded houses from which rise the hueless stone spires of the ever-present Church Orders. This scenic appeal apart, Derry at first sight seems to have little to tempt you to stay overnight, for all the richness of its history. Yet there are things worth seeing, all of them enclosed within the seventeenth-century walls, themselves the most significant reminder of the city's past. And four miles or so out of the center, across the border on the Letterkenny road, is an unmissable sight—the Griannan of Ailleach, a stone fort that is the oldest habitation left standing in Ireland.

Outside of Ireland, the name of Derry brings to mind the troubles of recent years, difficulties with which the Bogside and the Creggan are inextricably associated. Don't be put off by this. Unlike Belfast, the cutting edge of violence has receded here considerably in the past five years, and a resurgence of optimism is being felt for the first time since the early Sixties. Moreover, the southern border is no more than a few miles away, making the city handy for a day excursion that anyone should jump at.

The Historical Background

Derry's original name was *Daire Calgaigh* meaning "the oakwood of Calgach," a warrior who led the Caledonians at the battle of the Grampians. This name remained in use until well after the coming of Saint Columba (or Colmcille), who founded a monastery here in AD 546; then, in the tenth century, the settlers renamed the spot *Doire Colmcille*. As the annals of the city record, the settlement suffered frequent onslaughts, first from the Vikings, later from the Anglo-Norman barons de Courcy and Peyton. In 1566 Elizabeth I of England sent a small task force in a failed attempt to pacify such troublesome chieftains as Shane O'Neill, but at the end of the century the uprising of Hugh O'Neill, Earl of Tyrone, provoked another English invasion, this time successful. It paved the way for the first widescale "planting" of English and Scottish settlers in the reign of James I. Doire became anglicized to **Derry** and then, in 1613, "London" was bestowed as a prefix after

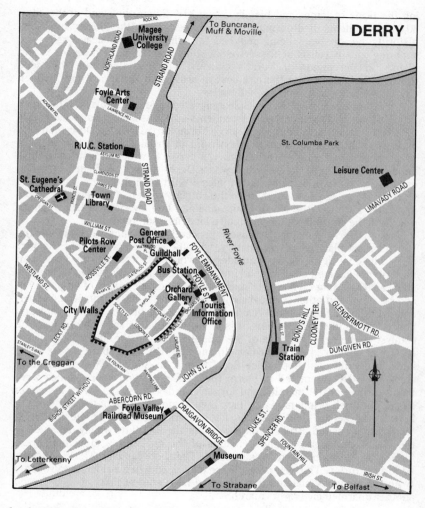

land within the newly drawn borders of the county was awarded to the Twelve Companies of the Corporation of London. Today the entrance routes to the city bear the two different names—"Welcome to Londonderry, an historic city" and "Welcome to Derry, a nuclear free zone"—reflecting the changing sectarian majority on the city council.

The seventeenth century was the most dramatic phase of the city's evolution. The city walls withstood successive sieges, the last of which (in 1688–89) played a key part in the Williamite army's final victory over the Catholic king James II at the Battle of the Boyne—the Derrymens' obduracy crucially delaying the plans of James and his ally Louis XIV. Seven thousand of the city's 30,000 inhabitants died during the fifteen-week siege (the longest in British history), the survivors being reduced to eating dogs, cats, and rats. The suffering and heroism of those weeks still have the immediacy of recent history in the minds of Derry's citizens, who commemorate the siege through the skeleton on the city coat of arms, and the lyrical tag "maiden city," a reference to its unbreached walls.

After the siege many Derry people emigrated to America to avoid the harsh English laws, and some of their descendants—such as Daniel Boone and Davy Crockett—achieved fame there. George Farquhar (b. 1678), a Derryman who chose to stay, became a major playwright in Britain. Derry's heyday as a seaport came in the nineteenth century, a period in which industries such as linen production also flourished. It was a Derry weaver, William Scott, who established the world's first industrialized shirt manufacturers, cutting the shirts in Derry and sending them to the cottage women of Donegal for stitching. After Partition, the North–South dividing line lay right at Derry's back door, and the consequent tariffs cut off a lot of its traditional trade.

Though Derry remained relatively peaceful, its politics were among the North's most blatantly discriminatory, with the substantial Catholic majority denied its civil rights by gerrymandering which ensured that the Protestant minority maintained control of all important local institutions. On October 5, 1968, a 2000-strong **civil rights march**—demanding equality of employment and housing, and other political rights, and led by a Protestant, Ivan Cooper, and a Catholic, John Hume—came up against the batons of the Protestant police force and the B Specials. It is an event which is seen by many as the catalyst of the present phase of the troubles: faith in the impartiality of the RUC was destroyed once and for all, and the IRA was reborn a year or so later. The Protestant Apprentice Boys' March, in August 1969, was another step—the RUC attempted to storm the Bogside (from where stones were being thrown at the march), and for several days the area lay in a state of siege. The Irish prime minister, Jack Lynch, moved units of the army to the border and set up field hospitals for injured Bogsiders. In the mounting tension that ensued, British troops were for the first time widely deployed in the North, and many of the demands of the civil rights movement were forced on Stormont from Westminster. Then, on January 31, 1972, came **Bloody Sunday**. Thirteen people were shot dead when British paratroopers (who subsequently claimed that they had been shot at first) opened fire on another unarmed civil rights march.

Arriving and Finding a Place to Stay

Northern Ireland Railroads runs about six **trains** a day from Belfast to Derry (information on ☎0504-42228), and there are also frequent **buses** to all parts of the North and the Republic. *Ulsterbus* (☎0504-262261) serves all the main Northern Ireland destinations and Dublin, at frequencies ranging between twice weekly to Dublin, and twelve weekly to Strabane; *Lough Swilly Bus Services* (☎0504-262017) also operates a good network, connecting Derry to towns as far away as Galway and Dublin. Good roads enter the city from all directions, making it very straightforward to **hitch**. You can also **fly**. *Aer Lingus* has just started operating a service from Dublin to Eglinton Airport (☎0504-810784), seven miles out on the A2 road, and there are also flights to Glasgow, with Manchester and Gatwick in the pipeline as future destinations.

The **tourist information** office is handily situated downtown, across from the bus station. Housed in a pagoda-like accretion, it contains both a *Bord Fáilte* office and a branch of the *Northern Ireland Tourist Board* (May–Aug Mon–Fri 9am–5:15pm, Sat 10am–5pm; Sept–April Mon–Fri 9am–1pm and 2–5:15pm; ☎0504-267284, *Bord Fáilte* ☎0504-369501). Grab a free pocket guidebook for up-to-date information.

Accommodation

The nearest **hostel** to Derry is run by the *Independent* group in MUFF, just across the border on the Inishowen Peninsula, five miles away; it's open until 11pm, and is connected to Derry by very regular bus services—hitching is easy enough too. **Cheap accommodation** is seasonally available at the university; student rooms are rented from approximately mid-June to mid-September, a week each side of Easter and a week each side of Christmas (£3.50 for students, otherwise £7.50 single, £12 double and £5 for children; Mon–Fri ☎0504-265621 ext 5218). *YHANI* is planning to open a new youth hostel in the St Columb's Park area on the east of the river—ask at the tourist office for a progress report. **B&Bs** are fairly thin on the ground within the city itself, but *Clarendon House*, 15 Northland Road (☎0504-265342; £10), has a good range of rooms. For extremely good value and comfort, reserve a room with Mrs Dunn of *Abode*, Dunwood Road (☎0504-44564; £8).

The City

The walls of Derry—some of the best-preserved historical defenses left standing in Europe—are the starting point for a walkabout of the city, though iron sheeting and rolls of barbed wire laid down by the military make it impossible to walk all the way around. A mile in length and never higher than a two-story house, the walls are reinforced by bulwarks and bastions, and a parapeted earth rampart as wide as any thoroughfare. Within their circuit, the original medieval street pattern has remained, with four gateways—Shipquay, Butcher, Bishop, and Ferryquay—surviving from the first construction, in slightly revised form.

You're more than likely to make your approach from the Guildhall Square, once the old quay. Most of the city's cannons are lined up here, between Shipquay and Magazine gates, their noses peering out above the ramparts. A reconstruction of the medieval **O'Doherty Castle** was built here a few years back, and is scheduled to house local history exhibits and act as an interpretive center; the exterior blends well with the walls, but inside only a very roughshod estimation of sixteenth-century style has been attempted.

Turning left at Shipquay Gate into **Bank Place**, access to the walls' promenade is pretty immediate and opens up an unhampered stretch that runs

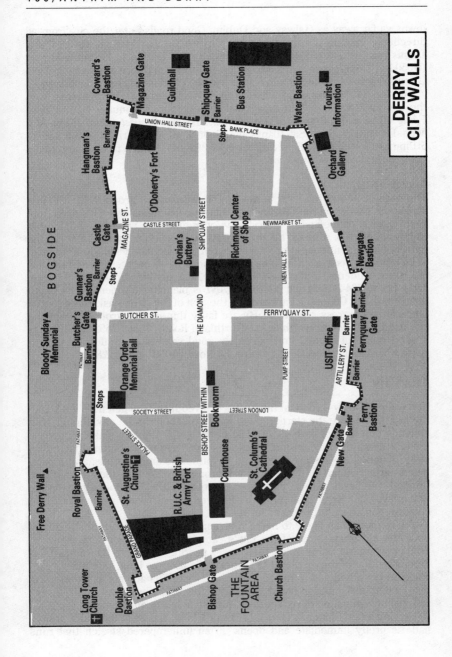

DERRY CITY WALLS

nearly to the Ferryquay Gate. On your way around you'll come across a cast-iron cruciform mold of two figures back to back. Several such sculptures have been placed at strategic points on the walls by the English artist Antony Gormley, their gaping eye sockets looking out in diametrically opposite directions from a single body—a frank comment on the city's ideological split. Vandals have daubed one body with paint and graffiti, an intervention which Gormley has let stand, seeing this spontaneous acknowledgment from part of the community as the ultimate final touch. Aesthetics aside, the figures provide essential visual relief against the office buildings that already swamp the immediate view.

St Columb's Cathedral and the Fountain Area

Between Ferryquay and Bishop's Gate there are two sights of interest: the Protestant cathedral, just within the south section of the walls, and the Fountain, the Protestant enclave immediately outside the same stretch of walls. **St Columb's Cathedral** was built in 1633 in a style later called "Planter's Gothic," and is not unlike many parish churches of the period built in London; it was the first cathedral to be constructed in the British Isles subsequent to the Reformation. On show in the entrance porch is a cannon shell fired during the siege by the besieging army, to which was attached their terms of surrender. The cathedral was used as a battery during the siege, its tower serving as a lookout post; today it provides the best view of the city. The present spire dates from the late Georgian period, its lead-covered wooden predecessor having been stripped to fashion bullets and cannon shot. Inside, an open-timbered roof rests on sixteen stone corbels carved with portraits of past bishops; hanging above the nave, flags brought back from various military expeditions give the interior a strong sense of the British realm and its regality. Other things to look out for are the finely sculpted reredos behind the altar, the eighteenth-century bishop's throne, and the window panels showing scenes as diverse as the relief of the city on August 12, 1689 and Saint Columba's mission to Britain. In the chapter house are more relics of the siege, plus the grand kidney-shaped desk of Bishop Berkeley and mementoes of Cecil Frances (1818–95), wife of Bishop Alexander and composer of the famous hymns: "Once in Royal David's City" and "There is a Green Hill Far Away".

To reach the **Fountain** area from here you'll first need to pass by the **Courthouse**, built of white sandstone in crude Greek revival style, and then cut down through a passageway tucked into the left of the Bishop Gate arch. The Gate itself was remodeled for the first centenary of the siege, but today is defaced by a mangle of fences and scaffolding, underneath which skulks an army cinder-block hut. Before passing the glare of the RUC men, take a glance at the surrounding pieces of eighteenth-century architecture, evident even in boarded-up Dean Street. The Fountain area is a housing estate that sticks into the Catholic west bank like a sore thumb, with a single road entrance close to the Craigavon Bridge. It's of interest solely for its Union-Jack curb paintings and huge wall murals—one reads *LONDONDERRY/ WESTBANK LOYALISTS/STILL UNDER SIEGE/NO SURRENDER* in direct reply to the more famous Catholic *FREE DERRY* mural in the next valley.

The Bogside

If you're intent on missing out the Fountain, backtrack down Bishop Street towards the Diamond, taking a left to the west section of the walls, or just follow the path around the outside. The Double Bastion on the west wall has now been taken over by the British army, its signal mast and cameras monitoring the activity in the valley below. The streets under surveillance are those of the Bogside, where, at the start of the Troubles, young Catholics were caught up in an advancing disarray of army and police, who replied to bricks and gas bombs with tear gas, rubber bullets, and careening Saracen tanks. The area at the foot of the escarpment has been redeveloped in the form of a divided highway, a new project of tenement flats, and empty concrete precincts. But clinging to the opposite hillside is one of the most attractive urban landscapes around, with turn-of-the-century rows of stucco facades, blue tile roofs, and red chimney stacks.

Most eye-catching in this panorama is an isolated wall bearing the slogan YOU ARE NOW ENTERING FREE DERRY—for the first two years of the Troubles the territory beyond was ruled by the IRA without incursion from the British army. (This is not the original frontier wall—that later fell afoul of the army.) This autonomy lasted until 1972, when "Operation Motorman" was launched; the IRA men who had been in the area were warned, though, and got across the border before the invasion took place. Farther across to the right of the wall stands the memorial pillar to the thirteen Catholic civilians killed on **Bloody Sunday** by British troops. The soldiers immediately claimed they were fired upon, a claim that was later disproved, though some witnesses have come forward to report seeing IRA men there with their guns. To the right of this area once stood the Rossville flats, by far the most infamous part of the Bogside—Derry's answer to Belfast's Divis. Farther up the Westland Road, which runs up by the *Bogside Inn*—a former IRA stronghold, where the gunmen would set their revolvers on the bar while drinking—is a busy mural grouping the silhouetted faces of Bobby Sands, Che Guevara, and Lenin; other murals are now faded, evidence of the greater stability of recent years.

Music, Entertainment, and Eating

Traditional music in the city is not as busy nor as attractive as it was twenty years ago. The venues that remain are all grouped in and around **Waterloo Street**, just outside the northern section of the walls. However, if you go into this area in the evenings, exercise caution as to which bars you enter. Being a strange face you might not receive the warmest of welcomes even in the ones listed here. The *Dungloe Bar* in Waterloo Sreet claims to be the most regular music-making place, with traditional stuff on Monday and Wednesday evenings and a two-piece folk band on Thursdays and Fridays. The *Phoenix Bar*, on Park Avenue in the Rosemount area, has traditional music on Tuesday evenings, as does the *Pilot's Row Centre* (7:30–9:30pm), which also offers classes in Irish dancing, music, and language. The *Bogside Inn* has music on Thursday evenings, but it's a dangerous place to venture in the evening. Other Thursday sessions take place at the *Rocking Chair Pub* and the *Gweedore Bar*, both in Waterloo Street (9:30–11:30pm; also Fri and Sat). Many local young people, though, head across the border on Friday and Saturday nights, to nightclubs at Quigley's Point, Redcastle, and the White Strand, Buncranna.

Classical music thrives in the city through the Londonderry Arts Association, with around a dozen concerts a year held in the Great Hall of Magee University College. Orchestral concerts by the Ulster Orchestra are held much less regularly in the Great Hall of the Guildhall. The vanguard of **theater** in the city is *Field Day*, one of Ireland's most notable companies, principally directed by a set of Derrymen (Seamus Heaney, Seamus Deane, and Brian Friel) and a few other artistic luminaries (Tom Paulin and Stephen Rea). Their repertoire comprises mainly new work by contemporary Irish playwrights dealing with historical-political themes, and Derry always receives the premiere, normally in the Guildhall during September. The **visual arts** in Derry are attracting a lot of international attention, thanks to the highly innovative contemporary art programming of the *Orchard Gallery* in Orchard Street; a visit there is a must—and watch out for the exhibitions it sometimes arranges in the *Foyle Arts Center*, off Lawrence hill, or at other forums around the city. The *Heritage Library*, on Bishop Street, occasionally has local artists' work on display.

Several **arts festivals** take place at regular times throughout the year, the most interesting of them being the *Foyle Film Festival* (late April) and the *North West Arts Festival* (early November). The tourist information office will have details. The **movie house**, at the city end of the Strand Road, shows current mainstream stuff.

Bars

For a purely sociable type of entertainment the **pubs** once again are the best bet. The student set congregates at the *College Arms* at the bottom of the Rock Road, and of course in the campus bar in Magee College grounds. The Waterloo Street pubs are principally used by the area's Catholic working-class community. Congenial and conversational pubs are *Badgers Place*, 18 Orchard Street; *The Clarendon Bar*, 44 Strand Road; and *The Mourne*, 53 Foyle Street.

Quizzes are a distinctive feature of pub life in Derry: on Monday evenings there's one at *Rosses Bar* in Waterloo Street, while the University Students' Union at Magee College holds one every Monday and Wednesday evening at 9:30pm—cheap beer being an additional attraction.

Food

Eating out in the city has improved dramatically over the last few years, though you still won't be put out by a bewildering choice. Shipquay Street has the widest variety, including *Dorian's Buttery* (Mon–Thurs & Sat 9am–5:30pm, Fri 9am–9pm), which does very tasty and reasonably priced home-style food. Even cheaper are *Annes Place* on William Street and the very sociable *Leprechaun* on the Strand. *Piemonte Pizzeria* on Great James Street is the only pizza place in town. The *Taj Mahal* on Strand Road offers cheap lunches.

Listings

Banks Principally situated on Shipquay Street and Waterloo Place.

Bicycle repairs *Sackville Cycles*, 5 Sackville Street (☎0504-268330); *McClean Bros*, 108 Spencer Road (☎0504-43171).

Bookshop *Bookworm* on Butcher Street is one of the best bookshops in the country, comprehensive and with excellent coverage of contemporary and historical Irish works.

Car rental *Hertz*, c/o *Desmond Motors*, 173 Strand Road (☎0504-360420).

Hospital Accident and emergency department, Altnagelvin Hospital on Belfast Road (☎0504-45171); contact this number also for **dental** emergencies after working hours or at weekends.

Laundromat 147 Spencer Road.

Library The Central Library (Great James Street) has a good selection on Irish studies and local history (Mon & Thurs 10am–7:30pm, Tues, Wed, & Fri 10am–5:30pm, Sat 9am–1pm).

Market Bottom of Orchard Street every Sat.

Newspapers The Catholic *Derry Journal* (Tues & Fri) is good for entertainment listings; the Protestant local paper is the *Londonderry Sentinel* (Wed).

Taxis Black cabs run from Foyle Street and most operate in a similar way to those in Belfast, functioning like minibuses to ferry the Catholic community to and from their housing estates. If you want a regular taxi, call: *Auto Cabs* (☎0504-45100); *Blue Star Taxis* (☎0504-264888); or *Quick Cabs* (☎0504-260515).

Police ☎0504-265161.

Women's Center 7 London Street, for information and advice (Mon–Fri 9:30am–5pm; ☎0504-267672).

Southern Derry: Dungiven and the Planned Towns

South of the A6, the Derry-to-Antrim road, the landscape settles down into a pattern more familiar to the Republic: fertile farming land, rising to the **Sperrin Mountains**, punctuated by small, planned towns. The pattern is subtly different from the south, though, because the grants of land here were not made to individuals, but to various London guilds or companies. Consequently, there isn't the strange, late-flowering feudalism that you see in the south, with its repeated archetype of big house and surrounding town, but rather entirely **planned towns**, often built on green-field sites selected by professionals, who specialized in doing just that.

Coming from the coast, **DUNGIVEN**, 18 miles east of Derry, provides a small shock, as it's the first place where there's an army control zone (no unattended vehicles) and (periodically) a heavy military presence. Originally an O'Cahan stronghold, Dungiven was given to the Skinners' Company to settle in the seventeenth century. The remains of the O'Cahan fortifications are incorporated into the ruined nineteenth-century **castle**, whose battlemented outline gives Dungiven a particular flavor when approached from the south. This was the scene of the 1971 attempt to set up an independent Northern Ireland parliament.

Dungiven Priory, signposted down a footpath a little way out of the town towards Antrim, gives a taste of the pioneering life of the early plantation settlers, and of the continuity of tradition. No more than a ruin, the Augustinian priory stands on an imposing, defensible site on a bluff above the river. Founded in 1100 by the O'Cahans, it belongs to the first wave of European monastic orders which arrived in Ireland to supplant the Celtic church. The church contains the tomb of Cooey na Gall O'Cahan, who died in 1385, rated as the finest medieval tomb in Northern Ireland. Beneath the effigy are six bare-legged warriors in kilts, presumably denoting Scotsmen, who represent the O'Cahan chieftain's foreign mercenaries from whom he derived his nickname, na Gall, or "of the foreigners." At some point, the O'Cahans added a defensive tower to the west end of the church and—when Dungiven was granted to the Skinners' Company, in the person of Sir Edward Doddington—this was later enlarged to become a two-and-a-half-story defensive manor house. There's an evocative artist's impression on the site of what that building looked like.

Although the church hasn't been used since 1711, Dungiven Priory remains a religious site of sorts. The tree knotted with rags—handkerchiefs, torn off bits of summer dresses, socks—stands over a deeply hollowed stone, originally used by the monks for milling grain, and now an object of pilgrimage for people seeking cures for physical illness.

Draperstown, Moneymore, Magherafelt, and Upperlands
South of Dungiven, well into the Sperrin Mountains, are more of the **plantation towns** of the London companies, most of them clearly planned, characteristically, around a central diamond.

DRAPERSTOWN, unsurprisingly founded by the Drapers' Company, is essentially a junction, with well-mannered houses facing each other in a very grand street plan. The real gem, though, is **MONEYMORE**, to the southeast, also built by the Drapers, and reconstructed by them in 1817; graceful, pedimented buildings oppose each other across a wide, main street topped by an Orange Hall (plenty of red-white-and-blue curbstones here). It was the first town in Ulster to have piped water, as early as 1615. Just outside Moneymore, **Springhill** (Easter week 2–6pm daily; May, June & Sept Sat & Sun 2–6pm; July & Aug Fri–Wed 2–6pm) is a typical example of the fortified manor houses built by the early planters. Dating from the late seventeenth century, it's a lovely bit of sober, whitewashed architecture, and inside there's a good collection of costumes.

MAGHERAFELT, granted to the Salters' Company by James I, has another wide, sloping main street with Union Jacks fluttering everywhere. Of more delaying interest, just north of MAGHERA, at **UPPERLANDS**, you can get some idea of the impact of the new eighteenth-century technology on the area. The **Middle House Museum** here is a private textile museum owned by the Clark family; in 1740, Jackson Clark dammed the river to provide power and installed linen-finishing machinery here. If you want to look around, then phone Wallace Clark (☎0648-42214 or 42737) in advance to arrange a guided tour.

South Antrim: Ballymena to Belfast

South Antrim is unlikely traveling country, largely rolling (and unexciting) farmland, with places whose names are familiar because you've heard them so often on the news: Ballymena, Antrim, and Lisburn. Still, you're likely to see something of most of these towns as the train from Belfast passes through them on the way to the northern coast.

Ballymena and Gracehill
BALLYMENA (pronounced, incidentally, "Ballamena," unless you're a BBC newsreader) is a fine, upstanding Protestant town that could have been transplanted straight from the Scottish lowlands. Indeed, most of its Plantation settlers came from the southwest of Scotland, and it's said that the Ballymena accent still retains traces of Scottish lowlands speech. Like many Northern Irish towns, its prosperity derived from the linen trade, while the alleged tightfistedness of its residents earned it the sobriquet of the "Aberdeen of Ireland." A mile and a half west of Ballymena is **GRACEHILL**, a reminder of the curious mixture of religious oppression and tolerance that has characterized Northern Ireland's history: at the same time as Ireland's Catholics were suffering heavy penalties, the country was welcoming dissenting Protestant groups, among them the Moravians (the United Brethren), who built a model settlement at Gracehill. The elegant square survives, with separate buildings for men and women, whose main trade was making lace and clocks. Segregated in life, the sexes remained divided in death, and in the graveyard you can walk down the long path that separates the graves of the men from those of the women.

Antrim
ANTRIM, by way of contrast, is a tacky and flyblown town, the sort of place that despite its recent growth—the population has trebled in the last fifteen years—isn't really given a chance by either the Troubles or the grim economics of Northern Ireland. If you've time to kill, there's a tenth-century **round tower** in Steeple Park, a mile out of town, indicating the site of an important monastery that flourished between the sixth and twelfth centuries; and a pretty, if unremarkable, eighteenth-century cottage, **Pogue's Entry**, off the main street (ask for the key at *Simpson's* newsagents at 32 Church Street). **Belfast International Airport** is actually four miles south of Antrim, but this doesn't mean that you have to stick around—the transportation links to Belfast are much better than to Antrim.

Lisburn

LISBURN, practically a suburb of Belfast, is also best ignored, with a grimy, uninteresting sprawl of cut-price shops. Again, there are few clues to its past as an important linen town. After the revocation of the Edict of Nantes in 1685, which removed French and Dutch Huguenots' freedom of worship, large numbers of them were persuaded to come to Ulster, where they founded the linen trade. Bleaching greens were set up along the banks of the Lagan River; the first of them started in 1626 at LAMBEG, a mile downstream from Lisburn. The place has given its name to the big drums which appear in the Orange marches, deriving from the military drums of Prince William's army. The **museum** (Tues–Sat 11am–1pm and 1:45–4:45pm; closed Sat in winter) in Lisburn's Market Square has a permanent exhibition on the development of the linen trade.

Long Kesh

The political prison of **Long Kesh**, or **the Maze**, which lies to the south of Lisburn, incorporates the notorious H-Blocks which were the focus of the 1981 Hunger Strikes, in which Republican inmates demanded the reinstatement of political status.The prison, erected on an old airfield soon after the Troubles began, housed hundreds of activists, Loyalist and Republican, interned without trial by the British government. Originally all inmates— convicted prisoners as well as internees—had special category status (a kind of POW status), in conjunction with the Emergency Powers legislation under which they had been convicted, but when the British Government phased out internment in late 1975, special status went with it. From March 1, 1976, the prison was in the peculiar position of housing the last of these special category prisoners as well as—in the H-blocks—those convicted after this cut-off date, who were now classified, and treated, as ordinary criminals.

The IRA campaign for the reinstatement of status began in 1976 when Kevin Nugent, in refusing to wear prison clothes, initiated what become known as the "blanket protest" (quite simply, draping a blanket around himself instead of wearing prison clothes). By 1978 this had escalated into the famous "dirty protest" in which Republican prisoners refused to undertake ordinary prison duties such as emptying chamber pots, resorting instead to smearing the cells with their own excrement in order to get rid of it. In 1981 a concerted hunger strike led to the deaths of ten men, including Bobby Sands, provisional commander of the IRA men inside the prison, who had, significantly, been elected MP for Fermanagh-South Tyrone six weeks into his fast. None of this succeeded in budging the government who steadfastly refused to back down in the face of what they believed was nothing more than moral blackmail. The motivation for the hunger strikes was made manifestly clear in a piece of contemporary graffiti that appeared in Republican areas:

I'll wear no convict's uniform
Nor meekly serve my time
That England might brand Ireland's fight
Eight Hundred years of crime.

Meanwhile, the system of justice that allows one law for the British and another (internment and the jury-less Diplock courts) for the Irish seems an altogether greater cause for concern. In November 1989 the Guildford Four, imprisoned after the 1974 spate of pub-bombings in Britain, were freed when it became clear that they had been convicted on the sole basis of fabricated police evidence. As we go to press there are renewed calls for a review of the similar case of the Birmingham Six.

travel details

Trains
From Derry to Dublin Connolly Stn. (6; 2hr 20min); Belfast (6; 2hr 20min); Portrush (6; 1hr); Coleraine (6; 40min); Ballymena (6; 1hr 20min).

Ulsterbus
From Derry to Dublin (3; 4hr 40min) Sligo (1; 2hr 45min); Donegal (1; 1hr 10min) Monaghan (3; 2hr 5min).

Private buses
Funtrek (☎01-730852) runs a daily service **from Derry** bus depot to Dublin via Monaghan, Omagh, and Strabane.

CHAPTER SIXTEEN

DOWN AND ARMAGH

D own and Armagh occupy the southwest corner of Northern Ireland, between Belfast and the border. It's territory where all too many of the names are familiar from the news, and certainly the border areas, especially South Armagh, have borne more than their share of the Troubles. But it's also very attractive country, especially around the coast, with a rich history which takes in **Saint Patrick**—who sailed into Strangford Lough to make his final Irish landfall in County Down, founded his first bishopric at Armagh, and is buried at either Downpatrick or Armagh, depending whose claim you choose—and the constant defense of Ulster from invasion.

Heading south from Belfast, the glowering **Mourne Mountains** dominate every view, and it's in this direction that most of the attractions lie. If you simply take the main roads in and out of Belfast—the A1 for Newry and the border or the N1 motorway west—you'll come across very little to stop for; it's in the rural areas, the mountains and coast that the charm of this region lies. Probably the best option is to head east from Belfast around the Down shore, through the **Ards Peninsula** or along the banks of **Strangford Lough**, towards **Newcastle**, the best base for excursions (on foot) into the Mourne Mountains. Along the way there are plenty of little beaches, early Christian sites, and fine houses to stop for. Immediately outside Belfast in this direction—easy day trips from there—are the **Ulster Folk and Transport Museum**, one of the best in the North, and the overblown suburban resort of **Bangor**. Beyond the Mournes a fine coast road curves around to **Carlingford Lough** and the border.

Inland there's less of interest, certainly in County Down. **Armagh City**, though, is well worth some of your time for its ancient associations, cathedrals, and fine Georgian streets. South Armagh has some startlingly attractive country, especially around **Slieve Gullion**, though its border position makes traveling here a less appealing proposition than it might otherwise appear.

COUNTY DOWN

In **County Down** it's the coast, and the Mourne Mountains at their southern extremity, that you're heading for. The big towns in the north, **Newtownards** and **Bangor**, are not at all attractive, but beyond them the A2 road clings to the coast all the way round to Newry, or lesser routes follow the shores of Strangford Lough towards **Downpatrick** and its associations with the arrival of Saint Patrick. There are numerous small resorts around the coast but **Newcastle** is the biggest, and in some ways the most enjoyable. It's also the ideal place to start your exploration of the mountains.

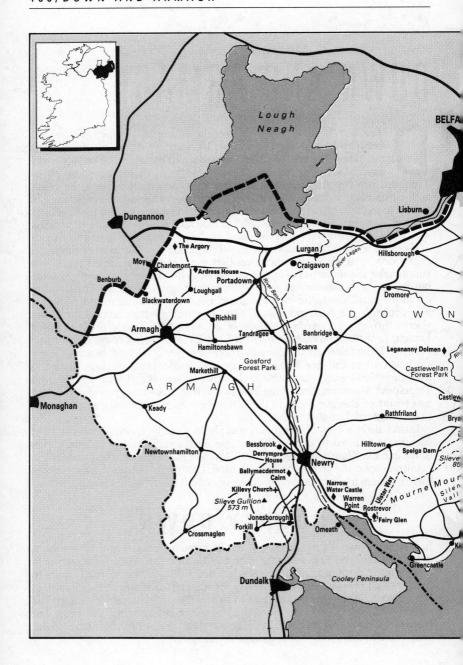

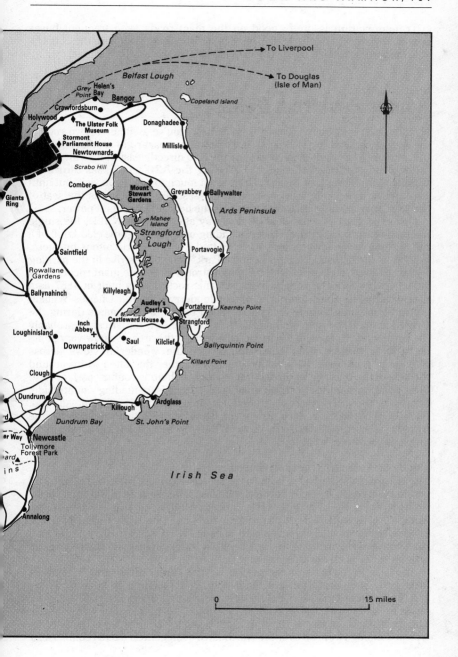

Transportation is pretty good on the main roads, with frequent buses connecting anywhere of any size, but again if you want to explore the country-side in any depth you'll need your own means—much of Down is ideal cycling country.

Routes East from Belfast

Heading east into County Down from Belfast, you've a choice of two routes: the A2, which heads up to Bangor and follows the coast right around the edge of the county, to wind up in Newry; or the A20 directly east to Newtownards, at the head of Strangford Lough. Following the **A20** you'll pass **Stormont Castle**, four miles out of Belfast. There's not much to see if you visit, but until 1974, when direct rule was imposed from Westminster, this was the seat of the Northern Ireland parliament, and thus the heart of Protestant power.

Once you get on to the dual carriageway after DUNDONALD, the single interesting sight is **Scrabo Tower**, standing on a rocky, gorse-clad knoll of a hill. Getting to the tower after you've spotted it is quite a circuitous business, but follow the signs to "Scrabo Country Park" and you'll arrive in the parking lot just below. Up close it looks quite monstrous, like some giant rocket in its launcher, hewn out of rough, black volcanic rock. It was built in 1857 as a memorial to the third marquess of Londonderry, General Charles William Stewart-Vane, in gratitude for his efforts on behalf of his tenants during the Great Famine. The spot was originally a Bronze-Age burial cairn, probably the resting place of one of the grand chieftains of the area. It's now very popular with sightseers, who come mostly for the wonderful views across Strangford Lough and the healthy, blustery weather that often whips around the side of the hill. The woodland immediately behind is country park open to the public; in contrast to the tamed, prosperous surrounding countryside, Scrabo is the only piece of ground for miles around to feel at all wild. **NEWTOWNARDS**, a place strong on manufacture but unexciting for the traveler, is evenly spread out below. What you see of it from Scrabo is as much as you'd ever want to.

The Ulster Folk and Transport Museum
The **A2** towards Bangor is both more scenic and more interesting, and still within easy reach of a day trip from Belfast. There's a beautiful fifteen-mile walk between HOLYWOOD (pronounced "Hollywood") and Helen's Bay, along a mildly indented estuary coast with some fine silvery sand beaches, especially the small crescent-shaped ones at Helen's Bay itself. The railroad runs between the path and the road, with a couple of stations where you can pick up services on towards Bangor.

At CULTRA station you can get off for the **Ulster Folk and Transport Museum** (May–Sept Mon–Sat 11am–6pm, Sun 2–6pm, until 9pm Wed May and June; Oct–April Mon–Sat 11am–5pm, Sun 2–5pm; £1; ☎0232-428428; buses to Bangor will also stop here), one of the most fascinating in the North. The main site is an open-air museum, still being added to, where about twenty typical buildings from all over the North have been gathered and rebuilt, as far as possible in authentic settings and with furnishings as they would have been at the turn of the century. The idea is that you can walk from one part of Northern Ireland to another, amid scenes typical to each: to this end traditional farms have also been created, and assorted livestock roams between the buildings. You start with a gallery where there are exhibitions, permanent and temporary, on Ulster's social history, and an introduction to the buildings you'll see. From here you walk around the grounds, visiting the various buildings (not all of which are always open); they include a small village street with church and rectory, two schools, various typical farm dwellings, and a forge and other buildings used in light rural industry. On the far side of the main road, across a bridge, are the **transport galleries** (an annex of the Belfast transportation museum), where the exhibits include every conceivable form of transportation from horse-drawn carts to lifeboats and a vertical-take-off plane, but especially veteran cars (and, of course, a De Lorean). Outside the galleries there's a miniature railroad, which runs on summer Saturdays, and back in the main section there's a handy restaurant in the Education Centre.

Helen's Bay

If you're not walking, **HELEN'S BAY** is signposted a mile off the A2, or it's another stop on the Belfast–Bangor rail line. It's a rather smug but restful little place, with a red-painted, baronial-style station and a truncated golf course course. **Grey Point Fort** (open Easter–Oct daily 9am–5pm; winter Sun 2–5pm; ☎0247-85362), a little to the left of the bay and on the walking path, is positioned to command the mouth of Belfast Lough, along with its sister fort at Kilroot on the other side. The fort has what you'd expect in the way of quarters, engine house, and stores, as well as an impressive battery of gun emplacements, ready to challenge the shipping that entered the lough during the two world wars. In the event, the two six-inch breech-loading guns were never fired except in practice, but they still look pretty impressive. The Battery Observation Post and Fire Command Post are today manned by dressed-up mannequins, like stills taken from a war movie—though they're now staring straight into a growth of trees that have sprung up to obscure the view. There's also a selection of photos showing the original guns and their positions; but it's really as a viewpoint with an atmosphere of military history, rather than as a panoramic citadel, that the fort is worth visiting nowadays.

The fort, and in fact the whole short stretch of coast from Helen's Bay, is actually part of the **Crawfordsburn Country Park**, an estate handed down from the Scottish Presbyterian Crawford family, then acquired by Lord Dufferin (whose mother Helen gave her name to the bay) and now in public hands. Its glens and dells are replete with beeches, cypresses, exotic conifers, cedars, the usual burst of rhododendrons, and also a Californian giant redwood. Perhaps the best walk (well marked) is to follow the pathway back from Grey Point to the top of the bay's beaches, and turn inland by the stream (Crawford's Burn). This will take you up through the best of the woodland, under a fine nineteenth-century rail viaduct (still in use), and up to a waterfall at the head of the glen. The **Park Centre** has a restaurant (a bit pricey) and a video show on the area's chief attractions; you can also **camp** on the estate.

CRAWFORDSBURN village is on one of Ireland's most ancient highways—now the B20—and has a nice but cutesy (as with many things in this part of the world) early-seventeenth-century **pub**, *The Old Inn*, which also serves cheap lunch specials.

Strangford Lough and the Ards Peninsula

The three most scenic routes south through County Down are all to the east. The **Ards Peninsula** stretches out an arm to enclose the waters of **Strangford Lough**, with only the narrowest of openings to the sea in the south, and it's around the lough's waters that most of the area's interest is concentrated. Ancient annals say the lough was formed around 1654 BC by the sea sweeping in over the lands of Brena. This created a beautiful, calm inlet, the archipelago-like pieces of land along its inner arm fringed with brown and yellow bladderwrack and tangle weed, and tenanted by a rich gathering of bird life during the warmer months. It makes a haven for small boats and yachts, and several attractive stopping-off places for the land-bound make the road along the lough's western bank the most interesting of all routes leading south from Belfast.

Surprisingly perhaps, the least interesting of the three possible routes is the coastal trip along the peninsula's outer arm from Bangor down to Portaferry. **BANGOR** has been a popular seaside resort for Belfast people since Victorian times, but today it's pretty dull—as much a suburb of Belfast as a vacation spot—and its attractions rather tawdry. There are, however, plenty of facilities for visitors, and scores of **B&Bs**, concentrated especially in Queen's Parade, Princetown Road, and Seacliff Road. What history the place has, as yet another ancient monastic settlement, has entirely disappeared, and Bangor's one claim to historical fame now lies in the Ambrosian Library in Milan. This is the *Antiphonarium Benchoreense*, one of the oldest known ecclesiastical manuscripts, consisting of collects, anthems, and some religious poems. It came originally from the great Bangor Abbey (one of the most powerful for nearly 800 years), though had it remained here it would surely have perished with the abbey's destruction.

Moving south along the Ards coast, you'll find many **campgrounds** along the A2—at DONAGHADEE, MILLISLE, BALLYHALBERT and CLOGHY, to name a few—but it's far from the most attractive coastline around here. Just about the only minor piece of interest is the late-eighteenth-century **Ballycopeland windmill** (April–Sept Tues–Sat 10am–7pm, Sun 2–7pm; Oct–March Sat 10am–4pm, Sun 2–4pm), a mile west of Millisle. This claims to be the only working windmill left in Ireland. You'll find a great deal more to detain you if you follow one of the shores of the lough.

Along the Western Bank

Leaving Scabro Tower on the A20, you'll pick up signs for COMBER (famous only for its potatoes) and then Downpatrick, with a turning to "Castle Espie Conservation" on your left, which you should follow. The *Old Schoolhouse*

Restaurant by the roadside, unmistakable with a fire engine lodged in its front garden, provides first-class eating with a fair-priced Sunday lunch (otherwise open Tues–Sat 7–11pm; ☎0238-541182). From here, you can wind along the very edge of the lough, on a series of minor roads. Traveling this route is enjoyable in itself, but there are a couple of spots worth making for.

First of them is **Mahee Island**, named for Saint Mochoe, the first abbot of the island, who died tragically, burned in his cell. Heading past crumbling Mahee Castle at the entrance to the island, and over the causeway, you come to the Celtic **Nendrum Monastic Site** a few hundred yards farther on. It's a gorgeous spot, surrounded by drumlins and the lough's waterways. This was once a massive establishment, with church, round tower, school, and living quarters all contained within a *cashel* of three concentric wards, which is itself probably even earlier. Today, the inner wall shelters the ruined church, and a restored sundial uses some of the original remnants. There's an illuminating reconstruction map at the site.

Back on the road along the lough, follow the signs to Ardmillan, Killinchy, and then Whiterock for **Sketrick Island** (which itself is not signposted). As with Mahee Island, there's a castle to guard the entrance, now no more than a shattered reminder. *Daft Eddy's Pub and Rest*, behind the castle, offers bar snacks as well as a more elaborate restaurant menu. An equally daft competition known as the **Hen Island race** takes place here in October, when craft made of oil drums and crates are ridden and paddled between Sketrick and the nearby Hen Island.

The tiny coves and inlets at the feet of little drumlins continue as far as Killyleagh, almost any of them worth a lazy exploration. The best would be to **rent a boat** for a day or more, which you can do at RINGAHADDY, about halfway down the lough, from Alan McGarvey at *Strangford Lough Charters* (☎0238-541186; £12–30 per day, £140–170 per week, depending on season).

Approaching **KILLYLEAGH**, what looks like a huge child's sand-castle comes into view, wholly out of character with the area. This began life as a John de Courcy castle in the late twelfth century, but went through a major overhaul by the Hamilton family in the nineteenth century to give it the Bavarian *schloss* appearance it has today. It's still a private house, and when viewed close up it's much more gaunt, with a squat mixture of high step crenellations, turrets, and cones. The stone outside the castle gates commemorates the town's most famous son, Hans Sloane (1660–1753), physician to King George II and founder of both the British Museum and Kew Gardens—London's Sloane Square is named after him. Through rather more obscure connections, Prince Andrew was created Baron Killyleagh on his wedding day in 1986, the Duchess of York having some ancestors from here.

The Lough's Eastern Shore

Over on the Ards Peninsula, the eastern edge of Strangford Lough is not as indented as its opposite shore, but betters it in having a major road (the continuation of the A20) that runs close to the water virtually all the way down. The scenery is pleasant enough, and there are two places to stop off en route to Portaferry—the Mount Stewart Gardens and Grey Abbey.

The National Trust-owned **Mount Stewart House and Gardens** (June–Aug Tues–Sun noon–6pm; May and Sept Wed–Sun 2–6pm; April and Oct weekends 2–6pm; ☎024-774387) lie five miles southeast of Newtownards. The **gardens**, only part of an eighty-acre estate, are laid out on a grand scale. The trees and shrubs here are no more than sixty to seventy years old, but they've grown at such a remarkable rate that they look twice this age. This is principally due to the microclimate, which is unusually warm and humid—the gardens get the east-coast sun, causing a heavy overnight dew, and the Gulf Stream washes the shores only a stone's throw away; surprisingly for so far north, conditions here rival those of Cornwall and Devon. It was Lady Londonderry, wife of the seventh marquess, who laid out these gardens from about 1920 on, and she made a thorough job of it; titles include the Mairi Garden (after her daughter), Italian Garden, Spanish Garden, Peace Garden, Sunk Garden, Shamrock Garden and many more—well worth visiting in the blooming season.

The **House** is also worth a visit. It was once the Irish seat of the Londonderrys, one of whom, Viscount Castlereagh, acted as Foreign Secretary under Pitt in the late eighteenth and early nineteenth centuries, and is best remembered for guiding the Act of Union into operation. Among the splendid (and occasionally eccentric) furniture inside, much of it once again the work of Lady Londonderry, is a set of 22 empire chairs used by the delegates to the Congress of Vienna in 1815, including the Duke of Wellington and the Prince de Talleyrand; the chairs were a gift to the Viscount's brother Lord Stewart, another high-ranking diplomat of the time. The European connection is flaunted farther in bedrooms named after various major cities: Rome, St Petersburg, Madrid, Moscow, and also Sebastopol (from the time of the Crimean war). One of the most notable and largest paintings in the house (and in Ireland for that matter) is *Hambletonian* (1799) by George Stubbs, showing the celebrated thoroughbred being rubbed down after a victory at Newmarket. A little to the east of the house, the **Temple of the Winds** is a remodeling of the Athenian *Tower of Andronicus Cyrrhestes* by James "Athenian" Stuart (1713–88), one of the pioneers of Neoclassical architecture. The Temple is set on a promontory overlooking Strangford Lough, making it a great place for bird-watching.

A short diversion from Mount Stewart will take you to CARROWDORE, in the middle of the peninsula, and the grave of the underrated Ulster poet **Louis MacNiece** (1907–63). Continuing on the shore road, however, **Grey Abbey** (April–Sept Tues–Sat 10am–1pm and 2–6pm, Sun 2–6pm; Oct–March Tues–Sat 10am–1pm and 2–4pm, Sun 2–4pm) is only a couple of miles farther on; approaching from the north, take a left turn in the village of GREY ABBEY. Typical of the Cistercian, or "white monks" order, of which Mellifont was the mother house, Grey Abbey sits in remote parkland beside the fresh-running water of a rivulet, a perfect example of the kind of idyllic setting the Cistercians used to seek. Even today, that setting is barely disturbed, and reason in itself to visit, with a substantial set of ruins to complete the picture.

The abbey was founded in 1193 by Affreca, daughter of the King of Man and wife of John de Courcy, in thanksgiving for having made a safe sea-crossing during a storm. Its plans conform pretty much to the same shape as all Cistercian abbeys, with a church at one end and the living and working quarters of the monks ranged around a cloister, and its structure was realized in a very plain manner, without distracting embellishments. Grey Abbey is unusual for Ireland, though, in showing early Gothic features at a time when late Romanesque work was still common here. Among the best-preserved remains are the **west door**, much of whose carved decoration can still be made out, and the church in general. Another unusual feature is that the church is a simple hall, with no aisles around which the monks could process. Outside the church, the guide notes on display help you to imagine the covered alleys and walks of the elongated rectangular cloister that would have been overshadowed on three sides by buildings which are now no more than stumps. These would have included the chapter house, dormitories and refectory. There's a **B&B** in the village (*Gordonall*, 93 Newtownards Road, ☎0247-74325) if you want to stay in these parts.

PORTAFERRY marks the bottom end of the peninsula and the only place of any real size beyond Newtownards. Even this doesn't amount to much, however, and besides the usual scattering of pubs there's not a great deal to hang around for. If you're looking for somewhere to **stay**, there's B&B with the Adairs (22 The Square; ☎02477-28412) or a little way out at *Millview Farm* (8 Abbacy Road, ☎02477-28030), and there's the *Portaferry Hotel* (10 The Strand; ☎02477-28231; about £18), which also has a decent restaurant. **Ferries** leave regularly (every half hour or so) for the five-minute ride across the lips of the lough to Strangford (see below).

The Lecale Peninsula

Jutting around the bottom of Strangford Lough, the **Lecale Peninsula** is above all Saint Patrick's country. Ireland's patron saint was originally a Roman Briton, first carried off as a youth from somewhere near Carlisle in northern England by Irish raiders. He spent six years in slavery in Ireland before escaping home again and, at the age of thirty, decided to return to Ireland as a bishop, to spread Christianity. Christianity had actually reached Ireland a while before him, probably through traders and other slaves, and Saint Patrick was not in fact the first bishop of Ireland (then on the edge of the known world)—but he remains far and away the most famous. He arrived in Ireland this second time, according to his biographer Muirchú (also his erstwhile captor, converted), on the shores of the Lecale region, and his first Irish sermon was preached at Saul in AD 432. Today the region commemorates the association with sites at Struell Wells and Saul, as well as at Downpatrick town itself.

Downpatrick

DOWNPATRICK, the county capital, is not somewhere you come for a vibrant nightlife. In modern times it seems depressed and rather lethargic, awaiting the invigorating kiss of economic revival. On the other hand its history is a rich and well-preserved one, with the major sites conveniently concentrated at one end of town, around the **Hill of Down** on which the cathedral now stands. This was once a rise of great strategic worth, fought over long before the arrival of Saint Patrick made it famous. A Celtic fort of mammoth proportions was built here, and was called first *Arús Cealtchair*, then later *Dún Cealtchair* (Celtchar's fort). Celtchar was one of the Red Branch Knights (see "Armagh," below), a friend of the then King of Ulster, Conor MacNessa, and, according to the *Book of the Dun Cow*, "an angry terrific hideous man with a long nose, huge ears, apple eyes, and coarse dark-gray hair." The *Dún* part of the fort's name went on to become the name of the county, as well as the town.

By the time the Norman knight **John de Courcy** made his mark here in the late twelfth century, a settlement was well established. Pushing north out of Leinster, and defeating Rory MacDonlevy, King of Ulster, de Courcy dispossessed the Augustinian canons who occupied the Hill of Down to establish his own Benedictine abbey. He flaunted as much pomp as he could to mark the occasion, and one of his festive tricks was to import what were supposedly the disinterred bodies of Saint Brigid and Saint Columba to join Saint Patrick, who was (supposedly again) buried here. One of the earliest accounts of Patrick's life asserts that he's buried in a church near the sea; and since a later account admits that "where his bones are no man knows," Downpatrick's claim seems as good as any.

The site of the three graves is meant to be just to the left of the tower entrance and is marked today by a rough granite slab, put there around 1900 to cover the huge hole created by earlier pilgrims searching for the saints' bones. The cathedral built by de Courcy was destroyed in the fourteenth century, and a new abbey erected in the early sixteenth century was even more short-lived. Today's **Cathedral** (open to visitors 9am–5pm) dates basically from the early part of this century, though it incorporates many aspects of earlier incarnations. Its most unique feature are the private box-pews, characteristic of the Regency period and the only ones remaining in use in Ireland.

Leaving the cathedral and retracing your steps a little down English Street, the eighteenth-century jail has undergone some renovation and now houses both the **Down Museum** and the **St Patrick Heritage Centre** (Mon–Fri 9am–5pm, Sat and Sun 2–5pm; ☎0396-5218). The heritage center occupies the gatehouse, and has a video and display of illustrations telling the Saint Patrick story, principally through his own words from his autobiographical *Confessions* (the short video also provides a handy summary of what the rest of the peninsula has to offer by way of relics of the saint). The three-storey Georgian **Governor's House**, in the middle of the walled courtyard, includes a local history gallery with a fascinating set of photographs of Loughinisland (see below) and its people at the beginning of this century. The cell block at the back of the enclosure (still awaiting restoration) once held the United Irishman Thomas Russell, who had already survived the 1798 uprising but was implicated in Robert Emmetts's rebellion and was duly hanged in 1803 from a sill outside the main gate of the jail.

Turn downhill between the jail and the fenced-up courthouse, and you come to the **Mound of Down**, a smaller prominence half submerged in undergrowth. It's in fact sixty feet high and inside its outer ditch is a horseshoe central mound of rich grass. Once a *rath*, or round hill-fort, it was considerably altered and enlarged to create a Norman motte-and-bailey style fortification, with a *bretasche* (a wooden archery tower) at the center. Its view back onto the Hill of Down illustrates clearly the attractions the Hill had for its earliest settlers.

Over to the other side of the Quole Marsh lie the remains of **Inch Abbey**. Unfortunately, you can't get over to it from here, due to the river, and it's vexing to be only a stone's throw away—its setting and atmosphere are amongst the most exquisite of all these Cistercian sites. The only access is a mile out along the Belfast Road, taking the left turn down Inch Abbey Road just before the *Abbey Lodge* hotel. It's signposted from here down another left turnoff. The site was once an island, and its early church was replaced by de Courcy with the Cistercian Abbey. The monks were shipped over from Furness Abbey in Lancasrent with the intention of establishing a strong English center of influence—no Irish monks were ever allowed to be part of it. Not unexpectedly, little of it is now left standing, having undergone its alotted burning in 1404, with monastic life completely finished off by the mid-sixteenth century. Still, it makes by far the most satisfying memory of the Downpatrick area, with a picturesque setting among small glacial drumlins and woodland, and strolling up the valley sides (now a nature reserve, created when a flood control dam downstream turned this part of the river from salt-water estuary to freshwater marshy lake) is a very pleasant way to pass time.

Downpatrick Practicalities

The **Tourist information**, for what it's worth, is based at the Leisure Centre out on the Clough Road (Mon–Fri 10am–10pm, Sat 10am–6pm, Sun 2–6:30pm). The **bus station** is also on the Clough Road. You won't find much exciting to **eat**, but you won't starve either: try the *Abbey Lodge Hotel* or the *Russell* pub, both on the Belfast road; the *Abbey Grill* out on the Newcastle road; or the lunchtime specials in the *Old Mart*, opposite the Downtown Shopping Centre. The only effort at **music**-making takes place in the form of jazz at the *De Courcy Arms* on Tuesday nights, although there may also be occasional performances in the excellent new **Down Arts Center** (in the refurbished old town hall on Irish Street; ☎0396-615283); there's also an art gallery, coffee bar and performance space here. Should you want to **stay** you've little choice—just the *Abbey Lodge Hotel* again (about £20; ☎0396-4511) or B&B at Mrs McCormick's *Rivendell* (69 Saul Road; ☎0396-2695).

On the Trail of Saint Patrick

The nearest of the surrounding Saint Patrick sites, within a couple of miles of Downpatrick, is **Struell Wells**. To get there, head out on the Ardglass Road, then turn left just past the hospital, then a right down a narrow track into a secluded rock-faced valley. The waters here were once a grand old center for pilgrimage and their miraculous healing powers recorded as far back as medieval times. In 1744 Walter Harris described the scene at their height: "Vast throngs of rich and poor resort on Midsummer Eve and the Friday before Lammas, some in the hopes of obtaining health, and others to perform penance." Mass is still said here on Midsummer's Eve, and people bring containers to carry the water home with them; but if you're not looking for health or penance, there's still the joy of spotting one of the tiny gems of Irish landscape beauty—a hidden rocky dell with an abundance of yellow-flowering whin, its underground stream rechanneled to run through the wells' purpose-built bath houses.

The next Saint Patrick landmark is at **SAUL**, not much farther from Downpatrick off the Strangford Road. Saint Patrick is said to have landed nearby, sailing up the tiny Slaney River, and it was here that he first preached, immediately converting Dichu, the lord of this territory. Dichu gave Patrick a barn as his first base (the town's name in Irish is *sabhal*, meaning barn), and the saint frequently returned here to rest from his traveling missions. Today a memorial chapel and round tower in the Celtic Revival style, built of pristine silver-gray granite in 1933, commemorate the place as "the most ancient ecclesiastical site in the land, the cradle of Christianity." Two cross-carved stones from between the eighth and twelfth centuries still stand in the graveyard, though there's not a trace of the medieval monastery built here by Saint Malachy in the twelfth century.

Back on the Strangford Road, a few miles farther on between Saul and Raholp, **St Patrick's Shrine** sits atop *Slieve Patrick*, a tract of hillside much like a slalom ski-slope, with the stations of the cross marking a pathway up. The summit (no more than a twenty-minute climb) offers a commanding view of the county, a vista of the endless little bumps of this drumlin-filled territory.

Loughinisland

Loughinisland lies in quite the other direction, inland from Downpatrick, but it's probably the most worthwhile of all the sites associated with Saint Patrick, and indeed one of the most idyllically tranquil spots in County Down. It comprises a reed-fringed lake contained by ten or so little drumlin hills, one of which forms an island in the lake. Here, across a short causeway, are the ruins of three small churches, set next door to each other. To get here from Downpatrick, take the Newcastle road out past the racecourse, then look for the right-hand turnoff to Loughinisland. The most interesting of the churches is the smallest one, **MacCartan's Chapel** (1636), which has an entrance door no taller than four or five feet. It was used by both Catholics and Protestants until they quarrelled on a wet Sunday around 1720 over which congregation should remain outside during the service. The Protestants left and built their church at SEAFORDE instead.

Around the Lecale Coast

If you're coming by ferry to Lecale from the tip of the Ards Peninsula, and following the A2 round the coast, you'll arrive at tiny **STRANGFORD** village, directly opposite Portaferry. Its small harbor makes a pleasant setting for watching the to and fro of the ferry boats, and the *Lobster Pot*, on the front, has mid-range prices for evening meals. But there's little else, and nowhere to stay.

Immediately around Strangford are a few houses and castles worth visiting, the first of them on the road back towards Downpatrick. **Castleward House** (July and Aug Wed–Mon noon–8pm; May and June Wed–Sun noon–6pm; April, Sept, and Oct Sat and Sun noon–6pm), the eighteenth-century residence of Lord and Lady Bangor, is now owned by the National Trust. It's a positively schizophrenic house, thanks to the opposing tastes of its creators (they later split up): one half (the Lord's) is in the Classical Palladian style, the other (the Lady's) in neo-Gothic, a split carried through into the design and decor of the rooms within. Outside there are pleasant gardens and preserved farm buildings. There's also a sixteenth-century tower house (Old Castle Ward) inside the grounds, and another, **Audley's Castle** (fifteenth-century), just outside on the lough shore. It has a superb view across the lough, though there's a better example of a tower house just south of Strangford. On your way back to the main coast road, **Audleystown Cairn** is marked across the fields to the right—though access isn't easy since it's in a field which is usually full of bulls.

A couple of miles south of Strangford, **Kilclief Castle** (Easter–Sept Mon–Fri 10am–7pm, Sat 10am–4pm, Sun 2–4pm) is another, slightly earlier fifteenth-century tower house, in much better condition than Audley's Castle. One of Ireland's earliest tower houses, this was originally the home of John Cely, Bishop of Down—until he was defrocked and thrown out for living with a married woman.

By now you're on the A2 heading down towards Ardglass, but there remain a couple of things worth stopping for. A half mile or so before you reach Ardglass, the ruin of fifteenth-century **Ardtole Church** is well signposted just a few hundred yards off the road. It's set on the spur of a hill, which gives it a fine perspective out to sea and back across the undulating flat of Lecale. Once dedicated to Saint Nicholas, patron saint of sailors, this church was used by English fishermen until a quarrel broke out with the Irish around 1650. The story goes that the fishermen tied a sleeping Irish chief to the ground by his long hair so that he couldn't get up when he awoke. Tradition has it that Swift adapted the similar episode in *Gulliver's Travels* from this tale, and certainly the Ardtole region is rampant with tiny drumlins—very much like the description of the Lilliputian mountains.

Also signposted off the Ardglass road (a mile's drive and a quarter of a mile's walk) is **St Patrick's Well**, set on a wonderful rocky shore. The well is easily spotted—it looks rather like a sheep-dip trench, but with a crucifix at its head. Its holy water has turned into something closer to stagnant consommé than an ever-youthful source of new life.

Ardglass

ARDGLASS is set on the side of a lovely natural inlet. Its domestic buildings, rising steeply from the harbor (*ard glas* in Irish means the green height), are interspersed with fortified mansions, towers and turrets. These date from a vigorous English revival in the sixteenth century, when a trading company first arrived to found a colony here. The best preserved of these fortifications, and the only one in the town open for visits, is **Jordan's Castle**, next door to the *Anchor* pub on the Low Road (Easter–Sept Mon–Fri 10am–7pm, Sat 10am–4pm, Sun 2–4pm). The most elegant and highly developed of all the

Down tower houses, this now contains the local museum. The tall, crenellated building with white plaster trimming up on the hill was once **King's Castle**; its nineteenth-century renovation is obvious, as is modern work to turn it into a nursery. The lone ornamental-looking turret on the hilltop is **Isabella's Tower**, a nineteenth-century folly created by Aubrey de Vere Beauclerc as a gazebo for his invalid daughter.

During the nineteenth century, Ardglass was the most thriving **fishing** port in the North; even today, as well as the prawns, herrings and whitefish brought in by the fishing fleet, there's very good rod-fishing off the end of the pier for codling, pollack, and coalfish. Even the *Spar* supermarket on the quay is wonderfully stocked with a fantastic range of seafood (scallops, monkfish, oysters, salmon, etc), enough in itself to entice a quick shopping visit. It's also sometimes possible to buy direct from the cannery on the quay. You can get **food** and a **room** (about £15) at the *Ardglass Arms* on Kildare Street (☎0396-841228).

From Killough to Clough

KILLOUGH, a few miles on, is an unworldly village stretching around a much larger harbor than Ardglass—but now silted up. The A2 passes through Killough's main street: a fine avenue of sycamores with a string of picturesque cottage rows at its southern end, this makes an unlikely major thoroughfare. It was the wards of Castleward who built the harbor in the eighteenth century, and there's still a direct road running inland, virtually in a straight line, from Killough to Castleward.

From the southern end of Killough you can head out to **St John's Point**, on which lie the ruins of one of the North's best examples of a pre-Romanesque church. It's an enjoyable two-and-a-half-mile walk. The tiny west door of the tenth-century church has the distinctive sloping sides, narrowing as the doorway rises, that were a common feature of these early churches. Also still apparent are the *antae*, enclosures created by the extension of the west and east walls to give extra support to the roof. Excavations in 1977 revealed graves that extended under these walls, indicating that an even earlier church existed from the early Christian period, probably made of wood. The red-white-and-blue lighthouse on the tip of the point is a needless reminder of the region's political complexion, no doubt intended to emphasise how far east and close to Britain this position is.

From here, the A2 passes long, sandy beaches at MINERSTOWN and TYRELLA STRAND before reaching **CLOUGH**, a crossroads village between Downpatrick and Newcastle and the inland ending of the Lecale region. It has a Norman *motte* and bailey, as pristinely preserved as a carpet of mown grass, with a poor remnant of a thirteenth-century stone keep stuck in the middle. The site, just behind a gas station at the Belfast end of the village, has surprisingly good views—considering its low-lying position—across Dundrum bay inlet towards the Mournes and back over to Slieve Croob in central Down. Presumably because of its situation astride several main roads, Clough has a number of cheap **B&Bs**: they include *Woodhill* (☎039-687240) and *Teac'cúilín House* (☎039-687662), both on Moneycarragh Road, and *Timakeel* (27 Claragh Road; ☎039-6778751).

The Road to Newcastle

Heading south along the coast from the Lecale region, **DUNDRUM** lies beside a hammer-head-shaped tidal bay, only a few miles down the road from Clough. Above the town are the quite spectacular ruins of a large Norman **castle** (summer Tues–Sat 10am–7pm, Sun 2–7pm; winter Tues–Fri 10am–4pm, Sat 10am–4pm, Sun 2–4pm); to get to it, take the steep turning up the hill from Dundrum village, a fifteen-minute walk. The castle has a central circular *donjon* (with a fine stairway in its walls), a fortified gateway, and drum towers, all set upon a *motte* and bailey. In its time it was described as the most impenetrable fortress in the land. Some say it was a de Courcy fortress, designed for the Knights Templar; but the circular keep, a rarity in Ireland, is not at all in keeping with the other fortresses de Courcy built to defend the stretch of coast from Carlingford right up to Carrickfergus. De Courcy's successor, de Lacy, is a more likely candidate—his Welsh connections tie in with the castle's similarity to the one at Pembroke, Wales. If you're lucky, your visit might coincide with the real McCoy soundtrack of live gunfire from the shooting range down by the Murlough Sand Dunes (a National Trust reserve beside the bay), which sharpens the atmosphere of the scene superbly.

There's a **B&B** in Dundrum (*Mourneview House*, 16 Main Street; ☎039-675457), and the *Dundrum Bay Inn* at the south end of the village serves good meals and snacks.

Newcastle and Around

NEWCASTLE, with its lovely stretch of sandy beach, is the biggest seaside resort in Down, and also the best base for excursions into the Mourne Mountains. The mountains' highest peak, **Slieve Donard**, rises just behind the town; at 2796 feet it's also the highest peak in Ulster, yet it makes an easy and safe climb. The town itself isn't exactly exciting, but it's well equipped to send you pony-trekking, or fishing on the river, and for the inevitable rainy day there are indoor alternatives at the *Newcastle Center and Tropicana Complex* on the promenade (summer only; ☎03967-22222), with swimming pools, water slides, and playgrounds.

Places to stay include the only official **youth hostel** in this region in a terraced house on the seafront (30 Downs Road, near the bus station; ☎03967-22133), and lots of **B&Bs**. The richest concentration of these is again along the seafront, on Downs Road and the South and Central Promenades: for much the same price you can stay at the **YMCA** (*Rathmourne House*, 143 Central Promenade; ☎03967-24488) or the **YWCA** (*Glenada Holiday Center*, 29 South Promenade; ☎03967-22402). The best of the more upmarket hotels is the very obvious Victorian red-brick *Slieve Donard Hotel* (☎03967-23681; about £30) on Downs Road near the youth hostel. There are also two semi-detached National Trust properties, *Murlough Cottages* on the shore of Dundrum Bay (sleep 4–6; longer periods only; contact Mrs Whatmough ☎03967-51311). Obviously, these get reserved well in advance, but you may be lucky out of season. There are a couple of **trailer parks/campgrounds** at the northern end of town. Newcastle's **tourist information office** is at 61 Central Promenade (☎03967-22222).

There's little to see in Newcastle itself—though the hideous modern Catholic church is hard to miss—but in the immediate surroundings are several pleasant **parks** created from the estates of old houses. The nearest is **Donard Park** on the slopes of Slieve Donard. There's a good walk along the Glen River from the town center to the park, and if you keep following this path uphill you'll emerge on the other side and eventually come to the Saddle, a col between the two mountains of Slieve Donard and Slieve Commedagh; from here, via Trassey Burn, you can go straight into the heart of the hills. **Tollymore Forest Park** is a little farther away, two miles inland along the Bryansford Road, and considerably bigger and better equipped. It also creeps up the northern side of the Mournes, and its picturesque trails wind through woodland and beside the river. You enter the park by one of two ornate Gothic-folly gates—there are more follies in BRYANSFORD nearby—and there's an information center and café in an elaborate stone barn.

Castlewellan Forest Park is also inland, outside the elegant market town of CASTLEWELLAN. A wonderful **arboretum**, dating originally from 1740 but much expanded since, is its outstanding feature; the sheltered south-facing slopes of its hills, between the Mournes and the Slieve Croob range, allow exotic species to flourish here. There's trout-fishing in its main lake and coarse fishing in the smaller lakes; there's also a café in the 1720 Queen Anne-style farmstead and courtyards, near the main entrance. The Baronial castle to which the grounds originally belonged is now the property of a Christian conference organization, and it offers a very few cheap rooms (☎03967-78733). Inside the park, **Dolly's Brae** (one of the westernmost hills) is often remembered at Loyalist celebrations as the site of one of the greatest victories against Catholic uprisings.

The Mourne Mountains

The **Mournes** are a relatively youthful set of granite mountains, which explains why their comparatively unweathered peaks and flanks are so rugged, forming steep sides, moraines, and occasional sheer cliffs. Closer up, these give sharp, jagged outlines; but from a distance they appear much more gentle, like a sleeping herd of buffalo. The wilder topography lies mostly in the east, below Newcastle, although the fine cliff of **Eagle Mountain**, to the southwest, is wonderful if you can afford the time and effort to get there, and the tamer land above Rostrevor has views down into Carlingford Lough that can rival any in Ireland.

Newcastle is by far the best base if you want to do any serious walking or climbing in the Mournes, and the route outlined above through Donard Park is the obvious starting point. A climb to the peak of **Slieve Donard** (a relatively easy ascent on a well-marked trail to a massive hermit cell on the summit) should be one of the first things you do, not least for its view across the whole mountainscape, which can help you pick out your preferred route. In summer at least (winters can be surprisingly harsh) there are plenty of straightforward hikes in the Mournes that require no special equipment, with obvious tracks to many of the more scenic parts. For further information, and maps, go to the Newcastle tourist office or to the youth hostel there. There are also, of course, more serious climbs: **climbing courses** in the Mournes are run by the *Northern Ireland Mountain Centre* in Newcastle (☎03967-22158), but they must be booked at least two weeks in advance (contact *The Sports Council for Northern Ireland*, House of Sport, Upper Malone Road, Belfast; ☎0232-381222).

Among the highlights are the route that follows Trassey Brook beyond Donard Park up towards the **Hare's Gap**, where minerals have seeped through the rock to form precious and semiprecious stones—topaz, beryl, smoky quartz, and emeralds—in the cavities of the **Diamond Rocks** (hidden behind an obvious boulder stone on the mountainside). Around this point in spring, you might get the chance to hear the song of the ring ouzel bird, which migrates from Africa to breed in these upland areas.

Other heights worth chasing include **Slieve Bingian**, beyond the Hare's Gap, and reached through the Brandy Pad passes by the Blue Lough and Lough Bingian; **Slieve Commedagh**, with its Inca-looking pillars of granite; and **Slieve Bearnagh**, up to the right of the Hare's Gap. Also, try and cross the ridge from **Slieve Meelmore** to **Slieve Muck**, the "pig mountain," descending to the shores of Lough Shannagh, where there's a beach at either end—useful for a swim, though the water's freezing. In the panorama beyond the Hare's Gap, the places not to miss are the eastern slopes of **Cove Mountain** and **Slieve Lamagan**. If you're sticking to the roads, all you can really do is circle the outside of the range, though there is one road through the middle, from Hilltown to Kilkeel.

Around the Western Slopes

There's really not much of interest on the landward side of the Mourne Mountains. **HILLTOWN** has a main street extraordinarily well provided with pubs (supposedly because it was once a smugglers' hideaway, where the spoils would be divided), and it's still a crossroads where numerous roads meet. But most of the time its atmosphere is that of a ghost town. Little over a mile from Hilltown on the Newcastle road is the handsome **Goward dolmen**, known locally as "Pat Kearney's big stone." It's well signposted off the road, though the last quarter mile of track is severely potholed.

Drumena Cashel, back in the same direction off the A25, is one of the better preserved ring-forts, or defended homesteads, in the area. It has a T-shaped underground chamber intended to give shelter from the Vikings—though it's only twelve yards long, and seems better suited to its peace-time function of providing cold storage for food. The stone foundations of a few circular beehive huts (known as *clochans*) also remain. The puzzling aspect of the cashel is its position *below* the summit of the hill—possibly a compromise between the needs of defense and those of comfort, affording some shelter from the harsh winds that whip through the area.

The Mourne Coastline

The A2 south along the coast from Newcastle, trailing the shore around the edge of the mountains and then looping inland around Carlingford Lough, is a spectacularly beautiful drive—though villages become increasingly politicized as you approach the border. There's no shortage of **campgrounds and trailer parks** along this coastal run—try *Annalong Marine Park* (☎03967-68736); *Ballymartin Caravan Park* (☎06937-62881); *Chestnutt Caravan Park*, on the beach at Cranfield near Kilkeel (☎06937-62653); *Kilbroney Caravan Park*, Rostrevor (☎06937-38134); or *Moygannon Caravan Site* at Warrenpoint (06937-72346). **B&Bs** are also plentiful in Annalong, Rostrevor, and Warrenpoint.

Annalong

The first place worth stopping at south of Newcastle is the small fishing harbor of **ANNALONG**. Its name in Irish is *ath na long*, or "ford of the ships"—though today it's mostly pleasure boats that moor here—and the town's a pleasantly relaxed seaside attraction during the summer, with a stony beach and Slieve Binnion providing a grandiloquent backdrop. There are a number of small **B&Bs** here (for example, Mrs Gordon, 32 Majors Hill, ☎03967-68348; Mrs Stevenson, 237 Kilkeel Road, ☎03967-68345; Mrs Whyte, 57 Kilkeel Road, ☎03967-68849) and a **campground/trailer park** (*Marine Park*, summer only) that's landscaped in the shape of a shamrock. The only drawback is the powerful smell of herring wafting up from the harbor.

The campground is just off the main road, and a path from it gives immediate access to an early-nineteenth-century **cornmill**, still in working order and open for visits (June–Aug Mon–Sat 11am–6pm, Sun 2–6pm; Easter–May Sat 11am–6pm, Sun 2–6pm; 50p), down by the walled harbor and the beach. The village itself goes about its maritime work in its narrow streets much as it always has done, and it comes as a surprise in this out-of-the-way part of the North to find the gray harbor walls adorned with the familiar ritualized Protestant graffiti—Ulster 1690, UVF and a Union Jack. The only Republican effort (IRA) is sneaked in on the seaward side of the walls, lending an almost humorous touch to the imbalance of the sympathies in this particular spot.

Kilkeel

Continuing south, there's a good small beach just outside the hamlet of BALLYMARTIN. **KILKEEL** is a much grander version of Annalong, remarkable mainly for the even heftier stench of fish from the canneries on the harbor. The biggest excitements here are the fish auctions that take place on the quayside when the fishing boats come home, and the annual summer **harbor festival**. Both Kilkeel and Ballymartin have places to stay: Kilkeel has a couple of hotels (*Cranfield House*, 57 Cranfield Road, ☎03967-62327; and *Kilmorey Arms*, Greencastle Street, ☎03967-62220), both of which also serve food, and numerous B&Bs (try *Morne Abbey*, 16 Greencastle Road, ☎03967-62426; *Homesyde*, 7 Shandon Drive, ☎03967-62676; or Mrs McKibben, 181 Moyad Road, ☎03967-63444); Ballymartin has just small B&Bs (for example Mrs McCormick, 3 Ballymartin Village, ☎03967-62077; or Mrs Bingham, 6 Ballykeel Road, ☎03967-62521).

Not far from Kilkeel, **Greencastle Fort** (April–Sept Tues–Sat 10am–1pm and 1:30–7pm), on a promontory at the mouth of Carlingford Lough, is worth a diversion off the main route. The fort is a comparatively well-preserved Anglo-Norman edifice, with a unique rock ditch, built in the same year (1261) as Carlingford Castle on the southern side of the lough. After succumbing to several attacks from the local Magennis clan, and falling to Edward Bruce in 1316, it fell into complete ruin after the Cromwellian invasion and today sits forlornly next to a working farmstead, for tourist use only. It's wide open to the blustery winds that sweep up the lough, and it takes great imaginative effort to summon up warmth from the great fireplaces, and fill the large window frames. But much of the structure is still here, to its full height (you can climb up the corner turrets and have full run of the top story), plus there's a sandy beach below, and photographic views up the mouth of the lough.

Rostrevor and Warrenpoint

Beyond Kilkeel the road turns inland to follow the lough shore around towards Newry. Four or five miles out of Kilkeel a signpost points to the **Kilfeaghan Dolmen**, a mile inland, then a short walk through a couple of fields and turnstile gates. This polygonal stone is enormous, and could only have got here during the retreat of the glacial drift. Farther up the lough, **ROSTREVOR** sits at the point where the waters dramatically begin to narrow towards Newry, and also where the population and political climate turns more in favor of the Catholic communities of County Armagh and those of the approaching border. It's a surprisingly picturesque town of Victorian terraces, clambering up the slopes of **Slievemartin**. A steep forest drive leads up the mountain from the back of the town, a long and winding ascent, really only of use to motorists, though rewarded at the top with wonderful views across to the Cooley Mountains over the frontier. Again there are just a couple of tiny B&Bs, the best of them probably *Still Waters* (14 Killowen Road; ☎06937-38743).

WARRENPOINT is equally picturesque, with a colorful esplanade of seafront housing and a spacious central square. It's much more of a traditional seaside resort than Rostrevor, with a **tourist information** kiosk occupying a pagoda-like hut on the shore, and good places to spend a night. There are handy **boat trips** across to Omeath on the opposite side of Carlingford Lough, leaving from just in front of the *Marine Tavern* (July and Aug only Mon–Sat 1–5pm, Sun 1–7pm, tides permitting; 5min).

If you do want to stay, **B&Bs** include the *Waterfront Guest House* (6 Seaview; ☎06937-73629), *Oran-Dara* (Princess Street; ☎06937-72746), and *Fernhill House* (90 Clonallon Road; ☎06937-72677). There's cheap **eating** at the *Diamond Restaurant* on the main square, and cosy **drinking** at *Molly McCabe's*, at the bottom of the road that runs uphill from the square, where the old boys gather to drink bottled stout only—it can accommodate twelve people at the most. Warrenpoint also has something of a tradition of singing pubs: there's regular **ceilidh** dancing in St Peter's Gaelic Hall and **tradi-**

tional sessions in the Forresters' Hall on the seafront (every Wednesday 9–11:30pm, with every third Wednesday being the big one). These days, though, there are even more **discos**, for which locals come from miles around: biggest are at the *Marine Tavern* (Wed, Fri and Sat 9:30pm–1:30am; £3; no admittance after 11pm) and the *Osborne Hotel*, also on the seafront (Thurs £1, Sat £2, Sun free). You can **rent bikes** at *Stewart's* (☎06937-73565).

Less than a mile from Warrenpoint along the Newry road is the ruined **Narrow Water Castle**, built in the sixteenth century to guard the entrance of the river that flows from Newry into the lough. In this serene setting, it's hard to imagine that sixteen British soldiers were blown up here by the IRA, on the same day that Lord Mountbatten was killed in Mulloughmore Bay in 1979. There are very slight remains of an earlier castle nearby, and on the other side of the road an avenue leads up to New Narrow Water Castle (a private residence) whose private **gallery** is worth checking out if you're interested in contemporary art (ring ☎06937-73940 for permission first).

Newry

Although **NEWRY**, astride the border of Down and Armagh, is this area's most important commercial center, it's the least attractive proposition for a visit. The town here has always been a garrison, guarding the borders of Ulster at the narrow point between the mountains known as the Gap to the North, but there's no trace at all of the early fortresses that were fought over so often. Rather what you see dates mostly from the eighteenth and nineteenth centuries, when a canal brought ships right up from Carlingford Lough into town, and with them trade and considerable wealth. This business has gone, however, and these days Newry is probably best known from the news; the town and its immediate environs were repeatedly bombed by the IRA in the 1970s, and even now it's frequently a hive of army and police activity. Given its central position you're highly likely to pass through Newry, and it does make a possible base for exploring Slieve Gullion and the south Armagh district, but you're unlikely to be tempted to stay.

Perhaps the most interesting building in town is the **Catholic Cathedral** on Hill Street, in the pedestrian mall. The rich mosaic pattern along its walls gives an oriental feel to the interior, which also has a striking vaulted ceiling of decorative sweeping plaster arcs. Not far away the **Town Hall** is remarkable mainly because it's built on a bridge over the Clanrye River—it's half in Down, half in Armagh. The **Newry and Mourne Arts Center**, next door on Bank Parade (with the classical facade), is really the only relief available if you find yourself facing a night here—except for a few nightclubs; check out *JPS* in the central precinct square (9:30pm–1am; closed Tues), where you'll also find the taxi rank. There's reasonably priced **food** at the *Ambassador* restaurant at the start of the pedestrian mall, near to the Town Hall, and a fair number of **B&Bs** should you want to stay—they include *Oisín House*, 4a Canal Street (☎0693-5715); *Ashton House*, 37 Fathom Road (☎0693-2120); and *Millvale House*, 8 Millvale Road (☎0693-3789). There's a **tourist information center** in Monaghan Row (☎0693-5411).

Heading south **towards Dundalk** in the Republic, you'll be struck by the multitude of gas stations crammed in along the route to the border—people stock up here before hitting the more expensive South.

ARMAGH

Armagh has a history as rich as that of any county in Ireland, especially in Armagh city with its associations with Saint Patrick and early Christianity. The county town still has a few reminders of this, but the county as a whole is quiet and rural, with little evidence that anything of significance occurred here before this century. What has happened in recent years has hardly heightened the appeal for tourists, since south Armagh, especially, is now best known for its leading part in the Troubles, and for cross-border incursions. Although it's peaceful enough most of the time—and you can travel entirely freely—the constant army presence does little to encourage peace of mind.

From Belfast the M1 motorway cuts across the north of the county, below Lough Neagh, giving easy access to the industrial towns in the north of the county, LURGAN, CRAIGAVON, and PORTADOWN. Virtually joined now by a single strip of development, these three offer little reason to stop, and you're far better off pushing on down to Armagh city instead, pretty much at the heart of the county.

Armagh City and Around

ARMAGH's small size disappoints some people, and certainly the city doesn't immediately present a greatly exciting prospect—but, rich in history at least, Armagh and its surroundings have plenty to keep you occupied for a day or two. The city offers cathedrals, museums, and a planetarium set in handsome Georgian streets, while the ancient site of once-grand Navan Fort and two stately homes, Ardress and Argory, are features of the excellent bicycling country nearby. Armagh has been the site of the Catholic primacy of all Ireland since Saint Patrick established his church here (it's also the seat of the Protestant Church of Ireland archbishop of Armagh) and has rather ambitiously adopted the title the "Irish Rome" for itself—like Rome, it's positioned among seven small hills.

Historical Background

Armagh (*árd macha*, the height of Macha) was first named after Queen Macha, wife of Nevry, who is said to have arrived in Ireland 608 years after the biblical flood. She's supposed to be buried somewhere in the side of the main hill, where the Protestant cathedral now stands. If this is true, it confirms Armagh as one of the oldest settlements in Ireland, a theory supported by the city's position on one of the most ancient roads in the land, the Moyry Pass. This once stretched from the extreme south of Ireland,

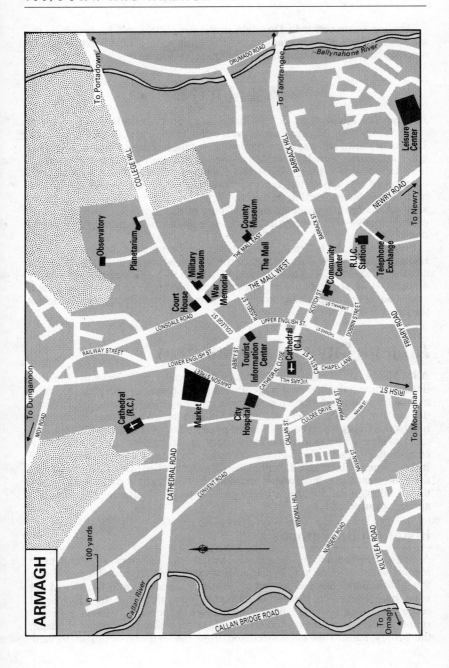

ARMAGH

To Portadown
To Tandragee
DRUMADO ROAD
Ballynahone River
BARRACK HILL
Leisure Center
COLLEGE HILL
NEWRY ROAD
To Newry
Observatory
Planetarium
County Museum
BARRACK ST.
THE MALL EAST
The Mall
THE MALL WEST
Community Center
R.U.C. Station
Telephone Exchange
Military Museum
War Memorial
Court House
RUSSELL ST.
SCOTCH ST.
LINENHALL ST.
THOMAS ST.
DOBBIN STREET
FRIARY ROAD
LONSDALE ROAD
COLLEGE ST.
UPPER ENGLISH ST.
RAILWAY STREET
ABBEY ST.
Tourist Information Center
Cathedral (C.I.)
CASTLE ST.
VICARS HILL
CHAPEL LANE
IRISH ST.
To Monaghan
LOWER ENGLISH ST.
CATHEDRAL CLOSE
To Dungannon
MOY ROAD
Cathedral (R.C.)
DAWSON STREET
Market
City Hospital
CALLAN ST.
CULDEE DRIVE
PRIMROSE ST.
NAVAN ST.
CATHEDRAL ROAD
CONVENT ROAD
WINDMILL HILL
NURSERY ROAD
KILLYLEA ROAD
100 yards
0
Callan River
CALLAN BRIDGE ROAD
To Omagh

through Tara, to the north. In about 300 BC, the center of power shifted westward across the Callan River to where another Queen (of the same name, Macha) built the legendary **Navan Fort.**

After nearly seven hundred years, the ruling dynasty at Navan was defeated by the Collas brothers, and the new rulers reestablished their main base back on the hill of Armagh. A hundred years later, in AD 445, **Saint Patrick** declared the hill the site of his primacy and first bishopric, and built his cathedral here (having first converted the local chieftain Daire, a descendant of the Collas brothers). Other churches grew up around the cathedral and Armagh became *the* great center of learning during the Dark Ages, the period when Ireland was known as the "Isle of Saints and Scholars." Armagh strongly challenges Downpatrick's claim to be the burial place of Saint Patrick; they argue that since the relics of Patrick's book, bell, and staff are here, his body must be too (though the burial site, somewhere on the main hill, is not identified).

Between the ninth and the eleventh centuries, the city was constantly pillaged by the Vikings, mainly from the Norse settlements at Lough Neagh. The Irish king who claimed final victory over the Norsemen, **Brian Boru**, is buried in Armagh Cathedral. Armagh's ecclesiastical power weakened in the Middle Ages, and its history ran in line with the rest of the north for the next several hundred years, with no lengthy periods of peace until the eighteenth and nineteenth centuries, when there was a final flourish of building (much of which survives today). Modern Armagh is a predominantly Catholic city— it's strong on Gaelic sports—and although physically it has borne up well under the Troubles (certainly in comparison to Newry and Derry), it has not avoided them. One local to fall victim to the IRA was the moderate Protestant chairman of the Council, Charlie Armstrong.

The City

The Mall, an elegant tree-lined promenade, is as good a place as any to begin looking around, and strongly sets the tone of the place. The handsome Georgian street architecture is by the early nineteenth-century Armagh-born architect Francis Johnson, and you'll come across more of his work in many of the central streets that shoot off The Mall (Johnson also designed many of Dublin's best Georgian buildings). In its late eighteenth-century heyday The Mall was used as a racecourse; nowadays there's nothing more athletic than the occasional Sunday cricket game. A former schoolhouse on the east side of The Mall houses the **County Museum** (Mon–Sat 10am–1pm and 2–5pm; free) with all the usual local miscellanea plus a little art gallery tucked away on the second floor. Here there are several mystical pastels, oils, and cartoon sketches by the Irish turn-of-the-century poet **George Russell** (alias AE, and a much-negected complement to Yeats). A local painter, J.B. Vallely, is also represented with a superb oil showing five musicians having a session— Vallely currently runs the town's *Armagh Pipers Club*. There's also a permanent exhibition of stuffed wildlife, alarmingly vivid. Farther along The Mall, beside the Classical Courthouse, the **Royal Irish Fusiliers Museum** (Mon–Fri 10am–1pm and 2–4pm; 20p) is pretty much as you'd expect: tons of weaponry, uniforms, medallions, and regimental silverware.

The road that leaves The Mall by the Fusiliers Museum will take you to the **Observatory** (not open to the public) and the **Planetarium** (Mon–Fri 2–4:45pm, Sat 1:30–4:45pm; "Star Shows" Sat 2 and 3pm), which are linked by a short, woodland path around the back. The Observatory is an ancient one, celebrating its second centenary in 1990, but it's still at the forefront of astronomical research. The Planetarium is much more recent—1968—and its best feature is a sophisticated video projection of a multitude of skies around the world onto its hemispherical ceiling, while you sit back on reclinable seats. It also has on display various antique astronomical instruments from the earliest days of the Observatory.

St Patrick's Church of Ireland Cathedral lays claim to the summit of the principal hillock, where Saint Patrick founded his first church, commanding a distinctive Armagh view across to the other hills and down over the shambles of gable walls and pitched roofing on its own slopes. The church is more spartan inside than you might expect from its noble past; there have been a string of buildings on the site, and although the core is medieval, a nineteenth-century restoration coated the thirteenth-century outer walls in stucco, and robbed the interior of many of its ancient decorations. Just as you enter from the highly distinctive timber porch, there are a few remnants of an eleventh-century Celtic cross, and inside, high up, you should be able to sight the medieval carved heads of men, women, and monsters. One other unusual feature is the tilt of the chancel, a medieval building practice meant to represent the slumping head of the dying Jesus. The **chapter house** has a small collection of stone statues (mostly gathered from elsewhere), the most noticeable of which is a *sheila na gig* with ass's ears—some reckon it's King Midas but most people guess it represents one of the three ancient Queen Machas who ruled Navan fort. The **cathedral library** (weekdays 2–4pm, closed July and Aug) has a copy of *Gulliver's Travels*, annotated by Swift himself, among many other rare tomes.

The **Catholic St Patrick's Cathedral**, on another knoll, is more recent, and at first sight little different to the many other nineteenth-century Gothic Revival Catholic cathedrals across the country. But it is impressively large and airy and inside, as befits the seat of the cardinal archbishop, every inch of wall glistens with mosaics, in colors ranging from marine- and sky-blue to terra-cotta pinks and oranges. Other striking pieces include the white granite "pincer-claw" tabernacle holder, reflected in a highly polished marble floor, and a statue of the Crucifixion which looks (deliberately or otherwise) like a Campaign for Nuclear Disarmament symbol.

Moving on, the final piece of ecclesiastical interest, the ruins of **Armagh Friary**, lie within easy walking distance of the city center, just off Friary Road in the grounds of the archbishop's palace (now the District Council Offices). This was a Franciscan friary, dating from around 1263; the Franciscans, known as Grey Friars because of the color of their robes, arrived in Ireland as soon as six years after Saint Francis' death in Italy, and their sect spread like wildfire through the country. The ruins here are those of the church alone; the site is an unfortunate example of how atmosphere can be destroyed when a noisy major road runs alongside.

Practical Details

Armagh does not offer a great deal of choice if you want to stay. There's **camping** at the playing fields on Cathedral Road (although you're supposed to apply to the District Council first); otherwise your best bet is to ask first at the helpful **tourist information office** on Upper English Street (☎0861-524052). **B&Bs** are scarce, but they include two on Cathedral Road: *Desart* (no. 99; ☎0861-522387) and *Padua House* (no. 63; ☎0861-523584). There's not a great deal of choice when it comes to **food** either, but many of the pubs will serve bar food at lunchtime, or you can always get a reasonably priced full meal at the *Drumsill Hotel* (25 Moy Road; ☎0861-522009). Other possibilities are mostly on English and Scotch streets: *Hester's Place* (Upper English Street) and *The Lantern* (Scotch Street) both serve good-value lunches, or you can pick up picnic supplies at *Armagh Fine Foods* (Scotch Street).

Navan Fort

Navan Fort is the Irish Camelot, with the one difference being that the Irish have kept better track of their ancient capital. For nearly 700 years this was the great seat of Northern power, the rival of Tara. It was here that the Kings of Ulster ruled and that the court of the **Knights of the Red Branch**, Ireland's most prestigious order of chivalry, was based. The knights, like those of the Round Table, are historical figures who have been entirely subsumed into legend, their greatest champion the legendary defender of Ulster, **Cúchulainn**. The stories of these warriors' deeds are recited and sung in what's now known as the *Ulster Cycle*. Their dynasty was finally vanquished in AD 332, when three brothers (the Collas), in a conquest known as the Black Pig's Dyke, destroyed Navan Fort, razing it to the ground and leaving only the earthen mounds you see today. The defeated Red Knights were driven eastward into Down and Antrim, but their glories withered away soon afterward.

THE GAME OF BULLET

On the roads just north of Armagh city, you may be lucky enough to witness an ancient road game by the name of **Bullet**, played by local men. It's played here and in County Cork—and virtually nowhere else in the world. The game consists of throwing an iron ball (the size of a cricket ball but 28oz in weight) along about two and a half miles of winding road, and the aim is to know your road well and get the ball to the end with the least number of throws—it takes approximately twenty. The game draws big local crowds and there's even some betting along the way. Oncoming cars are hastily stopped, and the crowd has to scatter as the ball hurtles along cutting corners or clearing the heights of hedges. Roads where you're likely to catch sight of the game include Napper Road, Blackwater Town Road, Rock Road, Tassa Road, Keady Road, Newtonhamilton Road, and Madden Road, usually on Sunday afternoons. The most reliable information on pending games is probably in local pubs. The "World Championship" takes place on the first Sunday in August in Armagh and the last Sunday in August in Cork: the Armagh world champion to look out for is Aiden McVeigh.

It's advisable to keep the old stories in mind, since when you arrive at the site (just a couple of miles west of Armagh on the A28) there's nothing more than an earthen mound to be seen. Excavation of the mound took place over a ten-year period (1961–71) and revealed a peculiar structure, apparently unique in the Celtic world. Archaeologists reckon that around 100 BC the buildings that had existed since the Neolithic period were cleared, and a huge structure 36 yards in diameter was constructed. An outer wall of timber surrounded five concentric rings of large posts, 275 in all, with a massive post at the very middle. This was then filled with limestone boulders and set on fire, creating a mountain of ashes that was then covered with sods of clay to make a high mound. It is anybody's guess what the purpose of the structure was—a temple, or perhaps a massive funeral pyre.

Loughgall, and Ardress and Argory Houses

LOUGHGALL, about five miles north of Armagh along the B27 in the middle of apple-orchard country, is worth visiting mainly for its **Orange Museum**. It was in Loughgall that the first Protestant Orange order was founded in 1795, and today the little village, like many others in Armagh's rural north, is a strongly Protestant enclave. The museum occupies a house at the northern end of the main street (key next door with Mrs Vallary) and includes such Orange paraphernalia as sashes, flags, and the banner from the Dolly Brae victory, and the first Orange order death warrant signed on a Catholic after the Battle of the Diamond. It was this fight just outside town, when the Protestant "Peep O' Day Boys" gave the Catholic "Defenders" a thrashing, that led to the foundation of the first Orange group; in its early days this was a crude organization whose aim was to drive Catholics from their homes by threats or actual violence, condemned by most Protestant landowners and politicians. Nowadays the village is deceptively quiet, its main street lined with antique shops, and with a nice tea-house parlor, *Emily's Cottage*. In 1988, however, it was the scene of a British Army ambush in which eight IRA men died. There's B&B at *Hillview*, 28 Grange Blundel Road (☎076-289679).

A farther five miles or so north, and only a few miles apart, are two National Trust properties worth visiting if you've more than a day in the area. **Ardress House** (April, May, and Sept weekends 2–6pm; June Fri–Mon 2–6pm; July and Aug Tues–Sun 2–7pm) is a seventeenth-century manor house with ornate plasterwork, a good collection of paintings, a sizable working farmyard, and wooded grounds. **Argory House** (same hours, except July and Aug Wed–Mon 2–7pm), built in 1820, is a fine Neoclassical building, containing the original furniture and lit by an original acetylene gas plant in the stable yard.

South Armagh

South Armagh is a tiny area, but a well-defined one, stretching from the border to a line drawn roughly between Newry and Monaghan. It's a completely different proposition from the more populated northern slice of the county. Today it's known to outsiders, if at all, primarily from news reports, and even locally it's often referred to as Bandit Country or The Killing Fields. Its towns, from Bessbrook through Newtownhamilton to Keady, are heavily defended with electronic barriers and manned by army or RUC billets. These are Protestant-dominated bastions, forced into a kind of internal exile, and their Union Jack flags fly defiantly in an area where the countryside is heavily Catholic. The IRA is waging a campaign here aimed at driving out the remaining Protestant landowners (their sons are favorite targets), in the long-term hope that they'll pack up and leave the land to the Catholics. The British Army seems equally hell-bent on using the territory as a trainee war zone, much better preparation than the German bases in the event of another Falklands.

With both forces now firmly locked into this combat, the innocent majority of the Armagh people have to carry on with their lives in as normal a way as they can, and it's incredible to see, from the outside, with what little fuss the people view the situation. It's this continuation of normal, everyday life that you'll come across as a passer-through, and probably little else. If you're bicycling the country roads, you'll sooner or later round a corner and come up against an army foot patrol, which nine times out of ten couldn't be more polite; if they immediately recognize you as a tourist they won't even bother you for identification. If you're moving round in a vehicle you might suddenly get the shock of a Chinook helicopter swooping down across the road only ten or so feet away from your windscreen. Once again, it's nothing to get bothered about—the sooner you run into the army, and the more often, the better, for then they'll be fully aware of your activity and purpose in the region and absolve you from any suspicion. It may not sound an attractive prospect, but in fact this is one of the most scenically beautiful parts of the North, where even the army encampments on the hill summits can come to seem weirdly atmospheric.

Around Slieve Gullion

Slieve Gullion (*sliabh gCuilinn*, "the mountain of Chullain"), which dominates the southeast corner of Armagh, is one of the most mysteriously beautiful mountains in the country. A store of romantic legends are attached to it, especially concerning **Cúchulainn**, who took his name here after slaying the hound (*Cú*) of his chief, *Chullain*; and **Finn Mac Cumaill***, who founded the *Fianna*, a mythical national militia whose adventures are told in the *Fenian Cycle*. Slieve Gullion itself is surrounded by a far-flung circular rampart of smaller hills that make up what is known as the **Gullion Ring Dyke**, which rises to no more than a thousand feet and encloses some of the most beautiful countryside of these two northern counties.

---

*One of the Finn Mac Cumaill legends refers to the little lake on the top of Slieve Gullion. A magic drinking-horn once disappeared here, near the "growth of slender twigs," and if you manage to look at the right area in the morning, having previously fasted, you'll instantly know everything that's going to happen that day.

Approaching the mountain from the north, you'll pass BESSBROOK, where the Union Jack flies, and then CAMLOUGH, where the Republican tricolor flies. As you turn off the main road to go down by the eastern slopes of Camlough mountain, you'll see a beautiful lake, inset like a jewel into its green sides. A little farther on, between Camlough Mountain and Slieve Gullion, are the **Killevy churches**. Two churches of different periods, they share the same gable wall: the west church is pre-Romanesque, and one of the most important survivors of its kind in the country; the other, larger church dates from the thirteenth century. The grave of Saint Blinne, the founder of a fifth-century nunnery, is here, and there's a holy well dedicated to her a little farther up the slopes of Slieve Gullion; pilgrims visit it on her feast day (the Sunday nearest July 6).

The official, asphalt entrance up into Slieve Gullion is on the mountain's forested southern face, after you've passed through the village of KILLEVY. Here there's a small forest park with a winding drive up to the summit, where various vertiginous viewpoints offer spectacular views over the Ring of Gullion and the surrounding countryside for miles around.

The Border

JONESBOROUGH, east of the mountain, is the scene each Sunday of a vast **market**, with traders and customers coming from north and south of the border to buy and sell a wide range of wares (11am–5pm, up at the school). If you're around, it's well worth experiencing. Two miles south of Jonesborough is the **Pillar Stone of Kilnasaggart**, a beautifully inscribed Christian monument and one of the earliest (AD 700) of its kind. Several small crosses are marked within circles on its back face, and the defaced markings on its edges are possibly ogham writing. It's surrounded by several other tiny stones with similar cross markings, all held within a pentagonal enclosure three fields away from the roadside, behind a farmhouse. Less than a mile west of here, on the other side of the railroad line, you should be able to see **Moyry castle** on the hill. It's a timid affair and not really worth even this slight detour; but among its interesting features are several musket loopholes; it was built by Lord Mountjoy, Queen Elizabeth I's deputy, in 1601 as the defense for the Gap to the North.

To get to FORKHILL, barely five miles west of Jonesborough, you'll have to take a long way around, back to the main Forkhill–Newry road; the obvious and quickest route passes along unapproved border roads. The more legitimate route will bring you to the **Three Steps Inn**, on the corner as you reach the main road. It's an ordinary-looking pub, but was the site of the abduction of an undercover British Army captain, **Robert Nairac**. Nairac was a regular visitor to pubs in the area during the mid-Seventies; it was well known that he was in the army, and no one could understand what he was up to. When handed the microphone in a singing pub, he once started singing a Republican song; at closing time, he was heard singing the Irish national anthem in Gaelic—while in uniform. It was also well known that when someone local was arrested and taken down to the army camp, Nairac aways tried to intervene for their release. What Nairac was in fact up to was a long-term intelligence survey, a phenomenally daring (not to say crazy) exercise. His luck ran out on May 14, 1977, when he was in the the *Three Steps Inn* with a large local crowd. That night he sang two songs on stage and the last anyone saw of him was when he left the pub. It's assumed that he was kidnapped in the parking lot outside and later executed by the IRA. His body has never been found.

Forkhill and Crossmaglen

FORKHILL is a tiny village right up by the border in the southwest foothills of Slieve Gullion, a simple, quiet, and remote-looking place—except for the massive army encampment stacked upon the crown of its hill, which entirely dominates everything else in sight. The village is strong on **traditional culture**; O'Neill's *Welcome Inn* has a storyteller, John Campbell, on Tuesday nights (check first on ☎0693-888552) and a singalong on Thursday nights. There's *ceilidh* dancing in the INF hall most Tuesday nights, and a two-day festival of singing (unaccompanied by instruments) takes place in late July; there's a lively musical tradition both here and in MULLAGHBANE farther north up the road.

Passing through Mullaghbane, you get back to the main Newry–Crossmaglen road, on which there's a small **Cottage Folk Museum**, a little up towards the Newry end. **CROSSMAGLEN**, however, dominates the southwestern corner of Armagh. Its reputation in print looks frightening—seventeen soldiers have died in its main square alone, and it's seen by all as the eye of the storm in south Armagh. It has been a hot-spot for so long largely because it's militantly Catholic (note the very powerful Republican sculpture in the square) and only a couple of minutes away from the border; the army has therefore positioned one of their stronger encampments on the main square. Helicopters are continually flying in and out, and their approach path is only feet above the players on the neighboring Gaelic soccer field—which, if you see it, is one of the most bewildering scenes you're ever likely to encounter here. All this said, on arrival you'll find the pubs much friendlier than you've been forewarned, and you're hardly likely to brush up against any trouble. Should you want to stay there's a tiny **B&B** at 6 Newry Street (☎0693-861630).

Darkley

There's little to lure you up the western side of Armagh except for the natural beauty of the route. Up near KEADY, the small village of **DARKLEY** is, tragically, worth mentioning because in November 1983 it was the victim of one of the most brutal attacks of the Troubles. The INLA arrived at the Mountain Lodge Pentecostal Assembly while a Sunday prayer-meeting was in progress and shot three men who were standing outside the main door, killing them all. They fired more shots through the door, then walked around the outside of the church, shooting low through its wooden walls in the hope of killing many more. In the end, they managed only to wound a number of the congregation.

travel details

Trains

From Bangor: to Belfast (2 an hour; 30min); Lisburn (2 an hour; 55min); Lurgan (every hour; 1hr); Portadown (every hour; 1hr).

Ulsterbuses

From Armagh: to Belfast (2 daily; 50min); Dublin (1 daily; 2hr 20min).

CHAPTER SEVENTEEN

TYRONE AND FERMANAGH

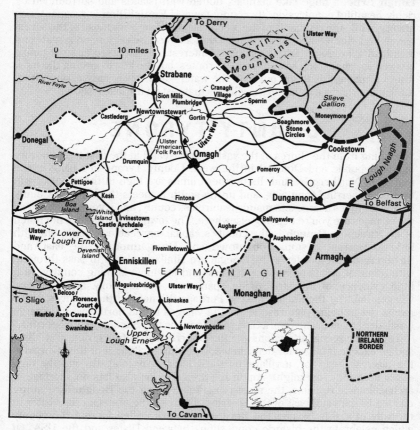

To Derry

Ulster Way

0   10 miles

Sperrin Mountains

Strabane

River Foyle

Sion Mills   Cranagh Village

Plumbridge   Sperrin   Slieve Gallion

Newtownstewart   Moneymore

Castlederg   Gortin   Ulster Way

Beaghmore Stone Circles

Donegal   Ulster American Folk Park   Omagh   Cookstown

Drumquin   Pomeroy   Lough Neagh

T Y R O N E

Pettigoe   Fintona   Dungannon   To Belfast

Kesh   Boa Island   Irvinestown   Auger   Ballygawley

White Island   Castle Archdale   Aughnacloy

Ulster Way   Lower Lough Erne   Fivemiletown   Armagh

Devenish Island

Enniskillen   F E R M A N A G H   Monaghan

Belcoo   Maguiresbridge   Ulster Way

To Sligo   Florence Court   Lisnaskea

Marble Arch Caves

Swaninbar   Newtownbutler

Upper Lough Erne

NORTHERN IRELAND BORDER

To Cavan

C ounties Tyrone and Fermanagh form the bulk of inland Northern Ireland. Though these neighboring counties are both predominantly rural, essentially their characters are quite different. **County Tyrone** is largely dull farming country; the chief scenic attractions are to be found in the wild and desolate **Sperrin Mountains**, to the north. It's remote country, and thinly served by the local bus network; unless you have a car it's very much a region for determined hikers and bicyclists only. In the lowlands the occasional castles, archaeological sites, and heritage centers are frustratingly scattered and difficult to get to—with the exception, luckily enough, of the Ulster American Folk Park north of the county town of **Omagh**. Overall it's an area where small villages dominate—none of enormous fascination, but most retaining an historical quirk or two which enliven the journey.

In contrast, **County Fermanagh** attracts plenty of visitors—chiefly for the watersports and fishing that are widely available. It has at its core the great **Lough Erne**, a huge lake complex dotted with islands and surrounded by richly beautiful countryside. Its county town of **Enniskillen** is resonant with history, while the remnants of the medieval past along with those of the seventeenth and eighteenth centuries are found all over the region, on islands and mainland alike. As in Tyrone, sights of interest are dispersed and the public bus service again only serves the main routes, but the key to getting the most from Fermanagh is to get out onto the water—and this is easy enough from Enniskillen, and a number of the villages that rest on the lakes' shores.

COUNTY TYRONE

Stretching from the shores of the vast Lough Neagh in the east to the border of the Republic and Donegal in the west, County Tyrone lies bang in the middle of Northern Ireland. Its northern limits are high in the desolate and beautiful Sperrin Mountains, and in the south it meets the lakes of County Fermanagh. It's a large and mainly featureless county, and if you are here at all the chances are you're heading elsewhere. The towns of Tyrone are not much of an attraction. **Omagh** is the county's capital, agreeable enough, but with little to warrant a stop. **Cookstown** and **Dungannon** in the east, and **Strabane** on the border with Donegal are similarly places to pass through, with minimal points of interest. It's first and foremost farming country, with little evidence of industrialization apart from the starchily neat planters' villages built by the linen industry. Perhaps the nearest the county's settlements get to being picturesque are the villages to the northwest of Omagh: Castlederg, Newtownstewart, Sion Mills, and the tiny hamlets of the Sperrins.

The major scenic attractions are the **Sperrin Mountains**, rich in wildlife, and an excellent target for determined, lonesome walking. For this, **Gortin** is the place to head for, a village on the **Ulster Way** footpath, and the only easily accessible overnight stop in the area. Tyrone also has no shortage of archaeological remains, the most remarkable being the **Beaghmore stone circles** in the southeast of the Sperrins. There's little to detain the visitor in the way of sights beyond the **heritage centers** dotted around the county which celebrate the historic connections between Ulster and the USA. Of these the **Ulster American Folk Park** near Omagh is by far the best.

The only **local transportation** in the region is *Ulsterbus*—reliable along main routes, and not as infrequent as you might expect in such a rural area; nonetheless, it makes sense to pick up a timetable in a major bus station before you head off into the country. However, the attractions of this largely empty county are so scattered that you're likely to see little of the most interesting parts without a car or a bike. The one exception, of course, is in the Sperrins, where **hiking** is the best way to get around.

Some History

Tyrone is the land of the O'Neills, a heroic clan celebrated in legend as the sons of "Niall of the nine hostages," who became chiefs of Ulster, ruling from Omagh, Dungannon, and Cookstown. The county was a key source of Gaelic resistance to English rule. It was in Dungannon that the first Gaelic Bible was printed in 1567, and Hugh O'Neill, Earl of Tyrone, and his ally the earl of Tyrconnell were the last of the great Gaelic chiefs to fight against Tudor control. Their continual wars with Elizabeth I inspired revolts throughout Ireland but, despite their Spanish Catholic allies, they were finally defeated at Kinsale in 1601. The earls' departure for Europe in 1607 has been enshrined in folk memory as "The Flight of the Earls," the final departure of the Gaelic aristocracy. The subsequent Plantation of Ulster during the reign of James I established the hegemony of the Crown, giving control of Tyrone to the Protestant immigrants from England and Scotland.

But this was not the end of Gaelic resistance, and it was again from this part of Ulster that the next serious threat to English control came. The **Great Rebellion of 1641** began in Tyrone with Phelim O'Neill's capture of Dungannon and Charlemont. The uprising spread throughout the country as Catholics all over Ireland joined together to claim their religious and civic rights. Undoubtably the rebellion was accompanied by considerable brutality, but horror stories grew to such an extent that settlers came to believe that there was a concerted plan to massacre the entire Protestant population, and the alleged scale of the violence gave Cromwell his justification for the massacre at Drogheda ten years later. Ulster remained in the hands of the planters, and it was they who introduced linen manufacture in the eighteenth century—the county's only experience of industry.

The first significant emigration from Ireland to America was that of Ulster men and women in the early eighteenth century, many of whom were of Scottish Protestant origin. Of all the USA's immigrant communities, it was the Irish who most quickly—and profoundly—made their mark: the three first-generation American presidents were all of Ulster stock, and another nine presidents could trace their roots here. Sit in any bar in Tyrone long enough and someone will tell you with pride that these men and women emigrated because they had ambition and vision, and that they were not, unlike later emigrants, forced out by famine and eviction.

Omagh

Tyrone's county town, and the most likable place of any size, is **OMAGH**—*Oigh Maigh* in Irish, meaning "the seat of the chiefs" or "the virgin plain." The glory days are gone now, though, and there's no trace of the O'Neill fortress which once overlooked the river and from where the clan ruled Ulster. Instead, today Omagh's main street leads up to a fine classical courthouse and the irregular twin spires of the Sacred Heart Catholic Church. Pleasant enough, but the only reason you'll spend time here is for a breather if you're on your way to or from the west coast, or heading north into the Sperrins.

Tourism in the region is generally geared to those with cars looking for scenery, and the **tourist office** in the main street (May–Sept Mon–Sat 9am–1pm and 1:30–5pm; Oct–April Mon–Fri 9am–1pm and 2–5pm; ☎0662-47831) promotes a very large area. Ask for **camping** and you'll be pointed towards the *Gortin Forest Park*, which is as pretty as is claimed, but lies six miles north of Omagh up the Newtownstewart road (6 buses daily). Better to ask a farmer if you can use a field. Alternatively several **B&B**s are registered with the tourist office. Mrs McCann's, 12 Tamlaght Road (☎0662-3381 or 46535; £10) is the nearest to the town center: from the tourist office walk up the main street, take the left fork in front of the Sacred Heart up to James Street, and Tamlaght Road is the second road on your right. Also near downtown is Mrs B. Cuddihy, 1 Georgian Villas, Hospital Road (☎0662-45254; £12): walk down the main street away from the courthouse, cross the river, and Hospital Road is to your right.

The town is a good place to stop for **food**, particularly during the daytime. *Pink Elephant* in the High Street is a local favorite, serving traditional daytime dinners in huge helpings. Almost as popular is the *Libbi Eating House*, open during the daytime Monday to Saturday. The *Fox's Lair*, John Street, serves a decent set lunch around midday (Mon–Fri), while *The Royal Arms Hotel* in the High Street serves excellent pub grub at midday, and limited hot snacks in the evening. There's no shortage of cafés.

In the unlikely event of you spending time here, *Bogan's*, in Mountjoy Road, churns out traditional Irish **music** on Saturdays, as does *The Deerhead Bar*, Railroad Road, on Thursdays, or *The Fox's Lair*, also on Thursdays. *The Fox's Lair* also has local bands on Tuesdays, Fridays, and Saturdays, and *Kelly's Bar* in Abercorn Street is a similar forum on Fridays and Saturdays. Occasional jazz sessions are to be found at *McElroy's* in Castle Street, though at weekends the place is generally devoted to teenage discos. *The Royal Arms Hotel* has jazz and blues sessions for free on a Thursday, and again discos at weekends. Despite this apparently promising list of options, there is no tangible "scene" here and what you get is very much the luck of the draw.

Omagh's *Ulsterbus* **bus depot** (☎0662-42711), for all country-wide and local connections, is just across the river in Mountjoy Road (north off the High Street).

The Ulster American Folk Park

About five miles north of Omagh, and a short ride on the Omagh–Newtownstewart bus, is the **Ulster American Folk Park**, Camphill, the most successful (and least cringe-worthy) of the American heritage projects dotted around the country (Easter to early Sept Mon–Sat 11am–6pm, Sun and public holidays 11:30am–6:30pm; mid-Sept to Easter Mon–Fri 10:30am–4:30pm; last admission 1hr before closing; £2). It makes a good afternoon away from Omagh, and is also on the **Ulster Way**, which to the northeast enters the scenic GORTIN area at the start of the Sperrins. Mrs Fulton, next door to the Folk Park's farm, does **B&B**.

The Folk Park tells the story of early emigrants: the first half is a typical eighteenth-century **Ulster village**; the second shows the communities they went on to build in America. The Ulster village is reconstructed around original buildings that include cottages, a schoolhouse, and an austere Presbyterian meeting house. There are plans to build a ship that will depict the grueling passage to America, a display that will form a link with the **American settlement**, which at the moment is reached by a walk through the trees. The buildings of the Irish village are modest, but the multi-purpose log barns of the Pennsylvanian settlers are massive. Again the attention to authenticity is excellent, and captures a sense of the ambition and hope these emigrants must have felt on their arrival in the New World. Whatever your feelings on the Ulster Presbyterian work ethic, this propagandist Folk Park does powerfully recreate something of the Ulster emigrants' experience. In the accompanying **museum** there's a comprehensive exhibition on the American War of Independence, the making of the Constitution, and more on the lives of the early pioneers.

Northwest from Omagh

Northwest Tyrone has some of the county's most attractive towns and countryside. The fastest route west—and the only feasible one if you're hitching (see *Basics*)—is the A5 through Newtownstewart, Sion Mills and Strabane. Far quieter is the route via Castlederg along minor country roads west to Castlefinn, County Donegal, which takes you through a much more remote and isolated border crossing point; it's only really possible by car or bike.

The friendly village of **CASTLEDERG** sits around a spruced-up square beside the river Derg, apparently trying to ignore its police barracks bristling with barbed wire. Across the river are the ruins of a Plantation castle, built in 1609, and not long after destroyed by Sir Phelim O'Neill; today it sits in picturesque innocence, as though it had nothing to do with the current state of affairs. Castlederg retains something of its traditional flavor as a staging post for travelers and wateringhole for pilgrims on their way to Lough Derg—its bars and cafés make this a good place to stop for food. If you're taking the fastest route west from Omagh you will pass through **NEWTOWNSTEWART**, settled in rich farmland, with its **castle**—another fourteenth-century O'Neill stronghold—looking clean and lonely on a hill to the south. There is a **tourist office** in the main street, next to the Church of Ireland (mid-June to Sept Mon–Fri 9:30am–5pm; ☎06626-61560).

The linen industry of the eighteenth century made a big impact in Tyrone, as it did all over Ulster, but its traces are mostly faint ones—such as the disused mills along the Ballinderry River near Cookstown. **SION MILLS**, a planned linen village just two miles south of Strabane, is the glaring exception. Here simple millworkers' cottages are neatly laid out around the mill, the quaintness of the village today belying the gruesome conditions of nineteenth-century factory work. The **tourist office** at Sion Mills (mid-June to Sept daily 9:30am–5:30pm; ☎06626-58027) is geared towards the car-bound tourist.

Strabane
Grim and congested, **Strabane** seems to glower over the Foyle River. Its recent history has been troubled, which is hardly surprising; not only does

the town sit right on the border, but it's a small Catholic enclave uncomfortably surrounded by largely Protestant-owned farmland.

In the eighteenth century Strabane was an important printing and publishing center. John Dunlap emigrated from here and went on to print the broadsheets of the American Declaration of Independence in 1776, as well as the *Pennsylvanian Packet*, America's first daily paper. All that is left in Strabane of these times is the cute, Georgian bow-windowed storefront of *Gray's* printing shop, which is now owned by the National Trust; there's a small printing **museum** upstairs (April–Sept Mon–Wed and Fri–Sat noon–6pm; 50p). Sadly the store's interior has been ripped out to provide maximum space for cards, completely destroying the scale and atmosphere the place must have once had.

Head east of Strabane two miles down the Plumbridge road, and you run into another tourist product of the Ulster-American connection: the **President Woodrow Wilson ancestral home** at DERGALT (open any reasonable hour—ask at the adjacent farm). The president's father, who was a printer in Strabane, lived in this small, traditional farmers' cottage. Stuffed with furniture and effects belonging to the family, it's now a target for American tourists, who dutifully meander through the hallowed rooms.

The Sperrins

The huge, undulating **Sperrin Mountains** form the northern limits of County Tyrone. Wild, empty, and beautiful, they reach 2240 feet at their highest, yet the smooth and gradually curving slopes give them a deceptively low appearance. The covering of bog and heather adds to this effect, suggesting nothing more than high, open moorland. For all this, views from the summits are panoramic, and the evenness of texture can make these mountains sumptuous when bathed in evening light. Once in the mountains it's impossible not to catch sight of the **wildlife** here. Hawks and kestrels hover above, and you might see buzzards or the far rarer hen harrier. They're attracted by rich prey in a landscape undisturbed by development—the mountains teem with assorted rodents, rabbits, stoats, and badgers, even the Irish hare. One threat to this fragile ecosystem has been the recent discovery of gold in the mountains. Their future is in the balance, but for the moment at least, the Sperrins offer a wilderness to be enjoyed.

For local sheep-farming communities, however, the underpopulation of the Sperrins is a real problem, and their traditional way of life is now slowly dying. The sparseness of the population and the lack of focal centers makes it difficult for an outsider to key into this culture. For the same reason, hitching isn't easy, and walkers should bear in mind that there's a shortage of places to buy food, so thinking ahead is *essential*. Rely only on large villages for provisions of any sort; hamlets often have nothing.

The Sperrin Centre, between CRANAGH and SPERRIN, five miles east of Plumbridge (see below), enables you to explore the area's environmental and cultural issues without getting your feet wet (June–Sept Mon–Fri 11am–6pm, Sat 11:30am–6pm, Sun 2–7pm; Oct–May Mon–Sat 11am–5pm, Sun 1–6pm;

£1). The video games and audio visuals of this interpretive center are of a decidedly educational bent. It's tricky to get to without transport, but worth bearing in mind for its very pleasant tea room if you are walking in the area.

Walking

The Sperrins offer good long-distance **walking**, without necessarily involving steep inclines. You can hike wherever you like in the Sperrins, but remember that despite appearances these *are* high mountains, and changeable weather makes them potentially dangerous. A map and compass are essential for serious walking. For those not equipped for the high ground, the **Glenelly** and **Owenkillen** river valleys run through the heart of this stunning countryside from Plumbridge and Gortin respectively (see below), and are particularly enjoyable for cyclists.

The signposted **Ulster Way** can be picked up three and a half miles east of SPERRIN as the road leaves the Goles Forest, and will take you into the heart of the mountains. The problem is that you'll probably have to walk that distance to join it, since this valley is almost impossible to hitch through. From the forest the Way climbs Crockbrack (1631ft), to fine, wide views, and then heads north through the Glenshane Forest to the A6 main road, four miles south of DUNGIVEN, County Derry—a walk of around twelve miles. Route guides to the Ulster Way can be bought from the *Sports Council of Northern Ireland* (see "Information and Maps" in *Basics*) or from tourist offices.

Plumbridge and Gortin

Once in the mountains, settlements are mere specks of houses, and if you're tackling the Sperrins from Tyrone, there are really only two places that'll offer you any amenities at all. And even these are comatose for much of the year.

The first, **PLUMBRIDGE**, doesn't look like it's changed much over the years, beyond encouraging the fishing fraternity to set down their rods and drink in its bars. Apocryphally, it gets its name from the building of the village bridge. The engineer in charge didn't have a spirit level and so, from his scaffolding, spat in the water, using his phlegm to take the perpendicular. Nearby **GORTIN**, three and a half miles south, though greatly promoted as a tourist center, is a one-horse town with a café and a pub. Mrs Kelly offers **B&B** for £9 at 34 Main Street (☎06626-48241), and you'll find a **campground** at *Gortin Forest Park* (☎06626-648217; tent space 30p). The **Ulster Way** passes through the village, though at the moment the signposting which should connect it with Goles Forest is incomplete, and stops at Craignaddy (930ft), just two and a half miles to the north. However, the signposted Way does continue to the south of Gortin through the pretty forest park, with its little loughs and wild deer, before swinging west to low farmland and the Ulster American Folk Park (see above).

Three and a half miles east of Gortin (on the B46 CREGGAN road) is the tiny village of **Rouskey**, with the ruins of a "sweat house"—a sort of early sauna. After the steam treatment, the luckless invalid was plunged into the icy stream nearby. The use of sweat houses died out after the famine years, possibly because the experience of typhoid which accompanied the famine dealt a severe blow to people's confidence in traditional medical treatments.

Prehistoric Remains, and the Beaghmore Stone Circle

County Tyrone is peppered with archaeological remains, the Sperrins themselves having their fair share—including over a thousand standing stones—and the county as a whole having numerous chambered graves. The **Lough Macrory** area, just east of MOUNTFIELD on the A505 (Omagh–Cookstown road), is particularly rich in dolmens and megaliths, though many of these are hard to find and of specialist interest only.

The uninitiated will get most out of the Bronze-Age **Beaghmore Stone Circle**, in the southeast of the Sperrins; it's well signposted seven miles west of Cookstown, and is just three and a half miles off the A505. Although most of the stones on this lonely site are no more than three feet high, the complexity of the ritual they suggest is impressive; there are seven stone circles, ten stone rows, and a dozen round cairns (burial mounds, some containing cremated human remains). All of the circles stand in pairs, except for one, which is unique in that it is filled with over 800 upright stones, known as Dragon's Teeth. The alignments correlate to movements of sun, moon, and stars. Two of the rows point to sunrise at the summer solstice; another may point to moonrise at the same period.

East Tyrone

The east of Tyrone is low-lying and uninspiring, and it seems even the legendary Finn Mac Cumaill (pronounced "McCool") was unimpressed. The tale goes that he took a massive lump of land from Ulster and hurled it across the Irish Sea. It landed and became the Isle of Man, and the hole it left behind became **Lough Neagh**. The lough's shores form the county's huge eastern boundary and provide excellent fishing and plenty of birdlife, but beyond this, both land and lake are almost featureless.

Slight relief from the shore's numbing tedium is to be found at ARDOE, ten miles east of Cookstown, where there's a tenth-century **high cross** heavily carved with Biblical scenes. Its size is exceptional—eighteen feet high—yet it lacks impact: so dull is this shore the cross stands devoid of spatial context.

Mountjoy Castle lurks behind a farm eight miles south of here on the road towards Dungannon. Built in 1602 as part of the English campaign against Hugh O'Neill, it was strategically important, but again the setting is disappointing.

Cookstown, Dungannon, and Around

The only places in the east of the county that could be described as being much more than villages are Cookstown and Dungannon. A planned planters' town, **COOKSTOWN** boasts the longest main street in Ireland, which in effect means the community now clings for dear life to the sides of a divided highway. There are a couple of places to **eat**: *The Royal Hotel*, Coagh Street, and *The Central Inn* in William Street. But the main attraction for the visitor is the *Edergole Riding School*, 70 Moneymore Road (☎06487-62924), whose one-hour-to-three-day treks wind up the slopes of Slieve Gallion and into the Sperrins. They can also arrange **canoeing** for you, and the school is attached to a friendly **B&B**.

Two miles out of Cookstown on the B520 is **Tullyhoge Fort**, the site of the inaugural ceremonies of the O'Neills. From the road it looks like nothing more than a copse of beech and Scotch pine on the top of a very gentle hill, but in fact these are very clear, comprehensible earthworks of the early Christian period—a circular outer bank with an inner oval enclosure. Ulster chiefs were crowned here from the twelfth to the seventeenth century, and it was in Tullyhoge forest that O'Neill tribesmen hid after the Flight of the Earls.

More recent history is on display three and a half miles west of Cookstown, at the National Trust-owned **Wellbrook Beetling Mill**, an eighteenth-century, water-powered linen mill (Easter, May, Sept, and Oct Sat, Sun, and bank holidays 2–6pm; June–Aug Wed–Mon 2–6pm; 2–7pm Sun in July and Aug; 50p). "Beetling" is a process whereby linen is given a sheen and smoothness by hammering with wooden "beetles." The mill is very well preserved, and all the engines still work. As you hurry through dreary **DUNGANNON** pause and briefly reflect on its illustrious history as the hilltop seat of the O'Neills, from which they ruled Ulster for over five centuries. Heading west by car you might want to visit *The Simpson-Grant Farm* (3 miles east of BALLYGAWLEY, signposted off the A4 road; Oct–April Mon–Fri 10:30am–4:30pm; May–Sept Mon–Sat 10:30am–6:30pm and Sun 12:30–7pm; 60p). Based around the nineteenth-century homestead of the maternal ancestors of President Ulysses S. Grant, it's of interest chiefly for the traditional livestock of the working farm.

COUNTY FERMANAGH

It is for the intense beauty of its lakes that Fermanagh is famous. A third of the county is water, the great **Lough Erne** complex swinging right across the region from Lower Lough Erne in the northwest to Upper Lough Erne in the southeast. Surrounding hills are wooded with oak, ash and beech, producing a scene of fresh, verdant greens in spring, and rich, rusty colors in autumn. The water's rippling surface reflects whatever light there is, mirroring the palest of skies through to the ruddiest of magenta sunsets. It's a breathtaking landscape, where land and water complement one another in a fine, stately harmony.

The **Lower Lough** in winter has the character of an inland sea, dangerous waves preventing even the locals from sailing. Fabulous vistas reach across to the uninhabited shores of richly wooded islands, on which are scattered early Christian ruins and evidence of earlier pagan cultures. The **Upper Lough** is quieter and less spectacular. The waterway here is a muddle of little inlets and islands, where waters are shallower and shorelines reedy. Fields have shocks of bristly marsh-grasses; definitions between land and water are blurred.

The county town of **Enniskillen** sits at the point where the Upper and Lower loughs meet, long an important bridging point; it's still the only real town in Fermanagh, and a good base for exploring the region. If you want hostel accommodation, you'll have to stay out in the country at Castle Archdale, ten miles north of Enniskillen, or in the extreme west at Garrison—both good options, set in magnificent scenery. If you've a vehicle, there are historical tracks to cover touring Fermanagh's impressive series of **Planters' castles**, while the county's two stately houses—**Florence Court** and **Castlecoole**—are both open to the public.

There are plenty of opportunities for **watersports**, and the less energetic can get out onto the lakes by renting a **boat** or taking one of the lough cruises. Surrounding hills are accessible to **walkers** along the Ulster Way, while **cyclists** will find the road surfaces smooth and empty. Boats aside, this last is perhaps the best way to get around the county, since **public transit** is limited to *Ulsterbus*—reliable enough, but only main routes from Enniskillen are served with any frequency. If you look like a foreign tourist, then **hitching** along main roads is possible during the summer months, though never easy; County Fermanagh is as friendly as anywhere in the North, but people tend to be more cautious because of the border.

History

The region's early history was dictated by the difficulties of the Lough Erne waterways, in earlier times even more confused and forested than today. Recorded history begins with the early Christians, who slowly permeated the culture and established religious foundations. They appreciated the seclusion of the lakes, and ruins of **medieval monasteries** remain. Centers of ecclesiastical power and learning were dotted on islands in the lough, and it is likely they were visited by pilgrims on their way to St Patrick's Purgatory, the shrine on Lough Derg. More brutal invaders found the lough complex difficult to infiltrate. The **Normans** never managed to control the region, and throughout the medieval and Tudor period the English similarly failed to subdue it. The surrounding land was unruly and hard to govern even for the Irish. The Maguires, who ruled the west of the kingdom of Oriel (Fermanagh, Monaghan, South Tyrone, and Louth) from 1250 until 1600, were originally based at Lisnaskea, but the cattle raids of neighboring chiefs forced them to move to Enniskillen in the early fifteenth century. The town was to become strategically crucial as the determination of the English to dominate Ireland increased during the sixteenth century. As the crossing point through the waterways it was one of only three land routes into Ulster available to the invaders, the others being over the river near Ballyshannon and the Moyry Pass between Dundalk and Newry. So Enniskillen and the Maguire castle became focal to the Irish resistance to the Tudors. It was taken in 1600, and in 1607, after the Flight of the Earls, the **Planters** arrived.

The usurpers were obliged to build a ring of **castles** around the lough in order to maintain control: Crom, Portora, Tully, Castle Archdale, Crevenish, Cauldwell, and, most important of all, the old Maguire castle at Enniskillen. Given sizable grants from the English crown, the Planters of Enniskillen built an Established Church, a fort, and a royal school, turning the place into a British colonial town. It became a Loyalist stronghold, which successfully defended itself against the Irish during the Great Rebellion of 1641, and against an attack by James's troops in 1689. The Loyalists of Enniskillen formed a regiment which William of Orange chose as his personal guard at the Boyne. In the late eighteenth century Enniskillen proved to be of key military importance, with the threat of a French invasion through the northwest of Ireland. By now the town had two royal regiments—a unique phenomenon.

At **Partition** Fermanagh became a part of the state of Northern Ireland, despite its predominantly Catholic population, and despite this majority's cultural affinities with Cavan in the Republic, with whom it shares the tail end of the Lough Erne complex. In 1921 the county returned a Nationalist majority in local government elections, an undesirable state of affairs for the British. The abolition of proportional representation in 1922 and the gerrymandering which followed ensured the subsequent Loyalist majority. With a history of such blatant injustices, a large Catholic population, and a lengthy border with the Republic, Fermanagh is a nucleus of Nationalist activity, and today has strong Sinn Fein sympathies. It was Fermanagh and South Tyrone that in April 1981 returned **Bobby Sands** as Westminster MP. At the time of the election Sands was serving a fourteen-year prison sentence for possession of weapons, and was leading a hunger strike for political status for IRA prisoners. His death from starvation after 66 days made him one of the most famous IRA heroes.

Enniskillen

Amid the innumerable atrocities that have scarred Northern Ireland in recent years, the name **ENNISKILLEN** has a special capacity to shock, after the IRA bomb attack on Remembrance Day 1987, which killed 11 and injured 61 people as they gathered to commemorate the dead of the two world wars. In a town of only 10,500, the bombing profoundly affected the lives of every citizen, and at once gave Enniskillen a reputation for sectarian violence that bears no relation to its true nature. In fact, this is a pleasant, conservative little town, rather relaxed and very friendly. Central to both Fermanagh and the lakes, Enniskillen is a focus for visitors and locals alike. It's the only place of any size in the county, and although you can see all that it has to offer in a day, if you're using B&Bs it makes a good base from which to explore the lakes.

The Town—and Castlecoole

The town sits on an island like an ornamental buckle, two narrow ribbons of water passing each side, connecting the Lower and Upper Lough complexes. The water loops its way around the core of the town, its glassy surface imbuing Enniskillen with a pervasive sense of calm, and reflecting the mini-turrets of the **Watergate**, so making a toy image of the military presence. Rebuilt by William Cole, the man to whom the British gave Enniskillen in 1609, the Watergate stands on the site of the old Maguire castle, next to the island's westerly bridges. Cole's additions show obvious Scottish characteristics in the turrets corbeled out from the angles of the main wall. It houses the **Fermanagh County Museum** (Mon–Fri 10am–1pm and 2–5pm; also May–

Sept Sat 2–5pm, July–Aug Sun 2–5pm; free), a fairly dull local collection, and **The Regimental Museum of the Royal Enniskillen Fusiliers** (same times), a proud and polished display of the uniforms, flags, and paraphernalia of the town's two historic regiments.

Much of Enniskillen's character comes from a wealth based on the care of a colonial presence. Evidence of British influence is widespread: on a hill to the west the stately Portora Royal School overlooks the town, discreetly reminding one of the continued elitism in the social order. It was founded by Charles I in 1626, and the present building dates from 1777; old boys include Oscar Wilde and Samuel Beckett. Over on a hill to the east a Wellingtonian statue keeps an eye on the town from a very British-style park; immediately below is the war memorial, scene of the bombing. The center invites strolling: the main street undulates gently, lined with confident Victorian and Edwardian town houses, thriving stores, and smart pub fronts. Lanes fall to either side down towards the water, and calmly sitting next to one another are three fine church buildings—Church of Ireland, Catholic, and Methodist.

Evidence of how the richest of the colonists lived is found on the outskirts of town at **Castlecoole**, the eighteenth-century home of the earls of Belmore (June Fri–Mon 2–6pm; July and Aug Wed–Mon 2–6pm; Sept Sat and Sun 2–6pm; £1.50; grounds open April–Sept, free). A perfect Palladian building of Portland stone, with an interior of fine plasterwork and superb furnishings, it sits in a beautiful landscaped garden, whose cultivated naturalness reinforced its owners' belief that the harmony of God's creation mirrored that of society. Castlecoole can be walked to either from the Dublin road (signposted close to the *Ardhowen Theatre*), or across the golf course from Castlecoole road.

Practicalities

The **tourist office** is housed in the *Lakeland Visitor Centre*, set among parking lots in the island's low-lying part, south of the main street (June–Sept Mon–Fri 9am–7pm, Sat 10am–6pm, Sun 10am–5pm; May and Oct Mon–Fri 9am–5pm, Sat and Sun 10am–5pm; Nov–April Mon–Fri 9am–5pm; ☎0365-23110 or 25050). The "Round O" jetty for lough cruises is signposted off the Derrygonnelly road. Enniskillen's **bus station** is next to the tourist office for buses to Belfast, Dublin, Dungannon, Sligo, Derry, Omagh, and local services.

Accommodation

The tourist office has comprehensive accommodation lists and will reserve for you (50p charge). Alternatively, **B&B** is easily found across the town's western bridges, along the A46 Derrygonnelly road and along the Sligo road. On the former, try *Willoughby Guest House*, 24 Willoughby Place (☎0365-25275; £11); along the latter there's Mrs Mulhern, *Carraig Aonrai*, 19 Sligo Road (☎0365-24889; £7.50), J & N Sheridan, *Rossole House*, 85 Sligo Road (☎0365-23462; £8.50), and Mrs Johnston, *Castle View*, 9 Henry Street (☎0365-27408). The nearest **hostel** is at Castle Archdale, ten miles north of town, and all local campgrounds are well out of town. The nearest, *Florence Court Park*, is off the A32, six miles south; *Blaney Caravan Park* (☎036564-634; £3.50) is ten miles to the northwest, off the A46, directly behind the BLANEY service station.

Eating, Drinking, and Entertainment

Enniskillen has a handful of good cheap places to **eat**. Currently everybody's favorite is *Franco's* in Queen Elizabeth Road, the northerly road that runs into East Bridge; open daily from noon til late, it has delicious pizza, pasta, and seafood. A lot of the bars along the central main street serve decent pub grub, particularly *The Vintage* and *Pat's Bar*. More upmarket is *The Royal Hotel*, East Bridge Street, which has good buffet lunches at midday during the week. The restaurant at the *Ardhowen Theatre* is worth visiting for the setting, should you be hungry after a traipse around Castlecoole.

Enniskillen is well provided with **cafés**, many of which do good cheap meals. The most popular of these are *Leslie's*, in the main street, and *As You Like It*, Head Street (off Queen Street), which serves plenty of delicious homemade dishes, including salads and vegetarian meals.

There is no shortage of cheerful **pubs** in Enniskillen, although there is little by way of entertainment. Musically, this is country-western country: bands play at *The Watergate* on Friday and Saturday, at *The Tipplers Brook* at the west end of town, and at *The Railroad Hotel* in Fort Hill Street. As ever **discos** occupy the hotels, in particular *The Fort Lodge Hotel*, Fort Hill Street, which also occasionally has local bands. *The Vintage*, on the main street, is a popular disco bar with video jukebox, while nearby *Blakes of the Hollow*, a traditional Victorian-style bar, is popular with visitors.

The hub of Enniskillen's **arts scene** is *The Ardhowen Theatre* (☎0365-25440), overlooking the lough a mile out of town on the Dublin road. It has a year-round program of top-quality drama, film, and ballet, and hosts a great range of music events—traditional Irish, jazz, opera, country, classical—as well as productions by local community groups. Ticket prices start at £2. Its annual **film festival** runs for a fortnight from the last week in August.

Listings

Bike Rental Mr Conor Foley, 146 Windmill Heights; £3.50 a day, £12.50 for five days; phone ☎0365-25783 between 7pm and 9pm the day before.

Boat Rental Mr P. Bailey, 103 Hillview Park (☎0365-26257); £18 for half a day, £28 a day, £125 a week, including fuel—and see the "Lough Erne" section below for more boat rental details.

Car Rental *Gilleeces Car Rental* (☎0365-23811), Kilmacormick Road, June–Sept only, minimum rent period one week; *Lochside Garages* (☎0365-24366), Tempo Road; *Modern Motors* (☎0365-22974), 74 Forthill Street. Drivers must be over 25 for all these companies.

Early Closing Day Wednesday.

Fishing Licences, permits and info from the *Lakeland Visitor Centre*.

Hospital *Erne Hospital* (☎0365-24711), Corngrade Road.

Laundromats *The Wash Tub*, East Bridge Street, Enniskillen; and in Castle Street, Irvinestown (see below).

Travel Agency *Erne Travel* (☎0365-24477), Paget Square; youth/student tickets available.

Lough Erne: Islands and Idols

Lough Erne has had a profound effect on the history of Fermanagh. The earliest people to settle in the region lived on and around the two lakes; many of the islands here are in fact *crannogs*—early Celtic artificial islands. Its myriad connecting waterways were impenetrable to outsiders, protecting the settlers from invaders, and creating an enduring cultural isolation. Evidence from stone carvings suggests that Christianity was accepted far more slowly here than elsewhere: several pagan idols have been found on Christian sites, and the early Christian remains to be found on the islands strongly show the influence of pagan culture. Here Christian carving has something of the stark symmetry and vacancy of expression found in pagan statues. Particularly suggestive of earlier cults is the persistence of the human-head motif in stone carving—in pagan times a symbol of divinity and the most important of religious symbols.

The most popular of the Erne's ancient sites—**White Island** and **Devenish Island**—are on the **Lower Lough**, as is the so-called **Boa Island**, which is actually attached to the mainland in the far north of the complex. The **Upper Lough** is less rewarding, but it too has spots of interest which repay a leisurely dawdle. Whichever you choose, the easiest way to go is on one of the **cruises** or **ferries** that operate from Enniskillen, the *Castle Archdale* hostel, and surrounding villages (see below), or by **renting your own boat** again from Enniskillen, Kesh or Belleek (see below). Renting your own boat will cost around £28 a day, including fuel, and you should let the owner know where you're going and ask to borrow navigation charts; this lough can be dangerous—outside of the summer months, not even the locals venture out.

Devenish Island

The easiest place to visit from Enniskillen, certainly if you don't have your own transportation, is **Devenish Island**, in the south of the Lower Lough. A monastic settlement was founded here by Saint Molaise in the sixth century, and became so important during the early Christian period that it had 1500 novices attached to it. The foundation was plundered by Vikings in the ninth

---

FERRIES

To White Island Boat from *Castle Archdale* jetty June–Aug Tues–Sat 10am–7pm, Sun 2–7pm, and less frequently during September. Fare £1. Phone ☎0365-22711 ext 40.

To Devenish Island *Devenish Island Ferry Service* (☎0365-22711 ext 40) operates a continual service to Devenish from TRORY, 4 miles north of Enniskillen (April–Sept Tues–Sat 10am–7pm, Sun 2–7pm. Fare £1.

A two-hour **cruise** of Lough Erne, stopping at Devenish for half an hour, operates from the "Round O" pier, Enniskillen. The *Kestrel*, operated by *Erne Tours* (☎0365-22882), sails May and June Sun 3pm; July and Aug Mon–Fri 11am and 3pm, Thurs and Sat 7pm, Sun 11am, 3pm and 7pm; first two weeks Sept daily 3pm. Fare £2.50.

century and again in the twelfth, but continued to be an important religious center up until the Plantations. It's a delightful setting, not far from the lough shore, and the ruins are considerable, spanning the entire medieval period. Most impressive are the sturdy oratory and perfect round tower, both from the twelfth century; Saint Molaise's church, a century older; and the ruined Augustinian priory, a fifteenth-century reconstruction of an earlier abbey. The priory has a fine Gothic sacristy door decorated with birds and vines; to the south is one of Ireland's finest high crosses, with highly complex, delicate carving. Other treasures found here—such as an early-eleventh-century book shrine, the *Soiscel Molaise*—are now kept in the National Museum in Dublin.

Killadeas, Irvinestown, and Castle Archdale

In **KILLADEAS** churchyard, seven miles north of Enniskillen on the B82, stands the **Bishop's Stone**, carved some time between the ninth and eleventh centuries. It's one of the most striking examples of the appearance of pre-Christian images in early Christian culture, having a startled pagan face on one side, and a bishop with bell and crozier on the other. There are other interesting carved stones in the graveyard too, including two cross-slabs and a rounded pillar, possibly a pagan phallic stone. If you want to get out onto the water, Manor House Marine, Killadeas (☎03656-21561), rents out **motor boats** from £28.

A few miles inland, in **IRVINESTOWN**, a head idol found in Enniskillen has been set in the wall of the lounge of *Mahon's Hotel*. It has an unusually long neck, long narrow face, wide slit mouth and two holes for eyes—almost certainly pre-Christian. If you want to stay in Irvinestown, there are a couple of **B&Bs** in the village: Mrs Morton's, *Drumcrin*, 20 Liscreevin Road (☎03656-28020; £7), and Mrs Hudson's, *Roseville*, on the DROMORE road (☎03656-21239; £8).

To thoroughly immerse yourself in the beauty of the lough scenery, you could hardly do better than stay in the **hostel** of **Castle Archdale** (☎03656-28118; £3.50, non-members £4.85; closed Dec 19–Jan 19), set in a forest park near LISNARRICK, around five miles west of Irvinestown. It makes sense to arrive here in daylight—look out for a small sign beside a church for the turn off from the main road. It's a An Óige hostel, with the attendant curfew restrictions, and three miles from the nearest shop, but the hostel warden sells milk, eggs, and potatoes, and it's a perfect place for getting out onto the lough. The ferry to White Island (see below) leaves from nearby, and you can also **rent boats**.

White Island

Mounted on the wall of a ruined abbey, the early Christian carvings of **White Island** look eerily pagan. Found earlier this century, they are thought to be caryatids—carved supporting columns—from a monastic church of the ninth to eleventh centuries.

The most disconcerting statue is the lewd female figure known as a *sheila na gig*, with bulging cheeks, a big grin, open legs, and arms pointing to her genitals. This could be a female fertility figure, a warning to monks of the sins of the flesh, or an expression of the demoniac power of women, designed to ward off evil. (In the epic *Táin Bó Cuailnge*, Cúchulainn was stopped by an army of 150 women led by their female chieftain Scannlach. Their only weapon was their display of nakedness, from which the boy Cúchulainn had to avert his face.) Less equivocal figures continue left to right: a seated Christ figure holding the Gospel on his knees; a hooded figure with bell and crozier, possibly Saint Anthony; David carrying a shepherd's staff, his hand towards his mouth showing his role as author and singer; Christ the Warrior holding two griffins by the scruff of their necks; and another Christ figure with a fringe of curly hair wearing a brooch on his left shoulder and carrying a sword and shield—here he is the King of Glory at his Second Coming. There is an unfinished seventh stone, and on the far right, a carved head with a downturned mouth which is probably later than the other statues. The church of White Island also contains eleventh-century gravestones; the large earthworks round the outside date from an earlier monastery.

Boa Island and Kesh

One of the most evocative of the carvings of Lough Erne is the double-faced Janus figure of **Boa Island**, at the northern end of the Lower Lough—barely an island at all these days, since it's connected to the mainland by bridges. The place to look out for is CALDRAGH cemetery, poorly signposted off the A47, about a mile and a half from the island's eastern bridge.

Down by the lake shore is an ancient Christian burial ground of broken, moss-covered tombstones, where low, encircling hazel trees enhance an almost druidic setting. Here you'll find the **Janus figure**, an idol of yellow stone with very bold symmetrical features. It has the phallus on one side, a belt and crossed limbs on the other. The figure was probably an invocation of fertility and a depiction of a god-hero—the belt being a reference to the bearing of weapons. Alongside it stands the smaller "Lusty Man," so called since it was moved here from nearby Lustymore Island. This idol has only one eye fully carved, which may indicate blindness—Cúchulainn had a number of encounters with war goddesses, divine hags described as blind in the left eye.

The nearest village, **KESH**, four and a half miles to the east, is a possible overnight stop, having some cheapish **B&B** accommodation. Try Mrs Lee, *Ernevale*, 26 Main St (☎03656-31668; £8), or Mrs Stronge, *Alaise*, 4 Station Road (☎03656-3196; £8). If you have a vehicle there's also the option of staying in the *Ardess Craft Centre* (☎03656-31267; B&B £12), housed in a fine Georgian rectory, which offers residential courses in spinning, weaving, and natural dyeing (courses start from £5 a half day). To find the center take the Enniskillen road out of Kesh, turn left just before police barracks, take a hard right, then follow the road for one and a half miles.

The chief recommendation of Kesh itself is its position on the lough. You can rent **motor boats** here from Mr R. A. Graham, Manville House (☎03656-31668; £20 a day); Mr J. E. Brimstone, Main Street (☎03656-31091 or 31527) rents out **fishing boats** for around £13.50 a day. If you want to combine **camping** with **watersports** it makes sense to stay at the *Lakeland Caravan Park*, Boa Island Road (☎03656-31025), which offers windsurfing, canoeing, and waterskiing. Alternatively, away from the lough shore, there's also *Clonelly Forest Campground*, three miles north of Kesh on the A35.

Upper Lough Erne

Upper Lough Erne holds nothing like the interest of the Lower Lough, nor the scenic splendor. The most you're really likely to do is disturb the fishermen or get lost among its crazy causeways and waterways—fun on a boat, but frustrating on dry land. Should you be tempted to venture farther into the maze of reed and water, it might be an idea to take the 45-minute **cruise** from the **Crom estate**, four miles west of NEWTOWNBUTLER. Run by the National Trust, the *Trasna Service* (☎03655-21221) operates from the Crom Boat House (June and Sept Sat and Sun 2–6pm; July and Aug daily 2–6pm; £1.50 each—group reservations only during the week).

Around the County

Around the islands and waterways there are innumerable stunning routes for both walkers and bicyclists, and as the county as a whole is geared towards fishing and boating, there's no problem finding somewhere to eat and sleep in villages around the lough. **Walkers** will find the countryside to be mostly gentle hills and woods, which rise to small mountains in the south and west of the county. For **cyclists**, there are well-surfaced (and empty) roads around the Lower Lough, though routes around the Upper Lough are harder to negotiate, with little lanes often leading to nowhere but some empty, reed-infested shore. Immediately around the entire lough complex is a ring of defensive Planters' **castles**, while the most assured achievement of the colonists, 150 years later, is evident in the magnificent eighteenth-century house of **Florence Court**, southwest of Enniskillen. If you've transportation, a visit to the house can be combined with an hour or so at the **Marble Arch Caves**—the finest cave system in Ulster. Throughout the county, there's a wealth of **wildlife** (particularly water fowl), and the lough, forest parks, and **Ulster Way** all make access to the riches of the countryside very easy.

The Planter Castles

The Lough Erne complex was ringed by a series of Planter castles early in the seventeenth century—a crucial part in the settlers' bid to control the region—and many of these are worth dropping in on as you travel around the county.

Monea Castle, on the west side of the Upper Lough, less than a mile off the B81, is a particularly fine ruin in a beautiful setting at the end of a beech-lined lane. Built around 1618, it bears the signs of Scottish influence in its design, with similar features to that of the reworked Maguire castle in Enniskillen. It was destroyed by fire in the Great Rebellion of 1641, and by Jacobite armies in 1689, and was eventually abandoned in 1750 after another fire. There's a **campground** (☎0365-89609; £3 per tent) here, on the Derrygonnelly road, or you can ask at the *Castle Inn*, right by the castle. Five miles farther north, beyond DERRYGONNELLY, the fortified house and bawn of **Tully Castle** sits down by the lough shore. Both castles are freely accessible at all times.

The best of the Planter castles on the Upper Lough is **Castle Balfour** at **LISNASKEA**, twelve miles southeast of Enniskillen. Again, strong Scottish characteristics are clear in the turrets, parapets, high-pitched gables, and tall chimneys. Lisnaskea itself is one of Fermanagh's few towns—and a small one at that. Its tiny nineteenth-century cornmarket yard has an early Christian carved cross depicting Adam and Eve beneath a tree, and in the library there's a tiny **folk museum** (Mon–Wed and Fri 9:15am–5pm, Sat 9:15am–12:30pm), with displays on local Gaelic traditions and festivals, including plenty of detail on the making of poteen. If you're **camping**, there are two campgrounds within three miles of Lisnaskea: one at Mullynascarthy, the other on the Derrylin road.

The Marble Arch Caves and Florence Court

Fermanagh's caves are renowned, and while some are for experts only, the most spectacular system of all—the **Marble Arch Caves**, south of Belcoo—is accessible to anyone. A tour of the system lasts around an hour and a half, taking you through brilliantly lit chambers dripping with stalactites and fragile mineral veils. **Tours** of the caves are sometimes filled up by parties, so it makes sense to phone ahead to check that your journey there will not be wasted (open last two weeks of June Mon–Sat 11am–4:30pm, Sun 11am–5pm; July and Aug Mon–Sat 11am–5pm, Sun 11am–6pm; Sept and Oct Mon–Sat 11am–4:30pm, Sun 11am–5pm; ☎0365-82777).

The caves are around eleven miles from Enniskillen, but there's no bus service. From Enniskillen follow the A4 Sligo road for three miles, branching off on the A32 Swalinbar road; the caves are well signposted from then on. Walkers can reach them along the Ulster Way, which from the A4 runs four miles south to the caves, past Lower Lough Macnean.

If you have a vehicle, the magnificent **Florence Court** (April–Sept Wed–Mon noon–6pm; £1.50; grounds free and open all day), eight miles southwest of Enniskillen and five from the caves, is worth a visit. A three-story mansion built in 1764, and joined by long arcades to small pavilions, it was owned by the Coles, descendants of the planters of Enniskillen. It is notable for its lavish Rococo plasterwork and rare furnishings.

The Ulster Way

The **Ulster Way** provides a signposted, long-distance path across the county. In the southwest it takes you through the bog and granite heights of the Cuilcagh mountains and Ballintempo Forest, offering fabulous views over the lough. The Way then continues north, through the **Lough Navar Forest**, a well-groomed conifer plantation with asphalt roads and shorter trails. Although a lot of fir-plantation-walking is dark and frustrating, this forest does, at points, provide some of the most spectacular views in Fermanagh, looking over Lower Lough Erne and the mountains of Tyrone, Donegal, Leitrim, and Sligo. The Lough Navar Forest also sustains a small herd of red deer, as well as wild goats, foxes, badgers, hares, and red squirrels.

It is advisable to follow the signposting rather than design your own route where the Way runs close to the border with the Republic. Route sheets on the Navar Forest and Big Dog Forest trails are available from local tourist offices; and you can get a route guide for the southwest section of the Way from *The Sports Council for Northern Ireland* (see *Basics*).

Accommodation possibilities along the Way are limited. There are a couple of B&B places in BELCOO, two and a half miles west from the trail's ascent to the Ballintempo Forest: try Mr and Mrs Thornton, *Fir Grove*, Enniskillen Road (☎036586-387; £9) or Mr Greene, *Lurgan House*, Belcoo Post Office, 8 Holywell Road (☎036586-278; £8). There's a **campground** in the Lough Navar Forest, five miles west of Derrygonnelly, off the A46.

Castle Cauldwell and Belleek

The forest of **Castle Cauldwell**, near the western extremity of Lower Lough Erne, is the main breeding site in the British Isles for the common scoter (a species of duck), and a habitat of rarities such as the hen harrier, peregrine falcon, and pine marten. A commercial, state-owned forest of spruce, pine, and larch, it's protected as an area of wildlife conservation. At the entrance look out for the giant stone fiddle in front of the gate lodge, the sobering memorial to Denis McCabe, a local musician who in 1770 fell off the Cauldwells' barge while drunk, and drowned.

BELLEEK itself, situated 24 miles from Enniskillen, has **B&B** accommodation—at Mrs McDonnell's, Main Street (☎036565-491; £8.50)—and several places from where you could **rent boats**. For rowboats call at Carlton Cottages (☎036565-8181; £10 a day); for motorboats contact Brian Hallett (☎036565-8174; £25 a day, fuel extra).

Five miles south of Belleek, at **GARRISON**, the *Lough Melvin Holiday Centre* (☎0365-658142) is a residential **outdoor pursuits** center, offering caving, canoeing, windsurfing, and hill-walking—prices from £3 a half day, £55 a weekend. The center has **hostel** accommodation open to all comers, from £4.50 per person, camping £3 per tent—though you should phone ahead to check on space if you want to stop here.

travel details

Ulsterbus
From Strabane three buses daily to Omagh (1hr 5min); Monaghan (2hr 5min); Dublin (4hr 40min).; two daily to Derry (50min).
From Enniskillen to Belfast (1 daily, 2 in summer; 2hr 35min); Dublin (3; 3hr 35min).

Private buses
Funtrek (☎01-730852) serves Omagh and Strabane on its daily Dublin–Letterkenny and Dublin–Derry routes.

THE HISTORICAL FRAMEWORK

The history of Ireland is an essential ingredient in any understanding of its troubled present. In these few pages we cannot do more than provide a brief outline of that history, in the hope that it will serve as a starting point for further reading and discussion, and encourage the visitor to become familiar with the patterns of the past.

EARLIEST INHABITANTS

It is generally believed that the first settled population of Ireland were the **Mesolithic** hunters and fishers who arrived in the northeast of the country from Scotland some time around 6000 BC. They probably crossed the water in skin coracles, and they lived close to the sea, rivers, and lakes; their flintwork has been found in Antrim, Down, Louth, and Dublin. In about 3000 BC the Neolithic people arrived. With skills in animal husbandry, weaving, pottery, and farming they used their stone axes to clear forest for cultivation.

These were the people responsible for the vast assortment of **megalithic remains** still to be seen throughout Ireland. Such sites can be found all along the Atlantic seaboard of Europe—not just the huge sites such as Carnac in Brittany, Stonehenge in England, and the Ring of Brodgar in the Orkneys, but also smaller examples from Galicia in Spain up to Scandinavia. It used to be thought that the

culture that produced them originated around the Mediterranean—many similar sites exist in Malta and Sardinia—and spread to the "barbaric outposts" of Europe, but radiocarbon dating techniques show that the progression was not so simple. The inhabitants of prehistoric Ireland are better considered as equal participants in a sophisticated and continent-wide culture, even at this early stage intimately connected with the peoples of Britain and Brittany.

Nonetheless, each area of Europe had its own distinct styles and traditions, and Ireland's contribution is exemplified by the great **passage-tombs** such as Knowth and Newgrange in County Meath, with their elaborate spiral engravings, cut into the stone entirely without the use of metal tools.

Little is known of the people themselves, although their civilization was long-lasting, with several thousand years separating the earliest and the latest megalithic constructions. Only rarely have skeletons been found in the graves, but what few there have been seem to indicate a short, dark, hairy race with a life expectancy of no more than 35 years. Legends call them the **Fir Bolg**, and speak of shambling subhuman giants who served as their slaves on such projects as the building of the Giant's Causeway on the coast of Antrim. The perpetual rivals of the *Fir Bolg* were the *Tuatha De Danann* (the Tribes of the Goddess Danu), who feature heavily in storytelling from this time on as the underground fairy people.

THE CELTS

The semimythical *Fir Bolg* were eventually supplanted by the **Celts**, an Indo-European group called *Keltoi* by the Greeks and *Galli* by the Romans, who had spread from central Europe south into Italy and Spain and west through France and Britain into Ireland. The main Celtic arrivals in Ireland probably happened during the late Bronze Age, around 700 BC, although dating is complicated by the fact that the Celtic tribes continued to use bronze for weaponry long after the appearance of iron.

It is hard to separate the truth about the Celts from the stories they told of themselves. Theirs was an oral culture, very much in the mold of the *Iliad*, in which the immortality to be gained from starring in an epic tale was prized above all else. With an enthusiasm for war little short of bloodthirsty, they celebrated battles decided by the single combat of great champions, guided and aided by the unpredictable whims of the gods. They swiftly appropriated the religion and beliefs already current in Ireland; the *Tuatha* were transmuted into Celtic gods, and although the Celts had nothing to do with the building of the megaliths, the sites continued to have great symbolic significance.

The Atlantic seaboard of Europe in the first centuries AD was largely populated by independent tribes who had been driven westward by the Romans. At a time when communications were much easier by sea than by land, a loose pan-Celtic trading confederation came into being. In Ireland itself, Celtic settlements took the form of ring-forts, with the island consisting of about one hundred small kingdoms or *Tuatha*, each with its own king. The *Tuatha* were grouped into the Five Fifths or provinces, which were Ulster, (*Ula. í*), Meath, (*Midhe*), Leinster, (*Laigin*), Munster (*Muma*) and Connaught (*Connacht*). In theory, the High King (*Ard Rí*) ruled over all from his throne on the Hill of Tara—a place long associated with mysterious power—although only rarely did any one figure of sufficient strength emerge to lay undisputed claim to that title. The two greatest heroes of the epics, **Cúchulainn** and **Finn Mac Cumaill**, have been tentatively identified with warrior champions of the second and third centuries, transformed by legend into semidivinities in much the same way as King Arthur was in England.

THE COMING OF CHRISTIANITY

The Christianization of Ireland began as early as the third century AD, well before the arrival of Saint Patrick (assuming he ever existed at all). Vestiges did survive of the previous religion of the Celts, but Ireland after the collapse of the Roman Empire assumed a position at the very forefront of European Christianity. Partly due to the sheer impassability of the landscape, it became a haven for religious orders, which were the only sources of learning at this time. Many of the great Irish monasteries such as St Enda's on the Aran Islands, Clonmacnoise in County Offaly, and Clonard in County Meath date from this period. Ogham, the Celtic line-based writing system seen on standing stones,

was rapidly supplanted by the religious scholars, who introduced Latin to a people distrustful of the written word.. The first—and best known—of their richly illuminated Latin manuscripts, the **Book of Kells**, can be seen in Trinity College, Dublin.

The traditional view of these as "Dark Ages" of terror and chaos throughout Europe bears little relation to what was happening in Ireland. Stable diplomatic and trading contact continued along the Atlantic seaboard, while Irish missionaries spread the Gospel onto the continent. St Columba's proselytizing took him to Germany and to Italy, where he founded a monastery at Bobbio, and Irish bishops were responsible for the virtual colonization of Brittany.

INVASION: VIKINGS AND NORMANS

Ireland however was increasingly plagued by pirate raids, wreaking great destruction which included the plundering and burning of the monasteries—hence the invention of the **round towers**, which were used as look out posts and places of sanctuary. The raids culminated in the **Viking invasion** of 795. The invaders then set about founding walled cities, usually at the mouths of rivers, such as Dublin, Wexford, Waterford, Youghal, Cork, Bantry, and Limerick. The decisive defeat of the Danes by the High King Brian Boru at the Battle of **Clontarf** in 1014 at least spared Ireland from the threat of becoming a colony. However, the murder of Brian Boru immediately afterward, and the subsequent fragmentation of his chieftains, meant that his victory was never consolidated by the formation of a strong unified kingdom. The Vikings that remained, as they did everywhere, soon merged fully into the native Irish population.

From the time of the Norman conquest onwards, the Norman kings of England coveted Ireland. The first of the Anglo-Normans to cross over to Ireland was something of a free-lance adventurer, Richard FitzGilbert de Clare (also called **Strongbow**). He came in 1169 at the invitation of Dermot MacMurrough, the exiled king of Munster, who sought Strongbow's help to regain his throne. Henry II, however, was concerned that Strongbow might establish himself in an ineradicable power base and therefore went personally to Ireland as overlord. He had earlier secured papal support and authorization over all powers—native, Norse, and Norman—from, ironically, the only English pope in history, Adrian IV.

In September 1172, Pope Alexander III reaffirmed Henry II's lordship. This seemed to open the prospect of an Anglo-Norman conquest in which Gaelic tribal kingdoms would be reshaped into a strong feudal system, but the native Irish resisted so effectively that royal authority outside the "English Pale" was little more than nominal.

The Statutes of Kilkenny

By the fourteenth century, this wave of Anglo-Norman settlers had integrated with the native Irish population to such an extent that the crown, eager to regain control, sought to drive a permanent wedge between the natives and the colonists with the introduction of **The Statutes of Kilkenny** (1366). This legislation prohibited intermarriage with the Irish, forbade the Irish from entering walled cities, and made the adoption of Irish names, dress, customs, or speech illegal. Despite these measures, Gaelic influence continued to grow until, by the end of the fifteenth century, the "Pale" had been reduced to a narrow strip of land around Dublin.

THE TUDORS: HENRY VIII

The continued isolation of Irish politics from English and continental influence during the fifteenth century, and England's preoccupation with the Wars of the Roses, helped Ireland's most powerful Anglo-Norman family—The FitzGeralds of Kildare—to establish and consolidate control of the east and southeast of the country. For the most part, their growing authority was left unchallenged by the early Tudor monarchy, whose policy towards Ireland was based mainly on considerations of economy (it was cheaper to accept Kildare's rule than establish an English deputy who would need expensive military backing) and security; Irish discontent with English rule should not be allowed to take forms which might be exploited by England's foreign enemies.

The Reformation

Henry VIII was able to retain this attitude of expedient caution until his break with Rome introduced several new factors: the clergy began to preach the necessity of rebellion against the schismatic king, while Henry was able to reward his supporters with the spoils from the dissolution of religious houses. Kildare's son, Lord Offaly ("Silken Thomas"), convinced that the family power was under threat, staged an insurrection in the summer of 1534. Aid from the Pope—who for the first time was seen as a potential supporter of opposition to England—was hoped for, but never came. Henry, inevitably, reacted forcibly, and changed his policy of prudence to one of aggression. War dragged on until 1540, by which time Kildare and his supporters, their power all but crushed, were forced to submit to the crown.

The Dublin Parliament enacted legislation accepting Henry's Act of Supremacy, which made the king head of the church. At least three distinct factions emerged in Ireland; the "Old English," who were loyal to the king but denied him spiritual primacy; the independent-minded and staunchly Catholic Gaelic Irish; and the new Protestants, many of whom had benefitted materially by acquiring Church property. (At this stage, those "recusants" who refused to swear the oath acknowledging Henry as head of the church were not yet subject to discrimination.) The crown, in an attempt to bind the chiefs and nobles of Ireland more closely to its authority, forced them to surrender their lands only to return them again with the reduced status of landlords. This was central to Henry's policy—the wish to rule Ireland cheaply, with least risk of foreign intervention, through Irish-born "deputies" whose loyalty was assured. But, of course, such loyalty could not be counted on and after Henry's death the authority of the English crown was again challenged.

ELIZABETH I

During the reign of Queen Elizabeth I (1558–1603), a growing number of "adventurers" (mainly younger sons of the aristocracy) arrived from Protestant England to pillage Ireland. For the first time, the supposed moral imperative to turn the Gaelic Irish away from papacy was used as an excuse to invade and dispossess. This justification for the suppression of Irish culture, religion, and language was to be the trademark of English occupation of Ireland for many years to come.

Elizabeth's aim was to establish an English colony. This policy of **"plantation"** had been started, albeit unsuccessfully, some thirty years before in the reign of Mary I when Laois—renamed "Queen's County"—and Offaly—"King's County"—were confiscated from their native Irish owners and given into the possession of loyal Old English. Elizabeth's first attempt, in the 1570s, to "plant" northeast Ulster, which was then the most Gaelic area of the country, failed miserably. Nonetheless, the colonization process, when eventually achieved, was to be instrumental in subjugating the entire country.

Hugh O'Neill and the Flight of the Earls

At least three major Irish rebellions were prompted by Elizabeth's policies. Two, led by the Desmonds of Munster, were easily put down, and their lands were confiscated and given to English settlers. The third, last, and most serious was in Ulster, led by **Hugh O'Neill**. O'Neill was originally a protegé of the English court, instrumental in crushing the revolt of the Desmonds, and had long been groomed to become chief of Ulster. He'd always imagined that in that role he would be an autonomous Gaelic chieftain; he turned against his Queen in 1595 when he appreciated to what extent he would be the pawn of English Protestantism. His forces won one major victory over the English at the Battle of the Yellow Ford in 1598, but were defeated in September 1601 when the Spanish reinforcements they were expecting at Kinsale failed to arrive in time.

The Tudor conquest of Ireland was completed when O'Neill signed the **Treaty of Mellifont** in 1603, ignorant of the death of Elizabeth just a few days before. Half a million acres of land were confiscated from the native Irish, including all the estates of O'Neill and O'Donnell. English plans to redistribute the land supposedly included generous endowments to the "natives." However, an abortive and unplanned insurrection in 1608 was enough to frighten them into abandoning any such idea, and English and Scottish "planters," many of whom were ex-soldiers, were instead brought over, to be ensconced in fortified enclosures known as "bawns." Chiefs such as O'Neill were still nominally landlords, but unable to accept

the loss of their ancient authority, and living under constant suspicion that they were plotting against the crown, many chose instead to leave their country as exiles. Their mass departure to continental Europe in 1607 became known as the **Flight of the Earls**.

It was at this time that the character of **Ulster** began to change. James VI of Scotland had just become James I of England, encouraging many Scots to emigrate the short distance to Ulster where so much newly-confiscated land awaited them. There was a great deal of bitterness on the part of the dispossessed native people, and little intermarriage with the Planters, so that the whole country, and above all Ulster, became divided along Catholic and Protestant lines.

CHARLES I AND THE ENGLISH CIVIL WAR

The widespread belief in England and Ireland that James' successor **Charles I** harbored pro-Catholic sympathies was one of the spurs for the armed rebellion in Ulster in 1641. Terrifying stories circulated in England of the torture and murder of Protestant Planters, and the rebels' (bogus) claim that they were acting with Charles' blessing did much to provoke the **English civil war**. The origins of the current situation in the six northeast counties of Ulster can be traced to the policy and events of this period.

During the civil war, the "Old English" in Ireland allied with the native Irish in the **Confederation of Kilkenny**, supporting the royalist cause in the hope of bringing about the restoration of Catholicism. It was an uneasy alliance, characterized by inadequate leadership and personal rivalries, in which the Irish felt they had nothing to lose in pursuit of liberty whereas the Old English lived in fear of a Protestant invasion should the forces of **Oliver Cromwell** achieve victory. The war did indeed end with the establishment of Cromwell's protectorate and the execution of the King, and the conquest of Ireland was Cromwell's most immediate priority.

CROMWELL IN IRELAND

Cromwell's ruthless campaign in Ireland remains a source of great bitterness to this day. He arrived in Dublin with 3000 "Ironsides" in August 1649, and was soon joined by a larger force under General Ireton. **Drogheda** was stormed in September, and thousands, including civilians and children, were slaughtered. Cromwell continued south and quickly took Wexford and New Ross, whereupon the towns of Cork, Youghal, and Kinsale in the southeast (all in the hands of Protestant royalists) swiftly capitulated. Although Waterford held out valiantly for several months, it was not long before Cromwell's forces had overrun the entire country and broken the back of resistance.

The Act of Settlement

By the time the struggle was over, almost two years later, one quarter of the Catholic population was dead, and those found wandering the country orphaned or dispossessed were sold into slavery in the West Indies. The **Act of Settlement**, drawn up in 1652, confiscatied land from the native Irish on a massive scale. All "transplantable persons" were ordered to move west of the river Shannon by May 1, 1654 on pain of death; in the famous phrase, it was a matter of indifference whether they went to "Hell or Connaught." The mass exodus continued for months, with many of the old and sick dying on the journey. Cromwell's soldiers were paid off with gifts of appropriated land, and, remaining as settlers, constituted a permanent reminder of English injustice.

KING JAMES AND KING BILLY

Irish hopes were raised once more by the **Restoration** of Charles II in 1660. He had regained the English throne, however, only as the result of lengthy negotiations with the Protestant parliamentarians of London and Dublin, and was in no position to give expression to any Catholic sympathies which he may have held.

Things only changed when Charles' brother James II succeeded him in 1685. He appointed a Catholic viceroy in Ireland, and actually got as far as repealing the Act of Settlement. Had this had time to take effect, the land confiscated by Cromwell would have been returned to its former (Catholic) owners. However, the Whigs and the Tories in England united to invite the Protestant William of Orange to take the throne. James fled and was soon raising an army in Ireland. He was successful until he came to lay siege to the city of **Derry** in Ulster, where his forces were held at bay by the young trade apprentices of the city (known thereafter as the "**Apprentice Boys**")—a victory of Protestant over Catholic which is still celebrated annually.

In July 1690 the armies of James and William met in the **Battle of the Boyne**, and James was defeated. The repeal of the Act of Settlement was therefore never implemented, but the very idea that the Catholics still had claims to their old property which they might one day be able to reassert became established in the Protestant consciousness. As William's victory was consolidated, measures were taken to ensure irreversible Protestant control of the country.

THE PENAL LAWS

In 1641 the percentage of land in Ireland owned by Roman Catholics was 59 percent. In 1688 it was 22 percent and by 1703 it was 14 percent. The Protestant population, about one tenth of the total, lived in fear of an uprising by the vast majority of dispossessed and embittered Catholics. In order to keep the native Catholics in a position of powerlessness, a number of acts were passed, collectively known as the **Penal Code**. Not only were Catholics forbidden to vote or join the army or navy, but it became illegal to educate a child in the Catholic faith; neither could they teach, open their own schools, or send their children to be educated abroad. Catholics could neither buy land, nor inherit it other than by the equal division of estates between all sons. There were vast rewards for turning Protestant; a male convert was entitled to all his brothers' inheritance, a female to her husband's property. Irish language, music, and literature were banned, as was the saying of mass. The intention was to crush the identity of the Irish people through the suppression of their culture but it had, in fact, the opposite effect. Clandestine "hedge schools" developed where outlawed Catholic teachers taught Irish language and music; mass was said in secret, often at night in the open countryside; and the culture remained as strong as ever.

GRATTAN'S PARLIAMENT

The next turning point in Irish history came in the late eighteenth century, when the increasingly prosperous merchant class ceased to identify its own interests exclusively with those of the English crown. The British in their turn were forced into the realization that an economically strong Ireland might be the best guarantee of its stability. This was an age of bourgeois revolution, and the events of the **American War of Independence** attracted much Irish attention. As early as 1771, Benjamin Franklin was in Dublin suggesting future transatlantic cooperation. Although the rebellion of the American colonies threatened Irish commercial interests, opposition to the war did not mean opposition to the American cause. Thus far, the bulk of Irish emigrants to the American colonies had been Ulster Presbyterians (Catholic emigration being subject to legal restrictions), and the Protestants of Ireland felt a deep sympathy with Washington's campaign. The demand for "no taxation without representation" struck an emotional chord with the parliamentarians of Henry Grattan's Patriot Party—not that Ireland was directly taxed by the British Parliament, but the relationship between Dublin and London was sufficiently inequitable for that to seem a possibility.

Protestants and Catholics in Ireland made common cause to the extent that Grattan declared "the Irish Protestant could never be free till the Irish Catholic had ceased to be a slave." Its resources stretched to the limit by war, the British government was intimidated enough by the thought of Irish rebellion to be in the mood for concessions. The land stipulations of the Penal Code were repealed in 1778, and in 1782 **Grattan's Parliament** achieved what was felt at the time to be constitutional independence for Ireland, beyond the interference of the London parliament although still subject to the veto of the king. In the "Renunciation Act" of 1783, the British parliament declared that the executive and judicial independence of Ireland should be "established and ascertained forever, and . . . at no time hereafter be questioned or questionable."

As it turned out, the independence of the Dublin parliament lasted for just eighteen years, and even those were long on dissent and short on achievement. Economic measures certainly benefitted the merchants, but such issues as the extension of voting rights to Catholics—despite Grattan's personal support—were barely addressed. A major reason for this disappointing performance was the influence of the **French Revolution** in 1789.

Wolfe Tone and the United Irishmen

In the 1770s, the threat of French invasion, coupled with the obvious inadequacy of the few British soldiers stationed in the country, had led to the formation throughout Ireland of bands of **Volunteers**. These were exclusively Protestant groups, at their strongest in Ulster and particularly Belfast, which rapidly acquired a political significance way beyond their supposed role as a sort of Home Guard.

The French Revolution transformed invasion from France from a menace to be feared to a prospective means of national liberation. Wolfe Tone's **United Irishmen**, built on the foundations of the Protestant Volunteers but attracting if anything more support from Catholics, rallied to the call of Liberty, Equality, and Fraternity. Tone himself was a Protestant lawyer, who saw equal rights for Protestants and Catholics in Ireland as the only route to independence from England. The United Irishmen were originally disposed towards non-violence, but for Tone the possibility of French aid was too appealing to resist. The British, and the majority of Ulster Protestants, were by contrast so alarmed by tales of the bloodshed in France, that they too prepared for war; it was at this juncture that the Protestant Orange Society, later the Orange Order, was established, with the aim of maintaining Protestant power. The uprising came in **1798**; disorganized fighting broke out in different parts of the island well before the French fleet—and Tone himself—arrived, and the scattered rebels were swiftly and bloodily suppressed. Tone was sentenced to be hanged, drawn, and quartered, but before he could be executed he was found with his throat cut in his cell. (See p.327 for more details). The limited advances which Henry Grattan had won for Catholics were withdrawn as a result of the rebellion.

THE ACT OF UNION

The destiny of Ireland during this period was largely subject to the whim of political factions in England, ever ready to make an emotional cause célèbre of the latest developments. The rebellion of 1798 provoked Prime Minister William Pitt into support for the complete legislative union of Britain and Ireland, and the dissolution of the Dublin parliament. Pitt argued at one and the same time that this offered the most hopeful road towards Catholic Emancipation while also ensuring the perpetuation of the Protestant ascendancy. In 1801 the **Act of Union** was therefore passed in London, and Ireland legally became a part of Britain.

All hopes of independence seemed crushed. Ireland itself housed an utterly divided people, a minority Protestant ruling class and a Catholic and politically powerless majority. Robert Emmet, a romantic figure in Irish history, made one last stand for independence, and, inspired by Wolfe Tone, attempted an uprising in 1803. His followers, however, were small in number and disorganized. The rising failed, and Emmet was executed.

DANIEL O'CONNELL

The quest for **Catholic Emancipation** by peaceful constitutional means was the life's work of Daniel O'Connell (1775–1847), the lawyer who became known as "The Liberator," and whom Gladstone called "the greatest popular leader the world has ever seen." He founded the Catholic Association in 1823, which attracted a mass following in Ireland in its campaign for full political rights for Catholics. O'Connell himself was elected to the British House of Commons as the member for Ennis, County Clare in 1828. As a Catholic, he was forbidden to take his seat in Westminster; but the moral force of his victory was such that a change in the law had to be conceded. Royal assent was given to the Catholic Emancipation Bill on April 13, 1829, granting voting rights (subject to fairly stringent property qualifications) to some, but not all, Catholics.

At the height of his success, O'Connell's popularity was phenomenal. He was elected Lord Mayor of (Protestant) Dublin for the year of 1841, and two years later embarked on an ambitious campaign for the **Repeal of the Union** with England. O'Connell addressed a series of vast "monster meetings" throughout Ireland; according to the conservative estimate of the *Times*, over a million people—one eighth of the Irish population—attended a meeting symbolically held at the Hill of Tara.

The climax of O'Connell's campaign was to be a meeting at **Clontarf** (where Brian Boru had defeated the Danes) on October 8, 1843. All Ireland was poised and waiting, conscious of the sympathy which O'Connell's profoundly peaceful movement had won from around the world. The pacifism which led him to say that "no political change is worth the shedding of a single drop of human blood," and his determination always to act within the law, were however exploited against him by the British. One day before the Clontarf meeting, it was declared to be an illegal gathering; O'Connell, remarkably, obliged by calling it off. The crowds which had already gathered, and the population at large, were baffled that O'Connell backed down from direct confrontation. His moment passed, and the stage was left to those who, having seen pacifism fail to secure independence, believed that armed struggle would prove the only way forward. The **Young Ireland movement**, once aligned with O'Connell, attempted an armed uprising in 1848, but by then there was little chance of mass support. The country was already undergoing a national disaster.

THE FAMINE

The failure of the Irish potato crop in 1845, 1846, and 1848 plunged the island into appalling famine. Where the blight hit elsewhere in Europe, it was a resolvable problem, but Irish subsistence farmers were utterly dependent on their potatoes, as all other foodstuffs were sold to pay exorbitant rents to English landowners. No disease affected grain, cattle, dairy products, or corn, and throughout the disaster Irish produce that could have fed the hungry continued to be exported overseas. Millions were kept alive by charitable soup kitchens, and certain individual landlords were supportive of their tenants; for millions more, the only choice lay between starvation and escape.

In the space of a decade, the population of Ireland was reduced by two million. Half of them died, the other half—over a quarter of the population—left Ireland for ever. Many were too ill to survive the journey on what became known as "coffin ships," some drowned when overcrowded ships sank, and still more died on arrival in the United States, Canada, Britain, Australia, and New Zealand.

A consequence of **mass emigration** was the creation of large Irish communities abroad, which from then on gave the struggle for Irish independence an international significance. Financial support from overseas Irish became crucial to such nationalist organizations as the Irish Republican Brotherhood, also known as the **Fenians**. Their attempted uprisings in 1865 and 1867 were little short of fiascos, but they nonetheless continued to have a loyal following both in the States and in England (where a number of bombings were carried out in their name).

The legacy of the Famine was such that the long standing bitterness aroused by the English connection now deepened to a new level of emotional intensity. Resentment focused on the failure of the British government to intervene, and more specifically on the **absentee English landlords** who had continued to profit while remaining indifferent to, if not ignorant of, the suffering of their tenants. Such landlords had little or no contact with the realities of life on their estates; rents were far higher than most tenants could pay and evictions became widespread.

PARNELL AND HOME RULE

The second half of the nineteenth century was characterized by a complex interplay of political and economic factors which contributed towards the exacerbation of religious differences. The most important of these was the struggle for land, and for the rights of tenants. A coherent nationalist movement, with modest aims, began to emerge, operating within the setting of British parliamentary democracy.

Charles Stuart Parnell (1846–91), a Protestant who was elected to Westminster in 1875 and became leader of the **Home Rule** Party two years later, was the tenants' champion. He insisted that only a parliament meeting in Dublin could be responsive to the needs of the people, and to that end consistently disrupted the business of the British House of Commons.

Parnell also organized the Irish peasantry in defiance of particularly offensive landlords, adding a new word to the English language when the first such target was a certain Captain Boycott.

A breakthrough seemed to be approaching when Parnell won the support of Prime Minister Gladstone, but the **Phoenix Park murders** in Dublin in 1882 (see p.57) hardened English opinion against the Irish yet again. Three Home Rule Bills were defeated in the space of ten years; instead the Prevention of Crimes Act (temporarily) abolished trial by jury and increased police powers. The transparent honesty of Parnell's denials of complicity in the murders for a while served to boost his career, but public opinion finally swung against him in 1890, when he was cited as adulterous correspondent in the divorce case of his colleague Captain O'Shea.

The attitude of many Irish Protestants to the agitation for Home Rule was summed up by the equation "Home Rule=Rome Rule"; such a threat was enough to unite the Anglican (broadly speaking, conservative gentry) and Presbyterian (liberal tradesmen) communities. These were certainly the people who were doing best from a modest boom in Ireland's economic fortunes, with Ulster, and specifically Belfast, having been the main beneficiary when the industrial revolution finally arrived in Ireland. Large scale **industrialization** in export industries such as shipbuilding, linen manufacture, and engineering gave the region an additional dependence on the British connection, while the fact that these industries were firmly under Protestant ownership increased social tensions.

The end of the nineteenth century saw a burst of activity aimed at the revival of interest in all aspects of Irish culture and identity. Ostensibly non-political organizations such as the **Gaelic League** and the Gaelic Athletic Association were founded to promote Irish language, music, and traditional sports, and these inevitably tended to attract the support of politically minded nationalists. As well as those who sought to encourage the use of Gaelic, a body of writers, with **W. B. Yeats** in the forefront, embarked on an attempt to create a national literature in English.

In 1898, Arthur Griffith, a printer in Dublin, founded a newspaper called the *United Irishman*, in which he expounded the philosophy of **Sinn Fein**, meaning "We, Ourselves." His was a non-violent and essentially capitalist vision, arguing that the Irish MPs should simply abandon Westminster and set up their own parliament in Dublin, where, with or without the permission of the British, they would be able to govern Ireland by virtue of their unassailable moral authority. Such political freedom was a prerequisite for Ireland to achieve significant economic development. Sinn Fein incorporated itself into a political party in 1905. Meanwhile, **socialist** analyses of the situation in Ireland were appearing in the *Workers' Republic*, the newspaper of **James Connolly**'s Irish Socialist Republican Party, pointing out that Ireland's frail prosperity rested on a basis of malnutrition, bad housing, and social deprivation.

Reaction and Counter-reaction

In reaction to the declared intentions of Asquith's Liberal government in Britain in 1911 to see through the passage of yet another (exceptionally tame) Home Rule Bill, the Protestants of Ulster mobilized themselves under the leadership of **Sir Edward Carson**. A Dublin barrister who at first glance had little in common with the people of Ulster, a region he barely knew, his one great aim was to preserve the Union, in the face of the "nefarious conspiracy" hatched by the British government itself. To that end he declared that, should the Home Rule Bill become law, the unionists would defy it and set up their own parliament. In preparation for that eventuality, they organized their own militia, the Ulster Volunteers.

James Connolly, who had spent the years from 1903 to 1910 in disillusionment in the United States, found himself on less fertile ground when he tried to convert the workers of Belfast to socialism. He was, however, impressed by the example of the Ulster Volunteers, and the brutal police suppression of a protracted and bitter strike in Dublin, organized by James Larkin's Irish Transport Workers Union, gave him the opportunity to form the **Irish Citizen Army**. Other militant Republicans had also resolved to create an armed force in the south to parallel the Ulster Volunteers, and almost simultaneously, in November 1913, the **Irish Volunteers** came into being. The Gaelic League and Gaelic Athletic association acted as prime recruiting places, and provided such leaders as Padraig Pearse. The movement should not however be seen in strictly sectarian terms; at least two of its most prominent leaders were Ulster Protestant nationalists.

REVOLUTION AND CIVIL WAR

The British Parliament did eventually pass the Home Rule Bill of 1912, and for a while Ireland seemed primed to erupt into civil war. Before this could happen, however, the outbreak of World War I dramatically altered the situation. An immediate consequence of war was that implementation of the bill was indefinitely postponed.

For the majority of the Irish Volunteers, the primary aim of their movement was to safeguard the postwar introduction of Home Rule. Not simply to that end, but also out of loyalty to the British Crown, many of them joined the British Army. Some, however, led by Owen MacNeil, in part supported the British war effort but were reluctant to commit too much of their strength towards defending Britain without a pledge of concrete rewards. These individuals in turn fell under the domination of a small and secret militant faction, the revived **Irish Republican Brotherhood**, to whom "England's difficulty was Ireland's opportunity." They made tentative overtures for German support (and even contemplated installing a German prince as king of Ireland); but went ahead with preparations for armed insurrection regardless of whether or not they received foreign aid—indeed all but regardless of the virtual certainty of defeat.

The Easter Uprising

The outbreak of fighting on the streets of Dublin on Easter Monday in 1916 was expected by neither the English nor the Irish Army, and was a source of bemusement to the Dubliners themselves. Republican forces swiftly took over a number of key buildings, although they missed an easy opportunity to capture the castle itself.

The leaders of the uprising made their base in the General Post Office on O'Connell Street, and it was from there that Padraig Pearse emerged to read the "Proclamation from The Provisional Government of the Irish Republic to the People of Ireland":

> *"Ireland, through us, summons her children to the flag and strikes for her freedom . . . The Irish Republic is entitled to, and hereby claims, the allegiance of every Irishman and Irishwoman. The Republic guarantees religious and civil liberty, equal rights and equal*

*opportunities to all its citizens . . . cherishing
all the children of the nation equally, and
oblivious of the differences carefully fostered
by an alien Government, which have divided a
minority from the majority in the past."*

To these fine democratic sentiments Pearse
in particular added a quasimystical emphasis
on the necessity for blood sacrifice; although
potential allies such as Owen MacNeil
declined to join them with so little prospect of
success, these were men prepared to give their
lives as inspiration to others.

So weak was the rebel position that they
only held out five days; at the time of their
surrender they were even less popular with the
mass of the nation than when they began, as a
result of the terrible physical damage Dublin
had suffered.

And yet, as the leaders of the Rising were
systematically and unceremoniously executed
by the British—the crippled James Connolly
was shot tied to a chair—sympathy did indeed
grow for the Republicans and their cause. In
the words of Yeats' *Easter 1916,*

*All changed, changed utterly.
A terrible beauty is born.*

War with England

When the British Government felt able once
again to turn their minds to Irish affairs, it was
to confront a dramatically altered situation.
Sinn Fein won a resounding victory in the elections of 1917, refused to take their seats at
Westminster, and met instead in Dublin as the
Dail Éireann (Assembly of Ireland). Leadership
had passed to **Eamonn de Valera**, the sole
surviving leader of the Easter Rising, whose
sentence of death had been commuted. Ireland
and England were therefore at war.

The main instrument of British power in
Ireland, the Royal Irish Constabulary, experienced severe difficulties in recruiting sufficient
new members (other than from Ulster). Newly-
demobilized British soldiers were therefore
brought over from England, and by virtue of
their distinctive uniforms became known as the
"Black and Tans." The Irish Republicans,
fighting on home territory, were well able to
hold their own in guerrilla fighting across the
country, while the "Black and Tans" acquired a
reputation as the last word in infamy which
still endures.

The Government of Ireland Act of 1920
created separate parliaments for "Northern
Ireland" (Derry, Antrim, Fermanagh, Down,
Tyrone, and Armagh) and "Southern Ireland"
(the 26 counties of the present-day Republic),
to remain under the nominal authority of the
British crown. Elections were held for the two
bodies in 1921, but the members elected to the
southern Parliament constituted themselves
instead as the *Dail Éireann*, with De Valera as
their president. With the Protestants of Ulster
still firmly pledged to the Union, a negotiated
settlement seemed to be the only way out. De
Valera sent emissaries to London, including
Arthur Griffith and Michael Collins, but Lloyd
George somehow persuaded them to think of
the Act as merely a stopgap solution until a
Boundary Commission could draw new
borders—borders which he strongly suggested
would be so drastic as to preclude the North
from being a viable entity. (That this never
occurred is largely attributable to the pressure
from Edward Carson).

Civil War

The **Anglo-Irish Treaty**, signed on December
6, 1921, was hailed by Lloyd George as "one of
the greatest days in the history of the British
Empire." Griffith and Collins had, however,
allowed their exhaustion after endless negotia-
tion to override the need to secure de Valera's
agreement in Dublin. De Valera's refusal to
accept the Treaty—he resigned from office and
left the *Dail*—plunged Ireland into a squalid
and sectarian **civil war**.

Men who had been fighting alongside each
other the year before were now pitched into
bitter conflict, the Free-Staters who supported
the Treaty against the Republicans who would
not. In the North, the understandably alarmed
Protestant community created the Ulster
Special Constabulary, including the "B
Specials" drawn from Carson's Ulster
Volunteers, ostensibly to control the rioting
which persistently broke out in response to
events south of the border.

De Valera and his supporters were eventually forced to capitulate; as he put it, "military
victory must be allowed to rest for the moment
with those who have destroyed the Republic."
The way was clear for a new constitution,
approved by both the *Dail* and Westminster,
formally creating the Irish Free State.

THE IRISH FREE STATE

The first government of the Irish Free State, under William T. Cosgrave, got on with the business of re-creating Ireland as an independent nation. The civil service was set up, along with a police force and the hydroelectric scheme on the Shannon River which was to lead to the establishment of the ESB (Electricity Supply Board).

Still an important political force, Eamon de Valera abandoned *Sinn Fein's* postwar policy of boycotting the *Dail* to form his own political party in 1926. This took the explicitly mythological name of **Fianna Fáil**, which means "Soldiers of Destiny," and was victorious in the 1932 general election. Under de Valera other state bodies were set up including *Coras Iompair Éireann* (road and rail transport), *Aer Lingus* (air transport) and *Bord na Mona* (peat production). In 1933 the rival **Fine Gael** (Tribes of Gaels) party was founded.

The recession of the Thirties was made considerably worse for Ireland by the **Economic War**. De Valera had withheld repayments to England of loans made to tenants to buy their holdings; the British responded by imposing heavy duties on Irish goods.

In 1938 a new constitution came into effect, which finally declared Ireland's complete independence by renouncing British sovereignty. The Free State, under the name of **Eire**, was to be governed by a two chamber parliament (the *Dail* and the *Seanad*), with a president (the *Uachtarán*), and a prime minister (the *Taoiseach*).

Ireland remained officially neutral during World War II, although considerable informal help was given to the Allies. De Valera on the other hand was the only government leader in the world to offer his commiserations to the Reichstag on the suicide of Adolf Hitler.

It took Ireland twenty years to recover from the economic stagnation brought on by the war. Vast numbers, disproportionately drawn from the young and talented, moved across to take advantage of Britain's labor shortage. Not until a break was made with the past, with the accession to the premiership in 1959 of the vigorous and expansionist Sean Lemass, was a sufficient level of prosperity achieved to slow down the process of chronic emigration. Foreign enterprises began to invest heavily in Ireland, unemployment dropped by a third, and this paved the way for the country's successful application to join the European Economic Community in 1972. The most immediate benefits were enjoyed by those employed in agriculture (20% of the working population), although Irish fishing waters had now to be shared with other EEC members.

Ireland's and Britain's membership in the EEC did not bring Southern and Northern Ireland closer together. Their membership was made official on January 22, 1972; eight days later came Bloody Sunday (see below), and on February 2 the British embassy in Dublin was destroyed by an angry mob.

The international recession hit Ireland very severely in the Eighties. Emigration rocketed once again and unemployment remained consistently high. The referendums on abortion in 1983 and divorce in 1986 reflected the Catholic Church's considerable influence in such matters, and both abortion and divorce remain illegal in the Republic. Ireland's president is elected every seven years and President Patrick Hilary, elected in 1983, is serving his second term in office. (The electoral system is one of proportional representation.) The 1987 general election, fought principally on the issues of taxation and unemployment, resulted in the *Fianna Fáil* party coming to power, led by the resilient and wily Charles Haughey. In the summer of 1989, Mr Haughey called another election with the intention of increasing his majority. The result had the opposite effect, however, and the present government is a *Fianna Fáil*/Progressive Democrat alliance (See "Contemporary Ireland," below).

NORTHERN IRELAND FROM 1921 ONWARDS

On June 22, 1921, the new political entity of Northern Ireland came into existence with the opening of the Northern Irish Parliament in Belfast's City Hall. In order to understand the present situation in the North it is necessary to grasp the political background to this development. Since the Plantation of the seventeenth century, the Protestant descendants of the settlers had been concentrated in the northern part of the island; they rarely intermarried with the local people or assimilated the native culture, feeling both superior to and threatened by the Catholics, who formed the vast majority of the population of Ireland as a whole. The economically dominant group in the northern counties was essentially Protestant, and when an industrial base developed in this part of the island, the prosperity of the region was inextricably tied to the trading power of Britain. In negotiating for their exclusion from the new Irish state, Carson and the Unionist Council decided to accept just six counties of Ulster out of a possible nine, because only in this way could a safe Protestant majority be guaranteed. Thus Westminster gave political power into the hands of those whose pro-British sympathies were certain.

The Unionists were not slow to exploit their supremacy: a Protestant police force and military were set up, and "gerrymandering" (the redrawing of boundary lines in order to control the outcome of elections) was commonplace, so securing Protestant control even in areas with Catholic majorities. Thus Derry City, with a two-thirds Catholic majority, returned a two-thirds Protestant council. Nothing was done to rectify the situation for several decades. The Catholic community was to benefit from the British welfare state, but they were discriminated against in innumerable ways, most notoriously in jobs, and in housing, an area controlled by Protestant local authorities.

In 1967, inspired by the civil rights movement in America, the Northern Irish **Civil Rights Movement** was born, a nonsectarian organization demanding equality of rights for all. Massively supported by the Catholic community, the campaign led to huge protest marches, some of which were viciously attacked by Loyalist mobs. The **RUC** (Royal Ulster Constabulary) rarely intervened, and when they did take action, it was generally not to protect the Catholics. The Apprentice Boys' march of 1969 proved to be the flashpoint. Taking their name from the apprentices who shut the gates of Derry in the face of James II's troops in 1689, this Loyalist order commemorates the city's siege with an annual march on August 12, a triumphal procession that goes through Derry's Catholic areas. The 1969 march provoked rioting that ended in the Catholic community barricading themselves in and Jack Lynch, the Irish prime minister, mobilizing Irish troops and setting up field hospitals on the border.

On August 14 British troops were sent to Derry to protect the besieged minority, and at first they were welcomed by the Catholics, who were relieved to see the troops pushing back the RUC and B Specials. Belief in the neutrality of the British army did not last long, however. Escalating violence between the two communities across the North forced the army into a more interventionist role, but confusion arose as to whether **Stormont** (the Northern Parliament) or Westminster was giving the orders. Before long the army was not acting as a protective force but as a retaliatory one, and it was clear that retaliation against the Catholics was far harsher than measures taken against the Protestants. With the Catholics again vulnerable, the resurgent IRA quickly assumed the role of defenders of the ghetto areas of Derry and Belfast. Within a few months the **Provisional IRA**, now stronger than the less militant **Official** wing of the organization (colloquially known as the "stickies"), had launched an intensive bombing and shooting campaign across the North.

At the request of Brian Faulkner, Prime Minister of Northern Ireland, **internment without trial** was introduced in 1971, a measure which was used as an indiscriminate weapon against the minority population. Then, on Sunday, January 30, 1972, thirteen unarmed civil rights demonstrators were shot dead by British paratroopers in Derry, an event that shocked the world and was to become known as **Bloody Sunday**. The Irish government declared February 2 a national day of mourning; on the same day an angry crowd in Dublin burned down the British embassy. Stormont was suspended and direct rule from Westminster imposed.

Sunningdale and After

In 1973 a conference was held at Sunningdale between representatives of the British and Irish governments and both sections of the community in Northern Ireland, a meeting that led to the creation of a power-sharing executive representing both Unionists and Nationalists. An elected executive took office in November 1973, but in May of the next year the United Ulster Unionist Council responded by organizing a massive strike which, enforced by the roadblocks of the UDA, crippled the power-stations and other essential services run by a strongly Unionist workforce. In the same week as the strike, three car bombs planted by the UDA exploded in Dublin, without warning, at rush hour—33 people were killed, the highest death toll since 1969. By the end of the month, the Sunningdale executive—the first ever to have Catholic representation—was disbanded, and direct rule from Westminster has continued to the present day.

Almost immediately a bombing campaign was launched in Britain by the IRA, aimed at destabilizing the government by provoking public revulsion. Twenty-one people were killed in a pub bombing in **Birmingham** in 1974, and in the same month seven people died in simultaneous pub bombings in Woolwich and Guildford. The British response was to introduce the **Prevention of Terrorism Act**, permitting lengthy detention without charge. Four people were arrested for the Guildford bombings, and convicted on the basis of confessions which even at the time were thought by many people to be unreliable. After fifteen years of imprisonment, all four were released when the judiciary finally conceded, with no hint of regret for the injustice, that they were indeed innocent. Six Irish people are still serving life sentences for the Birmingham attack, although their innocence seems equally indisputable.

In 1976 Special Category Status was abolished for future prisoners in Northern Ireland (previously those arrested for offenses connected with "The Troubles" enjoyed the status of political prisoners), and when Republican prisoners refused to wear prison uniforms in accordance with their change in status, prisoners were locked naked in their cells in Long Kesh—the beginning of the famous "**Blanket Protest**" (see p.463). In 1978 Britain was found guilty by the European Court of Human Rights of "inhuman and degrading treatment" of Republican prisoners. Soon afterwards in Northern Ireland the "Dirty Protest" began in Long Kesh and Armagh women's

prison (see p. 463), with Republican prisoners forcing the issue of political status by refusing to wear criminal uniforms or empty their slop buckets. In late 1980 a hunger strike for the same demands was called off when one of the strikers was close to death. The following March a **hunger strike** was begun by **Bobby Sands**, who on April 11 was elected as MP for Fermanagh and South Tyrone. By the day of his election, nine other Republicans had joined the hunger strike. All ten died, an outcome that brought widespread condemnation of British intransigence.

1982 saw the British government make a timid attempt to break the impasse, introducing the Northern Ireland Assembly, a power-sharing body with some legislative but no executive powers. It was boycotted by the Nationalists, and survived only until 1985, by which time the final stages had been reached in the negotiations over the **Anglo-Irish Agreement**. Largely drafted by John Hume, the leader of the moderate nationalist SDLP, and signed in 1986, it instituted official co-operation between Dublin on security and other issues, and strengthened the consultative part played by Dublin in Northern affairs. Immediately the majority of loyalist MPs withdrew from Westminster in protest, and still do not participate in any talks under the aegis of the agreement.

There is now some disagreement in Unionist circles as to whether they should continue to refuse to play a part in the latest attempt at a political accommodation. However, a lasting solution is still a long way off. Sectarian violence is still frequent, and the fundamental grievances of the Catholic minority in the North have not been assuaged. Unemployment was a major factor in the outbreak of trouble in 1969, and remains an area of acute injustice: discrimination by employers is still rife, and the rate of unemployment among Catholics is two and a half times greater than among the Protestant community.

CONTEMPORARY IRELAND

A second executive jet has been leased, public relations consultants have been put in place in Brussels and Strasbourg, teams of officials have been drilled—the Republic of Ireland aims to start the 1990s by creating the best possible impression during its presidency of the European Community. A formal duty which rotates every six months to each of the twelve member-states has been turned into a major challenge—that of a small nation on the periphery, making a distinctive mark on a fast-changing Europe.

Charles Haughey and European Ireland

The *Taioseach* (literally "chief"), Charles Haughey, intends to stamp his personality on the EC at a critical time both in the development of the community and in his own political career. Leader of his *Fianna Fail* party for a decade, he is now in his mid-sixties, and unlikely to carve himself the historical role he sought as the architect of Irish unity.

He did make a small bit of political history in 1989 when he was forced to abandon the deeply held *Fianna Fail* conviction that the party always governs alone. The party has a unique record among European political parties in consistently winning forty to fifty percent of the popular vote over the past five decades. But in six successive elections the party has failed to win an overall majority. It has had to adapt to the European mode of coalition, forming a government with the Progressive Democrats, led by Des O'Malley—who was expelled from *Fianna Fail* after repeatedly challenging Mr Haughey's leadership.

This enforced compromise still rankles with many in *Fianna Fail*, but Mr Haughey commands broad approval for some aspects of his administration. He is generally acknowledged to have raised confidence among Irish business people and thus boosted investment, and his government has come closer than any other of the past fifteen years to balancing its books.

Now, as Ireland's turn comes around in the EC lottery, Charles Haughey sees another means of writing himself into the history books as having accelerated the process of European union, and played a central role in other key areas—the formalization of the Community's Social Charter, the "greening" of Europe green, and the articulation of the EC's response to the changes in Eastern Europe.

In opposition up to 1987, *Fianna Fail* expressed grave concerns about the implications for Irish neutrality and sovereignty of the Single European Act, which legislates a post-1992 single market. In government, their preoccupation has been to secure as large a portion as possible of "the structural funds" being allocated to cushion weaker member-states against the effects of the new pan-European economy.

Facing harmonization of taxes throughout the EC, Mr Haughey's government has demanded to be allowed to retain, at least temporarily, its above-average VAT rates. Ireland has also indicated it could not implement provisions of the Social Charter on minimum wages. Unlike the Christian Democrats, Liberals and Socialists, *Fianna Fail* has no European identity. A bit nationalist, a bit populist, a bit conservative, it is aligned in the European Parliament with a motley crew of unenthusiastically European Gaullists, a lone Greek conservative, and a convicted Spanish fraudster, Jose María Ruíz Mateos.

In view of all these circumstances, Mr Haughey might not seem particularly well suited to the task of steering the Council of Ministers through this crucial period. That has not stopped him from indicating that he has his own agenda to bring to the task. On the eve of assuming the EC presidency, Mr Haughey stated that he wished to give the Irish tenure of the office an environment theme. Yet Ireland has failed to implement some EC environmental directives. Mr Haughey's own government has been unable to make much progress on reducing Dublin's choking winter smog, and has made no impact on the increasing number and intensity of summer "fish kills" from agricultural and sewage pollution. Behind these personal and political paradoxes are the deeper contradictions in Ireland's role in the wider world. They reflect the tussle between traditional Ireland and modern Ireland that underlies much of everyday life, showing itself in uncertainties of style and of language. The traditional and the modern coexist uneasily in public affairs—and in the obsessively talked-about personality of Charles Haughey. He cultivates the image of nationalist and populist and he pursues with resolute pragmatism policies chosen as most likely to succeed. Though a very recent convert to doctrines of fiscal rectitude and European economic integration, he is happy to take credit for any supposed gains they bring.

The Economy

Ireland's stunted political development and peculiarly unbalanced economy are, at least in part, a legacy of colonial rule. But both states are fully fledged members of an international club of (mainly) past and present colonial powers. The Republic, which built large sections of its own economy behind protective barriers, is guiding the EC through the next stage in the removal of tariffs. An economy based historically on strong state intervention—because of a weak native middle class—is being integrated further into an economic community where certain forms of state intervention may be proscribed.

On the conventional criterion of income per head of population, Ireland is among the two dozen most developed countries in the world. And on economic indicators of inflation, balance of trade, economic growth, and rate of investment, the Republic of Ireland is among the best-performing of the EC member-states. But over 300,000 people, equivalent to eight percent of the population, have emigrated since 1982, and nearly one percent of the population leaves every year. The official unemployment levels are officially seventeen percent in the Republic and fifteen percent in the North. They reach several times those figures in large pockets and would be much worse but for massive emigration. One-third of the population—the unemployed, farmers with meager holdings, workers on low wages—live in poverty.

The Republic's national debt is of Latin American proportions, and it costs nearly as much each year to pay the interest on the debt as it does to maintain the state's social welfare program. But Ireland, with a healthy balance of trade, remains a good bet for bankers. Nobody has been stung on bad debts here as in Latin America. Ireland also remains a good bet for mobile capital—and not just for those multinationals in search of cheap labor, either. Although between one-third and one-quarter of each year's crop of technical graduates leave to work abroad, enough stay or return to be a powerful magnet for high-technology companies. Equally beneficial are the open-handed tax regime and generous state handouts.

The flow is not entirely one way. The most successful Irish companies are themselves multinationals: Ireland is the base of Europe's biggest beef producer and the world's largest aircraft-leasing company. The two largest industrial groups together have investments in Britain, the Netherlands, Spain, United States, Mexico, and Colombia.

In this once-rural country, industrial production and exports now far outstrip agricultural production and exports, and more people live in towns and cities than in the countryside. As many live in the single Dublin suburb of Tallaght as in the large western county of Mayo.

The Northern Factor

Business gets good returns in the stable commercial and industrial relations environments—a stability that might seem a surprise in a country which for twenty years has been affected by violent conflict. The northern situation does raise problems for the two Irish states, but does not actually shake their foundations. Both states have been able to absorb the shocks, partly through repressive measures, and none of the forces active in the drama are strong enough to compel a new settlement.

The IRA apparently has the resources and the support to sustain indefinitely its campaign at about the present level, but neither it nor *Sinn Fein*, its political wing, has the capacity to steer developments on a particular course. By their own admission, the British government and the combined forces of the RUC and British Army cannot defeat the IRA. The Loyalists have disrupted settlement efforts, but are fractured and too unsure about their goals to impose their own. The rivalry of Ian Paisley's Democratic Unionists and the Ulster Unionists is barely disguised as they maintain their supposedly joint opposition to the Anglo-Irish agreement.

The British and Irish governments agree only on broad principles, cooperating closely on security—despite the rhetoric—but unable to enforce a new "solution." The Anglo-Irish Agreement of 1985 has been principally a mechanism for communication between the governments in Dublin and London. To many northern Nationalists, who were promised most from it, it is irrelevant. To northern Unionists, it is a constant source of provocation.

Over 2500 have been killed in the violence of the past twenty years. But the conflict still escapes the grasp of the wider international community—and the wider national community. For many of those living in the North the conflict with all its attendant daily disruption is the primary reality. It alienates large sections of them from the state and involves tens of thousands in personal turmoil and tragedy.

For several days in a row there may be scarcely a reference in southern newspapers to the continuing violence and political chaos. The *Dail*—which purports to legislate for all of Ireland—rarely debates the North. On one of those rare occasions, in late 1989, all of the political parties professed their concern that the political stalemate in the North—where the principal parties do not even talk to each other—should be broken. Mr Haughey repeated an invitation to unionists to talk to him. They could do so, he suggested, through having their MEPs (Members of the European Parliament) talk to him in his capacity as president of the European Council of Ministers, if that was more convenient. The shortest route from Nationalist Dublin to Unionist Belfast apparently runs through Brussels or Strasbourg.

Days after the invitation, the distance between even Nationalist South and Nationalist North became clear when a Northern-born *Dail* deputy joined in a parliamentary row. A politician on the government side was heard to shout "Go back." Nationalist rhetoric about uniting the country often masks a conviction that partition should remain.

The Catholic Church

Voters in the Republic, under the guidance of the main political parties and of the Catholic Church, have tended to reinforce Unionists' view of the state as church-run and priest-ridden. In 1983 a small, vociferous group of right-wing Catholics was able to stampede the two main political parties into supporting an amendment to the constitution which committed the state to do everything in its power to protect the life of the unborn. As a consequence of that amendment, approved in a referendum, women's groups providing advice to those with unwanted pregnancies have been forced underground. During 1989, student unions publishing information on abortion services in Britain were taken repeatedly before the courts by the *Society for the Protection of Unborn Children*, which has continued to be active as guarantor of the amended constitution.

In 1986, a proposal to remove the constitutional ban on divorce was defeated in a popular vote. *Fianna Fail* and the Catholic Church nominally stood aside, but their troops did the work. Traditional Ireland, dogmatic but inarticulate, triumphed; although, again through the Catholic Church, it can also be compassionate, deterring the modern gurus from even more drastic cuts in public services and highlighting poverty and oppression in Ireland and in the Third World.

Secular, radical thought, which is well represented in other European countries, is barely discernible in Ireland. The radical and revolutionary impulses of the war of independence and of the social upheavals which accompanied it were deflected in the division of the country. A party based on labor has been unable to survive in the North—because labor itself does not stand on a firm foundation.

During the June 1989 general election in the Republic, the Irish Labor Party and the Workers' Party, together with a few independent left-wingers, gathered a total of just fifteen percent of the vote. The small increase caused the left to celebrate and analysts to reflect on a decisive shift in Irish politics. But a center-right coalition government and a center-right opposition fill the largest part of the political stage. The government has already set about recuperating for itself the stray Green vote—hence, in part at least, Mr Haughey's "green" agenda for the EC. It already holds the trade union movement in check through a Program for National Recovery.

The embrace of the nationalist-populist-conservative mix is broad enough—or so it is implied—to contain all of these impulses. With seven daily papers, seven Sunday papers, two dozen radio stations and an independent commercial TV channel, there would seem to be plenty of room for diverse opinions. But they, too, fit in the embrace. Censorship, both formal and informal, helps to establish the boundaries. Yet the pains of modernization and of the northern conflict affect all the major institutions of the two states, and they keep opening cracks where more critical activity takes place, as much through music and film as through more directly political spheres. The contradictions of contemporary Ireland always make it possible to envisage a different future.

Brian Trench

ENVIRONMENT AND WILDLIFE

Ireland conjures up images of a romantic wild territory unscarred by human activity—a somewhat rosy picture, but with more than a little truth to it. Genuine wilderness may be scarce, but the centuries of economic deprivation have ensured that most of Ireland is a rural landscape in which the only intervention has come from generations of farmers.

IRISH LANDSCAPES AND HABITATS

The topography of Ireland is fairly homogenous: there are few high mountain ranges and most of the center of the country is covered by a flat, boggy plain. And with only four degrees of latitude from north to south it lacks extremes of weather, the enveloping Atlantic Ocean producing a mild, damp climate. Summers are rarely hot, winters rarely cold and in parts of the west it rains two days out of three.

In these conditions you'd expect to find broad-leaved woodland, but intensive pressure on the landscape during the centuries leading up to the Great Famine of 1845 denuded the country of its original tree cover. Now it is replaced mostly by a patchwork of small grass fields divided by wild, untidy hedgerows— these long lines of trees acting as refuges for the former woodland community of plants and animals. (In common with many islands, Ireland has a limited number of animal species—there

are no snakes, no moles, and no woodpeckers, for instance.) The low population in Ireland today means that over much of the country the intensity of land use is lower than in many other European countries. Mixed farms are still more common than specialized intensive units. Visitor numbers in the countryside are still low and it is possible to find long sandy beaches which are completely deserted even in summer.

Natural habitats such as peat bogs, dunes and wetlands still survive here, having all but disappeared elsewhere under the relentless pace of modern development. However the pressures are growing. The great midland bogs are being rapidly stripped for fuel. Mountainsides are disappearing under blankets of exotic conifers and shoals of dead fish are becoming all too frequent an event in Irish waterways.

The Coasts

With over 2000 miles of shoreline and hundreds of islands, there is plenty of variety along the Irish coast. There are spectacular cliffs, especially in the west and southwest, which hold large **bird colonies**. Razorbills, guillemots, kittiwakes, shags, and gulls (seven different types) are among the commonest species, and a few of the larger colonies hold puffins, gannets, and cormorants. After dark some of the uninhabited islands are filled with the sounds of Manx shearwaters and storm petrels. The best time to see breeding seabirds is in early summer (May–June), but later in the year you can watch large flocks on the move by positioning yourself on a prominent headland. In the right weather conditions some rare seabirds such as great shearwaters, which normally feed well offshore, will come within sight of the land. Patient seawatching from a western headland may also be rewarded with the sighting of a school of **dolphins** or porpoises or the occasional larger **whale** feeding in the rich inshore waters.

The remoteness of the western **islands** makes them ideal habitats, and several of their deserted villages are now tenanted only by seabirds. Grey **seals** breed on island beaches and in caves during the autumn months. Due to lack of disturbance, nocturnal animals like otters can be seen here during daylight, hunting for food among rocks and pools. Beachcombing can be a rewarding experience in the west of Ireland, where the waters of the Gulf Stream may yield up anything from tropical seeds to a massive turtle.

In some counties, notably Donegal, Mayo, Kerry, and Wexford, there are extensive **sand dunes**. In summer these are clothed in a profusion of **wild flowers** such as the yellow bird's-foot trefoil and pink sea bindweed. The exotic-looking bee orchid is one of the rarities sometimes to be found in the dunes. The absence of tree cover means few breeding birds, but **cuckoos** are a special feature of Irish sand dunes, as they exploit the nests of the ubiquitous meadow pipits. The **chough**, a comparatively rare crow, breeds extensively on the south and west coasts and can be seen in large flocks feeding in sand dune systems. The low, sandy coasts of the northwest, especially where they adjoin small lakes or marshes, are populated by breeding **waders** such as dunlin and lapwing.

The low coasts, especially on the east and south, are punctuated by **estuaries**, some with vast lonely mudflats. Despite their bare appearance, below their surface are uncountable shellfish and other burrowing animals, which attract feeding waders and wildfowl. From October to April the estuaries are alive with the calls of curlews, redshanks, godwits, wigeon, teal, and shoveler. Virtually all the pale-bellied brent geese to be seen in Europe are on Irish estuaries in winter, having traveled from their breeding grounds in northern Canada. The estuaries and inlets of the west coast are wider and sandier; at low tide herds of common seals often bask on the sand banks.

Lakelands and Grasslands

A traveler in the midlands and west of Ireland will see large numbers of small **lakes** and reed-fringed **marshes**. High rainfall and poor drainage ensure plentiful surface water, especially in winter. As a result, breeding **water birds** are extremely common and every waterway has its resident pair of swans, moorhens and herons. The lakes have a unique assemblage of plants and animals, but many of these special habitats have already been drained.

Limestone grassland, a special feature of the west of Ireland, is best exemplified by the **Burren** area in north Clare. Its main attraction is the wealth of wild flowers, which include a mixture of arctic-alpine species such as the mountain avens and Mediterranean species such as maidenhair fern all found at or near sea level. Perhaps the most striking feature is the large amount of bare rock, whose cracks and fissures give shelter to delicate plants.

The Boglands

Ten thousand years ago, when glaciers and ice sheets had stripped the soil from the Burren and retreated to the north, their melting ice left central Ireland covered by shallow lakes. As time went by the lakeside vegetation grew and died and partly decomposed, in a cycle which changed these lakes to fens, and then the fens to bogs. Ireland now boasts the finest selection of **peatlands** in Europe, but it's a terrain at risk. At one time there were 850,000 acres of raised bog in the country; by 1974 there were 175,000 acres, and by 1985 that area had shrunk to just 54,000 acres. Ireland's bogs are disappearing at a rate of 8000 acres per year, and it's only recently that environmentalists have secured protection for a few of the finest.

The exploitation of the boglands has been going on for centuries. Dried peat sod has always been used for fuel. The top layer of matted vegetation was used to insulate thatched roofs, and preserved timbers dug from the bog—some of them 5000 years old—provided stout beams for lintels. The lime-rich marl below the peat was used to fertilise the land. During World War I, sphagnum moss from the bogs was used for wound dressings, and extract of the carnivorous sundew was traditionally used to treat warts.

Because the bog preserves so well, it provides botanists with a calendar of plant history over the past 9000 years, and the archaeologist with a wealth of objects—dugout canoes, gold and silver artifacts, shoes, spears and ax heads, amber beads, wooden vessels, and of course bodies in an extraordinarily good state.

The best introduction to this landscape is to visit the **Peatland Interpretation Centre** in Lullymore, County Kildare; nearby is a fine expanse of **fenland—Pollardstown Fen**, two miles northeast of Newbridge. To see a **raised bog** of international importance, go to **Mongan Bog** in County Offaly. The bog is part of the *Clonmacnoise Heritage Zone*, which includes one of Ireland's most important monastic sites, situated on the banks of the Shannon. Ask at the tourist office at Clonmacnoise about the Shannon Callows, a wetland area of great importance to wildfowl, sadly now threatened by drainage schemes. If you are in this area in late summer and the evening is calm and fine, then go to the bridge in **Banagher**, and listen for the corncrakes as they search for mates.

For the finest example of relatively undamaged **blanket bog** you must go to the **Slieve Bloom** mountains, which straddle the counties of Laois and Offaly. The two mountain roads that divide the range rise to 1300 feet, with wonderful views in every direction across the flat plains to the distant horizons of Wicklow, Galway, Roscommon, and Waterford.

ENVIRONMENTAL ISSUES

Several of the areas of Ireland renowned for their rugged beauty—Kerry and the Dingle peninsula, Connemara, and Donegal—are now the scene of intense **gold-prospecting**. The gold finds at Croagh Patrick and Doo Lough (County Mayo) and Cornamona (County Galway) have brought an influx of mining companies. Local communities fear the economic impact of the new mines, which could damage the existing industries of farming, fishing, and tourism.

The ecological consequences are a contentious issue as well. Gold-mining is generally an activity of arid areas, and it is not clear how the technology will translate to an area of watery landscape with high rainfall. Local populations dependent on surface water for their water supply compound the problem. Of great concern is the risk of cyanide spillage and overflow, and long-term pollution from heavy metals released by mining and milling the ore. A coalition of concerned groups is now trying to raise the money to commission an independent environmental impact report.

Other environmental issues in the Republic include the **drainage of wetlands** and the consequential loss of wildfowl habitat; the **expansion of forestry**, both state and private; and the growth of the **chemical** and **pharmaceutical** industries. Over the past couple of years attention has turned to the damage being done to the country's **waterways**. A ridiculous situation had evolved whereby it was cheaper for a farmer to empty his tanks, pollute a waterway and pay the statutory fine, than to dispose of his effluent properly. Numerous fish-kills were reported, and many rivers were poisoned by effluent from silage pits and slurry tanks. A

DIRECTORY OF WILD PLACES

East

North Bull Island, Dublin Bay; NNR. Sand dunes, saltmarsh and mudflats. Large flocks of ducks, waders and brent geese in winter. Dune flowers and ferns in summer. Hares common on dunes and saltmarsh. Best months Nov–June. Interpretive center with free entry. Three miles northeast of Dublin city center on coast road to Howth.

Pollardstown Fen, Co. Kildare; NNR. Largest remaining limestone fen in Ireland. Open water surrounded by sedge and marsh vegetation. Best months June–July. No visitor facilities. Two miles northeast of Newbridge near Curragh racecourse.

Glendalough, Co. Wicklow; part NNR. Dramatic glaciated valley with two lakes and oak woodland. Rich in breeding birds. Best months April–June. Famous monastic remains. Visitor center in parking lot. Eleven miles west of Wicklow. *St Kevin's* private bus from Dublin.

Wexford Wildfowl Reserve, Co. Wexford; NNR. Flat farmland reclaimed from sea. Large flocks of Greenland white-fronted and brent geese in winter. Best months Nov–April. Visitor center with free entry open all year. Observation tower and bird-watching blinds. Two miles north of Wexford town on Gorey road.

South

Ballycotton, Co. Cork. Two coastal lakes with marshland. Famous for rare migrant birds especially North American waders in autumn. Wintering ducks and swans. Best months Sept–Oct. No visitor facilities. Southeast of Cork city.

Cape Clear Island, Co. Cork. Rocky offshore island. Famous bird observatory known for rare migrant songbirds. Good place to watch seabirds passage and occasional whales. Best months Sept–Oct. Booking necessary to stay at observatory. Daily ferry boat from Baltimore.

Skelligs, Co. Kerry; NNR. Two rocky islands. Large and spectacular seabird colonies containing mainly gannets, storm petrels, shearwaters and puffins. Best months May–July. No landing on Little Skellig but regular boat trips to Great Skellig to see early Christian monastic ruins from Portmagee and Valentia. Cost varies according to boat.

Killarney National Park, Co. Kerry. Extensive area of native woodland and bog surrounding famous lakes. Spectacular Torc waterfall and surrounding mountain ranges hold Ireland's only native herd of red deer. Best months April–May and Sept–Oct. Visitor center and nature trails. One mile south of Killarney town.

The abbreviation **NNR** signifies "National Nature Reserve"   /continues next page national outcry led to an increase in fines for such actions, and this, coupled with a campaign to educate the farming community to the effects of pollution, should improve the situation.

A recent nationwide dispute is the **rod license** dispute. The government has imposed a license fee to fish, which it says will provide funds to protect and restock the fisheries. Some anglers and angling clubs (but no means all) regard the fee as a tax and maintain that the money will not be used in the interests of fishermen. Various political bandwagons have been rolled out, and while the occupants of each hurl abuse at those of the other, the country's hotels and guesthouses lose an estimated £15 million in tourist revenue from visiting anglers. There are, however, still plenty of places to fish in Ireland, and an inquiry in the locality will indicate whether that area is levying the charge.

Tom Joyce and Richard Nairn

West

Burren, Co. Clare. Large area of limestone sidewalk famous for wild flowers. Many rare species of arctic-alpine and Mediterranean plants. Includes several turloughs (seasonal lakes). Best month May. Burren Display Center at Kilfenora. Easiest access from coast road between Ballyvaughan and Lisdoonvarna.

Cliffs of Moher, Co. Clare. Sheer limestone cliffs, spectacular in clear weather. Large colony of nesting seabirds—guillemots, razorbills, puffins, and kittiwakes. Best months May–June. Visitor center in parking lot near the cliffs is a good starting point for a walk. Six miles west of Lahinch.

Connemara, Co. Galway. Extensive area of mountain, bog, and lakes surrounded by deeply indented coastline. Interesting plant communities. High numbers of nesting herons. Mountains heavily overgrazed. Best months June–July. Visitor center and nature trails at National Park near Letterfrack, six miles north of Clifden. Oughterard–Clifden road gives good views of mountains and bogs.

Mullet Peninsula, Co. Mayo. Low, sandy spit of land linked by narow bridge to mainland. Low-intensity farming supports wild flower meadows, corncrakes, and breeding waders. Wintering barnacle geese and waders around shoreline. Best months May–June. No visitor facilities. Access via Belmullet, 38 miles west of Ballina.

North

Glenveagh National Park, Co. Donegal. Deep glaciated valley with lake surrounded by high mountain range and native woodland. Good for mountain birds and red deer. Best months April–June. Visitor center and minibus tours of park available. Twelve miles northwest of Letterkenny.

Horn Head, Co. Donegal. High sea cliffs topped by heather moorland. Large seabird colonies especially razorbill, guillemot, and kittiwake. First landfall for migrant birds from Iceland. Best months May–June. No visitor facilities. Three miles north of Dunfanaghy.

Rathlin Island, Co. Antrim; part NNR. Populated offshore island formed of chalk and basalt. Large seabird colony at western end. Good numbers of feeding buzzards. Best months May–July. No visitor facilities. Access by ferry from Ballycastle.

Strangford Lough, Co. Down; part NNR. Large land-locked inlet with numerous islands and shallows. Mudflats hold large winter flocks of waders, ducks, and brent geese. Breeding terns and common seals easily seen. Very rich marine life studies by research station at Portaferry. Best months Oct–Dec. Visitor facilities at Castleward (National Trust) six miles west of Downpatrick. Regular ferry from Strangford to Portaferry.

Central Ireland

River Shannon Callows, Athlone–Portumna. Most extensive flood plain in Ireland. Hay meadow flowers, breeding waders and corncrakes. Wintering waders, and wildfowl. Best months May–June & Nov–March. Birdwatching blind four miles west of Birr, Co. Offaly. Best access points at Banagher, Shannonbridge, or Clonmacnoise.

Clara Bog, Co. Offaly; NNR. One of largest remaining raised bogs in Ireland, with well-developed wet areas and hummock-and-hollow surface. Interesting plant communities. Best months June–July. No visitor facilities at present. One mile from Clara town.

Books

Watching Birds in Ireland, Clive Hutchinson (Country House, 1986).

IPCC Guide to Irish Peatlands, Catharine O'Connell (Irish Peatland Conservation Council, 1987).

Bellamy's Ireland: The Wild Boglands, David Bellamy (Country House, 1986).

Nature in its Place, Stephen Mills (Bodley Head).

The Personality of Ireland, E. Evans (Cambridge University Press).

A Connaught Journey, Desmond Fennell (Gill & Macmillan).

WOMEN IN IRELAND

As a female who grew up in the 1960s and 1970s, I was the unthinking beneficiary of the actions of a small group of Irish women radicals. I was also the beneficiary of a changed sociological climate and of legislation which Ireland was obliged to pass subsequent to its entry into the European Community and which conferred equal status on women as regards conditions of employment and, theoretically at least, pay. There was a farther intangible advantage to the chronological accident of my birth: an optimism rooted in the 1960s, a product of the pervasive mood of liberalism and egalitarianism, and—significant in a country that had experienced nothing but economic depression since the foundation of the state in 1921—of a growing economy. When I was growing up, there was the expectation that jobs were available for everyone. Standards of living were rising; with equal employment legislation and statutory maternity leave, more and more women were choosing to work after marriage. Circumstances such as this have a considerable impact on the way a teenage girl views her career prospects: a job then becomes not just a stop-gap between the end of education at eighteen or twenty-one and the mandatory marriage age of 25, but a career for life. In my case, the optimistic prospect was compounded by my own role model of a career mother, a rare phenomenon in rural Ireland in the 1960s.

Much of the zest of the 1960s and early 1970s has gone out of life, for many reasons: the resurgence of social and moral conservatism; economic recession and the renewed popularity of right-wing fiscal policy. For Irish women, the high unemployment rate (almost 20 percent) is bound to be an enormous obstacle to progress and fulfilment. Yet, interestingly, there have been very few public protests about married women "taking up a man's job," or about some families enjoying two incomes. The changes won dearly are not altogether lost, but progress has become slower for women. Facilities for child care are still grievously lacking and family legislation is another area where much remains to be done if women are truly to reach equal status.

No account that bears on family, social or sexual life in Ireland can omit reference to the role of the Catholic Church. Doctrinally, the Church has a curious and ambivalent position on women. It unequivocally denies them the priesthood, thereby distancing itself sharply from recent developments in the Anglican Church. In the Catholic liturgy, women are allowed only to assist the celebrant in tasks which the hierarchy glorifies but which are, in reality, menial. Like the rest of the laity, women are denied any voice in decision- or policy-making. But at least men can become priests if they want to run the Church. Simultaneously, the Catholic Church promotes the veneration of Mary, virgin mother of Christ, as a model for women, claiming that this degree of veneration elevates the status of all women. It is significant, however, that Mary is wife, mother and faithful follower, but completely asexual. This is seen as an essential aspect both of her complete sinlessness and her complete selflessness. For many Irishwomen, this role-model is a barrier to their fulfilment: not only do they have to learn to assert and enjoy their sexuality in the face of the Catholic Church's overt prohibition of sexual activity except within the bounds of marriage, but also in the face of their religion's loftiest model—an insidious pressure.

Ireland is unique among the countries of Europe in having no civil divorce—another example of the influence of the Catholic Church but not, it must be said, attributable solely to this. As recently as 1986, the Irish people voted in a referendum against introducing divorce legislation. There is no doubt that many of those who did not favor divorce were women, even though its absence greatly affects women's status and lives. Many women exist in a legal limbo of "irregular" relationships, or are abandoned by husbands who still have legal rights over them and their families. An earlier referendum allowed for the insertion of a prohibition on abortion into the constitution: a hypocritical action since Irishwomen travel freely and regularly to England to avail themselves of abortion services there.

There is a wide disparity between different women's perceptions of the Church, Irish society and the role of women. Some women, fortunate in their personal lives, fulfilled in their careers and happy in their personal relationships, wonder what all the fuss is about. Yet subtle sexism is rife, rape and molestation of women is far too common, and sexual harassment, especially in the workplace, has recently been receiving media and legal attention. Very few women, if they are honest and open their eyes, have never been on the receiving end of some form of sexist or discriminatory behavior, even if it expressed as benign paternalism. Most women shrug this off or allow themselves to be convinced by the common male argument that it is all in the spirit of fun; others take action in the courts, usually with the help of the Council for the Status of Women. A third category gives up all commerce with men, declares itself radical-feminist-lesbian-separatist and speaks of men only to denounce them. This is a small, albeit vocal minority in Ireland.

The last few years have also seen the growth of psychotherapeutic services in Ireland, mainly in the larger cities. These agencies are staffed largely by women and most of the clients are women. The kind of humanistic psychology which is generally practiced is specifically geared to combating the patriarchal model which sanctions the abuse and patronization of women. As women are much more prone than men to suffer so-called nervous breakdowns, it also provides a healing system far distanced from traditional psychiatry, which is male-dominated and conservative, like most branches of medicine. In a way, the liberation of women is a cause of many problems, in that many women are now unsure of their roles. Whereas in previous decades they were, by and large, resigned to keeping house, cherishing their husbands, and rearing their children, now their expectations are different but not always achievable. Add to this the practical problems women face in trying to combine a career and family life and the very serious problem of poverty—almost all single-parent families have a female head—and it will be understood that there is no easy solution.

Change in the status of women has not yet been reflected in the decision-making areas of Irish life. There are very few women members of the Dail, and only one female cabinet minister. Nor is the record of industry any better—women who succeed in the commercial world tend to make the headlines. There are scarcely any female professors in academic life; though girls out-achieve boys in school and as college undergraduates, they are outstripped at post-graduate and research level. The issue of the dearth of female representation is often aired in the liberal media, but change is very slow. On the other hand, women dominate the "caring" professions—teaching, nursing, and social work—and make up the bulk of the lowest-paid and temporary workers.

If you are a bright female eighteen-year-old in Ireland today you probably think that the world is your oyster. You are praised for excellence at school and can look forward to a brilliant college career. Nothing is barred to you, except full membership of certain golf clubs, and there is provision for you, in theory, to have both a family and a career. There is no point in disillusioning this bright young female—who knows, perhaps the 1990s will be a kinder decade to women in Ireland than the 1980s. So much has been done that it may only need some thousands of young people like her to achieve power and to remember her less fortunate sisters.

Jo O'Donoghue

ARCHITECTURE

BEGINNINGS

Although Ireland has a rich heritage of prehistoric remains, little of it can be discussed as "architecture," as the wealth of dolmens, burial chambers, and passage-graves are too remote to be fully understood in terms of construction, function, and use. Irish prehistoric remains do, however, attest to a highly sophisticated culture capable of astounding engineering feats. The passage-grave at **Newgrange** stands in a circle of large standing stones—similar to Stonehenge but now believed to be about 1000 years older. On the shortest day of the year, December 21, a shaft of light from the rising sun penetrates the tomb. In other words, the people who constructed this tomb were sufficiently sophisticated to have possessed an annual calendar.

The Bronze Age in Ireland (ca.2000-500 BC) is remembered more for its craft and decorative artistry (jewelry, tools, and pottery) than for its building. Little is known of domestic structures, which seem to have been constructed of wood and daub. Toward the end of this period a new type of fortified enclosure known as a hill-fort began to emerge. The great fortress of **Dun Aengus** on the Aran Island of Inismore is the most impressive piece of Iron-Age architecture, and dates possibly from the first century AD.

From the fifth century, when the island was Christianized, up to the Viking invasions of the ninth century, Ireland lived in relative peace compared with the rest of Europe. The country was divided into a series of bishoprics, which resulted in a system of scattered monasteries. As with domestic building of this period, the first churches were constructed of wood and daub, none of which have survived. The stone churches you can see now when visiting early monastic sites are of a later date. **Early Christian** monastic complexes often included round towers, a specifically Irish phenomenon. Sometimes as high as 100 yards, these towers were traditionally believed to have functioned as fortresses in times of danger, as the door was several yards off the ground. It now seems that these buildings were used as bell-towers and that the doorways were positioned high in the wall for structural purposes. One of the best-preserved towers is **Devenish**, on an island in the southeast corner of Lower Lough Erne, near Enniskillen, County Fermanagh.

FROM ROMANESQUE TO THE 17TH CENTURY

By the twelfth century the Romanesque style, imported from England and continental Europe, began to have an effect on Irish ecclesiastical building. **Cormac's Chapel** in Cashel, County Tipperary, erected between 1127 and 1134, is the earliest and best surviving example of an Irish church built in the Romanesque style, although very much a miniature version of its counterparts elsewhere. It was not until this century that Irish church builders stopped using the simple box design in favor of the basilica style—characterized by a nave, side-aisles, and a round apse at the eastern end. The religious orders such as the Cistercians, Augustinians, and Benedictines did much to propagate this change in taste. Monastic settlements such as the one at **Boyle**, County Roscommon, are very European in their layout of a cloister surrounded by church, chapter house, and dormitories. A wing of government called the Board of Works is the body responsible for most of the country's early and medieval remains; although chronically underfunded, it has achieved some major restorations.

By the end of the twelfth century much of Ireland had been brought under the control of the Normans. The Anglo-Normans, as they came to be known, introduced to Ireland the mighty stone castle of the European tradition. Good examples of the genre survive throughout the country, for example at **Trim** in County Meath and **Athenry** in County Galway. The

Anglo-Normans also introduced the Gothic style to Ireland. In Dublin, both **St Patrick's** and **Christchurch** are good examples of the early Gothic style.

Fortified dwellings of the fifteenth and sixteenth centuries tended to be smaller than their earlier prototypes. A good sixteenth-century example is **Dunguaire**, County Galway, which has been restored and is now open to the public. **Bunratty Castle**, which dates from the middle of the fifteenth century, has also been fully restored and can be visited by the public.

Rothe House in Kilkenny town, was erected in 1594, and is one of the very few examples of domestic architecture to survive from the period before 1600. It's now open as a museum. Nearly all domestic architecture of the seventeenth century has some provision for defense, reflecting the political unrest resulting from a succession of land confiscations, plantations of English settlers, and religious suppression. While tower houses were still the favored domestic building type, toward the end of the century a small number of unfortified purely domestic houses were built. **Beaulieu**, County Louth, is the best surviving example of this type. Built in red brick, Beaulieu reflects the influence of Dutch prototypes popular in England at this time.

At about the same period, the **vernacular thatched cottage** came into being. These dwellings were usually built of clay with only one or two rooms in total. Windows were small and whitewash was used both inside and out. As a type it is perfectly suited to the damp Irish climate. Its simple, humble design did, however, reflect a repressive social system based on the rights of the landlord. Often viewed as picturesque by tourists, the thatched cottage has fallen into disuse during the latter half of this century because of these unpleasant connotations.

THE 18TH CENTURY

In the 1680s the **Royal Hospital at Kilmainham**, Dublin, was built. Modeled on Les Invalides in Paris, the hospital catered for retired soldiers and consists of ranges around four sides of a courtyard. It is the first great classical building in Ireland and has recently been fully restored.

The eighteenth century in Ireland produced an unparalleled spate of building, both public and domestic. The Protestant Ascendancy, having consolidated their claim to the lands granted to them in the previous century, began to build unfortified dwellings. A parliament independent of, but subject to, Westminster sat in Dublin, the city subsequently often referred to as the second capital of the British Empire. It is still possible to get some idea of the great prosperity and confidence which emanated from this parliament by simply walking round Dublin and looking at the many splendid public buildings and elegant squares. This prosperity and confidence, however, was based on a repressive regime weighted very much in favor of the Ascendancy. The Penal Laws, as they were known, restricted Catholics from holding public office, owning property, and practicing their religion.

In the first half of the century the Palladian style (derived from the work of the sixteenth-century Italian architect Andrea Palladio) was the style favored by the Irish ruling classes, as it was by the aristocracy in England. The great **Parliament House** in Dublin (now the Bank of Ireland) was built to a design by Sir Edward Lovett Pearce between 1729 and 1739. It is the earliest large-scale Palladian public building in all Ireland or England, and was the model, a century later, for the British Museum in London. Palladianism was also the style favored for country-house architecture in the first half of the century. As a style it was extremely adaptable, producing on the one hand splendid houses that bear comparison with any in Europe, such as **Castletown**, County Kildare or **Russborough**, County Wicklow, and on the other, simpler houses built as much for utility as for ostentation, such as **Hazelwood**, County Sligo and **Ledwithstown**, County Longford.

Toward the end of the century the Neoclassical style, based on Roman and Greek prototypes, became popular. **Marino Casino** just outside Dublin was built by Sir William Chambers for Lord Charlemont during the 1760s. Intended as a country villa, the Casino is one of the most refined architectural creations in the city and is well worth a visit. **Castlecoole**, County Fermanagh, is arguably the finest Neoclassical house in Ireland. Designed by James Wyatt, it is now owned by the British National Trust and has recently been lavishly, if controversially, restored—the National Trust's new color scheme involves a shade of what the previous owner, who still lives there, calls "Mercurochrome Magenta"

Much of Ireland's Georgian architecture has disappeared. Thirty years ago Dublin was still one of the most perfectly intact eighteenth-century cities in Europe. Today, because of bad planning and inadequate legislation, much has been destroyed and lost. This century has witnessed a decline in the fortunes of the Anglo-Irish ascendancy, with many of them selling off their estates and houses, most of which are now in ruin. Because of their unsavory associations, many of these houses were destroyed by the people who for so long had been held in check by a political system completely identified with the houses. The Anglo-Irish plus their estates and mansions were viewed as alien to the country and since independence in 1922 much has been done to erase evidence of them. Happily, this situation is now changing and the Anglo-Irish heritage is beginning to be seen as something inherently Irish. A good example of this change can be seen at **Strokestown**, County Roscommon, where an outstanding Palladian house is being carefully restored by a small local mechanic's. The house is now open to the public.

Surviving eighteenth-century church architecture is not all that common. Rarest of all are surviving eighteenth-century Catholic churches, a notable exception being the **South Parish Church** in Cork, built in 1766.

THE 19TH CENTURY

In spite of the Act of Union (1800), which dissolved Ireland's independent government, building work flourished throughout the nineteenth century. An increasing number of Irish-born architects enjoyed patronage although, as in the previous century, many English architects also enjoyed considerable Irish practices. The Anglo-Irish Ascendancy, perhaps feeling farther isolated from their English contemporaries after Dublin ceased to be a center of power, embarked on vast building programs. In 1860, **Temple House**, County Sligo, originally a modest late Georgian residence, was turned into an enormous 100-room mansion which is now being run as a guesthouse.

Throughout the century, and in line with developments in England, revival of styles as diverse as Gothic, Tudor, Greek, and Oriental enjoyed great popularity. Much public architecture, such as jails, courthouses, and buildings to accommodate the fast-growing railroad system, was undertaken throughout the country. With the advent of Catholic emancipation in 1829, church architecture flourished. Although predating emancipation, the **Pro-Cathedral** in Dublin is worth mentioning. Catholic church design usually took as its inspiration Baroque French or Italian models. At the Pro-Cathedral a graceful but severe Greek revival influence is evident, a style more often associated with large-scale public building. The Victorian period, characterized by an unrestrained eclecticism, flourished all over the country and is particularly evident in much urban public and suburban building.

The Celtic Revival was also reflected in architecture, particularly church architecture. Hiberno-Romanesque was the style favored, and its influence can be seen in **Spiddal Church**, County Galway and **St Honan's Chapel**, University College Cork.

THE PRESENT

Because of the low density of population, Irish cities still possess low skylines; even today, Dublin can be said to have just one skyscraper. During the 1930s and 1940s a restrained Art Deco style made itself evident in the design of many hospitals, dance halls, and factories—for instance, the **Kodak building** in Rathmines, Dublin. Perhaps too often architects have opted to revive or invoke elements from earlier priods rather than embrace truly modern techniques, although this can also be the best option in certain cases. One side of Georgian **Mountjoy Square** in north Dublin is at present being completely rebuilt so that the street facades will at least have the proper appearance. A good example of the blending of old and new is **New Square** at Trinity College, Dublin, where modern buildings have been juxtaposed with existing ones. Perhaps the worst example of modern building is the recently erected **Civic Offices** at Wood Quay in Dublin. Commonly known as "the Bunkers," these offensive structures are doubly horrible in that they were constructed atop the most important early Viking archaeological site in Europe before it could be properly excavated.

Luke Dodd

THE MUSIC
OF IRELAND

Ireland is a very musical nation and offers plenty of opportunities to enjoy any one of its many different musical strands. The radio stations, clubs, and halls pump out an endless stream of derivatives of the country-and-western style whose popularity is ever-increasing. *Céilí (ceilidh)* bands are rented for the village weekend dances to bang out the boisterous rhythms of the set-dance tunes, and the pubs host raucous ballad-singing, the repertoire ranging from heartfelt love songs through to equally heartfelt rebel songs. (Some of the greatest date from the 1798 revolution—for example, "The Croppy Boy" and "The Wearing of the Green." However, it is what is termed the **traditional music** culture that is by far the most intriguing and characteristic musical aspect to Ireland.

The turn-of-the-century English composer Arnold Bax said of the traditional music that "of all the antiquities in the world Ireland possesses the most varied and beautiful music," yet of all countries Ireland is the worst in appreciating and looking after its tradition. But a great revival of the tradition did take place in the 1960s at the instigation of the Irish composer **Seán O'Riarda**, when "sessions" (an *ad hoc* group of players improvising together) took place in pubs all over the country. Interest has now waned once again, as publicans attend to more commercial interests. In fact the pub is not a very good environment in which to appreciate the full brilliance of the music, but it seems there is no alternative to the pub session available at the moment.

Some places hold "open sessions," which are open to outsiders—make sure you gauge the class of performers before joining in. If you're there to listen, you shouldn't sit right by the players, for it's probable that space is being kept for late arrivals.

The Forms and State of Irish Music

Although Ireland is part of Western Europe its music is much more akin to oriental forms. European classical music develops a very broad structure beginning with one idea (or two) that is taken through a crescendo eventually to arrive at a climax, which then resolves into a catharsis. Irish traditional music, on the other hand, unfolding in a cyclical pattern: the basic element of a song or tune remains the same in each repetition, with miniscule events of ornamentation and variation giving the music its distinctive texture (and testing the mettle of the player). Unlike the European tradition, there are no dynamics in the Irish tradition and you'll see this physically reflected in the emotionally uninvolved posture that most musicians assume while playing.

Unfortunately, the European dimension of modern Irish society has now all but suffocated the source of this culture, and most of the young players are unable to resist the influences of both European classical and popular music. This diagnosis may at first seem baseless, because you'll find plenty of lively-looking sessions on the midwest coast, especially around Clare. Yet enjoyable though these may be, few represent what was once the best of Ireland's musical culture. To begin with, the music is best heard from an individual musician, and groups of more than three cannot preserve the clarity of the pieces. Bands such as the **Chieftains**, the **Bothy Band** and **Clannad**, have produced interesting material spun off from the tradition, but the genuine product is more likely to come from a single musician playing in South Sligo, Wexford, or Clare.

The Style of Singing

The heart of the Irish traditional music ethic lies in the **sean nós** style of singing, in which the singer is not allowed to sing any two verses of a song in the same way—tantamount to asking him to act as a composer as well as performer. Some songs have only two lines, presenting the ultimate challenge to the interpreter's skill.

The variations must be distinctly audible and yet small enough to maintain the basic structure of the song. Singers instinctively call upon a variety of improvisational techniques: glottal stopping or clicking to shut off the voice in midphrase; drawing attention to a single note or group of notes by nasalizing the voice (but this should be used very sparingly); melisma; lengthening and shortening of intervals and notes; and changing stresses and speeds. Each region has its distinctive devices: the Connemara style, for instance, is traditionally very melismatic with a compressed vocal range, while the Munster style has a wider range and is slightly more nasal. These regional differences are becoming less marked; the older the singer, the more obvious they'll be. Sadly, it's not often that you'll come across *sean nós* singers, as they tend to perform in small social groups rather then public places. *Róisín Dubh* and *Eileinn Aroon* are among the most popular songs in the tradition.

The Uillean Pipes

The instrument best able to emulate the voice is the **uillean pipes** (elbow pipes) which came into being during the seventeenth century, but only took on their present shape early in the eighteenth. Nearly every country in the world has some form of bagpipe, but few are as complex as these. The seven-holed wooden tube held in the player's hands is known as the "chanter"; players cover the holes an inch down from the fingertip, a technique that enables the tone to be varied. The chanter is capable of a two-octave range, with the silver keys to the side of the holes creating extra semitone notes within the basic scale of D major. As for the mechanics of it—the double reed within the metal tubing is vibrated by dry air from the leather bag squeezed by the left elbow, which itself is fed from the bellows being squeezed by the right elbow. Notice how the chanter is sometimes pushed down on a popping pad, a piece of leather wrapped around the player's thigh. This produces the upper octave but is also used to great effect for clipping the notes, which is superb for the rhythm of the faster tunes.

This basic assembly of bag, bellows, and chanter is called a half set. The virtuoso instrument has an extra set of tubes providing regulators (keys for making up harmonic chords) and drones (offering three octaves of the fundamental note D). The stylistic flourishes to listen out for are the cranning (a repeated note preceded by a fast grace note) and the roll (dipping to a lower note to approach the main note from below). The mark of great piper is the judicious but imaginative use of the regulators, not too much popping and an ability to emulate the *sean nós* style—especially in the slow airs, for which the naturally plaintive sound of the instrument is so suitable. One of the finest players ever on the instrument was Johnny Doran; today both **Davy Spillane** and **Paddy Maloney** are excellent pipers.

The Fiddle

The violin in Irish music, commonly called the **fiddle**, differs from the classical instrument only in the way it's played. It is often held resting on the shoulder without chin support; only a small section of the bow is used (necessary for articulating the rapid notes); and the player stays mainly on the bottom two strings, with the bottom G string sometimes used as an intermittent drone or chord maker.

As with *sean nós* singing, nearly every cultural area of the country has its own approach to the instrument and its repertoire. (Although, similarly, there's a growing uniformity.) For instance, the Donegal style is characterized by a relatively smooth and slick sound, and a heavy leaning of the bow producing a louder volume. The Sligo style, only a little farther south in the country, is more flamboyant, with a liberal use of ornaments and a lightly pronounced tick-over in the rhythm. (The greatest fiddler Ireland ever had was a Sligoman, **Michael Coleman**.) In Clare the rhythmic component is much stronger than in any other area, the normal run of quaver notes nearly becoming a regular long–short, long–short sequence.

The fiddle should be heard on its own and certainly never with a piano vamping out chords to accompany it.

The Flute and the Whistle

The Irish **flute** is a wooden instrument, descended from the German model of a hundred years ago. Again it's pitched in the key of D with a range of a couple of octaves, though in Irish music it rarely leaves the bottom octave, producing a really mellow sound even in the fast tunes. Again there are regional styles of approach, the Sligo and Leitrim one being the best known. A native Sligo player tends to break up the phrases but also extend the phrase length, using little ornamentation – unlike the fiddle playing in the region. Clare, in comparison, uses gentle rolling ornamentation and is not as emphatic with its rhythm, but makes an interesting rhythmical peculiarity by accenting the offbeats. The **tin whistle** is regarded as the toy of Irish instruments only by those who have never heard a good player. Many pipers are also whistle-players, as both possess a sharp upper-frequency quality and permit the same types of rapid ornamentation. If you're buying a whistle to learn, the D whistle is the one to get, for most of Irish music is in this key. Before buying, give the instrument a try to make sure the plastic top allows a clear and unfuzzy tone—some don't. The higher octave is obtained by just blowing harder, and lots of in-between notes can be produced with cross-fingerings and half-covering. This latter technique is now used a lot to create little slides up to the main notes, especially for laments and slow airs.

The Accordion and Concertina

Two types of accordion are used for Irish music. The **piano accordion** is not highly thought of, because of the virtually complete lack of control the player has over its tone production and rhythmic articulation. However, its size of tone is used to great advantage as a "filler-in" sound for the *céilí* bands. Articulation on the **button accordion** is a little bit better, as the bellows produce a different note when being compressed from the one produced during extension. It's getting much more popular now with the young musicians and is a delight to listen to at first. Its limited musical scope soon becomes obvious, though. To get out of these inherent difficulties many players revert to excessive, sugary ornamentation. The **concertina**, also popular with the younger players, has a lightness of tone that makes it far more suitable for delivering the brittle bareness that is the predominant characteristic of most Irish tunes.

The Bodhrán, Bones, and Spoons

The most ancient of all Irish instruments is the **bodhrán**, which may date from the Bronze Age. It's a small, shallow circular drum with a skin on one side, usually goatskin, and is often played with a small stick that has beaters at both ends to facilitate double and triple rhythms. Sometimes the skin is played with the bare hand, producing a more subtle scale of sounds. Sounds are also struck on the wooden rim, and for pitch variation the left hand can be used to affect the tuning of the skin by pressing into it. The best of players will use the instrument sparingly to augment or rub against the rhythms of the pitched instruments rather than cloud everything with a continuous roll of beats.

The **bones** (rib-bones of a sheep, goat or cow) make another purely rhythmical instrument and are ideal for traditional music. Two bones are held between the thumb, index, and middle fingers and are played in a castenet style—usually using the left hand as a ceiling and the thigh as a base about nine inches below. **Spoons** are also used nowadays in a similar fashion, but they interfere with the timbre of the other instruments.

The Harp

The normal-sized **harp** rarely appears as part of an ensemble, owing to its weaker voice and its sheer size. (There's a smaller version, the *clarseach*, which appears at the occasional session.) Yet the harp began traditional music as we know it today. From 1100 to 1600 the harpists and the poets provided the "art music" for the Gaelic Chieftains, and it is not often acknowledged how intimately connected are the familiar tunes to those early Gaelic meters. With the demise of the Gaelic courts after the Battle of Kinsale in 1601 the native music became diluted by an influx of British tunes. The skill of the harpist flourished for another hundred years, but eventually perished in the mid-nineteenth century, leaving few details of performance styles.

The harpist of the seventeenth and eighteenth centuries would have traveled the new Anglo-Irish households with his freshly composed tunes, compositions that acknowledged the master's acquaintance with the mainstream European musical tradition. **O'Carolan** was the most famous of all the harpists and his love of the Italian composer Corelli is obvious in the hundred or so melodies left us.

Dancing

Irish dancing is inextricably linked to the music tradition, but nowadays it has become either too loose and uncreative—as at most *céilís* (although they're still great fun) —or too formal, largely through the competitive festivals (although they are better than nothing at all). Gone is the old tradition when a musician would have taken up a place at the village corner and couples would have arrived in ordinary dress to dance. The costumes you'll see today at every *feis*—green dress, embroidered Celtic designs, black stockings, white apron—only arrived on the scene at the time of the Gaelic revival at the end of the last century. In the opinion of the purists, the complexity and rigidity of movement seen in supposedly authentic performances is throttling the creative development of the art.

IRISH LITERATURE

Samuel Beckett, in an interesting turn of phrase, maintained that Irish writers had been "buggered into existence by the English army and the Roman pope." Oscar Wilde sighed to Yeats that "we Irish have done nothing, but we are the greatest talkers since the Greeks." Both were right. Politics, religion and literature in Ireland have always been inextricably linked, sometimes in a futile attempt to escape from each other. And the suppression of the Irish language did give rise to a fresh and vital use of colloquial English that somehow retained the musical rhythms of the dying tongue. But it's a more complex story than that, and any outline of Ireland's vast canon of very different literatures has to go back a long way.

THE GAELS

Irish writing first appeared in the fifth century AD when monastic settlers brought classical culture into contact with a Gaelic civilization that had a long and sophisticated oral tradition. Faced with the resistance of the pagan bards, the newcomers set about incorporating the Celtic sagas into the comparatively young system of Christian belief. These ancient tales told of war and famine, madness and love, death and magical rebirth—story sequences from deep in the folk memory. One of the earliest of these, the *Táin Bó Cuailnge*, deals with a ruckus between **Cúchulainn**, a prototypical Celtic superman, and the mighty Queen Medb over the theft of a prize bull.

Later Irish artists made much use of the early tales, sometimes with less than proper reverence—in Beckett's novel *Murphy*, for instance, a character attempts suicide by banging his head repeatedly against the buttocks of the statue of Cúchulainn which still adorns the lobby of Dublin's GPO. New versions still appear from time to time, Seamus Heaney's translation of the mythical wanderings of the mad king Sweeney Astray being particularly brilliant.

Fairy tales from this Celtic era reveal a world of witches, imps, and banshees, all cavorting around in a manichaean struggle with the forces of love, wisdom, and goodness—which, refreshingly, do not always triumph. Check out Kevin Danaher's *Folk Tales of the Irish Countryside* for full-blooded retellings.

In the eighth century **Finn Mac Cumaill** toppled Cúchulainn from the top of the folk hero charts, and stories of his exploits with his posse, the Fianna, began to appear. Finn was a more disturbing and sophisticated figure, and his antics can be read in various modern translations.

The first of many incursions from England took place in the twelfth century, when gangs of Norman adventurers invaded at the invitation of an Irish High King. But it wasn't until five centuries later that the English presence found its way into the literature, when the excesses of English rule began finally to provoke an early literature of resistance.

The high point of this Gaelic tradition is the 1773 long poem by **Eibhlin Dhubh Ni Chonaill** (1748–1800), *Caoineadh Airt Ui Laoghaire*. (In English, *A Lament for Art O'Leary*.) A traditional *caoineadh* or lament infused with a new political awareness, it deals with the execution of the poet's lover, who had refused to sell his prized white horse to the local redcoat and was therefore hunted down and killed. Even in translation it has a sparse and chilling beauty.

Other marvelous laments include the anonymous *Donal Og*, Lady Gregory's translation of which was included with cheeky but effective license in the 1985 John Huston film of Joyce's short story, *The Dead*. But the early written tradition wasn't all tears, and some pieces harked back to a pre-Christian earthiness. One such text from the later Gaelic era is **Brian Merriman**'s satirical *aisling* (vision poem), *Cuairt an Mhean Oiche* (The Midnight Court), a trenchant attack on the sexual inadequacy of the Irish male. One translation which preserves the raunch of the original is by Frank O'Connor, in *Kings, Lords and Commons*.

Despite persecution the Irish language persisted well into the last century and Thomas Kinsella's book of translations, *An Duanaire: Poems of the Dispossessed*, records the voices of those marginalized by foreign rule and famine. But thanks to the ineptitude of successive Irish governments, the Irish language is now in an advanced state of decay. Despite occasional revivals, contemporary Gaelic literature has been almost completely wiped out. Urban Irish schoolchildren are forced into reading **Peig Sayers** (1873–1958), a miserable native of the Blaskets whose sentences usually start with "God between us and all harm" or "Ah sure, life, what can you do?" Arguably the finest of modern Gaelic writers is **Padraig O'Conaire** (1883–1928), whose statue stands in Eyre Square, Galway. His *Scoithscealta* reads like Maupassant, capturing the stark cruelty of the Irish landscape and the petty malices of rural life. But unless you want to know about turf-cutting, hill-farming and getting up at five in the morning to milk your one mangy cow, recent Gaelic literature is generally unrewarding.

THE START OF A LITERARY TRADITION

Between the 1690s and the 1720s the hated Penal Laws were passed, denying Catholics rights to property, education, political activity, and religious practice. British misrule created widespread poverty which devastated the countryside and ravaged the population. It's in this period that Anglo-Irish literature began.

One of the most prominent of the early pamphleteers and agitators was **John Toland** (1670–1722) whom the authorities gave the dubious distinction of being the first Irish writer to have his work publicly burned. But the first big-league player arrived in the angry little shape of **Jonathan Swift** (1667–1745), Dean of Saint Patrick's Cathedral, Dublin. Swift was a cantankerous but basically compassionate man who used his pen to expose viciousness, hypocrisy, and corruption whenever he saw it, which in eighteenth-century Dublin, was pretty often. In one of his 75 pamphlets he proposed that the poor should be cooked to feed the rich, thereby getting rid of poverty and increasing affluence. His masterpiece is *Gulliver's Travels* (1726), a satire as terrifying now as it ever was. Following a life of unrequited love he died a bitter man, and in his will he left an endowment to build Dublin's first lunatic asylum, adding in a pithy codicil that if he'd had enough money he would have arranged for a twenty-foot-high wall to be built around the entire island. He is buried in the vault of Saint Patrick's, where, as his epitaph says, "Savage indignation can rend his heart no more."

The elegant prose of **Edmund Burke** (1729–97)—graduate of Trinity College, philosopher, journalist, and MP—argued for order in all things, decrying the French Revolution for its destruction of humanity's basic need for faith. He is a complex and difficult figure, and his ideas are claimed in Ireland both by the civil-liberties-trampling Right and by elements of the progressive Left.

1780–1880: THE CELTIC REVIVAL

A new interest in the Scottish and Welsh Celtic tradition was exported to Ireland, prompting a renaissance in Irish music and an interest in all things Celtic, vague, and misty. A couple of important books appeared, including **Joseph Cooper Walker**'s *Historical Memoirs of the Irish Bards* (1786) and **Edward Bunting**'s *General Collection of Irish Music* (1796).

Dublin at the time of the Act of Union with Britain (1801) had long been a truly European city, frequently visited by French, German, and Italian composers. Indeed, Handel's *Messiah* was first performed in Dublin's Fishamble Street. One Irish composer and writer who thrived under the European influence was the harpist **Turlough O'Carolan**, (1670–1738), who met and traded riffs with the Italian composer Geminiami.

At the turn of the century a series of Irish harp festivals began, their purpose being to recover the rapidly disappearing ancient music. With their evocation of the bardic tradition they became a focus not just for nifty fingerwork but for political agitation as well. The harpers harped on into the nineteenth century until **Thomas Moore** (1779–1852) finally appropriated many of their traditional airs, wrote words for them, published them as *Moore's Irish Melodies,* and made a lot of money. (Carolan had died in a hovel.)

The concomitant literary revival entailed a resurrection of the Irish language too, and although few went so far as to learn it, it became a vague symbol of a heroic literary past that implied a fundamentally nationalist worldview. **John Mitchell**'s Fenian movement, provoked by Britain's callous response to the Famine, was at least as influenced by the Celtic rvival as it was by the new revolutionary ideas being imported all the time from Europe. Particularly in their impact on Yeats, the

Fenians were to provide a bridge between the heroic past and the demands of modernism. One of their supporters, **James Clarence Mangan** (1803–1849), inaugurated in *My Dark Rosaleen* the image of suffering Ireland as a brutalized woman, awaiting defense by a heroic man. In a country where visual and literary imagery of the Virgin Mary is ubiquitous, the symbolism escaped nobody.

THE 19TH-CENTURY NOVEL

The unease generated among the aristocracy by growth of Irish nationalism and the Fenian Rebellion of 1848 found expression in novels showing the peasantry plotting away in their cottages against their masters up in the manse—the "Big House" sub-genre of Anglo-Irish writing, represented by such writers as **Lady Morgan** (1775–1859). Typically, such a book will involve an evil-smelling Irish hoodlum inheriting the mansion and either turning it into a barn or burning it to the ground. *Castle Rackrent* by **Maria Edgeworth** (1776–1849) is one of the few good "Big House" novels, its craftily resourceful narrator telling the story of the great family's demise with a subtle glee.

The Irish fought back, appropriating the well-made novel for themselves. **Gerald Griffin** (1803–1840), **John Banim** (1796–1874), **William Carleton** (1794–1869), and **Charles Lever** (1806–1872) emerged as the voice of the new middle class, protesting at the stereotyping of the Irish as savages, and demanding political and economic rights.

Meanwhile **Bram Stoker** (1847–1912) was busily writing his way into the history books with a novel that would enter modern popular culture in all its forms, from the movies to the comic book. *Dracula* is a wonderful book, more of a psychological Gothic thriller than a schlock horror bloodbath, and its concerns—the nature of the soul, for instance, versus the bestial allure of the body—are curiously Irish. But even this had its political implications. With its pseudo-folkloric style and its pitting of the noble peasants against the aristocratic monster debauching away in his castle, its symbolism is inescapably revolutionary and romantic.

E. O. Somerville (1858–1949) and **Violet** (alias **Martin**) **Ross** (1861–1915) close the century with *Some Recollections of an Irish RM*. The partnership's work is imbued with a genuine love of Ireland and the ways of the Irish peasantry, yet occasionally there's a chilling sense of things not being quite right. The Irish had invaded English literature. Previously marginalized in the tradition, the peasants now seem to keep intruding, sneaking into the upstairs rooms, interrupting their betters, conspiring behind the bushes in the well-kept gardens. And we see them in ominous prophecy of things to come, wielding ploughshares and scythes which slowly begin, in the gray light of Galway which the two genteel old ladies capture so well, to look like weapons.

THE STORY OF THE STAGE IRISHMAN

It's one of the delicious twists of fate which seem to beset Irish literary history that the country's most important early dramatist only took up writing by mistake. One evening a young Derry actor named **George Farquhar** was playing a bit part in the duel scene of Dryden's *Indian Emperor* at the Dublin Smock Alley theater when, in a moment of tragic enthusiasm, he accidentaly stabbed a fellow actor, almost killing him. Understandably shaken, Farquhar gave up the stage for good and went of to London to write plays instead.

Farquhar (1677–1707) is often credited, if that is the right word, with the invention of the stage Irishman, the descendants of whom can still be seen on many of the programs euphemistically referred to as "situation comedies" on British television. Effusive in his own way, but basically sly, stupid and violent, this stock character stumbled through the dramas of **Steele** (1672–1729), **Chaigneau** (1709–1781), **Goldsmith** (1728–1774), and **Sheridan** (1751–1816), tugging his forelock, bumping into the furniture and going "bejayzus" at every available moment. In fact Irish stereotypes had existed in the British tradition for many centuries before these chaps had at least the good sense to make some money out of them. The stage Irishman was brought to his ultimate idiocy by **Dion Boucicault** (1820–1890), whose leprechaunic characters seemed to have staggered straight out of the "Big House" novel and onto the London stage. Boucicault's chum, **George Bernard Shaw** (1856–1950) turned out to be the kind of stage Irishman the English couldn't patronize out of existence. A radical socialist and feminist, he championed all kinds of cranky causes and some very admirable ones, and lived long enough to be a founding member of the Campaign for Nuclear Disarmament. His cerebral and often polemical plays—of which *Saint Joan* is perhaps the best—have remained a mainstay of theater repertoire. Yet even Shaw paled in comparison to the ultimate king of the one-line put-down, **Oscar Wilde** (1856–1900). After a brilliant career at Oxford—during which he lost both his virginity and his Irish accent—Wilde went on to set literary London alight, creating the smiling resentment that would finally destroy him. In *The Picture of Dorian Gray* he expanded on the Gothic tradition of Stoker and Sheridan Le Fanu (1814–73) to explore the fundamental duality of the romantic hero. But it was in his satirical plays, particularly *The Importance of Being Earnest*, that he was at his most acerbic. A brilliant and gentle man, he poured scorn on his critics, openly espoused home rule for Ireland and lived with consummate style until the debacle of his affair with Lord Alfred Douglas. This self-obsessed bimbo persuaded Wilde into a foolish libel action against his thuggish father, the Marquess of Queensbury, which Wilde lost. Immediately afterwards he was arrested for homosexuality, publicly disgraced, and privately condemned by his many fair-weather friends. He served two years in prison where he wrote his finest works, *The Ballad of Reading Gaol* and *De Profundis*. In early 1900 Ireland's greatest, and saddest, comedian died alone and distraught in Paris. "I will never live into the new century," he declared;"The English would just not allow it."

IRISH MODERNISM: POETRY AND DRAMA

Shortly before Wilde's death, the myth of the fallen hero had entered the vocabulary of Irish literature with the demise of Charles Stuart Parnell, Protestant hero of the Irish nationalist community. Savaged from the pulpit and the editorial page for his adulterous involvement with Kitty O'Shea, Parnell had resigned in disgrace with only a few lonely voices in the literary world defending him. He died shortly afterwards and Irish constitutional politics died with him.

The changed atmosphere of Irish life is caught in the work of **J. M. Synge** (1871–1909) and **George Moore** (1852–1933), who wrestled to accommodate a tradition they now saw rapidly slipping into the hands of the priests. Synge's *The Playboy of the Western World*, with its patricidal hero, is the last and perhaps the most brilliant attempt at a fundamentally English view of Irish peasant life, and was greeted by riots when it opened at the *Abbey Theatre*. His friend George Moore identified Catholicism as a life-denying and authoritarian creed, and his extraordinary volume *The Untilled Field* in many ways anticipates much later writers.

Meanwhile the separatist *Sinn Fein* party made great advances, and in 1916, led by the poet **Patrick Pearse** (1879–1916) and **James Connolly** (1868–1916), an important socialist figure and powerful writer, mounted an armed insurrection in Dublin. It was crushed savagely. Connolly and all the other leaders were court-martialled and shot, thereby becoming heroes overnight, and leading Yeats to observe that everything had been "changed utterly" and that "a terrible beauty" had been born.

William Butler Yeats (1865–1939) is one of the most written-about but most elusive characters in Irish literature. A Protestant aristocrat who argued for Irish independence, he helped found the world's first national theater, *the Abbey*, before the nation even existed. He wrote early lyrical ballads about gossamer fairies and stunning sunsets until, stricken with desire for the beautiful Maude Gonne, he began cranking out some of the century's greatest works of unrequited love. Much of the work of his middle period lambasts the Dublin middle class for its money-grubbing complacency—*September 1913* is well worth a read if white-lipped rage is your thing. The late period is more problematic, producing a series of spare, lucid but complex meditations on the artist's task, but also some dubious marching songs for the fascist Blueshirt movement.

Until the 1920s Yeats maintained friendship with **Sean O'Casey** (1884–1964), who was that rarest of things, a working-class Irish writer. The Dublin slums in which he was born were later immortalized in his trilogy *Shadow of a Gunman*, *Juno and the Paycock*, and *The Plough and the Stars*. As with Synge, O'Casey's opening nights were occasions for rioting and his plays were usually attended by more policemen than paying customers. Indeed one night, in one of the more unusual moments in Irish literary history, Yeats had to lead the cops' charge into the stalls to break up the fracas. Later he harangued the audience, screeching that the very fact they had broken up his play meant that O'Casey was a genius, and that "this was his apotheosis." O'Casey's journal records that while he smiled nervously and twiddled his thumbs backstage he couldn't wait to get home so that he could look up the word "apotheosis" in the dictionary. O'Casey is currently the subject of a misplaced revisionism which condemns his plays as sentimental and preachy.

MODERN IRISH FICTION

As the tide of history turned towards nationalism and republicanism, and Yeats wondered glumly whether the tradition would die with the aristocracy, one of the seminal figures of literary modernism was emerging in Dublin. While still a student at the new University College—founded in 1908 by Cardinal John Henry Newman to provide a college for Catholic middle-class youth—**James Joyce** (1882–1941) set himself against the world of politics and religion, and announced that he would become, in his own phrase, "a high priest of art." His subsequent career was to be the epitome of obsessive dedication.

Dubliners, his first book, continued where George Moore had left off, evoking the city as a deathly place, its citizens quietly atrophying in a state of emotional paralyzis. *A Portrait of the Artist as a Young Man* is largely autobiographical and deals with Stephen Dedalus' decision to leave Ireland, criticizing the country as a priest-ridden and superstitious dump. After ten years of trying to get it published, Joyce finally had the bad luck to get it printed in 1916, year of the Easter Rising. Perhaps understandably, lack of patriotism was not fashionable. Joyce was condemned by just about everyone who mattered and quite a few people who didn't.

His next novel, *Ulysses*, came out in 1922, another flashpoint in Irish history, as the new Irish government turned its guns on its former supporters. Modeled on Homer's *Odyssey*, the book follows Stephen Dedalus and Leopold Bloom through one day and one night of Dublin life, recording their experiences with a relish and precision that repulsed the critics, including Virginia Woolf and D. H. Lawrence. The book was widely banned and its self-exiled author was condemned as a pornographer. *Ulysses* is a kaleidoscope of narrative techniques; Joyce's last work, the vast *Finnegans Wake*, is the only true polyglot novel, a bewitching—and often impenetrable—stew of languages, representing the history of the world as dreamed by its hero, Humphrey Chimden Earwicker (alias "Here Comes Everybody," "Haveth Childers Everywhere" etc). Critics of different persuasions see it as either the pinnacle of literary modernism, or the greatest folly in the history of the novel.

The other great Irish modernist, **Samuel Beckett** (b. 1906) emigrated to Paris and became Joyce's secretary in 1932. One writer has remarked that while Joyce tried to include everything in his work Beckett tried to leave everything out, and that's a pretty good summary. Beckett is bleak, pared down, exploring the fundamental paradox of the futility of speech and its absolute necessity. A modernist in his devotion to verbal precision, Beckett is on the other hand a dominant figure in what has been termed the postmodern "literature of exhaustion." As he said recently—"I have never been on my way anywhere, but simply on my way." Despite his reputation for terseness, Beckett has been a prolific writer—the best places to start are the trilogy of novels (*Molloy*, *Malone Dies*, and *The Unnamable*), and the play *Waiting for Godot*.

The absurdity of **Flann O'Brien** (1912–1966) goes a little easier on the desperation. His comic vision of Purgatory, *The Third Policeman*, includes the famous molecular theory, which proposes that excessive riding of a bicycle can lead to the mixing of the molecules of rider and machine—hence a character who is half-man, half-bike. O'Brien's other great book, *At Swim-Two-Birds*, is a weird melange of mythology and pastiche that plays around with the notion that fictional characters might have a life independent of their creators. Under one of his several pseudonymns, Myles Na Gopaleen (Myles of the Little Horse) he wrote a daily column for the *Irish Times* for many years, and his hilarious journalism is collected in *The Best of Myles* and *Myles Away to Dublin*.

Traditional fiction continued of course—for instance, **Brinsley MacNamara** (1890–1963) devastatingly portrayed small-town life in *The Valley of the Squinting Windows*. But many writers had moved away from social observation and into a kind of modernist fantasy that had its roots way back in the Celtic twilight. **James Stephens** (1882–1950), a writer with an unjustly insignificant international reputation, used absurdity as a route to high lyricism. His *The Crock of Gold* is a profoundly moving fantasy on the Irish mythological tradition, part fairy story and part post-Joycean satire—in a sense, a precursor of "Magic Realism."

POSTWAR LITERATURE

Ireland in the late Forties and Fifties suffered severe economic recession and another wave of emigration began. Added to this, the people had in 1937 passed a constitution—still operational today—which enshrined the Catholic church's teachings in the laws of the land. Intolerance and xenophobia were bolstered by an economic war against Britain and a campaign of state censorship which was truly Stalinist in its vigor. Books which had never been read were snipped, shredded, and scorched by committees of pious civil servants. No history of postwar Irish literature would be complete without at least a mention of *The Bell*, a highly influential but now defunct literary magazine. In the mid-Fifties it was a forum for writers like **Frank O'Connor** (1903–1966), **Liam O'Faolain** (b. 1900) and **Liam O'Flaherty** (1897 - 1984), all of whom were veterans of the Independence War, and all of whom became outstanding short-story writers. They chronicled the raging betrayal they felt at state censorship and social intolerance – O'Connor's *Guests of the Nation* is perhaps the most eloquent epitaph for Ireland's revolutionary generation, a terrifying tale of the execution of two British soldiers by the IRA that influenced Brendan Behan's *The Hostage* enormously. *The Bell* also opened its pages to writers like **Peadar O'Donnell** (1893–1985), a radical socialist who, only six months before he died in 1985, publicly burned his honorary degree from the National University of Ireland on the occasion of a similar honor being conferred on Ronald Reagan.

In an infamous speech President Eamonn de Valera envisioned a new rural Ireland full of "comely maidens dancing at the crossroads and the laughter of athletic youths." But writers such as **Denis Devlin** (1908–1959), **Francis Stuart** (b. 1902), **Mary Lavin** (b. 1912), and **Brian Moore** (b. 1921) took up the

fight for truth against propaganda. Their youths and maidens didn't dance. They were too busy packing their bags, or wandering in bewilderment across the desolate pages of an Ireland that had failed to live up to its possibilities. In their poetry **Austin Clarke** (1896–1974) and **Thomas Kinsella** (b. 1928) mourned the passing of hope into despair and fragmentation.

Patrick Kavanagh (1906–1967) was an exception to all the rules. His poetry is almost entirely parochial, celebrating what he called "the spirit-shocking wonder of a black slanting Ulster hill," and his contemplative celebrations of the ordinary made him perhaps Irelands's best-loved poet. But as time went on, the harshness of reality began to press in on his work. His long poem *The Great Hunger* portrays rural Ireland—the same Ireland that Kavanagh had extolled—as physically barren, with the blasted landscape an incisive metaphor for sexual repression. Its publication was widely condemned and the writer was even questioned by the police, an event he discussed with customary venom in his own newspaper, *Kavanagh's Weekly*.

The forces of reaction were again about to wage war on Irish literature. O'Casey's anti-clerical play *The Drums of Father Ned* was produced in Dublin in 1955 and received aggressive reviews. Three years later there was a proposal to revive it for the new Dublin Theater Festival. The Catholic archbishop of Dublin, John Charles McQuaid, insisted that the plans be dropped, and when the trade unions stepped into the fray on his behalf, His Grace got his way. The year before, the young director Alan Simpson had been arrested and his entire cast threatened with imprisonment for indecency following the first night in Dublin of Tennessee Williams's play *The Rose Tattoo*. The important novelist **John McGahern** (b. 1935) lost his teaching job in a Catholic school in 1966 following the publication of his second book *The Dark*. It's a marvelous novel, dealing tenderly with adolescence and clerical celibacy, and was immediately banned.

A more celebrated literary victim—in this case a self-destructive one—was **Brendan Behan**, who died in 1964, only six years after the publication of his first book, *Borstal Boy*. He spent the last years of his life as a minor celebrity, reciting his books into tape recorders in Dublin pubs, drunk and surrounded by equally drunk admirers, some of whom sobered up for long enough to try and save him from becoming the victim of his own myth.

CONTEMPORARY WRITING

It was only in the Seventies that the climate of repression began to lift, and a sophisticated and largely progressive generation began to publish. **Seamus Heaney** (b. 1939) came to prominence as the unofficial leader of an unofficial group of Northern Irish poets who combine a sophistication of technique with a thoughtful political commitment. **John Banville** (b. 1945) brought out his first book, *Long Lankin*, in 1970—a precocious debut that has been followed by a string of extraordinarily inventive novels.

The *Irish Writers' Co-Op* produced novelists such as **Desmond Hogan** (b. 1951), **Ronan Sheehan** (b. 1953), and **Neil Jordan** (b. 1951), the last of whom has gone on to major international acclaim as a film director (*Company of Wolves, Mona Lisa*). Courageous young publishing companies founded by writers began to appear, of which Peter Fallon's **Gallery**, Dermot Bolger's **Raven Arts Press**, and Steve McDonogh's **Brandon** are still going from strength to strength.

At the end of the decade **Paul Durcan** (b. 1944) emerged as the inheritor of Kavanagh's mantle. He is a quirkily witty and profoundly religious poet, whose work encompasses social issues such as IRA bombings and Ireland's prohibition of divorce and abortion, but always addresses them in personal terms.

Other important poets include **Richard Murphy** (b. 1927), **Brendan Kennelly** (b. 1936), **Michael Hartnett** (b. 1941), **Padraic Fiacc** (b. 1924), **Derek Mahon** (b. 1941), **Michael Longley** (b. 1939), **Medbh McGuckian,** (b. 1950) and **Eavan Boland** (b. 1944). Even more recently **Christopher Nolan** (b. 1965), a severely disabled writer, has proved to be an amazing talent, employing a rich language reminiscent of Dylan Thomas. His first book of poetry, *Damburst of Dreams*, received great acclaim and he later won the Whitbread Prize for his autobiographical novel *Under The Eye of The Clock.*

Drama has undergone a resurgence too, with Galway's *Druid Theater* doing groundbreaking reinterpretations of Irish classics under the guidance of its brilliant director Garry Hynes. Roddy Doyle and Paul Mercier's *Passion Machine* theater company offers plays about urban working-class experience in the manner of Stephen Berkoff or John Godber. Two other good young companies whose work is political and challenging, if more international in scope, are *Co-Motion* and *Rough Magic*. A more established and successful company is *Field Day*, a northern-based team founded by poets **Seamus Deane** (b. 1940) and **Tom Paulin** (b. 1949), and playwright **Brian Friel** (b. 1929). In addition to producing plays, *Field Day* publishes an excellent series of cultural and critical journalism pamphlets.

Any list of Ireland's innovative theater writers must include **Thomas Murphy** (b. 1936) and **Thomas Kilroy** (b. 1934), but in the opinion of many the most important dramatist to emerge in the last few decades is **Frank McGuinness** (b. 1953). His play *Observe the Sons of Ulster Marching Towards the Somme*, staged in Dublin as talks began on the Anglo-Irish agreement, focuses on the participation of a group of Northern Loyalists in the Battle of the Somme. Its imagery exploits the symbolism of the whole Irish tradition, permitting a range of readings, in which the Somme represents the current situation in the North, or the battlefield of the Boyne, or the slaughters of the early sagas. It was his 1987 piece, *Carthaginians*, a play set in his native Derry, which thrust him into the major league of Irish writers. The play found a vocabulary in which to explore ancient Irish themes—the nature of political allegiance, death and resurrection, the relationship between Britain, Ireland, and the North, sexuality, religion—in a way that seems to sum up the whole tradition while simultaneously threatening to demolish it. His work provides, if not some hope of unifying the various strands of Ireland's long cultural histories, at least an analysis of what divides them.

Joe O'Connor

BOOKS

This list is short by necessity, but anything you don't find here will be included in Maurice Harmon's, *Select Bibliography for the Study of Anglo Irish Literature* (Dublin 1977). Dates given below are those for most recent publication, not original publication. All these books are in paperback unless otherwise stated.

HISTORY AND POLITICS

J. C. Beckett *The Making of Modern Ireland 1603–1923* (Knopf). Concise and elegant, this is probably the best introduction to the complexities of Irish history.

David Beresford *Ten Men Dead* (UK; Grafton, 1987; £3.95). Revelatory account of the 1981 hunger strike, using the prison correspondence as its basic material; a powerful refutation of the demonologies of the British press.

Peter Ellis Beresford *Hell or Connaught* and *The Boyne Water* (UK; Blackstaff, 1989; both £5.95). Vivid popular histories of Cromwell's rampage and the pivotal Battle of the Boyne.

Terence Brown, *Ireland: A Social and Cultural History 1922 to the present* (Cornell Univ Press 1985; $12.95). Brilliantly perceptive survey of writers' responses to the utter hash made of post-revolutionary Ireland by its leaders.

James Connolly, *Selected Writings* (Unwin Hyman, 1988; $18.95). Classic texts from the father of modern Irish socialism.

Tim Pat Coogan *The IRA* (UK; Fontana, 1987; £4.95). Substantially revised since its first publication in 1970, this well-researched and even-handed study remains the authoritative book on the subject.

Liz Curtis, *Ireland: the Propaganda War* (Unwin Hyman, 1984; $14.95). An unanswerable indictment of the truth-bending of the British media.

John Devoy, *Recollections of an Irish Rebel* (UK; Irish University Press, 1979; £17.50 hardback). Excellent personal account from an old Fenian troublemaker.

Myles Dillon (ed.), *Lebor Na Cert: The Book of Rights* (UK; Irish Texts Society, 1962; £12). Fascinating and literary explanation of the early Brehon laws.

Michael Farrell, *Arming the Protestants: The Formation of the Ulster Special Constabulary and the Royal Ulster Constabulary, 1920–1927* (UK; Pluto, 1983; £6.95). Farrell is a fine journalist and veteran of Northern Ireland's civil rights campaigns. Argues, as the title implies, from a Republican standpoint.

Michael Farrell *Northern Ireland: The Orange State* (Unwin Hyman, 1980; $18.95). At times tendentious, but still persuasive account of the political development of Northern Ireland.

Roy Foster, *Modern Ireland 1600–1972* (UK; Allen Lane, 1989; £25 hardback). Superb and provocative new book, generally reckoned to be unrivaled in its scholarship and acuity. Not recommended for beginners, though.

Robert Kee, *The Green Flag* (Penguin, 1989; 3 vols; $7.95 each). Scrupulous history of Irish nationalism from the first Plantations to the creation of the Free State. Masterful as narrative and as analysis.

Joseph Lee, *The Modernization of Irish Society* (UK; Gill and Macmillan, 1973; £5.95; available in US in libraries.) Collection of learned but refreshingly jargon-free articles.

F. S. L. Lyons, *Ireland Since the Famine* (UK; Fontana, 1980; £6.95). The most complete overview of recent Irish history, either iconoclastic or revisionist, depending on your point of view.

T. W. Moody and F. X. Martin, *The Course of Irish History* (Dufour,1967; $23.95 hardback). Shows its age a bit, but still very good on early Irish history.

Cecil Woodham Smith, *The Great Hunger* (UK Hamish Hamilton; £6.95). Definitive, harrowing history of the famine.

A. T. Q. Stewart, *The Narrow Ground* (UK; Pretari; £4.95). A Unionist overview of the North's history from 1609 to the 1960s, providing a good background to the current situation.

GAELIC TALES AND MUSIC

Brendan Behan, *An Giall*; in English, *The Hostage* (UK; Methuen, 1975; £4.50). Behan's play is better in Gaelic, but still pretty damn good in English. The best work from an over-rated writer.

Breandán Breathnach, *Folk Music and Dances of Ireland* (Dufour, 1971; $9.95). All the diddley eye you could ever want, and in one volume.

Kevin Danaher, *Folk Tales of the Irish Countryside* (Dufour, 1985; $9.95). The best available volume on fairy and folk tales, recorded with a civil servant's meticulousness and a novelist's literary style.

Myles Dillon (ed.), *Irish Sagas* (Dufour 1985; $9.95). A good examination of Cúchulainn, Finn Mac Cumhaill etc, in literary and socio-psychological terms.

Myles Dillon, *Children's Book of Irish Folktales* (UK; Mercier Press, 1984; £4.95). Fairies, will o' the wisps, puckoons and nasty hags with pointy noses.

Seamus Heaney, *Buile Suibhne*; in English, *Sweeney Astray* (Farrar, Straus,& Giroux,1984; $7.95). A modern translation of the ancient Irish saga of the mad king Sweeney.

Thomas Kinsella and Sean O'Tuama, *An Duanaire: Poems of the Dispossessed* (Univ of Pennsylvania Press; O/P;). Excellent translations of stark Gaelic poems on famine and death. See also Kinsella's translation of one of the earliest sagas, the *Táin Bó Cuailnge* (Univ of Pennysylania Press; $34.95).

Thomas Moore, *Irish Melodies*, edited by Sean O'Faolain (Various nineteenth century US edns. in libraries). All the prettied-up tunes Moore ripped off from the harpers, along with lyrics of mind-numbingly perfect rhythm. Moore is an important historical figure, who expressed the nationalism of the emerging middle class and brought revolution into the parlour.

Padraic O'Conaire, *Finest Stories* (Dufour, 1982; $7.95). O'Conaire's dispassionate eye roams over the cruelties of peasant life.

Tomas O'Criomhthain (sometimes **Thomas O'Crohan**), *An tOileanach*; in English, *The Islandman* (Oxford University Press, 1986; $9.95). Similar to O'Conaire but non-fiction and, if possible, even more raw.

George Petrie, *The Petrie Collection of the Ancient Music of Ireland* (Gregg International, $33.12 hardback). One of the most important cultural documents in Irish history.

Mark J. Prendergast, *Irish Rock: History, Roots and Perspectives* (Dufour; $19.95). The only decent book on Irish rock music.

Peig Sayers, *An Old Woman's Reflections* (Oxford University Press, 1962; $8.95). Unfortunately, Sayers' complacent acceptance of her own powerlessness is still held up as an example to Irish schoolchidren. Still, it's a frightening insight into the eradication of the Gaelic language through emigration, poverty, and political failure. A very funny deconstruction of the Sayers style is Flann O'Brien's *An Beal Bocht*, in English *The Poor Mouth* (UK; Paladin, 1988; £3.50).

William Butler Yeats, *Irish Fairy and Folk Tales* (Hippocrene Books, 1987; $16.95). Yeats gets all misty-eyed about an Ireland that never existed.

FICTION

John Banville, *Birchwood* (UK; Paladin, 1987; £3.50); *The Newton Letter* (Godine, 1989; $9.95) *The Book of Evidence* (UK; Secker and Warburg, 1989; £8.95). Three novels from the most important Irish novelist since McGahern, including his 1989 Booker Prize nomination, a sleazy tale of a weird Dublin murder.

Leland Bardwell, *The House* (UK; Brandon Books, 1984; £3.95). Quirky, bleak prose, often dealing with domestic violence, male cruelty, drink, and poverty. But funny too, in a black way.

Samuel Beckett, *Molloy/Malone Dies/The Unnamable* (Grove, 1989; $9.95). Old Beady Eyes' wonderful trilogy of breakdown and glum humor.

Brendan Behan, *Borstal Boy* (Godine, 1982: $10.95). Behan's gutsy *roman à clef* about his early life in the IRA and in jail.

Elizabeth Bowen *The Death of the Heart* (Penguin; $5.95). Finely tuned tale of the anguish of unrequited love; generally rated as the masterpiece of this obliquely stylish writer.

Clare Boylan, *Nail on the Head* (Penguin 1985; $4.95). Elegant, powerful novel from an emerging star of contemporary fiction.

Maria Edgeworth, *Castle Rackrent* (Oxford University Press,1982; $4.95). Best of the "Big

House" books, in which Edgeworth displays a subversively subtle sympathy with her peasant narrator. Would have shocked her fellow aristos if they'd been able to figure it out.

Desmond Hogan, *A Curious Street* (UK; Picador, 1985; £3.50); *A New Shirt* (UK; Faber, 1987; £3.95). Closet gays, small-town runaways, IRA bombers holed up in London bedsits, Hogan's characters are always outsiders in a hostile world. One of the country's most lyrical and rhapsodic prose writers.

Neil Jordan, *A Night in Tunisia and Other Stories* (Random; $5.95). Jordan's Ireland is one where everything is implied and never said. The title story weaves together a painful evocation of lost innocence with the healing power of great music. See also his filmscript, with David Leland, for *Mona Lisa* (UK; Faber, 1986; £3.95).

James Joyce, *Dubliners* (Penguin, 1976 $4.95); *Portrait of the Artist as a Young Man* (Penguin, 1964; $3.95); *Ulysses* (Random, 1986; $15.95); *Finnegans Wake* (UK; Faber; £7.50). No novel written in English this century can match the linguistic verve of *Ulysses*, Joyce's monumental evocation of 24 hours in the life of Dublin. From the time of its completion until shortly before his death—a period of 16 years—he labored at *Finnegans Wake*, a dream-language recapitulation of the cycles of world history. Though indigestible as a whole, it contains passages of incomparable lyricism and wit; try the "Anna Livia Plurabelle" section, and you could be hooked.

Molly Keane, *Good Behavior* (Dutton, 1983; $8.95). Highly successful comic reworking of the "Big House" novel.

Mary Lavin, *The House in Clewe Street* (Penguin, 1988; $7.95); *Stories* (UK; Constable, 1985; 3 vols; £10.95 each). The best available works by this much-lauded writer. Try libraries for her classic *Tales from Bective Bridge*.

John McGahern, *The Dark* (Faber, 1983; £3.95); *The Barracks* (Faber, 1983; £3.95). *The Barracks* is classic McGahern: stark, murderous and not a spare adjective in sight.

Bernard MacLaverty, *Cal* (UK: Penguin, 1988; £3.95); *Lamb* (UK; Penguin, 1988; £3.95). Both novels of love beset by crisis, the first deals with an unwilling IRA man and widow of one of his victims. *Lamb* is the disturbing tale of a Christian Brother who absconds from a borstal with a young boy.

Brinsley MacNamara, *The Valley of the Squinting Windows* (UK; Anvil Books, 1984; £3.95). A brilliant title for a brilliant book, set in the author's Westmeath birthplace.

Deirdre Madden, *Hidden Symptoms* and *The Birds of the Innocent Wood* (UK; Faber, 1987 and 1988; £3.50 and £9.95). Evocatively grim novel of life in the North.

Brian Moore, *The Lonely Passion of Judith Hearne* (Little, 1988; $6.95). Moore's early novels are rooted in the landscape of his native Belfast; this was his first, a poignant tale of emotional blight and the possibilities of late redemption by love.

Christopher Nolan, *Under the Eye of the Clock* (Dell, 1989; $7.95) Extraordinary and explosive fiction debut, that won the Whitbread Prize in 1987. Largely autobiographical story of a handicapped boy's celebration of the power of language.

Edna O'Brien, *Johnnie I Hardly Knew You* (UK; Weidenfeld, 1977; £5.95); *The Country Girls* (New American Library 1976; $7.95). Sensitively wrought novels from a top-class writer sometimes accused, unjustly, of wavering too much towards Harlequin.

Flann O'Brien, *At Swim-Two-Birds* (New American Library $8.,95); *The Third Policeman* (New American Library; $7.95). Enter the world of Ireland's master of the ominously absurd; *At Swim-Two-Birds*, O'Brien's first novel is an exhilarating blend of Gaelic fable and surrealism.

Frank O'Connor, *Guests of the Nation* (UK; Poolbeg Press, 1979; £3.95). The best Irish political fiction of this century.

Peadar O'Donnell, *Islanders* (Dufour, 1988 $9.95). Evocative, mesmerizing prose from an important Republican figure.

Julia O'Faolain, *No Country for Young Men* (Adler & Adler, 1986; $15.95). Spanning four generations, this ambitious novel traces the personal repercussions of the Irish civil war.

Sean O'Faolain, *Bird Alone* (Oxford University Press, 1986; $5.95); *Collected Stories* (Little 1983; 1 vol set $29.95). A master of the short story form and the juiciness of rural dialect.

Liam O'Flaherty, *Short Stories:The Pedlar's Revenge* (Dufour; $7.95)). Best of the postwar generation of former IRA men turned writers.

E. O. Somerville and (Violet) Martin Ross, *Some Recollections and Further Experiences of an Irish RM* (Longman, Green; O/P). The needle pushes the begorrah factor a little too heavily here and there, but Somerville and Ross write with witty flair and are very significant for what they reveal, accidentally, about a dying class.

James Stephens, *The Crock of Gold* (Macmillan, 1986; $8.95); *The Charwoman's Daughter* (UK; Gill and Macmillan, 1972; £3.95). Two fabulous masterpieces from the country's most underrated genius.

Bram Stoker, *Dracula* (Penguin, 1979; $2.95). Stoker woke up after a nightmare brought on by a hefty lobster supper, and proceeded to write his way into the nightmares of the twentieth century.

Jonathan Swift, *Gulliver's Travels* (Oxford University Press, 1987; $2.50); *The Tale of a Tub and Related Pieces* (Oxford University Press, 1986; $3.95). Surrealism and satire from the only writer in the English language with as sharp a pen as Voltaire.

William Trevor, *Stories* (UK; Penguin, 1983; £4.99). Five of Trevor's short-story collections in one volume, revealing more about Ireland than many a turgid sociological thesis. Often desperately moving, Trevor is one of the true giants of Irish fiction.

Oscar Wilde, *The Picture of Dorian Gray* (Penguin, 1986; $2.95). Wilde's exploration of moral schizophrenia. A debauched artist maintains his youthful good looks while his portrait in the attic slowly disintegrates into a vision of evil.

POETRY

Eavan Boland, *The Journey and other poems* (Carcanet, 1987; $7.50). Thoughtful, spare and elegant verse from one of Ireland's most significant women poets.

Austin Clarke, *Selected Poems* (Wake Forest, 1976; $7.95). Clarke's tender work evokes the same stark grandeur as the paintings of Jack Yeats.

Anthony Cronin, *The End of the Modern World* (UK; Raven Arts Press, 1989; £4.95). Interesting attempt to sum up hundreds of years of history in one long poem series, Cronin's latest work is ambitious and skillful.

Seamus Deane, *History Lessons* and *Selected Poems* (UK; Gallery, 1983 and 1988; £4.95 each). Tersely precise poems about assassination victims, slowly fragmenting relationships, and the petty disasters of daily life in a divided island.

Denis Devlin. Amazingly, no collected volume of Devlin's work exists. But he's such an important poet that he must be mentioned. Selections from his work are included in most anthologies of modern Irish poetry.

Paul Durcan, *The Berlin Wall Café* (Dufour, 1985; $10.95). A lament for a broken marriage, recounted with agonizing honesty, dignity and ultimately, forgiveness. See also his *Selected Paul Durcan* (UK; Blackstaff, 1988; £4.95).

Padraic Fiacc, *Missa Terribilis* (UK; Blackstaff, 1986; £4.95). Fiacc's work is informed by the political and social tribalism of Northern Ireland, and explores personal relationships in these contexts.

Seamus Heaney, *Death of a Naturalist* (Faber & Faber; $5.95;) *Selected Poems* (Farrar, Straus & Giroux; O/P) *Station Island* (Farrar, Straus & Giroux; $6.95). The most important Irish poet since Yeats. His poems are immediate and passionate, even when dealing with complex intellectual problems and radical social divisions.

Patrick Kavanagh, *Collected Poems* (Norton; $7.95). Joyfully mystic exploration of the rural countryside and the lives of its inhabitants by Ireland's most popular poet. See also his autobiographical novel, *Tarry Flynn* (Devin; $12.50).

Brendan Kennelly, *Cromwell* (Dufour, 1985; $14.95). Speculative meditation on the role of the conqueror in Irish history.

Thomas Kinsella, *Poems: 1956–1973* (Wake Forest, 1979; $7.95. See also his translations from the Irish (above) and his first-rate anthology *The New Oxford Book of Irish Verse* (Oxford University Press, 1989; $9.95).

Patrick MacGill, *The Navvy Poet: The Collected Poetry of Patrick MacGill* (UK; Brandon, 1985 in Ireland; Caliban, 1985 in Britain; £5.95). Not exactly what modern audiences would call poetry, but MacGill's balladstyle verses are important social texts, recording with quiet outrage a migrant laborer's life of poverty and loneliness.

Shane MacGowan, *Poguetry* (UK, Faber, 1989; £6.95). Rock-solid debut by the Pogues' bardperson. Not for Yeats fans.

Medbh McGuckian, *Venus in the Rain* (Oxford University Press, 1984; $8.95). Trawling the subconscious for their imagery, McGuckian's sensuous and elusive poems are highly demanding and equally rewarding.

Louis MacNeice, *Collected Poems*, (Faber & Faber; £11.95). Good chum of Auden, Spender, and the rest of the "Thirties' generation," Carrickfergus-born MacNeice achieves a fruitier texture and an even more detached tone.

John Montague, *Dead Kingdom* (Wake Forest, 1984; $6.25). Terse, hard poetry concerned with history, community and social decay. See also his anthology, *The Faber Book of Irish Verse* (UK; 1978; £5.95).

Eileán Ní Chuilleanáin, *The Rose Geranium* (UK; Gallery, 1981; £3.90). A promising and constantly surprising young poet. Joint editor of *Cyphers*, a good Dublin literary magazine.

Nuala Ní Dhomhnaill, *An Dealg Droighin* (UK; Mercier, 1984) is published in Irish only, but haunting translations of her modern erotic verse by the fine poet Michael Hartnett are included in *Raven Introductions 3*, (UK; Raven Arts Press, 1984) and in Frank Ormsby's anthology (see below).

Frank Ormsby (ed.), *The Long Embrace: Twentieth Century Irish Love Poems* (Faber & Faber, 1989; $9.95). Excellent anthology with major chunks from the work of just about every important twentieth-century Irish poet from Yeats to the present day. See also his *Poets from the North of Ireland* anthology (Dufour, 1979; $14.95

Tom Paulin, *Fivemiletown* and *The Strange Museum* (UK; Faber; £4.95 and £3.95). Often called "dry" both in praise and accusation, Paulin's work reverberates with thoughtful political commitment and a sophisticated irony.

Oscar Wilde, *The Ballad of Reading Gaol* (Dutton, O/P). The great comedian achieves his greatest success, in tragedy.

William Butler Yeats, *The Poems of W.B. Yeats* (Macmillan, 1983; $24.95). They're all here, poems of rhapsody, love, revolution, and eventual rage at a disconnected and failed Ireland "fumbling in the greasy till."

DRAMA

Samuel Beckett, *Complete Dramatic Works* (UK; Faber, 1986; £12.50); *Collected Shorter Plays* (Grove, 1984; $11.95); *Waiting for Godot* (Grove; $5.95). Bleak hilarity from the laureate of the void. All essential for loitering around Dublin coffee shops.

Brendan Behan, *The Complete Plays* (Grove; $9.95). Flashes of brilliance from a talent destroyed by alcoholism. His *The Quare Fellow* takes up where Wilde's *Ballad of Reading Gaol* leaves off.

George Farquhar, *The Recruiting Officer* (St Martin, 1988; $13.50). The usual helping of cross-dressing and mistaken identity, yet this goes beyond the implications of most restoration comedy, even flirting with feminism before finally marrying everyone off in the last scene.

Oliver Goldsmith, *She Stoops to Conquer* (Norton, 1980; $6.95). Sparky dialogue, with a more English sheen than Farquhar. See also Goldsmith's novel *The Vicar of Wakefield* (Penguin, 1982; $2.50), an affecting celebration of simple virtue.

Augusta, Lady Gregory, *Collected Plays* (Dufour, 1971: 4 vols; $9.95. $11.95, $13.95, $30.00). The Anglo-Irish writer who understood most about the cadences of the Irish language. This gives not only her translations, but also her original drama, an authenticity lacking in the work of others.

Frank McGuinness, *Observe the Sons of Ulster Marching Towards the Somme* (Faber & Faber; $8.95); *Carthaginians* and *Baglady* (UK; Faber; £3.95). Three major works from Ireland's most important contemporary dramatist.

Sean O'Casey, *Three Plays* (St Martin, 1969; $4.95). Contains his powerful Dublin trilogy, *Juno and the Paycock*, *Shadow of a Gunman*, and *The Plough and the Stars*, set against the backdrop of the Irish civil war.

John Millington Synge, *The Complete Plays* (UK; Methuen, 1985; £2.95). Lots of "begorrahs" and "mavourneens" and other dialogue kindly invented for the Irish peasantry by Synge; but *The Playboy of the Western World* is a brilliant and unique work, greeted in Dublin by riots, threats and moral outrage.

Oscar Wilde, *Complete Works* (Harper & Row, 1989; $12.95). Bittersweet satire, subversive one-liners, and profound existentialist philosophy all masquerading as well-made, drawing room farce.

William Butler Yeats, *Collected Plays* (Macmillan, 1953; $17.95). Long-haired hunky Celts and gorgeous princesses, as Yeats inaugurates the Finian's Rainbow school of Irish History. Stick to the poems.

OTHER NON-FICTION

Sally Belfrage, *The Crack* (UK; Grafton, 1987; £3.95). Readable if romanticized anecdotes and impressions of an American journalist, covering the spectrum of Belfast communities.

A. M. Brady and Brian Cleeve, (eds.), *Biographical Dictionary of Irish Writers* (St Martin, 1985; $35.00). Succinct entries on all the greats, better used as a magical mystery tour through the lost byways of Irish literature.

Seamus Deane, *Short History of Irish Literature* (Univ of Notre Dame Press; $27.95). Deane brings a poet's sensitivity to a massive and sometimes unwieldy tradition, with skill and a profound sense of sociopolitical context.

Richard Ellmann, *James Joyce* (Oxford University Press, 1982; $18.95); *Oscar Wilde* (Random, 1988; $11.95). Ellman's *Joyce* is a major literary work in itself, a massive and brilliant book. His *Oscar Wilde* is at least its equal, an eloquent corrective to the image of Wilde as an intellectual mayfly.

Myles na Gopaleen, (aka Flann O'Brien), *Myles Away From Dublin* (UK; Grafton, 1988; £4.95). Hilarious journalism, pillorying petty bureaucracy, snobbery, and pretension.

C. Desmond Greaves, *The Life and Times of James Connolly* (UK; Lawrence and Wishard, 1972; £4.95). Slightly folksy biography of major Irish socialist in which Greaves makes no secret of his unqualified admiration for his subject.

Michael Holroyd, *The Search for Love* and *The Pursuit of Power* (vol 1, Random, 1988; $24.45; vol 2, 1989; $24.95, hardback). First two volumes of Holroyd's three-part biography of Shaw; unfairly slammed by the critics, this is a pretty successful stab at understanding one of the most difficult and complex authors in the whole Anglo-Irish canon.

Field Day Pamphlets, (available only in the UK), especially: **Seamus Deane**, *Heroic Styles: The Tradition of an Idea*; **Declan Kiberd**, *Anglo-Irish Attitudes*; **Michael Farrell**, *Apparatus of Repression in Ireland*; and **Seamus Heaney**, *An Open Letter*. Other pamphlets by Robert McCartney (a northern Unionist lawyer), Tom Paulin and other leading lights of the Irish cultural scene. (£2–3.50.)

T. Augustine Martin, *Anglo-Irish Literature* (UK; Irish Department of Foreign Affairs, 1982; £5.75). Readable scholarship and precise insight from the country's foremost Yeatsian scholar.

Nell McCafferty, *The Best of Nell* (UK; Attic Press, 1987; £3.95). Along with *Magill* magazine's Gene Kerrigan, Nell McCafferty is Ireland's best journalist. Read the article *The Accusing Finger of Raymond Gilmour* in this volume. It will tell you more about Northern Ireland's divisions than anything you've read before.

Tim Robinson, *The Stones of Aran* (UK; Viking, 1989; £12.95 hardback). In the opinion of some, the most perceptive book on Ireland yet produced by an English travel writer.

LANGUAGE

Irish is a Celtic language, evolved from a linguistic base of which ancient Gaulish is the sole written record.

The Celtic settlement of Ireland probably began in the seventh century BC; the later migration of Irish tribes to the Isle of Man and to Scotland established Irish-speaking kingdoms in those areas. With the rise of Rome the Celtic languages survived only in the peripheral western areas—today, Celtic languages are limited to parts of Scotland, Wales, and Brittany in addition to Ireland. Cornish, another Celtic derivative, died out in the eighteenth century and this century Manx ceased to be a community language. In Ireland a succession of invaders speaking Norse, French and English were assimilated into the population, with resulting cross-fertilization of languages. The first Anglo-Norman aristocracy became thoroughly Gaelicized, and even as late as 1578, the Lord Chancellor could report that "all English, and most part with delight, even in Dublin, speak Irish and greatly are spotted in manners, habit and conditions with Irish stains."

This situation soon changed, however. The Tudor and Stuart wars, Cromwells's campaign, the Orange invasion, and the subsequent Penal Laws resulted in the virtual elimination of the Irish aristocratic and learned classes and replaced them with English-speaking landowning middle classes.

Immediately after independence in 1921, Irish was installed as the first national language and steps were taken to revive it as a community tongue. It's now estimated that in the designated Irish-speaking (*Gaeltacht*) areas—in County Donegal, Galway, and north Mayo, and in Counties Kerry, Cork and Waterford—there are around 66,000 speakers of the language, which is 77 percent of the *Gaeltacht* population. The use of Irish is widespread in Irish society: on public notices and documents, on television and radio, in newspapers, books and magazines. Irish has been compulsory in Irish schools since independence, and until recently a qualification in Irish was required for university graduation and for entrance to the civil service.

Yet figures show that only thirty percent of the population is competent in the language, and that the native speaker category is still declining, paralleling the population decline in the Gaeltacht areas. Only half of Irish children are introduced to the language before they attend school. The modernization of Irish society is accelerating the decline of the native tongue, which has become associated with an economic status lower than that implied by the use of the international English language. The new social structures being introduced are threatening the existence of the tightly knit family communities on which the survival of Irish as a living language depends.

Phrase Books and Primers

Teach Yourself Irish, Miles Dillon/Doncha O Croinin (UK; Hodder, £2.50).
Archaic teaching methods, student needs to be a saint, southern dialects favored.

Learning Irish Michael O Siadhail (Yale University Press, $19.95 hardback)
Modern guide to language through speaking. Cassettes available. Strong on grammar. Connaught dialect preferred.

The Pocket Irish Phrase Book (UK; Apple Tree, £1.95)
Excellent introduction with useful background information. Brief on grammar but good on pronunciation. Dialect differences taken into consideration. Not possible to learn the language from this booklet but it is a valuable aid to any learner.

A GAELIC PRIMER

Although virtually everyone in Ireland speaks English, in the strong *Gaeltacht* areas you might hear almost no English at all. Obviously, people will speak with you in English when you arrive, but the greeting will be a lot warmer if you show even the most basic interest in the language. Should you take things a bit farther and attend a college *ceilidh*, bear in mind that any student caught speaking English to you could face expulsion. Below are listed the most basic vocabulary and phrases you may like to try and use, and a bibliography of text books is on the facing page if you're intent on taking it any farther.

Vocabulary

Yes	*Tá (ta)*	school	*scoil (scoyle)*
No	*Níl (neil)*	hospital	*ospideal(oss-pe-jall)*
I am not	*Nílim (néil'im)*	she	*sí(she)*
Hello	*Dia duit (jeea ditch)*	dry	*tur (tour)*
Hello (in return)	*Diás muire duit (jeea smoora ditch)*	cheers	*sláinte (sláyn-che)*
		Mass	*Aifreann (aff-rin)*
How are you doing?	*Ca dé mar ata tú (ka jay mar a ta too)*	ocean	*aigéad (eg-agg)*
Welcome	*Fáilte romhat (phal-tche rów-at)*	money	*airgead (are-eh-gidge)*
Goodbye (to the person leaving)	*Slán leat (slann lat)*	weather	*aimsir (am-sheer)*
		beautiful	*aoibhinn (even)*
		brown	*donn (don)*
Goodbye (to the person staying)	*Slán agat (slann ugget)*	black	*dubh (doo)*
		blue	*gorm (gáw-rrm)*
I would like..	*Is maith liom..(iss mwáích lum)*	red	*dearg (jár-rug)*
Would you like..	*Is maith leat..(iss mwáích lat)*	fort	*dún (doon)*
the	*an (an)*	two	*dó(daw)*
Who?	*Cé?(kay)*	bright	*geal (gal)*
Where?	*Cén ait? (kane átch)*	also	*freisin (frésh-een)*
Which?	*Cé acu (kay awkoo)*	another	*eile (elle-leh)*
morning	*maidín (mwai-jean)*	I listen	*Éistim (éhsh-cheem)*
day	*lá(laa)*	flute	*feadóg mór (fádyog more)*
here	*anseo (an-sháw)*	fiddle	*fidil (fíd-jill)*
work	*obair (úbur)*	perhaps	*b'féidir (báy-jer)*
quick	*luath/beo (looa/byaw)*	meat	*feoil (foil)*
OK	*ceart go leor (kyart go lower)*	hotel	*ostan (austin)*
food	*bia (bee-a)*	airport	*áerfort (air-fawrt)*
the famine	*an gorta mór (an gawrta more)*	street	*sráid (schraelídj)*
big	*mór (more)*	town	*baile (byle-yeh)*
small	*beag (bug)*	house	*teach (chachh)*
island	*inis (én-ish)*	pub	*teach tabhairne (chachh tao-war-nye)*
centre	*lár (lahr)*		
milk	*bainne (bayn-nye)*	poet	*file (feel-leh)*
but	*ach (ach)*	a romantic tale	*tale finscéal (feenscale)*
to	*do (daw)*	traditional music	*ceol tradisiunta (cyawl traa-dish-oonta)*
at	*ag (eg)*		
from	*ó(aw)*	story	*scéal (scale)*
he	*sé(shaay)*	tired	*tuise (toorsher)*
old	*sean (shan)*	thirsty	*tart (tart)*
young	*óg (ogue)*	water	*uisce (éschka)*
tea	*tae (tay)*	whisky	*uisce beatha (éschka bachah)*
cold	*fuar (fur)*	station	*stásiún (stá-shoon)*
pound	*punt (punt)*	post office	*oifig an phoist (áwfig am phwisht)*
accordion	*an bosca ceoil (an boxa kyoil)*	song	*amhrán (hour-run)*
monastery	*mainistir (man-iss-tyer)*	ten	*deich (jeichh)*

Some Useful Phrases

English	Irish
It's a nice morning	Tá sé an mhaidin deas (ta shay an waajean jass)
How much is that?	Ca mhead sin? (Ka vadj shin)
It's a warm day	Tá an lá te (ta an laa chay)
Does the train stop at Derry?	An stadann an traein ag Doire? (an sta-dan an train eg derrah)
Where is the man?	Ca bhfuil an fhear? (ka will an are)
Good night	Oiche mhaith (eeya wyych)
I understand	Tuigim (tig-im)
I don't understand	Ní thuigim (nee hig-im)
What's your name?	Cad é an t-ainm ata ort? (ka jay an tan-nym a ta awrt)
My name is Mary	Máire an t-ainm ata orm (my-ra an tan-nym a ta aw-rim)
Excuse me	Gabh mo leithsceal (gum awh lesh-kill)
I'm hungry	Tá ocras orm (ta aw-crus aw-rim)
I'd like a room	Ba mhaith liom seomra (bah wyych lum shawm-ra)
Can you play the fiddle?	An feidir leat seinm? (an fay-jure lat shennim)
I'd like a pint	Pionta leanna (peenta lanna)
Would you like to dance?	An bhfuil tu maith ag damhsa? (an will too mwáîch eg douse-ah)
Will there be any music tonight?	An mbeidh aon cheol ann anocht? (an may ian hyawl unn anocht)
Do you speak Irish?	An bhfuil Gaelige agat? (an will gail-i-geh uggat)
I don't speak English	Níl mé ag caint Bearla (neil may eg kentch Bare-lah)
I don't know	Níl a fhios agam (neil iss sawg-um)
What time is it now?	Cad é an t-am e anois? (ka jay an tam ay a-nish)
Where do you live?	Ca bhuil tu i do chonai? (ka will too eh daw chon-nay)

AN IRISH GLOSSARY

BAWN A castle enclosure or castlefold.

BODHRÁN (pronounced "bore-run") A hand-held, shallow, goatskin drum.

B-SPECIALS Auxiliary police force of the Stormont government, disbanded 1971.

CASHEL A kind of *rath* (see below), distinguished by a circular outer stone wall instead of earthern ramparts.

CEILIDH Traditional Irish barn dance.

CLOCHÁN A beehive-shaped hut, of tightly fitted stone without mortar; early Christian.

COMHALTAS National organisation for traditional music-making and teaching.

"THE CRACK" Good conversation, a good time, often accompanying drinking. "What's the crack?" meaning "what's the gossip?"

CRANNOG A manmade island in a lake, now usually indistinguishable from natural islands.

CURRAGH/CURRACH Small fishing vessel used off the west coast; traditionally made of leather stretched over a light wood frame, modern curraghs are of tar-coated canvas.

THE DAIL Lower house of the Irish Parliament.

DOLMEN (or "portal-tomb") A chamber formed by standing stones that support a massive capstone. The capstone often slopes to form the entrance of the chamber. Date from the Copper Age (2000 BC—1750 BC).

DRUMLIN Small, oval, hummocky hill formed from the detritus of a retreating glacier.

DUP Democratic Unionist Party, a Loyalist political party founded by Ian Paisley and Desmond Boal (Shankhill MP) in 1971. The party appeals to the hard-line Loyalists, staunchly defends the Union with Britain, and is typified by intense hostility towards Catholicism.

EIRE Gaelic name for Ireland, but officially indicates the 26 counties.

FEIS Festival, usually involving music.

FIANNA FAIL The largest and most successful of Ireland's two main political parties since Independence. Essentially a conservative party, it has its origins in the Republican faction of *Sinn Fein*, and fought against pro-Treaty forces in the civil war. During the Thirties the party did much to assert Ireland's separateness from Britain, and has always claimed a united Ireland. While still calling for British withdrawal, Fianna Fail co-operates with British military cross-border operations, and since coming to power Haughey has worked with Britain on the issue of the future of the North.

FINE GAEL Ireland's second largest political party, Fine Gael sprang from the pro-Treaty faction of Sinn Fein which formed the first Free State government in 1921. Since then it has not been able to gain a strong majority, and short periods in office have been in coalitions. It advocates more liberal policies than Fianna Fail in terms of social welfare, but there is little to distinguish the two main parties.

FIR Men's public toilets.

GAELTACHT Irish (Gaelic) -speaking areas.

GALLERY-GRAVE A burial chamber of squared stones, generally found under a long mound.

GARDAÍ The police force of the Irish Republic.

INLA Irish National Liberation Army. Fanatical, splinter group of the IRA.

IRA Irish Republican Army.

LOYALIST A person loyal to the British Crown, usually a Northern Irish Protestant.

MNÁ Women's public toilets.

MOTTE A circular mound, flat on top, which the Normans used as a fortification.

NAVVY Derogatory term for an Irish laborer.

NATIONALIST Those who want reland united.

THE NORTH Term refering to Northern Ireland used by most people, except Loyalists.

OGHAM (rhyming with "poem") The earliest form of writing used by the Irish (fourth to seventh century), and found on the edge of standing stones. Employing a twenty-character alphabet derived from Latin, the letters were represented by varying strokes and notches, and read from the bottom upwards.

ORANGE ORDER A Loyalist Protestant organization, found throughout Northern Ireland, which promotes the Union with Britain. The name comes from William of Orange, the Protestant king who defeated the Catholic James II at the Battle of the Boyne (1690). Most Unionist MPs are Orangemen, and outside of Northern Ireland Orange Lodges are found amongst Loyalist ex-patriates.

OUP Official Unionist Party, the largest elected Protestant party.

PASSAGE-GRAVE A megalithic tomb from the Neolithic period. A simple corridor of large, square, vertical stones leads to a burial chamber, and the whole tomb is covered with earth. The stones are decorated with simple patterns: double spirals, triangles, zigzag lines, and the sun symbol.

POTEEN/POITÍN (pronounced "potcheen") Highly alcoholic (and often toxic) and illegal spirit distilled from potatoes.

RATH or RING-FORT A farmstead dating from the first millennium AD. A circular timber enclosure banked by earth and surrounded by a ditch formed the outer walls, within which roofed dwellings were built and, in times of danger, cattle were herded. Today *raths* are visible as circular earthworks.

REPUBLICAN An extreme Irish nationalist.

ROUND TOWER Narrow, tall (65–110 feet), and circular tower, tapering to a conical roof. Built from the ninth century onwards, they are unique to Ireland. They are found on the sites of early monasteries, and served to call the monks to prayer. The entrance is usually a doorway 10–15 feet above the ground, reached by a wooden or rope ladder that could be pulled up for safety.

RUC Royal Ulster Constabulary. Northern Ireland's regular, but armed, police force.

SDLP Social Democratic Labor Party; a moderate nationalist party in the North.

SOUTERRAIN Underground passage that served as a hiding place in times of danger; also used to store food and valuables.

TAOISEACH Irish prime minister.

TD, Teach Dail. Member of the Irish Parliament

TRICOLOR The green, white, and orange flag of the Republic.

THE TWENTY-SIX COUNTIES Republican term for the south of Ireland.

UDA Ulster Defense Association. A legal, Protestant paramilitary organization the largest in Northern Ireland.

UDF Ulster Defense Force. Illegal paramilitary Protestant organization.

UDR Ulster Defense Regiment. A regular regiment of the British army recruited in Northern Ireland.

UFF Ulster Freedom Fighters. Another illegal Protestant paramilitary faction.

UNIONISTS Those (predominantly Protestant) who wish to keep Northern Ireland in union with the rest of the United Kingdom.

UVF Ulster Volunteer Force. Yet another illegal Protestant paramilitary organization.

INDEX